Christine Meyer
Questioning the Canon

Culture & Conflict

Edited by
Isabel Capeloa Gil, Catherine Nesci and
Paulo de Medeiros

Editorial Board
Arjun Appadurai · Claudia Benthien · Elisabeth Bronfen · Joyce Goggin
Bishnupriya Ghosh · Lawrence Grossberg · Andreas Huyssen
Ansgar Nünning · Naomi Segal · Márcio Seligmann-Silva
António Sousa Ribeiro · Roberto Vecchi · Samuel Weber · Liliane Weissberg
Christoph Wulf · Longxi Zhang

Volume 17

Christine Meyer

Questioning the Canon

Counter-Discourse and the Minority Perspective
in Contemporary German Literature

Translated from the original unpublished French
manuscript by Dustin Lovett and Tegan Raleigh

DE GRUYTER

Translation carried out with the support of the Université de Picardie Jules Verne and the Centre d'Études des Relations et Contacts Linguistiques et Littéraires (CERCLL)

ISBN 978-3-11-125843-0
e-ISBN (PDF) 978-3-11-067439-2
e-ISBN (EPUB) 978-3-11-067442-2
ISSN 2194-7104

Library of Congress Control Number: 2021935845

Bibliographic information published by the Deutsche Nationalbibliothek
The Deutsche Nationalbibliothek lists this publication in the Deutsche Nationalbibliografie; detailed bibliographic data are available on the Internet at http://dnb.dnb.de.

© 2023 Walter de Gruyter GmbH, Berlin/Boston
This volume is text- and page-identical with the hardback published in 2021.
Cover image: © Barbara Meyer; author portraits by Arne Wesenberg (Rafik Schami) and Isolde Ohlbaum (Feridun Zaimoglu and Emine Sevgi Özdamar); Goethe and Schiller statue in Weimar, Germany (marako85/iStock).
Printing and binding: CPI books GmbH, Leck

www.degruyter.com

Endorsements

"This book is a revelation. For too long, much literary study has been limited by a methodological monolingualism, refusing to acknowledge the creative potential of an emerging translingual poetics. Christine Meyer boldly questions this status quo. She has assembled a remarkable corpus of exophonic, diasporic writing in German, and her sustained focus on canonicity reveals the progressive hybridization of national literatures. The result is essential reading for all those interested in cultural transmission and literary creativity."
Charles Forsdick, James Barrow Professor of French, University of Liverpool, and UK Arts and Humanities Research Council Theme Leadership Fellow, Translating Cultures

"Meyer's monograph is a rare, sophisticated, and beautifully translated treatise that brings conceptual rigor to the complexity of migration literature in Germany since the 1970s, while situating it in broader Germanophone literary questions from the 19th century onward. Meyer's scholarly formation shines through here, showing us how critical vantage points on 'Germanophonie' from beyond German borders can be just as promising as parallel inquiries into 'Francophonie' have been throughout the postcolonial period. The monograph invites a new commitment to literary-historical clarity, as we enter the next half century of Germanophone literature of migration."
David Gramling, Professor of Central, Eastern, and Northern European Studies, University of British Columbia

"Theoretically sophisticated and historically situated, Questioning the Canon: Counter-Discourse and the Minority Perspective in Contemporary German Literature is a novel and welcome contribution to the study of 'migration literature' in contemporary German letters. By focusing on selected writers of Middle Eastern heritage, Meyer offers an indispensable in-depth analysis of the intertextual themes and strategies of their work and shows how they negotiate their own cultural inheritance with homage to German literary models."
Azade Seyhan, Fairbank Professor in the Humanities, Department of German, Bryn Mawr College

To my parents

Contents

Acknowledgements —— XIII

Abbreviations and Translation —— XV

Introduction —— 1
  Semantic Beacons —— 3
  The Canon Question —— 10
  Methodologies —— 14
  Presentations of Main Authors —— 17

PART I The Forms and Foci of Canon Critique

Chapter 1
Postcolonialism and the Canon —— 23
  Theorizing the Canon —— 27
  The German Canon at the Turn of the Twenty-First Century —— 30
  The German Canon of Authors of Migration Literature —— 34
  Decentering: A Hybrid and Anti-Nationalist Canon —— 34
  Re-centering: Making the "Heart" of the National Canon Beat Again —— 37
  A Typology of Canonical References —— 44
  Major Line: The "Representatives" —— 46
  Minor Line: The "Martyrs," the Marginal, the Rebellious —— 51

Chapter 2
Counter-Discursive Strategies: From Metatextuality to Rewriting —— 56
  Generic Hypertextuality ("Architextuality") —— 58
  Metafiction: Dialogues with the Dead —— 59
  Irreverent Dialogues with Goethe and Hölderlin (SAID) —— 62
  Complicit Conversations with Chamisso and Heine (Schami) —— 65
  Encounters in Fantasies and Dreams (Özdamar) —— 73
  At the Threshold of Rewriting: De- and Reterritorializing the Canon —— 77
  Conclusion —— 81

PART II The Canon and Its Discontents: Palimpsestic Re-Inscriptions in Schami, Özdamar, and Zaimoglu

Chapter 3
Writing Back from the East: Schami's Corrective Reading of European Classics —— 85
- Aesthetic Program and Work on the Canon —— 91
- Does Dracula Need Rehabilitation? The Stakes of a Marxist Rewriting —— 93
- Writing back to the "Grimm Bros.": A Plea for a Paradigm Shift —— 101
- Will Goethe Be Allowed into the Postcolonial Canon? The Deliberations of an Arab Jury —— 110
- Conclusion —— 121

Chapter 4
Özdamar's *Keloglan in Alamania:* The National Tradition Tested by Diversity —— 123
- Ethos and Posture of a "Left-Wing Oriental Libertarian" —— 123
- Genealogy and Solidarity: Özdamar's "Family" —— 127
- The Deterritorialization of the Turkish Patrimony —— 129
- What Becomes of Keloğlan "in Alamania"? —— 135
- An Intertextual Web —— 139
- Keloglan/Butterfly: Deconstructing the Orientalist Myth —— 142
- The Trials of Keloglan through the Lens of Mozart: A Disenchanted Flute —— 146
- Matrimonial Strategy: Queering *The Bartered Bride* —— 152
- The Deadly Subtext of National Folklore —— 154
- Positive Resonances: Under the Protection of Shakespeare, in the Footsteps of Heine —— 162
- Conclusion: Disorder in the Cultural Nation —— 169

Chapter 5
Reading against the National Grain: Özdamar's Commitment to Oppositional Literature —— 171
- *Karriere einer Putzfrau:* "Hamlet" Reread through the Prism of Heiner Müller —— 171
- Recontextualization and Transfocalization of *Hamlet* —— 172
- Ophelia, Story of a (Double) Resurrection: On the Shoulders of Heiner Müller —— 179

Opheliamachine: Giving a Voice back to the Subaltern —— 185
Intertextual Constellations in *Seltsame Sterne starren zur Erde:*
Searching for Beacons in the Night —— 188
In the Orbit of Else Lasker-Schüler, "Poetess of Arabia" —— 195
Osmosis with Heine: Germany 1975, a New Winter's Tale? —— 201
Refraction of Popular Mythology: Like in One of Grimms' Fairy tales —— 205
Conclusion – and Return to Heine —— 211

Chapter 6
Claiming Access to the German Canon: Zaimoglu's Conquering Down-Top Approach —— 213

The Life and Battles of an *Enfant Terrible* —— 213
Liebesmale, scharlachrot: Reconfiguring Pre-Romantic Heritage in "Kanak" Literature —— 223
A Coming-of-Age Novel and Its Canonical References —— 223
Pragmatic and Semantic Transformations: On the Importance of Social Ties —— 229
The Parody of *Werther:* An Intertext with a False Bottom —— 231
The *Kanak* Generation's *Sturm und Drang:* Male Trouble and Re-Narcissization through Language —— 250
The "New Sorrows of Young Ali," or Zaimoglu's Response to Plenzdorf —— 265
The Pirinçci Precedent: Developments and Limits of a Post-Ethnic Variation on the Wertherian Theme —— 279
By Way of Conclusion: *Sturm und Drang* Revisited, or Zaimoglu Versus *Popliteratur* —— 295

Conclusion —— 298

Bibliography —— 308

Index of Names —— 337

Index of Notions —— 342

Acknowledgements

First of all, I would like to thank Bernard Banoun for all his encouragement, advice, and support throughout the journey that led to the completion of this book. His openness, vast knowledge of scholarship, and methodological rigor enabled me to refine my analysis by providing it with the necessary perspectives.

My gratitude also extends to Michel Grimberg, who accompanied me with infinite patience every step of the way for this project. This book was made possible in large part thanks to his moral and material support, his precise revisions, and his readiness to enrich my ideas with his feedback and knowledge on a daily basis.

In addition, I would like to thank the first readers of the French manuscript, whose critical and gracious response served as encouragement to make it accessible to a broader public by having it translated: Anne Duprat, Charles Forsdick, Sylvie Le Moël, Fabrice Malkani, and Arvi Sepp.

I am also greatly thankful to my colleagues from the Department of German Studies at Amiens for having been so supportive and understanding of my reduced participation in our shared administrative duties for the last two years of this project: Clémence Couturier-Heinrich, Doreen Dziuballe, Michel Grimberg, Herta Luise Ott, Ludolf Pelizaeus, Christine Roger, Wolfgang Sabler, and Anne Sommerlat.

This book benefitted from the support of the Université de Picardie Jules Verne in several respects. Two semesters of sabbatical during the research and writing phase, as well as financial assistance for the translation, helped me to see the project to completion. I sincerely thank the members of the Commission de la Recherche at the Université de Picardie Jules Verne for their support. My gratitude also extends to all of my colleagues at the "Centre d'Études des Relations et Contacts Linguistiques et Littéraires" (CERCLL – UR 4283) for having generously supported the publication process.

I am incredibly grateful to my two translators, Tegan Raleigh and Dustin Lovett, whose scrupulous work, enthusiasm, and seamless collaboration made the development of the English text a shared and thought-provoking adventure.

Finally, I would like to acknowledge the contribution of the "Culture and Conflict" series directors and the publishing staff at De Gruyter. Above all, I would like to express my extreme gratitude to Catherine Nesci, who believed in the publishing project from the outset and supported its completion in numerous ways.

Abbreviations and Translation

AC   *Wer zwischen den Stühlen sitzt, verteidigt keinen. Ein Brief an Adelbert von Chamisso* (Schami 2009: 204–210)
AR   *Die Verteidigungsrede. Akte: Rotkäppchen* (Schami 2011: 90–96)
GB   *Der geheime Bericht über den Dichter Goethe, der eine Prüfung auf einer arabischen Insel bestand* (Schami 2001)
HH   *Zu Besuch bei Harry Heine. Ein Hörspiel* (Schami 2009: 211–226)
HM   *Hamletmaschine* (Müller 1978: 89–97)
KA   *Keloglan in Alamania* (Özdamar 2005)
KP   *Karriere einer Putzfrau. Erinnerungen an Deutschland* (Özdamar 1990: 110–127)
LS   *Liebesmale, scharlachrot* (Zaimoglu 2002c)
NL   *Die neuen Leiden des jungen W.* (Plenzdorf 1981)
SSE *Seltsame Sterne starren zur Erde. Berlin – Pankow 1976/77* (Özdamar 2003)
T   *Tränen sind immer das Ende* (Pirinçci 1980)
VK   *Die Wahrheit über Vampire und Knoblauch* (Schami 2011: 48–70)
W   *Die Leiden des jungen Werthers* (Goethe 2006: 349–465)

Unless otherwise indicated, all translations of foreign language quotations are those of Dustin Lovett and Tegan Raleigh.

Introduction

The question of transmission is at the heart of literary creation. Every writer becomes part of a genealogy, even if only to distinguish themselves from it. This act of positioning is subject to a construction that is more or less conscious and assumes a form that is more or less approving (mimetic, identificatory) or critical (polemical, adversarial). The relationship to tradition generally becomes problematic in modernity, and it is this same sense of rupture with the past ("crisis") that is fundamental to modernity as a project of emancipating the subject in keeping with the philosophical ideal of the Enlightenment. Moreover, nationally and internationally available literary reference points have diversified. Since the 1960s–1970s at the latest, alternative reference points have existed alongside the institutional canon of "great works": one or more "counter-cultures," bodies of texts reflecting the preoccupations of particular groups (women, ethnic minorities, gays and lesbians, etc.). In every instance, the construction of a genealogy, beyond its importance for the self-fashioning of the writer, includes those concerns that relate to the author's positioning within the cultural field, i.e. their legitimation vis-à-vis the public and critics, "literary posture"[1] (social), and authorial ethos[2] (discursive) in accordance with the principle: "Tell me who your models are, and I'll tell you who you are." All these elements that are constitutive of authoriality imply taking reception into account as a given that determines the structure of discourse.

Among the authors who write in a context defined by the coexistence of multiple cultures within a relationship of asymmetrical power ("contact zone"[3]) and who have opted for the language of the dominant group (a "major language" according to the distinction Gilles Deleuze and Félix Guattari established[4]) while only partially identifying with that group or only feeling partially represented by it, the appropriation of the cultural heritage conveyed in that language assumes additional stakes in terms of legitimization and the construction of identity. One may recall the scandal stirred up in Germany by the polemical use of the concept of *Leitkultur* ("leading/guiding culture") in the debate on integration. The word was put forward in Europe by political scientist Bassam Tibi, initially

---

[1] For Jérôme Meizoz (2007: 18), literary "posture" is "the unique way of occupying a 'position' in the literary field" ("la manière singulière d'occuper une 'position' dans le champ littéraire").
[2] According to Ruth Amossy (1999, 2000), an authorial ethos is the image of the self an author constructs within the text in order to establish credibility; it is created instantaneously for the specific situation and develops from discourse.
[3] On this concept, see Mary Louise Pratt (1991: 34).
[4] See Deleuze and Guattari, *Kafka. Pour une littérature mineure* (1975).

within the context of the rise of Islamism, to advocate for a republican consensus on European values (*europäische Leitkultur*) as an alternative to the cultural relativism conveyed in the concept of multiculturalism. Removed from its European context, appended to the adjective *deutsch* ("German"), and presumed to represent the ultimate objective of immigrants' social integration in Germany, the term experienced great success in the decade from 2000–2010 among journalists and politicians on the right (Theo Sommer, Friedrich Merz, Norbert Lammert, Alexander Dobrindt, Thomas de Maizière). This nationalist instrumentalization roused protests on the left, while Tibi himself denounced the distorted use of the concept he had coined. This controversy, however, did not manage to hold back the resurgence in popularity experienced at the same time of the representation of Germany as a *Kulturnation* ("cultural nation"). The idea of a German cultural community preceding the political nation and transcending state and religious borders had emerged in the second half of the eighteenth century following the revival of German literature. Its resurgence in the context of the reunification reveals the loss of inhibitions in nationalist discourse in this period, including in intellectual and artistic milieus.[5]

How are we to imagine an immigrant author or one descended from immigrants being able to establish a relationship with a culture imposed on them in this manner without some reservation – particularly given that the adoption of German as the language of writing does not erase any preexisting relationship to another language and another culture? The literature of the foreign-born is the site of interaction, overlapping, and mingling of multiple (at least two) languages, mentalities, and systems of reference *par excellence*. Hence, it is the site of a fusion or a reworking that leads to what Homi K. Bhabha (1994), wanting to move past the antagonism between dominant and dominated, called "hybridization." If all writers fashion themselves within a more or less dialectic relationship to tradition, then the situation is even more complex in the case of writers who occupy a peripheral position in the literary field by dint of their ethnocultural origins. What models, what figures of identification do they choose? By contrast, which authors do they choose to differentiate themselves from and why? How do they affirm their adherence to their national culture? How do they signal their difference?

---

[5] On the recent revival of a widespread nostalgic discourse about the German nation, see Weigel (2008).

Semantic Beacons

With the Adelbert von Chamisso Prize, awarded by the Bosch Foundation from 1985 to 2017 to writers "with a non-German mother tongue" who had made a significant "contribution" to German literature,[6] these writers "from elsewhere" saw themselves assigned an ad hoc model: the French count Louis Charles Adélaïde de Chamissot de Boncourt, whose family emigrated to Germany during the Revolution and who became one of the most celebrated representatives of German Romanticism, thus attaining the status of precursor to today's authors of "migrant literature." By initiating the prize, the Romance philologist Harald Weinrich established a place within the German literary system for a category of writers whom the country's philological institutes had not – and still have not – gotten around to "integrating" naturally, a category that had only existed until then under the name of *Gastarbeiterliteratur* ("guest worker literature"), the emergence of which resulted historically from the economic immigration that began in the 1950s.

A secondary effect of the arrival in Germany of these "workers," euphemistically labeled "guests," [7] this literary production initially joined in the politically engaged tradition of German workers' literature – thus already a kind of inscription into the national patrimony. It rapidly exhausted itself in this original form of militant social witnessing; the emergence of a new generation – this time born in Germany – and the arrival of new streams of immigration following the collapse of the Soviet bloc gave birth to a literature so mixed and varied that today one can no longer define it by objective criteria, whether ethnic, linguistic, religious, or "cultural" (in the anthropological sense of the term).[8]

---

[6] This initial definition was changed in 2012 so as to emphasize the literary quality of the works rather than the ethnic background of the authors.

[7] It should be recalled that the semantics of the word *Gast* has a long history of xenophobia in the context of anti-Semitic rhetoric, starting with Luther (*Von den Juden und ihren Lügen*, 1543), revived in the late 19th century by Édouard Drumont (*La France juive*, 1886), popularized in Germany by Heinrich von Treitschke, Eduard von Hartmann, Karl Eugen Dühring and others, then culminating in 1920 with the platform of the NSDAP ("Wer nicht Staatsbürger ist, soll nur als Gast in Deutschland leben können und muß unter Fremdengesetzgebung stehen"). Derived from the medieval aliens' law, the distinction between *Gastvolk* and *Wirtsvolk* contributed to *Gast* serving, within political discourse, as a euphemistic equivalent to the words *Parasit* et *Schmarotzer*, which achieved all-too-well-known popularity in National Socialist ideology. See Alexander Bein (1965: 121–149: 128, footnote 27; 1980).

[8] See especially Williams (1958, 1961) and Schöning (2000: 9–47). Schöning relies on Ernst Cassirer's definition of culture ("Welt der Bedeutungen") and theory of communication ("Eine Kultur wird folglich von einer Sprach- und Lebensgemeinschaft verwirklicht, die hinreichend homo-

From *Gastarbeiterliteratur* – a term initially coined in a spirit of ironic provocation by the writers Franco Biondi and Rafik Schami (1981) but taken at face value in criticism and hence judged to be too stigmatizing and proletarian – terminology moved on, first to *Ausländerliteratur* ("literature by foreigners"), rapidly discarded for the same reasons, then to the rather ambiguous *Literatur der Betroffenheit* ("literature of the affected" or "literature of effusion")[9] – which, despite taking a different tack, is not any less reductive. The 1990s witnessed the emergence of the concept of *Migrantenliteratur* ("migrant literature"), which continued to highlight the writers' allochthonous status and supposed instability. It was later partially supplanted by *Migrationsliteratur* ("literature of migration"), obviously more appropriate but also more generic if it is supposed to be understood as more than a simple euphemism. After all, would such a concept not also include travel and exile literature and the work of German writers abroad?

With the desire to avoid discriminatory appellations, some critiques have retreated to differentiation by default. Harald Weinrich, the initiator of the Chamisso Prize, for example, inaugurated the scholarly reception of German literature of immigration with an anthology coedited by Irmgard Ackerman entitled *Eine nicht nur deutsche Literatur* ("A Not Only German Literature," 1986). The Germanists Manfred Durzak and Nilüfer Kuruyazıcı opted for a definition no less evasive when they spoke of *Die 'andere' deutsche Literatur* ("the 'other' German literature," 2004), thus, by affixing quotation marks to bicultural writers' work, applying a qualification used by Wolfgang Emmerich ten years earlier to designate the literature of "the other Germany": the GDR, East Germany.

Afterwards, the concepts of "intercultural" then "transcultural" literature that are still in vogue today appeared, both responding to the desire to place the "cultures" involved on the same plane. Despite this worthy intention rooted in the recognition that German society has slowly but surely become a "globalized, poly-cultural culture" (Schmitz 2009: 7), the recourse to the prefixes "inter"

---

gen und hinreichend von anderen verschieden ist und die keine Übersetzungen braucht, damit sich ihre Träger untereinander verstehen", 23).

9 The expression was coined by Schami and Biondi (1981: 124–136) in order to emphasize the solidarity linking the writers to the non-native minority and their desire to address the issues concerning this minority in particular, irrespective of any aesthetic value. The general public took up the term to designate production characterized solely as a form of testimony, to the exclusion of any other (literary) aims and hence exempt from aesthetic judgement. The concept of *Betroffenheit* thus led to a disqualification of the literature of immigrant writers by reducing it to a form of production exclusively dedicated to the expression of affliction, concern, and self-pity. See also Amodeo (2009: 6–8).

and "trans" cannot but fail to reinforce, sometimes in spite of the authors' intentions, the problematic hypothesis according to which the different cultures at play in the processes described are a priori homogenous and independent.

Finally, the rise of postcolonial studies has fostered the emergence of terms such as *hybride Literatur* ("hybrid literature") and *Literatur des Dritten Raums* ("literature of the third space").[10] The advantage of such terms is that they encourage people to reconsider the literary field's cartography in terms of power relations while not confining texts to a seemingly homogeneous corpus or limiting them to a transitory in-between. The concept of hybridity involves more than just blending: it is a process that leads to a new identity for all components. However, the use of these terms has become so commonplace that in practice they frequently stand in for an underlying ethnic categorization. This has the perverse effect of reintroducing a distinction between a Germanophone literature that is "hybrid" and another that is not. Yet the work that has been conducted since the turn of the 1990s on cultural transfers in the European region has amply demonstrated how this essentialist vision of national culture is a fiction.[11] In general terms, the restrictive use of postcolonial concepts is incompatible with recent attempts by both historians and cultural studies theorists to deconstruct the premise that national communities are culturally homogeneous. Thus, Stuart Hall (1993: 356), drawing on the historians Benedict Anderson (1983), who sees nations as "imagined communities," and Eric Hobsbawm (1983), for whom nations are cemented by "invented traditions," defines national cultures as "discourses" and as "systems of representation" that serve to represent the ethnic amalgam, from which modern nationality actually results, as the primordial unity of "a people."

Among the most global and dynamic approaches to literature "from elsewhere," let us mention the one proposed by Ottmar Ette (2005), which emerged in the wake of the spatial turn. Ette attempts to overcome territorial partitioning and the anthropological concept of culture developed by area studies in order to reposition the issue of "migrant" literatures in the broader context of *Literaturen ohne festen Wohnsitz* ("literatures without a fixed abode"). Defined as "vectorial" and "fractal" and placed under the sign of dislocation and heterotopy, "literatures without a fixed abode" are at once transcultural, trans-linguistic, and trans-areal. Though the concept proposed by Ette proves to be fruitful for analyzing and connecting texts of diverse types and origins, the heuristic interest of this

---

10 See for example Yeşilada (2012).
11 On the concept of cultural transfer, see Espagne and Werner (1988, 1994) and Espagne (1999).

transdisciplinary approach nonetheless remains limited for the analysis of the German literary field as such.

In the face of all these semantic difficulties, it is understandable that journalistic criticism has hurriedly fallen back on the label *Chamisso-Literatur* to designate *en masse* the production of writers of uncertain identity, whether or not they have actually been awarded the eponymous prize. This phenomenon elicited protests from scholars like Dieter Lamping (2011) who criticize its inclusive and essentialist aim, as if Chamisso could be considered the instigator of a genuine "tradition" of bicultural writing in Germany, or even of an ideological movement to which all subsequent bicultural writers would naturally be attached. Some of the writers in question object to such a standardization of their production and their respective cultural origins, beyond the very fact that the term confirms and perpetuates the overexposure of their allochthonous status.[12]

If the problem of denomination is so persistent in the German context, it is because it refers to the still unresolved question of what really constitutes "German literature." The existence of such a corpus brings into question the very concept of a linguistic nation, which has, of course, been important in the construction of the German nation. Otherwise, why would these texts written in the German language need a particular label? Some critics have attempted to problematize the historiographic ethnocentrism that presides over this need for demarcation between the interior and the exterior, the autochthonous and the exotic, and have deemed it necessary to relax the very definition of what "German" is in terms of literature, which means opening up the national literary field and taking account of the reality of its diversification. Elke Sturm-Trigonakis (2007) has proposed *neue Weltliteratur* ("new world literature") to reflect cultural globalization while simultaneously performing a thoughtful return to Goethe. Myriam Geiser (2014) speaks of *Literatur der Postmigration* ("postmigration literature") to refer to the new generation of authors who, according to the official formulation, have a *Migrationshintergrund* ("migration background").[13]

---

12 On the concept of *Chamisso-Literatur* and the issues it raises, see also Natalia Blum-Barth (2013).

13 The term *Migrationshintergrund* became an official category in 2005 when the Federal Statistical Office of Germany (*Statistisches Bundesamt*) began publishing data regarding "the population with a migration background" based on the microcensus, a 1% household survey with mandatory participation. The phrase is tightly bound to citizenship and summarizes a number of older ethnic categories, but also excludes Germans who immigrated shortly after the Second World War and from the former German Democratic Republic. Therefore, the label "migration background" is misleading because the definition emphasizes inherited citizenship and ancestry rather than the migration experience. It thus became yet another stigmatizing euphemism, along with *Gastarbeiter, Einwanderer, Migrant*, etc., for non-native German citizens.

It is also worth noting that a breakthrough occurred in the use of the sociological concept of *diaspora* – a Greek term that was long reserved for the history of the Jewish people and that emphasizes the culture of origin, which is seen as a center (real or imaginary) from which the "dispersal" of a given population takes place – and the English term "community," for designating minority ethnic groups. These notions, stemming from the fight for the recognition of cultural diversity in the wake of the civil rights movement in the United States, respond to a dual desire to lay claim to the ethnic identification of corpora and to resist the tendency to standardize: one can thus speak of the Turkish diaspora, the Korean diaspora, the Asian or African community, and so on. The disadvantage of this militant approach, which also responds to an undeniable social reality (stigmatization creates objective bonds), is that it leads to a new compartmentalization and even fragmentation of the national literary field into a multitude of diasporic literatures that will develop on the margin of "German literature" proper, despite the fact that all bicultural authors do not necessarily claim to belong to a community defined this way – in fact, far from it.

A few years ago, I approached the question from another angle by proposing the neologism *Germanophonie* (2012) in order to emphasize the need to rethink the contours of what is called "German literature" so as to be able to integrate these textual corpora that still have not found their place, despite their strong presence on the market, richness, and success. In other words, this emphasized the need to decentralize research within German literature. Modeled on the term *Francophonie* – itself highly problematic – the concept of *Germanophonie* was to draw attention precisely to the specificity of Germany in terms of its colonial past (which hardly left any linguistic imprint on the areas involved) and the persistent assumption of an equivalence of language, territory, and ethnicity in its definition of itself as a nation: a way of highlighting that at first glance this country, partially along with Austria – which has yet another history – thus far has only defined itself as a homogenous community both ethnically and linguistically. This was, in part, a provocation: it is obviously impossible, for these very reasons, to perceive all this behind the word *Germanophonie* (especially in German). But it was a way to question the relations between the center and the margins, between a culture that dominates and those that are subjugated, and thus to place the question of semantic classification within the political context of the asymmetrical balance of power that exists in German society at all levels. It was also a way to approach the problem from the angle of postcolonialism, a school of thought that was born in previously colonized countries and has spread over the last forty years throughout American universities under the impetus of scholars who came from the former British and French colonial empires. The vogue for postcolonial theory then spread to Europe, where it is currently flourishing, or at least appears to be, in the sense that its key concepts (hybridity, subalternity, third space, othering, writing back, etc.) have been readlily picked up by scholars from many disciplines without always being related to a global comprehension of its underlying thought.

This all-encompassing approach falls in line with quite a number of works by Germanists who, while not always explicitly assuming a postcolonial stance, have approached the production of bicultural writers in a way that differs from the first generation of scholars who were interested in the same phenomenon. Unlike the members of this first generation, who were often specialists of Romance literatures or of pedagogy relating to German as a foreign language, they considered for the first time this corpus "from within": no longer as a marginal and minor object, unusual and exotic, liable at best to make a humble contribution to national patrimony, but as a literary production in its own right that, in fact, inscribes itself within this field and is therefore able to shift the center of gravity in its entirety. It is certainly no coincidence that this new way of considering the question was inaugurated by teacher-researchers and intellectuals with foreign origins such as Immacolata Amodeo, who, in her book *Die Heimat heißt Babylon* ("The Homeland is called Babylon," 1996) draws on the concepts developed by Deleuze and Guattari (rhizome, minor literature) who – like other French thinkers such as Foucault, Bourdieu, Derrida, and Lacan – largely inspired the pioneers of postcolonialism in the context of the transfer of "French theory."

Other important work has been done by Germanists abroad, primarily in the United States. This includes Azade Seyhan's seminal work *Writing outside the Nation* (2001) and, most importantly, Leslie A. Adelson's critical study *The Turkish Turn in Contemporary German Literature. Toward a New Critical Grammar of Migration* (2005), which assesses the historical, aesthetic, and political issues of German literature of Turkish migration after 1989. A specialist in German minority literatures, Adelson draws significantly on work from the postcolonial school and from gender studies. This is also the case for the Comparatist Liesbeth Minnaard (Leiden University), who works on migration literature that is primarily German and Dutch (2008).

Lastly, it is necessary to mention the numerous reflective texts published in recent years in Germany by authors who take a critical, lucid, and nuanced look at the situation in the country and the way in which public debate is conducted on socio-ethnic issues (integration of ethnic minorities, Islam, conflict of cultures, etc.): essays like those by Zafer Şenocak (1992, 2006, 2012) and Navid Kermani (2009, 2012b), or even popular treaties like the one co-signed by Ilija Trojanow and the English-speaking Indian critic Ranjit Hoskoté under the title *Kampfabsage: Kulturen bekämpfen sich nicht, sie fließen zusammen* ("Truce: Cultures Don't Clash; They Intermingle," 2007). For some time, it has been possible to see a flourishing in various traditional disciplines (literary studies, political and social sciences, study of religions, etc.) of various works situated in this anti-culturalist and anti-essentialist movement, inspired in some way by cultural studies and postcolonial studies. This trend is firmly established in Germany now that many universities have created entire departments devoted to intercultural studies.

For the purposes of the present investigation, I will provisionally use the term "migration literature" to designate this body of works defined by its inclusion within a national literary field where its reception from the outset is determined by its grounding in an "other" context. Applying one of the numerous terms already in use for discussing minority literatures serves to acknowledge the fact that it would be vain to introduce yet another designation to describe literary productions characterized most saliently as "othered" due to their authors' immigration backgrounds. If the ethnocultural origin of writers is indeed relevant to the way they attain their position in the field, the importance such an origin assumes for their writing does not so much result from their personal trajectory (immigrants or not, for how long, and under what conditions), nor from the perception they have of themselves and their level of acculturation (are they "more" this or that), but rather the public's expectations of them and the place assigned to them from the outside in the national intellectual field, according to their origins. Whether or not a writer is "immigrant," "refugee," "migrant," or "post-migrant" is thus not of interest in this context; however, if we want to get a real understanding of the texts, we must instead consider whether the works testify to one position or another with regard to institutional codes, from a point of view defined (by themselves, by their competitors, or by the institution) as that of a minority in the national context.

In this approach to the question, the distinctive criterion separating "migration literature" from other bodies of works does not reside in the biography of the authors, but in the type of literature they produce: a category of texts indistinguishable from the national mainstream in terms of thematic constants (including migration, uprootedness, and exile, for example), by a style of writing or peculiar (i.e. more or less "deviant") uses of language, or even by a framework of exogenous cultural references, but rather first and foremost by the place it occupies in the field by virtue of its perception as being partially exogenous. In other words, the aim is not to endorse the classification of one part of German literature – which is by no means homogeneous – as "peripheral," but noting that some authors are confronted with their origins more than others and in different ways, and that there is a need to (re)negotiate their relation to the canon, according to a line of questioning that could be formulated as follows: do the works praised by the institution as timeless classics also represent me, an Arab Christian from Syria / Turkish Muslim feminist / son of immigrant workers / Japanese expatriate, etc.? To what extent can I adhere to values whose fetishization attests to a supposed universality, and to what extent can I – or can I not – inscribe my own writing into their development?

The Canon Question

The question that concerns us here, that of the construction of a literary filiation in the German field against the backdrop of migration, has barely occupied scholars' attention to this day, which is all the more surprising given that reflections on the canon, its hegemonism, ethnocentrism, its impact on subjugated and minority cultures, its revision, renovation, etc., form the core of the preoccupations that undergird postcolonialism as a theory and practice. While Germanists may still be struggling to move past the schismatic opposition of colonized and colonizer in their approach to relationships of domination in literature, the writers themselves have been sketching much more complex and ambiguous configurations in their works for a long time now. It thus appears fruitful, even necessary, to mix the conceptual tools developed within the framework of postcolonial studies with the analytical methods that have proven their worth in the traditional disciplines (literary hermeneutics, semiotics, sociology, philosophy, aesthetics, history, anthropology, psychoanalysis, cultural studies, etc.) in order to represent the literary treatment of questions such as identity and alterity, cultural memory and tradition, the social construction of the subject, the canon, the nation, etc. Studies carried out in Anglophone fields demonstrate the fecundity of such approaches, as in Monika Reif-Hülser's work *Fremde Texte als Spiegel des Eigenen. Postkoloniale Literaturen und ihre Auseinandersetzung mit dem kulturellen Kanon* ("Foreign Texts as a Mirror of one's own. Postcolonial Literatures and their Conflict with the Cultural Canon," 2006) – combining the concepts developed by Wolfgang Iser, Hans-Robert Jauß, Bernard Waldenfels, Jürgen Habermas, Walter Benjamin, Michel Foucault, Jacques Derrida, Jan and Aleida Assmann among others – devoted to the rewriting of the canon in Anglophone postcolonial literature.

To date, no comparable study exists for the Germanophone world. At best, one could cite the study by Petra Fachinger (2001) entitled *Rewriting Germany from the Margins: "Other" German Literature of the 1980s and 1990s*, which takes an intertextual and "counter-discursive" approach to different categories of minority literatures in the Germany of the 1980s: feminist literature (B. Frischmuth, Hanne Mede-Flock), the new Jewish-German literature of the second generation post-Shoah (Barbara Honigmann, Lea Fleischmann, Richard Chaim Schneider), post-GDR literature (Thomas Brussig, Kerstin Jentzsch), and literature of immigration or related to immigration (Franco Biondi, Akif Prinçci, Zehra Çirak, José F. A. Oliver, Feridun Zaimoglu). The present study, drawing inspiration from postcolonial theory and forging links to similar discursive strategies tested in other national contexts, demonstrates the utility of a transnational approach for apprehending literature "from the margins" – which in Germanophone contexts here, as elsewhere in the world, appears as a privileged space of empowerment. One might likewise mention the dissertation Maha El Hissy defended in 2010 in Munich concentrating on the "carnivalesque" mode in the contemporary cultural products of German-Turkish artists. Focused specifically on the performing arts (theater, cinema, political cabaret, and comedy), this work, which rests on the Bakhtinian notions of polyphony and the carnivalesque, the theory devised by Bhabha for approaching subversive writing strategies in the postcolonial field (mimicry, trickster, hybridity, etc.), as well as the concept of "gender performativity" developed by Judith Butler, places a particular emphasis on comic subversion and parody. El Hissy demonstrates, much like Fachinger, the pertinence of concepts developed within the frame of postcolonial studies for approaching minority literatures in Germany, notably in their rapport with German literary tradition.

In order to explain why such approaches still remain marginal in the context of Germanic studies, it might be tempting to invoke the relative insignificance of the body of German texts that support this type of analysis. Such a hypothesis, however, does not stand up to even a superficial scrutiny of the last thirty years' literary production. On the contrary, from SAID to Navid Kermani via Galsan Tschinag, Kemal Kurt, Emine S. Özdamar, Yoko Tawada, Feridun Zaimoglu, Zafer Şenocak, and many others, bicultural authors draw sustained attention to both the national and international canon, and a number of them carved out a lasting place for their works in a productive dialogue with the "great authors." Granted, they do not always do so as confrontationally as their Anglophone and Francophone colleagues. Hence, one would search in vain for a German counterpart to literary ripostes as explicit and targeted as Jean Rhys's *Wide Sargasso Sea* (1966, based on Charlotte Brontë's *Jane Eyre*) or J. M. Coetzee's *Foe* (1986, a rewriting of Daniel Defoe's *Robinson Crusoe*) – to cite merely two of the numerous rewritings that have themselves become "classics" in the postcolonial context – or, to take a more recent example from the Francophone context, the novel *Meursault, contre-enquête* ("Meursault, Counter-Inquiry", 2013; Engl. trans. *The Meursault Investigation*, 2015), a response to Camus's *L'Étranger* "The Stranger" by Algerian writer and journalist Kamel Daoud. Nevertheless, this difference between the German literary corpus and those of English and French warrants examination with textual support, both in terms of its literary modalities and aims, its strategies and stakes.

The relative isolation of works like those of Fachinger and El Hissy thus seems to confirm that the lack of interest in these questions evinced by the German and French Germanists does not arise so much from the paucity of the available corpus as from a more or less deliberate sidelining of this field of research. Clearly, the pertinence of the postcolonial paradigm for Germanophone space has yet to establish itself in continental Germanic studies. There are very different reasons for this on the one side of the Rhine and the other. In France, the academic reception of postcolonial theories is the object of a knee-jerk "theoretical bristling" (Baneth-Nouailhetas 2009: 25) that renders these voices practically "inaudible" (Joubert 2009: 154), at least outside the disciplines where their institutionalization on an international scale has made them more or less incontrovertible (English and comparative literary studies, anthropology, history, geopolitics). In Germany, on the other hand, where postcolonial theory enjoys great popularity, it is all the more striking to note the persistent reticence of researchers to apply the postcolonial framework to works by ethnic minorities situated in the national territory – as if the relations of domination existing within German society between the nation's "center" and "margins" were inaccessible per se to this type of approach. Arguably, this is for historical reasons: the German colonial empire, of course, ceased to exist in 1918, and the immigrant populations of today come largely from territories that were either never colonized by the West (Turkey) or were colonized by powers other than Germany (France, Great Britain, the Netherlands, etc.). This argument is nevertheless just as weak when one considers, firstly, that postcolonial theorists themselves never claimed to limit their approach to a single geopolitical configuration (that corresponding to colonialism in the stricter sense) and above all that this narrow definition of the postcolonial investigative field has not stopped a number of Germanists in Germany over the past few years from exploring – increasingly and profitably – native corpora from an ethnographic angle reflective of the colonial condition.[14] All of which draws attention to the blind spot in current German studies research on German soil surrounding the perceived relevance of a postcolonial approach, in the larger sense of the term, to the literature of non-natives. For our part, it seems – and this is what motivates the present study – that it is not only justified but necessary to apprehend the texts of certain German writers through the post-

---

14 See, for instance, Uerlings and Patrut (2011), Beck (2011), and Osthues (2017). To date, only Diallo and Göttsche have sought to broaden the scope of investigation with their work *Interkulturelle Texturen. Afrika und Deutschland im Reflexionsmedium* der *Literatur* (2003).

colonial prism if one wants to comprehend how, why, and to what end(s) they situate themselves with reference to the literary canon.

By that we mean that even the possibility of a counter-discourse,[15] a modality in postcolonial configurations favored for what has been called the appropriation of the canon, constitutes a heuristic hypothesis permitting an approach to immigrant authors writing in German from the angle of their own strategic concerns, namely in terms of legitimation and positioning (ideological and textual) in the national intellectual milieu. This hypothesis in no way prejudges the results that might arise from such research. The fact that some writers question the canon does not mean that they reject or contest it, merely that they are interrogating the criteria of selection that guided its construction and, in the cases that interest us, doing so from the nation's margins – that is, from the point of view of those who until now have not had any say in the matter because they were "the other," the object of discourse. It is a matter of historicizing the process of canonization in order to make a confrontation with the texts themselves possible, stripped of the aura of universality a tendentious and normative "tradition" has conferred on them.

This critical reevaluation of the canon might perfectly well lead to a *reinforcement* of the subjective link to this or that "great work." It is precisely this renewed link to tradition, understood as a critical bond against a backdrop of calculated detachment, that is at play in the act of appropriation. The diffusion of postcolonial critique has had the effect of overexposing the polemical dimension of this process of renegotiation to the detriment of its approbative dimension. In fact, even in the postcolonial context, the authors most "rewritten" (Shakespeare, Defoe, Conrad, Jane Austen, Charlotte Brontë) are not exactly the most cartoonishly xenophobic or imperialist of the colonial era, far from it. It is rather their semantic complexity that makes them interesting for the former subjects of empire to confront. Ultimately, a number of postcolonial texts testify instead to a prevailing adherence to the canon over its subversion, and it is not at all certain that this nuanced position, the polar opposite of the iconoclasm in the works most readily studied in postcolonial critique (like those of Salman Rushdie), must be systematically interpreted as a sign of alienation and blind submission to authority.[16]

It is on the basis of these premises that we propose to examine the conditions, forms, and issues of the work to (de)construct the canon as it is carried

---

15 On the concept of (postcolonial) counter-discourse, see especially Helen Tiffin (1987).
16 On this frequently overlooked aspect of Anglophone postcolonial literature, see especially Girardin and Whyte (2014).

out by the representatives of that German literature we call, for lack of a better word and conscious of the limits of every act of naming, "migration literature." In doing so, we have deliberately chosen to concentrate on those authors coming from countries that find themselves in a distinctly asymmetric relationship of power with Germany and that are seen by majoritarian society as problematic, e.g. Turkey, Iran, and the Arab states. In truth, it is in this configuration, more so than in the context of immigration from Southern and Eastern Europe, that the question of the minority position presents itself with greater insistence because it is there that rejection and marginalization are the most virulent in society for both ethnic and religious reasons. For our primary corpus, we will present three of the most representative authors in this subcategory of migration literature: Emine Sevgi Özdamar, Rafik Schami, and Feridun Zaimoglu. Aside from these three principal authors whose work we will examine using several examples chosen with regards to the connection they establish with the Western, and especially the German, literary canon, our analysis will also draw support from a number of texts – fiction, essays, poems, articles, speeches – from other authors such as Zafer Şenocak, Navid Kermani, SAID, Yoko Tawada, Galsan Tschinag, Kemal Kurt, and Akif Pirinçci, which will help put its findings into perspective.

Methodologies

We thus set out in search of footprints. By noting the traces left in literary and paraliterary texts by readings and hints of a response or an homage – citations, allusions, pastiches, parodies and other intertextual references, which we think of as so many signposts in the charting of these authors' literary projects – we will endeavor to uncover the modalities according to which a literary genealogy develops within the specific conditions of migration literature in the German language.

From a methodological point of view, this investigation largely draws inspiration from the typology of hypertextual practices established by Gérard Genette for "literature in the second degree" in his foundational work *Palimpsestes* ("Palimpsests," 1982). However, this internal approach to texts fits into the more expansive context of studies conducted on relationships to the canon in the postcolonial field and clears significant space for questions of ideological and strategic positioning. In this respect, analysis of the processes of textual derivation finds support in notions issuing from literary sociology: notably, it is useful to consider the literary field (Bourdieu) as a space structured by positions that mutually define each other and by means of which writers *likewise* situate themselves in presenting their reinterpretation of a canonical text. To the extent that the structure of an intertextual reference responds to specific concerns (legitimation, acknowledgment, demarcation, polemic, etc.), the choices authors make in this regard are bound together with their battle to impose themselves on the field and thus with their literary "posture" (Meizoz 2007). These choices likewise participate in the construction of a more-or-less-internal *discourse* that constitutes what one could call, following Dominique Maingueneau (1993, 1999) and Ruth Amossy (1999, 2010), an author's discursive ethos, the totality of values by which they demonstrate belonging.

Thus, attention will be focused on the purpose, that is to say the semantic concerns of cultural appropriation these interventions represent, rather than on the nature of what they accomplish. In this sense, studying work on the canon in migration literature presents certain similarities with the method articulated by Michel Espagne and Michael Werner for analyzing transfers between different cultural spaces (national and/or linguistic/ ethnic/ religious). By declining to operate with the classic comparative categories (facile analogy and uncovering "sources" and "influences," categories that postulate the original's superiority over the copy), the theory of cultural transfer approaches the reception of texts, of knowledge, and of ideas in terms of importation, adaptation, and re-interpretation. From this perspective, the accent is placed on the context of reception more so than the context of production, and it becomes a question of appreciating the semantic transformations that occur during the passage from one code to another. Our approach espouses this point of view, with the proviso that, here, the dynamics of translation and re-semantization operate apart from any spatial circulation. At most, immigration is a background datapoint in the trajectory of authors who write texts in German on German soil destined for the German market – but from a cultural horizon that defines itself in part, at least, by its foreign character within the national context. The presence of references to the national literary canon (which includes the "international," i.e. essentially the Western, canon) in these texts can therefore be understood essentially as *intra*cultural importation on the part of authors who consider the context within and for which they write through the prism of a partial extraneity (more or less assigned).

Such an approach defies spatialized representations of borders between cultures and relations between "center" and "periphery." The notion of center – already largely relativized from the perspective of cultural transfers – is definitively emptied of meaning the moment the point of departure and the point of arrival for importation become identical. The same is true for the idea that literary creation originates, in principle and quasi-naturally, in a tradition inscribed within the confines of a given (national, religious, ethnic, cultural) territory. From this study's perspective, there are only constructed traditions, as much through intermixing as through "invention" (Hobsbawm and Ranger 1983), and the idea of spatial identity (of cultural "roots") yields the field to rhizomatic representation of transmission. Granted, deterritorialization/ reterritorialization, in the sense Deleuze and Guattari (1980) gave this conceptual pair, enters as a factor in the process of cultural appropriation as this study construes it, but there the question is of an abstract spatiality, as it were, which inserts itself into "spatial thinking" largely detached from geography and reconfigured "in the category of the discrete, the disjointed" (Regnauld 2012: 199).

Taking all of these parameters into account relativizes up to a certain point the formal distinctions between the different types of hypertextual derivation. In fact, as Paul Aron (2013: 23) remarks, in a work dedicated to mimetic practices in international exchanges, from the moment wherein "that which is at issue concerns itself less with formal principles than the complex realities of the production and reception of texts," it is no longer necessarily essential "to identify the differences between transformation and imitation." It thus suffices to adjust one's theoretical tools to the evolution of practices and notably, when dealing with writers whose situation forces them to renegotiate their position regarding an institutionalized literary corpus, to give up describing in minute detail the relationship between a canonical text and one or multiple new text(s) that is/are partially derived from it in order to focus more attention on the reference's goals and *raisons d'être.*

It is within this context that the present work situates itself, studying the modalities of the canon's inscription within the works of the present corpus, following an approach that crosses narratological analysis with the concepts elaborated in other fields of knowledge like sociology of literature, discourse analysis, the study of cultural transfers, and anthropology. In this manner, the present work endeavors to demonstrate that productive dialogue with the canon, such as that which develops within the configuration of migration literature, is undergirded by the specific concerns that form it into a means for positioning oneself within the field and a particularly apt argument in support of an ethical and political discourse. As Lise Gauvin (2013) observes: "If writing is always in some manner rewriting the world and its literature, one can reverse the statement and say that rewriting is also *writing* in the first degree, reinventing literature and its models, even making itself a model in the infinite chain of texts that make up the global library."[17] It is to this process of generating a "global library"

---

[17] "Si écrire est toujours, de quelque façon, réécrire le monde et sa littérature, on peut renverser la proposition et dire que réécrire est aussi *écrire,* au premier degré, réinventer la littérature et ses modèles, voire se constituer en modèle dans la chaîne infinie des textes qui constituent la bibliothèque mondiale" (Gauvin 2013: 15).

that *Questioning the Canon* turns to by examining the ways in which canonical literary texts have been reread and reworked by authors of German migration literature.

Presentations of Main Authors

Emine Sevgi Özdamar and Rafik Schami are members of the first generation of post-war immigrants to become writers in German. Both born in 1946, they arrived in Germany in the 1960s at the beginning of their adult lives, fleeing dictatorships in their respective countries and finding better living and working conditions in a democratic society. They were both engaged in Marxist movements, first in their countries of origin then in Germany, and worked for a time as laborers before turning to an artistic profession. Both originally from the Muslim world, they are, nevertheless, in a minority position even within the immigrant population.

Rafik Schami who was, along with Franco Biondi, one of the pioneers of *Gastarbeiterliteratur* in the 1980s, comes from Syria's Christian minority and received a traditional Western education in an establishment run by Greco-Catholic monks in Lebanon. As a student in Damascus studying French and English, he immersed himself in contemporary Western literature early on before exiling himself to Europe to escape military service and the repressive regime in Syria. He first aimed for France, but it was Germany that accepted him in 1971. Thus, he settled in, learned German, and worked as a laborer before resuming his studies in chemistry, from which he graduated with a doctorate in 1979. At the same time, he began a work of literature in German composed essentially of short prose pieces centered first and foremost on the situation of immigrant workers in Germany and the problematics of exclusion particular to the German society of the "economic miracle." His activist engagement alongside workers and outcasts gave way in his writing little by little to a growing focus on "bicultural" thematics (German – Syrian; Occident – "Arabia"), then to a re-centering of his literary universe upon the Syria of the 1950s. Since 1982, the success of his books, some of which are meant for an audience of children and adolescents, has allowed him to make his living solely from writing.

For her part, the actor and novelist Emine Sevgi Özdamar, like the majority of immigrants living on German soil, comes from a country linking Europe and Asia that, though never colonized, has nevertheless long found itself in an underdeveloped and dependent situation vis-à-vis the Western world and Germany in particular: Turkey. As a woman coming from the Westernized urban bourgeoisie, a non-practicing Muslim steeped in Kemalist secularism, Özdamar corresponds no more than Schami to the stereotype of an immigrant from the "(Middle) East," i.e. an uneducated, usually male, worker of rural origins. Her double mooring in the worlds of literature and live performance distinguishes her even more with regards to the other immigrant writers of her generation. All these biographical elements occupy a central place in her work, which consists essentially of novels and short stories that retrace, on various levels and in various modes, her own trajectory as a woman and immigrant (at once worker, engaged intellectual, theatrical performer, and feminist) at the crossroads of a story of emancipation, a picaresque novel, and the nostalgic quest for one's origins.

Despite the atypical profiles of these two authors, or perhaps rather because of them, the works of Schami and Özdamar have both achieved brilliant success in Germany as well as abroad. Translated into several languages, they represent the object of study at a growing number of universities. In this manner, Rafik Schami has managed to carve out a fitting place for himself in the German literary field at the intersection of several seemingly opposite poles: political literature (sub-field of limited production), what gets called "foreigner" literature (niche within the culturally dominated pole, but which in becoming "literature of migration" and then "intercultural literature" is gaining more and more in institutional recognition and visibility), young adult and children's literature (its own domain, characterized by the contrast between its wide readership and limited prestige among peers and institutions), and finally mass market "Orientalizing" literature (sub-field of the culturally dominant bloc). His immense popular success rests essentially on his reputation as an "Oriental storyteller" and as a promoter of "intercultural dialogue" between Germany and the Arab world.

Despite utilizing radically different literary techniques, to a certain extent Özdamar also turned her Eastern origins and her status as a "cultural intermediary" into a brand. Her texts take a more difficult tack from the start and meet with a more modest commercial reception, but they have been awarded numerous prizes and arouse, much more than Schami's, a keen interest in intellectual and academic milieus, where they are readily interpreted according to a postcolonial framework. However, like Schami, Özdamar is part of that generation of Easterners inspired by Edward Said, who embarked on the path of an "anti-Orientalist Orientalizer."[18] This common background exposes them to the reproach, expressed by a number of their peers, of giving in to the ease of complacent exoticist writing well-suited to feeding the German public's worst clichés

---

[18] I borrow this expression from historian and Arabist Bernard Heyberger (EHESS), who coined it to describe Schami's position in his referee report for Ellerbach's 2014 doctoral thesis "L'Arabie contée aux Allemands: Fictions interculturelles chez Rafik Schami" (unpublished source).

in matters of Orientalism ("Uncle Tom literature" according to Maxim Biller, 2014).

The third author of this work's primary corpus, Feridun Zaimoglu, belongs to the second generation of immigrants coming from Turkey. Born in 1964, he came from a working-class background and arrived in Germany at the age of one with his parents, who had been recruited as immigrant workers for subaltern labor. As a journalist and writer, he gained renown in 1995 thanks to *Kanak Sprak. 24 Mißtöne vom Rande der Gesellschaft* ("Kanak Speak. 24 Discordant Notes from the Margins of Society"), a collection of monologues shining a light on young Turkish-Germans relegated to the margins of society. This book-manifesto, the immense success of which went a long way towards revealing the creative potential hitherto unsuspected of the "post-migration" generation, established his reputation as an *enfant terrible* in German letters. No less recognized than his two literary elders by the public and critics, he poses the interesting case of a writer simultaneously activist (in 1998, he cofounded the movement *Kanak Attak*, which fights against racism and defends immigrants' rights to assert themselves politically and culturally), happily adopting an iconoclastic posture with regards to his own camp (he defends wearing the hijab and embraces his Muslim faith), but simultaneously determined to be recognized as a "serious" author. Considered from the start as the "Malcolm X of German Turks" (Lottmann 1997), Zaimoglu has bit by bit established himself as one of the most noteworthy figures in the whole German literary field. This visibility is due in part to the provocative potential of his texts, in part to his divisive, and sometimes contradictory, public stances, and in part to his strong media presence as well. Zaimoglu, who tellingly eliminated the breve on the ğ of his Turkish patronym (the unpronounced "soft g," which lengthens the preceding vowel[19]), asserts his German cultural identity and refuses to be classified as a representative of a minority literature.[20] He equally, and more clearly than his two elders, keeps his distance from any exoticism. Like them, he has indeed succeeded up to a certain point in emancipating himself from the sub-field of the literature of immigration, which nevertheless helped him secure his standing in his early career.

In the first chapter, I define what the term "canon" entails within the postcolonial framework of this study and propose an initial classification of different degrees of canonical status. In the second chapter, I turn to various modalities of discourse on the canon, using a narratological framework, and set the concep-

---

[19] Some critics fail to respect this choice. I will use the spelling preferred by the author throughout this study and the spelling *Zaimoğlu* will appear only in quotes where it is originally used.

[20] See especially the interview "Ich bin ein begeisterter Deutscher" (Zaimoglu 2008b).

tual framework for my case studies. The following chapters are devoted to close analyses of works by each of the three main authors of my Germanophone corpus so as to shed light on the forms, functions, and values of canonical references in their respective texts. Along the way, I will also address issues of gender and class in relation to ethnoracial differences, in the fabric of characters, and will approach various modes of re-creation of the canonical hypotexts: change of genre, intermedial and performative adaptations, and parody, among other modes of transposition.

PART I **The Forms and Foci of Canon Critique**

Chapter 1
Postcolonialism and the Canon

> "Literary history is the great morgue where everyone seeks his dead, those whom he loves and to whom he is related."
> Henrich Heine (1833)[1]

Reflection on the literary canon, understood as the collection of texts that constitute the cultural patrimony of a given community as it is passed on by scholarly, academic, and cultural institutions, initially falls to those who do not feel themselves represented by this communal corpus: firstly women and ethnic minorities, i.e. African-American descendants of the enslaved in the US, immigrant populations throughout the Western world composed essentially of former colonial subjects, and finally sexual minorities such as those in the LGBTQ+ community. Starting at the end of the 1970s, these population groups designated as minorities brought the problem of the representation of minorities in schools and on the literary market to the surface in Anglo-Saxon universities. They could not identify with either the subject of discourse presented in the texts taught, i.e. the white Western male who held economic, institutional, and symbolic power, or its object, in which they found themselves described with the traits of the absolute Other, at once provoking fear, fascination, contempt, and revulsion.[2]

Reread through the eyes of former colonial subjects, of the descendants of the enslaved, of oppressed women – that is, of every individual situated in a position of inferiority in relation to the supremacy of the white Western male – the text that formed the object of general consensus, thus revealed themselves to constitute an exclusive normative discourse whatever the grand ethical, humanist, or republican values they otherwise embodied. What was called into question by this reading "against the grain" from the point of view of the excluded and dominated was the pretension of canonical authors to represent the whole of humanity, moreover, the aptitude to do so attributed to them by institutions.

---

[1] "Die Literaturgeschichte ist die große Morgue wo jeder seine Toten aufsucht, die er liebt und womit er verwandt ist" (Heine 1976: V, 373; trans. Charles G. Leland, London: Heinemann, 1892, 260).

[2] For this presentation of the "postcolonial turn" in literary studies, I draw heavily on Bardolph's analysis (2002).

In the academic world, the first texts indicted in this manner were those that directly addressed the confrontation with the Other: travel literature of the colonial period as well as ethnological studies and the works of art inspired by these voyages. The work that comparatist Edward Said, originally from Palestine, devoted to Orientalism in 1978 became the foundational reference for postcolonial studies. Relying on a critical analysis of texts by Nerval, Flaubert, Maupassant, Daudet, Byron, and Conrad among others; the operas of Verdi, Mozart, and Beethoven; the films of Rudolph Valentino, etc., Said affirms that the "Orient" is a fiction created by the West and demonstrates that the colonizer's discourse, in depicting the dominated as the ultimate Other and in constructing it as an object of knowledge, at once justifies and exercises power. Literary works contribute, just as scientific treatises do, to reinforcing and extending the domination of socio-economic institutions and even governments over subjugated peoples: in representing a culturally backwards East, archaic and degenerate, cruel, barbarous, or lascivious, writers validate and strengthen the economic, military, and religious stranglehold on these territories. The history, anthropology, and literature constructed for intellectually understanding the colonies are cultural productions with real historical power, and the vision of the "Orient" that resulted is extensive and coherent, though without any connection to extra-linguistic reality. The East described in these documents is an object, never a subject of its own discourse. Said underlines how the East has endured as a spectacle, even after decolonization, for the West. Although the tone has changed and many of the texts of that era appear caricaturish with distance, most of the stereotypes remain. Part of Said's goal is thus to explain how this power dynamic persisted, and to chase the traces of Orientalist representations out of contemporary discourse. Undergirded by Foucault's work on "the order of discourse," Said's study rests on a project of awareness: the aim is to bring to light, in a constant back-and-forth between the past and present, what today's world is made of and what representations we have of it. This epistemological and hermeneutic project doubles as a political project. By means of this awareness, the long-term objective is to break away from the power dynamic between "the West" and "the Rest," that is to say: to leave behind the colonial paradigm.

It is for this second point that Said is most often attacked by his successors. They, beginning with Bhabha, do not question *Orientalism*'s presuppositions and likewise approve of its anti-establishment aims, but they point to the reductive aspect of an analysis that reveals itself to be, on the whole, incapable of transcending the binary vision instilled by colonialism. By imputing the entire responsibility for the problems inherited from colonialism to "the West" (just as monolithic and undifferentiated a concept in its way as the "Orient"), Said ultimately did nothing more, in their eyes, than comfort formerly colonized peoples in their victimhood. To free themselves from the mental framework imposed by the former "centers" of the colonial world, however, they would have to adopt a point of view that permitted them to think differently about alterity. This is what Bhabha first attempted to do in 1994 with *The Location of Culture* by indicating that the relationship between the colonized and the colonizing culture is not one-way but rather dialectic. Thence Bhabha developed a theory of "hybridity," which pays as much attention to the role of imitation among the colonized ("mimicry," the art of copying as strategic duplicity) as to the transformation the colonizer undergoes in turn from contact with the foreign country. According to Bhabha, this reciprocal influence gives rise to the desire to change and permits the relationship to evolve; the ambivalent intimacy between the colonizer and colonized opens a hybrid space, an "in-between-space" or "third space" where forms of resistance are discovered. The analysis Bhabha performs on stereotypes in the colonial and neocolonial discourse sheds a light on the ambivalent, fundamentally unstable, and precarious character of the colonial identity and its hegemonic pretensions. These reflections thus present the basis of an ethnological critique of the West.

Another American scholar from the Indian subcontinent, Gayatri Chakravorty Spivak, has attempted to develop a concept of "subalternity" inspired by Antonio Gramsci's theory of cultural hegemony. A Marxist and disciple of Derrida, Spivak pursues the analyses inaugurated by Said and Bhabha from a perspective at once more political and more feminist. In particular, she insists on the disparities that exist even within post-colonial spaces and on the gap that separates the intellectual elites from the truly "subaltern" social strata (peasants and paupers), but even more so from the lower-class women subjected at once to imperialist power and that of the colonized men. *Can the Subaltern Speak?* Spivak asks in the title of her now most famous work published in 1988. The answer is: no. Poor women of formerly colonized countries do not have access to the subject position claimed by postcolonial writers.

What is at stake in postcolonial studies and, beyond them, in the cultural practices of the places concerned, is precisely the question of knowing how to transcend that incapacity to speak, how to leave the position of object to attain dignity, a voice, and "agency" (another key concept in postcolonial studies) as a free and sovereign subject. Owing to the inherent schizophrenia of the colonized position,[3] this reappropriation of the status of subject comes by way of a confrontation with the interiorized colonizing discourse. Precolonial "purity," a hypo-

---

[3] On the diagnostic category of schizophrenia as a reading of colonization, see Frantz Fanon's essay *Peau noire, masques blancs* (1952).

thetical state of innocence supposed to predate colonization, cannot be reconstituted. Postcolonial creators must therefore invent new strategies, e. g. defining the contours of the dominant discourse by exposing its presuppositions and mechanisms, dismantling that discourse, and destroying it. In the literary domain, this happens by means of work on the "canon" by which the postcolonial writers are simultaneously nourished, notably through scholarly institutions, and dispossessed of their proper cultural identity. The fourth foundational work in postcolonial studies, a book-manifesto published in 1989 by Bill Ashcroft, Gareth Griffiths, and Helen Tiffin entitled *The Empire Writes Back*, is dedicated to such responses. In order to detail the strategies of resistance from the periphery against the center, the authors analyze several texts that serve as an example from this perspective: the re-readings of Shakespeare's *Tempest* by Caribbean or Australian authors who adopt the point of view of Caliban, the rewriting of *Robinson Crusoe* by South African author J. M. Coetzee from the point of view of a woman and taking for its true hero a Friday with his tongue cut out (*Foe*, 1986). These texts are *responses*, at once analytical and polemical, to Shakespeare and Defoe.

"Re-reading" and "re-writing": these intertextual procedures are at the core of literary creation in the postcolonial context. Contrary to the ludic forms of intertextuality that developed in the Western world as an effect of "anything goes" 1980s postmodernism, there is nothing gratuitous about these practices. Quite the opposite: for postcolonial subjects, like for women in Western countries, rewriting the canon is a question of survival.[4] Born of the need to establish oneself as subject, these discursive techniques distinguish themselves from the postmodern game by their political and dialectic character; they are essentially subversive modalities of writing. As Jacqueline Bardolph notes, there is a radical opposition between the postcolonial approach founded on the conquest of agency, "the subject's assumption of responsibility for the collective future," and the "pessimistic but impotent contemplation of contemporary disorder," which nourishes postmodernism. The postmodern, Bardolph adds,

> places the problem of representation at the heart of production, favoring the metafictional and reflexivity in works while the postcolonial is ultimately seeking a representation better suited to the awareness that would enable social change. Postcolonial theory as a whole refutes the postmodern vision of cultural mixing as too close to the dominant consensus,

---

[4] As Adrienne Rich noted in the early 1970s, "Re-vision – the act of looking back, of seeing with fresh eyes, of entering an old text from a new critical direction – is for women more than a chapter in cultural history: it is an act of survival" (1972: 18).

which causes the discourse on multiculturalism to slip into a demobilizing cultural relativism.[5]

For writers in the postcolonial context, working on the canon is thus working on history, in the sense that it consists of (re)reading the texts of a past wherein they find themselves represented, but not from their own point of view. The critical, corrective reading of these texts is a means of responding to the other's pretensions of domination and so of re-appropriating one's own history. This work has nothing to do with strategies of integration or acculturation. Nor is it reducible, contrary to the image one might glean from its detractors like Harold Bloom (1994), to a simple repudiation: one does not take the time to "retort" in like manner to texts unless one thinks their impact withstands the test of time, that is, unless deep down one recognizes their authority, even beyond the fact that they have been perverted by institutions as instruments of domination. It is a matter precisely of historicizing the very process of canonization to make possible a confrontation with the text itself, stripped of the aura of universality that confers on it a tendentious and normative "tradition."

Theorizing the Canon

The concept of a canon implies a dialectic rapport between permanence and evolution, inclusion and exclusion, and the universal and particular. Considered as a selective corpus of texts withdrawn from the historicity of thought and human endeavors, the canon is itself subject to the evolution of taste, values, and representations. "The canon is nothing other than a list of enduring works, or what are supposed to be," Jean-Jacques Lecercle notes (2006: 11). This claim of resisting time is nevertheless regularly reevaluated within literary history with a mind toward updating the canonical corpus, which was explicitly prescriptive for centuries, without the ethical and aesthetic bases of the normative apparatus provoking discussion. At the end of the twentieth century, however, following the unprecedented acceleration of the rhythm with which literary movements succeeded each other after the turn of the nineteenth century (al-

---

5 "Le postmoderne met au cœur des productions le problème de la représentation, favorisant le métafictionnel et la réflexivité de l'œuvre, alors que le postcolonial cherche finalement une représentation plus adaptée à la prise de conscience qui permettrait le changement social. La théorie postcoloniale dans son ensemble réfute la vision post-moderne du mélange des cultures comme trop proche du consensus dominant qui fait glisser le discours sur le multiculturel à un relativisme culturel démobilisateur" (Bardolph 2002: 47).

ways in more or less stark opposition to the aesthetic norms prevailing until then), consciousness of the canon's relativity and the questions raised by its malleability and subjectivity began to take hold – so much so that, as Fabrice Malkani, Anne-Marie Saint-Gille, and Ralf Zschachlitz argue, "archetypical forms of research into canonical truths gave way to conceptions of truth in progress" (2007: 526). This outcome, corroborated by the work of Pierre Nora among others on "sites of memory," translated itself into a new understanding of the canon. Henceforth, "[i]t is the aptitude to recontextualize themselves beyond the original situation that bestows status on patrimonial works or objects. Canons establish themselves according to the societies or milieus that cultivate them."[6] Thus, the cultural patrimony is no longer thought of "as an immutable canon" (*Textkanon*), but "always considered a renewable canon" (*Deutungskanon*) (2007: 527).

Inversely, this new approach resulting from the transgressive experiences of modernity honed the perception one might have of the residual normativity inherent in any canon. Like it or not, the body of works passed on and circulated through institutional channels is always "the site of a sedimentation of fetishized texts and dead interpretations" (Lecercle 2006: 11). Moreover, the process of canonization takes place according to selection criteria, which while in no way inappropriate, do imbed themselves within cultural politics, the object of which is to justify and propagate the dominant group's values. As Ralf Zschachlitz observes, the perception of the mechanisms of power that determine a society's cultural memory parallels the model of the literary field developed by Pierre Bourdieu:

> It is the struggle within the literary field that forms the history of the field [...], struggle for the monopoly to impose legitimate categories of perception and appreciation; it is the "combat between those who have made their mark on history and fight to endure and those who cannot in turn leave their mark without relegating those with an interest in stopping time, in eternalizing the present, to the past."[7]

For, Zschachlitz continues: "[I]n Bourdieu's model of the literary field, a canon of stable works and points of view cannot exist. Every successful canonization im-

---

6 "[...] c'est l'aptitude à se recontextualiser au-delà de la conjoncture originelle qui donne leur statut aux œuvres ou objets patrimoniaux, les canons s'institutionnalisant selon les sociabilités ou les milieux qui les cultivent" (Malkani et al. 2007: 526).
7 "[...] c'est la lutte à l'intérieur du champ littéraire qui fait l'histoire du champ [...], lutte pour le monopole de l'imposition des catégories de perception et d'appréciation légitimes, c'est le 'combat entre ceux qui ont fait date et qui luttent pour durer, et ceux qui ne peuvent faire date à leur tour sans renvoyer au passé ceux qui ont intérêt à arrêter le temps, à éterniser le présent'" (Zschachlitz 2007: 548).

mediately calls forth a reaction meant to destabilize the new canon; every new element, every new arrival destabilizes the ever-precarious harmony of the field and established canons."[8] Across the consolidation of a cultural system that forms an integral part of the social system as a whole, ensuring group cohesion also matters. In this manner, the canon serves as much to legitimate a form of society and regulate the mechanisms of distinction within the social field as to delimit the symbolic space by which one community defines itself vis-à-vis the outside, offering its members a relatively stable collection of values and representations on which to found their collective identity. Notwithstanding its pretense of universality, the canon not only varies from one epoch to the next but also between each national or supranational community – even, in an increasing fashion, from one sociocultural or political milieu to another.

It is therefore impossible to speak of "the" canon in the singular, without understanding thereby an ideal-typical category that never materializes except in an infinity of variants, in flux and subdivided themselves into partial canons or sub-canons. The gap between the idea that one might form (or might have formed) of a normative canon, universal and ahistorical, and the reality of what the members of a given community actually read is abyssal. However, even if there is no longer consensus either within a nation or on the scale of multiple continents on the subject of a unique or hegemonic canon, the total disappearance of the canon is inconceivable. The concept designates the principle of cultural memory itself. On the other hand, it has become necessary to designate different types of canons. So, one could contrast, as Irmgard Ackermann (2009: 50) does, for example, the "official" canon, representing the object of a voluntary and targeted transmission through biased scholarly and academic programs, manuals, anthologies, rituals of commemoration, etc., with a "secret" canon, having no tangible existence attested to in published lists but rather reflected in the perception citizens intuitively have of their national literary patrimony on the basis of a tacit and partially unconscious consensus.

This distinction coincides more or less with the nuances that other researchers draw between the "prescriptive canon," the normative scholarly instrument, and the "real" or "factual" canon, which would forever be the transitory fruit of an ongoing process of development and renovation of the works of reference ("Kanonbildung").[9] In either case, it is a matter of confronting an institutional

---

8 "[D]ans le modèle du champ littéraire de Bourdieu, un canon stable d'œuvres et de points de vue ne peut exister : chaque canonisation réussie appelle tout de suite la réaction qui vise à déstabiliser le nouveau canon, chaque nouvel élément, chaque nouveau venu déséquilibre l'harmonie toujours précaire du champ et des canons établis" (Zschachlitz 2007: 548).
9 See for example Zymner (1998).

corpus resting on an objective list, tangible and preestablished, of representative works, which the powers that be in a society decide to pass down to subsequent generations (i. e. a conscious construction, however collective), with a virtual and implicit corpus that can only be reconstituted by deduction from the image – made concrete in cultural practice – real individuals have of their literary patrimony at a given historical instant.

The fact remains that, according to the common perception, as formulated by Manfred Schneider (1997), "[t]he canon is not what one reads but what one knows is supposed to be read."[10] Yet, this prescriptive canon has a tendency itself to blur as the body of works taught and consecrated enlarges and, what is more, as the consensus about the criteria of literary value crumbles. Thus, no a priori definition of what the "German canon" or "Western canon" should mean at the turn of the twenty-first century will be offered; plenty of ink has already been spilled over the question. It remains open and cannot be treated on a theoretical plane within the framework of a study that aims to comprehend the idea(s) of the national canon that emerge(s) empirically from observations of the works under examination. And yet, it is worth briefly recalling the premises and concerns of the debate that question sparked in Germany during the 1990s in order to demonstrate how the positions adopted on the subject by the authors of this corpus fit into the national debate.

The German Canon at the Turn of the Twenty-First Century

When feminist American academics, quickly joined by other minority groups rising up against their marginalization, called for the expansion of the list of works taught at universities in the 1990s and demanded programs that did not singularly reflect the point of view of white bourgeois heterosexual men, the campus debates they set off were so violent that they are referred to the "canon wars." The polemics pitted the conservative right, which rebelled against the devalorization of the national literary patrimony, aesthetic leveling, and the dismantling of classical European heritage, against adherents of a less elitist conception of literature, which would validate the evolution of programs towards greater pluralism and social representativity. The latter saw in the canon a normative system that included and excluded as much with regard to the outside as to a hierarchical mode within the literary field itself (works considered "minor") whereas the

---

[10] "Der Kanon ist nicht das, was man liest, sondern das, wovon man weiß, dass es gelesen werden sollte" (Schneider 1997).

former, unconditional defenders of the supposedly timeless and universal aesthetic values (and despite, or even because of that, explicitly "Western"), rose up against a politicization of academic environments, which they attributed to the diffusion of Marxist, feminist, structuralist, new-historicist, and postmodern ideas by way of cultural studies. From this point of view, ardently defended by Harold Bloom (1994), any questioning of the canon, whether on a theoretical or practical level, could only be perceived as a "provocation" for literary studies, an affront to the deontological code of a discipline dedicated to the exegesis and transmission of a heritage considered the natural expression of great men's genius.[11]

These controversies remained mostly ignored in France, where even the notion of a canon in the sense understood here was (and continues to be) largely rejected, so strong is the consensus on the authority of the institutional corpus. In Germany, the canon wars were followed with interest, but, in a much less divided academic landscape (and a society less ethnographically heterogenous), the question was first treated on the level of abstraction. The canon thus became the object of critical reflection, which opened a new field of research (*Kanonforschung*), at the crossroads of literary history, literary pedagogy, sociology, and cultural studies, to study the institutional mechanisms involved in the formation of the canon (canonization, de-canonization, and re-canonization) as well as the possibilities for the emergence of counter-canons and secondary or community canons alongside (or in place of) the dominant canon, no longer secure.[12] This notion, in effect, opened the way for the expansion of corpora taught and researched that henceforth would welcome, alongside the "great works" of the traditional canon, works and genres until then brushed aside, especially contemporary works.

This *Kanondebatte* ("canon debate") was the occasion for, among other things, taking the measure of the inevitable character of a canon's very existence – for some agreement has to be reached about the cultural material to pass on to future generations. Once there is no longer a declared consensus around the body of works that deserve to be studied in class, published in everyman editions, performed on the stage, etc., the revision of the canon becomes a societal concern. The interdisciplinary reflection on the relativity of the canon has firstly fostered efforts in literature pedagogy: What should one have children read now

---

[11] See in particular Aleida Assmann, "Kanonforschung als Provokation der Literaturwissenschaft" (1998).
[12] See Johannes Janota (1993) and Renate von Heydenbrand (1998). For the Austrian context, see Schmidt-Dengler, Sonnleitner and Zeyringer (1994). On the possibility of an Austrian canon, see also Stieg (2010).

and how? The question of content becomes articulated on the one hand by criteria (should ideology or aesthetics be privileged, and how does one distinguish between the two?), on the other by research into new pedagogical approaches aimed at encouraging students to appropriate the texts instead of submitting passively to authority. The development of less front-loaded methods of instruction suited to promoting a critical spirit go hand in hand with research into a more open and less normative canon. It is not a question of abolishing the canon – an impossible task – but of softening it and making its historical relativity and ideological implications visible in the process of transmission itself. Such is the truth that, as Peter Gendolla and Carsten Zelle stated, "the negation of the canon is always a new canon" (2000: 7–16).

Hence, the German canon debate, a consequence of successfully confronting the norms established in the 1960s and 70s, paradoxically led to renewed interest among the public at large for national culture, i.e. this iconoclasm precipitated an appeal to restore the canon on a new basis or to define a new canon. This quest for landmarks met an even stronger need in Germany as the loss of certainty in this matter coincided with the end of its political partition. At the beginning of the 1990s, the question of the canon recalled the immediate necessity to (re)define a common cultural basis for the German citizens now reunited. What was to be conserved from the culture of the now defunct GDR, what was to be rejected from that of the former – and now no less defunct after all – FRG? Each of these political entities born in the ruins of Nazi Germany had chosen references from the communal patrimony best suited to supporting and legitimizing its own political project, in part by opposing the nationalist basis on which Hitler's dictatorship had been erected and in part those of the rival state. The universal questioning of German cultural patrimony in 1945 had thus led to a doubling of national literary historiography whereby the two states bitterly contested their humanist heritage and its most agreed upon representatives (Lessing, Goethe, Schiller) while dividing up the others according to ideological criteria: in the FRG, Romanticism, the grand bourgeois tradition, and the avant-garde aesthetic (Kafka, the expressionists); in the GDR, the revolutionary tradition of literature (from the *Vormärz* to the proletarian theater of the Weimar Republic), the antifascist and exile literature (Heinrich Mann), and above all Brecht. The collapse of the GDR as a distinct and competing state would undermine, including in the former FRG, the foundations of that postwar intellectual construction. At the very moment Germany sought to redefine itself as a *Kulturnation*, it became urgent to look back anew in order to sort through what literary history offered as common points of reference beyond the ideological and political cleavages.

The conjunction of these two factors – the crisis of authority for the prescriptive canon, such as it was, and the challenges raised by the two separated German histories (literary and political) since 1945 – brought about a veritable explosion in interest regarding the canon in Germany at the end of the 1990s. Editors and the media seized upon the subject and made a profitable commercial niche out of the appeal for "re-canonization." The surge in interviews and polls, in tests and polemics, launched by that supra-regional press was accompanied by a multiplication of everyday editions meant for a public in need of cultural landmarks.[13] This editorial boom reached its apogee with the publication, between 2002 and 2006, of critic Marcel Reich-Ranicki's monumental anthology, soberly named *Der Kanon* ("*The Canon*"). In Reich-Ranicki's selection, one finds the "great authors" of the traditional canon, to which are now added a number of authors who were anti-establishment and/or contested or little-known figures in their day, such as J. M. R. Lenz, Büchner, Kafka, and Robert Walser. Women, by contrast, are still hardly represented. As for those authors whose distance, whether territorial or ethnic, from the "center" of the German nation could provoke a consideration of them as representatives of an expanded, "hybrid," Germanophone culture, they are tacitly incorporated into the German corpus by dint of belonging to the linguistic nation. Chamisso, Kafka, Canetti, and Celan thus become German authors no different than Goethe, Benn, and Brecht: canonization stands in for naturalization.

Such attempts at canonical restoration could not, however, halt the discrediting of the very idea of a single canon. Alongside this increasingly vast general canon, the formation of canons specific to a political or social group took root, e.g. a "leftist" canon (beginning with Lessing), an "avant-garde" canon (privileging aesthetic innovation), sub-culture canons, etc., with each one delimiting its particular territory based on available touchstones.

Throughout this debate, the question of ethnic representativity, a crucial concern of the American canon wars, played no role to speak of. Yet, on the side of the immigrants still fighting – even more than ever before – for their legitimacy in the literary field of a reunified Germany, authors are likewise searching to position themselves using these touchstones. There, too, everyone works hard to mark their territory according to their own values. It is, notwithstanding, possible to tease out at least two key threads that traverse the assemblage of approaches across differences of an ideological nature. Before proposing a structure for the assemblage of mobilized canonical references, I will briefly present these two tendencies, envisioned as topoi or recurrent argumentative schema in

---

[13] See for example Schwanitz (1999) and Zschirnt (2002).

the appropriative strategies the authors of my corpus implement toward the canon.

The German Canon of Authors of Migration Literature

Decentering: A Hybrid and Anti-Nationalist Canon

One primary tendency is to "denaturalize" the references that national literary historiography has annexed in such a way as to make reappear, behind the cultural homogenization induced by the canonizing process, the asperities that this process has – deliberately or not – erased. Training an eye unencumbered by nationalist ideology on canonical authors, the authors of migration literature highlight, if only by discovering points in common with some of them, the fact that German literature is, as Navid Kermani suggested, much less "German" in its totality than one tends to believe. This author and essayist of Iranian descent, born in 1967, also a scholar trained in Islamic studies, expressed this point of view in 2006 in an address entitled *Was ist deutsch an der deutschen Literatur?* ("What's German in German Literature?").

It is worth pausing on this address, not only because of the view on the German canon, which matches the one taken by many foreign-born intellectuals, but also because of the political and institutional context in which it is embedded. Voiced within the framework of a series of conferences organized by the Konrad Adenauer Foundation and dealing with the question *Was eint uns?* ("What unites us?"), Kermani's address presents the post-reunification debate about national identity with a countercurrent to the rightist discourse (maintained in that era by the luminaries of the CDU) with regards to *Leitkultur*. This stance is all the more striking in that it came from an esteemed personality (contrary to someone like Zaimoglu, Kermani is no provocateur) and unfolded thoughtfully a sort of reverse definition, perfectly coherent and appropriate, of the "cultural nation."

Kermani develops his "anti-German" reading of the German canon with reference not only to the ethnic diversity of a corpus that evinces strong representation from Jewish writers resistant to assimilation such as Heine, Kafka, and Celan. To that trio he joins a larger circle of writers coming from territories outside the political nation (Joseph Roth, Rilke, Horvath, Robert Walser), without forgetting the case of the French refugee Chamisso. Through the ideas they hold, he argues, the vast majority of the authors Germany takes the most pride in today – Lessing, Schiller, Hölderlin, Heine, Börne, and Büchner – represent each in their own way, when it comes to identarian assignment and ideological appropriation, an intellectual tradition that lends itself rather poorly to nationalist hijacking. In truth, "Germany's literati had long since turned their thoughts beyond Germany by the time Germany finally crystalized as an intellectual and later as a political entity."[14] At a time when their contemporaries were still dreaming of national unification, it was European unity, Kermani emphasizes, that "the great German poets and philosophers" had aspired to since the end of the eighteenth century, citing Kant and Goethe for support: "In Germany, the Enlightenment was, from the beginning, not a national but a European program. In literature, too, one did not follow available German models but adhered to foreign literature from Homer via Shakespeare to Byron. German literature specifically did not want to be *German* – and yet was exactly that in its adoption of non-German subjects and models."[15] Even Goethe, the "national poet" (Kermani 2008: 87) *par excellence*, could not be hijacked for the purposes of patriotic edification without profoundly misunderstanding his work. Kermani supported this stance with several citations testifying to the skeptical, if not outright hostile, attitude of the most eminent representative of German letters with regard to the idea of national unification – among them the phrase, already cited by Thomas Mann in his speech from 1945 on "Germany and the Germans," the interpretation of which is far from clear: "The Germans should be uprooted, scattered throughout the world, like the Jews, in order to develop the good that lies in them, fully, and to the benefit of all nations."[16] What distinguishes the German literary tradition from other national traditions is, according to Kermani, a widely shared penchant for fundamentally "cosmopolitan" humanist approaches undergirded by an avowed refusal of any national particularism. His speech underlines that this reluctance to claim identification with the German nation in many cases went as far as a fierce desire to distance oneself from a collective to which one would be ashamed to belong:

---

[14] "Deutschlands Literaten [dachten] längst über Deutschland [hinaus], als Deutschland sich endlich als ein geistiges und später als politisches Gebilde herausgeschält hatte" (Kermani 2008: 84).

[15] "In Deutschland war die Aufklärung von Beginn an kein nationales, sondern ein europäisches Programm. Auch in der Literatur folgte man nicht etwaigen deutschen Vorbildern, sondern hielt sich an die außerdeutsche Literatur von Homer über Shakespeare bis Byron. *Deutsch* wollte die deutsche Literatur gerade nicht sein – und war es doch gerade durch die Aneignung nichtdeutscher Motive und Muster" (Kermani 2008: 84).

[16] "Verpflanzt, zerstreut wie die Juden in alle Welt müssten die Deutschen werden, um die Masse des Guten ganz und zum Heil aller Nationen zu entwickeln, die in ihnen liegt." This quote (Kermani 2008: 87) refers to a remark that Goethe made during a conversation with his friend Chancellor von Müller on 14 December 1808 (Grumbach and Grumbach 1999: 605).

> The critique and even rejection of Germany is a leitmotif of German literary history (Mayer, Das unglückliche Bewußtsein). This national self-critique, in its sharpness and comprehensiveness, can hardly be found in any other literature. It is by no means only a product of the postwar period but rather characteristic of German literature long before National Socialism. No matter how often one claims finally to have found a "normal," unstrained relationship to Germany – Germany's writers have often set themselves apart particularly through their strained relationship to Germany. They are great Germans even though, or rather because, they argue with Germany. Put another way: Germany may be proud of those who were not proud of Germany.[17]

From this paradoxical approach to national cultural identity, Kermani can fully claim to belong to "the same literature as the Prague Jew Franz Kafka." "His Germany unites us," Kermani says, and it is Kafka's heritage that he responds to as a writer.[18]

The case for inverse patriotism Kermani pleads here, supported not by his experience or his vision of the world but by incontestable representatives of the canon such as Lessing, Schiller, Goethe, Kafka, and Tucholsky, corresponds to a point of view shared by many of the authors of migration literature. It is from such angle that a number of them prefer to seek their references. Without necessarily going as far as Kermani in his panegyric for a literary tradition that for him was established "in hatred for Germany," they endeavor with a certain constancy to scratch, so to speak, the varnish of canonization from these authors in order to reveal, in rereading them through the prism of "minoritarian" and "hybrid" writing, those aspects of their texts their consecration had so far concealed.

In this appropriation of a German canon defined by tolerance, humanism, and cosmopolitanism and from which authors who gave in to the siren song of Nazism or were coopted by Hitlerian ideology (e.g. Benn and Heidegger) are explicitly excluded, identification with German-Jewish writers, often bilingual and bicultural, is central. There is, of course, nothing revolutionary about such stance, as Kermani was paying homage to the values the two Germanies

---

17 "Die Kritik und sogar Absage an Deutschland ist ein Leitmotiv der deutschen Literaturgeschichte (Mayer, *Das unglückliche Bewußtsein*). In ihrer Schärfe und Durchgängigkeit ist diese nationale Selbstkritik wohl in keiner anderen Literatur zu finden. Sie ist keineswegs erst ein Produkt der Nachkriegszeit, sondern schon lange vor dem Nationalsozialismus charakteristisch für die deutsche Literatur. Mag man noch so oft fordern, endlich ein "normales", ein unverkrampftes Verhältnis zu Deutschland zu finden – Deutschlands Dichter haben sich häufig insbesondere durch ihr angespanntes Verhältnis zu Deutschland ausgezeichnet. Sie sind große Deutsche, obwohl oder gerade weil sie mit Deutschland haderten. Anders gesagt: Stolz darf Deutschland auf jene sein, die nicht stolz auf Deutschland waren" (Kermani 2008: 88).

18 "Zugleich gibt es für mich keine größere Verpflichtung, als derselben Literatur anzugehören wie der Prager Jude Franz Kafka. Sein Deutschland eint uns" (Kermani 2008: 98).

had been professing officially since 1945. However, in the context of the "de-tabooization" of nationalism that had taken root since reunification, making such an appeal was not insignificant.[19] Iranian-German and Muslim by religion, Kermani defended the values of a democratic Germany, to which he asserted his adherence over the voices of those ready to liquidate that heritage and rehabilitate the culture of backlash and intellectual nationalism with its customary whiff of antisemitism and xenophobia.

Re-centering: Making the "Heart" of the National Canon Beat Again

Another topos of the reception of the German canon by authors of migration literature appears in the revival of a national tradition postwar writers more or less consciously left by the wayside, if not outright renounced: very broadly, literature devoted to utopian expressions and sentiments in quest of the mystic absolute and the cult of interiority. Here, conversely, taking up anew a heritage disavowed by its rightful historical heirs meant to lift a taboo and fill a gap in contemporary literature.

The Romantic-idealist paradigm, which has run through German literary history since the eighteenth century and crystalized into several representative branches – *Empfindsamkeit*, *Sturm und Drang*, Romanticism, Expressionism, *Jugendstil*, and neo-Romanticism – was brought into discredit in the aftermath of the Second World War. The damning evidence of the culture's failure to fulfill its promises of emancipation, on the one hand, and the complicity of intellectuals in Nazism's rise, on the other, certainly called into question the definition of literature as an opposite to "barbarism." Yet this ethical delegitimization of "Belles-Lettres" particularly concerned the lyric-Romantic tradition. (Mis-)construed as an anathema, Adorno's famous declaration about the impossibility of writing poetry after Auschwitz served as a justification to construct a literature on the ruins of war and fascism unsullied by aestheticism, mannerism, and sentimentalism.[20] If it was not created ex nihilo at the "zero hour" of the new era in

---

19 Leading politicians of one of the two majority parties were speaking without irony about a *Leitkultur* and a writer as well-known as Martin Walser was railing publicly against the "instrumentalization of our shame" ("Instrumentalisierung unserer Schande") in the Church of Saint Paul in Frankfurt and calling for the rehabilitation of national honor after years of expiating Nazi crimes. See Martin Walser, "Erfahrungen beim Verfassen einer Sonntagsrede" (1999).
20 It is worth recalling Adorno's frequently misunderstood dictum in its entirety: "Kulturkritik findet sich der letzten Stufe der Dialektik von Kultur und Barbarei gegenüber: nach Auschwitz ein Gedicht zu schreiben, ist barbarisch, und das frisst auch die Erkenntnis an, die ausspricht,

German history as some at first wanted to believe, this new literature nourished itself on foreign references (drawn from the Anglo-Saxon world for West Germany) and resumed the tradition of the *Aufklärung* (Lessing) or, notably in the East, the revolutionary, proletarian, and antifascist traditions. Poets whose style did not conform to this imperative of affective restraint, aesthetic asceticism, and laconicism, such as Paul Celan, met with violent rejection on the part of the bodies of cultural legitimization.[21]

Even though this distrust toward the sentimental register faded somewhat thereafter, notably under the influence of a current that brought "interiority" back into fashion in the 1970s (*Neue Innerlichkeit*), it never completely disappeared. One of the most defamatory labels for a German writer to this day is to be considered part of that "non-literature" or "pseudo-literature" known as *kitsch*. The concept of *kitsch*, in Hermann Broch's analysis a principle of "dishonesty" that forms the basis of "totalitarian art," has run through the history of the German intellectual field since the first decades of the twentieth century.[22] Broch developed his theory of *kitsch* at the beginning of the 1930s in the wake of Walter Benjamin's "culture critique" and his famous aphorism: "There is never a document of culture that is not at once one of barbarism."[23] It is in continuation of this tradition that Austrian-Jewish writer Jean Améry, for example, could say in 1966 that "the German youth cannot cite Goethe, Mörike, and the Baron vom Stein while bracketing Blunck, Wilhelm Schäfer, and Heinrich Himmler."[24] The postulate of a continuation between Romanticism – or even the currents that preceded it – and totalitarian "pseudo-literature" shaped literary and artistic practice in the German field in such a manner as to create, according to Frédérik Detue (2012), a veritable "schism," "forming a critical relationship and dialectic toward the idea of Romantic literature" and "defining a new literary mode of being." It is to the overcoming of this schism that many authors of migration literature have directed their efforts, establishing a code of references at once aes-

---

warum es unmöglich ward, heute Gedichte zu schreiben" ("Cultural criticism finds itself faced with the final stage of the dialectic of culture and barbarism. To write poetry after Auschwitz is barbaric. And this corrodes even the knowledge of why it has become impossible to write poetry today") (Adorno [1951] 1998: 30; trans. 1997: 34).

21 On the Group 47's very cold reception of Celan, see Briegleb (1997b, 2003).
22 See especially *Einige Bemerkungen zum Problem des Kitsches. Ein Vortrag* [1950] and *Das Böse im Wertsystem der Kunst* [1933] (Broch 1955: 295–310 and 311–350).
23 "Es ist niemals ein Dokument der Kultur, ohne zugleich ein solches der Barbarei zu sein." In *Über den Begriff der Geschichte* [1940] (Benjamin 1972–1989, I: 691–701), 696.
24 "Die deutsche Jugend kann sich nicht auf Goethe, Mörike, den Freiherrn vom Stein berufen und Blunck, Wilhelm Schäfer, Heinrich Himmler ausklammern" (Améry 2002: 140).

thetic and ethical within which the incriminated lines of tradition have a new rightful home.

According to the essayist and poet Zafer Şenocak, who was born in Ankara in 1961 and arrived in Germany with his parents at the age of eight, the crisis that German lyrical poetry has endured since 1945 makes it difficult for native-born writers to access a heritage compromised by the nationalist and bellicose anthems of which culminated in Nazism. This, however, has left an open space for those who, because they come from elsewhere, have not been conditioned by national trauma and have remained in contact with the living forces of *Weltdichtung* ("world poetry"). In this poetry from which the majority of German writers of his generation – the *Dichter ohne Lieder* ("poets without songs") – were irrevocably cut off, Şenocak discovered "the international language" among others in Goethe (notably in the *Divan*), Nietzsche, Rilke, Rimbaud, and subsequently in Celan – a poet whose disastrous history of reception in Germany he recalls as symptomatic (Şenocak 2011: 75–85).

The interest of Şenocak's analysis is that it does not content itself with viewing the aridity of German literature after 1945 as a backlash motivated by the ethical questioning of the national literary tradition, instead tracing its source back to the emotional and linguistic atrophy caused by Nazism itself.

> The literary, above all lyrical, crisis of the '68 generation was probably unavoidable. Important social struggles were in the offing and politicized consciousness; they created a theoretical language, which is the greatest foe of poetry. The crisis was, however, also a flight from the responsibility of people for their feelings, for the mysterious hole within them. The generation before had failed in this responsibility. This failure left wounds on the Germans that scarred over without truly healing.[25]

For Şenocak, the "glacial cold" given off by "the father figures of the 68ers" was really a "steel-helmet cold,"[26] a shadow cast much further back than 1945 and beyond which the shameful predilection "for the sensual, for the nameless, for

---

[25] "Die literarische, vor allem lyrische Krise der Generation von '68 war wahrscheinlich unvermeidbar gewesen. Wichtige gesellschaftliche Auseinandersetzungen standen an und politisierten das Bewusstsein, sie schufen eine theoretische Sprache, die der größte Feind der Poesie ist. Die Krise war aber auch eine Flucht vor der Verantwortung des Menschen für seine Gefühle, für die geheimnisvolle Höhle in seinem Inneren. An dieser Verantwortung waren die Generationen zuvor gescheitert. Dieses Scheitern hatte dem Deutschsein Wunden geschlagen, die vernarbten, ohne wirklich zu heilen" (Şenocak 2011: 77).

[26] "Die Vaterfiguren der Achtundsechziger strahlten eine eiserne Kälte aus, eine Stahlhelmkälte sozusagen" (Şenocak 2011: 77–78).

the darkened landscape within" could prosper.²⁷ In this unhealthy climate, liberation came for him, he says, in the discovery of the works of Celan, Bachmann, Trakl, and Rilke – and he underlines that it is surely no coincidence that these four poets came from territories situated "on the linguistic frontier of German space" and that they were steeped in an intermingling of different languages and cultures. In the case of Celan, the Ashkenazi culture with its Hebraic roots intermixed with European modernity.

This analysis could be extended to other literary genres, like the novel or drama, wherein affective expression has not become less problematic for the generations following Nazism. There, too, authors from a mixed culture can, it would seem, make their voice heard, however imprinted with Romantic pathos, without actually crossing the red line – if only because those lyric accents are more acceptable to the public coming from them. Given what could be called an "Orientalist bonus," they are able to make the barren land – too depleted for their monocultural contemporaries – of literature "of the heart" bear fruit. This interpretation could partly explain the success of an inspired creator like Zaimoglu who has adopted in all of his writing since *Liebesmale, scharlachrot* ("Love Marks, Scarlet Red," 2000),²⁸ a posture and tendency toward an assumed anachronism. In his public pronouncements, Zaimoglu claims a "Romantic" sensibility, the origin of which he situates expressly in the German tradition and which he defends with all the more ardor because it has been discredited by that national institutions of legitimization. In contrast to Şenocak, Zaimoglu (2008b) categorically rejects any imprint of his familial culture, vigorously insisting on a Romanticism labeled "made in Germany":

> Many people believe because of my Eastern ancestry that I must be familiar with the fairy tales from *The Thousand and One Nights*. But I grew up with the Grimms' fairy tales, with old German sagas and popular legends. There people are always vulnerable and surrounded by the inexplicable. The forest is full of dangers. Hence the attempt to bind the world with spells. That is the language that made the world come alive to me. The experimental literature of the seventies, on the other hand, darkened the world for me. I saw no color and felt no temperature.²⁹

---

27 "Hinter der Fassade der Distanzierung gegenüber bildhafter Sprache und der Ablehnung poetischer Mittel steckte ein brennendes Interesse für das Sinnliche, für das Namenlose, für die verdunkelte Landschaft im Inneren" (Şenocak 2011: 78).
28 See chapter 6.
29 "Viele Leute glauben, wegen meiner orientalischen Herkunft müsste ich vertraut sein mit den Märchen aus Tausendundeiner Nacht. Dabei bin ich aufgewachsen mit den Grimm'schen Märchen, mit alten deutschen Sagen und Volkslegenden. Da sind die Menschen immer verwundbar und umstellt von Unerklärlichem. Der Wald steckt voller Gefahren. Daher der Versuch, die Welt mit Zaubersprüchen zu bannen. Das ist die Sprache, die mir die Welt anschaulich gemacht hat.

A year later, upon the release of his novel *Hinterland*, Zaimoglu outdid even that Romantic declaration of faith. To the question of a journalist who asked where all the supernatural creatures – elves, gnomes, genies – that populate his novel come from, he responded: "From German magical realism!" As he elaborated:

> Here in Germany people always acted as if magical realism had been invented by Gabriel García Márquez. That was ignorance. That was the conscious desire to block out everything those beautiful German folktales achieved. Some have called me a "multicultural German-nationalist" because I've gestured toward the beautiful old stories. There is a German magical realism. It was everywhere people were made anxious and frightened, saddened, in premodern times. My inspiration as storyteller doesn't come from the Orient but from the German – digressions, the baroque, everything the modern had cut us off from. Don't get me started on the modern. The modern is disdain for what you don't understand. What someone doesn't understand gets declared old. The modern trivializes what people once believed themselves surrounded by.[30]

These impassioned declarations prompted literary critics to praise Zaimoglu's work's embeddedness in the one German tradition that is simultanously the most emblematic and possibly the most denigrated in Germany itself. The critics then extended this line of interpretation by applying the same critical framework to his following novels, even though these conjured a radically different imaginary. Hence, one can read in a critique of the novel *Isabel* (2014) from the pen of Jens Jessen (*Die Zeit*) the following panegyric:

> It is the artificially brusque speech of Expressionism. In *Isabel*, we are only topographically in present-day Berlin. Atmospherically, we've gone a hundred years or so back into the young Brecht's steamy, even in its aphorisms extatically heated, world of expression, that of Ernst Toller, Georg Kaiser, and Carl Sternheim in its brutish truncation. It's an as-

---

Die experimentelle Literatur der Siebzigerjahre dagegen verdunkelte mir die Welt, ich sah keine Farben und fühlte keine Temperatur" (Zaimoglu 2008b).

30 "Es wurde hier in Deutschland immer so getan, als wäre der magische Realismus von Gabriel García Márquez erfunden worden. Das war Ignoranz. Das war der bewusste Wille, all das, was die schönen deutschen Volkserzählungen geschaffen hat, auszuklammern. Mich hat man schon als 'deutschnationalen Multikulturellen' tituliert, weil ich auf die schönen alten Geschichten hingewiesen habe. Es gibt den deutschen magischen Realismus, es gab ihn überall, wo die Menschen in Angst und Schrecken versetzt, betrübt waren, in der vormodernen Zeit. Meine Inspiration als Geschichtenerzähler kommt nicht aus dem Orient, sondern aus dem Deutschen – die Abschweifung, das Barocke, all das, von dem die Moderne uns abgeschnitten hat. Die Moderne kann mich gerne haben. Die Moderne ist die Verachtung gegenüber dem, was man nicht versteht. Was man nicht versteht, wird für alt erklärt. Die Moderne verniedlicht, womit die Menschen früher sich umgeben glaubten" (Zaimoglu 2009c).

tounding, but not arbitrary choice of style. *Isabel* was written directly from an agitated soul with a voice gasping for air amidst the billows just before drowning. One should not too quickly pass over the fact that it was, of all things, a Turkish immigrant author who rediscovered this completely forgotten, most German of German literary styles. Feridun Zaimoglu can do what no other author of his generation can. He commands the whole arsenal of German literature; he can pick and choose what he likes. Already, at the very beginning of his career, he made eighteenth-century parlance, that of the sentimental epistolary novels, his own.[31]

In the course of these successive metamorphoses, Zaimoglu has indeed appropriated a whole series of traditions each more emblematically German than the last, from *Sturm und Drang* and *Empfindsamkeit* to working-class neo-Romanticism (*Ruhrpotromantik*) in his novel *Ruß* ("Soot," 2011) – not forgetting the legacy of the Reformation, to which he addresses a literary monument in a novelistic homage to Martin Luther (*Evangelio – Ein Luther-Roman*, 2017) published just in time to celebrate the 500th anniversary of the nailing of the "95 Theses." A single constant implicitly suffuses these stylistic and thematic mutations: an antimodern posture, sustained by a rebellion directed pell-mell against secular universalism, instrumental reason, consumerism, and the "politically correct" of the left.[32]

At the same time, other authors have inserted themselves more discretely, in a manner much more nuanced and less offensive, into the breach opened up by the delegitimization of pathos in the German literature of the second half of the twentieth century. At least, that is one way of understanding the "declaration of love" to the German language delivered by the novelist and essayist Ilija Trojanow (born in 1965 in Sofia) at his conference on poetics in Tübingen. References to the lyrical paradigm are deployed here, if not explicitly on the level of theme (the object of this declaration being the German *language* and not a specific lit-

---

[31] "Es ist die künstlich verknappte Sprache des Expressionismus. Mit *Isabel* sind wir nur topografisch in der Berliner Gegenwart, atmosphärisch sind wir um hundert Jahre zurück in der dampfenden, selbst in der Sentenz noch ekstatisch erhitzten Ausdruckswelt des jungen Brecht, bei Ernst Toller, Georg Kaiser und in der brachialen Verkürzung bei Carl Sternheim. Das ist eine erstaunliche, aber nicht willkürliche Stilwahl. *Isabel* ist direkt aus der aufgewühlten Seele, mit einer in den Wogen nach Luft schnappenden Stimme kurz vor dem Ertrinken geschrieben. Man sollte den Umstand, dass ausgerechnet ein Autor mit ebenfalls türkischem Migrationshintergrund diesen gründlich vergessenen, deutschesten aller deutschen Literaturstile wiedergefunden hat, nicht zu schnell übergehen. Feridun Zaimoglu kann, was kein Autor seiner Generation kann. Er verfügt über das ganze Arsenal der deutschen Literatur, er kann sich bedienen, wo es ihm geboten scheint, er hat bereits, ganz zu Beginn seiner Karriere, sich die Ausdrucksweise des 18. Jahrhunderts, des empfindsamen Briefromans, anverwandelt" (Jessen 2014).
[32] See the analysis by Michael Hofmann (2012: 239–257).

erary tradition), then at least between the lines in the choice of register and the address's position:

> Now the time has come to sing the praises of my beloved, the German language [...] You will not, however, hear a pragmatically motivated plea for German from me, because I'm moved [...] to a declaration of love. [...] What separated me from many other young readers, was the intense feeling of wonder and admiration at my discoveries, this astonishment with eyes wide open and ears pricked at the beauty and riches of this language, which I had only just [...] learned. Nothing of what revealed itself to me in shimmering variety was obvious. I treasured my early discoveries of Trakl and Celan like miners once did the first diamond they found. This astonishment has stayed with me. A wonderful quality of my beloved encouraged my infatuation: she is open and tolerant. Yes, German is more welcoming to foreigners than the Germans.[33]

What Trojanow inserts playfully and so cleverly here into his laudation of the "hospitality" of the German language – a quality the Orientalist cliché usually reserves for traditional societies in exotic countries – in contrast to the collective xenophobia of Germans as a people, their lack of curiosity and openness to the other, which goes hand in hand with a distorted relationship to their own past, is that Germany has need of "foreigners" – of their new perspective filled with wonder at the beauties of German language and literature – in order to make good use of its own patrimony and reconnect with its history. The reason why he nonetheless willingly agrees to take on the role of intercultural mediator that thus falls to immigrants, is that it involves an exchange where both parties can only win. "No affliction of modernity is so grave that it can't be healed with a little nomadization," Trojanow notes a bit later by way of conciliation (2008: 79).

Doubtlessly, the convergence of a crisis of the German literary tradition and an "Orientalist bonus" given to minority writers played no small part in the great popularity of the novelist and storyteller Rafik Schami. Practicing a genre abandoned by most of his colleagues, the fantastical tale, Schami makes use, along-

---

[33] "Nun ist es an der Zeit, ein Hohelied auf meine Geliebte, die deutsche Sprache, zu singen. [...] Von mir werden Sie allerdings kein pragmatisch motiviertes Plädoyer für das Deutsche vernehmen, denn es drängt mich [...] zu einer Liebeserklärung. [...] Was mich von vielen anderen jungen Lesern unterschied, war das intensive Gefühl des Wunderns und der Bewunderung über meine Entdeckungen, dieses Staunen mit weit aufgerissenen Augen und tief offenem Ohr über die Schönheit und den Reichtum dieser Sprache, die ich ja erst kurz zuvor [...] erlernt hatte. Nichts von dem, was sich mir in schillernder Vielfalt offenbarte, war selbstverständlich. Ich hegte frühe Trouvaillen von Trakl oder Celan wie einst Schürfer ihren ersten Diamantenfund. Dieses Staunen ist mir geblieben. Gefördert wurde diese Vernarrtheit von einer wunderbaren Eigenschaft meiner Geliebten: Sie ist offen und tolerant. Ja, das Deutsche ist ausländerfreundlicher als die Deutschen" (Trojanow 2008: 76–77).

side Eastern references (*The Thousand and One Nights*), of a series of models drawn from German literature. If the themes, motifs, and narrative structures outline an imaginary and a topography anchored in the Arab East, his poetological program in turn stands at the confluence of several canonical German models. Indeed, the rehabilitation of popular and oral culture he is undertaking is in line with the Romantic project as it was successfully realized by story collectors Jacob and Wilhelm Grimm. As for the theoretical support for this program and his conviction that it responds to a vital need in today's industrialized world, Schami owes a great deal to Walter Benjamin on the art of storytelling. Additionally, Schami is one of those immigrant writers who have taken on the task of reconciling East and West, at once on the thematic level, by informing the German public about the Arab world from which he comes, and on an aesthetic level by accomplishing a synthesis of the two cultures' narrative forms – a project for which he overtly aligns himself with the Goethean model.[34]

These two key threads – "denaturalization" of the canon on one hand, and re-centering along the lines of tradition left without an heir, on the other – are in no way incompatible. In Şenocak just as in Kermani, Trojanow, Schami, and Özdamar, one finds at once a valorization of the *Aufklärung*'s "internationalist" heritage (openness to the other, tolerance, utopia of emancipation, and social progress), with its extensions into modernity (Marxism), and the reclaiming of a sensibility and expressivity, which these authors themselves locate within the continuity of the grand Western tradition particularly as it developed in German literature from the eighteenth to the beginning of the twentieth century.

A Typology of Canonical References

Using the categories outlined by critic Hans Mayer in his 1971 *Der Repräsentant und der Märtyrer* ("The Representative and the Martyr"), I propose a descriptive, and necessarily cursory, classification of the representatives of the "dominant" or "conservative" canon, on one side; on the other, I list those whose canonicity is constructed from a "subaltern," "progressive," or "marginal" position that arises from their social origin or their convoluted trajectory or just as well from a deliberate ideological position. This very cursory distinction, which rests on an approach to canonical authors in terms of "configurations" or "con-

---

[34] See especially "Von der Flucht eines Propheten: Zu Goethes Liebeserklärung an den Orient" (Schami [2006] 2009: 196–202) and *Der geheime Bericht über den Dichter Goethe, der eine Prüfung auf einer arabischen Insel bestand* (Schami and Gutzschhahn [1999] 2001). Regarding the latter, see also chapter 3 ("Will Goethe Be Allowed into the Postcolonial Canon?").

stellations," in the sense given to this term by Hans Mayer, crosses the sociological perspective – taking the subjective point of view of the creators into account, their social *habitus* and status – with the objective analysis of the orientations outlined in their works.

> Constellation means the subjective factor, represented through artistic and scientific creativity, as much as the objectivity of texts, doctrines, and political positions. In the ideological situation of our day, characterized by the overripeness and disintegration of bourgeois normativity, in art and literature, too, but just as much by the defilement of former utopias, constellations of all sorts present themselves. Either as – relative – attributions to the bourgeois world or to those forces undertaking the task of reordering society. Then one constellation, which – with reservations – would be attributed to the established bourgeois world, distinguishes itself from the other one, which comes into its own in struggle, in negation, in the – often unconscious – intellectual anticipation of future conditions.[35]

To distinguish the two ideal-typical configurations sketched here, Hans Mayer takes back up the terms Thomas Mann used in a bitter letter he wrote from his English exile to the dean of the faculty of philology at the University of Bonn in 1937 after witnessing the revocation of his professorial title *honoris causa:* "I was born much more to be a representative than a martyr."[36] In his illustration of so close an affinity with the established order and power that it was difficult for Mann to disengage from them even after he had passed into the camp of the regime's opponents, this declaration effectively reveals a positioning consubstantial with the literary project of its author. It shows both that, if this stance and the presumption of occupying the center of the literary field that flows from it is determined to a certain degree by social origins, it is not in so far directly correlated to the material, social, and political conditions of the moment. Even in exile, Thomas Mann remains a "representative" in his heart and

---

35 "*Konstellation* meint den subjektiven Faktor, repräsentiert durch künstlerische und wissenschaftliche Kreativität, ebenso wie die Objektivität von Texten, Lehrmeinungen, politischen Positionen. In der ideologischen Situation unserer Tage, die gekennzeichnet ist durch Überreife und Zersetzung bürgerlicher Normativität, auch in Kunst und Literatur, nicht minder aber durch Verschmutzung einstiger Utopien, präsentieren sich Konstellationen aller Art. Entweder als – relative – Zuordnungen zur Bürgerwelt, oder zu jenen Kräften, die sich die Aufgabe einer gesellschaftlichen Umgestaltung stellen. Dann unterscheidet sich eine Konstellation, welche – mit Vorbehalten – der etablierten Bürgerwelt zuzurechnen wäre, von jener anderen, die sich im Kampf erfüllt, in der Negation, in der – oft ohnmächtigen – geistigen Vorwegnahme künftiger Zustände" (Mayer 1971: 11–12).

36 In his letter to Karl Justus Obenauer dated 1 January 1937, Thomas Mann wrote: "Ich bin weit eher zum Repräsentanten geboren als zum Märtyrer, weit eher dazu, ein wenig höhere Heiterkeit in die Welt zu tragen, als den Kampf, den Haß zu nähren" (as quoted in Wysling und Schmidlin 1997: 336).

cannot wrap his head around the idea that the call (certainly late) of his political conscience has placed him – provisionally – on the side of those used to fighting and whose self-image is consequently compatible with the destiny of a "martyr."

The classification of "representatives" and "martyrs" (or "rebels") thus rests on a subjective assessment, as much on the part of the authors themselves as on their readers – and on the interpreter as well. From this point of view, it could only be in equal measure approximative and provisional, knowing that the author's historiographic status is subject to important fluctuations. Thus, the position occupied by this or that writer in today's canonical hierarchy is, needless to say, not identical with that occupied in their day. In many cases, the process of canonization (or inversely de-canonization) itself has created a considerable divide between the recognition a creator enjoys while alive or at the moment of death, let alone fifty or a hundred years later, and the current degree of canonicity. Think of the cases of Lenz, Büchner, Hölderlin, or Heine (or Nestroy in Austria), all "rediscovered" or elevated to the ranks of the classics more or less belatedly – and of the opposite destiny of authors who enjoyed a considerable prestige in their day, like Klopstock, Wieland, Uhland, or Heyse, but whose imprint is hardly perceptible today except as the names of streets or scholarly institutions, the names on statues and in the accounts of more famous contemporaries. Since *Questioning the Canon* does not undertake a sociohistorical study of reception, it is not those paradigm shifts that will take priority in this book, but rather those authors consecrated within the contemporary national canon.

Major Line: The "Representatives"
At the forefront of the emblematic figures of official culture is Johann Wolfgang Goethe (1749–1832), who offers the archetypal image of the "representative." Along with Friedrich Schiller, he is the only German writer of international renown, and because of the richness of his work and personality, he lends himself to extremely diverse approaches.[37] He was born into a patrician family and occupied high political offices in the Duchy of Weimar, leaving his mark on an entire era. More than anyone else, he embodies the proximity of the intellectual to the established order. Goethe was responsible for creating the immense body of work

---

37 The second paradigmatic figure of Weimar Classicism, Friedrich Schiller (1759–1805), appears to hold less interest for authors of migration literature. Although his ballads and his revolutionary plays still have a prominent place in academic curricula and his works are still very much present in the theater, the author of *William Tell*, *Intrigue and Love*, and *Mary Stuart* does not appear, at least for now, as a central figure in the critical debate taking place about the national canon.

from which the mythical heroes Werther, Meister, and Faust emerge. He was also the first to instigate an intercultural dialogue with the East in his *West-Eastern Divan* and was the most eminent advocate for the notion of *Weltliteratur*. At a time when other intellectuals and artists were unapologetically throwing themselves into the European enterprise of colonial domination, Goethe instead opened up perspectives that have made it possible, up through the present day, to think about the cultural reconfiguration of the world. Consequently, he serves as a reference point for critical approaches ranging from enthusiastic acceptance to thorough objection, though more frequently a nuanced approach tempering praise with a dose of critique, or vice versa.

While at the turn of the twenty-first century Goethe may no longer be central to intellectual debate in Germany, he nonetheless remains by virtue of his undisputed canonical status an unavoidable figure for authors who follow an intercultural trajectory, especially those coming from the "Oriental" world. The poet SAID, born in 1947 in Tehran, notes that the *Divan* is "practically required reading for Iranians" (1999), and awareness of its reputation in his country preceded his own reading of Goethe's works, which he discovered well after moving to Germany at the age of seventeen. Because of this positive reception, when he later became acquainted with the positions that Goethe had adopted in his personal and political life, he responded with such disappointment and "indignation" that his admiration morphed into "antipathy."[38] Schami describes a reverse process in admitting that he "only learned to love Goethe gradually" (1999a), disheartened as he was initially by both Goethe's fetishization and counterrevolutionary political positions. Schami claims that it was necessary for him to experience the frivolity and provincialism that prevail in the so-called progressive circles in Germany today – the chauvinism, arrogance, and ignorance of official cultural conduits in the media (which take pride in their environmentalism and anti-authoritarian education and worship postmodern literature) in order to appreciate, by contrast, the degree of intellectual audacity that Goethe had shown in his time. Alongside the authors whose position towards Goethe is ambivalent, there are those who unreservedly claim Goethean heritage. These include, for example, Galsan Tschinag, who was born in Mongolia in 1944 and admits in no uncertain terms that Goethe is his "god."[39]

---

[38] On this text entitled ""Sehr geehrter Herr Geheimrat'. Zwischen Orient und Okzident: Zum Ende des Goethe-Jahres ein Brief an den Dichter", see chapter 2, "Metafiction: Dialogues with the Dead", subsection A.

[39] "Goethe ist mein Gott. Natürlich, jeder Germanist hat einen Hauptgott, und ob er das will oder nicht, er heißt Johann Wolfgang von Goethe," Tschinag said in an interview (Saalfeld 1998: 85–108, here 100). On the reception of Goethe by Tschinag, see Koiran (2009: 222–248).

Gotthold Ephraim Lessing (1729–1781) is the main representative of the pre-Classicist period and, as a literary figure of the *Aufklärung* who embodied a discourse of tolerance and ethical responsibility, is certainly a major reference point. While easily identifiable, however, he does not elicit much controversy – except in calling into question the optimism of the humanistic ethical discourse as such. Zaimoglu's rewriting of *Nathan the Wise* under the title *Nathan Messias* (co-authored with Senkel, 2006) serves here as an exception that confirms the rule. Re-reading Lessing's dramatic poem against the currents of the *Aufklärung*'s message, Zaimoglu no longer places the main character above the melee but at its center: the Jew Nathan becomes a guru claiming himself to incarnate the Messiah.[40] This very free adaptation, which reconfigures the original plot in light of the current religious wars in the Middle East, can be considered as little more than an act of isolated "cannibalism."[41] By inverting the gaze of literary history's most positive Jewish character, Zaimoglu doubtlessly chose the most provocative angle possible in order to denounce the unilateral discourse about Islamic fanaticism that spread throughout the West following 9/11, but this challenge to public opinion by an inveterate critic of the "politically correct" was destined to miss the mark in the context of a general resurgence of racism in Germany.

Friedrich Hölderlin (1777–1843), on the other hand, is an author at once fascinating and intriguing, as much for his enigmatic œuvre as for his contradictions and his tragic destiny. Inspired by Schiller's ideas and aesthetic project as well as by the philosophical constructions of Hegel, Schelling, and Fichte, he followed an unusual trajectory, went long unrecognized, and was in conflict with his times. He ardently supported the liberation of the people and, an enthusiastic witness of the French Revolution, he transferred his disappointed hopes for emancipation to Greece's mythical past. He isolated himself from artistic and intellectual circles and foundered in insanity and silence. Hölderlin, belatedly canonized at the beginning of the twentieth century, was upheld as a model by Heidegger, who saw in him a precursor to the tragic fate of the modern individual with no homeland and a visionary bard awakening national identities. This partial reading allowed him to be instrumentalized by the National-Socialist regime, which served as a new obstacle to the objective reception of his work. Because of this unusual biographical and historiographical trajectory, the author

---

40 Written for the Düsseldorf Schauspielhaus, *Nathan Messias* was first staged by Anna Badora in 2006. It was revived in 2009 at the Ballhaus Naunynstraße in Berlin under the direction of Neco Çelik.
41 See Cheesman (Cheesman and Yeşilada 2012: 118–144, here 124).

of *Hyperion* is as likely to inspire admiration (for his lyrical spirit, radically innovative language, and revolutionary aspirations) as he is compassion (for his radical isolation and suffering), but also incomprehension and disapproval – even rejection.[42]

Another unclassifiable figure of the "classical" canon, the prose writer Johann Paul Richter (1763–1825), known as "Jean Paul," was well-connected within the literary circles of his time, and he occupies a long-standing and undisputed place in the canon. However, his monumental and generically hybridized work, which embraces Laurence Sterne's art of digression and arabesque, upsets the codes of classical aesthetics and has known no real posterity in Germany. For this reason, it offers a few anchoring points for reception along the "minor" line. Kermani draws particular inspiration from Jean Paul's model in constructing *Dein Name* ("Your Name," 2014), a polyphonic monolith of colossal dimensions (1229 pages) that is located at the confluence of journal, autobiography, novel, philosophical essay, travel narrative, and reportage.[43]

As a group, the Romantics benefit somewhat from collective canonization. Yet this label brings together authors with a wide variety of profiles. Novalis, Arnim, Brentano, Eichendorff, and (to a lesser extent) Tieck embody the dominant canon in different ways, while Kleist and E. T. A. Hoffmann form a more deviant line. Probing the depths of the human soul and exploring the duality of the world with an ironic gaze, Hoffmann (1776–1822) represents a version of Romanticism at its most bitter and subversive – what Goethe considered "sick" compared to a classical aesthetic of the beautiful and "healthy."[44] The same is true of Kleist (1777–1811), a tortured and tragic writer who vainly solicited the support of the "Olympian" and who, at the end of his short life, left behind a feverish work with finely-wrought language. He did not enjoy much recognition during his lifetime, and it was not until the beginning of the twentieth century that he received some attention after the rediscovery of his work. These two precursors of modernity have been the subjects of an intense contemporary reception, especially by the German-Japanese writer and essayist Yoko Tawada (born

---

[42] See the analysis of SAID's radio play *Friedrich Hölderlin empfängt niemanden mehr* below.
[43] On this work, see Kermani, *Über den Zufall. Jean Paul, Hölderlin und der Roman, den ich schreibe* (2012).
[44] In a letter to Eckermann on 2 April 1829, Goethe claimed, "Das Klassische nenne ich das Gesunde und das Romantische das Kranke" ("The classic I call the healthy, and the romantic the sick") (Goethe 2006, Vol. 19: 300).

in 1960), who considers their work from a decentralized point of view, oriented in particular by her readings of Kafka and Benjamin.⁴⁵

As for Chamisso (1781–1838), the very fact that there is a literary prize in his name for authors with a "non-German mother tongue" attests both to the degree of his canonicity and a form of persistent marginality. An eminent figure from the dominant literary system, the intimate friend of Friedrich de la Motte Fouqué and Germaine de Staël, he nonetheless presents the image of an ambivalent personality due to his atypical cultural and social trajectory. Taking refuge in Berlin during the Revolution, this French aristocrat was a representative of the *ancien régime* who chose to serve in the Prussian army and wrote all his works in German despite retaining his French nationality. As such, he was certainly no more destined to be a "martyr" or "rebel" than was Thomas Mann. Nevertheless, Chamisso stands for a certain social and cultural marginality because he was torn between nations, religions, and social classes (all his life he was "caught in the middle," as Schami said of him⁴⁶) – an experience that doubtlessly also brought him closer to the Jewish worl. The key figure of the *schlemiel*, borrowed from Ashkenazi folk culture and made into the protagonist of his only prose fiction, testifies to this identification with, or empathy for, the Jewish people. And it is indeed this parable about the dissociation of the individual from his social identity, *Peter Schlemihls wundersame Geschichte* ("The Wondrous Story of Peter Schlemihl"), rather than the poetic cycle *Frauenliebe- und leben* ("A Woman's Life and Love"), that has gained him recognition from authors for whom his career has in some ways served as an example.

In the Romantic pantheon, there are special places for the philologists Jacob (1785–1863) and Wilhelm (1786–1859) Grimm, who distinguished themselves by promoting literature that was simultaneously "popular" and "national." The Grimms participated in the normative remodeling of oral tradition in the service of the values of the bourgeoisie and, as such, the two brothers strongly embody the dominant ideology of their time, which is widely perceived today as reactionary. However, their legacy is still very much present in the collective imagination thanks to their *Kinder- und Hausmärchen* ("Children's and Household Tales"), which ranks first among the works of the German patrimony accepted into the world canon. This international consecration (the UNESCO International Register "Memory of the World" has included the work since 2005), combined with a nationalist orientation that has persistently permeated the folk and educated cul-

---

45 See especially *Spielzeug und Sprachmagie: Eine ethnopoetische Poetologie* (Tawada 2000) and "Kleist auf Japanisch" (Tawada 2003: 241–244).
46 See the analysis of Schami's text "Wer zwischen den Stühlen sitzt, verteidigt keinen" (Schami [2006] 2009: 204–210) in chapter 2.

ture of Germany, makes the "Grimm Bros." prime targets for the questioning of the national canon. Nevertheless, as initiators of a "literarization" of folklore, it is also possible to view them from the potentially multicultural and translational angle of the rehabilitation of orality and popular culture. This ambivalent reception is notably present among writers like Schami and Özdamar who critique dominant discourses in search of a literature that is socially relevant and that gives voice to the "people" in its dimension of political subalternity.[47] It is worth noting that in counterpoint to his critical reception of the Brothers Grimm, Schami refers positively to another representative of the German tradition of folk storytellers, the author of "oriental" tales Wilhelm Hauff (1802–1827), a member of the Swabian poetic school.

This list should also include a number of representatives of the Western canon like Homer, Dante, Cervantes, and especially Shakespeare, whom the German national canon assimilated so long ago that it is no longer possible to consider them as entirely foreign. Shakespeare in particular has had almost the status of a national author since the eighteenth century. In addition, his dominant position in the Western canon makes his work a first choice for "writing back" in the postcolonial context.[48] German writers make their own contributions to this endeavor, especially playwrights Özdamar[49] and Zaimoglu.[50] There is also Rafik Schami, who uses *Romeo and Juliet* as a backdrop for his novel on the clan wars in Syria, *Die dunkle Seite der Liebe* ("The Dark Side of Love," 2005), though this is not a major point of reference.

Minor Line: The "Martyrs," the Marginal, the Rebellious

Of the authors characterized by their remove from political and institutional power and their resistance to the dominant thought of their time, Jakob M. R. Lenz (1751–1792) and Georg Büchner (1813–1837) are especially noteworthy. Lenz, a key figure in the *Sturm und Drang* movement, was Goethe's contemporary

---

47 On Schami's rewriting of *Little Red Riding Hood*, see chapter 3. On the critical reworking of the Grimms' tales in Özdamar, see chapter 4.
48 Beyond Aimé Césaire's *Une tempête* (1987), let us recall in particular Derek Walcott's *A Branch of the Blue Nile* (1986), Suniti Namjoshi's *Snapshots of Caliban* (1989), Salih Tayeb's *Season of Migration to the North* (2003), and the productions of *The Merchant of Venice*, *Hamlet*, and *Macbeth* directed by Salim Ghouse. On these "Native Shakespeares," see Dionne and Kapadia (2008).
49 See the analysis of Özdamar's *Keloglan in Alamania* in chapter 4.
50 Together with Senkel, Zaimoglu has co-authored adaptations of *Othello*, *Hamlet*, *Romeo and Juliet*, and *Julius Caesar*. See "Feridun Zaimoglu adaptateur de Shakespeare" (Meyer 2014).

and friend and enjoyed support from intellectual circles. However, he led a wretched existence and ultimately became an outcast. A defender of social reforms and creator of a devastatingly critical theater, he sank into madness and died in exile, unknown and alone. It was not until the twentieth century that Lenz's work was rediscovered, following the likewise belated canonization of Georg Büchner, who had dedicated a short story to him. Büchner had been a militant revolutionary and, falling under the censors' axe, faced prosecution; he took refuge in Strasbourg and then in Switzerland, and died at just twenty-three years of age. The playwright, pamphleteer, and satirist was also a translator of Victor Hugo and a doctor of medicine and left behind a significant body of work – three plays (*The Death of Danton, Leonce and Lena*, and *Woyzeck*), a revolutionary tract, and the radically innovative short story *Lenz* – now considered one of the most remarkable of the time.

Continuing with this "minor" line of German letters, the Jewish poet, satirist, and polemicist Heinrich Heine (1797–1856) likewise left behind a pioneering body of work. He is simultaneously the most widely received author of the Romantic corpus – with his lyric works set to music more than any others in the German repertoire – and perhaps the most unclassifiable German writer, the most challenging to fit within national frameworks, and the one with the most eventful reception history. An admirer of the French Revolution schooled as a Romantic, Heine was a staunch opponent of the monarchy and the Restoration but also had ruthless disdain for the "politically engaged" writers of the Vormärz who dreamt of national unification. Lambasting conformity and nationalism, he persistently challenged authority and denounced oppression in all its forms, rooting out hypocrisy in the discourse of all the factions flourishing around him. Because of this rebellious spirit, he spent his entire lifetime at odds with censorship, personal attacks, and antisemitism. Having converted to Protestantism without ever denying his affiliation with Jewish culture, Heine went into exile in France in 1831 and spent the last part of his life there. Nonetheless, his work remained popular enough for Hitler to take the trouble of personally banning it and having all his books tossed into the fires lit on 10 May 1933. Yet this stigmatization was not enough to facilitate his recovery following 1945. It was not until 1988 that the University of Düsseldorf, located in his home town, agreed to adopt his name. Heine's contemporary reception is based on the rich body of work he left behind as well as on the recognition it received from later Jewish poets such as Paul Celan.[51] As for authors of migration

---

[51] See for example the poem "Eine Gauner- und Ganovenweise, gesungen zu Paris emprès Pontoise von Paul Celan aus Czernowitz bei Sadagora" (Celan 1996: 40–45).

literature, he enjoys the most positive (and resolutely empathic) reception among those who, like Schami and Özdamar, invoke a tradition of political (in the broadest sense of the term), radically anti-nationalist, and "leftist" literature.

Heine inaugurates the long and heterogeneous series of Jewish writers who successfully established themselves in the twentieth century literary field, generally by way of a detour through the international stage. Because these authors belonged to a historically persecuted minority and were kept, by extension, at a remove from the centers of power even after its progressive political liberation over the course of the nineteenth century, they have a marginalized status that reveals itself in various forms throughout their works. The most illustrious of this group is undoubtedly Franz Kafka (1883–1924), who served precisely – though not entirely appropriately – as the basis for Deleuze and Guattari in their formulation of the notion of "minor literature."[52] Born into the Bohemian Jewish community (a "subaltern" cultural minority within a politically dominant linguistic minority, the German-speaking population of the provinces of the Habsburg Empire), the Prague writer left an œuvre that explores the isolation of a radically marginal intimate experience to reach the universal, to such a point that today, along with Proust, Joyce, Woolf, Pessoa, and Beckett, he epitomizes twentieth-century European modernity. Through this exceptional and seminal œuvre, which flourishes well beyond the frontiers of German cultural space, Kafka illustrates better than anyone else the artistic fertility of peripheral territories and cultural minorities. His claustrophobic universe provides an inexhaustible reservoir of potentially identificatory images for writers in a subaltern or minority position – particularly in postcolonial settings, where his work is one of the most popular in the German canon.[53] For Kermani, Kafka best embodies the greatness of German letters because of his remove not only from power, but also from Germany as a nation. It is worth noting that, in the early twentieth century, the reception of Kleist – whose work is no less unclassifiable and who served as Kafka's greatest model in German literature – was largely through the prism of Kafka.

---

[52] On their misappropriation of Kafka's thoughts regarding "small literatures" and their subsequent misinterpretation of Kafka himself as a "minor writer," see Jamison (2003), Corngold (2004), and Lauer (2006).
[53] Through his works based directly on colonial motifs (*In der Strafkolonie, Ein Bericht für eine Akademie*), in particular, Kafka found a considerable reception among postcolonial writers. These include, for example, Coetzee (whose work, practically in its entirety, bears the marks of Kafka) and Mario Vargas Llosa (*El Hablador*, 1987). See Engélibert (2007) and Luste Boulbina (2008).

A contemporary of Kafka, poet Else Lasker-Schüler (1869–1945) occupies a unique position in the canon for a number of reasons. She came from a bourgeois Jewish family in a small town but freed herself both of her original class and the social constraints related to her status as a woman to assert a culturally and sexually hybrid identity in an environment that was mostly male and "native." Playing with stereotypes, she established herself in expressionist circles by developing an original type of writing that summoned a syncretic imaginary with a mixture of folklore and the avant-garde, of kitsch and mysticism. In this respect, her work opens an "Orientalizing" line in contemporary immigration literature by giving an example of a voluntary, ambivalent, and rebellious appropriation of the discourse on alterity, but also writing at once from a feminine and feminist, anti-conformist, and fundamentally "embodied" viewpoint. Unsurprisingly, women have paid most attention to her: Özdamar,[54] Tawada,[55] the poet Zehra Çırak (born 1960 in Istanbul), and the novelist and poet Olga Martynova (born in 1962 in Doudinka, Siberia).

The Nazis' rise to power in 1933 brutally interrupted the great Judeo-German tradition, though there were some poets who survived the Shoah and were able to contribute to prolonging the tradition. Romanian Jew Paul Celan (1920–1970) wrote all his lyric works "in memory of the genocide," thereby exposing himself to the hostility of many of his German contemporaries within the context of a general repression of the Nazi past. Celan provides an example of internal resistance that is both obstinate and demanding. His work paves the way for a critical reappropriation of the national canon that outlines the contours of possibilities for "writing back" from within the German context itself. Celan is a major point of reference for many authors and representatives of migration literature, from Zafer Şenocak to Yoko Tawada to Zehra Çırak by way of Khalid A-Maaly, a poet and publisher who translated Celan into Arabic for the publisher Al-Kamel, founded in Cologne in 1983.

Another Jewish writer from the margins of the former Austro-Hungarian Empire, Elias Canetti (1905–1994) offers the complex image of a personality that is both entirely atypical – because of his origins, his career, and some of his intellectual positions – and less controversial than many others aesthetically and politically. The only Sephardi to have made a career in German letters, Canetti was a descendant of Jews expelled from Spain in 1492 and was a latecomer to the German language. He became stateless following the annexation of Austria by Nazi Germany in 1938 and presents a figure of the marginal among the marginalized.

---

[54] See chapter 5.
[55] See especially "Zu Else Lasker-Schülers *Mein blaues Klavier*" (Tawada 2003: 45–47).

Exile had cut him off from his public, and he wrote for several decades in the shadows, preferring – despite his polyglossia – to count on achieving renown in posterity rather than to renounce German as the language in which he wrote. It was thus in a context of great precariousness that he constructed an ambitious body of work, generically heterogeneous but of remarkable thematic coherence, by which he hoped to "take this century by the throat." His perseverance paid off and he received the Nobel Prize for Literature in 1981 the ultimate of accolades for an exile born in Bulgaria whose first language was Judeo-Spanish. Exemplary in his unfailing acculturation and his assimilation of the classic European canon, Canetti nonetheless constantly asserted his opposition to all forms of domination and advocated for a "minor" line of literature, which he found most admirably illustrated by Kafka and Robert Walser.[56] According to Ilija Trojanow (2000: 13), this writer with cultural roots submerged in the Ottoman Empire could, better than Chamisso, serve as the patron figure for contemporary literature by German-speaking immigrants.

In addition to the entirely discontinuous line of twentieth-century Jewish writers in the German literary field, the "minor" canon is dominated, on its revolutionary side, by the figure of Bertolt Brecht (1898–1956). To a certain extent, the Marxist poet and playwright perpetuates the tradition born with Lenz and Büchner by making "distancing" the foundation of a social theater and critique diametrically opposed to Western dramaturgy based on the principle of illusion and mimeticism. An essential reference for all playwrights of the late twentieth century, he is of particular importance for a writer like Özdamar, whose works – including her narrative corpus – are nurtured by her theatrical practice.

This list is necessarily schematic and quite incomplete, both in terms of the authors identified and their readers. Yet it sketches the dominant lines of possible reconfigurations the German canon embodies for authors of migration literature.

Examining some of the discursive strategies used by those authors to position themselves toward canonical writers and texts, the following chapter will outline and illustrate the main levels of "second degree" writing that can be observed within this corpus, from generic references and critical commentary to more complex forms of textual transposition.

---

[56] See "Elias Canetti als Ahne?" (Meyer 2012b).

Chapter 2
Counter-Discursive Strategies: From Metatextuality to Rewriting

In the introduction to *Palimpsestes*, Genette establishes a typology of trans-textual relations that he divides into five categories: "intertextuality" in the strict sense (quotation, allusion, plagiarism); "paratextuality" ("relation that binds a text properly speaking, taken within the totality of the literary work, to what can be called its paratext: a title, a subtitle, intertitles; prefaces, postfaces, notices, forewords, etc."); "architextuality" (relation of belonging or, on the contrary, of exclusion, between a text and an entire category of earlier texts); "metatextuality" (the "relationship most often labeled 'commentary' [that] unites a given text to another, of which it speaks without necessarily citing it"); and finally, "hypertextuality," which Genette defines as "any relationship uniting a text B (which I shall call the *hypertext*) with an earlier text A (I shall, of course, call it the *hypotext*) upon which it is grafted in a manner that is not that of the commentary." However, the boundaries between these categories are far from distinct, as Genette himself concedes, listing all kinds of possible interference:

> [o]ne must not view the five types of transtextuality as separate and absolute categories without any reciprocal contract or overlapping. On the contrary, their relationships to one another are numerous and often crucial. For example, generic architextuality is, historically, almost always constituted by way of imitation (Virgil imitates Homer, Mateo Aleman's *Guzman* imitates the anonymous *Lazarillo*), hence by way of hypertextuality. The architextual appurtenance of a given work is frequently announced by way of paratextual clues. These in themselves often initiate a metatext ("this book is a novel"), and the paratext, whether prefatory or other, contains many more forms of commentary [...]; the critical metatext can be conceived of, but is hardly ever practiced, without the often considerable use of a quotational intertext as support. The hypertext tends to avoid this practice, but not entirely, for it makes use of textual allusions [...] or of paratextual ones [...]. Above all, hypertextuality, as a category of works, is in itself a generic or, more precisely, *transgeneric* architext [...] Like all generic categories, hypertextuality is most often revealed by means of a paratextual sign that has contractual force [...]. (Genette 1997: 7)

It therefore bears keeping in mind that the categories Genette establishes refer only to reasonably homogenous sets. Indeed, the other types of relation include intertextuality in the strict sense of the term (quotation and allusion) as well as paratextuality, which most frequently serve to establish a contract of hypertextuality that develops throughout the body of the text in other forms. Thus, the title of Özdamar's auto-fictional novel, *Seltsame Sterne starren zur Erde* ("Strange

Stars Stare to Earth"),[1] which is a direct quote from a poem by Else Lasker-Schüler, places the work under the patronage of a poet who is emblematic of the expressionist avant-garde of the early twentieth century, and thereby indicates perspectives for its reading. Some of Schami's titles even more explicitly orient reading by establishing at the outset a reading contract including discourse about canonical authors in one form or another. These titles include *Die Verteidigungsrede. Akte: Rotkäppchen* ("Plea for the Defense: The Little Red Riding Hood File"), or *Der geheime Bericht über den Dichter Goethe, der eine Prüfung auf einer arabischen Insel bestand* ("The Secret Report on the Poet Goethe, Who Passed a Test on an Arabian Island," 1999), with the first work constituting a rewriting and the second a commentary coupled with a continuation. This is likewise the case for Kemal Kurt's novel, *Ja, Sagt Molly*, ("Yes, Says Molly," 1998), where the name "Molly" is a nod to the character Molly Bloom, the source of the renowned soliloquy in Joyce's *Ulysses* – thus announcing a complex transfictional game that has as its governing theme the explorations that Gregor Samsa, the hero who wakes up as a bug one morning in Kafka's *Verwandlung* ("Metamorphosis"), makes of Molly's body.[2]

Genette, however, devotes the body of his work to hypertextuality, and to it alone – if it is even possible to isolate it, which is far from easy, as we have just seen. It is worth recalling his definition of hypertext, the type of text that "is more frequently considered a 'properly literary' work than is the metatext" because "generally derived from a work of fiction (narrative or dramatic), it remains a work of fiction":

> By hypertextuality I mean any relationship uniting a text B (which I call the hypertext) to an earlier text A (I shall, of course, call it the hypotext), upon which it is grafted in a manner that is not that of commentary [...] To view things differently, let us posit the general notion of a text in the second degree [...] i.e., a text derived from another pre-existing text. This derivation can be of a descriptive or intellectual kind, where a metatext (for example, a given page from Aristotle's Poetics) "speaks" about a second text (Oedipus Rex). It may yet be of another kind such as text B not speaking of text A at all but being unable to exist, as such, without A, from which it originates through a process I shall provisionally call transformation, and which it consequently evokes more or less perceptibly without necessarily speaking of it or citing it. (Genette 1997: 5)

Below, I address specific developments for those of Genette's categories that are most relevant to *Questioning the Canon:* architextuality, belonging to a genre or

---

[1] All further references to this work will appear as SSE plus page number in the text.
[2] See Moray McGowan's discussion of this work (2010).

subgenre; metatextuality or commentary; and hypertextuality – that is to say, very broadly, rewriting.

Generic Hypertextuality ("Architextuality")

Among the modalities of inscription, the architextual relation is a priori the one least loaded with semantic issues. However, it merits further scrutiny in a context where, as is the case for "oriental" writers in Germany, the publishers' marketing policy is preponderantly directed towards an interpretive framework with *The Thousand and One Nights* as more or less the sole generic reference. However, even among authors like Schami and Özdamar who do not challenge such inclusion in the (or an) Eastern tradition, other references are often just as significant.

It is therefore necessary to evoke, in Schami's case, the European tradition of the story with multiple narrative levels (*récit à tiroir*) going back to Boccaccio – a way of portraying a society through a series of short stories connected by a narrative frame that brings together characters, against a backdrop of disaster, who in close quarters are to take turns telling stories to the group. The *Decameron* inaugurated this tradition and among those who used it were Goethe (*Unterhaltungen deutscher Ausgewanderten*, "Conversations of German Refugees," 1795) and Wilhelm Hauff (*Die Karawane*, "The Caravan," 1825), and it also provided Schami with the compositional principle of his first novel *Erzähler der Nacht* ("Damascus Nights," 1989). The novel takes place in Damascus in the 1950s and is divided into a series of nights in which seven characters gather to tell each other one story after the next intended to restore the faculty of speech to their friend, the coachman Salim, an outstanding storyteller who has mysteriously lost his ability to talk. This obvious reference to a European tradition did not prevent commentators from invoking here, as with all of Schami's other "Syrian" works, Scheherazade and *The Thousand and One Nights*.[3]

When it comes to the tales as such, Schami refers to several European traditions apart from the (criticized, deconstructed) tradition of the "popular" tales à la Grimm or Perrault: the fantastic tale in the Romantic vein of E. T. A. Hoffmann, the philosophical tale of the Enlightenment (Voltaire), and even the European "oriental" tale of the Biedermeier period as represented by Wilhelm Hauff. Liter-

---

[3] See for example Schami's presentation as "the companion from Damascus" by Ineichen (2006). On the "orientalist" reception of Schami, see especially Ellerbach's monograph *L'Arabie contée aux Allemands. Fictions interculturelles chez Rafik Schami* (2018).

ary motifs invoke certain traditions, as is the case for German Romanticism in the novel *Sieben Doppelgänger* (1999). Here, the narrative context brings the central motif closer to strategies of resistance against cultural domination Bhabha interpreted using the concepts of mimicry and hybridity.[4]

Özdamar also draws inspiration from certain elements of the folk culture of her country of origin, particularly with regard to her narrative style, recognizable by the use of recurring formulas that are more or less fixed. Yet, her autobiographical novels have specifically European models as direct generic references, both for the themes and structures, in the picaresque novel, on the one hand, and the German coming-of-age novel (*Bildungsroman*), specifically the *Künstlerroman* on the other.[5] And if she also relies on the popular tradition of *karagöz* shadow theater, in particular in her dramatic works, it is precisely with the intention of "revitalizing" this ancient Ottoman tradition of puppet theater in a spirit of carnivalesque transgression and very modernist distancing. Apart from this reference, and even through the usage she makes of it, Özdamar's literary and dramatic landmarks are primarily located in the European avant-garde of the 1920s through the 1970s and 1980s.

Zaimoglu fell in line with the classical tradition of the epistolary novel with *Liebesmale, Scharlachrot* ("Love Marks, Scarlet Red," 2000), and then with his subsequent novels *Liebesbrand* ("Blazing Love," 2008) and *Hinterland* (2009) endeavored to rehabilitate the aesthetics, imaginary, and philosophy of the first German Romantics.

Metafiction: Dialogues with the Dead

On the generic level, metatextuality is located a priori within the scope of paraliterary texts or paratextual elements such as essays, poetics conferences, awards speeches, prefaces, press forums, and other public statements. By its very definition, the attribution of a literary distinction in particular offers laureates the opportunity to situate themselves in relation to the individual to whom the prize is dedicated. This is the reason why Chamisso, Büchner, Kleist, and Bachmann, whose names were given to prestigious literary awards, are in a way predestined to be the object of generally laudatory discursive developments in this context. The analysis of this category of texts certainly merits its own spe-

---

[4] Regarding these concepts, see Pizer (2004) and Arnds (2005).
[5] See Michael Hofmann's analysis in *Interkulturelle Literaturwissenschaft* (Hofmann 2006: 214–225).

cific study. For the purposes of my inquiry, I will refer only occasionally – as has been the case so far – to a meta-discursive evocation of a given author, in parallel with the analyses of these more "properly literary" texts: the rewritings.

Before addressing this final category, however, it is necessary to reflect for a moment on a mode of reference that is an intermediary between commentary and re-creation and that does not appear in the typology established by Genette. Nonetheless, it seems sufficiently significant in the context of the present study to deserve special attention. It is an enunciative device that consists of setting up (or occasionally even on a stage) a fictional dialogue with a canonical personality. Often employed in reflexive (meta-discursive) or paratextual (prefaces) texts, this rhetorical process can also give rise to an entire work of fiction or just as well appear in a fragmentary state within a narrative work – in the form of dreams or hallucinations, for example. Whatever the context into which it enters, it introduces a critical relationship to its object while consisting of a significant element of fictionalization.

I will refer to this rhetorical device that combines self-referentiality and meta-discursiveness as "dialogue with the dead," with reference to the ancient tradition of the "dialogue of the dead." In this genre dating back to the second century AD (Lucian of Samosata), historical and/or mythological characters converse, usually with one another, either in the Elysian Fields or in the Underworld. This device, which enjoyed renewed popularity in Europe during the classical period (from the 1680s to the end of the eighteenth century) following a long period of neglect, presents a certain number of analogies with the texts that are under investigation below. The "dialogues of the dead" from the classical age are dedicated to debating ideas and related to pamphleteering literature, journalism, and chapbook literature. They thus belong to the literary trend of the dialogue of ideas (Pujol 2005, Cazanave 2007), though they represent, according to Lise Andries, "an autonomous category with its own history" (2013: 134).

The purpose of the "dialogues of the dead" was to entertain and edify, but also to bear judgment on the contemporary period by playing with the comic effects of bringing together "characters you wouldn't expect to find in the same place, either because they belong to different social categories, epochs, or countries that prevent them from meeting on earth" (Andries 2013: 135). Born of "the double tradition of the burlesque genre and the moralists" (148) these dialogues had a subversive character, which became even more pronounced over the course of the eighteenth century, because they made it possible to "have people make all sorts of reflections, more or less insolent, about the situation here below, with their words having the gravitas of a message coming from beyond the grave," writes Andries (137). "Their aim" in these texts, "rests on a paradox: these are uchronia against a backdrop of eternity whose primary concern is to know what is happening on earth. Indeed, the dead have a lively interest in news […], which explains the rapprochement of the genre with journalistic writing: the ones who have been there a long time ask the newcomers for news of life on earth."[6] The genre fell into disuse in the nineteenth century but was occasionally revived in the twentieth, especially in Germany by authors like Arno Schmidt (*Dichtergespräche im Elysium*), Bertolt Brecht (*Das Verhör des Lukullus*), Hans Magnus Enzensberger (*Ohne uns*), and Walter Jens (*Der Teufel lebt nicht mehr, mein Herr!*).

Contrary to authors who explicitly refer to the classical tradition and reproduce its well-identified rhetorical framework, Schami, SAID, and Özdamar do not cite a particular genre when imagining fictional encounters or dialogues of their alter ego with a writer of the past. The process, however, is not fundamentally different; the authors also play with the dynamics of the burlesque paradox and uchronia. It is possible to see what interest the use of such a device can hold for them, given their marginal position on the national literary scene: namely, it allows them to position themselves in the field by giving credence to the connections that unite them, despite their foreign origins, with a well-identified native tradition. By asserting their legitimate position as successors to the authors they invoke, they also allow themselves, under the authority of these authors, "more or less insolent" reflections about modern-day Germany. Beyond its rhetorical potential, the process is an exercise in erudition through which minority writers provide proof of their expertise in German and world literature by demonstrating familiarity with the work of great authors.

It is worth noting that this modality of discourse about the canon also has some points in common with the motif in theatrical productions of the resurrection of the dead, as seen in the late twentieth century with the "post-dramatic" works, for example, of Heiner Müller and Elfriede Jelinek, with ghosts and other phantoms who attest to the persistence of the past. For Özdamar, who is situated partly in this current, the theater is the site *par excellence* for the resurrection of the dead, a place where one goes to see and hear those who came before (the playwrights and the characters to whom they have given life) "to meddle in the future stories of the world."[7]

---

6 "Leur propos […] repose sur un paradoxe: ce sont des uchronies sur fond d'éternité dont la préoccupation principale est de savoir ce qui se passe sur terre. En effet, l'intérêt des morts pour l'actualité est vif […], ce qui explique le rapprochement du genre avec l'écriture journalistique: les anciens demandent aux nouveaux venus des nouvelles de la vie sur terre" (Andries 2013: 137).

7 Returning to East Berlin in 1976 after obtaining the visa that permitted her to resume her activity at the Volksbühne, the narrator of *Strange Stars* reports that she "rushed back to the dead":

Irreverent Dialogues with Goethe and Hölderlin (SAID)

On the occasion of the 250th anniversary of Goethe's birth, German-Iranian poet SAID contributed to the celebrations in the form of an open letter published in the *Berliner Zeitung* under the title *Sehr geehrter Herr Geheimrat* ("Dear Mister Privy Councilor"). In this text, SAID addresses the Weimar poet directly, painting a half-hearted portrait of the commander of German letters, whose openness to the Orient – illustrated by the *Western-Eastern Divan* – does not manage to exonerate him in SAID's eyes of his compromises with power and a deep conservatism, both political and aesthetic. The tribute paid to the author of the *Divan* is an opportunity for the exiled writer to make a disillusioned assessment of the current state of relations between the West and East. The reminder of the rare openness that Goethe exhibited in this work by "going to meet our Hafez" and "building a cultural bridge between two worlds"[8] allows him to measure the chasm that has broadened between these two places: condescending indifference and navel-gazing in the West and alienation and servile imitation in the East.

While Goethe certainly cannot be held responsible for this development, SAID nonetheless harshly attacks him for his allegiance to monarchical power. He wonders how the author of the *Divan* and *Faust* could have written a farce as flat as *Der Bürgergeneral* ("The Citizen General"). "I was horrified. It sounded petty, conservative, and reactionary. Precisely the opposite of what Thomas Mann once said of you: 'he who affirmed all that is vast and great.'"[9] The self-importance with which Goethe defended his counter-revolutionary positions ("Mr. Privy Councilor is trying to ridicule the French Revolution"),[10] weighs all the more heavily from the point of view of SAID – who himself had remained in Germany, where he had come to study in 1965, in order first to flee the regime of the Shah, then that of the mullahs – because it cannot be attributed to a passing folly. Indeed, the "prince of poets" was also disconcertingly small-minded in

---

"Ich war zu den Toten zurückgekehrt. Zum toten Goethe, zu Märten, Röse, Görge, dem armen Dorfbarbier, der wegen eines Kruges Milch Revolution spielte, dem Edelmann, der wie ein Förster aussah und das Volk belehrte. Im Theater stehen die Toten auf. [...] Die Toten wollen weiterleben, um sich in die kommenden Geschichten der Welt einzumischen" (SSE 169–170).
8 "Ein deutscher Klassiker geht unserem Hafiz entgegen [...] und schlägt eine kulturelle Brücke zwischen zwei Welten" (SAID 1999: 1).
9 "Ich war entsetzt. Das klang bieder, konservativ und reaktionär. Exakt das Gegenteil dessen, was einmal Thomas Mann von Ihnen behauptete: 'der jede Weite und Größe bejahte'" (SAID 1999: 1).
10 "Der Herr Geheimrat versucht die Französische Revolution lächerlich zu machen" (SAID 1999: 1).

his aesthetic judgments. To substantiate this verdict, the author cites statements that Goethe made attesting to his misunderstanding of the genius of Beethoven and Hölderlin and his condemnation of everything that was not consistent with his serene hedonism. "But the history of the world is not made only of pleasure and tranquility," SAID protests. And in response to Goethe's devotion to authority, he reminds him of "Mr. Luther" and his doctrine of absolute submission to the State, the power of which emanated from God himself.[11] He accuses him of, like Luther, "[having] always supported authority in decisive moments, a German attitude that has proved fatal to this very day."[12]

With such foundations, even the incontestable greatness of *Faust*, the poetic power of which SAID admires, cannot quite be credited to Goethe, insofar as this work feeds on an ambivalent fascination with evil. If Goethe is indeed the national poet in his eyes, it is effectively in part because in this work he presented the archetypal formula of the "German tragedy." "Here the German tragedy is anticipated: it only takes a Mephisto for Faust to emerge, quintessentially German, from his room, 'hemmed in by all the masses of books' in order to enjoy life. [...] He falls in love with Margarete's golden hair, commits a murder, and from then on is no longer fit for love."[13] Surprising in this context, the metonymy of "Margarete's golden hair" can only be understood as a reminiscence of Celan's famous poem, *Todesfuge* ("Death Fugue," 1948), which contrasts the "golden hair of Margarete" with the "ashen hair of Shulamith" in its evocation of the extermination of Europe's Jews as directed by a "master from Germany" who personifies death itself (Celan 2004: 55–59). Discreet but eloquent, the intertextual reference confirms the connection, already established by Celan, between the myth of Faust and the genocide, thereby indicating the author's diametrically opposite positions towards the two poets: SAID's relation to "Mister Privy Councilor" is as distant, tense, and polemical as his relation to Celan is intimate.

The way this reference is slipped between the lines of an ambivalent tribute to the author of *Faust* makes it clear beyond a shadow of a doubt that Celan, unlike Goethe, serves as a model for SAID. His solidarity and empathy with Celan speak for themselves. He appropriated Celan's words because he had been en-

---

11 "In Ihrer unbedingten Verehrung der Obrigkeit erinnern Sie mich an Herrn Luther: 'Gott ist es selber, wenn die Obrigkeit straft'" (SAID 1999: 1).
12 "Wie Luther haben Sie immer in der Stunde X zur Obrigkeit gehalten; eine fatale deutsche Haltung bis heute" (SAID 1999: 2).
13 "Hier wird die deutsche Tragödie antizipiert: Es braucht erst einen Mephisto, damit Faust urdeutsch aus seiner Stube 'beschränkt von all dem Bücherhauff' herauskommt, um das Leben zu genießen. [...] Er verliebt sich in das goldene Haar von Margarete, begeht einen Mord und taugt fortan nicht mehr für die Liebe" (SAID 1999: 2).

riched by his work and embraced his approach wholeheartedly. He thus shows that his criticism of Goethe, and by extension a confident, domineering, and conservative Germany, does not come "from the outside" but that it is rooted in a tradition, itself German or at least Germanophone (intracultural despite being peripheral, minority and subordinate), of demystifying the German language and culture. The Jewish poet from Czernowitz, survivor of the Shoah and inventor of a "counter-poetry" (Bollack 2001) shaped by the search for the cultural and mental sources of genocide, represents this tradition better than anyone else.

Two years later, SAID started a new post-mortem dialogue game. This time, he considered the case of Hölderlin, one of the two artists he mentions in his letter to Goethe as having been discredited by the poet of Weimar due to their failure to adhere to classicist aesthetics. In this radio play produced by the SWR in 2001, *Friedrich Hölderlin empfängt niemanden mehr* ("Friedrich Hölderlin Is No Longer Receiving Anyone"), however, he exhibits hardly any further indulgence towards the poet-philosopher. He stages an impromptu visit from a "stranger" to Hölderlin, aged 37, holed up in his "ivory tower" in Tübingen after having succumbed to madness. SAID himself performs the role of this anonymous visitor, who speaks German with a pronounced accent but reveals himself to nonetheless be a fine connoisseur of his host's work. Provocative and cynical, the stateless visitor is not afraid to point out the contradiction that results when the "most German of German poets" upholds his love of the fatherland. He blames him for betraying his revolutionary ideals and taking refuge in a mythological Greece, replacing reality with dreams, even though "to dream without a pulsating earth is self-annihilation."[14]

The fictitious resurrection of this other classical figure with a far more complex canonical status thus provides SAID with a new opportunity to address the writer's social role, this time from the perspective of his relationship to the nation and his right to withdraw from worldly affairs. Hölderlin, who does not listen to his visitor, recalls the advice that Goethe had given him to write "little poems" and observes with bitterness: "He loves his little poems, the privy councilor does; he believes German misery can be vanquished from within. He really believes that, the privy councilor, and he calls us a European with the soul of a

---

14 "träumen möchtest du, doch träumen ist selbstvernichtung ohne eine pulsierende erde" (SAID 2002: n.p.).

negro."[15] The author borrows the terms of this harsh and disillusioned retort, which he attributes to Hölderlin, from a famous verdict by Friedrich Engels:

> Thus Goethe is at times a colossus, at times small-minded; at times defiant, mocking, and disdainful of the world, at times a considerate, contented, narrow-minded philistine. Even Goethe was not able to overcome German misery, on the contrary, it overcame him, and this victory of misery over the greatest of Germans is the best proof that it cannot be overcome "from the inside out."[16]

In response to the illustrious poet's remark, the "stranger" played by SAID angrily replies, "what do you understand of German reality? You who have elegantly removed yourself from it, abandoning us for the ether..."[17] The exchange ends here, and there will be no debate between the dead German poet and the living poet with no country. Hölderlin will not or cannot hear anything anymore and his foreign visitor can only provide retrospective comments from the outside about his exalted escape into esotericism.

Complicit Conversations with Chamisso and Heine (Schami)

Writing the preface to a new biography of Chamisso in 1990 provided Schami with the opportunity to engage in a dialogue with one of his illustrious "colleagues." He opted for the epistolary mode, and it is with malice-tinged affection that he addresses him familiarly as "grandfather," justifying himself with the distinction conferred on him by the jury of the Adelbert von Chamisso Prize in 1985:

> Dear Grandfather,
> Erika Klopp Verlag turned to me, one of your great-grandchildren, with the request to write a foreword for your biography. I agreed immediately, even though I'm in the middle of a

---

15 "er liebt kleine gedichte, der herr geheimrat, / er glaubt, die deutsche misere könne von / innen besiegt werden. / so glaubt er, der geheimrat. / und der nennt uns einen europäer mit der / seele eines negers" (SAID 2002).
16 "So ist Goethe bald kolossal, bald kleinlich; bald trotziges, spottendes, weltverachtendes Genie, bald rücksichtsvoller, genügsamer, enger Philister. Auch Goethe war nicht imstande, die deutsche Misere zu besiegen; im Gegenteil, sie besiegte ihn, und dieser Sieg der Misere über den größten Deutschen ist der beste Beweis, daß sie 'von innen heraus' gar nicht zu überwinden ist." Engels, "Über Goethe vom menschlichen Standpunkte" [1847], as quoted from Mandelkow (1977, II: 297).
17 "was verstehst du von deutscher wirklichkeit? du hast dich ihr elegant entzogen und uns dem äther überlassen" (SAID 2002).

narrative journey that has taken me through hundreds of places, including those where you yourself once lingered.[18]

Schami then admits that his knowledge of Chamisso's life and work is recent; it was not until he was awarded the prize bearing his name five years before that he started to look into the poet and botanist originally from France. Until then, all he had known of him was *Schlemihl*. Yet, he adds, "there was a book that appeared about you and about us. It was entitled *Chamisso's Grandchildren*. And so, you came to be my ancestor, Grandfather!" In order to update his information, he then read the most recent biography – the very one for which he is writing the preface[19] – and he explains his decision to employ the epistolary form.

> Since I hardly read forewords and don't like to write things nobody wants to read, I threw my original drafts of a serious and very pompous preface into the wastebasket. It would be best, I thought, for you to write a letter to Grandpa. Yes, Grandfather, you live on fresher than ever, 152 years after your physical death. Rest assured, I wouldn't write to the dead, even if they were still breathing. Yet you live. A year ago, I read your poem in a literary journal about the drunkard Hans Jürgen and how his crafty wife punished him. A clever poem.[20]

Following this introduction, the text assumes the form of a travel diary, with dates and locations accompanying the entries, though it remains in the dialogical mode, addressed to its "recipient." It covers the period from 2 February to 6 March 1990 and follows the stages of the author's readings for a book tour.

By adopting the enunciative posture of a letter-writer, "the friend from Damascus" affirms his second position in relation to his subject. At the same time, the comic premise of being related to Chamisso, as suggested by the anthology

---

18 "Lieber Großvater, Der Erika Klopp Verlag wandte sich an mich, einen Deiner Urenkel, mit der Bitte, ein Vorwort für Deine Biographie zu schreiben. Ich stimmte sofort zu, obwohl ich mitten in einer Erzählreise bin, die mich durch Hunderte von Orten führte, auch an solche, an denen Du auch einmal verweilt hast" (Schami [2006] 2009: 204–210), 204. Further references to this work will appear as AC plus page number.
19 Robert Fischer, *Adelbert von Chamisso: Weltbürger, Naturforscher und Dichter* (Berlin: E. Klopp), 1990.
20 "Da ich auch kaum Vorworte lese und nicht gerne schreibe, was kein Mensch lesen will, habe ich meine anfänglichen Entwürfe zu einem ernsten und sehr geschwollenen Vorwort in den Papierkorb geworfen. Am besten, dachte ich, schreibst Du [sic] dem Opa einen Brief. Ja, Großvater, Du lebst frischer denn je, und das 152 Jahre nach Deinem physischen Tod. Sei sicher, ich würde Toten nicht schreiben, auch wenn sie noch atmeten. Du aber lebst. Vor einem Jahr noch las ich in einer Literaturzeitschrift Dein Gedicht über den Säufer Hans Jürgen und wie ihn seine listige Frau bestrafte. Ein kluges Gedicht" (AC 204–205).

Chamissos Enkel. Zur Literatur von Ausländern in Deutschland ("Chamisso's Grandchildren. On Literature by Foreigners in Germany," 1986) compiled by Heinz Friedrich, allows him to situate his tribute in a discursive space that is at the intersection of public and private, ceremonial and intimate: despite all the respect that should be shown to a grandfather, a grandson has the right to good-natured impertinence. By pretending to take the anthologist's genealogical metaphor literally and noting as proof the homophonic link that exists between his own *nom de plume* and the name of the Romantic poet – Schami/ Chamisso – Schami subverts the protocol of the writer's preface, a site of legitimation *par excellence*, not in order to place himself in the position of disciple or epigone, but as a direct descendent. Incidentally, he also points with feigned innocence to the literary critics' tendency to dwell on the foreign origins of writers and to homogenize their varied works by assigning them a generic term ("Chamisso literature").

Using a direct tone that enables him to assume this ironic stance, Schami demonstrates that what he sees in the tutelary figure of Chamisso is above all a flesh-and-blood individual rather than a monument. Focusing on the difficulties that the Franco-German author had finding his place between two warring countries and within the society of each, Schami claims the legacy of these poets who were "strangers everywhere" (AC 209)[21] and who have experienced exile and persecution, have known what it is like to be torn between countries, languages, and religions, and for whom these trials have made it possible to create great works of art. By deliberately inserting himself in a line of poets who have been tossed back and forth between nations and communities, he in fact affirms a notion of literary filiation borrowed not from biological descent but a common destiny and elective affinity – an idea that invites a reference to Canetti's formula "A poet needs ancestors."[22] By elaborating on Heinz Friedrich's genetic metaphor, Schami simultaneously sheds a sardonic light on the national claim to give precedence to "blood" over other criteria in the process of transmission. He suggests rather the image of a network, a kind of transnational and transhistorical fellowship of writers who are united both by a shared fate of cul-

---

[21] Schami refers to this famous passage from a letter that Chamisso wrote to Germaine de Stael in 1820: "je suis français en Allemagne et allemand en France, catholique chez les protestants, protestant chez les catholiques, [...]. Je ne suis nulle part de mise, je suis partout étranger – je voudrais trop étreindre, tout m'échappe. Je suis malheureux..." ("I am French in Germany and German in France, Catholic among Protestants, Protestant with the Catholics [...] I am at home nowhere, a stranger everywhere – I would like too much to embrace everything, everything escapes me. I am unfortunate..."). Quoted from Parmentier (2002: 170–171).
[22] "Ein Dichter braucht Ahnen" (Canetti 1994: 276).

tural marginality and closely related ethical and aesthetic concepts. In this sense, this text is also an invitation to reread Chamisso's works through the "minor" and "exogenous" lenses that his canonization has helped to obscure.

Solidarity does not, however, mean allegiance. While Schami professes boundless admiration for *Peter Schlemihls wundersame Geschichte* ("The Wonderful History of Peter Schlemihl"), he takes a critical yet benevolent look at the sentimentalism of Chamisso's lyrical works. In turn, he does not hesitate to criticize his "ancestor" for his political positions, deploring his nationalist blindness, which Schami attributes precisely to the uncomfortable situation of a lieutenant of French origin in the Prussian army at war against Napoleon. The Syrian exile who had once been a communist activist sees in *Memoire über die Ereignisse bei der Kapitulation von Hameln* ("Memoir of the Events of the Surrender of Hamelin") – which Chamisso wrote after the surrender of the city in 1805 to document his shame at being involved in such a quick capitulation, even as a subordinate – nothing more than a pathetic documentation of the need for recognition by those who have been displaced. In Schami's mind, neither the extenuating circumstances, nor the distance that Chamisso subsequently established between himself and the army, exempt Chamisso from the responsibility for such patriotic misguidedness. And it is in a tone of affectionate severity that he airs his reproaches to him:

> It's too bad that you were at such odds with yourself until you turned your back on the military. [...] As with every emigrant, your inner conflict has no limits. You, the one with nothing to defend whenever rulers would divide territory among themselves, were ready to die. Thank God this didn't happen. One verse or fairy tale that you later wrote for posterity is more valuable than all that nationalist nonsense. That's why you'll understand that I didn't at all like what you did in Hamelin or your fiery statement in defense of the city's honor. Later in Berlin, you didn't allow yourself to be impressed by such nationalist hullabaloo. Disgusted, you retreated to your estate at Kunersdorf, and we got Schlemihl. What a good decision this was, Grandfather! Whoever is caught in the middle defends no one.[23]

---

23 "Schade, dass Du so lange mit Dir gerungen hast, bis Du dem Militär den Rücken gekehrt hast. [...] Deine Zerrissenheit hat wie bei jedem Emigranten keine Grenzen. Du, derjenige, der nichts zu verteidigen hat, wenn Herrscher Gebiete unter sich aufteilen, wolltest in den Tod gehen. Gott sei Dank ist Dir das nicht gelungen. Ein Vers oder ein Märchen, die Du später für die Nachwelt geschrieben hast, ist wertvoller als der ganze nationalistische Schwachsinn. Deshalb würdest Du mich verstehen, wenn mir Dein Auftritt in Hameln und Deine flammende Rede zur Verteidigung der Ehre der Stadt überhaupt nicht gefällt. Später in Berlin hast Du Dich vom ganzen nationalistischen Rummel nicht beeindrucken lassen. Du hast Dich angeekelt auf das Landgut bei Kunersdorf zurückgezogen, und wir haben den *Schlemihl* bekommen, wie gut war hier Deine Entscheidung, Großvater! Wer zwischen den Stühlen sitzt, verteidigt keinen" (AC 208–209).

It is because of the deep solidarity he feels with Chamisso and the fact that he credits him with the ability to learn from bitter experience that Schami allows himself to apostrophize his "grandfather" about his nationalist position during the Napoleonic wars. From then on, he can share with the author of *Schlemihl* his anxiety about the nationalist fever that had Germany in its clutches while he was writing the preface, during the era of reunification, and call him as a witness to ridicule this patriotic relapse leading to mindless xenophobia. This phenomenon is described in allegorical form as the revenge of the Berlin Wall, outraged by its demolition, its remains having been collected, preserved, and exposed as relics, even in leftist circles:

> The hateful wall soon had its revenge. My friend Herrmann [sic] had a piece of it on his bookshelf. We were drinking wine in his room in Kreuzberg. He was sitting with his back to the shelf and didn't notice anything. I, however, saw that the chunk of wall was growing by the minute. He just laughed at me. A sharp corner struck Herrmann in the left [sic] temple. He bled a little. Suddenly, he began to tell me, his eyes flashing, about Germany and the worldwide conspiracy that had formed in opposition to a great and peaceful Germany.[24]

It is on the basis of his profound solidarity with the Franco-German Romantic poet that Schami then includes Chamisso, with a new play on his last name, in the country's minority community of critical intellectuals empowered to express their shame in the face of this collective misguidedness, in terms he attributes to the Bavarian satirist Gerhard Polt: "I scham mi so!" (AC 207), which means, "I am so ashamed!" ("Ich schäme mich so") in the southern dialect but can also be heard as "I, Chamisso" ("Ich, Chamisso").

The second of Schami's two texts that stage a "dialogue with the dead" contextualizes the relationship he has with Heine. This was another commissioned work: a radio play produced in 1997 by the public broadcaster *Süddeutscher Rundfunk* as part of a series of programs broadcast on the occasion of the bicentennial of the poet's birth. Founded on the same principle of anachronism as SAID's radio play about Hölderlin, the dialogue entitled *Zu Besuch bei Harry*

---

24 "Die hasserfüllte Mauer rächte sich bald. Mein Freund Herrmann [sic] hatte ein solches Stück auf dem Regal. Wir tranken Wein in seinem Zimmer in Kreuzberg. Er saß mit dem Rücken zum Regal und bemerkte nichts. Ich aber sah, wie der Mauerbrocken von Minute zu Minute größer wurde. Seine scharfen Kanten näherten sich dem Kopf meines Freundes. Ich schrie, er solle weg von der Mauer kommen, doch er lachte mich aus. Eine scharfe Kante stieß Herrmann an die linke [sic] Schläfe. Er blutete leicht. Plötzlich fing er an, mir mit glänzenden Augen von Deutschland zu erzählen und von der weltweiten Verschwörung, die sich gegen ein großes und friedliches Deutschland gebildet hatte" (AC 207).

Heine ("A Visit to Harry Heine")²⁵ portrays a visit by writer-journalist "Rafik Schami," who immigrated to Germany to escape the dictatorship and military service in Syria, to his distant predecessor exiled to Paris and stricken with poor health. Separated by two centuries, the writers exchange their impressions of Germany, literature, life under authoritarian rule, censorship, and literary criticism.

This time, the use of the interview as staging device allows Schami to have his fictionalized addressee speak, instead of being content with a one-way interrogation. Here, he gives Heine the floor by having him answer his questions, usually with authentic quotations from his texts. Because of its dramaturgy as well as its content, this radio play testifies to a much stronger adherence to the recipient's ideas than does the letter to Chamisso. The relationship established with Heine is friendly, collegial, and complicit. The evident solidarity leaves no place for any critical reserve as Heine is taken to task in an exchange that has a polemic subtext entirely directed against the reactionary forces of contemporary Germany and draws a historical parallel with the Prussia of the Restoration. The mixture of self-referentiality and metadiscursiveness also combines with a level of self-fictionalization, since Schami gives himself a role in the scene.

At the beginning of this "interview," Schami again resorts to the genealogical metaphor by elaborating on a postulated kinship with Chamisso. His alter ego greets Heine in these terms: "Good morning, dear Mr. Heine. My name is Rafik Schami. I come from Damascus and am Chamisso's great-grandson."²⁶ This introduction leads to an initial comical misunderstanding, as Heine is entirely astonished by the unexpected lineage of his friend: "What? That old globetrotter fathered children in Damascus, too?"²⁷ Beginning in such a lighthearted manner, the conversation soon becomes animated as the two interlocutors discover how much they have in common. Not only have they both been subjected to political persecution that forced them into exile, but they have also been marked for life by belonging to a historical minority subject to the racism of the society in which they live. In this respect, the empathy that Schami, coming from the Aramaic minority in Syria, has for the Jewish *Harry* Heine (the preference given to the original name over its Germanized version is powerful) is immediate and visceral.

Have things changed in two centuries? Asked in turn by Heine about the state of Germany at the turn of the twenty-first century, Schami answers him

---

25 Subsequent references to this work (Schami 2009: 211–226) will appear as HH plus page number.
26 "Guten Tag, lieber Herr Heine. Mein Name ist Rafik Schami, ich komme aus Damaskus und bin ein Urenkel Chamissos" (HH 211).
27 "Was? Hat der alte Weltenbummler auch in Damaskus Kinder gezeugt?" (HH 211).

point blank with the very sentences Heine himself wrote two hundred years before. For example: "Other peoples may be wiser and funnier and more amusing, but there are none as faithful as the German people. If I did not know that loyalty is as old as the world, I would believe that a German heart had invented it."[28] By describing provocative parallels between Restoration Prussia and present-day Germany in this way, Schami testifies not only to his empathy with Heine but also to his ability to be both incisive and light, irreverent and sentimental, enthusiastic and skeptical – a way of proving that he is Heine's equal in terms of wit and repartee. As with Chamisso he likewise calls on Heine, by virtue of the solidarity he feels with and his esteem for his illustrious "colleague," to explain why he yielded to pressure from his family – he who had stood up to kings and despots – by agreeing to censor his own memoirs. The reproach does not weigh very heavily when balanced against the understanding that prevails between the two men regarding the flaws of their respective contemporaries, and Schami's main interest seems to be to show that the "journalist" is not in a position of exaggerated deference towards the individual he is interviewing. Heine, whom Schami informs on this occasion of the quarrel for succession that followed his death and the probable betrayal of his wife Mathilde, defends himself with fatalism: after all, he has already expressed all that was in his heart in his prose and even better in his poems. Schami shows himself capable of reconsidering his position and allowing himself to be persuaded. The dialogical form allows, even better than the epistolary one, for an illustration of the intellectual understanding – consisting of empathy, of open debate, and also of listening – that the author feels binds him to Heine.

The two main themes of the interview, however, are the writer's relationship to political power and belonging to the German nation. Recalling Heine's difficulties in Metternich's Europe allows Schami to shed light on the global expansion of terror regimes since the nineteenth century, made possible by technological advances. "Compared to our current dictators," he tells a scandalized Heine, "you really still had benign rulers." In turn, this affords him the opportunity to explain that the rulers were able to evolve faster than their opponents and that, thanks to the progress of the technologies available to them, they can now exert "universal terror" (HH 218). Although there is no explicit mention of Salman Rushdie, the case of *The Satanic Verses* and the *fatwa* that the Ayatollah Khomeini pronounced against Rushdie in 1989 are obviously in the background of this

---

28 "Andere Völker mögen gewandter sein, und witziger und ergötzlicher, aber keines ist so treu wie das deutsche Volk. Wüsste ich nicht, dass die Treue so alt ist wie die Welt, so würde ich glauben, ein deutsches Herz habe sie erfunden" (HH 213). Quoted from *Harzreise* [1824], in *Reisebilder* (Heine 1976, III, i: 101–166), 118.

tribute to the German satirist for whom the Prussian State issued an arrest warrant in 1844 because of blasphemous writings against the fatherland.

The other central subject of the text is the relation to the German nation and the impossibility of assimilation. In the face of Heine's insistence on claiming his identity as a "German poet,"[29] Schami argues that deep down, the true homeland (*Heimat*) of his interlocutor is "the language of Germany, rather than the degrees of latitude." The following sounds like a profession of faith:

> So we are, Chamisso, you and I, again countrymen. And there is something else common to all of us. However close we come in spirit to the heart of society or how much we write about it, we remain outsiders. And when people jabber about the foreigner problem, the last thing they have in mind are the problems that a foreigner in a sea of natives has. Instead, what they mean is simply the unrest a stranger brings into his adoptive society. To give an example: a stranger may be polite, industrious, and honorable and even exhibit many other attributes of bourgeois society's moral exemplars, but as long as he insists on remaining an outsider, none of this counts, and society would rather have a foreign panderer who has Germanized himself beyond recognition than him. I think this is what your problem was, and it's mine still.[30]

Heine then agrees with his interviewer by evoking his bitterness about having converted to Protestantism, expressing himself using the same terms as in his letter to Moses Moser on 9 January 1826: "It's crazy, isn't it? I've just been baptized, and I'm decried as a Jew. Nothing but hassles since then, I'm telling you…"[31] And

---

[29] "Ich bin ein deutscher Dichter" (HH 220), which is a quote from the poem *Wenn ich an deinem Hause*, in *Buch der Lieder* (Heine 1976: I, 114–115). Then, in response to a remark about the fact that he at least, unlike Schami himself, can still be read in his homeland, Heine declares in the very words he wrote in *Retrospektive Aufklärung* [1854] (Heine 1976: IX, 480): "Wir wollen auch kein Blatt davon aufgeben, und der Steinmetz, der unsre letzte Schlafstätte mit einer Inschrift zu verzieren hat, soll keine Einrede zu gewärtigen haben, wenn er dort eingräbt die Worte: 'Hier ruht ein deutscher Dichter'" (HH 221).

[30] "So sind wir, Chamisso, Sie und ich, wiederum Landsleute. Und noch etwas ist uns allen gemein. Sosehr wir auch mit unserem Geist dem Herzen der Gesellschaft nahe sind und darüber schreiben, so bleiben wir doch Außenseiter. Und wenn man von dem Ausländerproblem quasselt, meint man am allerwenigsten die Probleme, die ein Ausländer in einem Meer von Einheimischen hat, sondern man meint schlicht die Unruhe, die ein Fremder in die Gastgesellschaft einbringt. Um ein Beispiel zu bringen: Ein Fremder kann höflich, fleißig, ehrenhaft sein und noch viele andere Merkmale der moralischen Vorbilder der bürgerlichen Gesellschaft vorweisen, doch solange er darauf besteht, Fremder zu bleiben, zählt das alles nicht, und die Gesellschaft zieht ihm einen fremden Zuhälter vor, der sich bis zur Unkenntlichkeit eingedeutscht hat. Ich glaube, darin lag auch Ihr Problem, und es ist meines immer noch" (HH 221–222).

[31] "(Er lacht ironisch) Ist es nicht närrisch, kaum bin ich getauft, so werde ich als Jude verschrien. Ich sage Ihnen, nichts als Widerwärtigkeiten seitdem…" (HH 222).

Schami chimes in with his own experience: "Exactly, and it is useless for a Jew to be baptized or a man from the South to dye his hair or to join the majority parties. Foreigners bear their stigma on their foreheads."[32]

Though dialogues with the dead are playful, they also may serve a very serious purpose. They provide an opportunity to honor a role model, to claim an intellectual affinity and thereby become a part of the (or at least a) literary tradition in Germany, and also to denounce an intellectual attitude or failings in contemporary German society: the resurgence of nationalism, intolerance towards ethnic and religious minorities, and hypocrisy in the debate about "integration." If immigrant authors do not want to expose themselves to xenophobic accusations of maladjustment and ingratitude, they will need guardians from within the German pantheon itself in order to formulate such critiques. It thus makes sense to have such figures articulate the worst attacks in order to then temper them with a more balanced approach. Thus, for example, when on the topic of the liberating function of humor and its poor acceptance in German majority society, Heine attacks the intolerance of German literary critics and describes them as "lackeys stationed at the entrance to a court ballroom" (HH 223), Schami can magnanimously defend the Germans by replying to his elder's impetuosity with a more measured explanation: it is because "there is no comedic tradition of wit in Germany" and that "it is not attributable solely to the climate but also the form of government" since Germany has never known centralism, as France and Egypt have.[33]

Encounters in Fantasies and Dreams (Özdamar)

Beyond the rhetorical process, the summoning of a dead writer can also take the form of a foundational encounter that is the product of a fantasy or dream. In her autobiographical story *Mein Berlin* ("My Berlin," 2001: 55–61), Özdamar recounts a dream that her heroine-narrator has following a visit to the Dorotheenstadt cemetery, where she had gone to pay her respects at Brecht's grave. Returning from this site of remembrance for German literature where famous writers' graves are arrayed like "giant books" (60) on the ground, the young Turkish

---

[32] "Eben, und es hilft einem Juden keine Taufe und einem Südländer kein Haarfärben und kein Eintritt in die Parteien der Mehrheit. Das Stigma trägt der Fremde auf der Stirn" (HH 222).
[33] "Sinnreiches Lachen hat in Deutschland keine Tradition. Das hat nicht nur mit dem Wetter, sondern mit der Staatsform zu tun. Völker, wie die Franzosen oder Ägypter, die in ihrer Geschichte lange in einem zentralistischen Staat lebten, neigen eher zur Satire, vor allem gegen den übermächtigen und doch fernen Herrscher" (HH 223).

woman, who fled the military regime in her country to study Brechtian theater in Berlin, has a dream wherein she visits the great playwright but arrives too late: Brecht is stretched out in his bed, lifeless. Disappointed at not being able to speak with him, she asks his wife Helene Weigel, who is keeping watch over the deceased, to give her "something of his"; Weigel then gives her Brecht's pillowcase.[34] The dream ends with the narrator departing by boat, leaving the "fascists of Turkey" behind her.

The meaning of this dream is clear: in search of "ancestors" in the pantheon of German writers, the young woman requests and obtains a transitional object that establishes a symbolic connection with Brecht. The pillow, a symbol of oneiric activity and thus also artistic creativity, likewise refers to security, rest, and amorous intimacy. Although the episode is just a rough sketch, it has the value of an initiatory scene for Özdamar, who is both a thespian and writer. The fact that the inventor of epic theater had, like her, fought against the dictatorship in his country before going into exile plays an important role in this identification, as the end of the dream indicates. The posthumous gift consecrates the transmission of the spiritual heritage through the intermediary of a great actress and anticipates the happy outcome: Brecht's pillowcase serves as a talisman that protects the young activist from her pursuers.

Expressed here in the condensed form of a dream, the existential value of the reference to Brecht for Özdamar has been made explicit in other contexts, notably in her acceptance speech for the Chamisso Prize (1999). In this speech (2001: 125–132), she tells how Weil and Brecht's songs, which she listened to over and over on the records she had brought back from Berlin in 1966, helped her cope with the fear and harassment she endured following the coup d'état of 1971. Arrested for her militant journalism, she spent three weeks in prison and, she said, "there, in Istanbul, in that black hole, Brecht's words helped me." She quotes the chorus from *Nanna's Lied* – "Gott sei Dank geht alles schnell vorüber" ("Thank God, it all goes by quickly") – and explains that these German words helped her in Istanbul "like an Arabic prayer helped thirty years ago in Paris: bismillahirahmanirahim" (2001: 128).

The translation of this episode into the personalized form of the dream in *Mein Berlin* shows how Özdamar creates *incarnations* of her literary mentors' works, representing them as friends or relatives, as tutelary presences who serve as figures of consolation, encouragement, and emulation. This device is pervasive throughout her works, though she usually does not elaborate on it

---

34 "'[...] bitte geben Sie mir etwas von ihm. Seine Krawatte oder seinen Kopfkissenbezug.' Weigel gab mir Brechts Kopfkissenbezug" (Özdamar 2001: 60).

in great detail. There is another example from the same acceptance speech: to honor the poet whose name is on the award she has just received, she begins by paying homage to Chamisso. This poet does not seem to represent much for her, as she only has sparse, superficial knowledge of him, as opposed to Heine, whose esteem for his friend Chamisso she immediately mentions as a recommendation. "It appears that Heinrich Heine really cherished him. I love Heinrich Heine, and that's why I also love Adelbert von Chamisso, and I've often seen before me Heine and Chamisso conversing with one another."[35] After this, Özdamar brings them into a literal dialogue by alternating the poetry of one with that of the other.

> Heinrich Heine says:
> My child, we were two children,
> Small, merry by childhood's law;
> We used to crawl to the hen-house
> And hide ourselves in the straw [...][36]
>
> Chamisso says:
> I was also young and now am old
> The day is hot, the night is cold.
> Be off, off with you,
> And drive such thoughts from your head. [...][37]
>
> And Heine replies:
> It drives you on round and round,
> Without your knowing why;

---

[35] "Heinrich Heine soll ihn sehr geschätzt haben. Ich liebe Heinrich Heine, deswegen liebe ich auch Adelbert von Chamisso und sah vor mir Heine und Chamisso oft zusammensitzen" (Özdamar 2001: 125).

[36] "Mein Kind, wir waren Kinder, / Zwei Kinder, klein und froh; /Wir krochen ins Hühnerhäuschen, / Versteckten uns unter das Stroh [...] / Chamisso sagt: / Ich war auch jung und bin jetzt alt, / Der Tag ist heiß, der Abend kalt. / Geh du nur hin, geh du nur hin / Und schlag dir solches aus dem Sinn. / Und Heine antwortet: / Es treibt dich fort von Ort zu Ort, / Du weißt nicht mal warum; / Im Winde klingt ein sanftes Wort, / Schaust dich verwundert um." (Özdamar 2001: 125) Özdamar quotes the two first stanzas of the poem XXXVIII from Heine's *Buch der Lieder* (1976: I, 126–127). English translation by Elizabeth Barrett Browning, in *Last Poems – Paraphrases on Heine*.

[37] "Ich war auch jung und bin jetzt alt, / Der Tag ist heiß, der Abend kalt. / Geh du nur hin, geh du nur hin / Und schlag dir solches aus dem Sinn" (Özdamar 2001: 126). Here Özdamar quotes both stanzas of the short poem *Geh du nur hin!* (Chamisso 1975: 188), which in turn was inspired by a text from Achim von Arnim and Clemens Brentano's collection of songs, *Des Knaben Wunderhorn*.

> In the wind a soft word sounds
> Look around you in surprise.[38]

After bringing the two poets "to life" by transforming them into characters for the theater, drawing them into her own poetic universe – where wandering and sorrow are spoken in the simple words of childhood and everyday life – Özdamar tackles the subject that is truly close to her heart: the vital function that certain German figures served for her when she was living in Istanbul under the military regime. And it is then not Chamisso and Heine, but rather Heine and Brecht she evokes. The episode of double resurrection serves only as an introduction to the real tribute; however, her dramaturgy reveals the position of the author as a thespian, and the poems she chooses to quote from indicate just as clearly her aesthetic bias.

The topos of the imagined (dreamed, fantasized) encounter is more poetic than the rhetorical game of the interview or of the letter, which are also exercises of erudition and eloquence, and is therefore only naïve on the surface. In the case of Özdamar, it participates in an aesthetic that prioritizes emotional intensity and symbolic force over rational discourse. In this sense, the scenes described above illustrate her search for writing that is more "theatrical" than literary, inspired by the seemingly opposed models of Brechtian *gestus* and Stanislavski's emotional identification. Özdamar presents herself both in form and substance as a disciple of the German playwright. The difference with the letter or the dialogue is not, however, as great as it seems. These are also, fundamentally, theatrical processes based on simulated naïveté. In all three cases, the author referenced is both "incarnated" and "brought up-to-date" so as to give the living writer, the subject of the enunciation, a literary guardian to help her establish a position as a writer who is authentic but also legitimate in the eyes of the German public. Behind the gesture of devotion and respect is an act of appropriation. The construction of a fictional co-presence between the author and the "ancestor" is a setup that has the effect of transforming the latter into a literary character. These processes found a particular form of cultural transfer that includes the dimension of time: through the cultural and historical "import" of writers who serve as guardians, authors question the dominant discourse of the culture in which they live and thereby delimit a territory.[39]

---

38 "Es treibt dich fort von Ort zu Ort, / Du weißt nicht mal warum; / Im Winde klingt ein sanftes Wort, / Schaust dich verwundert um" (Özdamar 2001: 126). This is the first stanza of the poem "In der Fremde," published in 1844 in *Neue Gedichte* (Heine 1976: VII, 369–370).
39 According to the typology proposed by Udo Schöning (2000: 24), this may be considered a case of direct *diachronic* transfer – except for the fact that we are not actually dealing with an

At the Threshold of Rewriting: De- and Reterritorializing the Canon

The concept of deterritorialization, created by Deleuze and Guattari in *Anti-Œdipe* ("Anti-Oedipus," 1972) and then developed in *Kafka: Pour une littérature mineure* ("Kafka: Toward a Minor Literature," 1975) and especially in *Mille Plateaux* ("A Thousand Plateaus," 1980), refers to a process of decontextualization (declassification, decoding) of a system, allowing it to be updated ("reterritorialized") within other contexts. The heuristic interest of this concept, the subsequent fate of which led to a certain semantic weakening but which is used here in its original sense, lies in the questioning (deconstruction) of dominant discourses. The key challenge in the process of decontextualizing the "great works" of the national literary tradition, as seen in the authors of the corpus, is to confirm the universal scope of these works – as also claimed by the staunchest defenders of the Western canon – while simultaneously questioning the West's claim to exclusivity in the matter of literary value. To challenge this prerogative of dominant (Western) cultures to express universality (and thus their claim to intellectual domination over the rest of the world), these authors strive to deconstruct the fetishist character of the canonized work by re-evaluating it in light of social and political contingencies that differ from those that gave birth to it. Deterritorialization performed in this way prepares or even constitutes a form of reappropriation of the canon by (or on behalf of) population groups that would otherwise be only passive and subjugated receivers.

Prior to the rewriting as such, the operations of transfer effectively pass through a more or less targeted deterritorialization of the national or Western canon, which constitutes, to a certain extent, a critical reassessment. Thus, Özdamar reads – and shows herself reading – the texts of Lenz, Kleist, and Büchner through the lens of 1970s Turkey, leading her to juxtapose that country's situation with that of eighteenth- and nineteenth-century Germany. When receiving the Chamisso Prize in 1999, she pointed out, for example, that the character of Woyzeck, the model for whom was an anachronism in contemporary Europe, still existed at that time in Turkey. Thus, it was in the theater (in a Germany that seemed at first sight, from what she observed in the street, "not to have any history") that she "discovered history."[40] This history was familiar to her because it was that of her own country: "I saw Woyzeck on the stage, but no longer in German streets. Woyzeck still existed in the streets of Turkey. There you saw

---

"intercultural" relationship but rather the reception of a German writer by an author who has a foreign background but also writes in German as well.

40 "Auf der Straße sah Deutschland aus, als ob es keine Geschichte hätte, aber im Theater fand ich die Geschichte" (Özdamar 2001: 130).

men who moved me just like Büchner's character, Woyzeck. Perhaps that's why I did not feel like I had emigrated. German theater was an extension of my country."⁴¹ In (re)discovering the historical truth of Büchner's play through her own experience, Özdamar initiates a re-evaluation of his text from the point of view of eccentric, post-, or neocolonial spaces.

She has a similar experience with Goethe's *Bürgergeneral* ("The Citizen General"), noting that the social and political function of the barber shop as a space of freedom is still alive and well in Istanbul, even though it has completely disappeared in modern European democracies.

> Schnaps rips into the cupboard where the full milk jug stands. But the speeches he makes in front of the cupboard about freedom and revolution are essentially the speeches of a chatty village barber. Today his topic is revolution. The barber shops in Istanbul are also places where people can easily vent their ideas about politics, morals, and economics in front of the mirror as they are getting a shave. Goethe in Istanbul.⁴²

This example clearly demonstrates how work on the canon, even if just in an embryonic state as it is here, represents work on history. What it reveals could invalidate an entire contemporary Orientalist discourse about Turkey, in this instance regarding the cliché that the country's culture, imagined to be traditionalist and Islamic, would be intrinsically incompatible with the supposedly "Judeo-Christian" heritage of modern Germany.

Özdamar sometimes inserts deterritorializing experiments of this type into a novel without comment, as with *A Midsummer Night's Dream* at the very beginning of *Die Brücke vom Goldenen Horn* ("The Bridge of the Golden Horn"). An analepsis shows the narrator as a high school student prior to leaving for Germany, playing her first role in the theater and dreaming of becoming an actress. This passion worries her mother, who wants her to pursue higher education and become a lawyer. In the dialogue that pits mother against daughter, the latter haughtily responds to her mother's arguments with apropos Shakespeare verses she has memorized for her performance in the role of Titania. The first quote,

---

41 "Ich sah Woyzeck auf der Bühne, aber nicht mehr auf den deutschen Straßen. Woyzeck existierte noch auf den türkischen Straßen. Dort sah man Männer, die einen wie Büchners Figur Woyzeck berührten. Ich kam mir vielleicht deswegen nicht emigriert vor. Deutsches Theater war die Verlängerung meines Landes" (SSE 130).
42 "Schnaps geht auf den Schrank los, in dem der volle Milchkrug steht. Aber die Reden, die er über Freiheit und Revolution vor dem Schrank führt, sind im Grunde die Reden eines schwatzlustigen Dorfbarbiers. Heute ist sein Thema die Revolution. Auch die Barbiersalons in Istanbul sind die Orte, wo die Leute ihre Ideen über Politik, Moral und Ökonomie vor dem Spiegel einfach loswerden können, während sie rasiert werden. Goethe in Istanbul" (SSE 171).

taken from act II, scene 2 and still in connection with the heroine's work for the drama club, is given in Turkish in the German text and followed by A. W. Schlegel's translation, with everything set apart in italics and arranged on the page in verse.[43] The next quote, given this time as a retort the girl makes to her mother, is presented in the same way, though without the italics, serving as an indication that the teenager is reappropriating the proud words of the queen of fairies ("I am a spirit of no common rate"),[44] although her mother does not necessarily notice. From this moment, the quotations from *Dream* are given directly in German and sometimes fully incorporated into the text.

The effect is irresistible. The reader, initially disconcerted at finding quotes in a foreign language in a German novel, discovers in a second phase, undoubtedly with some amusement, that this is a text from the Western canon that the young heroine learned in Turkish, and finally sees quotes from the same text cleverly embedded in the dialogue between mother and daughter. The identification of these inserts is favored by the reader's likely familiarity, if not with the "classical" translation of Schlegel, at least with the exalted register that characterizes the authors of his period. The effect of the initial disorientation thus leads, through a kind of mirror effect, to a no less unexpected effect of recognition.

The comedic nature of this highly effective scene is attributable to the surprising alignment between the subject, a young girl's revolt against parental authority and bourgeois ideology in Turkey in the 1960s, and its doubly parodic treatment. The teenager's reinvestiture of the Shakespearian discourse in the universe of the novel responds, at the level of writing, to the author's reinvestiture of the Western canon (Shakespeare / Schlegel). In both cases, it is a parody at once playful and "serious," according to Genette's typology, meaning that the purpose is not to ridicule the source text but rather to "renovate" it by reinvesting it in a new context. If it works, it is because the Romantic majesty of Shakespearean verse as translated by Schlegel is reappropriated by the girl and resonates with the "Oriental" pathos of the mother's speech. Thus, when the sobbing mother exclaims, "Meine Tochter, du bist so entsetzlich wild und noch so jung" ("my daughter, you are so terribly ferocious and still so young"), the girl answers her with aplomb by adapting – just slightly – one of Helena's retorts to her rival Hermia in III, 2 (in italics in the text):

---

43 "*Haydi, halka olun, bir peri şarkısı söyleyin / (Kommt! Einen Ringel, einen Feensang!) / Dann auf das Drittel 'ner Minute fort! / Ihr, tötet Raupen in den Rosenknospen!...*" (Özdamar 1998: 12)
44 "*Adi olmayan cinsten bir ruhum. (Ich bin ein Geist nicht von gemeinem Stande.)*" (Özdamar 1998: 13; cf. Schlegel 1797, III, 1: 224).

> No, no, Mother, I will not trust.
> Nor longer look on your curst company.
> Your hands, than mine, are quicker for a fray;
> My legs are longer though, to run away!⁴⁵

This exchange, which would in no way be plausible in the context of a modern-day bourgeois German family, seems scarcely incongruous in the atmosphere of exuberant and distanced vitality that characterizes the novel. Incidentally, Özdamar indicates that the generational and ideological conflicts at work in Turkish society in the early 1960s were not so far removed from those that shook the pre-democratic societies of western Europe, and that the fight of a young girl from the Turkish bourgeoisie to be free presents certain parallels with the revolt of Romantic heroes against an imposed order. Situated in the incipit of the novel, this scene sets the tone for the whole story. An autobiographical novel of immigration, *Die Brücke vom Goldenen Horn* presents itself from the outset as a novel of growth and learning, a story of liberation, and an intercultural novel about theater and literature (the choice of *Dream* is in itself significant since it is a play about theater and *mise-en-abyme*). Located at the threshold of the narrative, this intertextual game also gives the reader all the information about the heroine needed not to fall into the trap of naïveté that the narrative technique adopted might suggest. It therefore serves to set the character in contrast to the cliché about the Turkish immigrant as a traditionalist, uneducated, and stupid peasant.⁴⁶

These spatio-temporal transfers and initial re-readings sometimes lead to the work of rewriting, as when Özdamar began adapting *Hamlet* to the contemporary Turkish context to make it a peasant drama. This intervention, already successfully carried out by the Swiss writer Gottfried Keller in the short story *Romeo und Julia auf dem Dorfe* ("A Village Romeo and Juliet," 1856), would have worked well because of the historical gap separating Turkey from western Europe. While this adaptation did not come to fruition, it did make way for more indirect rewriting, inspired by Heiner Müller's *Hamletmaschine* ("Hamletmachine"), discussed in detail in the fifth chapter of this study.

---

45 "Nein, nein, Mutter, ich will nicht trau'n. / Noch länger Eu'r verhaßtes Antlitz schauen, / Sind eure Hände hurtiger zum Raufen, / So hab' ich längre Beine doch zum Laufen!" (Özdamar 1998: 13; cf. Schlegel 1797: III, ii, 244) The single modification from Schlegel's text is the insertion of the word "Mutter."

46 For more details on Özdamar's intertextual treatment of Shakespeare's *Dream* in this passage, see Meyer (2019).

This is indeed the field of the hypertextual transformation itself, which is the realm of writing back *par excellence*. In the colonial and post-colonial context, rewriting is invested with a deconstructing function that targets not only the canon as such – i.e., the hegemonic culture perceived as an instrument of domination – but also, more generally, the ideological discourse that tends to essentialize notions of authenticity, cultural roots, nation, and identity instead of considering them as being determined by a given space-time.[47] Thus, Aimé Césaire adapts Shakespeare's *Tempest* "for a negro theater" (1969), adopting the point of view of Caliban and Ariel, as Derek Walcott "creolized" the *Odyssey* in his epic poem *Omeros* (1990). These manifesto-texts both create a synthesis between the classical European tradition and Caribbean folk culture and counter the Eurocentric and colonialist worldview conveyed by the classic texts by virtue of their canonization. By appropriating the language and culture of the colonizer, writers from the West Indies, Africa, or India free their own words and access cultural autonomy. Germanophone authors of immigrant origins also return to classic models (Homer, Shakespeare, Lessing, Goethe, the Brothers Grimm, etc.). Drawing on concrete examples, the following chapters will show how they effect such returns, why, and to what ends.

Conclusion

The aim of this general presentation was to demonstrate that intertextual dialogue with the authors of the Western canon is very much alive and well among Germanophone writers from the Eastern world. Their references are not limited to a "minor" line within literary history, to this mixed, marginal, and subversive side of the canon represented by authors such as Heine, Chamisso, Lasker-Schüler, Celan, and Kafka. Some of the most illustrious representatives of the pantheon of world literature such as Shakespeare, Goethe, and the Brothers Grimm are likewise valuable interlocutors in this dialogue, which includes giving new meaning to the concept of "world literature" among its aims. One way to achieve this is to draw out the convergences, or even the common backgrounds, of Eastern and Western cultures. Yet the opposite movement is equally present, i.e. offering perspectives to better emphasize differences, make distinctions, set oneself apart, and open a third way.

---

47 Anil Bhatti (1998: 345–346) stresses this fundamental issue of the palimpsest for postcolonial literature. See also Karine Chevalier (2008: 135).

At first glance, the work of Germanophone writers on the canon seems more "constructive" than dissident or critical. Rarely polemical, they seek less to reveal the ideological subtext (colonialist, racist) of canonical texts, as do many postcolonial or African-American authors, than to "denaturalize" or "de-ethnicize" the German canon by revealing its "hybrid" and cosmopolitan components. They look not for mothers and fathers to kill but rather willingly seek allies, guardians, ancestors, and godfathers.

And doubtlessly with good reason: the dominant discourse they face is not the same in nature as the one deconstructed by English writers. Unlike British imperialism, which – like French colonial discourse – availed itself of a universalist and humanist conception of culture to establish its claim of "civilizing" the rest of the world, the German discourse of the "cultural nation" is not built on an expansionist and missionary mode. Turned inwards in a context of homogenization, it is likewise not anchored in an American-style syncretism. The German nation is not thought of as a melting pot, but rather as a monocultural, largely mono-ethnic totality that is closed in on itself, with language its only crucible. In the words of Zafer Şenocak, the German concept of culture is "constructed like a monologue," practically a "forbidden zone" and a "labyrinth for trespassers."[48] According to this discourse, Heine, Chamisso, Kafka, Rilke, Canetti, and Celan are German writers, whatever the other parts of their identity may be. By highlighting the hybridity of these writers from the margins of the Germanophone world but also the cosmopolitanism claimed by some of the dominant canon's most representative authors like Goethe, immigrant writers challenge the very conception of national culture.

It is now necessary to refine these conclusions in light of specific texts by situating the discourse about the canon within the context of each writer's work. The following close analyses will shed light on the aesthetic and ideological stakes of these intertextual operations

---

[48] "Der deutsche Kulturbegriff ist als Selbstgespräch aufgebaut, nicht missionarisch nach außen, eher als Sperrbezirk mit ungewisser Tiefe, ein Labyrinth für Unbefugte" (Şenocak 2011: 71).

PART II **The Canon and Its Discontents:
Palimpsestic Re-Inscriptions in Schami,
Özdamar, and Zaimoglu**

Chapter 3
Writing Back from the East: Schami's Corrective Reading of European Classics

Schami, an asylee in the FRG since 1971 because of his opposition to the regime in power in Syria, made his entrance on the West-German literary scene as a voice for immigrant workers. Despite coming from a well-off family, receiving an advanced education, and coming to Europe with the intention of pursuing the studies he had begun in Damascus, he first made contacts in working-class circles through the jobs he was forced to take while learning German and finishing his studies.[1]

The *Gastarbeiter* ("guest workers"), the first population group to settle in large numbers in West Germany, then formed a particularly marginalized minority within the working class because they had been contracted by the German industry, primarily on a temporary basis. When, at the beginning of the 1980s, Schami founded the writers' collective Südwind and the PoLiKunst ("Polynationaler Kunstverein") association with the Italian Franco Biondi and several others, it was with an overtly militant outlook. Even the concept of *Gastarbeiterliteratur* he coined in a manifesto cowritten with Biondi in 1981 demonstrates the two authors' intention to inscribe their work within the Marxist tradition of *Arbeiterliteratur* ("workers' literature"), a branch that grew out of Russian proletariat art and developed in Germany during the 1920s. In contrast to earlier forms of political literature, this "workers'" or "proletariat" literature had the peculiarity of being written by the workers themselves and not by professional writers. Its principal representatives are Hans Lorbeer, Emil Ginkel, Willi Bredel, and Hans Marchwitza. At the beginning of the 1960s, there were attempts to revive the pre-war tradition in both Germanies: in the GDR with impetus from the Ulbricht government, itself aligned with the model of the Soviet Union (*Bitterfelder Weg*); in a much more marginal manner in the FRG and in opposition to the prevailing power structures (Group 61).

By affixing the root *Gast* in the guise of a prefix to the lexical compound *Arbeiterliteratur*, Schami and Biondi did not just repurpose a stigmatizing term (*Gastarbeiter*) in order, as they later explained, to better "unmask the irony it contains" (1981: 134) but also in an attempt to change the public's view of their literary production by inscribing it in a *native* genealogy, a proletarian

---

[1] Between 1971 and 1979, Schami worked various temporary unskilled jobs in industries such as production, construction, and catering.

https://doi.org/10.1515/9783110674392-006

one to be sure but one that had earned its patents of nobility during the Weimar Republic. *Gastarbeiterliteratur* would thus not only be understood as the "literature of immigrant workers," as the term had most often been understood, but first and foremost as "workers' literature written by immigrants." Like the proletarian authors of the 1920s and their successors in Group 61 such as Max von der Grün or Günter Wallraff, Schami and his comrades took a militant and documentary approach, depicting in their texts the immigrant workers' living conditions and their specific problems, linked on the one hand to being uprooted and to the xenophobia of German society on the other: loneliness, homesickness, disorientation, isolation, and an emergent solidarity. The ultimate objective was to provoke a feeling of involvement (*Betroffenheit*) within the group concerned but also within the majority of the population, capable of breaking through the wall of indifference and opening the way for a real transformation of society.

It was in the wake of this collective entry into the field that Schami developed his personal writing project. Until the end of the 1980s, his texts positioned themselves unambiguously as a continuation of the Marxist revolutionary project. Even if starting in 1979 he could seek lucrative employment in the pharmaceutical industry thanks to his doctorate in chemistry, and from 1982 on establish himself as an independent writer, he continued to lay claim to a combative and emancipatory conception of literature. No longer able to claim a directly documentary stance, he developed a more personal writing style that integrated imagination and poetic construction without, however, ceasing to cast a critical eye on society and discourse. Having become a professional writer, Schami understood how to continue to play his part in the struggle against exploitation and in changing mindsets.

His relationship with "established" culture, whether prestigious and selective or commercial and mainstream, was essentially of a polemic nature at the time. Through a series of satirical pieces of metafiction, he scrutinized the ideological subtext of works preferred by the public at large: Bram Stoker's *Dracula* (with all its adaptations and rewritings) and even the Grimms' fairy tales – two texts we will return to in detail – but also *Momo* (1973), for example, Michael Ende's fantasy novel for young readers, which Schami endeavors to show actually conveys a skewed (Eurocentric and apolitical) vision of capitalism under the veneer of a critique of the alienation produced by industrial society by obscuring the mechanisms of exploitation that lead to this alienation. In his short story "Warum Momo sich in J. R. verliebte" ("Why Momo Fell in Love with J. R."), he gives Ende's bestseller a sequel that calls into question the hypotext's humanist and pacifist message as well as the conditions of its global success (2011a:

94–108).² Schami still had not made a brand of his ethnocultural origins at the time. Nevertheless, his anti-capitalist engagement in this period cannot be separated from a critique of the Global North's exploitation of the South and the Eurocentrism that dominated Western culture.

After his novel *Eine Hand voller Sterne* ("A Hand Full of Stars," 1987), which relates in diaristic form how the life of a young man making his way in 1960s Syria – like himself – leads to writing by way of journalism and to commitment against the dictatorship, Schami began to distance himself, at least to judge by appearances, from the specific social problematics of Germany, and the Western world at large, in order to return to the world of his youth. Through stories and novels set in pre-Assad (Hafez) Syria, he outlined the contours of a Middle East relatively unknown to Germans: multiethnic, multifaith, and multilingual, still profoundly anchored in the preindustrial world with strong family structures and traditional forms of sociability. This "Arabia," partially dreamed-up (or at least largely vanished under the strain of successive dictators), represents at once the inverse of the industrialized West and an image of what could be, in certain respects, its future – particularly in a country like Germany where "multiculturalism" was then the object of so much imagining and so much fear. At the same time, the "Arabia" that Schami "recounts to the Germans"³ draws largely – in terms of subjects, motifs, and styles – from sources within an Orientalist imaginary that has long had a place in European literature.

In reviving the Orient of *The Thousand and One Nights* by way of fiction set in the twentieth century, Schami presents himself as a first-class "native informant." Coming himself from the world he describes, he cannot be accused of either blind complaisance or paternalistic arrogance. Arab *and* Christian – like Edward Said – he is living proof of the complexity of a world the West tends often to reduce to the equation Arab = Muslim. Adding story upon story of intercultural friendship and love with his books, Schami contributes to deconstructing the public discourse structured around this conflation and gives form to the utopia (not necessarily chimerical) of a harmonious coexistence between peoples and cultures. He likewise frustrates the stereotypes spread in the West about Islam by showing that, even within the Muslim community, there exist a great variety of configurations and attitudes. Women, notably, are not necessarily oppressed or condemned to chastity and silence. They can be strong and "emancipated"

---

2 See also the essay "Über Illusionäres und Revolutionäres in der Phantasie" published four years earlier in two issues of *Linkskurve* (Schami 1983a; 1983b).
3 For Arabia "recounted to the Germans," see Benoît Ellerbach, whose doctoral thesis *L'"Arabie" contée aux Allemands. Fictions interculturelles chez Rafik Schami* provided me with precious information about Schami's trajectory, work, and reception.

– or more to the point, since that term hardly applies in a context that remains despite everything incontestably patriarchal: free.

It is these works of fiction set in the Syria of the 1950s and 1960s, or between Syria and Germany, that have earned Schami the favor of the public at large and an enduring place in the German literary scene. His success is due in good measure to the stagecraft of his public performances and readings. Schami turns the book tour, that unavoidable extracurricular aspect of the life of a German writer, into a performance art all his own because he *tells* his stories instead of reading them. Thus, to the appeal of his narrative style he adds that of his performance. Consequently, he has established himself in the literary field as a *Märchenerzähler* ("storyteller") in the vein of the *hakawati*, itinerant tellers of fables, fairy tales, and myths comparable to the troubadours of the European Middle Ages.[4] However, this anachronistic posture likewise attracts critiques from a number of journalists and colleagues, notably among those who share the field of migration literature with him and who reproach him for exploiting the public taste for exoticism for venal ends by purveying essentialist clichés.

Obviously, Schami's "reorientation" along the East/West axis represents, at least in part, an intellectual construct. As Ewers (2000) and Ellerbach (2018) in particular have observed, this self-reinvention in the role of the "authentic" Arab storyteller is the fruit of a critique of modern Western culture anchored in a thought tradition itself eminently modern – and Western. Thus, the "self-Orientalization" of Rafik Schami, in so far as one can observe it during this period simultaneously in his texts – constructed like "mosaics," often around characters that are themselves storytellers who employ the art of digression and nested stories – and in his public appearances, results paradoxically from a conception of authoriality that is the very principle of the modern moment in European literary history. In celebrating the art of (oral) storytelling as an art of communication and dialogue, i.e. of listening and openness to the Other in opposition to a literature that cuts itself off from the living sources of creation in fixing the word on the page, the disciple of Walter Benjamin in Schami is knowingly following in the footsteps of the German Romantics. For him, too, it is a matter of reconciling "high" with "popular" culture. He does not pretend to be a naïve creator any more than the Romantics did; on the contrary, the high degree of self-reflexivity in his texts indicates he means to make it clear to anyone paying attention the level of construction (i.e. artifice and play) in his narrative productions.[5]

---

4 On Schami's "cunning" appropriation of the hakawati tradition, see Annette Deeken (1995).
5 See, for example, the novel *Sieben Doppelgänger* (1999), which develops the Romantic theme of the double by linking it to questions of self-Orientalization, self-promotion, and (post-) colonial mimicry, through a tale about the game of masks played by a writer named Rafik Schami.

Decried by some as a sham, in reality, the "Arab turn" in Schami's work results from a reconfiguration of his references. The persona of the militant author promoting *Gastarbeiterliteratur* and fighting on the side of the workers using a Marxist-inspired revolutionary approach ceded its place to that of the affable "storyteller," well-versed in all the illusionist's tricks and playing the Romantic irony card for all its worth. For all that, did he really change his discursive ethos, as those who see another writer in this "second Schami" would suggest? Surely not. If one is willing to see this repositioning as something other than a marketing ploy (though that may *also* play a part), some credit must be given to what the texts say, implicitly or explicitly, about his intentions. Namely, Schami has given himself a specific cultural and social mission with several facets: for one, "to recount Arabia to the Germans," as Ellerbach put it, meaning to provide them with serious, reliable, and useful information through a fictional (and sometimes fairy tale) lens about the "Orient" that attracts them as much as it repels them, and which they still know so little about though they have contact with it now more than ever; for another, and often simultaneously, to enlighten the Germans about their own society and their own culture by looking at it through the feigned naïveté of an "Oriental," that is by describing them from a decentered point of view against the grain of the national system of references. This discursive approach consisting in "Orientalizing Germany" (Ewers) is perceptible to different degrees in a number of his texts since the end of the 1980s. The reader finds a particularly eloquent illustration of this in the third and final text we will be addressing in this chapter, the novel for young adults *Der geheime Bericht über den Dichter Goethe, der eine Prüfung auf einer arabischen Insel bestand* ("The Secret Report on the Poet Goethe, Who Passed a Test on an Arabian Island"). Finally, the mission Schami assigned himself comprises a third part, which he recognizes himself as having something of a utopian quality and which has increased in importance as his books have been exported throughout the whole world: to rehabilitate the traditional (particularly popular and oral) culture from his home region, as much in the eyes of other peoples as in those of its rightful inheritors whom Western colonial domination has dispossessed of it.[6]

Whether consisting of "recounting Arabia to the Germans," "Orientalizing Germany," or reigniting the faith of peoples robbed of their cultural patrimony in their own creativity, the three parts of Schami's "intercultural" program serve the same objective. They mean to work toward a rapprochement between

---

6 On this matter, Schami (2012: 99–156, here 109) refers to his books as his "ambassadors" in regions of the world he himself never has visited and never will visit.

peoples and toward their emancipation by promoting a better understanding of the self as well as the other, strengthened by information not intended to be merely factual but first and foremost cultural. This program represents the taking of a position no less "political" than the first even if the accent is placed elsewhere. In Schami's movement from an authorial persona "committed" on the side of immigrant workers (which often expressed itself, as Ellerbach has said, in a "frontal" assault on German society) to the ethical persona of a cultural mediator conveying his political message through fantastical stories and heroic sagas, there is a change in perspective that no doubt owes much to the evolution of the political context itself. The two pivotal events of the 1990s and 2000s, the collapse of the Soviet bloc and the murder-suicides at the World Trade Center in New York, with all their consequences on the global and national levels, have left profound marks on the public discourse in Germany. Let us simply recall some elements of this evolution: the rebirth of a strong "national sentiment" in the wake of reunification (on the one hand, euphoria at Germany's victory in the soccer world cup in 1990, but racist pogroms on the other), the abandonment of optimistic discourse regarding "multicultural society" in the course of the 1990s, the launching of a debate around the integration of groups of people who had immigrated and the place of Islam in German society during the 2000s (the creation of the German Islam Conference, the DIK, in 2006), and finally the appearance of an "anti-system" hard right increasingly openly flirtatious with national socialist ideology on the political scene, which reshuffled the cards and set a general rightward drift in discourse in motion.

In light of this context, it seems hard to interpret the evolution one observes in Schami – in his writing as in his discursive and social "posturing" – as a simple disengagement, a retreat from politics dictated by personal interests. Let us take the opportunity to highlight that Schami continued to fight against the Assad regime (père and fils) using his contacts within the Syrian and greater Middle Eastern diaspora, and he never stopped involving himself in the international dialogue of intellectuals about the Israel-Palestine conflict.[7] Since the outbreak of the "Syrian spring," soon suppressed with horrendous violence and amidst general indifference, he has given innumerable addresses and interviews about the situation in the country. At the Hans Schiler publishing house in 2011, he inaugurated a collection dedicated to the publication of contemporary Arab literature in German, Swallow Editions. In 2012, using the name Schams, he cre-

---

7 In 2001, at the beginning of the second Intifada, he organized a meeting in Zurich between Israeli and Palestinian writers. The nine lectures resulting from this debate are assembled in the volume *Angst im eigenen Land. Israelische und palästinensische Schriftsteller im Gespräch* (2001). See also his open letter to David Grossmann (Schami 2009: 227–240).

ated a humanitarian association destined to help children victimized by the war in Syria.

So, there is at its core a strong coherence in Schami's approach, which remains eminently Marxist on one point at least: the confidence he has in the capacity of the "common people" to evolve, to attain political maturity, and to take their destiny into their own hands. The constancy Schami has shown throughout his creative career in dedicating himself to writing books for young people is an eloquent proof of this conviction, which led him to bet on education. The main reproach one could make against him is perhaps only that he has worked this program into his writing a little too systematically, leading to a sometimes reductive didacticism. In any case, Schami remains faithful to his intention of "producing entertainment, sure, but high-class entertainment."[8]

Aesthetic Program and Work on the Canon

Schami's aesthetic reflections find their source in a double realization. On the one hand, colonial and postcolonial domination has dispossessed subjugated peoples of their own cultural heritage by inciting them to imitate obsequiously the Western model.[9] On the other, the former colonial powers whose economic and cultural might extends over the rest of the world are themselves cut off from their roots by an alienation brought on by industrialization and the evolution of technology, just as they are cut off from the populations of other continents, from which, however, they have drawn a certain number into themselves, voluntarily or not, and which they do not know how to integrate. This analysis leads Schami to explore the sources common to the different systems of reference in order to locate the points of convergence and overlap that constitute the forgotten common basis of civilization. One of these anchoring points is the tale, a genre that comes out of popular mythical stories in the oral tradition. For Schami, tales represent a "magic bridge,[10]" not merely between different cultures and so potentially between peoples, but also between the past and the present, the world of childhood and that of adults, "high" and "popular" culture, the producer (or storyteller) and the receiver.

---

8 "Unterhaltung sollte es sein, ja, aber von großer Klasse" (Schami 2012: 109).
9 Schami made his position on this issue abundantly clear, above all in the essay "Eine Hand allein kann nicht klatschen. Über die Lage der arabischen Literatur" (Schami 2009: 151–183).
10 His poetological essay "Eine zauberhafte Brücke nur für Kinder" (Schami 2012: 47–70) builds on this metaphor.

In order to realize this largely unrecognized potential, it is important to Schami to revive and revitalize the fairy tale genre. Not, however, as he affirms, in a backward-looking and nostalgic way but from a constructive and jocund, if also critical and subversive, perspective – as Cervantes did, for example, in drawing on material from archaic genres for what would become "the first novel of the modern era" (Schami 2012: 100). From a technical standpoint, it was a matter of appropriating the fairy tale genre by adapting its contents for the modern world, on the one hand, and by extending it across the entire genre spectrum, on the other. Schami himself gives the example of just such a modernization and hybridization by integrating the thematic and narrative elements of a fairy tale into texts that, at first glance, belong to other genres like the novel, short story, or even essay. He hopes in this way to dynamize literature and escape the dead end of mimeticism and realism – following a path of "poeticizing the world," modeled by the German Romantics.

Alongside his research into the common cultural basis of the East and West, Schami engages in a critical rereading of the Western canon from his point of view as an exiled writer marked by his postcolonial experience. His reading functions on two levels. Firstly, it explicitly claims "elective affinities" with certain writers and thinkers in the Western tradition, Cervantes, Goethe, Chamisso, Heine, and Benjamin among others. These canonical authors, chosen based on their aesthetic and political positions, serve for him as guarantors and models, even witnesses against the social and cultural system in which he places himself – with sometimes important differentiations in status between them, as we have been able to see from the examples of his occasional works about Chamisso, Goethe, and Heine. Secondly, he turns his rereading into work in its own right, performing a hypertextual transformation of individual texts.

The first two of the three texts I will discuss, *Die Wahrheit über Vampire und Knoblauch* ("The Truth about Vampires and Garlic," 1987) and *Die Verteidigungsrede. Akte: Rotkäppchen* ("Plea for the Defense: the Little Red Riding Hood Files," 1988), represent hypertextual transpositions that present themselves as "rectifications" of canonical palimpsests. This method of derivation that establishes a critical and ironic relationship with the source text is characteristic of the modalities for rewriting the classics that developed in Europe during the twentieth century, long before the counter-discursive practices (rewriting, writing back) asserted themselves as privileged modes of expression within the postcolonial contexts. Let us consider Gide's *Le Prométhée mal enchaîné* ("Prometheus Illbound," 1920), texts by Kafka like *Die Wahrheit über Sancho Pansa* ("The Truth about Sancho Panza") and *Das Schweigen der Sirenen* ("The Silence of the Sirens"), Brecht's *Berichtigungen alter Mythen* ("Corrections of Ancient Myths," 1933), or Christa Wolf's *Kassandra* ("Cassandra," 1983) and *Medea* (1996) for that matter. These texts written in the form of apologues offer more or less parodic versions of mythic tales, generally in favor of contesting the established social order and its moral legitimacy, often from the angle of class and/or gender relations. The short stories that Schami devoted during his first creative period to Dracula and Little Red Riding Hood, respectively, fall into this tradition of polemic transvalorization. Yet, by submitting the texts of the global canon to critical revision from the point of view of those whom contemporary society exploits and belittles – principally, but not exclusively, immigrants – he is already pleading for a decentering of Western, and more specifically German, literary historiography.

If these first rewritings were still relatively barebones, Schami's fictionalizing of his work on the canon found a much more fulsome expression in his 1999 text written for an adolescent readership: *Der geheime Bericht über den Dichter Goethe, der eine Prüfung auf einer arabischen Insel bestand* ("The Secret Report on the Poet Goethe, Who Passed a Test on an Arabian Island"). The decentering of the perspective on the canon supplements a vibrant homage to the most emblematic representative of German letters in the world. I will turn last to this original work whose pedagogical goal is bound up with a postcolonial counter-discourse supported by Said's thesis.

Does Dracula Need Rehabilitation? The Stakes of a Marxist Rewriting

The short story entitled *Die Wahrheit über Vampire und Knoblauch* ("The Truth about Vampires and Garlic") proposes, as the title indicates, the "rectification" of a modern myth, the most popular foundation of which is the novel *Dracula* (1897) by the Irishman Bram Stoker. The thrust of the story involves the reestablishment of a "truth" as opposed to the legend about vampires circulating since the end of the nineteenth century through multiple works of popular, literary, and cinematic fiction. The paratext thus designates an entire genre tradition as the target of its rectifying discourse, that of the horror story rooted in popular mythology, culminating in Stoker's novel, and transmitted throughout the twentieth century by cinematic adaptations, from Murnau's expressionist *Nosferatu* (1922) to Roman Polanski's off-the-wall-comedic *The Fearless Vampire Killers* (1967). Schami expressly cites this tradition in the first line ("Many horror stories have been written about Count Dracula [...]")[11] before depicting his story's narrator, an exiled Jordanian journalist whom the editor-in-chief of a major German magazine asks to launch an investigation aimed at revising Dracula's negative personal image: "It's high time the true story of a count who respects the environment and loves peace was brought to light."[12] The irony of this introduction clues the reader in that the "correction" Schami is undertaking will not quite deliver the revelation expected.

To accomplish his mission, the narrator-protagonist sets out on the trail of the historic personage who had previously inspired Stoker, the bloody medieval hero Vlad Tepesch, son of Dracul, who had become Prince Vlad III of Wallachia in 1448, better known by the sobriquet Vlad the Impaler. Just like Stoker's novel, Schami's short story has the style of a travelogue, relating in the first person an investigative journey stretching from one end of Europe to the other. His purpose is not so much to contradict the hypotext but to put its historical and ideological dimensions into perspective.

Stoker's latecomer gothic novel presents itself as a travel narrative composed of journal entries, letters, and telegrams relating an expedition into Eastern Europe from London to the heart of the Carpathians. The journey toward Transylvania brings with it a progressive loss of reference points for the English protagonists that causes them to experience a regression of civilization. As they progress eastward, they are forced to utilize increasingly rudimentary means of transportation while the nature that surrounds them becomes increasingly inhospitable and disquieting, the local languages increasingly incomprehensible to British ears, and the inhabitants increasingly rustic and superstitious. At this harrowing journey's end, they find themselves confronted by a pitiless, bestial creature, devilishly cunning and gifted with exceptional strength and supernatural powers. Count Dracula, to whom the young notary clerk Jonathan Harker has been sent to negotiate a real estate transaction, is nothing less than a monstrous avatar of the national hero Vlad Tepesh, a medieval warrior wrapped in dark legends. He is a *nosferatu* ("living dead")[13] feeding on the blood of his victims and transforming them in turn into vampires. He nevertheless has several weak points, which his adversaries endeavor to exploit: the necessity of return-

---

[11] "Über Graf Dracula wurden viele Horrorgeschichten geschrieben." (Schami [1987] 2011: 48–70, here 48) Subsequent references to this work will appear as VK plus page number.

[12] "Es ist an der Zeit, daß die wahre Geschichte dieses umweltfreundlichen und friedliebenden Grafen ans Licht kommt" (VK 48).

[13] One of many suggested etymologies of the term is that it is derived from the Romanian *nu sfîrșitul* ("not ended"). Internal evidence in *Dracula* suggests that Stoker believed the term meant "not dead," and thus he may have intended the word *undead* to be its calque.

ing to ground sheltered from the light of day between dawn and dusk, as well as a pronounced vulnerability to garlic, to natural light, and to sacred objects such as the communion host or a crucifix. After barely escaping the cursed castle, Harker manages to return to England, but in so doing, he attracts the vampire toward the civilized world where he continues to strike until he is defeated once and for all.

The immense success of this thriller, which was to become the work of reference for vampire literature, results essentially from the complexity of its primary character. Dracula is not just a sanguinary monster but also an outcast, a creature rejected by God and deprived of his humanity, for which the author (with Mina Harker as a spokeswoman) explicitly exhorts the reader to pity. The ambivalence in the conception of the character explains why the reception of Stoker's novel was split between interpretations that made Dracula into the archetypical dominant figure and those that made him into the model of the pariah, the marginal figure. The postcolonial reading of the myth has been no less divided owing to the rather polysemic character of the novel in the context of colonial era literature. As Olivier Lubrich (2004: 99–147) has highlighted, Dracula could just as easily incarnate the colonial exploitation and sprawling power of empire as its inverse, subversive postcolonial hybridity. He represents an "ideological master key" that lends itself to interpretation according to one's point of view as either a symbol of the aggressive colonizer or as a figuration of the Other, of the "Oriental" barbarian, or of the "primitive," the object of rejection and contempt on the part of the Western colonialist. Placed in the paranoid perspective of Western Europe toward the diffuse menace of an "inverse colonialism" emanating from Pan-Slavist movements ("revenge of the East"), even of an "invasion" from the colonies within Europe, it could equally well represent racism, antisemitism, nationalism, cosmopolitanism, hedonism, decadence, irrationalism, the return of the repressed, etc.[14]

The "rectification" of the myth carried out by Schami operates on several levels and across two timeframes. Firstly, it selects as its narrator a man who, equipped by virtue of his connection to the Muslim world to glean new revelations about the character of Dracula,[15] sets out to bring to light a document that gives a concrete historical basis to this dark legend: the history of Vlad III the Impaler who broke the peace his father had concluded with the Ottomans

---

14 See also Tabish Khair and Johan Höglund (2013) on *Transnational and Postcolonial Vampires*.
15 "'Warum gerade ich?' [...] 'Also nehmen wir an, ein christlicher Reporter macht einen Bericht, irgendeine Story, daß das Kreuz doch heilig ist und Wunder vollbringt. Das kauft uns doch keine Oma mehr ab, da muß schon ein Muslim ran!'" (VK 49).

and waged war against them without mercy. In Romania, where this sinister figure is still venerated as a national hero even though, as Schami reminds his readers, his descendants made a pact with the Nazis,[16] the research carried out by the narrator reaches a dead end. However, the trail leads him to Istanbul, where he has a scholar translate a document in Ottoman Turkish from the fifteenth century, which is none other than the authentic testimony of a victim regarding the abuses carried out by the count on his Turkish prisoners. Contrary to the declared objective, arbitrarily fixed by his boss in the German press, the investigation in no way leads to the revelation of facts capable of rehabilitating the honor of a historical person unjustly defamed (and so to work as a "Defense of Western culture," VK 48). Instead, it leads to a resounding confirmation of the sanguinary penchants of Dracula's historical model. This finding is not the kind capable of sating the editor-in-chief's hunger for sensationalism and so he refuses to publish the article.

Nevertheless, a few years later, the journalist whose interest had been piqued and who identified with the victims of the barbarous torturer has a chance encounter in a train with a Moroccan immigrant worker, Ali Turki, who has bite marks on his neck, which he confesses are the work of a mysterious persecutor. This man's tale represents a new version of the end of Dracula's story. The horrible predator is not dead, or he at least has descendants still striking right in the middle of the civilized world. However, they now prefer to attack, with much more refined methods than before, defenseless working-class individuals. It's "at the assembly line and in the bars" that the new Dracula finds his "main course for the day."[17] Instead of killing his prey with a single spectacular blow by draining them of their blood, the vampire now contents himself to remove a half-liter of the fluid from different victims, thus ensuring his own subsistence while simultaneously prolonging the lives of his victims (who in this manner remain at his mercy, living reservoirs growing ever weaker) as well as the torment and terror they endure.

The sole point where the truth differs from the myth, according to Ali, is that modern vampires fear neither garlic nor the cross. On the contrary, being a free spirit, the distinguished parasite is above such prejudices and laughs at the spirituality attached to religious symbols of any provenance. Indiscriminately attacking German and foreign workers, he only lets his prey go by caprice when

---

[16] Schami insists on the ideological continuity between the struggle of Vlad Tepesch and the Romanian Royal family's links to the Nazi regime during the 1930s–1940s (VK 50).

[17] "'Ja, dann geh' doch in die Nebenhalle. Dort sind mehrere kräftige Kerle, da kannst du dich vollsaugen.' 'Das habe ich schon, weißt du's noch nicht? Am Fließband und in den Kneipen. Das ist mein tägliches Hauptgericht, und jetzt will ich meinen Nachtisch [...]'" (VK 62).

he has found something better elsewhere. Thus, the German worker Günther errs in thinking that he owes finally being released from his tormenter to his cross. When Ali, following his advice, begins wearing a crescent moon pendant, the amulet offers him no succor. Dracula not only shows nothing but contempt for this superstition, but he takes amusement in twisting the pendant into a cross – in so doing, proving that he has no more respect for Christian symbols (VK 66). As for garlic, contrary to a considerable number of Germans who, like the editor-in-chief, think of it as a stinking exotic food characteristic of cultures stigmatized as foreign,[18] far from repelling this gourmet cosmopolitan with its strong odor, he enjoys it to the point of seeking it out, borne as traces in immigrant workers' blood (like from eating harissa), as a little treat. Hence, the German worker undoubtedly does not owe ultimately being spared to his cross so much as his blander blood.

The reader can approach Schami's interventions in the hypotextual material along three axes involving different levels of reading: historical revision, reconfiguration of a myth, and a critique of the utilization of sources that calls into question the legitimacy of official sources. On the level of the historical substratum, the author seems at first to be adopting a counter-historical point of view. His character-narrator, a Syrian-German like himself, undertakes the reestablishment of the "historical truth" (well-known in actuality) about Prince Vlad III on the basis of a fragmentary document of the fourteenth century that partially restores the victims' obscured perspective. The exhumation of this "authentic" testimony transmitted by a "native informer" contemporary to events might at first blush open the door to a reappropriation by those who were the first (and real) victims. This way out is blocked, however, with the truth being once more obscured by the German magazine editor who refuses to publish the facts revealed by his investigator. As an added bit of irony, the editor had specifically asked the journalist he had chosen because of his "Oriental" origins to deliver an article that could contribute to the *rehabilitation* of Dracula. With this detail, Schami simultaneously denounces the appetite of opinion-makers in German society for anything that can compete with historical revisionism (fascination with barbarism and hunger for sensationalism) and the paradoxical and perverse injunction addressed to intellectuals, particularly those who are immigrants (whether or not

---

18 The editor-in-chief declares from the outset to his reporter: "'Daß der Graf den Knoblauchgeruch gehaßt hat, das versteht jeder vernünftige Mensch, diese üble Pflanze kann einen Feinschmecker richtig anwidern'" (VK 48). It is precisely – and only – this racist and stubborn certainty that will be refuted by the inquiry, revealing that the historical Dracula ordered that his prisoners be served nothing but water and fresh garlic in the days prior to their execution (VK 55).

they are Muslim[19]), from those same institutions to pay homage to Western culture and denounce the "primitive" societies whence they come.

On the level of myth, Schami devotes himself to a modernization of the literature about vampires, to which he gives a different political content. By having the oral testimony of a contemporary victim "reveal" to his narrator that Dracula still lives, he extends his fantastical hypotexts. The reader is no longer in the distant past but in a modern factory during Oktoberfest in Munich. Schami gives the contemporary witness a name that reflects, for one, on German stereotypes about foreigners and, for another, an overemphasis on his exogenous status: Ali is the quasi-generic name of immigrant workers in Germany,[20] and the family name Turki indicates that his family already had a foreign status in Morocco (VK 61). This unlucky man's story provides the narrator with the ultimate proof of barbarism's triumph over modern European civilization. Schami explains this final victory of Dracula's, a secret victory unbeknownst to society, in two ways. Firstly, the vampire evolved. He freed himself of religion and prejudice, learned to appropriate modern technologies (notably electric lights,[21] computers,[22] and disinfection techniques[23]), and learned moderation, which prevents him from resorting to such a spectacular method of murder and thus putting himself in danger. This civilized evolution, which the new Dracula acknowledges self-importantly ("Drain them to death! Oh, how brutal and primitive! It was my ancestors who would drain away whoever fell into their clutches [...] Oh, the fools!"),[24] revises the gothic novel wherein the medieval monster was vanquished with the aid of Christian faith and modern technology.

---

[19] Schami's narrator actually happens to be an atheist, which doesn't bother his boss in the least (VK 49).
[20] This association has been considered a commonplace at least since the journalist Günter Wallraff published *Ganz unten* (1985). The resounding success of this undercover reporting on the situation of immigrant workers, for which Wallraff disguised himself as a Turk named Ali in order to penetrate Germany's illegal labor market, definitively linked this first name to the figure of the immigrant, one decade following the release of Rainer Werner Fassbinder's film *Angst essen Seele auf* (1974), which was originally to be entitled *Alle Türken heißen Ali*.
[21] The modern vampire is an active supporter of electricity (VK 62).
[22] Computer science provides Dracula the means of information and research he needs to select his victims based on their origin (VK 61).
[23] The vampire is a hypochondriac who is sure to disinfect the necks of his victims before sinking his teeth into them (VK 63).
[24] "Zu Tode saugen! Oh, wie brutal und primitiv! Das waren doch meine Vorfahren, sie haben drauflosgesaugt, bei allem, was ihnen in die Hände fiel, ob Katze oder Mensch, Alkoholiker oder Hepatitiskranker, ihnen war alles egal" (VK 63).

Secondly, the vampire now benefits from the complicity of the majority society because he is careful to select his victims from among the pariahs of the modern capitalist world, those whose disappearance or disintegration no one would notice: unskilled workers, preferably (though not exclusively) immigrants. His actions are concealed by institutions and particularly propitiated by popular celebrations like Oktoberfest. Mixing a funfair with heavy drinking and costumed parades, the grand, open-air Bavarian festival permits the monster to show himself in the middle of the day on a factory floor without raising suspicions in spite of his archaic dress and extravagant manners. He unapologetically wears the emblematic costume of the nineteenth century victimizer, a black cloak, top hat, and white gloves, paired with exquisite manners and a perfect mastery of foreign languages (VK 60).

Here, Schami returns to the old Marxist metaphor of vampirism as capitalistic exploitation. With the aid of aspects of modernization represented by Dracula's rationing of blood withdrawals, he joins the character of myth to the Marxist allegory of capital as "dead labor" draining the "living labor" that is the proletariat.[25] Victims are no longer emptied of their blood to the point that death is certain, instead being killed little by little without disturbing anyone. Meanwhile the superficially happy-go-lucky setting of Oktoberfest serves as the ideal cover for these misdeeds since the victims cannot count on any compassion on the part of drunk passers-by for whom their cries for help provoke at most xenophobic mocking (VK 67). "Everyday people" thus make themselves complicit with the blood sucker, the demon with the sardonic laugh who represents their objective ally by way of their herd-like rejection of weakness, of the foreign, of the uprooted marginalized (VK 63). No more than Chamisso's "man in gray," this devil has nothing to be afraid of from the middle and working classes once he throws himself – with a perfect mastery of the cultural, social, institutional, and linguistic codes – upon the "schlemiels" of the modern industrial world. This lackluster outcome of the "process of civilization" (to use Norbert Elias's coining) at the end of the twentieth century, not just among the descendants of Vlad the Impaler but also, if one believes this depiction, among the German populace, calls into question the valorization of "progress" in and of itself in Western ideology.

To this transposition, which inscribes the myth of Dracula into the domain of ideological parable, Schami ultimately adds a media-critical dimension. Throughout his story, he not only confronts two ways of life and modes of perception but also two modes of communication: the archaic (oral culture, dia-

---

25 "Das Kapital ist verstorbene Arbeit, die sich nur vampyrmässig belebt durch Einsaugung lebendiger Arbeit und um so mehr lebt, je mehr sie davon einsaugt" (Marx 1867: 200).

logue) and the technological (written culture, science) mode. The common theme is constituted by the "living traces" of the old, authentic exhumed document and the oral testimony of the worker opposed to the pseudo-communication imposed by the possessors of economic and political power (the press and advertising).

In reexamining the Dracula myth from the point of view of a Middle Eastern intellectual living in Germany today, Schami draws attention to the historical basis of the myth, a particularly bloody episode in the wars that pitted Christian Europe against the Ottoman Empire at the end of the Middle Ages, and questions the ambivalent fascination with the legend that made Vlad the Impaler into an immortal monster but also an outcast inspiring as much pity as fear. However, by subverting the model of the Victorian gothic novel, the mirror of the anxieties born of the industrial revolution and colonial expansion, Schami also joins in the continuation of the tradition, adding a fantastical-comic epilogue to Stoker's novel evoking the vampire myth as a metaphor for capitalism.

Moreover, Schami points out the perverse dialectic at work in this globalized exploitation, which subjects its victims to a double punishment. Ravaged body and soul, hurled into the sorrow of loneliness, they are not only denied their traditional points of reference and the comfort of religion (the Arab immigrant loses his faith when he is robbed of the crescent and has it returned by the vampire as a cross, VK 66) but eventually and equally of all the hard-won ethical gains of civilization. Driven to his wits' end by the diabolical vampire who fears neither crescent nor cross, Ali regresses morally to the point of beating his wife, breaking the oath he once swore to his mother never to reproduce the brutality she had been forced to suffer from her husband. Dispossessed of his original culture and nevertheless thrown back into a "primitive" state of civilization, that of his own father, Ali understands that he has become what he had "never wanted to be" and curses the immigrant destiny, which has reduced him to the cliché of the Arab man oppressing and mistreating his wife (VK 70). The barbarism / civilization axis is irrevocably scrambled.

Beyond its critique of neo-imperialism, at stake in the novel is the question of the ambiguous fascination exerted by emblematically evil characters in contemporary Western society, especially so in Germany. Denouncing – just a few years after the scandal around the fake private journals of Hitler – the function of a yellow journalism in love with scoops capable of calling into question a presumed doxa (not yet termed "political correctness"), Schami points the finger at a culture of spectacle that mixes a thirst for transgression, the aestheticization of violence, and a taste for the bizarre and monstrous. Finally, in the context of the *Historikerstreit* ("historian's dispute") (1986–1989), the reader can find in the text a form of satirical commentary on the pernicious attractions of a historical relativism, which might extend, as contemporaneous examples from Ernst Nolte,

Michael Stürmer, and Andreas Hillgruber show, to the point of denying the singularity of the Nazis' crimes.[26]

Some of the thematic concerns of this rewriting – the theft of victims' speech, the critique of official sources, and the rehabilitation of oral popular tradition – likewise form the heart of Schami's second rewriting in the same period.

Writing back to the "Grimm Bros.": A Plea for a Paradigm Shift

Published in 1988 with the title *Die Verteidigungsrede. Akte: Rotkäppchen* ("Plea for the Defense: The Little Red Riding Hood File"), the rewriting of the Grimms' fairy tale Schami offers readers also presents itself as a story with corrective intent, playfully mixing transposition, continuation, and commentary. However, in a reverse of "The Truth about Vampires and Garlic," here the point is to rehabilitate a literary character with a big, bad reputation: the wolf, the mythic incarnation of childhood fears, and the favored allegory for being devoured. Yet, the process is much simpler. It has less to do, properly speaking, with a corrective than a sheer refutation, an operation of negative transvalorization that consists of dismantling a hypotext by reversing the point of view and casting the first author as an imposter.

In this story presented from the point of view of the wolf, Schami takes, without much originality, the opposing side of the famous Romantic-era tale, basing his on the final version of the text settled on by the Brothers Grimm (1857: 140 – 144) who worked from a supposed transcription made in 1697 by Perrault (*Contes de ma mère l'Oye*, "Mother Goose's Tales") of a European fairy tale in the oral tradition. In Schami's modernized version, the roles are reversed, and the elementary tale transforms into a parable of excluding the "stranger" in contemporary German society. Here the wolf, the paradigmatic figure of the "opponent"[27] in the upset schema of the hypotext, speaks up to plead, orally and in the first person, his own case in the trial brought against him by his supposed victim. Ad-

---

[26] Regarding this polemic that appeared on the pages of *Die Zeit* on 11 July 1986 when the philosopher Jürgen Habermas responded to an article by historian Ernst Nolte in the *Frankfurter Allgemeine Zeitung* entitled "Vergangenheit, die nicht vergehen will," see Augstein et al. (1987).

[27] The term "opponent" refers to the actantial model established by Vladimir Propp in *Morphology of the Tale*, first published in Russian in 1928 and translated into English in 1958. According to Propp, the opponent is the character who hinders the hero in the fulfilment of a quest, in contrast with the "helper." The pattern of the Grimms' *Little Red Riding Hood* is atypical compared to other coming-of-age tales since its heroine is an utterly passive victim.

dressing the tribunal in an equanimous and courteous tone using terms that denote a perfect mastery of judicial rhetoric, he proclaims from the very start that he bears no responsibility for the crimes of which he stands accused by the girl supported by "her army of propagandists." Instead, he proposes "to accuse the plaintiff," informing the jurors that he does not need their mercy but a "just verdict" once they have heard "the true story" and that he will defer, if such a verdict is denied him, to history's judgment for his "rehabilitation."[28]

Throughout this *pro se* apologia, the wolf characterizes himself as a pacifist outcast who feeds himself from the surplus of consumer society and is more than content to leave humans alone. A debonair bon vivant, he leads a good life in the woods that surround a retirement home, living in harmony with the elderly relegated there by their families who come to see them on the weekends with factory-made cakes and cheap wine to soothe their consciences. Helping himself to the rabbits that thrived all around, overfed by the home's retirees who in this manner disposed of the bad pastries they were brought, he lived a peaceful life until the day when, while he was flirting with a female wolf, he found himself being shouted at by a "fat girl" regarding his "big ears" and "big nose" (AR 92). Driven over the edge by the little pest's malicious bullying and abandoned by his sweetheart whom the invective had filled with disgust for him, he ended up biting the child on the derriere. He thus earns reprisal from a hunter who took the opportunity to accuse him baselessly of a second crime, that of kidnapping and murdering the girl's grandmother. The hunter then set off in pursuit of both the wolf and grandmother, who in reality had run away from the retirement home with a young man and whom the hunter returned by force after having caught her in her lover's arms, claiming to have saved her from the wolf's belly along with her granddaughter. The "official" version of the tale, which the wolf – and through him Schami – flatly deny, is that of a dangerous braggart, self-proclaimed defender of the weak, backed up and promoted by the little girl:

> Little Red Riding Hood, however, told her parents how the hunter had freed her and her grandmother from my stomach, and these simple parents believed her story and repeated it, and whenever a grandmother disappears, many wolves bite the dust because the bipeds

---

[28] "Verehrte Geschworene, Exzellenz, meine Damen und Herren! Das Hohe Gericht hat in seiner großen Gnade mir gestattet, mich gegen die Klägerin Rotkäppchen und das Heer ihrer Propagandisten zu verteidigen. Ich lehne jedoch jede Verteidigung ab und möchte höflichst Ihre Aufmerksamkeit auf die wahre Geschichte lenken und die Klägerin anklagen. Ich erhoffe mir nicht Ihre Gnade, sondern Ihr gerechtes Urteil, und sollte es mir verwehrt bleiben, so wird die Geschichte mich rehabilitieren" (Schami 2011b: 90–96, here p. 90). Further references to this work will appear as AR plus page number.

cut them open and look for their grandmothers there as if our stomachs were retirement homes.²⁹

By transposing the popular myth to contemporary German society, Schami on the one hand denounces the distancing of the old and the marginal in a society ruled by the law of the strongest and obsessed by the quest for profits, on the other the theft of minority voices in a society that hypocritically claims to protect the weak. The mock speech furthermore permits Schami to interrogate once again the status of oral tradition and the conditions of its distortion by institutions during the passage from writing to canonization. The role of self-referential correction in this story likewise makes an ideological commentary on the Grimms' fairy tale, the moral of which, supposedly "sugarcoated" compared to earlier versions, rests in reality on a mix of puritanism and cruelty.³⁰ In drawing attention to the semantic misappropriation that the two German philologists submit the traditional cautionary tale to in their final edition of the *Kinder- und Hausmärchen* ("Children's and Household Tales"), Schami puts the cultural roots of the social discrimination and stigmatization of the foreigner in Germany into perspective.

This last aspect resonates with the reflections Schami, like other politically engaged authors of his generation, developed in the 1980s around the poetics of the fairy tale. Duly noting the symbolic efficacy that predestines tales of wonder to be exploited as an instrument for transmission and education, the exiled Marxist writer opposed traditional popular tales with their moralistic and reactionary Romantic literary versions. While still paying homage to those scholars like Perrault and the Brothers Grimm who saved an inestimable cultural patrimony from oblivion, he draws attention to the instrumentalization that they submitted it to by serving, wittingly or not, their class interests. "In transcribing these tales, the writers performed a selection, generally in the interest of the bourgeoi-

---

29 "Rotkäppchen aber erzählte ihren Eltern, wie der Jäger die Großmutter und es selbst aus meinem Bauch befreit hätte, und die einfältigen Eltern glaubten die Geschichte und erzählten sie weiter, und immer wenn eine Großmutter verschwindet, müssen viele Wölfe dran glauben, weil die Zweibeiner sie aufschlitzen und ihre Großmutter dort suchen, als wären unsere Bäuche Altersheime" (AR 96).

30 In Perrault's version the tale ends with the disobedient heroine and her grandmother slaughtered by the wolf. The Grimms substituted this cruelly moralizing ending for a happy one. In their two separate versions, Little Red Riding Hood and her granny are saved. But while in the 1812 edition of the *Children's and Household Tales* they manage to trap and defeat the wolf by themselves, the 1857 version reduces them to total passivity. Deceived and swallowed by the wolf, they are ultimately rescued by a hunter who happens to pass by and cuts open his belly.

sie and aristocracy, *à la* the Grimm Bros.,"[31] he declared in saluting the work of the American Germanist Jack Zipes on the fairy tales and their "socialization function," particularly for the Brothers Grimm. He continued:

> Everyone here knows "Little Red Riding Hood," but what do we really know? In his excellent work, Jack Zipes establishes the original form of this fairy tale, in which a brave peasant girl who does not at all shy away from sensual experiences with a stranger but enjoys them until they become too tiresome, and she, on her own, gets rid of him using her rustic cleverness. The French civil servant Charles Perrlaut [sic], an admirer of Louis XIV, took up the fairy tale and turned it into moral pap. He replaced the clever peasant girl with a noble maid and put a red riding hood on her that does not appear in the old folktales. He now has Red Riding Hood come into danger, because the stupid girl leaves the marked path and messes around with a stranger (probably a guest worker) whom Perrlaut [sic] gives the form of a wolf. In the end, Red Riding Hood gets eaten. That's the official version. So, a French girl shouldn't be encouraged to be brave, to be independent, to enjoy sensuality but to be obedient. The Brothers Grimm later scrubbed the fairy tale of any French horniness and its brutal ending. Red Riding Hood is a child, and she's merely the victim of her naïveté, and naturally, a German hunter rescues grandmother and granddaughter in the end. Zipes's research clearly shows the transformation of women's role over the course of history."[32]

Stemming from this analysis of the Grimms' fairy tales' genesis, the critical rewriting Schami delivers of *Little Red Riding Hood* is an invitation to interrogate the historical and ideological reasons for their success and the timelessness of the values they convey. The stakes of this question are commensurate with the

---

31 "Die Schriftsteller wählten die Märchen bei ihrer Niederschrift aus, meist im Interesse des Bürgertums und des Adels, à la Grimm-brothers" (Schami 1983b: 20).
32 "*Rotkäppchen* kennt jeder von uns, aber was kennen wir eigentlich? Jack Zipes wies in einer hervorragenden Arbeit nach, wie das Märchen über eine tapfere Bäuerin, die durchaus sinnliche Erfahrungen mit einem Fremden nicht scheut und genießt, bis es ihr zu lästig wird und sie sich eigenständig durch ihre bäuerliche Schläue von ihm befreit, ursprünglich ausgesehen hat. Der französische Beamte Charles Perrlaut [sic], ein Bewunderer Ludwig XIV., griff das Märchen auf und wandelte es zu einem moralischen Brei. Er ersetzte die schlaue Bäuerin durch ein Edelfräulein und setzte ihr ein rotes Käppchen auf, das in alten Volksmärchen nicht vorkommt. Er ließ nun Rotkäppchen in die Gefahr kommen, weil das dumme Fräulein den vorgezeichneten Weg verließ und sich mit einem Fremden (womöglich einem Gastarbeiter), dem Perrlaut *[sic]* die Gestalt eines Wolfes gab, einließ. Rotkäppchen wird am Ende aufgefressen. So die offizielle Version. Also nicht zum Mut, nicht zur Selbständigkeit, nicht zum Genuß ihrer Sinnlichkeit soll die Französin ermuntert werden, sondern zum Gehorsam. Die Grimm-brothers säuberten nachträglich das Märchen von jeder französischen geilen Sexualität und dem brutalen Schluß. Rotkäppchen ist ein Kind, und sie ist nur Opfer ihrer Naivität, und, wie es sich gehört, rettet am Schluß ein deutscher Jäger Großmutter wie Enkelin. Zipes' Untersuchung zeigte deutlich den Wandel der Frauenrolle im Laufe der Geschichte" (Schami 1983b: 20).

interest Schami brings to the fairy tale in itself, the generic universality of which, according to him, predestine it to serve as a "bridge" between individuals and peoples.[33] Because he is convinced that the fairy tale responds to the existential needs of the human being and, more than any other genre, is capable of developing precious social competences in the reader (and the more so in the listener), Schami places importance on sensitizing his audience to the tendentious morals in the stories they have been fed since infancy and the degree to which the very values that undergird these stories permeate the society in which they live. By reversing the perspective of a tale like *Little Red Riding Hood*, he reminds his (German) readers that, beneath its inoffensive exterior (an illusion maintained by its recent restriction to an exclusively infantile target audience and its deceptive use of puerile diminutives: *Rotkäppchen* ("*Little* Red Riding Hood"), *Märchen*,[34] the moral it advocates serves a fundamentally antihumanist, sexist, and xenophobic ideology. This ideology is neither eternal nor universal. It is the product of the conservative and nationalist thinking of nineteenth-century Germany, and its survival in today's Germany does not foster the evolution of mentalities toward increased political maturity, open-mindedness, and solidarity. Indeed, far from encouraging children to develop their imagination and become autonomous subjects, fully realized and critical, stories that cultivate fear of the unknown in all its forms (the Other, sex, changes, the "wild") hold them in a dangerous state of infantilism that prepares them to accommodate themselves to an unjust and virulent society ruled by egotism, stagnation, obsession with security, and the interest of the strongest.

This focus and value-shifting rewriting locates itself in a contemporary context of the critical reception and counter-canonical adaptation of fairy tales tracing back to the experimentations of the 1930s. One very fertile branch of young-adult literature developed in the Weimar Republic, notably under the impulse of Benjamin's theories on the art of storytelling.[35] Authors like Edwin Hoernle[36] and Hermynia Zur Mühlen[37] attempted at the time to oppose the indoctrination of

---

33 See especially the essay "Eine zauberhafte Brücke nur für Kinder" (Schami 2012: 47–70).
34 Schami has repeatedly emphasized the axiological shift induced by the use of the diminutive *Märchen*, as opposed to the old German word *Mär*, which situated the tale within the field of legend and myth, noble genres that weren't reserved for children. See for instance 1983b: 52.
35 On Schami's debt to Benjamin, see the chapter "Das Erzählen / Der Erzähler: Benjamin et Schami" in Ellerbach (2018), 180–198.
36 The Marxist theoretician Edwin Hoernle (1883–1952) was also one of the KPD's literary and educational pundits. See especially his *Grundfragen der proletarischen Erziehung* (1929), to which Benjamin wrote a preface entitled *Eine kommunistische Pädagogik*.
37 Hermynia Zur Mühlen (1883–1951), *née* Gräfin Folliot de Crenneville, became the GDR's leading writer of revolutionary fairy tales for children. Her major publications include: *Was Pe-*

young people by far-right ideologues with an emancipatory culture based in a Marxist analysis of society. Taking a position opposed to the national-socialist instrumentalization of Germanic folklore wherein the Romantic-era tales and most especially the Grimms' literary fairy tales held a key place,[38] these writers strove to offer children positive models rooted in worker culture and capable of preparing them for the class struggle. While the writers of the GDR quickly revived this tradition, itself consistent with the model of revolutionary tales imported from the Soviet Union,[39] the critical reception of the Brothers Grimm would not become productive again in the FRG until the 1960s in the context of the student revolt and the increase in "alternative" (pacifist, antiracist, feminist, ecologist, etc.) movements. Two polemic rewritings of "Hansel and Gretel" inaugurated this change of perspective on the Romantic repertoire (Traxler 1963; Maar 1968: 29–33). As for *Little Red Riding Hood*, it became the object of numerous parodic transformations in the 1970s passing a more or less fierce verdict on contemporary German society.[40]

Schami's reflections on the fairy tale thus reveal his position in a national debate that made the folklore canon, and particularly the Grimms' *Kinder- und Hausmärchen*, a major issue in the semantic battle opposing the adherents of the established order and the defenders of an emancipatory and anarchistic concept of literature (Zipes 1996). In the majority of his later fictional works, of which many take inspiration from the generic schema of the fairy tale,[41] Schami endeavors to advance the poetics of the genre to place their pedagogical resour-

---

terchens Freunde erzählen ("What Little Peter's Friends Tell," 1920), *Das Schloss der Wahrheit* ("The Castle of Truth," 1924), *Es war einmal… und es wird sein* ("One Upon a Time… and It Will Be," 1930).

38 Once in power, the Nazis continued to systematically exploit the popularity of the Grimms' tales by producing big-budget studio adaptations with well-known actors, sumptuous costumes, and magnificent real-life settings. In the explicitly ideological adaptation *Rotkäppchen und der Wolf* (Fritz Genschow and Renée Stobrawa, 1937), the hunter, played by Fritz Genschow himself, wears the insignia of the Nazi eagle and swastika on his hat.

39 However, the determination of the East German political leaders to perpetuate the tradition of the revolutionary fairy tale did not prevent them from exploiting the moralizing message of the Grimms' tales for their own purposes. Thus, the author of an instructional manual for "teachers, educators, pioneering leaders, and parents" writes: "Für ältere Kinder ist die Herausarbeitung der bewußten Disziplin besonders wichtig: Rotkäppchen lernt selbst durch ihren Gehorsam und auf Grund ihrer eigenen Erfahrung mit dem listigen Wolf, daß gehorsam zu sein auf die guten und weisen Lehren der erfahrenen Erwachsenen achten heißt" (Siebert 1952: 15–16).

40 Notable examples are Janosch's *Das elektrische Rotkäppchen* [1972] (Janosch 1983), Max von der Grün's *Rotkäppchen* [1972] (Mieder 1986), and Margaret Kassajep's *Rotkäppchen mit Sturzhelm* (Kassajep 1980).

41 See Khalil (1990), Arens (2000b), and El Wardy (2007).

ces in the service of a critical and engaged perspective capable of promoting values which the world needs now more than ever: curiosity, adventurousness, openness to others, and the ability to listen and converse.

This may partly explain why his "anti-Little Red Riding Hood" has remained an exception in his œuvre. It works as an illustration of the intellectual and moral perversion across modern Western culture by revealing what shams lay at the root of the tales that had so shaped it. The quill of the Brothers Grimm, like the animated films of Walt Disney later,[42] perverted the liberative potential of the fairy tale in order to subordinate the individual and domesticate the imagination. Schami's demonstration opens the gates to the creation of tales for our time, which situate themselves in the tradition of what he calls "the other tale": that which does not feed the "reactionary illusion" but the "revolutionary imagination," i.e. "the rebellious fairy tale, which sends the happy ending to hell and only feels morally obliged to the exploited."[43]

If the majority of the fairy tales Schami has written since then draw more from the depths of the Arab-Islamic culture than the Western tradition, it is therefore not due to cultural preference or ideological partiality but because he has assigned himself the mission of "saving the Arab art of storytelling" – which he knows best and which his audience in turn knows very little about – by unburdening it of the weight of superstition and the spirit of subjugation, of the decorum "of the palaces, princes, and princesses," and of an artificially ornamental language in order to inject it with the fresh blood of "enlightenment, insolence, and the themes of our own time."[44] The two traditions he places in opposition in his 1983 essay, the rebellious tradition and the reactionary tradition, exist everywhere around the world and have always (co)existed. The critique of the European canon is, in this context, not an end in itself. It only serves to demonstrate to his readers the historicity and relativism of every official cul-

---

42 Schami (1983b: 21) addresses the case of Walt Disney's animated feature *Pinocchio* (1940) shortly after discussing the work of the "Grimm-bros."
43 "Sein [Franz Fühmanns] Plädoyer für den Mythos ist aber tatsächlich ein Plädoyer für das andere Märchen, [...] das rebellische Märchen, das das Happy-End zum Teufel jagt und sich moralisch nur den Ausgebeuteten verpflichtet fühlt. [...] Zu allen Zeiten gab es, gibt es und wird es revolutionäre Phantasie und reaktionäre Illusion geben. [...] Ich behaupte, die Illusion verhält sich zur engagierten Phantasie [...] wie ein Gegenpol" (Schami 1983b: 21).
44 "Ich aber wollte mit einer unerschrockenen Naivität einfach die arabische Erzählweise retten, sie vom Aberglauben und Untertanengeist und vom Ballast der Paläste, der Prinzen und Prinzessinnen befreien und ihr durch Aufklärung, Aufmüpfigkeit und Themen unserer Zeit frisches Blut spenden" (Schami 2012: 99–156, here 109).

ture with the goal of opening their eyes to the indoctrination that culture transmits.

From this angle, the paradigm shift implied by the rewriting of *Little Red Riding Hood* has a general significance. A fairy tale always says something about the world, but the validity of its message depends on the rapport it maintains with the real. According to the point of view of the system it expresses, it can just as easily propagate deceptive illusions as lucid knowledge. Thus, no one will move beyond the Manicheanism of traditional tales either by sugarcoating their morals or by renouncing the irrational and marvelous, only by re-appropriating these powerful resources for critical and rebellious ends. "The roots of the revolutionary imagination run deep into reality, into embattled reality, into the repressed but really attainable reality," Schami writes in his 1983 essay.[45] This is the path he follows, writing or rewriting to immense popular acclaim fairy tales inspired by the Arab-Persian tradition.

As for the Brothers Grimm, Schami later tempered somewhat the virulence of his discourse on the ideological refurbishment they undertook on the German folklore tradition, perhaps in part in order not to minimize the value of what they did to formalize tales that without them would have been lost to oblivion. The formerly militant writer, pioneer and spokesperson for the *Gastarbeiter*, who had meanwhile assigned himself the mission of cultural mediator between "the West" (and particularly Germany) and "the Orient" (i.e. "Arabia"), could more readily recognize their value because their project had several points in common with what he was undertaking with regards to the oral tradition of his homeland[46] – in order to accomplish which, he was relying on the transcriptions already done by German Orientalists.[47] However, more than a reversal, this restraint likely indicates a (diplomatic) concern about not running up against the institution by blaming authors who remain unassailable in Germany to this day. At least that is how one might understand the ambivalent status Schami assigns Jacob and Wilhelm Grimm in a recent essay dedicated to the "orality of our era." Published in 2011 in the collection *Die Frau, die ihren Mann auf dem Flohmarkt verkaufte* ("The Woman Who Sold Her Husband at the Flea Market") after having been read as his inaugural speech on receiving the prestigious

---

[45] "Die Wurzeln der revolutionären Phantasie schlagen sich tief in die Realität, in die bekämpfte Realität, die unterdrückte, aber real erreichbare Realität" (Schami 1983b: 20).
[46] See especially the collection *Malula: Märchen und Märchenhaftes aus meinem Dorf*, first published by Neuer Malik Verlag (Kiel 1987) and re-issued by DTV in 1990, which since 1994 has been released under the title *Märchen aus Malula*. By 2014, there had been nineteen editions.
[47] See the chapter "Traditions orales de Maaloula: Schami, tributaire des orientalistes allemands?" in Ellerbach (2018: 199–226).

"Brothers Grimm" chair at the University of Kassel, this text (2012: 99–156) presents itself as a debate in four voices between Schami himself, Don Quixote, Sancho Panza, and a certain Ibn Aristo. The homage he pays the two German philologists within this framework is equivocal to say the least, since the author puts his compliments into the mouth of the "very serious Mr. Ibn Aristo," a stuffy academician who he has make the following remarks:

> And since you are speaking here as Brothers Grimm Professor, perhaps it is fitting first to recall the great Brothers Grimm and their value to the German language and the treasury of oral tales they heard from storytellers and wrote down. However, it is also certainly necessary to recall that the Romantics as a whole were the ones to recognize the importance of oral traditions: James Macpherson (1736–1797) in Scotland, Thomas Percy (1729–1811) in England, the brothers Jacob (1785–1865) and Wilhelm Grimm (1786–1859) in Germany, and Francis James Child (1825–1869) in the USA.[48]

Not content to make his slightly ridiculous alter ego make his endorsement of the Grimms instead of assuming the full responsibility himself (the scholar Ibn Aristo, Arab "great-grandson" of Aristotle, is presented from the first as a pontificating, stodgy personage),[49] Schami further relativizes the compliment by asserting that the work of the two German scholars occurred within a general movement of rehabilitation for oral traditions brought on by Romanticism. Without overtly distancing himself from his illustrious predecessors – to whom, furthermore, he does not return afterward – he still manages in spite of everything to chip away discreetly at their image and to minimize the value of their work to affix in writing the rich tradition of oral culture they collected. One might call it an homage given through gritted teeth, a form of concession to his employers and editors, really the whole of his German readership, which one can imagine had been raised from infancy on Grimms' fairy tales. It is in the transition from the militant rhetoric of the 1980s (the frontal critique of the "falsification" at

---

[48] "Und da du hier im Rahmen einer Brüder-Grimm-Professur den Vortrag hältst, ist es zum einen vielleicht passend, an die großartigen Brüder Grimm zu erinnern und an ihr Verdienst um die deutsche Sprache und um das mündliche Erzählgut, das sie von Erzählerinnen und Erzählern hörten und niederschrieben. Geradezu notwendig ist es aber zum anderen, daran zu erinnern, dass die Romantiker insgesamt diejenigen waren, die die Wichtigkeit der mündlichen Traditionen erkannten: James Mac Virsen (1736–1797) in Schottland, Thomas Persi (1729–1811) in England, die Brüder Jacob (1785–1865) und Wilhelm (1786–1859) Grimm in Deutschland, Francis James Child (1825–1869) in den USA" (Schami 2012: 140–141).

[49] The name Aristo clearly evokes both a claim to the authority of the great Greek philosopher and a more generally "aristocratic" arrogance.

work in the Brothers Grimms' enterprise) to the discreet irony Schami employs today from the angle of a rhetorical plan based on polyphony and allusion, a change of tactics that might be revelatory of the limits of canonical critique for an author who has already "made it" on the literary market and who intends to defend his position.

In closing, let us note that the critical dialogue the young Schami engaged in with the European genre traditions widened to include marvelous tales of medieval origin by way of a brief allusion to *Reynard the Fox* slipped into the "Plea." Despite his aversion to foxes in general, the wolf Schami reinvents cannot help feeling pity for one when he sees his young persecutor going after "Meister Reineke" the same way she went after him.[50] In this unexpected wink from Isengrim to Reynard, Schami seems to gesture to a path of possible solidarity among the outcasts of the literary canon, across their reciprocal ancestral (though possibly only alleged) enmity.

Will Goethe Be Allowed into the Postcolonial Canon? The Deliberations of an Arab Jury

Der geheime Bericht über den Dichter Goethe, der eine Prüfung auf einer arabischen Insel bestand ("The Secret Report on the Poet Goethe, Who Passed a Test on an Arabian Island," 1999) counts among the commissioned texts Schami wrote – or in this case co-wrote with Uwe-Michael Gutzschhahn – in homage to a canonical German author. Conceived as a mass-market work meant for young readers, it is also the first text of Schami's that was translated into Arabic (2005). The work consists of the "secret report" itself, a discussion of Goethe's principal works by a fictional German-Arab scholar of the turn of the twentieth century, and a frame narrative establishing the beginning of an alternate history.

In the story, the young sovereign of an imaginary Persian Gulf island called Hulm ("dream" in Arabic) decides when he inherits the throne in 1897 to send emissaries throughout Europe to gather information about Western literature, the teaching of which he wishes finally to introduce in his realm, in order, he says, to prepare the next generation to welcome and understand the people who will inevitably invade the region. According to him, this is the only means of survival for the small, independent, and peaceful society to survive

---

50 "Also suchte ich diese verfluchte Rotznase, und da sah ich sie vor einem Fuchsloch knien. Sie rief gerade hinein: 'Oooh, was für einen dreckigen Pelz du hast!' Ich sah rot, und obwohl ich Füchse nicht ausstehen kann, bekam ich an jenem Tag Mitleid mit Meister Reineke" (AR 93).

the arrival of the Europeans without losing its own culture. He explains rather precisely to his subjects what awaits them in the years to come:

> The Ottoman Empire will fall, and the English will reach out toward Arabia [...]. The German Emperor Wilhelm II visited the Orient for the second time two years ago to show Istanbul that the Germans are reliable friends. [...] The Europeans will come. It's not malice, just the march of time, and we should prepare ourselves to take what suits us from them and leave the rest. That's the only way we'll be strong enough to be able to open our doors to the whole world and welcome them [...].[51]

On their return, the experts sent to Europe are charged with recommending to a commission of (male *and* female) scholars presided over by the sultan the names of writers from that continent they believe worthy of inclusion in the syllabus of authors to study. A group of well-paid translators, meeting in a grand "House of Wisdom" where they can work under the best conditions, are then to translate the works selected.[52] The man chosen to explore the German territories, Thomas, or Tuma as he was known in Hulm, is someone close to the sovereign. The son of a British colonial administrator in India and a Hanoverian aristocrat, Martha von Suttner, who disembarked on the island ten years before due to a mutiny at sea (which allowed her to slip out from under the thumb of the spouse she hated), he was raised in the closest confidence of the prince, whose instruction had been entrusted to Martha by his father such that the two young men, benefiting from the same education, had grown up like two brothers and become inseparable.

When he returns from Germany in 1901, Tuma recommends Goethe, and he justifies his choice by orally presenting a representative selection of his candidate's works. Of the nine chapters that make up the nested story, the first eight represent the reports delivered for each session of the eight nights that make up his defense. Tuma proceeds methodically, dedicating each night to a different work in chronological order: *Die Leiden des jungen Werthers* ("The Sor-

---

[51] "Das Osmanische Reich wird zerfallen, und die Engländer strecken die Hand nach Arabien aus [...] Der deutsche Kaiser Wilhelm II. besuchte vor zwei Jahren zum zweiten Mal den Orient, um Istanbul zu zeigen, dass die Deutschen zuverlässige Freunde sind. [...] Die Europäer werden kommen. Das ist kein böser Wille, sondern der Lauf der Zeit, und wir sollten uns darauf vorbereiten, das von ihnen zu nehmen, was uns passt, und das Übrige zu lassen. Nur so werden wir stark genug sein, um der ganzen Welt die Tür öffnen zu können und sie willkommen zu heißen [...]" (Schami and Gutzschhahn 2001: 18 – 19). All subsequent references to this work will appear as GB plus page number.

[52] This fictive institution is obviously modeled on the historical *Buyūt al-Hikmah* ("Houses of Wisdom" or "Houses of Science") that became widespread in the Arab-Muslim world during the Golden Age of Islam, as a part of the "translation movement" whose aim was to enrich Muslim thought with different knowledge and sciences. See Algeriani and Mohadi (2017).

rows of Young Werther"), *Wilhelm Meisters Lehrjahre* ("Wilhelm Meister's Apprenticeship"), *Reinecke Fuchs* ("Reynard the Fox"), *Der Zauberlehrling* ("The Sorcerer's Apprentice"), *Faust*, *Die Wahlverwandtschaften* ("Elective Affinities"), *Zur Farbenlehre* ("Theory of Colors"), and finally *West-östlicher Divan* ("West-Eastern Divan"). This personal synthesis, a pedagogical and apologetic digest of a monumental body of works, is not delivered plainly but as the centerpiece of an official document edited by the palace secretary that recounts in detail the proceedings of each of the commission's meetings. Thus, it is staged throughout, with scrupulous notes of every reaction, including non-verbal ones, that Tuma's reports provokes in the auditorium: questions, objections, attempts to explain, displays of enthusiasm or impatience, down to the clinking of spoons placed on the saucers after stirring the perfumed tea in the cups – for the debates take place in a hedonistic and good-natured atmosphere that does not prevent serious business. As the reporter defends his candidate with eloquence and the members of the commission are not averse to commentary, it presents a veritable *mise en scène*, animated and picturesque, of the (re)reading of a canonical body of works in a precolonial context. The interruptions of the members of the jury most often accentuate the closeness, as surprising for them as for Western readers, they perceive at every stage in the proceedings between classical Arabic literature and Goethe's thinking and sensibilities.

Thus, the cult of absolute love as it is depicted in *Werther* naturally reminds them of the legend of the star-crossed lovers, Layla and Qays, called *Majnûn Layla* ("Layla's Mad Lover"). This popular story is widespread throughout the area of Islamic cultural influence and has been the object of adaptations on the part of the greatest representatives of classical Arab-Persian literature. "By God, but Goethe's heart beats like that of an Oriental,"[53] Hakim exclaims while listening to his friend's summary, leaving it to an older scholar to express a more nuanced position: "Werther may have been a typical product of his time, but this unconditional devotion to love is just as much Arab as German."[54]

The jury is no less impressed by the finesse of the storyteller and fabulist whose verse adaptation of *Reinecke Fuchs* "particularly delights the Oriental heart and soul"[55] because it provided the poet disappointed by the French Revolution with an elegant means to critique "the rapacity of governments in gen-

---

53 "Der Sultan lächelte: 'Bei Gott, Goethes Herz schlägt ja richtig orientalisch, denn die Hälfte unserer Dichtung berichtet von unerfüllter Liebe [...]'" (GB 27).
54 "Werther mag ein typischer Sohn seiner Zeit gewesen sein, aber diese bedingungslose Ergebenheit an die Liebe ist ebenso arabisch wie deutsch" (GB 37).
55 "Heute ist es mir eine Freude, euch von einer Seite Goethes zu berichten, die Herz und Seele des Orientalen besonders erfreut [...]" (GB 56).

eral,"⁵⁶ while elevating this political message to a point of universality. The audience's admiration reaches its apex when Tuma, playing his trump card, presents the *West-östlicher Divan*, the summary of which elicits, as expected, appreciation mixed with astonishment and regret. "If only all Europeans thought of the Orient with so much respect,"⁵⁷ one lettered old man sighs. Unsurprisingly, Goethe's candidacy for canonization is ultimately accepted unanimously.

Alas, the ambitious reform project cannot be seen through: it is too late to save Hulm. The Sultan Hakim might well evict the European emissaries who disembark at Hulm starting in 1902, dispatched by French, Dutch, Canadian, and British oil companies to buy drilling rights. But there is nothing he can do against the military assault that follows soon after the failure of negotiations. Stormed by British troops with the support of Bahraein, Hulm is conquered before being able to perfect its techniques for defense. The Western powers begin drilling and line their pockets until the day the island, like a new Atlantis, is swallowed by the flood following a mysterious earthquake. Two annexes complete the tale: an intradiagetic appendix from the report delivered by Tuma that places the biography of Goethe straightforwardly in his historical context and, to conclude, a succinct bibliography intended for an adolescent audience provided by the extradiegetic authors in the form of a reading recommendation.

Beneath the apparent simplicity of its intent, this work of fiction, which opens the way for a rethinking of East-West relations using the exemplary case of a canonical German author, contains discursive and tactical shifts rich in discursive possibilities. First, Schami puts in place a fictional means of reevaluating the Western canon (the review of European literature ordered by Sultan Hakim on European literatures and the ad hoc deliberations of the commission), within which Goethe's reception by a lettered Arab audience as devoid of prejudice as of inferiority complexes regarding Europe situates itself. Initiated for the purpose of a well-considered, strategic opening of the domestic canon, this critical revision, which incidentally parodies the debate since launched in other parts of the world about the opening up of the Western canon to texts coming from the (post)colonial world, is only imaginable because it occurs in the privileged historical context of a microcosm having miraculously been preserved from colonial trauma.

---

56 "Aber am Ende war ein Werk entstanden, das eben doch politisch Stellung bezog. Es zeigte nicht nur den Betrug der Revolution am Volk, sondern klagte auch allgemein die Gier von Regierungen an" (GB 60).
57 "'Wenn nur alle Europäer so respektvoll vom Orient dächten', warf ein alter Gelehrter ein und seufzte" (GB 138).

Furthermore, the exam is more severe than it appears. If it has a favorable outcome for Goethe and for Heine as well (whom, the reader is told, the commission accepts "enthusiastically" into the scholastic syllabus), this not the case for either Hegel or Marx, and only partially for Nietzsche and Schopenhauer, though Tuma argues equally for all of them. As for Goethe, although accepted, he finds himself in a position that is the reverse of the one he himself adopted in the *Divan*. No longer the sovereign subject of intercultural discourse, he has become the object. Thus, even if there is nothing iconoclastic at first glance in this work of Schami and Gutzschhahn's, as eulogistic as the portrait they paint of the first among German "thinkers and poets" may be, it no less infers a change of perspective that has significant implications. Is not the unilaterality of the "dialogue" Goethe engaged in with the Orient, in truth, the only serious reproach one can make against his *Divan*?[58] From this point of view, Schami's work of fiction opens fecund perspectives on what could be a postcolonial critique and literature in Germany. We will return to this point.

The second shift effected in this text concerns precisely the exceptional situation Schami invents for the ideal society of Hulm. Long preserved from invasion by its geographic isolation and paucity of natural resources, quite literally "forgotten" by the great powers,[59] the island enjoys the privilege of having "almost never known foreign domination" (GB 13), because even the Ottoman Empire had spared it interference in its affairs.[60] It is this slight historical shift, this loophole in history, wherein Schami situates Hulm, that establishes the discursive credibility of this work of fiction and makes this truly *u*topic location into an experimental space favorable to the deployment of an alternate postcolonial history. The point of divergence for the alternative history presented here effectively occurs precisely at the moment when industrialized Western Europe seizes on the (premodern) Arab East in order to pillage its natural resources, a fleeting point of divergence because historical reality regains the upper hand even within

---

58 This reproach was formulated most explicitly by Mirjam Weber in her doctoral thesis *"Der wahre Poesie-Orient"; Eine Untersuchung zur Orientalismus-Theorie Edward Saids am Beispiel von Goethes 'West-östlichem Divan' und der Lyrik Heines* (2001). Other researchers such as Anil Bhatti (2007) have taken a more nuanced view.

59 This is the lesson the Abbasid caliph Al-Nassir learned from his defeat against Hulm in 1182. "Kalif Alnassir gab nach der schmächtigen Niederlage einen Befehl, der noch Jahrhunderte gelten sollte: 'Vergesst die Insel Hulm, tilgt sie aus eurem Gedächtnis, denn sie existiert nicht mehr'" (GB 14).

60 "Die Insel gehörte, als der englische Einfluss am Golf zunahm, offiziell zur osmanischen Zone, obwohl noch nie ein osmanischer Beamter seinen Fuß auf Hulms Boden gesetzt hatte" (GB 14).

this fictional world. Does this story then simply evoke in a nostalgic mode a missed opportunity on the eve of colonization? Or does it implicitly indicate a path to be explored for the possibility of renewal? Schami has confirmed this latter reading by stating in an interview that "the frame tale is a vision of the future, a dream for tomorrow."[61] As for the rest, as Sultan Hakim says: "reality was always a dream at first."[62]

By imagining that an alternate course for history could be possible based on a tradition anterior to the West's imperialist conquest of the East, it is surely a progressive utopia that Schami outlines. And what if, he implies between the lines, one were to take up again the long tradition of openness that characterized medieval Islam, a tradition founded in respect for and understanding of the other? Would not that spirit of openness and tolerance, of welcome and exchange be the strongest rampart against all the forms of exploitation and barbarism today as well? In a society inspired by these humanist values, the role of cultural mediators of every sort (nomads, travelers and other migrants, children born of ethnic and cultural mixing, scholars and translators) would be essential, as personified by Tuma and Hakim, the British-German raised in Arab culture and the Arab taught about European culture by a German refugee, two men diametrically opposed in birth and temperament but made bosom brothers who "completed each other like two halves of a picture"[63] by the intertwining of their destinies.

In such a society, women, too, would have a prominent role to play, like Martha von Suttner, whom the previous sultan had the wisdom to entrust with the education of his son. Rebellious and strong, gentle and resolute, the heir apparent's tutor is more than a simple governess. A cultured and multilingual German, Tuma's mother herself inherited a familial tradition characterized by open-mindedness responsible for her learning Arabic earlier thanks to an old Arab friend of her father's. It is to this cosmopolitan cultural background that she owes the intellectual resources and practical competencies that permitted her to escape her husband and the imperialism dominating Europe, taking advantage of a mutiny on the ship taking her to India to seize navigational instruments and find the way to the "indomitable"[64] Island of Hulm with her son.

---

61 "Die Rahmenhandlung ist eine Zukunftsvision, ein Traum vom Morgen" (Schami 1999b).
62 "[...] die Wirklichkeit war am Anfang immer ein Traum" (GB 21).
63 "Kronprinz Hakim war zwölf Jahre alt und das Gegenteil von Marthas Sohn [...] Trotzdem waren Hakim und Tuma bald unzertrennlich. Sie nannten sich gegenseitig 'Bruder' und ergänzten einander wie zwei Bildhälften" (GB 16).
64 "Die Fürstin wusste, wenn überhaupt ein Fleckchen Erde sicher vor dem Zugriff des britischen Militärs war, dann Hulm, die unbeugsame Insel im Persischen Golf" (GB 13).

Tasked with educating Prince Hakim, she finds herself likewise entrusted with the mission of developing the educational and health sectors of the kingdom, founding its first elementary school and first pediatric clinic. All of these activities (and her status as a married woman) do not prevent her from forming a free and lasting intimate relationship with a citizen of Hulm, the diplomat Salih Ben Akil.

This utopia at once retrospective and progressive that the story depicts thus not only leans on the historical trajectories cut short in the Arab world but also on the outdated or dissident traditions in European history – such as the enlightened cosmopolitanism rooted in eighteenth-century philosophical universalism that, fittingly, Goethe embodies so well, and which extended into the age of imperialism in internationalist and pacifist movements that tried in vain to oppose increasing nationalism. Possibly for this reason, as a form of homage, Schami bestows Martha, a key figure in this utopian story, with the family name of the author and journalist Bertha von Suttner (1843–1914), a great figure of fin-de-siècle pacifism and feminism. Endowed with a vast cultural upbringing and master of four languages, this descendent of a grand Austro-Hungarian aristocratic family argued for a radical ethical pacifism based on respect for human beings and the search for dialogue. As a feminist, she agitated for a perfect equality of rights and actual conditions between men and women in a spirit inspired by Enlightenment philosophy and the universalism of the French Revolution. Just like Schami's heroine, her life reads like a novel. Accustomed to traveling from early on, obliged to earn her living after her mother squandered the family fortune gambling, she worked as a governess and tutor before becoming the private secretary of the Swedish industrialist Alfred Nobel, then a journalist, novelist, and essayist. Her work promoting the 1891 creation of the International Peace Bureau, of which she was the first vice president, earned her the Nobel Peace Prize in 1905, an award she also helped create.[65]

Like Bertha, Martha von Suttner is an emancipated woman who struggles against the bellicose values of society in her day. By giving her the first name Martha, Schami simultaneously distinguishes her from the celebrated historical personality and bestows on her a name of Jewish origin the meaning of which, "lady" or "mistress," accords better with the function he has laid out for her. She soon translates this first name into "Saide," the feminine form of Said, which means "master" but also "fortunate" – and which it is possible to see as a form of homage to Edward Said.

---

[65] On Bertha von Suttner, see for example Harald Steffahn (1998) and Barbara Helm (1997).

It is worth noting that here Schami once again employs in a systematic manner descriptive names, the practice of which is common in didactic and popular literature and has the effect of undercutting the illusion of verisimilitude by drawing attention to the artificial nature of the story. Hence Martha's only son likewise bears a name of Aramaic origins (Thomas), Tuma in Arabic, which designates his function in the narrative framework: to be the "twin" of Prince Hakim, his cultural double and special envoy to the West. As for the prince himself, he receives a traditional Arab first name, the meaning of which ("wise") indicates in just as clear a manner his status as a shrewd and enlightened monarch. The diplomat with whom Martha chooses to partner is named Salih ("honest, upright, pious"), which sufficiently demonstrates the values underlying their happiness. As for Thomas's absent father, should the name of the British senior official Lord Morley, whose profile is summarily sketched in the background of the action but casts an ominous shadow of colonial expansion by an authoritarian and phallocratic Europe over Hulm, be read as an allusion to John Morley (1838–1923), the liberal politician who took over as Secretary of State for India when his party assumed power in 1905? Not only do the dates not concur but John Morley advocated for racial equality and effected all sorts of reforms, among them the election of Indians to provincial councils. Thus, he was far from representing the worst that European colonialism had to offer. Perhaps, however, by choosing a name associated with a rather moderate colonial administrator, Schami wanted to avoid lapsing into caricature – and so give more force to the evolution of a character for whom the narcissistic blow of having lost his wife in the troubled waters of the Gulf mutates into a "swelling anger at England's humiliation."[66]

Among the numerous strategic displacements employed in this text with regard to the Eurocentric vision of the world, the inversion of terms in the relationship that develops between the story's German and Arab protagonists must also be noted. Beyond even the *mise en abyme* of Goethe's works, which leads to a deliberately confusing – hence charming and stimulating – Arabization of the author, the narrative framework Schami puts in place implies a general reversal of the relationship of power between Europe and the Arab world, if not on the level of the geopolitical context, at least on that of the protagonists in the first-degree narrative. This reversal takes place as much in relationship to the Orientalist movement of Goethe's era (when the West made voyages of exploration and discovery into the East) as in relationship to the geopolitical reality of

---

[66] "Immer mehr trat bei Morley die Trauer hinter den wachsenden Zorn über die Demütigung Englands zurück" (GB 10).

the massive migrant flow today as inhabitants of the postcolonial world emigrate to Europe. Here, there are two Europeans, a woman and a child who escape a society that has become repressive and suffocating and find refuge in a kingdom in Eastern Arabia characterized by its humanism, political maturity, and pragmatism. Welcomed with open arms into this enlightened monarchy that only wants to integrate them, these Western "immigrants" blossom in their adopted home without giving up their own cultural richness, which they use to benefit their hosts in return. Thereafter, it is Hulm, a small, isolated Eastern Arab kingdom, that organizes its own expeditions of discovery into Europe to collect information on the unknown riches of that civilization. This reversal is certainly a bit contrived: as a model of well-reasoned openness to other cultures, Hulm is not only "since ages past a refuge for the dissenting and persecuted"[67] but also offers an exceptional degree of equality between men and women that the narrator admits has never been attained anywhere else in the Arab world (GB 15).

However, even if Hulm is a "dream," an "earthly paradise" (GB 17) that never existed in such a form, Schami insists on making it known that his invention is not totally without foundation. The religious fundamentalism that led to the enslavement of women in a number of Muslim countries does not lie at the heart of Arab culture. It is only one of its modern avatars, one perverse effect among many of colonial conquest. Conversely, Western culture cannot be reduced to the aggressive, nationalistic, patriarchal, and xenophobic ideology that motivated colonization. It also holds some of humanity's treasures, from which the Eastern world would do well to draw inspiration. Yet in order to be able to do so, the latter must rid itself of all feelings of inferiority towards those nations that have historically been agents of its subjugation and alienation. This is precisely the problem, and the alternate history Schami imagines rightly consists in depicting a situation in which that alienation did not take place. It is only thanks to suppressing that fatal moment in the history of the Arab people that Hulm, an ideal, autonomous Arab society, can draw entirely freely from the cultural wellsprings offered by the two exceptional native informers Martha von Suttner and her son Thomas, serenely examining the question to decide what components of European culture it would be well-advised to introduce into its children's academic curricula and which it is preferable to avoid.

It is on this basis of mutual independence, and on this condition alone, that Hakim and Thomas can form a truly equal pair of "twins" ultimately representing Schami's "realistic" counter to Goethe's older model of dream twins, where-

---

[67] "Schwer zugänglich für große Schiffe und ungastlich durch die Kargheit der Vegetation, war die Insel seit Urzeiten eine Zuflucht für alle Abtrünnigen und Verfolgten" (GB 13).

by he imagined a spiritual amity with a Persian poet of the fourteenth century, Hafez.[68] The cultural osmosis between the East and West, which the German writer merely dreamed of in the *Divan* by projecting his ideal of intercultural dialogue onto a far-off fellow poet, could not happen in reality except through the mutual listening and understanding rendered possible in turn by an authentic experience of the other.[69] The historical situation in which Schami and his readers find themselves today offers precisely these conditions when occasions for coexistence among individuals from different cultures and the practical means for them to cross paths and to develop an intercultural dialogue are multiplying – as is particularly the case in a classroom, the habitual setting of this "junior" audience to whom this work is primarily intended. The majority of students growing up in Germany at the turn of the twenty-first century truly have, at least theoretically, the possibility of forming friendships like the one that unites the two protagonists of *Der geheime Bericht*, Hakim and Thomas. Thus, the fictional contextualization of Goethe's work in a "pre-postcolonial" Arab context makes it possible, among other things, to hold a mirror up to German secondary schoolers, forced to study this or that text by Goethe in class, and inviting them to reflect on the relations that exist within their own group between non-minority German children and children of immigrants of diverse origins. It is also this very interculturality that these adolescents are asked to question by the "oblique" presentation of the most unavoidable of German canonical poets in their textbooks.

A popular literary work, a postcolonial alternate history, a political and intercultural fable with utopian overtones, Schami and Gutzschhahn's book is obviously a less simplistic work than one might think. Despite the didacticism of its execution and the one-dimensionality of its characters, it never falls into a reductive Manicheanism. Thanks mostly to the complexity of its narrative framework, by playing with the interweaving of first- and second-degree fictive identities, it manages to make the reader reflect on the overlap between reality, literature, and literary representation(s), all of this in a context that opens the way for a truly critical and unprepossessed (re)reading of classic works. Thus, the confrontation between the concept of intercultural dialogue Goethe imagined and that is embodied by the Thomas / Hakim pair in the story allows the text to

---

68 This is outlined in the poem *Unbegrenzt* ("Unbound") from "Buch Hafis," in which Goethe's poetic persona praises the greatness of Hafez's spirit, identifying him as his only worthy rival and poetic "twin-brother": "Und mag die ganze Welt versinken/ Hafis mit dir, mit dir allein / Will ich wetteifern! Lust und Pein/ Sei uns, den Zwillingen, gemein!" (Goethe 2006: XI, I, 2, *West-östlicher Divan:* 25).
69 See Pizer (2005).

raise the delicate question of Goethe's Orientalism, which rested on a far-off and largely idealized vision of the Orient. This question comes to the fore in the story itself since certain poems Tuma cites in the *Divan* cannot help but draw amused and even sarcastic responses from his audience, so effusive does the admiration Goethe professes for Oriental poets strike them: "'Well,' cried a scholar, 'isn't Goethe a little too kind to us? I don't mean any disrespect, but no doubt he's never seen an Oriental poet up close.'"[70]

In this manner, the fictional tribunal to which Schami subjects the German "prince of poets" reflects, in another mirror effect, the necessity to consider "for real" the legitimacy by which classic authors, even the German ones, occupy the place accorded them in the Western pantheon today. The framework established here suggests such a critical appraisal must at the very least take into consideration the point of view of those students whose families come from formerly colonized regions of the world and onto which these same authors were often pleased to project their dreams of a mythical, archaic, and primitive Orient. Although Goethe passes his exam with flying colors, thus becoming the first German writer to be "taught in all the schools and universities" of Hulm (GB 159), it should be borne in mind that other representatives of the grand German tradition fail to convince the commission. Hegel is rejected without appeal, and apparently without need of justification, no doubt in view of the indefensible positions the philosopher of reason adopted regarding Africa in his *Vorlesungen über die Philosophie der Weltgeschichte* ("Lectures on the Philosophy of World History," 1830–1831). The verdict is a little less severe when it comes to Marx, whose candidacy was only held up pending a "thorough deliberation" based on his status as the "prophet of modernity" ("but the Jews have produced better prophets," as the sultan maliciously observes, GB 159). As for Nietzsche, he is accepted with very serious reservations, the study of his work only being advised for the most advanced students (GB 159). Schopenhauer, too, despite being welcomed by the jury for his aesthetic thought (they were clearly thinking of the emancipatory virtues he attributed to poesy), finds himself nevertheless rejected because of the "sinister pessimism" of his philosophy (GB 159).

If Heine is the only one after Goethe to receive "enthusiastic" support from this fastidious tribunal (GB 159), it is surely not only because he, too, was a poet and not a philosopher (which certainly seems *a priori* to be a serious disadvantage). Heine, who in certain regards represents a tradition opposed to that of his illustrious elder, embodies a cosmopolitanism and an openness to the other

---

[70] "'Na', rief ein Gelehrter, 'ob Goethe da nicht zu gnädig mit uns ist? Mit Verlaub, aber er hat wohl doch nie orientalische Dichter aus der Nähe erlebt'" (GB 134).

based not in a cheerful humanism, but in intimate and sorrowful personal experience of the ravages of the dominant way of thinking. Although situated in a deviant (contested, controversial, marginal) line of national literary history, the commission places him in the same category as the obvious consensus choice, Goethe. It would be interesting to know the arguments Tuma advanced to argue for Heine's inclusion, but that angle is not developed in the book, the point of which is solely to celebrate the work of Goethe.

The information succinctly presented in the epilogue regarding the historiographic context is all the more revelatory of the position Schami adopts on the question of the canon. It is not because the superiority of Goethe has been established once and for all that he deserves to figure into the curriculum for future generations, but because his texts stand the test of critical reading, even coming from non-European intellectuals highly sensitive to the issues of power bound up in intercultural relations and the transmission of knowledge. Goethe's acceptance is not at all a given – he was very nearly eliminated straightaway at the presentation of his *Faust*. The "certainly very impressive" content of this tragedy about an intellectual seduced by satanic immorality does not convince the Arabic scholars who consequently begin contemplating whether to reserve (as with Nietzsche) the reading of the great writer for "older and more mature" students, in order to prepare them to receive "a glimpse of European Enlightenment thought" (GB 103). The fact that this work, generally considered Goethe's masterpiece because of the strength of its characters and the profundity of the questions it addresses, does not manage to win over the commission shows precisely that the "prince of poets" is not accepted because but rather in spite of his position in the official canon. Above all, it is as a lyrical poet, popular storyteller, universal wit, and champion of intercultural dialogue ("wanderer between cultures," GB 70) that Goethe merits being taught to new generations, not as the representative of tragic depths reputedly typical of German culture. The commission welcomes the relevance of his concept of "world literature" in particular, seeing in it an idea "very similar to our concept of a House of Wisdom" (GB 71).

Conclusion

Studying these three texts sheds light on the ambivalence of Schami's relationship to the literary canon. A certain appetency for writing back, understood as a counter-discourse to the master narratives and, buttressed by an essentially Marxist approach to social questions, led him to investigate canonical "proceedings" from the angle of discursive postures propped up by judicial models (revision, plea, examination). However, "the friend from Damascus," as he chose to call himself, has tempered this tendency through his desire to lean on his cultural alterity to make space for himself on the national literary field as a creative and conciliatory force. In his 1999 book on Goethe, conceived with a pedagogical goal, these two tendencies arrive at a productive synthesis, involving the reconciliation of the Germans with their own tradition by way of an identification with the (Middle-Eastern, Arab, Muslim) Other, distancing them from the nationalistic and Eurocentric point of view and opening the way to a lucid and critical (in the best sense of the term) reevaluation of the cultural patrimony equidistant from indictment and panegyric. By means of a narrative framework that offers young people an original perspective on the "Orient," which the political and media discourse continues by and large to present as radically other, backwards, and menacing in many respects, Schami decenters readers' perspective on official culture. His recourse to alternate history simultaneously allows him to give his young audience a positive image of this "Arabia" at once so exotic and so close to German contemporary society without falling into a retrospective idealization of colonization and a denial of its ravages.

Chapter 4
Özdamar's *Keloglan in Alamania:* The National Tradition Tested by Diversity

Ethos and Posture of a "Left-Wing Oriental Libertarian"

The public debate on Islam as it has developed in Germany over the course of the last twenty years places culturally Muslim authors within a reduced range of possible "postures," if one understands the concept in Jerôme Meizoz's sense as "the singular manner of occupying a 'position' in the literary field" (2007: 18). Fixated on the question of knowing if "Islam is part of Germany,"[1] which is to say whether practicing that religion is compatible with the ethical and civic foundations of German society, contemporary public discourse in effect constrains any intellectual originally from the Muslim world to take a position, whether or not they want to, on this question by "laying their cards on the table" regarding their personal relationship with Islam as a culture and religion.

If this injunction to situate oneself in terms of religious and cultural identity is addressed to any personality no matter how closely or distantly linked to the Muslim world, it imposes itself particularly on women, who are primarily affected by the key question in this debate: the status of women. The alternative for them could be summarized like so: either demonstrate their (sexual and religious) emancipation by denying any affiliation with a community, the archaic structure of which they themselves reveal by their own life course, or plead for a "reform" of Islam on the basis of a distinction between political and religious Islam, just as Christianity is intrinsically capable of evolving toward forms of practice compatible with the fundamental principles of German democracy (philosophical and spiritual neutrality of the state, equality of rights for men and women). Those who opt for the first solution run the risk of being instrumentalized as prosecutorial witnesses against the community of their origins – assuming they do not take on this role themselves by joining their voices to

---

[1] The phrase was coined by then interior minister Wolfgang Schäuble at the opening of the first German Conference on Islam in 2006 ("Der Islam gehört zu Deutschland"). It was echoed four years later by Federal President Christian Wulff in his address to the nation on the twentieth anniversary of German reunification and has since become a bone of contention for those who oppose mass migration from Muslim countries. In March 2018, Chancellor Merkel and her new interior minister Horst Seehofer (both from the conservative CDU party) clashed publicly over the issue, with Seehofer claiming that "Islam does not belong to Germany"and Merkel asserting that "Muslims are also part of Germany, and so their religion is just as much a part of Germany."

those of the most virulent *Islamkritiker* ("critics of Islam"), as has the journalist trained in sociology Necla Kelek, making a name for herself in the media as the close ally of xenophobic polemicists like Thilo Sarrazin. The others are drawn into a more or less active engagement for the development of a liberal Islam in Germany, sometimes exposing themselves to reprisals from fundamentalist quarters. This was the case, for example, with the lawyer Seyran Ateş, who specialized in criminal and family law and was threatened to such an extent that she was forced to close her offices after publicly expressing her views in favor of "religious liberty not at the cost of women and girls" (2004) and arguing that "Islam needs a sexual revolution" (2009) – which supposes that such a revolution is possible but still needs to be formed. Both sides claim to be feminists, but whereas the former argue for a universalist conception of the Enlightenment's heritage (separation of church and state, human dignity, the rights of women, etc.) and accuse the latter of a blind complaisance toward an essentially, they claim, obscurantist, patriarchal, and misogynist religion, these latter women assert the right to religious liberty and cultural difference, accusing the former of Eurocentric alienation.

Faced with this sort of polarized discourse around Islam, including that among the culturally Muslim intellectuals themselves, the position long held by Emine Sevgi Özdamar appears all the more singular. Without ever making public pronouncements on the question of Islam, the writer and dramatist has managed to carve out an ideological territory that invalidates the premise of a seemingly implacable choice between universalism and culturalism. Throughout her stories, plays, and public speaking, Özdamar has presented an image of herself that proves it is possible to be *at once* an avant-garde libertarian (with a lowercase "l") leftist intellectual ferociously attached to sexual emancipation and a secular model of society *and* an "Oriental" asserting her ethnocultural differences amidst a national collective preponderantly imagined to be white and "Judeo-Christian."

The originality of this position does not reside in the postulate of a possible synthesis between the two options, which appear opposed at first glance, but in the perfect nonchalance with which Özdamar evades the obligation to take sides. Rejecting for herself even the existence of a dilemma between tradition and the avant-garde, the East and the West, she is not looking for a compromise, instead asserting with a sort of self-evidence an "Eastern libertarian leftist" posture made, so to speak, to thwart automatically any attempt to assign her an identity. Although she presents herself – notably in her autofictional (fictionalized autobiographical) dramatizations and her writing style (German sprinkled with Turkish formulas, elementary syntax, references to Islam and tradition, etc.) and even in the visual presentation of her books' front covers – as an "exotic" personality in the national cultural landscape, she avoids communitarian misappropriation by clearly distancing herself from social conventions, sexual morality, and the patriarchal model. Conversely, she cannot be suspected of Eurocentrism despite her attachment to values coded as "Western" because she does not reject her communitarian attachments and, most importantly, because her approach to the "Western model" is itself critical. Özdamar inscribes herself unambiguously in a tradition of (Marxist, Brechtian, and postcolonial) resistance against all forms of domination and exploitation. Hence the two components of the "role" she plays on the literary scene, those of "Oriental (or transcultural) writer" and "disciple of Brecht,"[2] far from canceling each other out, complement each other in sketching a *persona* as original in the contemporary German context as it is, on the whole, coherent.

The key to this hitherto unseen formula, which only appears to be paradoxical, does not derive from some sort of promotional strategy but from a fundamentally political approach to social questions. When asked her opinion about the debate on Islam, Özdamar denies having any authority on the question by making it clear that she considers herself a "leftist."[3] In truth, these few words say it all. From her point of view, religion (any religion) is neither a problem nor a solution. Much like with inequality between men and women, the difficulties that coexisting with its minorities poses to Germany are structural. Hence, Özdamar does not allow herself to be drawn into a debate that excludes the question of power relations. She is engaged through her writing, theater work, solidarity with political resistance movements, and last but not least, through her personal trajectory of emancipation from repressive familial and social structures, which has thrust her as an artist into milieus dominated by men. If there is no – apparent – violence in her detachment from religion nor pain (although her novels tell a different story), it is because what she struggles against are, first and foremost, bourgeois morality, patriarchal domination, and exploitation, not the structures of solidarity that can exist within families and popular collectives.

Beyond this commitment at once – and inseparably – political and artistic, Özdamar is not suited to playing the spokeswoman for just anybody, which may be one of the reasons she is hardly present on television platforms and rarely expresses herself to the press. This reticence has been even more pronounced after

---

2 On Özdamar's relationship to Brecht with regard to her literary "posture," see especially Fischer (2014).

3 "Ach, wissen Sie, ich bin eine Linke..." (personal conversation with the author, 2 November 2010). The statement was made during a face-to-face meeting in Berlin, in the midst of the polemic following the publication of Sarrazin's pamphlet *Deutschland schafft sich ab* (2010).

a controversy that pitted her against Feridun Zaimoglu following the latter's publication of his novel *Leyla* in 2006. Sparked by an anonymous source, the affair centered on the numerous similarities between his text, which tells the story in the first person of a female Turkish immigrant born in Anatolia in the middle of the 1940s, and Özdamar's first novel *Das Leben ist eine Karawanserei hat zwei Türen aus einer kam ich rein aus der anderen ging ich raus* ("Life Is a Caravanserai, Has Two Doors, I Came in One, I Went Out the Other," 1992). A comparative literary analysis submitted to the press anonymously inventoried these parallels and concluded that Özdamar's work, set in the same spatial-temporal frame and retracing the course of a woman's life punctuated by anecdotes, some of them identical, had been ripped off by her young male colleague.

The first installment in an autofictional cycle followed by *Die Brücke vom Goldenen Horn* ("The Bridge of the Golden Horn," 1998) then *Seltsame Sterne starren zur Erde* ("Strange Stars Stare to Earth," 2003), *Das Leben ist eine Karawanserai* had been a pioneering work. Awarded the prestigious Ingeborg Bachmann Prize, it had inspired a whole generation of "postmigration" writers, including Zaimoglu. He claimed, however, to have done nothing more than faithfully transcribe his own mother's story in his novel – which he attempted to prove by presenting audio recordings of conversations with her as a defense. The affair threatened to end in legal action, with the publisher Kiepenheuer & Witsch (which published both writers) summoning Zaimoglu to explain himself and him bringing his lawyer, when Özdamar put an end to the scandal by publicly distancing herself from the rumor that imputed to her the accusation that he had plagiarized her book. Having never formally made the accusation, she did, however, say with conviction – off the record – that Zaimoglu had "stolen the story of her life" (Weidemann 2006).

This rather sordid affair stoked for six months by the literary columns in the major newspapers shed light on a symptomatic element in the reception of immigrant literary authors in Germany: the focus of – particularly though not solely journalistic – critique on the quality of texts' "authenticity" to the detriment of their formal construction, their style, or the narrative techniques employed. As Yasemin Dayıoğlu-Yücel (2012) has noted, everything seems to revolve, when it comes to immigrant authors, around a single issue: cultural capital. Authors are forced to compete on the basis of a strictly referential reading of their writing as if what was at stake in the struggle for literary recognition was not rather *symbolic* capital – which does not derive from right but from appreciation in academic milieus. In the present case, the quarrel was settled by an analysis on the part of the publisher concluding that it was sheer coincidence attributable to the fact that both writers were drawing inspiration for their works from a shared history and cultural patrimony. This meant ruling in Zaimoglu's favor, whose defense was their common cultural basis and who accused his elder of claiming as intellectual property what was in reality a "cultural matrix of superstitions and daily practices" largely shared by the Kurdish population of Anatolia (Breitfeld 2006).

Although it silenced the polemic, this "conciliatory" verdict was clearly not meant to satisfy Özdamar, who came out of the affair looking like a fool after her position had been torpedoed by this culturalist approach. Really, as Tom Cheesman (2013: 4) writes: "The point is not that he might have plundered *Karawanserei* for certain textual motifs or even narrative incidents: his more important putative crime lay in appropriating in *Leyla* the whole substance of Özdamar's story, the totality not of her text but of the experience out of which she created the text." In fact, the affair illustrates a fundamental difference in the way the two most highly-esteemed representatives of migration literature from Turkish backgrounds occupy their positions in the field. Zaimoglu has asserted himself as the creator of a protean body of work for which he draws primary material from diverse documentary and/or literary sources, and he "fictionalizes" and "poeticizes" (Cheesman 2013: 4) this material by adapting the form to each of the subjects he treats. The novel *Leyla*, for example, is constructed in a polyphonic manner, and the heroine's "I" – which is in no way superimposable with that of the author – assumes the function of illustrating the path of a whole generation, namely the one that immigrated to Germany in the 1960s. The work thereby acquires the quality of a socio-historical tableau doubling as the sensitive portrait of a woman. Özdamar, in turn, commits utterly to each of her texts, starting from a substratum of lived experience to create a form of poetic autofiction like nothing seen before. The work of fictionalization and poetization she effects on the material never totally eclipses the authorial point of view. If her narrator-protagonists never disappears – even in the autofictional cycle opened by *Karawanserei* – into her social persona, their "I" still does not quite efface her own voice, which they incarnate in more or less distorted and altered forms. Thus, the unity of foundation and form in her writing outlines the contours of a homogenous writing project, the coherence of which relies entirely on the ethos expressed therein – a "leftist" ethos, as she said herself, liberal and feminist situated in the tradition of a non-dogmatic Marxism inspired by the critical theater of Brecht and the protest movements of the 1960s and 1970s.

Genealogy and Solidarity: Özdamar's "Family"

Özdamar's texts articulate a critical analysis of society and its discourses with a carnivalesque aesthetic of joyous transgression. The personae in her autofictional novels perform a type of hedonistic and rebellious marginality rooted in an individual experience that is, first of all, that of a body in space. Through these transfigured projections of herself at different stages in the course of her personal emancipation and the advent of her writing, Özdamar nonetheless takes an approach that is to be understood as an ongoing and collective adventure, making it seem like she is a member of a transnational and transhistorical extended "family." Whether that be the "big family of the theater" – and more particularly the troupes with which she has worked directly – or, in a more general sense, that of artists around the world committed like her to the pursuit of a poetic-political ideal of resistance and liberty, her reference points place her in a boundless space-time.

Her dialogue with the canon is conditioned on this conception of a sort of Internationale at once horizontal (contemporaries) and vertical (mentors and ancestors) of dissident "poets" (in the larger sense), anarchists, revolutionaries, and the persecuted. In the theater, her artistic genealogy traces from Shakespeare and Molière to Brecht and Heiner Müller by way of Büchner and Kleist – not to forget the anonymous creators of a tradition of popular theater that took the form in the Ottoman Empire of *Karagöz* ("shadow theater").[4] As for novelists, essayists, and poets, her points of reference are principally modernist, whether in the German language (Heine, Lasker-Schüler), Turkish (Ahmet Hamdi Tanpınar, Nâzım Hikmet, Can Yücel, Cemal Süreya, Ece Ayhan), or international (Frederico García Lorca, Pablo Neruda, etc.).

All of these reference points designate a sort of transnational "anti-canon" that evokes less the Goethean concept of *Weltliteratur* than the image of the "meridian" claimed by Paul Celan in his award speech for the Georg Büchner Prize in 1960 (see Celan 1999). They represent, each in their own way, a literature that "is seen, written, and read [...] in solidarity with the oppressed of *all* times and in *all* countries" (Lauterwein 2014: 403). From the perspective of this writing against the grain of the cultural history of domination, the vectoral concept developed by Ottmar Ette (2005) of "literatures without a fixed abode" seems particularly pertinent for describing the manner in which Özdamar devises her work. We shall see, with the notable exception of the text discussed in the next chapter, *Seltsame Sterne starren zur Erde* ("Strange Stars Stare to Earth"), how this network of solidarity comes into being and what its stakes are in the context of her work. The intertextual frame of reference is dominated in this text by the figure of Else Lasker-Schüler, a Jewish poet from whom Özdamar

---

4 See below: "The Deterritorialization of the Turkish Patrimony."

claims descent as much in terms of gender positioning as from the perspective of her status as "Oriental" in the national field.

Özdamar's work on the canon also has a critical, indeed a polemic, side. The playwright and novelist handles the art of the satirical twist with perspicacity and playfulness, aiming at a demystification of ideologies with her model provided by Heine. This chapter's analysis of the play *Keloglan in Alamania* (2000) will illuminate the operations of deconstruction she carries out on dominant "canonical" works (operas by Puccini, Mozart, Smetana, Grimms' fairy tales, and the repertoire of folksongs), while always maintaining resonance with her tutelary "friends," in this case Shakespeare and Heine.

Shakespeare's œuvre furnishes Özdamar with a seemingly inexhaustible reserve of textual reference points, which she utilizes as generative matrices for her writing. Another central aspect of her rewriting practice is the productive dialogue with those of her contemporaries she considers allies and masters. The second text examined in this chapter, *Karriere einer Putzfrau* ("A Charwoman's Career"), will show how these two aspects of her reflection on the canon articulate themselves.

The Deterritorialization of the Turkish Patrimony

Özdamar's second theatrical work, *Keloglan in Alamania Oder die Versöhnung von Schwein und Lamm* ("Keloglan in Alamania, Or the Reconciliation of Pig and Lamb"), presents such a superabundance of intertextual callbacks that it is difficult to identify all of them and attribute a meaning and function to each. This section aims to unravel this tangle by concentrating on what appears to be the connecting thread in this work written on the eve of reunification: the questioning of the ideological foundations of the German nation, particularly in the relationship it has had historically with individuals and groups considered one way or another "foreign" – and as a consequence, the place ethnic minorities occupy in German society today. This complex questioning develops out of a plot that sheds light on the cruel absurdity of the nationality laws in force until 2007, which refused citizenship to immigrants and their children, even those born on the country's soil. [5]

---

[5] Katrin Sieg (2002: 239–240) enumerates the matters discussed in the play as follows: "The opposing orientations toward separatism versus assimilation, the experience of rightful belonging versus unjust exclusion, the celebration of multiculturalism versus the exploitative economics of race, the rejection of identity politics versus the legal uncertainties of migrant existence, the clash of collective ascriptions versus individual aspirations."

The critical examination to which the playwright subjects the German nation's self-presentation, using its own cultural patrimony, takes the form of joyous and ferocious demolition of many works featuring in the national cultural pantheon. For this intervention deploying a carnivalesque aesthetic that calls into question "identities," whether ethnocultural or generic, Özdamar relies on other reference points, drawn particularly from Middle-Eastern (and more particularly from Ottoman Turkish) cultures, but also from other German literary traditions: Brecht, Heiner Müller, and Heine among others, to back up her offensive against the good conscience of a nation fed on an entire tradition of Eurocentric and essentialist thought suited to legitimizing the worst forms of ostracism, xenophobia, and sexism.

All of these elements – the concrete situation of second-generation immigrants threatened with expulsion, the reactionary ideology underlying the "official" culture of reunified Germany, a popular cultural patrimony at once local and supra- or transnational (fairy tales, traditional songs, etc.), and ultimately a critical and satirical German literary tradition – are layered in such a manner as to make the emergence of a culturally hybrid and inclusive identity in Germany seem a chimerical goal. As Helga Kraft summarizes it, "it is a pessimistic work" where "only a *deus ex machina* can, not particularly convincingly, bring about the 'reconciliation of the pig and lamb,' and so make a utopian Turkish-German identity possible."[6] Which intertextual framework does the author craft to produce such disillusioning message?

In her first play, *Karagöz in Alamania: Ein türkisches Stück* ("Karagöz in Alamania: A Turkish Play," 1982), which depicts in a mode of comic detachment the complex reality of Turkish economic migration to the FRG, Özdamar relied on the generic model of the Turkish shadow theater, known by the name of its principal protagonist Karagöz.[7] Performances of *karagöz*, meant for adults and traditionally devoted to burlesque diversion and social satire, take place during the Ramadan holidays and offer a space for social critique. The classical repertoire for this popular genre, which more or less disappeared in the twentieth century with the arrival of movies, consists of about forty plays that over the course of the centuries have reached their definitive forms. However, these are more like canvases on which the actor-presenters can improvise, permitting them to introduce allusions to contemporary events and critique their own era. As with the

---

6 "Es ist ein pessimistisches Stück, und nur ein Deus ex machina kann, wenig überzeugend, die 'Versöhnung von Schwein und Lamm' herbeiführen, also eine utopische türkisch-deutsche Identität möglich machen" (Kraft 2011: 126).

7 On this specific tradition see especially Jeanneret (1969: 162–164), Smith (2004), and Öztürk (2006).

French Guignol or *Commedia dell'arte*, the decorations and costumes are codified, and the characters represent types more than living persons. The principal characters are Karagöz ("Black Eye") himself, a man of the people who is illiterate and always complaining but clearly full of guile with whom the audience is invited to identify itself, and Hacivat, a representative of the cultured class who speaks in Ottoman Turkish – the language of the elites, unintelligible to the majority – and affects a flowery form of speech, drawing the ridicule of his antagonist and the complicit public.

In Özdamar's play, Karagöz is a Turkish peasant who emigrates to Germany accompanied by his faithful companion Şemsettin, a donkey gifted with speech who drinks wine, smokes Camels, and expresses himself in literary and philosophical quotations, with a predilection for Marx and Socrates. The collision of languages (Turkish, German, and English), but above all of different language levels, *Gastarbeiterdeutsch* and literary language, and between language registers (the lyrical, religious, and philosophical), and even between poetry, prose, and variety songs, give the play – along with its situational comedy likewise inspired by traditional *karagöz* – one of its principal sources of comedy.

As for the plot, the Karagöz whom Özdamar delocalizes and saddles with the last name *Schicksallos* ("Fateless") takes a job as a laborer in Germany to pay his father's debts. He spends the better part of his adult life in this country where his wife joins him and gives birth to several children. Yet, the play shows next to nothing of their life in Germany. It portrays Karagöz almost exclusively "underway," going endlessly back and forth between his place of work and his home village where he returns between jobs and for vacation. This configuration, which pushes off stage all the events that occur in Germany, gives the impression that really the protagonist spends his whole existence commuting between these two locations: the village in Anatolia that remains his life's principal setting and the country where he works to meet his needs and those of his family – or, more precisely, the "door" to that country (*Deutschlandtür*), as Özdamar labels the liaison's office placed in Istanbul in 1961 by the Federal Office of Labor to select "guest workers" recruited as labor for German industry. With its focus on Karagöz's movement within the interstitial space between the Anatolian village and the German liaison's office in Istanbul, Germany's entrance and exit, which – based on a medical checkup and a perfunctory aptitude exam – swallows up or turns away aspiring immigrants, then spits back out those it has taken on, the play offers a view of the multiple facets of first-generation immigrants' uprootedness and the still strong ties that bind them to their homeland. Though Karagöz gains prestige in the eyes of the villagers back home who envy his success, neither he nor his wife manage to get their footing in their new country. The popular comedy and two-dimensional characters of the *karagöz*, an old genre fallen into desuetude in modern Turkey, are revisited in a spirit of avant-garde excess to point out *ad absurdum* the alienation and loss of reference points among rural immigrant workers. The treatment of this major reference source, which not only underlies this play's framework and that of the eponymous short story but also plays a role in Özdamar's other texts, has been astutely analyzed by, among others, Norbert Mecklenburg (2006) and Azade Seyhan (2016). Özdamar brought this work, the first dramatic work in German by a writer who immigrated as a *Gastarbeiter*, to the stage herself in Frankfurt am Main in 1986.

When she wrote her second play five years later, a "musical comedy" produced in 2000 at the National Theater in Oldenburg directed by Murat Yeginer, the political context had radically changed. The new generation of immigrants found itself suddenly confronting the massive threat of exclusion that was equal parts institutional, social, and physical from a Germany now complemented by the former GDR and focused on the goal of its own (re)unification. By approaching in *Keloglan in Alamania*, again from the perspective of Turkish immigrants, the then-burning question of redefining the German nation and German citizenship, the playwright portrayed the dangers of civilizational regression represented by the resurgence of German nationalism. Its title, once again bringing a figure of hybridization to the fore, underscores its connection with her first play. However, Karagöz, that somewhat simple-minded Anatolian peasant, hero of the Ottoman Empire's shadow theater, is no longer the protagonist, replaced instead by Keloglan ("Bald Boy") who has spent his whole life in Germany and does not even speak Turkish. Yet, this time too Özdamar has taken inspiration from a well-known comedic type. The original Keloğlan, hero of a whole series of Turkish folktales, is a country boy without a father who lives with his mother and grandfather. Afflicted by premature baldness (which, depending on the version, is either innate or caused by disease), he manages to get himself out of every bad situation thanks to his imagination, trickery, as well as luck and magic powers. Honest, mischievous, and courageous, he does not hesitate to fight against those stronger than himself, and he proves generous toward his adversaries. Despite his faults, he is a sympathetic character whose common sense makes one forget his ugliness and who represents in an allegorical fashion the Anatolian people as a whole.[8]

In Özdamar's musical comedy, this folk hero is also transplanted to a place designated by the words "in Alamania," which is to say, neither "in Deutschland", as one might expect in a play written in German, nor "Almanya'da,"

---

8 See Boratav and Eberhard (1953: 381–410).

which would be the correct spelling of this geographic reference in Turkish. Nevertheless, this time the dramatic action does take place – exclusively so – in Germany. Keloglan[9] is no longer the son of peasants but a second-generation immigrant who has grown up in Germany, which is now threatening to deport him when he reaches the age of majority for lack of employment that could extend his right to stay. The subtitle, *Die Versöhnung von Schwein und Lamm* ("The Reconciliation of Pig and Lamb"), points ironically to the contrast between the tense reality of the relationship that the country maintains with its culturally Muslim immigrant population[10] and the hypocrisy of official discourse about integration. In order to address this question, Özdamar works more resolutely within the terrain of the Western canon. Without abandoning the generic models of the Ottoman tradition, she deterritorializes them in order to replant them – reterritorialize them – into the German cultural context. In the same way the characters (and the author) left Turkey for Germany, their original frame of reference is disconnected from its territorial substratum and reinserted into interactions with another frame of reference, at once national (German) and transnational (Western), where it functions as a sort of indicator, because, as Özdamar says of her hero: "[Keloglan] is my brother, so I can do with him whatever I want."[11] This operation performs deterritorialization as decontextualization (*décodage*), which consists of first "uprooting," then "decoding" materials (objects, animals, gestures, signs, texts, etc.), and thus liberating them from their conventional associations in order to permit new ones.[12]

It is this double movement of de- and reterritorialization that the play sets into motion with its use of elements drawn from the Turkish cultural patrimony, because the whole point of the operation rests in the "recoding" they pass

---

9 In the published version of her play, Özdamar adopted a Germanized spelling (without a breve on the G). It is therefore the form that will be used throughout this chapter to designate her protagonist, as opposed to the folktale archetype.
10 Such frictions are regularly conveyed through sensational reports on the halal meat market, ritual home slaughter of lambs and sheep, Turkish families barbecuing illegally in the parks and public gardens of German cities, or simply the refusal of German Muslims to eat the nation's favorite meat, pork. By way of example, see headlines such as "Lammfromm – Muslimischer Schlachthof" (Fröhlich 2010) or "Hamburger Händler verkauft kein Schweinefleisch – nun nimmt Edeka ihm die Körbe weg" (anonymous, 2016).
11 "Das ist mein Bruder und mit dem kann ich ja dann machen, was ich will." Personal communication, cited in Boran (2004: 154).
12 See Deleuze and Guattari (1972, 1975, and 1980). As stressed by Guattari in an interview released in April 1992, the process of deterritorialization, which involves detaching a sign from its context of signification, goes hand in hand with an opposite movement of *reterritorialization* (Guattari and Zahm 1994: 8).

through once disconnected from their original frame of reference and implanted in the German cultural field.[13] In a theatrical space so open to the "glocal" dimension (Robertson 1995)[14] – in the sense that it transcends, by its very aesthetic code, the dichotomy between "local" and "global" – the deterritorialized elements are reinserted into the exploration of the characters and myths that populate the collective unconscious, as much on the national as on the European level and on the level of the rapport between East and West.

In any case, it must be noted that by the time Özdamar appropriated the character of Keloğlan, he had already been the object of adaptations/transposition into the German context. As early as the beginning of the 1980s, the author of children's literature Yücel Feyzioğlu inaugurated a series of illustrated books with *Keloğlan in der Bundesrepublik* ("Keloğlan in the Federal Republic"), turning the hero of folktales into a figure of projection for bicultural children confronted with the difficulties of finding their place in Germany.[15] In 1998, Kemal Kurt likewise published a collection of twelve tales entitled *Als das Kamel Bademeister war – Keloğlans lustige Streiche* ("When the Camel Was A Bath Attendant – Keloğlan's Merry Pranks"). Three of them were dramatized two years later in the form of a musical tale by the ATZE theater of Berlin in a syncretic composition mixing lyrical songs, Middle Eastern sounds, jazz rhythms, and musical comedy, with several incursions into German popular music and Hollywood soundtracks.[16] This work, the plot of which takes place in the indeterminate space of folktales and ends with the hero's triumph not only over forty brigands but also the despot who throws him in prison and whom he manages to turn into a good sovereign, achieved great success. Ultimately, the playwright, Erman Okay – actor, author, and director – exploited the popularity of Keloğlan for his work promoting integration and biculturality. In 1991, he produced an audiobook for children, *Keloğlan und der Riese* ("Keloğlan and the Giant") wherein the folktale character's tangles with the giants are related by a bilingual narrator in a mix of Turkish and German. This audiobook, accompanied by an educational booklet entitled *Zwischen Keloğlan und Rotkäppchen* ("Between Keloğlan and Little Red Riding Hood"), was followed in 2004 – four years after the production of *Keloglan in Alamania* in Oldenburg – by a second, *Keloğlan und Rotkäppchen*

---

13 See the chapter "*Rewriting* und Rekontextualisierung" in El Hissy (2012a: 97–101).
14 On the adequacy of the concept of glocalization to Özdamar's theatrical work, see Valera (2015).
15 See Feyzioğlu 1984, 1992a, 1992b, 2017 (non-exhaustive list).
16 Kemal Kurt, *Keloğlan und die Räuberbande*, music by Sinem Altan, ATZE Musiktheater, Berlin, 7 November 2010. The show received the "Junge Ohren Sonderpreis," an award for compositions for young audiences, in 2011.

("Keloğlan and Little Red Riding Hood"), that combined the popular folktales emblematic of the two countries. These works are still being successfully used as educational aids for bilingual intercultural education.

Hence, in seizing on the character of Keloğlan for herself, Özdamar was setting off on a path others had trod before. Not only had the hero of the tales already been introduced in Germany – although to a primarily very young audience – but he was a figure commonly seen there as emblematic of Turkish popular culture, really of the Turkish people as such, in the same way Little Red Riding Hood represented *pars pro toto* the German nation in its traditional dimension. Thus, this character, granted whom readers might place between Taugenichts ("Good-for-Nothing") and Till Eulenspiegel, became the Turkish – or more broadly the "Oriental" – counterpart to the Grimms' little heroine. In order to understand the originality of Özdamar's contribution to this process of cultural transfer, it would help to summarize the plot of her play and then examine the Western cultural references introduced into her deterritorialized and political version of the adventures of Keloğlan "in Alamania."

What Becomes of Keloğlan "in Alamania"?

Without work, young Keloglan, who will turn eighteen at midnight, seems irremediably condemned to be deported to Turkey, a country where he has no reference points and would be "even more foreign" than in Germany.[17] His mother, Kelkari ("Bald Woman"), a "former opera singer"[18] turned "cleaning woman at the opera" (KA 3), endeavors by hook or by crook to prevent him from leaving. In the face of his failure to find employment, she encourages him to find a German woman who will agree to marry him so that he can obtain the right to remain indefinitely. When he shows himself to be less than cooperative, she decides to use all of her savings to "buy" him a fiancée. The half-witted first

---

[17] "Er ist aber hier aufgewachsen, er kann nur die Sprache dieses Landes sprechen, er kann nicht mal mit seiner Mutter Kelkari sprechen. Das Flugzeug, das ihn als Fremden aufnimmt, wird ihn in einem fremden Land als noch fremder ausspucken." (Özdamar 1991, Scene 2 [Tekir's prologue], 6) All subsequent references are to this edition and will appear as KA, followed by the scene and page numbers.
[18] The name of this character is obviously modelled after that of her son, even though the "real" Keloğlan's mother doesn't bear this name, and isn't bald at all. But nothing prevents us from also seeing in this name a tongue-in-cheek allusion to Ionesco's absurdist play *La Cantatrice chauve* ("The Bald Soprano"). By giving body (and voice) to Ionesco's arbitrary and abstract invention, Özdamar somehow extends the joke, thus expressing her affinity with the codes of Absurdist Theater, and more generally with the avant-gardist mindset.

candidate proves difficult to convince because, for one, the 15,000 DM Kelkari set aside has been stolen out from under Keloglan's nose by two burglars labeled as *Räuber* ("robbers"), for another, the audience learns later that she has already been bought by another immigrant for just 5,000 DM.

The threat of deportation, illustrated in the background by the projection of a documentary showing "the deportation of one or more foreigners struggling with the police,"[19] becomes clearer when a desperate Keloglan falls asleep on one of his mother's tools, a floor polisher. Then the stagehands "bring a German fairy tale forest on stage with Little Red Riding Hood and the wolf inside."[20] "The author's voice" speaks up, accompanied by the clicking of a typewriter, to aver her impotence and declare that "in the real world" there would be no way out for Keloglan because the police would surely come find him early in the morning and put him on the first plane to Turkey.[21] Thus, what follows is located unequivocally in the ludic space of utopia and conjecture that the theatrical experience opens up. The audience sees two men in Elizabethan clothing take the stage, anonymous "trolls" who present themselves as having "been sent by Shakespeare" (KA 6.43) to save Keloglan, this young man who they say was "born of a tribe of asses" (6.43), by temporarily substituting his head with that of a "graceful young Teutonic woman" (6.43–44). The audience understands that the term designates Little Red Riding Hood, who has just been set up on stage like a sort of prop for the "German forest" as was the wolf, her aggressor in the Grimms' fairy tale. Taking advantage of the "veil of night" (6.43) with which they cover the German forest, the Shakespearean trolls proceed as in *A Midsummer Night's Dream* to swap the "heads" in the form of a spell that makes the two characters fall in love. Little Red Riding Hood finds herself in the arms of Keloglan who awakes desperately in love with her. Out of fear she would reject him if she were to discover that his "name is Keloglan and [he is] a man," he introduces himself to her with the name Butterfly, one of his mother's favorite roles.[22] With-

---

[19] "Ein Dokumentationsfilm zeigt die Ausweisung eines Ausländers oder mehrerer Ausländer, die sich gegen die Polizei wehren" (KA 6.42).

[20] "*Die Bühnenarbeiter bringen einen deutschen Märchenwald auf die Bühne, darin sind Rotkäppchen und der Wolf*" (KA 6.42).

[21] "Die Schreiberin dieses Stückes wusste keine Lösung, wie dieser Ausländerjugendliche Keloglan seine Probleme bis Mitternacht lösen könnte. Deswegen ließ sie ihn schlafen. In der Wirklichkeit wäre er gegen Morgen wachgeworden und nach Hause zurückgekehrt, hätte vielleicht ein Glas Tee getrunken, die Polizei hätte ihn abgeholt, und er hätte mit dem ersten Flugzeug dieses Land verlassen. Aber hier...?" (KA 6.42).

[22] "ROTKÄPPCHEN: Sag mir, wie heißt du? – KELOGLAN: Wie? Ja, wenn es nicht so dunkel wäre, wollt' ich dir's schon sagen, aber so – o weh, o weh! wenn ich nur wüsste, was mir lieber wäre? Dass ich Keloglan heiße und ein Mann bin. Wenn es nicht so dunkel wäre, ja. In der Fins-

out any trouble, the young woman falls for the young man wearing a blond wig and dressed like a girl and begins rattling off traditional children's songs. The wolf, transformed by the trolls into a common house dog, accompanies her on this number.

At this juncture, Kelkari, who has recovered the stolen money, offers Little Red Riding Hood the sum of 5,000 DM on the condition she marry her son. Not knowing that this son is none other than the blond she has just fallen in love with, she seeks counsel from Keloglan/Butterfly. He intimates she should accept the deal if she loves him, i.e. as Butterfly.[23] Giving up on marriage with her lover, she ultimately accepts, following his own advice, to marry Keloglan in exchange for the money. Saved, the hero then removes his "Butterfly" disguise and, at the risk of being rejected – let alone deported – he shows her his true face. Despite the disappointed reaction this unmasking provokes ("ein glatzköpfiger Türke," KA 56), he gets what he wanted: Little Red Riding hood's hand and, at the same time, the right to continue living in the country where he grew up. In this sense, the story ends happily, but Özdamar takes care to underscore once again the false nature of his happy ending. After removing her own mask, Little Red Riding Hood appears with the features of an old woman, and it is with an acquiescent pragmatism that this old woman resigns herself to marrying a man both ugly and of foreign origin. The audience recognizes in this final twist, simultaneously the comic image of the little girl from the fairy tale fused with her own grandmother and the inverted reflection of the scene in Mozart's *Zauberflöte* ("Magic Flute") (II.4) where Papageno, after accepting under duress to marry an old and ugly woman, watches that woman transform before his eyes into Papagena, a gorgeous young woman "eighteen years and two minutes" old.

This tale, painted in broad strokes onto the canvas of Smetana's *Prodaná nevěsta* ("The Sold Bride," German trans. "Die verkaufte Braut," Engl. "The Bartered Bride"), is introduced in a prologue delivered by a character – to be precise a cat, and to be more precise a "Turkish cat" – named Tekir ("Tabby Cat"). Performed on stage by an actress, Tekir takes on multiple roles over the course of the play. As the overarching narrator, she provides spectators elements of information she gleans from keeping close company with the two principals, carrying out a mediating function between the stage and house. However, she also gets involved in the dialogues and coordinates the speeches, playing among other

---

ternis kriegst du vor einem Mann sicher Angst, Angst ist manchmal größer als die Liebe, dann läuft sie weg von mir, aber wenn ich für sie eine Butterfly bliebe, so wird sie mich, o weh, an ihren heißen Busen drücken [...]" (KA 6.47).

23 "Wenn du mich liebst, heirate ihn, Rotkäppchen" (KA 8.56).

roles that of interpreter, and so of intermediary, between Kelkari and her son (since the latter does not understand Turkish). Finally, Tekir is also blessed with an aptitude for lyric singing that permits her to play opposite the former opera singer when she intones passages from *Don Giovanni*. Expert in narration, mediation, and translation, she is among those anthropomorphized animal characters who, like the Marxist donkey Şemsettin in *Karagöz*, borrow as much from the marvelous in folklore as from the Brechtian aesthetic in epic theater. Smarter and often wiser than their human companions, they introduce a comic inversion of roles that calls into question the superiority of humans over animals. Compared to them, it is the humans who come off as "beasts": Keloglan, who is depicted by his mother (in the matchmaker Kegal's terms from *The Bartered Bride*) as "a little lamb" because of his good-naturedness, is nothing in the eyes of Tekir and the trolls but an "ass" – the same as Kelkari herself[24] and all her "tribe." Worse, the humans are reduced to the condition of objects by an omnipresent capitalism. Ready to do anything to find work, Keloglan does not hesitate when he stumbles upon two adolescents dressed, one as lettuce, the other as a bottle of vinaigrette, for an advertisement to apply for his own role as a vegetable (KA 4.22). Informed not long after about the matrimonial plans his mother has made to get him out of his difficulties, he admits that he has no other choice – and no more worth than a "steak" (KA 5.32).

The cat and centerpiece of the narrative framework, Tekir, has the wolf from the German fairy tale as an antagonist – and foil – who has become the faithful companion of Little Red Riding Hood in the form of a pug. Likewise capable not only of speaking but singing, she expresses herself almost exclusively in scraps of folksongs. In the final scene, when the central conflict resolves in the marriage of Keloglan and Little Red Riding Hood, the pug tries (in the manner of the domestics in classical comedy) to profit from the occasion himself and kiss Tekir – who refuses him despite his telling her that he can only be released from the spell by a kiss from a "virgin maid" (KA 8.57–58). As the authorial figure, Tekir combines the ethics and cognitive competencies necessary to project beyond the play a lucid, mischievous, and liberal vision of the world in contrast to the darkness of the "realist" tableau of social relations.

Finally, beyond the pair of trolls that represent the positive forces of magic and art (Shakespeare), there are other secondary characters that act in pairs and are only designated by their function and a number: police officers 1 and 2 from scene 4 and robbers 1 and 2 from scene 5. Constructed in opposition (forces of order versus outlaws), the two pairs are in fact interchangeable. Equally hostile

---

[24] "TEKIR: Ihr seid Esel, ich gehe in die Kneipe" (KA 5.34).

to Keloglan, they humiliate and attack him one after the other, the former because he cannot show his papers, the others in order to rob him. Collective characters representing mainstream society in all of its cynical brutality and xenophobia, they take the place of the ogres, sorcerers, and other evildoers who confront the Keloğlan of the traditional folktales. In Özdamar's work, the hero does not emerge victorious from these assaults, and if the two scenes in question do not descend into pathos, it is solely because their violence is counterbalanced with buffoonery. Hence, the officer who strikes Keloglan does so at his own request – does Keloglan really have a choice, though? There is as much fatalism as tactical calculation in his expectation of the blows, because he knows he is risking much more than a beating. No sooner has the officer complied (he was only "doing his job" according to the sadly conventional formula, KA 4.25) than he begins taking his boots off for a farcical fight with his partner, both of them suddenly wearing boxing gloves and boxer shorts "in the colors of the German flag" – assisted in the roles of referees and trainer by a beggar and Keloglan himself, who have just been their victims. The burglary scene follows this slapstick interlude and finds the hero, defenseless in his bathtub, fallen into the clutches of two "robbers" disappointed to not find the money on him. Convinced that, even if the place does not exactly reek of opulence, it must still hold some treasure because "there's always gold in Oriental households" (5.35), they try everything they can to extract its location from him. In this scene that turns into a nightmare for Keloglan, the – dark – comedy results from the two robbers' military *habitus* and the crude, dietary, and scatological nature of the torture to which they subject, in vain, their punching bag.[25]

An Intertextual Web

Consisting of eight scenes of unequal length, the play presents itself as a simultaneously intertextual and intermedial montage, which spins out a web of references to European cultural heritage around its central figure, a delocalized version of the popular hero of Turkish folktales. These references are neither of the same nature nor on the same level, whether in terms of quantitative importance, generic status, or semantic value. Among the main references, one can pick out three operas (Smetana's *Prodaná nevěsta*, Puccini's *Madama Butterfly*, and Mo-

---

[25] "2. RÄUBER: Chef, melde gehorsamst, es ist keine Scheiße zu sehen. Der Feind bleibt mit dem Gold in seinem Versteck. – 1. RÄUBER: Gut, wir wenden härtere Maßnahmen an. Hier die drei Apfelkuchen, Sauerkraut, füttere ihn!" (KA 5.36). Then they start goose-stepping: "Links Rechts, Links Rechts, Eins Zwei, Eins Zwei..." (37).

zart's *Zauberflöte*), Shakespearean theater (primarily represented by *A Midsummer Night's Dream*), fairy tales (the Grimms' version of *Little Red Riding Hood*), and the repertoire of German folksongs. Several more discrete allusions join these major, explicit references. For example, the play alludes to other works in the lyrical repertoire, like *Don Giovanni* (KA 15) and *Manon Lescaut* (KA 54), only once, making their hypotextual value more anecdotal. The same can be said for the operetta *Gasparone* (1884) by Viennese composer Carl Millöcker, to which this chapter will return.

For its part, the treatment of the animal theme provokes associations with several works of German literature wherein anthropomorphized animals play a role. Tekir the cat, for example, evokes other celebrated felines in European literature, particularly those from the fantastical-ironic vein of the German Romantic tradition, such as Puss in Boots from Tieck's eponymous comedy (*Der gestiefelte Kater*, 1797, inspired by Perrault's tale) or E. T. A. Hoffmann's poet cat Murr. As for the fate reserved for the Big Bad Wolf, it clearly represents a nod to Heine, whose epic-lyric poem *Atta Troll*, itself inspired by Shakespeare (its subtitle: *Ein Sommernachtstraum*, "A Summer Night's Dream"), already contained a character transformed into a pug ("Mops"), not a wolf, true, but a figure emblematic of a certain type of German despised by the satirist – a "Swabian poet" whom Heine delights in imagining enchanted by a sorceress and crying for his lost country.

These references do not at all have the same semantic status. The works of Mozart, Puccini, Smetana, and the Grimms embody a canonical cultural patrimony from which Europe derives profit and glory, a pretension broadly derided in Özdamar's work. In turn, however, not Shakespeare, nor Hoffmann, nor Tieck, and certainly not Heine are ever the targets of irony. On the contrary, the play calls upon them as tutors, guarantors, and the masters of the subversive imagination whom it makes its accomplices. All the elements that constitute direct or indirect borrowings from Shakespeare – the "trolls" granted magic powers, the motifs of enchantment, the transvestitism, the debauching of the passions (the young girl in love with an "ass") – ultimately contribute to helping Keloglan and support him in his struggle to be able to remain in Germany. They are the means, not the targets, of parody. The "German fairy tale forest" is specifically not the enchanted forest of *A Midsummer Night's Dream* that enables fulfillment in dreams and nocturnal regeneration but a closed place, rigid and suffocating, a nightmare of paranoiac order and deadly violence that can only be transcended by Shakespearean magic. Özdamar thus underlines the way in which Shakespeare's works provide a universal and emancipatory aesthetic framework of references still valuable to modern theater. This conviction, which she shares with Tieck among others, is crucial for the whole work. The Shakespearean conception of theater – particularly as illustrated in *Midsummer's Night* by the doubling of the theatrical game, the opposition of night, the space of fantasy and dream, and day, the space of reality and order, but also by the theme of conflict between the individual and society – remains exemplary in her eyes even if, like Brecht and Müller, she thinks its foundations require adaptation and correction. References to these two authors can occur both in the somewhat clownish episodes of boxing and beatings as well as the epic motifs and processes that structure the piece, situating it within the framework of the open and heterogenous aesthetics of postdramatic theater.[26] The rhapsodic construction in eight scenes, the author's intervention at the end of scene 6, as well as the opera doorman's appearance at the very end, coming to announce (as *deus ex machina* and with corroborating evidence) to the hero that he is not only to be saved but congratulated and rewarded by the highest authorities, thus all point to an omnipresent Brechtian intertext.

References to Shakespeare and Heine are skillfully interwoven into the piece. Not only does *Atta Troll*, invoked by the transformation into the ridiculous form of a pug, already point back to Shakespeare's *Midsummer Night's Dream*, but it also provides the only key to the presence in the play of two "trolls" supposedly dispatched by Shakespeare. One may indeed be surprised that these characters appear on Özdamar's stage only to evoke a play involving a variety of supernatural creatures – fairies, elves, and hobgoblins – but not a single "troll." The choice of this word with Scandinavian origins that rather evokes the monstrous and evil characters from Nordic mythology[27] to designate these "men from Shakespeare's time" only makes sense if one makes a detour through Heine's satirical work.[28] By the same token, the sinister and artificial "German fairy tale forest," which in Özdamar's work supplants the murky and fascinating sylvan world of *Midsummer Night's Dream*, seems to pass through the ironic filter of Heine, whose poem "Das ist der alte Märchenwald" ("This is the Old Fairy Tale Forest") had already skewered this specter of ossification and death from behind the elegiac tone of its frame, which employs this emblematic motif of German Romanticism (Heine 1976: I, 14–15). Thus, *Keloglan in Alamania* is deeply embedded in an intertextual framework, the two principal positive reference points of which are Shakespeare and Heine.

---

26 On postdramatic theater, see Hans-Thies Lehmann (1990) and Gerda Poschmann (2007).
27 There is also the possible suggestion of the trolls in *Peer Gynt* (1876), but the reference to Ibsen, if it exists at all, is doubtlessly weaker and less specific than the one to Heine.
28 Unless we consider "Troll" to be a deformation of "Droll," the name Schlegel gives to Puck. Yet this is not sufficient to explain the use of this proper noun – in an altered form – as a generic name for the two characters "sent by Shakespeare" in Özdamar's play.

It is against this backdrop of adhesion to a fundamentally liberatory aesthetic, at the confluence of Romantic irony, anti-philistinic satire, and Marxist social analysis, that the play's other hypotexts, those forming the object of critique, reveal themselves. If these first works form the philosophical, ethical, and aesthetic framework in which Özdamar locates her dramatic project, the others constitute its very material: the props of the ideological discourse that she uses to proceed with the project of deconstructing the canon. I will thus analyze her work of deconstruction by beginning with an examination of the references that produce in that play a corrective to the high Western canon supported by a realist approach to social problems, namely the operas *Madama Butterfly*, *Die Zauberblöte*, and *Prodaná nevěsta*. The subsequent section will turn to those that more specifically outline a nationalistic and reactionary imaginary focused on identity, i.e. the folkloric patrimony including fairy tales and the repertory of popular songs and Romantic operettas. Finally, I will address the significance and meaning of the interwoven references to Shakespeare and Heine in order to determine their function in Özdamar's theatrical project.

Keloglan/Butterfly: Deconstructing the Orientalist Myth

A monumental work of lyrical Orientalism, *Madama Butterfly* (1904)[29] particularly lends itself to a critical rereading from the postcolonial point of view. This poignant story of love betrayed reveals some of the horror of imperialism (the white man's disdain for the populations of conquered territories) but also reinforces the conception of the Far East as timeless, abounding in exotic refinement and sensuality, but paralyzed by tradition. It is thus hardly surprising that, in the wake of the deconstructive work undertaken in 1978, a number of authors, female authors especially, sensitized to the question of Orientalism by their own ethno-social position, seized on this work to pick it a part with caustic and contextualized readings. In Germany, this was notably the case with Yoko Tawada, who made use of Puccini's opera in an original manner in her novel *Ein Gast* ("A Guest," 1993) before returning to it in the context of her poetics course in Hamburg (2012: 101–121). Özdamar made a central motif of it in two of her works written a year apart: the short story *Karriere einer Putzfrau* ("A Charwoman's Career") and the "musical comedy" *Keloglan in Alamania*.

---

29 *Madama Butterfly*, opera in three acts by Giacomo Puccini, libretto by Giuseppe Giacosa and Luigi Illica after a play by David Belasco (1900) based on a short story by John Luther Long (1898).

This latter work introduces the reference to *Madama Butterfly* as soon as the curtain rises when the audience takes part in the end of a German rehearsal for Puccini's celebrated opera. This liminary *mise en abyme* is almost immediately followed – after Tekir's prologue – by the appearance of Kelkari in the costume of Madame Butterfly, aka Cio-Cio-San's (the Italian transliteration of "Ms. Butterfly" in Japanese), taking up again one of the songs the audience just heard, all while scrubbing the stage left by the actors who are at lunch. By showing a Turkish immigrant in the middle of singing *Madama Butterfly*, ruined by cares, alcohol, and the demeaning work she is doing in costume, at the beginning of her play, Özdamar unexpectedly confronts the libretto's theme of a geisha's passion abused by an unscrupulous white man with the brutal reality of the treatment today's Europe reserves for its immigrants. The immense success of Puccini's opera over other works of the colonial period that handled the same theme[30] results in part from the magnification of the humility of the heroine, a pure, naïve woman-child, and her unshakable passion for Pinkerton, the American officer who seduces her, marries her, and then leaves her cynically. Complacently drawing out the painful gauntlet Cio-Cio-San runs until her ultimate sacrifice, the work pulls out all the stops to earn the audience's identification and empathy.

This sentimentalism is cruelly challenged by the parodic treatment to which Özdamar's play subjects its material. Incongruous at first glance, the superposition of the tragic heroine and the trivial figure of the cleaning woman kneeling on her floor polisher is, in truth, sadly coherent. This grotesque collision imposes a reading conjoining two facets of Western ways of looking at the East, and more particularly Eastern women, on the audience, those of exaltation and abasement. In a sort of eloquent condensing of Said's thesis, this palimpsestic image brings to light a similar sort of dispossession. Whether she be sublimated by art or instead degraded by her social instrumentalization, the foreign woman has her intrinsic human dignity taken from her and reduced to its servile relationship to a "master." Even idealized, as Cio-Cio-San is in *Madama Butterfly*, it is by these qualities of abnegation, submission, and self-renunciation that she transcends her condition and attains a tragic dimension. The superposition of these two figures retrospectively removes any dimension of personal tragedy from Puccini's sentimental fable about relations between East and West. The parodic allusion places the hypotext in a political framework and so bluntly reveals the simultaneously sexist and racist violence colonialist exoticism conveys (while concealing it). It also denounces the continuation into our own day of

---

30 See for example Pierre Loti's novel *Madame Chrysanthème* (1888), which served as the basis for the opera of the same name by André Messager (1893).

the violence inherited from colonialism, and hence its survival as a system of exploitation and ideology within European democracies at the dawn of the twenty-first century – among others, within the newly reunified Germany, wrapped up in celebrating the triumph of individual liberty over communist dictatorship.

The reprise of the theme from *Madama Butterfly* in scene 5 in connection with the love affair between Keloglan and Little Red Riding Hood further amplifies its political significance. When the hero, to disguise both his origins and his sex, dons the trappings of Cio-Cio-San, wearing his mother's stage costume and taking on the English (sur)name of Puccini's heroine in a bid to seduce the German girl with whom he has fallen in love, the palimpsest takes on a new dimension. It is no longer just the cleaning woman who is identified with the sacrificial figure of Western exoticism but her son as well, that is, all immigrants and children of immigrants, all those Germany considers "other." This transvestism on Keloglan's part responds to a desire (a need?) to distance himself from the stereotype of the aggressive Eastern male. In order to neutralize the potential menace associated in the national imagination with the figure of the Muslim man – comparable to what once emanated in the past from the Big Bad Wolf of fairy tales – he falls back on the reverse side of Orientalist prejudice: the figure of feminine submission. In this way, he subjects himself to a feminization that is, according to Said, at the very foundation of the Orientalization that inferiorizes by miniaturizing, infantilizing, and sexualizing the Other.[31] It is only at the price of this subterfuge that Keloglan – whose Anatolian model was already a character of ambiguous sexuality – thinks he has a chance of becoming an object of desire for Little Red Riding Hood. Through this, and only through this, detour does "she become [his] child" and accept him as "her man."[32]

This reuse of the operatic hypotext on the levels of metatheatricality and gender inversion presents certain analogies with David Henry Hwang's play, *M. Butterfly*, performed on Broadway in 1988 and adapted for the screen by David Cronenberg in 1993.[33] In this rewriting, where the action begins at the start of the 1960s, the Sino-American playwright inverts the relationship of

---

[31] Said (1978: 206) summarized the "basic content" of the ideas he observed among nineteenth-century authors writing about the Orient as follows: "its eccentricity, its backwardness, its silent indifference, its feminine penetrability, its supine malleability."

[32] "Aber wenn ich für sie eine Butterfly bliebe [...] wird sie mein Kind und ich ihr Mann" (KA 6. 47–48).

[33] *M. Butterfly* won numerous awards, including a Tony Award and the Drama Desk Award, and was named as a finalist for the Pulitzer Prize for Drama in 1989. It inspired a novel by Serge Grünberg, *Le roman de M. Butterfly* (1984). See also the entry "M. Butterfly" in Xu (2012: 175–176).

power within the couple. The Western man, a married French diplomat, René Gallimard, falls hopelessly in love with a Peking opera diva famous for her interpretation of Madame Butterfly – to the point of losing everything for her. He manages to make Song Liling his mistress, but his dream is cut short when the Cultural Revolution sends him back to France and Song to a reeducation camp. After returning to Paris, Gallimard admits his affair to his wife and asks for a divorce. Song reunites with him after she leaves the camp with a child she says is his, and they pass their days happily until, fifteen years later, the truth comes to light: Song is really a man, a secret agent of the Chinese communist government. Her transvestism was merely a cover and her liaison with Gallimard a means to obtain information on the military strategy of the Western powers in Vietnam and gain a foothold in Europe without raising suspicions. Devastated by this revelation, which lifts the veil on his own sexual ambivalence, Gallimard is thrown in prison for high treason. He finally understands that, far from calling the tune in an adventure he experienced from the start as a new version of *Madama Butterfly*, he was merely a puppet in the hands of his "ideal woman." He reenacted the drama, not in the role of Pinkerton, but in that of Cio-Cio-San. Understanding the consequences of this belated discovery, he dons Butterfly's costume and commits suicide like her, by *seppuku*.

The intrigue in this play – based on an actual case of espionage – lies in its subtle analysis of the psychological effects of colonial ideology, which compounds stereotypes of race and gender. If the French diplomat made it easy for Song to fool him, it is because the imperialist illusion of the gentle, fragile, and self-effacing Chinese woman blinded him. Inhibited, he attempts to assert his virility by subjugating a creature as helpless and docile as Cio-Cio-San for whom he will play the new Pinkerton. Unable to imagine another type of intimate relationship than that of domination, he takes pleasure in humiliating Song, certain that she – like Puccini's heroine – will only be the more devoted to her seducer. Even though this conviction goes against the positions championed at the beginning of their relationship by Song him/herself (who vigorously rejects the sentimental clichés conveyed by that opera and deplores the subaltern role reserved for women in Chinese traditional society), nothing can dissuade him from his illusion.

The transposition of *Madama Butterfly* undertaken in *Keloglan in Alamania* rests on a similar analysis of the significance of Orientalist and (neo)colonialist representations but presented this time from the point of view of an Eastern man. By dressing up as Butterfly to please Little Red Riding Hood, Keloglan makes use of the cliché of the exotic, delicate, and defenseless woman-child in order to protect himself from the inverted and complementary (and much more dangerous for him in his present circumstances) stereotype of the primitive and bestial Eastern man. Rather than appear to his ladylove as a potential predator, he chooses – in spite of, or perhaps because of, his own sexist prejudices[34] – to take advantage of the only other stereotype at his disposal, in accordance with the reasoning that a Turkish man can only be eroticized in Germany by means of his feminization.[35]

This tactic would seem grotesque if it did not work. But throughout this scene of "seduction," Keloglan hardly has to do anything else to turn Little Red Riding Hood's head than listen attentively to her in a duet with the wolf transformed into a pug reeling off the repertoire of old German folksongs – which reveals itself to be rather violent toward marginal people like himself. Özdamar's non-psychological dramaturgy does not really seek to resolve the question of whether this posture of submission traditionally reserved for women is more the supplementary sign of alienation for the son of marginalized immigrants, or if it contributes, from the perspective of carnivalesque reversal, to subverting the ethnically gendered representations it brings to light. It is both at once. Either way, Keloglan's dressing up as Butterfly, as funny as it may appear, fits within the logic of his social position and the priorities it imposes on him, as it indicates his willingness – conscious or not – to let himself be used by Little Red Riding Hood in the same manner Cio-Cio-San was, in spite of herself, by Pinkerton: with a marriage contract that might be worthless. Indeed, fundamentally, it does not matter much to him if their union is purely formal. He just needs an official document.

The Trials of Keloglan through the Lens of Mozart: A Disenchanted Flute

The intertextual status of Mozart's *Zauberflöte* (1791) is more complex than that of Puccini's opera. This is primarily due to the fact that although this work, which – along with *Zaide* (1780) and *Die Entführung aus dem Serail* ("The Abduction from the Seraglio," 1782) – is among Mozart's "German" operas and also depicts a fantasy Orient, its Orientalism greatly differs from *Madama Butterfly*'s. First of all, *Die Zauberflöte* belongs to the genre of the Viennese *Singspiel*, which is closely related to the comic opera and is intended to be performed on popular stages (*Theater auf der Wieden*) before a sociologically heterogene-

---

34 Keloglan, for instance, is not surprised to hear that Little Red Riding Hood likes to talk about love for she "is a girl" (KA 7.47).
35 On the treatment of masculinity in our corpus, see also chapter 6.

ous audience.³⁶ From the outset, its generic affiliation places *Die Zauberflöte* in the world of play, lightness, "fantasy" – that is to say, at a far remove from the tragic pathos of Puccini. On the other hand, the image of the Orient presented in this work, composed for a libretto by Emanuel Schikaneder (probably co-written by Mozart) based on an Oriental tale by A. J. Liebeskind, is anything but univocal. Its eclectic, colorful, and magical exoticism intertwines with the esoteric gravity of an evocation of the "wisdom of the Orient" viewed from the ethical and philosophical perspective of Freemasonry, with which both composer and librettist were affiliated. This singular treatment of the Oriental theme, combining the conventional fantasies of sensuality, cruelty, and irrationality with a Masonic symbolism connected to "visions of a benign Orient" (Said 1979: 118), makes *Die Zauberflöte* an extremely ambiguous work. This ambivalence goes hand in hand with the uncertainty regarding its semantic purpose. Is it pure entertainment or a coded plea in favor of the Enlightenment values of tolerance, justice, kindness, and reason? What are the boundaries among baroque fantasy, Masonic mysticism, and rationalism? If it is absolutely necessary to identify a message in this "childish and solemn myth" (Starobinski 1978: 435) structured around the conflict between good and evil, rationality and obscurantism, masculine and feminine, and body and spirit, it can be summed up as a lesson about being mistrustful of appearances in order to access the truth found in fraternity and wisdom.

When Özdamar draws elements from this "hieroglyphic" (J. Assmann 2006: 769) work and integrates them into her own "musical," she thus turns to a work that presents a portrayal of the Orient that is a far cry from other stereotypical, simplistic, and Eurocentric visions. Nevertheless, according to historian David Do Paço, who examines the relevance of the categories of play and fantasy to address Mozart's Orientalist "fantasies,"

> [t]he Mozartian *Phantasie* is characterized by its deep Orientalist nature, which, from a dramatic point of view, provides the composer and his librettists with the dramatic repertoire for the expression of fantasy. [...] Furthermore, the content of the Mozartian *Phantasie* allows for some distance from the connection too hastily established between fantasy and moral transgression. The fantasy can actually impose a morality just as easily as it can vilify it and so can constitute a tool for controlling society.³⁷

---

36 See Jean and Brigitte Massin (1970), 1136–1137, footnote 4.
37 "[l]a *Phantasie* mozartienne se caractérise bien par sa profonde nature orientaliste qui, d'un point de vue dramatique, fournit au compositeur et à ses librettistes le répertoire dramatique de l'expression du fantasme. [...] Par ailleurs, le contenu de la *Phantasie* mozartienne permet de prendre une certaine distance à l'égard du lien trop vite fait entre fantasme et transgression mo-

It is undoubtedly in terms of this tension between play and moral order – in other words, between fantasy as transgression on the one hand and as a tool of social control on the other – that it is necessary to look for the point of articulation in Özdamar's rewriting. There is no methodical deconstruction of a homogeneous axiological system, and for good cause, but rather the exploitation of a symbolic system. With the allegorical, playful, and fantastic elements of *Die Zauberflöte* as supports, Özdamar pushes the limits of the Mozartian game of masks and mirrors that progresses in keeping with reversals of fortune, blurring cultural and ethical points of reference, mixing the sublime and the grotesque, plunging the dream into nightmare and vice versa. The spiritual element that she thus introduces obliquely into her hero's pedestrian drama makes the absurdity of the situation and the total absence of morality in the story stand out all the more starkly.

Keloglan appears through the Mozartian prism successively as the avatar of Tamino, Papageno, Pamina, and even Papagena. Having embarked on a quest that turns out to be no less arduous than Tamino's, he is nonetheless not seeking to achieve any moral or sentimental objective, but simply to obtain the right to remain where he has always lived. The battle he must wage to accomplish this and emerge from his initial state of helplessness in some respects resembles the initiatory journey Tamino takes to enter the Temple of Wisdom (winning a fiancée and passing various trials, including that of silence),[38] and these analogies shed an ironic light on the pitfalls that young people encounter in their path when their sole aim is to legitimize their presence within a collective to which they belong. Materially, this "path" is the exact opposite of a voyage since what is at stake is *not* to leave a place where one already is. Thus, the Mozartian intertext makes the children of immigrants' access to German citizenship appear as an improbable quest for the Grail, the static nature of which further emphasizes an absence of meaning and rationale. The parodic reworking draws a line between the national community and the circle of the Initiates presided over by the high priest Sarastro, emphasizing the gap that separates the ideals of wisdom and fraternity preached in the *Zauberflöte* from the petty principles governing the acquisition of civil rights in Germany at the end of the twentieth century. But the satire of an exclusive democracy reflects back on the musical tale's high morality and the elitism of a utopia reserved for exceptional individuals.

---

rale. En effet, le fantasme peut imposer une moralité, comme la vilipender, et peut alors constituer un outil de contrôle de la société" (Do Paço 2010: § 25).

[38] "[...] ich schlage vor, ihr schweigt, und wer zuerst spricht, der sucht die Braut" (KA 5.32).

Beyond the general inflection it gives to Keloglan's adventure, the intertextual game muddies the waters in terms of the semantic and pragmatic categories that structure the *Zauberflöte*. After all, if Keloglan is indeed the subject of a quest, he is simultaneously the object of the negotiations that it involves. While Tamino must liberate his beloved in order to be admitted to the brotherhood of Sarastro, which puts his virile qualities (courage, perseverance, respect for his word once given) to the test, Keloglan must *sell himself* to find a wife. And yet, even with money (provided by his mother), he has extreme difficulties accomplishing this and ends up capitulating in the face of the task's difficulty. Leaving it to others, i.e. Kelkari and the supernatural powers, to do the selling in his place, Keloglan does not "conquer" anyone, as Little Red Riding Hood is practically handed to him on a platter. As already seen, in his relationship with her, he is not the one who plays the active role – and for good reason, since their respective positions in the social field establish an asymmetrical balance of power that is to her advantage. Thus, the similarity of Keloglan's situation to Tamino's, as suggested by the former's repetition of the aria "Dies Bildnis ist bezaubernd schön" ("This image is enchantingly lovely")[39] to express his delight at the sight of Little Red Riding Hood in his arms, is misleading. His situation is in no way the same as Tamino's when he is before Pamina's portrait. The conventional vision of woman that this quotation elicits, reducing her to an enigmatic and fascinating "image,"[40] is soon contradicted by Red Riding Hood's behavior, since she whom he delights in seeing as the "daughter of the Queen of the Night"[41] then begins to mechanically intone her nursery rhymes, each one crueler and more naïve than the last.

The play also sketches a connection between Keloglan and Papageno. This analogy culminates in the denouement with the engaged couple's double transformation. From an intertextual perspective, this final twist also operates an inversion of genders. Here, the parodic reversal occurs on several levels. On the one hand, it is not the young man – Keloglan – who agrees under duress to

---

[39] "Dies Bildnis ist bezaubernd schön / wie noch kein Auge sie je gesehn / ich fühl's wie dies Götterbild / mein Herz mit neuer Regung füllt / dies Etwas kann ich zwar nicht nennen / doch ich fühl's hier wie Feuer brennen / soll die Empfindung Liebe sein / ja, ja! Die Liebe ist es allein" (KA 46–47). These are the opening words of the third aria of Mozart's opera (I.4).
[40] Just before singing Tamino's aria, Keloglan (KA 46) exclaims, "Sieh! Das schöne Fräuleinbild!", thus comically merging the honorific *Fräulein* ("young lady") with the old-fashioned expression *Weibsbild* (literally "picture of a woman") for "woman", "female", which is still used today in a derogatory sense.
[41] "Du, Tochter der Königin der Nacht. Die Augen braun... richtig, braun. Die Lippen, rot. Blonde Haare, blonde Haare..." (KA 46).

marry a repulsive old woman and then has the happy surprise of seeing her transform into a young beauty, but instead the "graceful Teutonic woman" who has the nasty surprise of discovering an ungrateful "bald Turk" beneath the mask of the sweet young blond man she's promised to marry. On the other hand, and as if to complete the disillusionment represented by this twisted happy ending, the "young girl" transforms in turn into an old woman. There is therefore no compensation for the hardships endured, no reward for the sacrifices made on either side, and no morality.

This parody "squared" of Papagena's transformation points in turn to a structural resemblance between Keloglan and the *Zauberflöte*'s bird-catcher. A successor to the Keloğlan of Turkish tales, Özdamar's hero has a childlike, rough, and naïve side that places him in the generic proximity of the traditional type of theater buffoon embodied by Papageno. In addition, like the latter, he only knows a limited corner of the world – precisely the one from which he risks being banished – and is content with little and lives from one day to the next without making plans for the future. Moreover, like Papageno, he has an animal component (he is "of the donkey tribe"), though he lacks the Mozartian bird-man's erotic power, the virile health that makes of Papageno an assistant who in the end is indispensable to Prince Tamino.[42] At the level of the gendered construction of the characters, the gap further widens. Unlike the complementary Tamino-Papageno couple, Keloglan in no way embodies the principle of male domination, but is rather a combination of the characteristics traditionally associated with femininity and masculinity.

The strict dichotomy constructed in *Die Zauberflöte* between the world of women and that of men is therefore undermined by a framework that does not just assume a view opposite to that of the opera's libretto but also undermines the Manichean simplicity (which the music in Mozart already disrupts) through a dialectical game of mirrors. Thus, the maternal figure embodied by Kelkari can be read as the positive inverse of the Queen of the Night, a harmful and demonic mother who annexes and annihilates her daughter, preventing her from leaving and going so far as to deliver her to the fearsome Monostatos and inciting her to murder. Energetic and resourceful, Kelkari is a "Mother Courage" who does everything in her power to save her son from deportation, not because she wants to keep him, but to save him. The interpretation of this mother/son pair as the inverted reflection of the *Zauberflöte*'s mother/daughter pair indirect-

---

[42] "Si Papageno est sans pouvoir direct, son innocence, sa gaîté, – escortée du flûtiau et du glockenspiel – se renversent en un pouvoir indirect: Papageno fera tourner la roue du destin, à son insu" (Starobinski 1978: 438).

ly underscores the absence of a paternal figure capable of embodying – for good or ill – a patriarchal power that would oppose, as with Mozart, the matriarchal power of the Queen of the Night. This does not mean that the male element is removed from the balance of power the play portrays – far from it. As we will see later, the theme of male domination is very present, especially in the repertoire of folk tales and songs. However, it does not structure the dramatic framework, and just like Keloglan, Kelkari combines attributes supposedly specific to women (protective mother) and men ("head of the family" who provides for her child's material needs, initiating a positive strategy), without this duality being perceived as paradoxical in relation to philosophical, moral, or even social norms. If Mozart's *Zauberflöte* can be seen as a "family drama," as proposed by Nikolaus Harnoncourt (1987: 14–15), *Keloglan in Alamania* is ostensibly something else, and the conflict that is staged does not find its resolution in a harmonious social order driven by wisdom, reason, and truth.

The parody of the Mozart hypotext culminates in the impossible "reconciliation of the pig and the lamb" situated on the horizon of the play. Here again, the parallel highlights a contrast between ideal and reality while indirectly casting doubt on the validity and consistency of a utopia that bases the advent of universal harmony on an authoritarian power that is theocratic and inherently unequal. The very end of *Keloglan in Alamania* – which, we will recall from the author's foreword, does not correspond to what would have happened "in reality" – thus makes it possible to see, behind the obvious Brechtian palimpsest, an ultimate satirical wink at *Die Zauberflöte*. When the opera doorman gives the hero his residence permit accompanied by a giant clipping from the *Bild-Zeitung* announcing that, after all was said and done, "Keloglan must not die," and adding congratulations from the Minister of Labor and the Federal Chancellor, along with a 100 DM note as a "wedding gift,"[43] is not the audience invited to a finale that is on par with that of the *Zauberflöte?* Compared to the apotheosis of Tamino and Pamina who are solemnly received by the circle of the Initiates under the benevolent eye of Sarastro, enthroned majestically against a resplendent backdrop of the sun, this more modest consecration, which seals Keloglan's admission among the legitimate residents on German territory, also confirms a no less utopian triumph of harmony over chaos. The detail of the 100 DM offered by the federal government, a redolent, completely imaginary counterpart to the "welcome gift" given to the citizens of GDR after the fall of the Wall, serves

---

[43] "*Der Opernpförtner bringt die Aufenthaltserlaubnis für Keloglan und eine übergroße Bildzeitung. Überschrift: Keloglan muss nicht sterben!* – PFÖRTNER: Hier ist die Aufenthaltserlaubnis und hier Glückwunschbotschaften vom Arbeitsminister und Bundeskanzler und ein 100-DM-Geschenk für eure Hochzeit" (KA 60).

as a reminder in the last moments of the play that, while access to the right of residence remained strictly regulated for immigrants and their children, this same state welcomed nationals of the other Germany with open arms.

Matrimonial Strategy: Queering *The Bartered Bride*

Still considered a national institution in Czechia today, the comic opera *Prodaná nevěsta* (1866) by Bedřich Smetana (1824–1884) has become "the standard example of 'folk' opera" worldwide" (Kobbé). Smetana was the founder of the Czech national school, having joined the nationalist movement following the 1848 revolution. Drawing inspiration from folk dance, he wanted to provide a joyful and picturesque representation of village life in Bohemia by staging scenes featuring peasants. Just like the tales of the Brothers Grimm, his work thus participates in the shaping of national identity by returning to the sources of folk culture. The opera, initially considered outdated in form, struggled to establish itself on the stage of the all-new national theater in Prague before experiencing a triumphant, enduring success on German and Austrian stages. Its proper recognition dates from the international exhibition of theater and music organized in Vienna in 1892. Canonized in the musical metropolis of classicism, *Die verkaufte Braut*, although an "exotic work," also integrated the European – and particularly Germanic – musical pantheon.

The libretto relates a fairly conventional story of thwarted loves against the backdrop of arranged marriage. Marenka (Marie in the German version) is secretly engaged to Jeník (Hans), but her parents have planned a better match, Vašek (Wenzel), who is likely to inherit the family fortune because his older brother has disappeared. The suitor her parents favor turns out to be a stuttering simpleton and Marenka refuses to marry him. On the father's behalf, the village matchmaker, Kecal (Kezal), attempts to make Jeník change his mind by offering a large sum of money in exchange for giving her up. Unexpectedly, Jeník accepts the arrangement on the condition that Marenka marry Vašek's missing older brother. Furious at having been rejected, Marenka learns only at the very end that Jeník is himself the eldest son and that he has been manipulating Kecal. The two lovers can finally get married, and they are financially comfortable thanks to the profit that Jeník made from the deal.

In addition to the folkloric color and its immense popularity in the German-speaking region, it is obviously the theme of arranged marriage that attracted Özdamar to this opera, and the libretto provided the framework for her play. She borrowed the theme and the main episodes, specifically that of the fiancé commanding the beloved to marry someone else, knowing very well, unlike the beloved, that they are that someone else. But Özdamar's use of this traditional comedic theme is entirely original. First, because she reverses gender roles yet again. It is Keloglan who takes the place of the girl who is to be married (Marenka) and who is, according to his mother, as sweet and innocent as a "little lamb,"[44] while Kelkari is the one to play the active role in the marriage arrangement that is assumed in the hypotext by the professional matchmaker (Kecal) enlisted by the bride-to-be's father. Here, arranged marriage is not treated as a social (patriarchal) institution to be fought in the name of individual freedom, but rather as a salutary ploy invented by a defenseless mother to thwart the system established by the state to regulate immigration. For the Turkish characters, the scabrous calculations regarding marriage are motivated not by a desire for personal enrichment (finding a "good match" for a daughter, marrying into a wealthy family), but by the need to circumvent a perverse and inhumane law that prohibits a man from remaining in the country where he grew up and where his mother resides.

By assimilating what contemporary society condemns with the term "marriage of convenience" with the ancient institution of arranged marriage, the author offers a perspective that contrasts with the tone dominating public debate in Europe at the turn of the twenty-first century. The transgressive dimension of this new palimpsest appears even more clearly if we relate the play's theme to the political and media hysteria that appeared a few years later in Germany regarding "forced marriages" and "honor killings" in Turkish immigrant communities. At that time, a number of intellectuals started demanding repressive measures be taken against what they viewed as antiquated practices, which they explained with reference to these immigrant populations' "traditions" and "culture" – even measures against Islam itself. The campaign was led in the name of women's rights and the values of an enlightened Europe by figures who substantiated their critique of Islam both with professional expertise and intimate knowledge of the field. Necla Kelek, a sociologist by training, became famous when in 2005 she published the controversial work *Die fremde Braut* ("The Foreign Bride"), which includes an account of her personal struggle to free herself from her father's authority. She received the support of prominent feminist figures in mainstream society such as Alice Schwarzer and Monika Maron, who – like Elisabeth Badinter in France – reinforce a discourse that makes it necessary to choose between the fight for women's rights and the fight for freedom and against ethnic discrimination. A few years later, the campaign against the "Islamization of Ger-

---

44 "ja, mein Keloglan ist lieb und bescheiden /und was die anderen Jungen tun/ mag er nicht leiden/ ein wahres Lämmlein an sanftem Mut/ ohne Fehler ist er, zweifelsohne" (KA 2.10 – 11).

many" resumed, amplified by the banker, politician, and polemicist Thilo Sarrazin, whose high-profile, anti-Muslim pamphlet *Deutschland schafft sich ab* ("Germany Is Abolishing Itself," 2010) contributed to the rehabilitation of political racism, thus setting the stage for populist movements like PEGIDA.

Özdamar has always kept her distance from this debate, refusing to look among those affected for the cause of the (alleged) failure of multiculturalism and immigrants' social integration and, most importantly, refusing to intervene as a witness for the prosecution against the (alleged) obscurantism of the "culture" from which she comes. In this context, it is interesting to note that just a few years before the outbreak of this polemic, this feminist intellectual of Turkish and Muslim origins seized on the literary theme of arranged marriage to illustrate the pressure exerted on children of immigrants not by their own families but by the German state. Without giving the cliché of the cultural backwardness of Turkish society a second glance, with this play she contents herself with reminding Germans both that arranged marriages were an everyday reality in Europe not so long ago – and a reality it was possible to laugh at and even, with a little luck and skill, take advantage of in order to achieve one's personal aims – and that, threatened with expulsion, today's immigrants are doing nothing else in their efforts to circumvent the German nationality law by whatever means.

Smetana's opera is thus used to counter the very nationalist ideology it emblematizes. Such a contrapuntal reading participates in the more general context of the deconstruction of the European folk canon, which I will now address in terms of the treatment of Grimms' tales and traditional German songs.

The Deadly Subtext of National Folklore

When they wake up in the German forest that has been enchanted by the trolls, the new lovers Keloglan and Little Red Riding Hood have a dialogue of the deaf wherein Keloglan's lines, comprised of quotes from the great lyrical tradition, elicit folk song excerpts from the "graceful Teutonic woman." While the repertoire quoted by Keloglan (Mozart, Schubert)[45] sings of love's rapture, the selection of Little Red Riding Hood, who is invited to tell him in turn "something nice" (KA 48) focuses on refrains that invoke nature and bucolic life. With the

---

[45] "Mir ist es, denke ich nur an dich als in den Mond zu sehen, ein stiller Fried kommt auf mich, weiß nicht wie mir geschehen" (KA 48). This is the final stanza of Goethe's *Jägers Abendlied*, set to music by Schubert in 1827.

exception of *Wenn ich ein Vöglein wär* ("If I Were a Little Bird"),[46] where the animal theme serves as a metaphorical expression of nostalgia for the beloved, her repertoire focuses exclusively on the motif of hunting. Keloglan's putative fiancée makes a brief foray into the elegiac register with *Häschen in der Grube* ("Little Rabbit in the Hole"), though she only recites the first stanza before proceeding abruptly – encouraged by the former who shouts, "Schön, mehr, mehr!" ("Lovely, more, more!") – with *Ein Jäger aus Kurpfalz* ("A Hunter from Kurpfalz"):

> A hunter of Kurpfalz
> Is riding through the green woods;
> He shoots the wild game,
> Just the way he likes it best.
> Trara, trara
> How good it is to go hunting,
> All over the green fields,
> All over the green fields.[47]

The confrontation of the two repertoires highlights how these traditional songs, under their innocuous appearance (catchy rhythms, simple lyrics, and melodic construction), communicate a violent fantasy. These verses that are generally only half-listened to and continued to be taught to children in kindergarten smell of gunpowder. Composed for educational purposes (*Häschen in der Grube*)[48] or recycled as military marches (*Ein Jäger aus Kurpfalz*),[49] their central motif is hunting and killing, sometimes an animal (often anthropomorphized), sometimes a criminal. Their recurring hero is the hunter, the archetypal incarnation of a conquering virility,[50] in whom, as Özdamar's montage recalls, it is possible to recognize the model for the police officer and soldier charged today with

---

46 Only the first stanza is quoted (KA 48). The poem is taken from the collection of folk songs by Brentano and Arnim, *Des Knaben Wunderhorn* ([1805] 1987: 415).
47 "Ein Jäger aus Kurpfalz / der reitet durch den grünen Wald / und schießt sein Wild daher / gleich wie es ihm gefällt / Juja, gar lustig / ist die Jägerei / all hier auf grüner Heid ' / all hier auf grüner Heid'" (KA 49).
48 This nursery rhyme, composed by Friedrich Fröbel in 1840 to the tune of *Fuchs, du hast die Gans gestohlen* (which is the version by Ernst Anschütz of the folk song *Wer die Gans gestohlen hat, ist ein Dieb*, 1824), is commonly used as the basis for games such as tag or hide-and-seek.
49 The military march *Ein Jäger aus Kurpfalz* is part of the repertoire compiled for the Bundeswehr, *Deutsche Armeemärsche* (1970: II, 145).
50 The original text (Ludwig Erk/Franz-Magnus Böhme, *Deutscher Liederhort*, vol. 3, Leipzig 1893: 315) consists of five stanzas, the last two of which feature the rape of a "little girl" (*Mägdelein*) by the bold, energetic hunter and are generally omitted today. In Büchner's *Woyzeck*, the song is among those intoned in unison by drunken journeymen in the inn scene, just before Woyzeck discovers Marie dancing with the Drum Major (Büchner 2012: 28).

overseeing respect for order and the national community's well-being. At this point, the police officers who brutalized Keloglan in scene 4, just like the brigands who attacked him in the subsequent scene, appear retrospectively as avatars of this figure of national identification: men whose ego ideal developed in accordance with an ancestral pattern drawing on this common cultural background, the product of an unconscious nostalgia for feudal Germany.

That it is Little Red Riding Hood rather than a man who recites verses extolling the martial values of the hunter and his carefree existence based on the freedom to shoot game "just the way he likes it best," is perfectly consistent both with the position that this character occupies – as we have seen – in her asymmetrical relationship to Keloglan/Butterfly, and with the internal logic of the canonical text from which she originated. The heroine of the Grimms' tale (in the last and best-known version) is saved – or resurrected – at the end by the good hunter after being eaten alive by the Big Bad Wolf. It is therefore natural that she should sing his praises when she wakes up in Keloglan's arms. She is on the side of innocence, order, and the law in contrast to the shadows and the dangers of the deep forest.

It may seem more surprising, however, to find her on good terms with the wolf. But this too is less outlandish than it initially seems, firstly because the trolls have rendered the tale's aggressor harmless by transforming him into a dog, but also because in the axiological economy of the tale, the evil predator is just as useful as the good one. By referencing the two figures back to back, Özdamar draws attention to their complementarity with regard to the moral that the Brothers Grimm imparted to the traditional French tale. What triumphs here is not humanity but civilization in its most brutal form. Transformed into a pug, the wolf not only makes peace with his former victim, but becomes his most faithful servant (using Propp's terminology, his "helper"). This doesn't mean that he becomes harmless to someone like Keloglan – far from it – because in his world, the hunter and the wolf, like their modern avatars the police officer and the watchdog, can only incarnate hostile powers. Keloglan's ancestor from the Turkish tales, the bald teenager who would fly courageously to the aid of the weak, had nothing to hope for from the powerful. The meeting of the two universes, that of the traditional Keloğlan tales and that of Germanic folklore as reshaped by the Brothers Grimm, highlights the incompatibility of two codes of values: on the one hand, the deliverance of the beautiful ingénue who is the passive and defenseless prey of a monstrous and cunning aggressor thanks to the intervention of a superior virile force embodying law and order; on the other, the unsightly child's (active) triumph thanks to his own cunning and assistance from supernatural powers. The marvelous manifests in *Rotkäppchen* only in the improbability of the wolf's strategy (i.e. his success in passing for his own victim's grandmother) and of the heroine's ultimate resurrection, which serves as a fulfillment of the hunter's act of bravery. In Keloğlan's tales, on the contrary, it is the child himself who is invested with supernatural forces that make it possible for him to triumph over his adversaries. Indeed, this is what will happen here, since Keloglan will eventually be fine, saved by his mother's money and the intervention of the trolls sent by Shakespeare.

In the intertextual configuration of this scene, the role assigned to the wolf turned into a pug is illuminating. His contribution, which consists of playing opposite Little Red Riding Hood, is divided into two songs. The first, *Auf einem Baum ein Kuckuck* ("A Cuckoo on a Tree"), using just its refrain, and the second, "Dieb, o Dieb, ich will dich fassen" ("Thief, O Thief, I Want to Catch You"), is modified to "Dieb, o Dieb, ich muss dich hassen" ("Thief, O Thief I Must Hate You") whereby he articulates the verses consecutively, alternating with his partner's replies. The refrain from *Auf einem Baum ein Kuckuck*, which he uses to punctuate Little Red Riding Hood's recitation, is an enigmatic formula, apparently devoid of meaning: "Simsalambimbam, Basaladusaladim." The enchanted animal gradually leads the other two to join him in a chorus, which leads to the following "exchange":

> LITTLE RED RIDING HOOD: What else can I sing?
> Wolf-turned-Pug: Cuckoo.
> Little red riding hood: Thank you. On a tree a cuckoo
> Wolf-turned-Pug: Simsalabim Basaladusaladim
> Little red riding hood: On a tree a cuckoo sat
> Wolf-turned-Pug: Simsalabimbam Basaladusaladim
> Little red riding hood: Along came a young hunter
> Wolf-turned-Pug: Simsalabimbam Basaladusaladim
> Little red riding hood: Along came a young huntsman
> Wolf-turned-Pug: Simsalabimbam Basaladusaladim.
> Little red riding hood: He shot the poor cuckoo dead.
> Wolf-turned-Pug: Simsalabimbam Basaladusaladim
> Little red riding hood: And after a year'd gone by
> Wolf-turned-Pug: Simsalabimbam Basaladusaladim
> Little red riding hood: And after a year'd gone by, the cuckoo had returned
> Wolf-turned-Pug: Simsalabimbam Basaladüsaladim
> Keloglan: More, more![51]

---

51 "ROTKÄPPCHEN: Was kann ich noch singen? / WOLF ALS MOPS: Kuckuck. / ROTKÄPPCHEN: Danke. Auf einem Baum ein Kuckuck / WOLF ALS MOPS: Simsalabim Basaladusaladim / ROTKÄPPCHEN: Auf einem Baum ein Kuckuck saß... / WOLF ALS MOPS: Simsalabimbam Basaladusaladim / ROTKÄPPCHEN: Da kam ein junger Jäger / WOLF ALS MOPS: Simsalabimbam Basaladusaladim / ROTKÄPPCHEN: Da kam ein junger Jägersmann / WOLF ALS MOPS: Simsalabimbam Basaladusaladim. / ROTKÄPPCHEN: Der schoss den armen Kuckuck tot. / WOLF ALS MOPS: Sim-

The two words that are tirelessly repeated by the wolf-turned-pug – and finally repeated by Keloglan himself – are indeed the actual refrain from the song *Auf einem Baum ein Kuckuck*, spelled "Sim sa la dim bam ba sa la du sa la dim" in the version by Erk and Irmer (1838: 21). But within the context of the play, they resonate as a comic hybridization (an "Orientalization") of the famous magic formula of German tales, *Simsalabim* (equivalent to the English "abracadabra"). Today we now know that this "original" formula, or what the German public perceives as such and that passed into common parlance as a purely onomatopoeic performative turn ("Simsalabim – und es geschah," "Simsalabin – and it came to pass"), likely has Middle Eastern origins, just like abracadabra. Simsalabim is presumably derived from classical Arabic and constitutes an altered form of the ritual incantatory formula of the *Qur'an*, *Bismillah ir-rahmani r-rahim* ("In the name of Allah, the most gracious, the most merciful"), which is found at the beginning of almost all the suras (113 out of 114) that make up the sacred book of Islam.[52] The cultural weight of this formula, pronounced by pious Muslims before all undertakings of any importance and commonly used as a protection against the jinn, is emphasized by Özdamar in her first novel, *Das Leben ist eine Karawanserei*.

It is specifically a Turk whom a wolf turned pug presses to repeat the formula in its distorted German version, and this context for the play surreptitiously invites the viewer to speculate about the origin of this once familiar word – and perhaps to sense in it, more than just a loan word from a foreign language, the fruit of a negative re-semantization of otherness. In fact, the nominal form of the term *Simsalabim* in German has, just like its synonym *Hokuspokus*, disparaging connotations. This probably dates back to the importation of *bismillah* into the West at the end of the Middle Ages by the Crusaders, who truncated the formula sacred to the Arab tradition in order to mock the speech of the Infidels, incomprehensible to their ears, and to denigrate their scientific and technological superiority, preferring to equate it with witchcraft.

What seems at first glance in Özdamar's play to be an incongruous Orientalization of an old German formula can thus be interpreted on another level as a

---

salabimbam Basaladusaladim / ROTKÄPPCHEN: Und als ein Jahr vergangen / WOLF ALS MOPS: Simsalabimbam Basaladusaladim / ROTKÄPPCHEN: Und als ein Jahr vergangen war, da war der Kuckuck wieder da / WOLF ALS MOPS: Simsalabimbam Basaladüsaladim / KELOGLAN: Mehr, noch mehr!" (KA 49–50).

[52] See Hartmut Heller (1998: 245–254). This recent hypothesis has not been echoed by the Duden dictionary, which instead cites the Latin "simila similibus" (from the phrase "*simila similibus curantur*," "like is cured by like") as a possible origin for *Simsalabim* (described as pejorative).

form of re-appropriation. Yet, for the young Keloglan, who is forced to repeat these apparently empty words on pain of losing his only chance of being able to stay in Germany, the sequence constitutes an alienating experience. He is induced to approve a discourse that implicitly disparages and excludes him. Indeed, in the second part of the song, where we would normally expect the reappearance of the cuckoo shot dead the previous year by the hunter, it is Keloglan, alias Butterfly, rather than the cuckoo whom Little Red Riding Hood suddenly designates as the next potential target of the hunter's murderous whims. The line from the original version, "Da war der Kuckuck wieder da" ("Then the cuckoo had returned"), is first replaced by the unexpected, incomplete variation: "Da kam ein junger Butter-" ("Then a young butter-"), before giving way to the full and explicit version: "Da kam ein junger Butterfly vorbei" ("Then a young butterfly came by"). The rest remains unfinished because the reply Keloglan searches for seems to catch in his throat:

> LITTLE RED RIDING HOOD: And after a year'd gone by, / the cuckoo had returned
> WOLF-TURNED-PUG: Simsalabimbam Basaladüsaladim
> KELOGLAN: More, more!
> LITTLE RED RIDING HOOD: Then a young butter-
> KELOGLAN: Simsalabimbam Basaladusaladim
> LITTLE RED RIDING HOOD: Then a young butterfly came by
> KELOGLAN: Simsalabimbam Basaladusaladim
> LITTLE RED RIDING HOOD: Then a young butterfly came by. Butterfly is so fine
> KELOGLAN: Simsalabimbam Basaladusaladim
> LITTLE RED RIDING HOOD: Butterfly is so fine and pretty
> KELOGLAN: Simsa...[53]

The recurring role within the scenic framework for the wolf-turned-pug is therefore to articulate a threat. His enchantment did not pacify him, instead just making him switch sides. This is eloquently confirmed by the variation that he introduces into the song, a dance song he is repeating at this precise moment in the scene. By replacing the declaration of intent "Dieb, o Dieb, ich will dich fassen" ("Thief, O thief, I want to/will catch you") with an expression of emotion, "Dieb, o Dieb, ich muss dich hassen" ("Thief, O thief I must hate you"), he changes his enunciative positioning, not his attitude. The drive of hatred expressed in this

---

53 "ROTKÄPPCHEN: Und als ein Jahr vergangen war / Da war der Kuckuck wieder da /WOLF ALS MOPS: Simsalabimbam Basaladüsaladim / KELOGLAN: Mehr, noch mehr! / ROTKÄPPCHEN: Da kam ein junger Butter – / KELOGLAN: Simsalabimbam Basaladusaladim / ROTKÄPPCHEN: Da kam ein junger Butterfly / KELOGLAN: Simsalabimbam Basaladusaladim / ROTKÄPPCHEN: Da kam ein junger Butterfly vorbei. Butterfly ist so schön / KELOGLAN: Simsalabimbam Basaladusaladim / ROTKÄPPCHEN: Butterfly ist so schön und fein / KELOGLAN: Simsa..." (KA 50).

variant – towards a "thief" who took "[his] damsel" – is not even repressed, as momentarily suggested by the subsequent verse, "Aber nein, ich kann dich lassen" ("But no, I can leave you"). Rather, it is only suspended through emotional withdrawal. As in the traditional song, the speaker abandons the pursuit of his adversary by losing interest in what's at stake in this competition between predatory males. He will merely have to look for "another damsel" ("Such mir eine andere Maid"). From the point of view of Keloglan, who is right in the midst of courting a "damsel" to whom the animal is particularly attached, this bravado should nevertheless be taken seriously as a form of intimidation. Despite having been transformed into a bouncy puppy with a sullen expression, the wolf has kept his hunting instincts; he has become a guard dog, trained to defend the property of humans (men), and in particular their women. The result of all this for "poor Butterfly" is clearly articulated in his subsequent replies, which alternate with the others' (Little Red Riding Hood has now joined in with the wolf) last "*Simsalabim Basaldusaladim*)": "As for poor Butterfly/ Things didn't turn out so well [...] / Soon he'll be accompanied / [...] By the choirs of the police."[54]

In this seventh scene, there is thus a new perspective on East/West relations, once again with the inversion of genres (the Turk as Butterfly confronted by a Little Red Riding Hood who sings the praises of hunting's virile virtues), and also the vision of an acculturation presented as an aggressive onslaught of stereotypes that communicate a reactionary ideology characterized by racist and sexist violence. The viewers, in the face of the actor-singers' attempt to drag them along into this regressive chorus,[55] are thus relieved to see this scene close with a liberating storm that a stage direction explains has an explicit cause, though technically difficult to represent: "Die Bühne kann diese Volkslieder nicht mehr aushalten" ("The stage can no longer bear these folk songs"). The personified stage "shivers" at the flashes of lightning and claps of thunder while a train station clock shows that it is five to midnight, and consequently becomes not only the site but also the vector of an exorcism organized in the name of the common good.

It is against this backdrop that "the aria of the bandits of Gasparone" rises like a final signal, following the convulsions that took hold of the stage itself, intoned by the play's two "bandits," the thieves-torturers from Scene 5, who "come out of a grand piano with a white flag."[56] The rough, simple, and male

---

54 "KELOGLAN: Dem Butterfly ginge *[sic]* es schlecht, dem armen [...] Wir werden ihn bald begleitet sehn [...] Mit Chören von Gendarmen" (KA 51–52).
55 "*Die Schauspieler versuchen die Zuschauer zum Chor zu machen*" (KA 52).
56 "[...] die zwei Räuber kommen aus Flügel *[sic]* mit weißer Fahne und singen mit Flügelbegleitung das Gasparone-Räuber-Libretto" (KA 52).

overtones of Germanic folklore have given way to the light, parodic register of Viennese operetta: "Nur Gold will ich haben / und Edelgestein. / Welch herrliches Leben, / ein Räuber zu sein" ("I only want gold/ and precious stones. / What a glorious life/ being a robber"). It is the triumphant song of the gallant and unscrupulous thug, who in Millöcker's play (II, 6) is the figure of Count Erminio, who has just duped the wealthy widow Carlotta by courting her for the sole purpose of taking her money. But the vile Erminio, who is actually a minister's son, has been impersonating the legendary – equally fictional and fearsome – Sicilian smuggler Gasparone. Here we have *Räuberromantik*, but in the second degree: a commonplace braggart assumes the scandalous air of the high-profile criminal to seduce a countess and lead decent folk on a wild goose chase. This ultimate reference therefore plays on the ambiguity that reigns in European cultural tradition, especially in Germany, from Schiller to Brecht by way of Schinderhannes, regarding the figure of the brigand, oscillating between anarchist utopia and repressive ideology, the embodiment of power and opposition to power, respectively.

Serving as a high point in the demystification of Germanic folklore that takes place throughout scene 7, the reference to *Gasparone* is an ironic twist, much like the degeneration of police control into buffoonery in scene 4. The two thieves, who were just aping military codes and methods by torturing Keloglan, reappear in the doubly ambiguous role of petty bourgeois peacemakers (the white flag) who dream of being operetta hoodlums – but who could just as well be real thugs with impeccable social camouflage rejoicing at being able to scapegoat a notorious bandit. Should we thus see in this trapdoor palimpsest a final illustration of the affinity among the different incarnations of the predator, or rather (after the pug's aggressive interpellation of the "thief") an ironic mockery of the deadly ideology honored in the nineteenth century by proponents of cultural nationalism like the Grimms, Brentano, Arnim, and others?

It is perhaps futile to search for dramatic coherence at all costs. The postdramatic aesthetic of the play undoubtedly accommodates the indeterminacy that simultaneously affects the transgressive fantasy pushed by the figure of the brigand (between despotic predator and anarchist rebel) and the actor's dramaturgical status (actor or performer?). Yet, the fact that Millöcker's operetta was brought to the screen in the 1930s by Georg Jacoby, one of the most prominent directors of the National Socialist film industry, makes it possible to view this episode more as a denunciation of the ambiguous relations of reactionary ideology to morality and the law. The film was a huge success when it was released in 1937, in a context where the cinema – especially in the category of "light" entertainment – was a major axis of the Hitler regime's cultural policy. This musical comedy, which featured immaculate aesthetics and the stars Marika Rökk and

Johannes Heesters in the main roles, adds an extra layer to the intermedial palimpsest created by Özdamar's play. In this big-budget production from UFA studios, which remained popular in post-war Germany, the exoticism of the Dalmatian coast (a tourist paradise that supplanted picturesque Italy in Viennese operettas) serves as an alibi for the exaltation of an attractive and sensual criminality, with the charming male heroes confronted by women portrayed as aggressive seductresses. Although not foregrounded in the reminiscences evoked by this scene's finale, the film undoubtedly takes part in the exotic imagination that the German public is likely to associate with the figure of the "bandit."

At any rate, Keloglan is only implicated in this jumble of childhood clichés, murderous gestures, and fantasized transgressions to the extent that he risks paying the price for them. His position as an illegitimate foreigner makes him the designated victim of the capricious hunter and the heroic brigand, the police officer as well as the thief, the wild wolf and the pet dog. And yet to what extent does Özdamar's critical decryption of the national unconscious in this play itself participate in indigenous literary tradition?

Positive Resonances: Under the Protection of Shakespeare, in the Footsteps of Heine

In her fight against cultural nationalism, Özdamar finds two major allies in Shakespeare and Heine. In addition to Brecht, who remains a constant tutelary figure in her work, these two authors' imprint features in *Keloglan in Alamania*, notably in its tangled patterns of dream, chaos, and enchantment. As seen above, scene 7 unfolds under the sign of Shakespearean enchantment by its reference to *A Midsummer Night's Dream*. The intertext with Heine is less perceptible at first, primarily because it concerns ideas (internationalism), a *manner* (satirical), and themes (the criticism of Germany) rather than focusing on an individual, clearly identified text. Secondly, if there is a text to which it is possible to detect precise allusions, it is indeed the satirical epic *Atta Troll*, which does not have a prominent place in the global canon and has even become rather inaccessible to the average German spectator because of its numerous allusions to the personalities and events of its time. However, the references to Heine's work in general and to *Atta Troll* in particular are no less critical for understanding the play than the references to Shakespeare's œuvre, with which they are tightly interwoven.

A Midsummer Night's Dream (1600) combines elements of the comedic and the marvelous to explore the power of the imagination in the face of the arbitrariness of the law. Hermia and Lysander, the couple whose love is thwarted because Hermia's father wants her to marry somebody else, flee the court of Athens to escape his despotic authority. In the forest, they fall into the hands of a nation of elves and fairies who have their own troubles and who settle them in their own way, with magic – leading the two young people into a fabulous and disturbing adventure that makes them momentarily lose their bearings entirely before bringing them back, reassured and more mature, to civilized life. By inserting the meeting between Keloglan and Little Red Riding Hood into a scenic arrangement expressly borrowed from this tale, Özdamar gives everything that happens in this scene the character of a universe of fantasy and unconscious impulses. Notably, it is after the hero falls asleep, despairing at not having found a solution to extend his right of residence, that he is assailed by these half-idyllic, half-terrifying visions. If the pastoral turns to nightmare, it is because the cardboard forest in which his dreamlike escape takes place, although very different from the one that served as a refuge for Hermia and Lysander, is also a place of license and of chaos, where suppressed desires are revealed. Yet, the unconscious that appears here is not liberating. The passions that the abolition of social barriers gives free rein to are oppressive and deadly, and they only disrupt the order of the City in the sense that they suspend the rules that prohibit attacking the weakest. The anarchic affects that flourish in this "German forest" participate, as we have previously seen, in a fantasy that is regressive, unhealthy, as well as – paradoxically – totalitarian. The projection of the poetic excesses of the Shakespearean *Dream* onto the backdrop of these frightening chimeras only brings out all the more starkly, a contrario, their emotional, linguistic, intellectual, and ethical poverty. The Shakespearean intertext is therefore much more here than a simple game of associative erudition but functions instead as an instrument of investigation, almost a developing agent in the photographic sense of the term: That is, it serves as a critical tool. With the reference to *Dream*, there is also a broader invocation of Shakespeare's entire body of work as a standard for the dramatic arts due to its social realism, its themes (the love of power versus the forces of imagination and poetry, games of identity), the considerations it encourages regarding theatricality itself, and finally, the irreducible ambiguity of its discourse: elements that the preceding pages have shown are fundamental to Özdamar's theatrical writing.

It is with the extension of this foundational reference that the work of Heine, himself a great admirer of Shakespeare, is inscribed into the piece. Heine devoted one work entirely to him, *Shakespeares Mädchen und Frauen* ("The Women and Girls of Shakespeare," 1838) and it was not by chance that his two large pamphlets from the early 1840s about Germany were created to echo *A Midsummer Night's Dream* and *Winter's Tale*, respectively. These poetic cycles, entitled *Deutschland, ein Wintermärchen* ("Germany, a Winter's Tale," 1844) and *Atta*

Troll: ein Sommernachtstraum ("Atta Troll: A Midsummer Night's Dream," 1846), form the complementary panels of a bitter and caustic diptych about the state of Germany on the eve of the 1848 revolution. The first is a general and vitriolic picture of "German misery" (society, philosophy, religion, art, literature, folklore), while the second, started in 1841 and published as a fragment in 1846, more specifically targeted literary circles. Heine mocked all the currents opposing the dominant reactionary forces – the bourgeois-liberal movement, radical republicanism, socialism, and communism – to defend poetic freedom and the autonomy of art against all comers. His *Atta Troll* can thus be read implicitly as an attempt to negotiate a viable position between poetry and politics, poised on the razor's edge between aesthetic solipsism ("art for art's sake") and *Tendenzdichtung* ("politically engaged poetry"), which offers a way of being in touch with the real while keeping ideology at bay.

Heine's satire primarily plays out in the field of discourse, and references to Germany are stamped with the seal of "magic."

> The French and the Russians own the land,
> And the British reign over the sea,
> And we are the undisputed masters
> Of the lofty realms of dreams.[57]

According to Heine, this country more than any other is literally haunted by the myths of medieval folklore: "Seit ich auf deutsche Erde trat,/ Durchströmen mich Zaubersäfte" ("Since setting foot on German soil,/ Magical juices have been coursing through me"). These verses at the start of *Deutschland, ein Wintermärchen*, immediately situate the analysis in the domain of mythocriticism. Like Özdamar, Heine took myths seriously as archetypal tales explaining a society's cohesiveness. He was particularly interested in Jacob Grimm's *Deutsche Mythologie* ("German Mythology," 1835), which served as inspiration for certain motifs in his pamphlets, notably the trio of Amazons in *Atta Troll* comprised of the goddess Diana (incarnating Greek Antiquity), the fairy Habonde (Nordic mythology exalted by German Romanticism), and the queen of Judea Herodias (the Biblical legend of the Jewish people).[58] Likewise, he found material in Grimm to fuel his fascination with the theme of animals, which is of such

---

[57] "Franzosen und Russen gehört das Land, / Das Meer gehört den Briten, / Wir aber besitzen im Luftreich des Traums / Die Herrschaft unbestritten." *Deutschland, ein Wintermärchen*, Caput VII, l. 21–24 (Heine 1976: VII, 592).

[58] According to Atsuko Ogane (2011), the combination of these three figures originates in Chapter XIII of Grimm's *Mythologie*, from which Heine also draws the story of Tannhäuser and Venus.

great importance to folktales. This motif is at the heart of *Atta Troll*, a "humorous epic" based on the chivalrous model recounting the life of a bear, Atta Troll, who is captured and trained as a circus beast. He then breaks his chains and returns to nature to advocate for a revolution against the human race. Ultimately, he is killed by a hunter and meets a miserable end as a decorative carpet in front of a fireplace. The allegory of the erudite bear serves to mock the militant writing of the Vormärz poets, these *Tendenzdichter* whom Heine deplores for having abandoned all aesthetic ambition in order to serve a political utopia. Like them, Atta Troll is a "Tendenzbär" ("politically engaged bear"), an "authentic sans-culotte of the forest" who "dances very badly" but is possessed by strong convictions and, though perhaps not talented, is also endowed with "character."[59]

The satirist set his sights in particular on the representatives of Young Germany: Ludwig Börne, Ferdinand von Freiligrath, and Georg Herwegh. But these proponents of civil liberties and a unified Germany were not the only subjects of Heine's ridicule. His charge is even stronger against the "apolitical" liberals of the Swabian School, which between 1820 and 1850 gathered the epigones of Romanticism around Ludwig Uhland, Gustav Schwab, and Justinius Kerner. These champions of the rural idyll, chaste loves, and nature's beauties, nostalgic for the glorious past of "Old Germany," are portrayed in the guise of a domestic dog – a pug the narrator encounters in the witch Uraka's cave while he is wandering the Pyrénées. The pet confides to him that before being bewitched by Uraka, he was a "Swabian poet" who devoted his time and talents to praising virtue. The witch had, he lamented, inflicted this demeaning metamorphosis – she "pugged" (*vermopst*) him – to punish him for not having yielded to her attempts at undermining his virtue.

This charge against provincial writers draped in superb indifference to public affairs and protective of their "virtue" (rather than their talent) offered a counterpart to the criticism of the political utopia of the *Tendenzdichter*. While Heine may not have spared his politically engaged peers, even the ones who took political risks, he did not lose sight of the fact that their common enemy, sent after them to keep them from expressing themselves freely, was this "hunter" – the repressive apparatus of the Germanic Confederation. Yet, the most loyal servants of a repressive regime are those who turn away from politics to serve an aesthetic ideal and escapist ethic. With the figure of the pug, Heine reserved his most hurtful barbs for these objective allies of reactionary Germany. This short-haired

---

59 "Atta Troll, Tendenzbär; sittlich / Religiös; als Gatte brünstig; / Durch Verführtsein von dem Zeitgeist, / Waldursprünglich Sansküllotte; // Sehr schlecht tanzend, doch Gesinnung / Tragend in der zott'gen Hochbrust; / Manchmal auch gestunken habend; / Kein Talent, doch ein Charakter!" *Atta Troll*, Caput XXIV, v. 41–48 (Heine 1976: VII, 563).

breed with a squashed muzzle is the supreme embodiment of the symbol of loyalty to a master that is generally associated with the dog, and it becomes an emblematic figure of servile attachment to authority. Because he did not want to give in to the witch's advances, the bigoted rhymester, whose muse "is morality in the flesh" (wearing drawers of "the stoutest leather"), is condemned to stir the satanic mixture which boils in Uraka's cauldron. He will not be freed of this curse until the day when a chaste girl "who has never touched a man before" can read to him the poems of Gustav Pfizer – a representative of the Swabian School the author particularly despised – on New Year's Eve without falling asleep.[60]

In *Keloglan in Alamania*, it is not a well-meaning poet who is transformed into a pug but rather the wicked wolf of fairy tales, designated as humanity's public enemy number one (that is, of bourgeois society), the menacing Other *par excellence*. However, the national imagination invoked in the play joins and extends the one already present in Heine's satirical poem as an object of derision. The pug as an allegory of debasement and submission to power, certainly more disturbing than ridiculous in Özdamar, serves as a device for castigating a mindset considered as representative of a certain Germany, falsely innocuous: conformist, snarling, and incapable of looking beyond itself. It is the result of bewitchment and as such is a form of impairment just as in Heine, functioning in the play as a marker of intertextuality. The thematic allusion is reinforced on a formal level by verbatim quotations from *Atta Troll* and is followed by identical details regarding the condition claimed by the pug for breaking the magic spell and the reaction this demand triggers in his counterpart. Learning that the animal can only be saved by a virgin willing to give in to his desire, the cat Tekir responds with a refusal that is formulated in exactly the same terms as those of the narrator in Heine: "Alas, in this case, I cannot undertake the work of redemption."[61] The intentional and emphatic parallel provides an incentive to interpret all the "folk" characters of the play – Little Red Riding Hood and the wolf, the hunter of the musical repertoire, and all the innocent victims from little rabbit to the cuckoo and the thief – as elements that constitute one and the same

---

[60] "Ja, nur eine reine Jungfrau, / Die noch keinen Mann berührt hat, / Und die folgende Bedingung Treu erfüllt, kann mich erlösen: / Diese reine Jungfrau muß / In der Nacht von Sankt-Sylvester / Die Gedichte Gustav Pfizer's / Lesen – ohne einzuschlafen! / Blieb sie wach bei der Lektüre, / Schloss sie nicht die keuschen Augen / – Dann bin ich entzaubert, menschlich / Athm' ich auf, ich bin entmopst!" *Atta Troll*, Caput XXII, v. 133–140 (Heine 1976: VII, 557).

[61] "TEKIR: Ach in diesem Falle kann ich das Erlösungswerk nicht unternehmen" (KA 57–58). Cf. *Atta Troll*, Caput XXII, v. 145–147 (Heine 1976: VII, 557): "'Ach, in diesem Falle' – sprach ich – / 'Kann ich selbst nicht unternehmen / Das Erlösungswerk.'"

myth. It could not have been made any more obvious that these references have the same function as the constant references to mythology in Heine: they provide a model of intelligibility for analyzing the state of a society.

An additional point of convergence between the work of deconstruction in *Keloglan in Alamania* and what Heine accomplishes in *Atta Troll* relates to the demystification of Orientalism. One of the works the satirist attacked most head-on was a ballad by Ferdinand von Freiligrath entitled *Der Mohrenfürst* ("The Moor Prince," 1836). This poem, emblematic of the young Freiligrath's enthusiasm for exotic themes, is a pathos-laden account of what befalls an African prince who is defeated in battle to then be sold as a slave and wind up as a drummer in a circus. A perfect illustration of the "poetry of the desert and the lions" that characterizes the first collection of poems by Freiligrath, the work could be read – in keeping with the author's own interpretation[62] – as a harbinger of his subsequent commitment to the revolution of the proletariat.[63] Yet the poem is less a denunciation of colonialism and slavery than a racist representation of the African man: prior to his capture, the king was a proud warrior who spread terror by beating the call to arms on a drum decorated with the skulls of his enemies. Such cruelty was evidently necessary for Freiligrath to provide the scene with credibility or picturesque details, since it does not prevent the poet from urging compassion for his hero. In *Atta Troll*, Heine set his sights on this text in particular. He explicitly designates it as a satirical target by quoting its fifth stanza as an epigraph, providing it, as he specifies in the foreword, with the comical palimpsest that "sometimes pierces with a sneer" beneath the surface of its verses.[64] Mocked by repeated winks at its symbolism of the contrast between black and white, the Freiligrath ballad is the subject of a parodic hijacking on several levels that points to the racist blind spot of its emancipatory pathos. Defined as an other who is not like the lyrical subject but rather its radical opposite, with a "black" face opposed to the subject's whiteness, the African man is stripped of his humanity. Relegated to the rank of beast, he is the passive

---

[62] "Ich begreife gar nicht, wie man sich nur wundern mag, daß ich ein Dichter der Revolution geworden bin. Schon meine erste Phase, die Wüsten- und Löwenpoesie, war im Grunde auch nur revolutionär. Es war die allerentschiedenste Opposition gegen die zahme Dichtung wie gegen die ganze Gesellschaft." Letter to F.A. Brockhaus (Buchner 1882: 264).
[63] See for example Josefine Nettesheim (1969: 105).
[64] "'Aus dem schimmernden, weißen Zelte hervor, / Tritt der schlachtgerüstete, fürstliche Mohr; / So tritt aus schimmernder Wolken Tor / Der Mond, der verfinsterte, dunkle, hervor.' – (Der Mohrenfürst von Ferd. Freiligrath)." *Atta Troll* (Heine 1976: VI, 492). Heine later provided his own outlook on the issue in the poem *Das Sklavenschiff* ([1852/1855] 1976: VI, 194–199), written in response to Harriet Beecher Stowe's 1852 novel *Uncle Tom's Cabin*.

object – an alibi, in the literal sense – of an aesthetic construction and a condescending emancipatory discourse. By revealing the mechanism of dehumanization at work in this construction of an exotic and primitive otherness, Heine – who himself experienced cultural stigma as a Jew – does not of course attack Freiligrath's political convictions, but their literary expression and how Freiligrath reveals his paternalistic position through involuntary obscenity. He revels in this posture so much not because he takes issue with the ideas upheld by Freiligrath but the ethical imposture represented by giving them an artistic form. In his parodic hijacking of the *Mohrenfürst*, it is not difficult to detect the same process of creation as in Özdamar's postcolonial texts, especially in this play written in response to the sentimentalism of works like *Madama Butterfly*. It is a question of using derision to bring to light the cogs of the ethnocultural arrogance that lurk beneath fine sentiments and generous ideas. In this sense, *Atta Troll* is indeed the principal model, if not an intertextual matrix, for *Keloglan in Alamania*.

To conclude, let us emphasize that the overexposure of Freiligrath's poem in this satirical epic no doubt reveals Heine's desire to oppose the literary ideal caricatured by this poem with another conception of literary engagement. His own ideal of emancipation, which he also intends to promote via literary means, is not communicated through the illustration and the sensationalism of a demonstration, but instead the awareness that he hopes to arouse in his reader by exposing pompous rhetoric and replicating contradictory critical points of view. It is this reflexive process, which requires readers' participation and enlists their sense of responsibility, that Heine endeavors to instigate through irony and perspectivism. As Gerhard Höhn correctly points out, this emancipatory aesthetic represents the "superior form of engagement" that *Atta Troll* implicitly describes *because* it is devoid of any pre-established political or moral purpose (1997: 91). It is to defend this very particular conception of an autonomy of art, which owes nothing to aesthetics, that Heine invokes the Shakespearean model: "Summer night's dream! Fantastic/ Aimless is my song. Yes, aimless/ Like love, like life./ Like the Creator together with creation!"[65] This intuition of a "superior form of engagement" aimed at emancipating readers rather than edifying them is also, fundamentally, what will lead Brecht to replace the teachings of *Lehrstücke* ("didactic plays") with the dialectical model of epic theater. Shakespeare, Heine, Brecht: it is in such lineage that Özdamar's work is rooted.

---

[65] "Traum der Sommernacht! Phantastisch / Zwecklos ist mein Lied. Ja, zwecklos / Wie die Liebe, wie das Leben, / Wie der Schöpfer sammt der Schöpfung!" *Atta Troll*, Caput III, v. 1–4 *Troll* (Heine 1976: VI, 501).

Conclusion: Disorder in the Cultural Nation

While there are relatively few references to Heine in *Keloglan in Alamania*, they are quite powerful. Starting with the "forest of German tales" set up on the stage of a "real" opera before a sleeping Keloglan crying on his mother's floor waxer: the cheaply-decorated stage where Little Red Riding Hood and the wolf lay like accessories is nothing but a degraded form of the "old enchanted forest" dramatically evoked in the opening of the poem *Das ist der alte Märchenwald* ("This is the old enchanted wood") the abandoned realm of Romantic muses who long ago gave up their place to mythological chimeras (Kortländer 1995). Likewise, the motif of the wolf turned into a pug is a sarcastic one-upmanship of the post-Romantic poet's metamorphosis into the same animal in *Atta Troll*. By inscribing herself in this tradition, Özdamar supports the defense of a humanist and lucid cosmopolitanism committed to unmasking ideologies. She stands resolutely alongside the Jewish satirist to laugh with him, in keeping with the playful, jubilatory art of Shakespeare, at the clear conscience that the defenders of the established order share with the most radical of their adversaries who are obsessed with their struggle for a better world.

In addition to the nod to the parodic art of *Atta Troll*, this intertextual marker signals an adherence in principle to Heine's poetic program, which is understood as an attempt to make literature "the vehicle of emancipatory thought" (Espagne 2014: 31), in particular through the critical deciphering of the myths that shape a society. Mobilized by Heine against the nationalist thinking he saw flourishing in *all* political factions of the intellectual field on the eve of 1848, this critical strategy is applied in the play to confront the euphoric discourse after the Berlin Wall fell about the revival of national sentiment with the reality of the increased rejection that non-native populations suffered in reunified Germany. By bringing to light the elements of continuity in contemporary popular culture with a nationalist ideology that developed in the nineteenth century on the foundations of political Romanticism and colonial ethnocentrism, Özdamar challenges the political and media consensus that was establishing itself during this period regarding the emergence of an open and civic national identity unsullied by nationalism.[66] *Keloglan in Alamania* dismantles the sham of this pacifying dis-

---

[66] See the statement Chancellor Gerhard Schröder made upon taking office in 1998 to celebrate the reunification: "Dieser Wechsel ist Ausdruck demokratischer Normalität und Ausdruck eines gewachsenen demokratischen Selbstbewußtseins. Ich denke [...], wir können alle darauf stolz sein, daß die Menschen in Deutschland rechtsradikalen und fremdenfeindlichen Tendenzen eine deutliche Abfuhr erteilt haben. [...] Was ich hier formuliere, ist das Selbstbewußtsein

course by showing that the national feeling flourishing then did so at the expense of individuals and groups stigmatized on the basis of ethnocultural criteria – as confirmed by the bloodshed in racist attacks during the early 1990s (Hoyerswerda, Rostock, Mölln, Solingen, to name only the most publicized).

At a time when Germany was celebrating its reconciliation with its past, glorifying itself for finally being a "cultural nation" like others, meaning that it was "adult and responsible" (Schwilk and Schacht 1994), and anchored in an "enlightened" tradition borne by a common literary, artistic, and philosophical heritage, the "reconciliation of the pig and lamb" did not arrive under the best auspices. Only the magic of a revisited Shakespearean *Dream* seems to allow for a happy romantic ending for Keloglan and Little Red Riding Hood. It is possible to deduce that the emergence of a truly hybrid society has a chance – for Özdamar does not a priori despair of integrating ethnocultural minorities in Germany – outside the framework of national thought, as long as we agree to fearlessly confront the ideological substrate of exclusion on which cultural tradition has developed.

---

einer erwachsenen Nation, die sich niemandem über-, aber auch niemandem unterlegen fühlen muß."

Chapter 5
Reading against the National Grain: Özdamar's Commitment to Oppositional Literature

Karriere einer Putzfrau: "Hamlet" Reread through the Prism of Heiner Müller

The brief tale *Karriere einer Putzfrau. Erinnerungen an Deutschland* ("A Charwoman's Career. Memories of Germany," 1990) is the first-person account of the life of a divorced Turkish woman. Abandoned by her husband following a military coup, she leaves Turkey to go to Germany as an immigrant worker and becomes a cleaning lady. Obliged to accept jobs, one more degrading than the last, she starts to imagine another life as an actress in the theater. Letting her mind wander, she invents incredible encounters between a whole series of famous personalities, some imaginary and some historical, protagonists of stories that she rearranges in her own way. Finally, she goes to a theater to apply for a role, but of course she just winds up with a new cleaning job: it is the end of her career as an actress, and it is her "career" as a cleaning lady that continues.

The narrative is structured chronologically around three moments: emigration to Germany and the events leading up to it, the first calamitous experiences as a cleaning lady, and finally a fantasy sequence that may be the result of psychotic delirium or transgressive imagination – it is not clear which. This long transition to the present, composed in italics, ends with a kind of epilogue that marks a brutal return to reality in just a few lines.

This short narrative text weaves a net of theatrical references, the principal one being Shakespeare's *The Tragedy of Hamlet, Prince of Denmark* (1601). The intertextual game established with the famous Shakespearean drama unfolds according to a strategy that involves the underlying intervention of a second, contemporary palimpsest: Heiner Müller's *Hamletmaschine* ("Hamletmachine," 1977). This chapter will explore this double imprint by showing that these intertwined references constitute both the text itself and its "literariness." First, I will examine how Özdamar appropriated the Shakespearean material and then analyze the stakes for her transposition in light of her aesthetic and political project.

Recontextualization and Transfocalization of *Hamlet*

Published in 1990 in the collection *Mutterzunge* ("Mother Tongue"), *Karriere einer Putzfrau* is the fruit of years of reflection on *Hamlet* dating back to Özdamar's work as an assistant at the Volksbühne in East Berlin after she fled Turkey in 1976. Bearing a letter of recommendation from the Zurich bookseller Theo Pinkus for the director of the theater at the time, Benno Besson, the young actress and admirer of Brecht received authorization to follow the rehearsals for *Der gute Mensch von Sezuan* ("The Good Person of Szechwan"). She translated Besson's staging notes and made pencil sketches for her friends who had remained in Turkey. Her contract was renewed for Fritz Marquardt's staging of Heiner Müller's *Die Bauern* ("The Farmers"), a play in which she also obtained a silent role. Özdamar was subsequently assistant director for Goethe's *Bürgergeneral* ("The Citizen General") staged by Karge/Langhoff, and then she was first assistant director for the *Hamlet* staged by Besson in 1977 in a translation produced for the occasion by Heiner Müller and Matthias Langhoff. Meanwhile, the GDR Theaterverband purchased her sketches from the *Bürgergeneral* rehearsals, which enabled her to buy a typewriter. She intended to use it for her first writing project: a transposition of the Shakespearean tragedy to contemporary Turkish society. This dramatic project, which she called *Hamlet/Ahmet*, was never to see the light of day, but the succinct description she gives of it in *Seltsame Sterne starren zur Erde* provides a rather precise idea of it:

> Hamlet is a local Turkish history. Hamlet is a Turkish farmer. His father was a big landowner and his own brother poisoned him so he could get his land. For this reason, he also married his brother's wife, Hamlet's mother. These kinds of things happen all the time in Turkey. When a man dies, the brother marries his wife. The title of my play is *Hamlet/Ahmet*. His dead father appears to the shepherds as a ghost and the shepherds fetch the village teacher. The teacher claims that the ghost is showing itself to the shepherds because there are no tractors in the village. The farmers in the neighboring villages have tractors from Germany that they brought back from there. When Ahmet speaks to his father's ghost and learns that his uncle murdered him, he vows vengeance. When he starts to give bewildering speeches, his uncle sends him to Germany as a worker. He brings back a tractor from there, and in the end he owns an apple orchard and lets his uncle, his mother, and his wife Ophelia work there. His father's ghost is in the field as a scarecrow.[1]

---

[1] "*Hamlet* ist eine türkische Dorfgeschichte. Hamlet ist ein türkischer Bauer, sein Vater war Großgrundbesitzer und ist von seinem eigenen Bruder vergiftet worden, damit dieser den Grund und Boden seines Bruders bekommt. Dazu heiratet er die Frau seines Bruders, Hamlets Mutter. Solche Ereignisse gibt es immer wieder in der Türkei. Wenn ein Mann stirbt, heiratet der Bruder dessen Frau. Mein Stück heißt *Hamlet/Ahmet*. Sein toter Vater erscheint den Hirten als Geist, die Hirten holen den Dorflehrer. Der Lehrer behauptet, daß der Geist sich den Hirten

This first rewriting project was still very Brechtian. Marxist in inspiration, it emphasizes socio-historical transfer (transition from an aristocratic feudal society to an agrarian society subsisting on the margins of twentieth-century industrialized Europe) and the decisive nature of the economy for the geopolitical context of the 1970s (the asymmetrical relationship between a rural, poor Turkey, and a Germany in the midst of an economic boom, with Turkey exporting a workforce to produce machines that it will itself import). Human relationships are class relationships and family tragedy is resolved by – or dissolves in – economic exploitation.

In her new project that would culminate in the story *Karriere einer Putzfrau. Erinnerungen an Deutschland*, Özdamar frees herself of both Shakespeare and Brecht. She goes from dramatic action to first-person narrative, displaces the center of gravity of the hypotext, and gives it a sequel. The hero is no longer Hamlet but Ophelia, and the theme of the Shakespearean tragedy (the imperative of revenge that stems from regicide, the sacrifice of the romantic relationship, and the rejected lover's suicide) is only evoked in the background of a story that presents itself as the "posthumous" story, in the metaphorical sense, of Ophelia, or more precisely of a woman who says of herself: "In meinem Land war ich Ophelia" ("In my country I was Ophelia").² At first, this statement could be understood as "I played the role of Ophelia" (in the theater) as well as "I was in a situation comparable to Ophelia's" (in life). However, it becomes clear that this second interpretation is the case here, since the narrator's husband, who is the son of a family affected by a "unique childhood drama" (KP 110), decides to leave his wife, who is young and of lower social status. He makes this decision following the military coup that establishes the dictatorship in Turkey on the pretext of participating in the resistance against the tyrannical regime.

It is worth noting that some critics such as Norbert Mecklenburg (2006: 91) and Gisela Ecker (2012) have favored the first reading, thus making – against all

---

zeigt, weil es im Dorf keine Traktoren gibt. In den Nachbarsdörfern besitzen die Bauern Traktoren aus Deutschland, die sie von dort mitgebracht haben. Als Ahmet mit dem Geist seines Vaters spricht und erfährt, daß sein Onkel ihn ermordet hat, muß er Blutrache schwören. Als er anfängt, verwirrte Reden zu halten, schickt ihn sein Onkel als Arbeiter nach Deutschland. Von dort bringt er einen Traktor mit, und am Ende ist er Besitzer einer Apfelplantage und läßt seinen Onkel, seine Mutter und seine Frau Ophelia dort arbeiten. Der Geist seines Vaters steht als Vogelscheuche auf dem Acker" (SSE 194–195).

2 "Karriere einer Putzfrau. Erinnerungen an Deutschland" (Özdamar 1990: 100–127, here 110). Subsequent references to this work will appear as KP plus page number.

textual evidence[3] – the heroine-narrator a projection of the author's "real" self. However, in the absence of explicit or implicit indicators that would make it possible to conclude that an autobiographical writer / reader contract in fact exists, the postulate of an identity between the character and its creator leads to results that are haphazard at best. Admittedly, the themes of Özdamar's literary work in its entirety are rooted quite strongly in her personal experience, but the existence of this biographical substrate does not justify reading each of her texts as a confession. While the subheading *Erinnerungen an Deutschland* ("Memories of Germany"), can, if push comes to shove, leave some doubt about the nature of the writer / reader contract, the title is unequivocal. Özdamar never worked as charwoman, so this character cannot represent her in the story. Nor are there clues within the body of the text to identify the heroine as an alter ego of the author, no more than to liken her to Kelkari of *Keloglan in Alamania* (who is, nevertheless, both a former singer and thus partly actress, and a cleaning lady in a theater). It is undeniable that Özdamar did not pull these characters out of thin air and that she forged them from her personal experience, but the link between fiction and reality does not come under the category of replication but rather of transposition and recomposition. In this case, the idea of combining the professions of actress and cleaning lady in an immigrant's lifestory resulted from a misunderstanding. At the beginning of her theatrical career in Germany, Özdamar was given very small roles – and in particular, on several occasions, silent roles as a cleaning lady. Her performances often went unnoticed, however, because when spectators and critics saw this young woman kneeling silently at the front of the stage alongside a pot and a mop while the other actors interpreted the dramatic action, they thought she was a "real" Turkish cleaning lady, and the press would comment more or less indulgently on this untimely intervention by a service employee in the midst of a performance. Özdamar, who laughed with the other members of the troupe over this mistake, drew inspiration from this anecdote for career paths like Kelkari's. For *Karriere einer Putzfrau*, the biographical trigger was even more precise. One day, the director Matthias Langhoff shook up her routine by giving her a vacuum cleaner instead of a mop and pail prior to a performance. This novelty inspired her with the ironic comment that she had indeed "made a career" as a cleaning lady!

There is no reason to infer from the author's own theatrical career that the cleaning lady she brings to life in this story would likewise have been an actress before leaving for Germany. The statement "In meinem Land war ich Ophelia" cannot therefore be understood as anything other than as a retrospective con-

---

3 For further details about this interpretation, see my article (Meyer 2017).

struction of the narrator, who translates her personal drama by means of a literary metaphor. This metaphorical reconstruction is reinforced by a tight network of references to the Shakespearean drama, concentrated on the first two pages. Obviously, she was the wife of a rich man who was opposed to the military regime and left her to protect himself from punishment in case she was arrested. Commited to "silence" and the "restoration of democracy" in his country, this weak-willed and selfish bourgeois intellectual followed the advice of a friend, "the son of a doctor and a medical student himself," who after having seen his own wife die under torture learned the lesson that "he who keeps quiet lives longer." Sacrificing his marital happiness to a strategy for fighting against a usurping power, like Hamlet he rid himself of a companion who had become cumbersome by urging her to go and shut herself up "in a convent." Then he obtained a divorce with the active help of his mother, who rushed to testify in court against the daughter-in-law she despised, accusing her of having been a bad wife and a sneak: "This woman destroyed my husband. The bed linen was black. She's a gypsy girl but unfortunately we didn't notice."

Here, Özdamar has once again incorporated the geopolitical context and made immigration to Germany a central pragmatic element in her transformation-continuation of *Hamlet*. Her Ophelia, "drowned in the black stream of [her] bed linen," leaves the dictatorship-ravaged country and takes refuge in Germany where she "resuscitates" by earning a living as a cleaning lady. She provides a disjointed account of her experience under these new conditions in a falsely detached tone that is half naïve, half mischievous, in rough German strewn with onomatopoeias and non-idiomatic formulations. The account consists of sordid anecdotes interspersed with dreams to draw a somber portrait of an immigrant woman's experience in a prosperous country. Filled with repugnant and grotesque details about the inhabitants' vulgarity and contempt, this first sequence of the narrator's "memories of Germany" gives pride of place to a musical repertoire, here with a cacophonous succession of scraps of songs inspired by German variété from the 1930s to 1970s.

Having become a "Frau Scheiße" ("Mrs. Shit")[4] who makes her contribution through degrading work to "keep Germany clean" (KP 114), the narrator nonethe-

---

4 Before emigrating, the narrator hears the story of "Frau Scheiße" (KP 112–113) from her grandmother: A woman whose house has been plundered goes after the "bandits" to get back her money. She reaches an inn where they have taken refuge and introduces herself to them under the name *Scheiße*. While they are sleeping at night, she fills their boots with a mixture of water and flour. On awakening in the morning, they are furious for getting trapped and call out and denounce her, but their alarm calls are mistaken for expletives. This story of revenge is reminiscent of Ulysses' famous trick against Polyphemus and turns out to be premonitory in

less escapes from the curse of Ophelia. Here, "nobody notices [that she is] the castoff of a man who wanted and had to play Hamlet."[5] That is, until one day she comes across an old antique dealer who tells her that with her beauty, she "could have become an actress in the theater." She then begins to fantasize about an acting career that would allow her to exorcise the humiliations she has endured. So, the one who "drowned to death as an Ophelia in [her] country" and who "returned to the world as a cleaning lady in Germany" takes her revenge by throwing herself – in her imagination – into the fictitious space of the theater: "I thought – Why not – Why not. Bedsheet in hand, I thought of all the other dead people who play their parts on stage! The bad guys win in life, but the dead can play around on stage."[6] In addition to Ophelia, she lists the dead who come back to life in the theater, those who lost in life because they were crazy, outcasts, suicides, victims of assassination, or cursed poets but who all the same had a literary destiny, either as characters or as creators: "*Hamlet, Ophelia, Richard III, Nathan the Wise, Georg Heym, mute Kathrin [sic], Woyzeck, the horse, Danton, Robespierre, Miss Julie, Van Gogh, Artaud, Marie, Rimbaud, the gravedigger, all the fools from Shakespeare, all dead messengers, sailors, Medea, Caesar…*" (KP 120) The first "factual" phase of her memories of Germany is succeeded by a hallucinatory narrative introduced in these terms: "*Blödsinn habe ich selbst genug*" ("I have enough nonsense myself"). The narrator launches into a description of a riotous dramatic action located on a theater stage transformed into a gigantic "public urinal for men" – a hellish commotion that brings in pell-mell all the characters mentioned above as well as Cleopatra, Messalina, Brutus, Adolf Hitler and Eva Braun, plastic snakes with boxing gloves, etc. All these characters interact in a burlesque frenzy, which is not without a certain historical logic. The fact that Julius Caesar appears there as "Hauptpisser" ("pisser-in-chief") to announce in a press interview his intention to fight so that the public urinal might stink less, and that for this purpose he has had the urinals cleaned by Cleopatra, is certainly zany but not entirely absurd – just as it is not completely extravagant to imagine a Cleopatra treated in this manner taking her revenge

---

several respects: not only will the narrator, too, become a sort of "Frau Scheiße," in the sense that she will have to clean up other people's excrement, but this professional retraining will also be for her a kind of camouflage (a "false flag" in the military sense of the term) as part of a survival and revenge strategy.

5 "Keiner merkte, daß ich die ehemalige Leiche von einem Mann bin, der Hamlet spielen wollte und sollte" (KP 113–114).

6 "Ich dachte – Warum nicht – Warum nicht. Das Bettlaken in der Hand, dachte ich an alle anderen Toten, die auf der Bühne ihre Rollen spielen! Die Bösen gewinnen im Leben, aber die Toten dürfen auf der Bühne ihren Blödsinn machen" (KP 120).

by sleeping with all the men who come to relieve themselves at the urinal so as to infect them with venereal diseases.[7] The class and gender struggle is described with a merciless magnifying mirror, rich in possibilities for reversals and incongruous confrontations.

It is, however, impossible to reduce the entire sequence to a single interpretative pattern. Özdamar took care to foil any attempts to intellectualize excessively the "delirium" of her narrator, in which we can at most isolate the leitmotif of power and order, caricatured and challenged in multiple variations. Thus, Medea becomes a feminist activist who "fights so that women also have the right to enter the urinal for men," and in so doing "she caresses the balls of Brutus."[8] Hamlet "occupies" the urinal with Horatio, Medea's children, and the extras, which causes Hitler and Eva Braun to intervene by reprimanding the extras and telling them that if they do not stay in their place "on the other side of the wall," they will not be entitled to use "the beautiful highway."[9] Nathan the Wise, as "Nobel Peace Prize Laureate," is bitten by the dog of Eva Braun, who exclaims, paraphrasing a notorious statement usually attributed to Hermann Göring: "I'm the one who decides who is the Jew, everyone is Jewish, everyone is Jewish." This obscene and grotesque vision of a story completely taken off its hinges mixes in a carnivalesque distortion of historical and literary characters, motifs borrowed from fictional narrative of the first degree (characters and anecdotes, snatches of songs, etc.), significant events from European and especially German history, and elements of popular mass culture (Coca-Cola, television, soccer, etc.). A frenzied *mise en abyme* sequence nestled in a story that itself is partially phantasmagorical, the passage can be read as a transposition of the theatrical spectacle where Hamlet, in the Shakespearean tragedy, replays the scene of his father's murder before the very ones who committed it: his uncle and his mother (III, 2).

The passage ends with a brutal return to reality: "Dann ist Ende" ("Then it's over," KP 126). The brief epilogue, which recounts the narrator's quickly disap-

---

[7] "Die Bühne ist ein einziges Männerpissoir, Cäsar, der Hauptpisser, gibt drei Journalisten ein Interview: Daß er dafür kämpfen wird, daß dieses Pissoir weniger Gestank haben wird als vorher, und läßt Kleopatra die Pißbecken saubermachen. Sie tut es, und als Rache fickt sie mit mehreren Männern, die dorthin pissen kommen und alle kriegen Trichomonaden – wie Limonaden." (KP 120)
[8] "Medea kämpft dafür, daß die Frauen auch ins Männerpissoir reinkommen dürfen und streichelt dabei die Eier von Brutus" (KP 120).
[9] "Dann besetzt [Hamlet] mit Horatio und Statisten und Medeas Kindern das Männerpissoir. Da treten Hitler und Eva Braun auf und sprechen zu den Statisten: 'Wenn ihr so weitermacht, geht lieber in die andere Hälfte, Euer Platz ist hinter der Mauer, und die schöne Autobahn könnt ihr dann nicht mal in euren Träumen betreten'" (KP 122).

pointed attempt to obtain a "real" role as an actress, highlights the circularity of a "career" desperately mired in a destructive routine. The impersonal injunction that seals her fate, "Hier ist die Bohnermaschine, die Bühne wird täglich gebohnert, haben sie gesagt" ("Here is the polishing machine, the stage must be waxed every day, they said," KP 126–127), is a reprise almost identical to an instruction she received at a previous job, at the very beginning of her stay in Germany: "Die Treppen werden täglich geputzt" ("The stairs must be cleaned every day," KP 117). As the narrator repeats this phrase to the point of delirium,[10] the story seems to suggest that this Ophelia, though "resuscitated," will only set foot on the boards of the stage to wax them, in an eternal renewal of her degrading work, but that she will probably not escape descending into madness. Thus her flight will only have postponed the final foundering. The Shakespearean heroine's fate catches up to her, and she was only saved from direct violence – political and marital – to sink all the better into the silent and banal dementia reserved for the ordinary.

Shakespeare's tragedy therefore serves in this work as an anchor for a disillusioned parable about the inglorious "career" of a woman who had to flee her country ravaged by the dictatorship. She who leaves "so many dead behind" (KP 113) is "reborn" in Germany under conditions that are not enviable either. It is a country that initially presents itself as a "verdant garden"[11] only to reveal itself, when seen close up, as also being marked by violence and hatred. At the same time, the political problem of the hypotext (whether to submit to unjust power or rise up?) remains central, so that it acquires the status of a matrix for a multitiered reflection on the dynamics of power throughout history.

In her modernizing, transgenetic and transfocalizing rewriting of *Hamlet*, Özdamar adopts a point of view that can be defined in more than one way as "subaltern." Added to geopolitical inferiorization (East / West, South / North, countryside / city relations) are sexual and societal inferiority (male/female relationships) and social and political subordination (immigrants' loss of social position, exploitation, and marginalization in wealthy countries). The story is also anchored programmatically in a low-angle perspective that projects a harsh light on everything related to bodily materiality, excretions, and cesspits (overexposure of the semantic field of filth, with the white / black opposition that runs through the text from one end to the other). This point of view, reflected in the physical posture of the cleaning lady working on her knees to scour the

---

10 "[...] nein, hier ist die Bohnermaschine haben sie gesagt, die Bohne wird täglich gebühnert, die Bohne wird täglich gebohnert, nein, nein, die Bühne wird täglich gebohnt" (KP 127).
11 "Und ich Wasserleiche bin in einem grünen Garten angekommen. Als Ophelia ertrunken in meinem Land, wieder in die Welt gekommen in Deutschland als Putzfrau" (KP 113).

floors and collect waste, is further emphasized by the occasional and contrastive evocation of the noble register of the tragedy, as when the narrator responds to her husband's hollow speech explaining why he is leaving her by quoting verbatim Ophelia's famous reply to Hamlet (in the translation of Schlegel): "Oh welch ein edler Geist ist hier zerstört" ("Oh, what a noble mind is here o'erthrown!," KP 111). Whether through direct quotes, allusions, or metaphorical turns borrowing from the motifs of Shakespeare's drama (dream, madness, ghosts), the Hamletian palimpsest is constantly perceptible through the narrative framework of Özdamar's text.

The following section will now show how this approach is linked to the work accomplished for the same hypotext by Heiner Müller, who was a translator of Hamlet but above all also author of a rewriting-continuation, *Hamletmaschine*.

Ophelia, Story of a (Double) Resurrection: On the Shoulders of Heiner Müller

In *Hamletmaschine*, a short play in five scenes written in 1977 that premiered the same year at the Münchner Kammerspiele, the hero of the Shakespearean drama is already gone as a character. By way of opening the first scene, entitled "Familienalbum" ("Family Scrapbook"), a character designated as "Hamletdarsteller" ("Hamlet-Actor") comes on stage to announce point blank in the past tense: "Ich war Hamlet" ("I was Hamlet")[12] before briefly sketching, like a bygone inaugural scene, the well-known synopsis of the Shakespearean drama: "I stood at the shore and talked with the surf BLABLA, the ruins of Europe in back of me. The bells tolled the state funeral, murderer and widow a couple, the town councillors goose-stepping behind the highranking carcass's coffin bawling with badly paid grief."[13] The same "actor" further explains his status in relation to the original Hamlet by declaring, in the mode of denial and the unreal scenario: "I'm not Hamlet. I don't take part any more. My words have nothing to tell me anymore [...] My drama doesn't happen anymore. Behind me the set is put up.

---

[12] *Hamletmaschine* (Müller 1978: 89). All subsequent references to this work will appear as HM plus page number, followed by page numbers, within brackets, from the English edition (*Hamletmachine and Other Texts for the Stage*, 1984).
[13] "Ich stand an der Küste und redete mit der Brandung BLABLA, im Rücken die Ruinen von Europa. Die Glocken läuteten das Staatsbegräbnis ein, Mörder und Witwe ein Paar, im Stechschritt hinter dem Sarg des Hohen Kadavers die Räte, heulend in schlecht bezahlter Trauer" (HM 89 [53]).

By people who aren't interested in it anymore either. I won't play along anymore."[14]

Heiner Müller's play was itself the culmination of a long-term reflection on Hamlet. Before writing *Hamletmaschine*, the East German playwright had developed an initial adaptation he had entitled *Hamlet in Budapest*, with the plot of the Elizabethan drama set in the context of the 1956 uprising in Hungary. The transposition to Communist Europe was to denounce the stagnation of the socialist system and the petrification of utopia. Müller abandoned this initial project after translating Shakespeare's play for Besson's production. In *Hamletmaschine*, the transposition of the drama to a contemporary setting was no longer considered except as a counter-factual premise: "My drama, if it still would happen," declares the Hamlet-Actor, "would happen in the time of the uprising."[15] This is a premise that Müller develops by referring to the insurrections of 1956 in Budapest and 1953 in East Berlin, in the following terms:

> The uprising starts with a stroll. Against the traffic rules, during the working hours. The street belongs to the pedestrians. Here and there, a car is turned over. [...] The call for more freedom turns into the cry for the overthrow of the government. [...] My place, if my drama would still happen, would be on both sides of the front, between the frontlines, over and above them. I stand in the stench of the crowd and hurl stones at policemen soldiers tanks bullet-proof glass. I look through the double doors of bullet-proof glass at the crowd pressing forward and smell the sweat of my fear. Choking with nausea, I shake my fist at myself who stands behind the bullet-proof glass.[16]

In the scenario of an uprising like those experienced by the sclerotic regimes of the Soviet bloc in the 1950s, the Shakespearean hero's hesitation would therefore be conceivable only as an inability to take a stand on one side or the other of the frontline, or even as total indifference to positioning. Today's Hamlet would be

---

14 "Ich bin nicht Hamlet. Ich spiele keine Rolle mehr. Meine Worte haben mir nichts mehr zu sagen. [...] Mein Drama findet nicht mehr statt. Hinter mir wird die Dekoration aufgebaut. Von Leuten, die es nicht interessiert, für Leute, die es nichts angeht. Mich interessiert es auch nicht mehr. Ich spiele nicht mehr mit" (HM 93 [56]).
15 "Mein Drama, wenn es noch stattfinden würde, fände in der Zeit des Aufstands statt." (HM 93–94 [56]).
16 "Der Aufstand beginnt als Spaziergang. Gegen die Verkehrsordnung während der Arbeitszeit. Die Straße gehört den Fußgängern. Hier und da wird ein Auto umgeworfen. [...] Aus dem Ruf nach mehr Freiheit wird der Schrei nach dem Sturz der Regierung. [...] Mein Platz, wenn mein Drama noch stattfinden würde, wäre auf beiden Seiten der Front, zwischen den Fronten, darüber. Ich stehe im Schweißgeruch der Menge und werfe Steine auf Polizisten Soldaten Panzer Panzerglas. Ich blicke durch die Flügeltür aus Panzerglas auf die andrängende Menge und rieche meinen Angstschweiß. Ich schüttle, von Brechreiz gewürgt, meine Faust gegen mich, der hinter dem Panzerglas steht" (HM 94 [56]).

on all sides, meaning he would really be on no side at all. The evacuation of the tragic hero is a reference to the bankruptcy of ideologies in a Europe in "ruins" where the man who wanted to be the subject of history is no more than its pawn, a frightened individual who is involved, more or less in spite of himself and without his own motivation, in events over which he has no control. As such, the Hamlet-Actor continues: "My drama didn't happen. The script has been lost. The actors put their faces on the rack in the dressing room. In his box, the prompter is rotting. The stuffed corpses in the house don't stir a hand. I go home and kill the time, and one/with my undivided self."[17] The tragic hero's retreat is described in the rest of the monologue as a resignation to be deadened by the entertainments offered in abundance by modern society:

> Television The daily nausea Nausea
> Of prefabricated babble
> Of decreed cheerfulness
> How do you spell GEMÜTLICHKEIT
> Give us this day our daily murder
> Since thine is nothingness Nausea
> Of the lies which are believed
> By the liars and nobody else Nausea [...]
> I go through streets supermarkets faces
> With the scars from the consumer battle poverty
> Without dignity poverty without dignity
> Of the knife the knuckles the fist
> The humiliated bodies of women
> Hope of generations
> Stifled in blood cowardice stupidity
> Laughter from dead bellies
> Hail COCA COLA
> A kingdom
> For a murderer[18]

---

[17] "Mein Drama hat nicht stattgefunden. Das Textbuch ist verlorengegangen. Die Schauspieler haben ihre Gesichter an den Nagel in der Garderobe gehängt. In seinem Kasten verfault der Souffleur. Die ausgestopften Pestleichen im Zuschauerraum bewegen keine Hand. Ich gehe nach Hause und schlage die Zeit tot, einig / Mit meinem ungeteilten Selbst" (HM 95 [56]).

[18] "Fernsehen Der tägliche Ekel Ekel /Am präparierten Geschwätz Am verordneten Frohsinn / Wie schreibt man GEMÜTLICHKEIT / Unsern Täglichen Mord gib uns heute / Denn Dein ist das Nichts Ekel / An den Lügen die geglaubt werden / Von den Lügnern und niemandem sonst Ekel [...] / Geh ich durch Straßen Kaufhallen Gesichter / Mit den Narben der Konsumschlacht Armut / Ohne Würde Armut ohne die Würde / Messers from der Schlagrings der Faust / Die erniedrigten Leiber der Frauen / Hoffnung der Generationen / In Blut Feigheit Dummheit erstickt / Gelächter aus toten Bäuchen / Heil COCA COLA / Ein Königreich / für einen Mörder" (HM 95 [56–57]).

The weariness expressed by the Hamlet-Actor, his disgust at his own cowardice, leads also to the disgust of the Author, whose photo appears on the stage at the precise moment when the actor pronounces these words:

> In the solitude of airports
> I breathe again I am
> A privileged person My nausea
> Is a privilege
> Protected by Wall
> Barbed wire Prisons[19]

This lucid vision of the Author's own revulsion, which in the communist system represents a "privilege" of the writer in the same way as the right to travel, gives rise to a self-destructive response – "Zerreißung der Fotografie des Autors" ("Tearing up of the photograph of the author," HM 93) – followed by an even more marked withdrawal by the Hamlet-Actor, which takes the form of a radical refusal to live:

> I force open my sealed flesh. I want to dwell in my veins, in the marrow of my bones, in the maze of my skull. I retreat into my entrails. I take my seat in my shit, in my blood. Somewhere bodies are torn apart so I can dwell in my shit. Somewhere bodies are opened so I can be alone with my blood. My thoughts are lesions in my brain. My brain is a scar. I want to be a machine. Arms for grabbing Legs to walk on, no pain no thoughts.[20]

This central monologue is located in the fourth scene, entitled "Pest in Buda/ Schlacht um Grönland" ("Pest in Buda/ Battle for Greenland"). Before this, the second scene, "Das Europa der Frau" ("The Europe of the Woman"), introduced in counterpoint the role of Ophelia, assumed by an actress who declares herself in the present: "Ich bin Ophelia" ("I am Ophelia"), and who describes her status as follows:

---

19 I have modified the translation of "Beschirmt mit Mauer...". "In der Einsamkeit der Flughäfen Atme ich auf Ich bin / Ein Privilegierter Mein Ekel / Ist ein Privileg / Beschirmt mit Mauer / Stacheldraht Gefängnis" (HM 93 [57]).

20 "Ich breche mein versiegeltes Fleisch auf. Ich will in meinen Adern wohnen, im Mark meiner Knochen, im Labyrinth meines Schädels. Ich ziehe mich zurück in meine Eingeweide. Ich nehme Platz in meiner Scheiße, meinem Blut. Irgendwo werden Leiber zerbrochen, damit ich wohnen kann in meiner Scheiße. Irgendwo werden Leiber geöffnet, damit ich allein sein kann mit meinem Blut. Meine Gedanken sind Wunden in meinem Gehirn. Mein Gehirn ist eine Narbe. Ich will eine Maschine sein. Weapon zu greifen Beine zu gehen kein Schmerz kein Gedanke" (HM 93 [57]).

> The one the river didn't keep. The woman dangling from the rope. The woman with her arteries cut open. The woman with the overdose. SNOW ON HER LIPS. The woman with her head in the gas stove. Yesterday I stopped killing myself. I'm alone with my breasts my thighs my womb. I smash the tools of my captivity, the chair the table the bed. I destroy the battlefield that was my home. I fling open the doors so the wind gets in and scream of the world.[21]

Faced with the empty shell that in a previous time "was" Hamlet but who today has surrendered all hopes of influencing the course of history, the resuscitation of "Ophelia" as a collective figure who brings together all the women sacrificed throughout history with the allusive evocation of some (Inge Müller, Rosa Luxemburg, Ulrike Meinhof),[22] is a way of giving victims a voice and having them proclaim their refusal to submit along with their determination to take their destinies into their own hands ("Yesterday I stopped killing myself"). With this rehabilitation of the female character, it is possible to see a feminist positioning of the author,[23] who in the third tableau ("Scherzo") has a character, who this time is named "Hamlet," declare: "I want to be a woman." However, it is difficult to support this optimistic reading when we see "Ophelia" changing at the very end into a decrepit "Electra" in a wheelchair, her body wrapped in bandages, delivering a speech of murderous madness behind which looms the figure of Susan Atkins, who was the accomplice to the murderer Charles Manson.[24] If this revenge of women on history as written and committed by men represents a vision of the future, it is difficult to see it as particularly hopeful. Rather, this outcome should probably be seen as a warning to those who play their parts in history against having contempt for victims and being unaware of their potential for de-

---

21 "Die der Fluß nicht behalten hat. Die Frau am Strick Die Frau mit den aufgeschnittenen Pulsadern Die Frau mit der Überdosis AUF DEN LIPPEN SCHNEE Die Frau mit dem Kopf im Gasherd. Gestern habe ich aufgehört mich zu töten. Ich bin allein mit meinen Brüsten meinen Schenkeln meinem Schoß. Ich zertrümmere die Werkzeuge meiner Gefangenschaft den Stuhl den Tisch das Bett. Ich zerstöre das Schlachtfeld das mein Heim war. Ich reiße die Türen auf, damit der Wind herein kann und der Schrei der Welt" (HM 91–92 [54]).
22 See the chapter "Une utopie négative? *Hamlet-machine* de Heiner Müller" in Baillet (2004: 67–103), 86.
23 See for example Raddatz (1991: 22).
24 "Hier spricht Elektra. Im Herzen der Finsternis. Unter der Sonne die Folter. An die Metropolen der Welt. Im Namen der Opfer. Ich stoße allen Samen aus, den ich empfangen habe. Ich verwandle die Milch meiner Brüste in tödliches Gift. Ich nehme die Welt zurück, die ich geboren habe. Ich ersticke die Welt, die ich geboren habe, zwischen meinen Schenkeln. Ich begrabe sie in meiner Scham. Nieder mit dem Glück der Unterwerfung. Es lebe der Haß, die Verachtung, der Aufstand, der Tod. Wenn sie mit Fleischermessern durch eure Schlafzimmer geht, werdet ihr die Wahrheit wissen" (HM 97). The last sentence of this tirade is an exact quote from Susan Atkins.

struction, as well as perhaps an appeal to the public to seek at last – beyond the horizon of the text – a viable alternative to the inextricable cycle of violence.[25]

Like Müller, Özdamar went through a first phase of rewriting in which she still followed the dramatic hypotext fairly closely. Her *Hamlet/Ahmet* is "Hamlet in Turkey" in the same way that Müller's first *Hamlet* was "Hamlet in Budapest." In a second phase, she left behind theatrical writing for first-person narration, just as Müller distances himself from the traditional dramatic form (with dialogue)[26] in *Hamletmaschine*, since *Hamlet* is no longer performed but instead narrated in the form of monologues and in this way "destroyed."[27] Finally, she does not transpose the hypotext's action to the contemporary era and instead proposes a "sequel."

This rewriting in the form of a sequel is based on two major pragmatic modifications that likewise coincide with those that Müller made in *Hamletmaschine:* the removal of Hamlet as a central figure and the "resurrection" of Ophelia. Though the status accorded to these two main modifications and the consequences that result are different in each of the two cases (a perspective overlooking history versus a low-angle view), the enunciative mode that dominates in the two texts is nonetheless very similar. The form of diction is artificial and detached, which stands out in Özdamar simply through a jerkier rhythm and a "foreign" tinge. The first words of *Karriere einer Putzfrau* nonetheless resonate as an echo to the tirades of *Hamletmaschine:* "I am the cleaning lady, if I do not do the cleaning here, what else would I do? In my country I was Ophelia."[28] In both

---

25 See the chapter "Hamlet-machine, 'Adieu à la pièce didactique'?" in Maier-Schaeffer (1992: 237–273). Challenging the assumption that *Hamletmaschine* marks Müller's final distancing from Brecht's *Lehrstück* aesthetic, Maier-Schaeffer observes: "La vue d'Ophélie/Electre réduite, après la proclamation de sa liberté, dans son fauteuil roulant à l'immobilité et au silence, produit plus d'effet sur le spectateur que la démonstration d'une libération réussie. La retombée insoutenable de l'élan libérateur – 'rouler toujours la même pierre au sommet de toujours la même montagne' – est infiniment plus productive dans le sens même de Brecht, où le spectateur est appelé à imaginer une 'contre-proposition'" (264).
26 "Was ich schon in Bulgarien gemerkt hatte, war die Unmöglichkeit, mit dem Stoff zu Dialogen zu kommen, den Stoff in die Welt des sogenannten real existierenden Sozialismus-Stalinismus zu transportieren. Es gab da keine Dialoge mehr. Ich habe immer wieder zu Dialogen angesetzt, es ging nicht, es gab keinen Dialog, nur noch monologische Blöcke." (Müller 1992: 294)
27 "Mein Hauptinteresse beim Stückeschreiben ist es, Dinge zu zerstören. Dreißig Jahre lang war Hamlet eine Obsession für mich, also schrieb ich einen kurzen Text, Hamletmaschine, mit dem ich versucht habe, Hamlet zu zerstören" (Müller 1982: 81).
28 "Ich bin die Putzfrau, wenn ich hier nicht putze, was soll ich denn sonst tun? In meinem Land war ich Ophelia" (KP 110). This first statement already leads to a rhetorical question that does not quite correspond to the reader's expectations. One would rather expect a question such as: "Wenn ich hier nicht putze, wer soll es denn sonst tun?" ("If I didn't clean here, then

cases, Shakespeare's drama only remains on the horizon of the new activity as a contrasting frame of reference for the spectator and as a now-unattainable model for characters reduced to performing phantasmagorical "roles."

Opheliamachine: Giving a Voice back to the Subaltern

If the play *Hamlet/Ahmet* was an update of Shakespeare's tragedy reread through the Brechtian prism, the story *Karriere einer Putzfrau* can then be read as a response to Heiner Müller's rewriting of the same play. The point of view that is represented is, first of all, that of a woman (and not a male projection of a supposed female position), and furthermore, it is that of a woman who comes from a country that is doubly inferiorized because it is both exploited economically by Europe and abandoned to the military dictatorship by an indifferent and cynical international community.

This time, the removal of Hamlet is complete. Once the separation has been made, there is no further mention of him until he reappears in the dream sequence in the guise of a puppet who makes absurd speeches while getting drunk on brandy and simulating orgasms (KA 124). The regressive structure, developed not without pathos, in Müller's work as an attitude of disgusted withdrawal reaching the point of self-annihilation ("I withdraw into my intestines [...]"), here takes the otherwise banal form of "mama's-boy" infantilism. In the eyes of the woman he repudiated out of opportunism, "Hamlet" is only a spineless man obsessed with his personal comfort who, wanting to "think about his future, about the day when he imagines his own funeral," lets himself be distracted by the prosaic preoccupations of the petty bourgeois who are force-fed by consumer society.[29]

The individual who takes center stage throughout the story, this woman who "was Ophelia" in her country, is not a revolutionary either. Neither is she suici-

---

who else would do it?"). By replacing the commonplace discourse about immigrants (to whom society delegates "dirty work" while also easing its conscience) with a question centered on the speaker herself, Özdamar focuses on the social conditions of the cleaning woman rather than on the interests of the national collective.

29 "Ophelia sagt zu ihm: 'Hamlet, tue nicht so – gib dir nicht Mühe, ich weiß, du willst gerade an dein [sic] Morgen, wo du dir dein Begräbnis vorstellst, denken – aber du denkst, daß du bei der Sparkasse vorbeigehen sollst und vom Delikatessenladen den Expresso-Cafe holen sollst, weil du denkst – warum nicht, wenn ich es mir leisten kann, dann willst du mit deiner Mama telephonieren, weil sie jemand kennt, der die Adresse weiß von einer Dreizimmerwohnung, und du willst deinen Lieblingskäse holen, bevor du mit deiner Mama telephonierst [...]'" (KA 124).

dal, however, nor a terrorist, and she is by no means "the future of man," whether for good or ill. She is just a woman who literally has her hands in garbage, urine, and feces. Reduced herself to the status of refuse by her pseudo-intellectual husband, she must turn to the most subaltern job there is: that of cleaning up others' "shit." Serving as a projection surface for male and imperialist domination fantasies, she struggles to survive through all the violence she suffers and to make her way in this world of abjection through practical intelligence and derision.

The point of view the author offers us of the world through this frenzied "Opheliamachine,"[30] enshrined in a hopelessly trivial narrative framework, is not at odds with the one provided by Heiner Müller in *Hamletmaschine*; actually, it completes it. Özdamar thus engages in an intertextual dialogue of equals with an innovative writer and playwright whom she esteems and admires[31] and whose work has been a source of inspiration for her, particularly insofar as it encouraged her to look at history (especially German history). What she adds to the disillusioned play by the East German author is not, strictly speaking, a message of hope, but it does not serve to escalate its pessimism either. The focus is at the ground level, where the gaze of a cleaning woman for whom the world is reduced to an interminable parade of feet is fixed,[32] and this perspective acts as an obstacle to any heroization – of either the powerful or the victims – but also any melancholy grandiloquence.

Seen from this angle, the story is not so much a matter of revolution, blood, and tears as of excrement, urine, and sperm, and the "dream" (or "scherzo") of the one for whom this is the sole horizon takes the form of an anarchic disarray of the immense "public urinal for men" to which the drama of the world is reduced for her. All the gravity and all the pathos still persisting in Müller, even in a nostalgic form, have disappeared. When the "shit" we get stuck in is not

---

30 A play bearing this title was written by the Polish-born American playwright, dramaturgue, and scholar Magda Romanska. Designed as a ic response to Müller's *Hamletmachine*, Romanska's work premiered at the City Garage Company, Santa Monica, CA, June 2013.

31 On Özdamar's perception of Müller's work, see for example the diary entry dated 20 May 1976 in *Seltsame Sterne*: "Er zeigt die Realität hinter der Realität" (SSE 118), or her reflections after the dress rehearsal of Müller's *The Farmers* (24 May 1976): "Der erste Durchlauf hat fünfeinhalb Stunden gedauert. Man sieht, daß eine intensive Arbeit gemacht worden ist, aber was werden die Zuschauer denken? Ich kann darauf keine Antwort geben. Können sie diese Länge aushalten? Wollen sie etwas über die Geschichte der DDR sehen? Ich kenne die deutschen Zuschauer nicht. Der Text von Müller ist hinreißend" (SSE 126).

32 "[...] da habe ich einen Eimer gekriegt. Die Treppen. Lange, lange Treppen. Viele Füße. Füße rauf, Füße runter. Eine Nacht habe ich geträumt, im Zimmer liefen zwei Füße nur bis zum Knie" (KP 117).

only metaphorical, the only way out is through laughter. The disgust is not a disgust at one's own cowardice and does not result in the temptation to return to nothingness and to become oneself "a machine" or to flat out destroy the world, as with Müller's Ophelia/Electra, but only the desire to resist the humiliations somehow without sinking into madness or death. The question that then arises is not so much whether it is possible to overthrow an unjust regime but whether those, especially women, who have the most reasons to rise up even have the means to articulate their bitterness and their outrage. Or, more precisely: Under what conditions could they articulate their revolt *so as to be heard?*

In short, the question that Özdamar poses in this corrosively candid narrative more or less echoes the one raised by Gayatri C. Spivak in the well-known text, *Can the Subaltern Speak?* (1988). As Spivak subsequently explained in a less metaphorical fashion, this question is asked with the knowledge that subalterns, i.e. those who are excluded from the public sphere, actually "speak for themselves" because they have "as much of an interior life as anyone else" (Milevska 2003: 36). Yet they do not have the means to have their resistance recognized as such because there is "no infrastructure to produce recognition" (Milevska, Chakravorty, and Barlow 2006: 72). The answer is therefore no: because subalterns are by definition those whose lack of access to the public sphere prevents them from being heard, they cannot "speak" *so as to be heard*.

As far as Özdamar is concerned, the answer is not provided in the text. Following a Brechtian logic, it is left to the discretion of the reader, who is free to deduce that the answer, if there is an answer, lies partly in the very composition of this short story, whereby the author was able herself to escape, in life as in the theater, from working as a cleaning woman and thus give a "voice" to the proletarian immigrants relegated to the margins of German society through her work as a playwright and writer on the German literary scene. Yet even more significantly, the answer – since again Özdamar is not speaking about herself in this text, as she was never a subaltern in the Spivakian sense of the term – is up to the readers because the answer depends upon them above all: when women like this Turkish Ophelia speak, they only have the chance to be heard if society is ready to listen. It is precisely towards this goal, eminently Brechtian indeed, that the story leads.

The reference to *Hamletmaschine* is therefore constitutive of this story, and it is only by accounting for the intertextual game with Müller's play that it becomes possible to assess the central inquiry. Such a reading undoubtedly makes it impossible to subscribe to a judgment like that of Norbert Mecklenburg, who, obviously embarrassed by the scatological excesses of the text, attributed the heroine-narrator's "desperate aggressiveness" to a blow to the ego that Özdamar the *actress* suffered due to the temporary interruption of her career following her voluntary emigration from Turkey. Believing that there was not enough emphasis in this text on the emancipatory effects of immigration that the author nevertheless benefited from, he argues that "all Turkish cleaning women in Germany were not Ophelia in their country of origin" and warns against the disrespect that he believed was involved in such a caricatural depiction of immigrants' working conditions.[33] This biographical and moralizing interpretation appears to reveal the blindness that resulted among even the most discerning critics due to the overexposure of the "ethnic" component in the works of writers from immigrant backgrounds, to the detriment of poetological reflection and of contemporary Western references.

Intertextual Constellations in *Seltsame Sterne starren zur Erde:* Searching for Beacons in the Night

As the third volume of the reputedly "autobiographical" – one might more cautiously apply the term "autofictional"[34] – cycle that begins with *Das Leben ist eine Karawanserei* and continues with *Die Brücke vom Goldenen Horn*, *Seltsame Sterne starren zur Erde* (2003) presents itself as the reconstruction of an initiatory journey spanning 1976–1977 that leads the narrator, a young actress who has escaped the Turkish military dictatorship, into divided Berlin. The cultural excitement that prevails in this city and the alternative lifestyles being experimented with there make it possible for her to emerge from her existential crisis. Germany is no longer the country she had encountered ten years before as a contract immigrant worker in the flourishing industry of the FRG. It is the epicenter of the Cold War, and in the West, there is a superficially pacified society, divided in the aftermath of 1968 between fatalistic resignation, libertarian utopias, and terrorist excesses, and in the East a society with an economic stabilization obtained at the cost of international isolation and ideological regimentation. There is a

---

33 See Mecklenburg (2006: 92–93)
34 The best explanation of the narrower *sense* in which *I use this term, which was coined by Serge Doubrovsky in the late 1970s,* is provided by Martina Wagner-Egelhaaf (2006: 361) ["Autofiktion ist dann nicht mehr zu verstehen im Sinne defizitärer 'nur'-Sprachlichkeit, 'bloßer' Konstruiertheit, als Ausstellen von Differenz, sondern im produktiven Sinne einer möglichen Selbstsetzung, die es einem Subjekt erst erlaubt, sich mittels der und im Spiegel der Sprache zu positionieren. Dies bedeutet aber auch, dass es autofiktionalem Schreiben heute nicht mehr um die Alternative 'Wirklichkeit' oder 'Fiktion' geht. [...] Das heißt aber auch, dass die autobiographische Lesart eine Option ist, eine Option neben anderen. Wir können den autobiographischen Pakt schließen, müssen es aber nicht."].

progressively broadening gap between the intellectuals and a majority of the population on the one hand, and an increasingly repressive state apparatus ignoring the aspirations for democracy and the establishment of "socialism with a human face," on the other. This split, accentuated by the Socialist Unity Party's support for the Prague Spring crackdown, culminated in the Biermann affair that began in November 1976.

Meanwhile, the narrator is no longer the intrepid young girl in search of autonomy and new experiences as portrayed in *Die Brücke vom Goldenen Horn*. Her theatrical training and the political turmoil she has encountered have made her more mature. She has experienced the stage, an initiation into Marxism-Leninism, fighting alongside the poor peasants of eastern Turkey, powerful romantic relationships, and the military coup of 12 March 1971 together with the wave of repression that followed. She arrives in Berlin ravaged by the experience of prison and a romantic separation that is all the more painful because it resulted from forced isolation and political terror. Now, the reason for her departure is not the need for money or thirst for adventure, but the desire to escape a state of exhaustion resulting from a noxious lack of mobility. In Istanbul, she was condemned to go underground and to live in isolation, and when she goes to Germany she leaves behind a man she loves (and who is himself in distress), along with her family and friends, most of whom are incarcerated. She chooses Berlin this time with the plan to "learn Brecht's theater"[35] with the director Benno Besson, who had been Brecht's disciple and is then working as director of the Volksbühne in East Berlin. Her plan is thus not just to resume her activity and give meaning back to her life, but also to make some contribution to the resistance movement in Turkey against the military by letting her friends in the theater benefit, upon being released from prison, from the inspiration she hopes to draw on there.

It is therefore both a lifeline and, paradoxically, the breath of freedom that the narrator seeks in East Berlin, in the heart of a state in the midst of political glaciation – the freedom of artists and intellectuals who are in conflict with the authorities of their country yet perpetuate the very revolutionary ideals on which the GDR was founded and which underlie the fight her friends are waging in Turkey. In a very subjective manner that, nonetheless, refrains from idealization, Özdamar portrays the atmosphere of the avant-garde intellectual circles of East Berlin – so very stimulating for her – that has arisen from these unusual circumstances. The way she looks at their situation, and at the city in general,

---

35 "'Herr Besson', sagte ich, 'ich bin gekommen, um von Ihnen das Brechttheater zu lernen'" (SSE 34).

is determined by the exceptional freedom conferred on her by her own foreign status in Berlin at the time. Fleeing a military dictatorship, she comes to work in East Berlin but must find a place to stay in West Berlin for the amount of time needed to obtain the official commitment required to authorize a stay in the GDR. For several months, she lives in a student community in the Wedding district of West Berlin and leaves every morning for East Berlin to work at the Volksbühne. The ease with which the young woman is able to pass through the Iron Curtain every day in both directions gives this border, then dividing Germany and the world, an unreal and almost ridiculous character in light of the issues that come to the fore elsewhere: resistance against the military regime in Turkey, learning "Brecht's theater," the end of her personal crisis. This does not mean that the treatment of Germans' concerns (East and West) is indifferent or condescending. The subjective nature of the point of view does not lead to selfishness, and there is the constant presence of attention to others, be they unknown or famous. All the interest of the path described in this third part of the trilogy resides in these multiple paradoxes, which could be traced to a fertile asymmetry between the positive valuation of a personal experience of Germany at a given moment (it is the actualization of a "dream" for the narrator)[36] and the total absence of indulgence in the gaze directed at the country's political and social situation.

If she had illusions about Germany, especially regarding the East German regime, prior to her arrival, Özdamar lets none of them appear in this book, nor the disappointment resulting from her confrontation with the real. Faithful to the narrative mode that characterize her previous texts, she limits herself to reporting "facts" that are raw but in no way objective (meetings, dialogues, readings, impressions, visions, dreams, etc.) and refrains from providing commentary or rational analyses. In this way, she extends the illusion of a "naïve" form of writing that the text nevertheless denies on several levels. The impression of guilelessness that emerges from this account, which is simultaneously chatty and laconic, is in fact contradicted not only by the very content of the story – the state of mind, the level of contemplation, and the concerns it reflects – but also by the

---

[36] "Josef saß auf meinem Bett und fragte mich: 'Und dein Traum, in Berlin das Brechttheater zu lernen?' – 'Nur dieser Traum kann mir helfen. Wenn die Zeit in einem Land in die Nacht eintritt, suchen sogar die Steine eine neue Sprache'" (SSE 28). This dream comes true at the end of the first part, as she starts taking an active part in the staging: "Auf dem Korridor sah ich Benno Besson. Er gab mir die Hand, in der Hand hielt er eine Schachtel Gauloises. Als er ging, sah ich ihm nach, als ob ich in einem Träum wäre, der Traum, den ich in der Türkei gehabt hatte. Diesen Traum wollte ich aufschreiben und begann in den Nächten, ein Tagebuch zu führen" (SSE 84).

sophistication of a narrative technique that calls for different levels of reading. This complexity is mainly due to the entanglement of the first-degree narrative with multiple intertextual references that have different statuses. While the evocation of literary works and artists' personalities has always been an important part of Özdamar's narratives, here the inter- and metatextual dimension occupies such a central position that at times it takes precedence over the narrative itself. The narration is interspersed with so many references to literary works of all kinds that it would end up being crushed under the mass of quotes, comments, summaries, sketches and portraits of artists if this metatextual component did not constitute, now more than ever, an integral part of the story that is being told. For what is at stake here, now more than ever, is the becoming of an artist, the genesis of a creative personality that builds on the productive reception of diverse literary impulses. And it is to the extent that it is an artist's autobiography – or autofiction – that this book stands out in generic terms from its two predecessors, *Das Leben ist eine Karawanserei* and *Die Brücke vom Goldenen Horn*. This specificity is indicated in the title, since the enigmatic and poetic statement "strange stars stare to Earth" is taken from a poem by Else Lasker-Schüler (1869–1945). This "planetary" title (Ette 2005: 191–192), borrowed from an early twentieth-century German poet, thus functions in several respects as a writer / reader contract. It indicates that the text is a writer's autobiography and that the inter- or metatextual dimension is decisive. It also underlines that the quest for markers traced there is anchored in German literary history.[37] Finally, the ethico-poeticological project asserts itself therein while building on an individual work by an eminently atypical German Jewish writer and artist, and precursor of Expressionism. We will address the meaning such a multifaceted reference assumes within the context of the story.

Beforehand, it is worth pointing out that the way in which the inter- and metatextual references are incorporated into this seemingly autobiographical tale induces a generic fluctuation between the narrative mode of "classic" autobiography and memoir (which emphasizes the historical and intellectual context rather than the "development of the [author's] personality,"[38] and diaristic writing. The

---

[37] This contrasts with the self-Orientalizing gesture that characterizes the titles of both previous novels, *Life Is a Caravanserai* and *The Bridge of the Golden Horn*.
[38] Philippe Lejeune (1975: 14) defined autobiography as "le récit rétrospectif en prose qu'une personne réelle fait de sa propre existence, lorsqu'elle met l'accent sur sa vie individuelle, en particulier sur l'histoire de sa personnalité" ["A retrospective prose narrative produced by a real person concerning his own existence, focusing on the individual life, in particular on the development of his personality." Lejeune, "The Autobiographical Contract" (Todorov 1982: 192–222, here 193)].

book is in fact made up of two parts and only the first, which is divided into three chapters, consists of a retrospective, first-person narrative conforming to the traditional model of autobiography; the second presents itself as a diary kept by the author after the period covered by the first part. Both a diary and "logbook" of her participation in Fritz Marquardt's staging of Heiner Müller's *Die Bauern* ("The Farmers"), which was her first experience of direct collaboration with the Volksbühne troupe, this second diaristic section takes over as the narrator disappears so as to make way for the "authentic" account of her experiences of the time and cannot be considered ancillary since it makes up more than two-thirds of the book. Yet the formal heterogeneity does not stop there. Within this quasi-documentary second part, the writing is accompanied and complemented by the reproduction of numerous pencil sketches, most of which represent scenic configurations and were produced by the assistant-trainee as part of her work at the Volksbühne, while others are portraits of artists taken from life on the sidelines of rehearsals. The "diary" or "logbook" provided in the second part of the book is therefore in reality a mixture of text and images, and this places it in the line of a type of autobiography inaugurated in France by Stendhal with *Vie de Henry Brulard* ("The Life of Henry Brulard") and notably exemplified in the German context by the half-poetic, half-graphic work of Else Lasker-Schüler.

The inter- and metatextual component of *Seltsame Sterne starren zur Erde* thus is placed within the context of a generalized formal heterogeneity that can be viewed as programmatic. Adding to the linguistic-cultural hybridity that prevailed, at least in appearance, in Özdamar's previous works (if not by the choice of titles alone: *Karagöz in Alamania, Keloglan in Alamania, Mutterzunge, Das Leben ist eine Karawanserei, Die Brücke vom Goldenen Horn*), is the affirmation here of a much more extensive hybridization that concerns the literary genres involved (poetry, theater, novel, autobiography, memoir, diary) as well as the modes of expression employed (writing, drawing) and even the status of the discourse (literary or documentary, self or foreign, individual or collective). The montage technique actually goes so far as to question the individual status of the work since the border between the author's autonomous expression and what relates in one way or another to reported speech is blurred by the omnipresence of all kinds of intertextual references: staging notes, readings, direct quotes from author's verbal statements or texts, allusive or explicit references to literary works, etc. This "scrambling" has programmatic value in itself. The work, which recounts a personal adventure that is both very lonely and eminently collective, a woman's experience working for her comrades-in-arms in Turkey from Berlin, where she joins new groups, is in its very form a profession of faith in favor of intellectual emulation, political solidarity, and "elective affinities" of all kinds.

In accordance with this program, this time the references to literary heritage are in no way acerbic. The purpose is not to demystify official culture by denouncing the violence of certain latent contents, but to recount a human experience that can be described as a rebirth, or more precisely the reconstruction of a devastated subject through a process of cultural, and especially literary, education. The devastated state in which the narrator finds herself on the eve of her departure for Germany is described very directly, in the flashback of the second chapter, as a loss of the voice, of the ability to communicate through speech. The daily experience of police brutality, arrests, executions, and brutal "disappearances" plunges individuals into an existential distress much deeper than despair because it annihilates them as subjects. The trivialization of murder and torture creeps into the unconscious:

> I'm miserable in my language. For years we've only said sentences like: They're going to hang them. Where were the heads? Nobody knows where their grave is. The police have not released the body! The words are sick. My words need a sanatorium, like sick shells. [...] How long does a word need to get well again? They say you lose your mother tongue in foreign countries. Can't you also lose your mother tongue in your own country?[39]

Deprived of the possibility of expressing themselves, individuals are severed from their internal lives and literally stupefied, to the point of losing all their points of reference. "The fruit on the stands in the street seemed strange to me. What was the pomegranate doing there? The grapes? Who was going to enjoy them? Like the people on the streets who had fallen from bullets, the fruit fell from the bags of a man who ran away in fear."[40] Dehumanized individuals can lose the ability to love: "[E]verything stands still during a military putsch. Even love."[41] But the narrator attributes the fundamental need she has to leave Turkey to a loss of her cognitive and especially linguistic bearings

---

39 "Ich bin unglücklich in meiner Sprache. Wir sagen seit Jahren nur solche Sätze wie: Sie werden sie aufhängen. Wo waren die Köpfe? Man weiß nicht, wo ihr Grab ist. Die Polizei hat die Leiche nicht freigegeben! Die Wörter sind krank. Meine Wörter brauchen ein Sanatorium, wie kranke Muscheln. [...] Wie lange braucht ein Wort, um wieder gesund zu werden? Man sagt, in fremden Ländern verliert man die Muttersprache. Kann man nicht auch in seinem eigenen Land die Muttersprache verlieren?" (SSE 23).
40 "Das Obst auf den Ständen in den Straßen kam mir komisch vor. Was suchten dort ein Granatapfel, die Weintrauben? Wem sollten sie schmecken? Wie die Menschen, die auf den Straßen durch Kugeln umfielen, fiel auch das Obst aus den Tüten eines Mannes, der vor Angst davonrannte" (SSE 26).
41 "Josef, während eines Militärputsches steht alles still. Auch die Liebe" (SSE 26–27).

(the possession of which is a condition for the ability to love): "When in a country time enters into the night, even the stones seek a new language."[42]

The subject setting out on the journey recounted in this book is thus "disoriented" and "petrified." While it is not yet known what form this journey will take, its objective is determined in advance. It is a question of acquiring a "new language," not in the narrow linguistic sense of the term, but a system of expression and communication making it possible to come out of a state of shock and to come to grips with reality. In other words, the "new language" that is sought is not a foreign language. It is, more specifically – and at this stage still, only – "Brecht's theater." The learning process thus initiated will not stop with Brecht, though he can function as a landmark, as a beacon in the night, because the narrator is already very familiar with his work and his theory of theater, which at the time enjoyed great popularity in leftist intellectual circles in Turkey. Above all, Brecht can serve as a model because he developed a notion of theater based on a revolutionary ideal of emancipation of the individual through an awareness of one's alienation. Moreover, because Brecht's biography in Europe for the years 1930–1950 (fight against Nazism, exile, commitment to a reconstruction of Germany according to democratic and socialist principles with his settlement in the GDR and the establishment of the Berliner Ensemble) presents some similarities to the narrator's. Brecht's status as "master" is reaffirmed throughout the narrative, in particular with the evocation of a dream in which the narrator sees herself visiting the great man, whom she finds deceased on his deathbed with his wife, Helene Weigel, watching over him. In this new variant of a dream already reported in very similar terms in *Mein Berlin* (2001: 60–61),[43] Brecht then "awakens" and the narrator can address him directly (using the familiar "du"), asking him to give her "something of [his]," his tie or his pillow. The symbolic power of this gift, which seals the bond of transmission between the German dramaturge and the young actress, is further accentuated on the formal level by the fact that this time, the very narration of this dream is addressed to Brecht himself.[44]

This first reference point remains essential, and a number of others, with varying statuses, appear subsequently in the work. I will mainly examine the two that, after Brecht, constitute the major references for Özdamar's *Bildungsroman:* Lasker-Schüler and Heine. My inquiry into these references encapsulates

---

[42] "Wenn die Zeit in einem Land in die Nacht eintritt, suchen sogar die Steine eine neue Sprache" (SSE 28).

[43] On this episode, see chapter 2: "Encounters in Fantasies and Dreams."

[44] "Brecht, als du starbst, war ich zehn Jahre alt. Ich von Dir geträumt, vor ein paar Wochen" (SSE 115).

my approach to the canon and its discontents in this book. First, I will examine the case of Lasker-Schüler; then I will explore the path that leads to a reaffirmation of the links with Heine, woven in a more subterranean way into the framework of the story, in a minor and very ironic mode. I will end with the ways in which this second, more or less encrypted reference, echoing the knowing allusions that are interspersed throughout the play *Keloglan in Alamania*, appeals to (and includes) a third, which has a very different intertextual and axiological status: the tales of the Brothers Grimm.

In the Orbit of Else Lasker-Schüler, "Poetess of Arabia"

The very words of the verse quoted in the title, *Seltsame Sterne starren zur Erde*, place the story under the sign of a quest for direction or meaning that immediately characterizes itself as "planetary," as noted above. More precisely, these words create the troubling vision of an upended world where it is not people who scan the sky for luminous bodies and constellations but the reverse. This vaguely disturbing image of a dehumanized and disoriented world will take on its full meaning in relation to the situation of terror and chaos evoked in the second chapter of the narrative. Within the story, reading Lasker-Schüler is anchored in this context of shock, since the narrator discovers her work shortly after leaving Turkey, in "her" Wedding flat, thanks to a roommate, Peter, who will become her first Berlin lover (SSE 58). Lasker-Schüler's fiery and melancholy poetry thus functions as a second "beacon" in the night, the promise of another possible world where desire might regain its rights.

If the context in which the narrator was initiated into this poet's work is not explained until the third chapter (the action of which is chronologically anterior), the image elicited by the title is clarified with the first lines of the story, which resituate the statement "Strange Stars Stare to Earth" in the context of the poem *Sterne des Fatums* ("Stars of Fatum," 1902), reproduced here in full:

> Your eyes before my life
> Like nights, that long for the day,
> And the humid dream lies on top of them
> Unfathomed.
> Strange stars stare to the earth,
> Ironcolored with trails of desire,
> With burning arms, that are looking for love

And reach for the cool of the air.
Star in which the fate flows.⁴⁵

The first three lines of the second stanza – "Seltsame Sterne starren zur Erde,/ Eisenfarbene mit Sehnsuchtsschweifen,/ Mit brennenden Armen die Liebe suchen" – are explicitly quoted by Özdamar at the beginning of the first chapter, which opens with a scene of insomnia. Huddled up in bed on a freezing winter night in a large, unheated West Berlin apartment, the narrator is kept awake by the sorrowful barking of a dog in the courtyard.⁴⁶ "Else Lasker-Schüler's book" (SSE 9) is on her pillow; she had learned a few verses by heart before falling asleep and begins to recite them now, louder and louder, to drown out the sound of the dog's cries. The apartment is a part of "her" student community, which has replaced a community affiliated with the Actionist movement in the building.⁴⁷ The inhabitants have gone to spend the holiday season with their families in West Germany, leaving the building empty.

Like a magic ritual designed to ward off danger, speaking "Elses Wörter" ("Else's words," SSE 9) aloud has a soothing effect, if not on the dog, then at least on the young woman. The process is then resumed with other poems that are even more explicitly associated with the experience of the sacred, such as *Sterne des Tartaros* ("Stars of Tartarus"), which is also provided in partial quotation, detached from the running text.⁴⁸ The function assigned to the expressionist poet's work is thus located in the sphere of affect, with its lyrical power invoked as a remedy against anxiety, despair, abandonment, and loneliness. Its power comes from the identification of the young narrator, who finds herself alone in Berlin far from her family and loved ones, with the individual who wrote these verses.

---

45 "Deine Augen harren vor meinem Leben / Wie Nächte, die sich nach Tagen sehnen, / Und der schwüle Traum liegt auf ihnen unergründet. / Seltsame Sterne starren zur Erde, / Eisenfarbene mit Sehnsuchtsschweifen, / Mit brennenden Armen die Liebe suchen / Und in die Kühle der Lüfte greifen. / Sterne in denen das Schicksal mündet" (*The German Student Movement and the Literary Imagination* 2013: 143).
46 The incipit reads: "Der Hund bellte und hörte nicht auf" (SSE 9).
47 "Vor diesen sieben Leuten hatten hier andere Menschen gewohnt, die AA-Kommune" (SSE 10). This refers to the "Aktionsanalytische Organisation," a commune founded by the Austrian performance artist Otto Mühl in 1972. Its stated aim was free love, the destruction of bourgeois marriage and private property, and the collective education of children. The group fell apart in the early 1990s after Mühl was convicted of sexually abusing minors and sentenced to seven years of imprisonment.
48 "Warum suchst du mich in unseren Nächten, / In Wolken des Hasses auf bösen Sternen! / Laß mich allein mit den Geistern fechten" (SSE 15).

The niece of a rabbi and daughter of an assimilated Jewish banker from Wuppertal, Lasker-Schüler freed herself after a first marriage from her original bourgeois milieu to pursue a bohemian's vagabond and raucous lifestyle among avant-garde writers and painters. She had created the persona of an exotic and androgynous character whom she sometimes called "Tino, Princess of Baghdad" (AKA "Poetess of Arabia"), sometimes "Youssouf, Prince of Thebes," based on Joseph from the Hebrew Bible, known for his gift of dream interpretation and his ability to survive in exile as a Jew. She sketched these two alter egos in the margins of her texts and personified them throughout Berlin by sporting billowy pants and extravagant jewelry in cafes. This hybrid figure was at the center of an imaginary world she created from the kitschy images and tales that communicated a mythical Orient prevailing in the popular culture of the time (see Kirschnick 2007), and around this figure there gravitated friends and lovers who also had fancy nicknames and honorary titles. Her first collection of poems, *Styx* (1902), is haunted by mourning, the pain of failed romances, and a metaphysical nostalgia that takes shape in the motif of wandering. This initial publication was long before Hitler's takeover lead to the banning of her books and forced her into exile. In 1945, she died utterly destitute in Jerusalem, leaving behind a body of work with prophetic and visionary overtones, inextricably linked to her painful personal trajectory, where the annihilation of European Judaism (first by stigmatization and exclusion, then by forced acculturation, and finally extermination) was experienced as a personal catastrophe.[49]

If "Else," as Özdamar refers to her in a familiar tone, can be the reassuring and friendly presence that the first pages of her initiatory tale summon, it is surely because she exemplifies the model of an emancipated woman who is rebellious and passionate, but also because of the nature of her artistic project. The narrator emphasizes this aspect by citing the laudatory remarks of Gottfried Benn (who remains unnamed) about the woman who had once been his lover: "This was the greatest female poet Germany has ever had. Her subjects were often Jewish, her imagination Oriental, but her language was German, a luxuriant, sumptuous, tender German..."[50] Beyond the biographical context invoked at this point in the story (the narrator's situation in 1976), this homage by a renowned poet to the work of Lasker-Schüler, reproduced on the back cover of her volume of poetry, contains a number of elements that echo the subjects

---

[49] See in particular the collection *Hebräische Balladen* (1920), comprised of poems written between 1905 and 1913.
[50] "Dies war die größte Lyrikerin, die Deutschland je hatte. Ihre Themen waren vielfach jüdisch, ihre Phantasie orientalisch, aber ihre Sprache war deutsch, ein üppiges, prunkvolles, zartes Deutsch..." (SSE 15).

that interested the Turkish-German writer when she wrote this text: the expressionist poet's committed stance to assume her Jewishness through her thematic choices, the predominating "Oriental" nature of her sources of inspiration and, last but not least, her particular treatment of the German language, characterized by emotional intensity (pathos/ecstasy), the suggestive power of metaphors, and the subject's complete commitment to the writing project. It is partly in the wake of this model that Özdamar situated her own writing project, which she developed book after book with more or less romanticized variations to enact a transfigured subjectivity.

The strategic insertion of this episode in the incipit of the autobiographical narrative suggests that the homage is directed at the expressionist aesthetic and imagination, which Lasker-Schüler was a pioneer in and which Özdamar claims her affinity with in her writing as much as in her way of thinking, as well as at the unique position the poet occupies in the German literary and social landscape of the early twentieth century, this specific "outsideness" that she experienced simultaneously as poet, woman, Jew and nomad. As Ottmar Ette writes,

> Where Brecht stands for the theatricality in Özdamar's writing – for her attentiveness to the materiality and substantiality of the stage props; the epic distance of the representational process; the intertwining of aesthetics with political action and, last but not least, the alienation effects that emphasize the frictionality of Özdamar's writing time and again and undermine any potential identification – Else Lasker-Schüler, migrant, Jew, and woman, stands for that intense exotopy that the chosen 'planetary' title of the novel signals: Strange stars stare down upon the Earth.[51]

For a young woman in the 1970s who was passionate about theater and literature, loving Lasker-Schüler also and inextricably meant being fascinated by the "shimmering, exotic, and extravagant"[52] character she had invented, this fig-

---

[51] "Steht Brecht für die Theatralität des Özdamarschen Schreibens, insbesondere für die Aufmerksamkeit gegenüber der Materialität und Stofflichkeit der Bühnenrequisiten, für die epische Distanz der Darstellungsverfahren, die Verschränkungen von ästhetischem und politischem Handeln und nicht zuletzt für jene Verfremdungseffekte, welche die Friktionalität des Özdamarschen Schreibens betonen und stattfindende Identifikationsprozesse immer wieder unterbinden, so steht Else Lasker-Schüler als Dichterin, als Migrantin, als Jüdin und als Frau für jene intensive Außerhalbbefindlichkeit, von welcher der gewählte ‚planetarische' Romantitel kündet: *Seltsame Sterne starren zur Erde*" (Ette 2005: 191).

[52] These are the opening words of the "Declaration of love" to Lasker-Schüler that Elfriede Jelinek pronounced at the award ceremony upon receiving the Else Lasker-Schüler Prize in 2003 ["Als Schülerin habe ich eine bunte exotische extravagante Gestalt geliebt: Else Lasker-Schüler. Ich wollte solche Gedichte schreiben wie sie, und ich habe sie, als ich noch Gedichte geschrieben habe, sicher oft nachgeahmt. Ich wollte interessant angezogen sein und wunderbare Sachen

ure of a woman writer with a pageboy haircut, half-Amazon, half-imp, costumed as a prince from *The Thousand and One Nights* and adorned with ankle bells, whose narcissistic exhibition mixed provocative swagger with an assumed fragility. From a country with an "Oriental" culture herself, Özdamar was less likely than anyone else to be taken in by the element of mystification this folkloric scene entails. On the other hand, she would be all the more receptive to the profound implications of such self-stylization. The posture that Lasker-Schüler developed for herself in her own time by "self-Orientalizing" as a Jew in a German society that was becoming more violently antisemitic, transgressing cultural, social, and sexual codes by multiplying masks and travesties as so many survival tactics in reaction to the contradictory injunctions of her environment, resonated with Özdamar's own strategies for existing in the face of the cultural stereotypes confronting her in Germany – strategies that were for the most part pugnatious, aiming to subvert the clichés about the "Oriental woman" and to overdo and undermine them.

Returning to this literary precedent in the third part of her autofictional cycle is thus also, up to a certain point, to establish a position regarding the thorny question of exoticism. The Turkish-born novelist, exposed during the first two parts of her trilogy to suspicions that she was taking her chances with the public's expectations in terms of Orientalism, thus argues for the compatibility of a writing with accents that are literally "strange" and thus challenging for the average German reader, with the conscious development in the German language of an aesthetic of play and subversion that is rooted in German modernity itself. She thus affirms her legitimacy with a touch of provocation, as if to say: "So you think I exploit Orientalist clichés? Well, read your national literature again: Didn't these German writers you are so proud of often draw on the same sources? Didn't their genius consist of taking advantage of these 'productive misunderstandings' between cultures, even forging an identity and a writing that resulted from the appropriation of the Other and the exoticization of the self?"

In this context, it is worth noting that Özdamar's discovery of Lasker-Schüler, as reported in *Seltsame Sterne starren zur Erde*, comes at a period that marks a turning point in the reception of the expressionist poet. Until the early 1970s, the image of Lasker-Schüler that prevailed in criticism, particularly in Germany, was that of an "inspired" and "naïve" poetess who drew unthinkingly on Jewish cultural heritage (from which she was in reality very distant), which served as the

---

schreiben. Aber so herumzulaufen wie sie, mit Glöckchen an den Knöcheln, im Gewahrsam einer Prinzentracht, gleichzeitig vor der Öffentlichkeit geschützt und ihr bis zum Parodiertwerden ausgeliefert, das habe ich mich nicht getraut"].

inspiration for a visionary, irrational, instinctively "Oriental" work fueled by poetic and childhood images.[53] Ignoring the ironic and defiant elements of the writer's transgressive role-playing, this ethnicizing and sexist reading confused Lasker-Schüler's biography with the image (or images) that she liked to project of herself, in her work as well as in life. Her remove from political debates in Weimar Germany favored such an apolitical and sublimated interpretation of her work, which was very convenient in the post-war context for keeping the memory of the Shoah at arm's length in favor of an idyllic image of the Judeo-German literature that emerged from *Jugendstil*.

The invocation of this precedent in Özdamar's account draws attention to the fact that the Turkish-German novelist was (and still is, in part) the victim of a similar misunderstanding. Just as Lasker-Schüler was long disadvantaged by her reputation as a "naïve" poet, Özdamar initially found herself confronted by a first-degree reading of her texts that disregarded the self-parodic dimension of her writing. The ingenuous, carefree, and joyfully bohemian accents of her work have often been highlighted to the detriment of the work of literary construction and the resulting ideological deconstruction. This error is likely attributable to the same prejudice according to which a woman writer, all the more so if she is culturally different from those around her, can derive her creative potential only from a natural, unconscious, and innate "gift," clinging to a felicitous combination of feminine sensibility and cultural otherness. Lasker-Schüler and Özdamar both play with this dual sexist and ethnocentric prejudice, in a constant ironic distancing from gendered roles and cultural difference. As Anke Gilleir (2011: 394) points out, theatricality is a distinctive and transgeneric quality that occupies a central place in both of their works: "The *mise en scène* that is so present in the work of both women, and so disturbingly out of context, can be read as an instance of theatrocracy that disrupts concepts of community time and again. As such, it equally appears as a refusal to undergo the melancholia inherent to community belonging."

In both cases, these are deliberate strategies to escape the grip of identity discourse."[54] This theatrical resistance implies the quest for a writing anchored in the materiality, carnal and spatial, of the body. Hence, for example, the impor-

---

[53] On this biased reception of Lasker-Schüler, see Dieter Bänsch (1971). Bänsch's critical examination is based on a close reading of studies by, in particular, Heinz Politzer (1950), Karl Josef Höltgen (1955), Clemens Heselhaus (1961), and Meïr Wiener (1922).

[54] "Like Özdamar's use of Brechtian theatre principles outside of their proper sphere and institution, the Artaudian mise en scène in Lasker-Schüler can be read as literature's resistance to being mobilized in the service of identity discourse, by whichever part" (Gilleir 2011: 399). It seems unlikely, however, that Artaud's work would have directly inspired Lasker-Schüler.

tance of the sketches that accompany the text, which are in no way mere illustrations.[55]

The reference to Lasker-Schüler is thus constructed in this narrative in order to support a poetological project and to demarcate a territory. By inscribing her artistic trajectory in the wake of this Judeo-German poet with an assumed marginality, Özdamar asserts her singularity while claiming a heritage that legitimizes her own position in the German literary field. The second tutelary figure after "Master" Bertolt Brecht, within this intertextual galaxy, Lasker-Schüler embodies a model of combative femininity, poetic resistance to stigmatization, and liberation through the imagination and the power of desire. It is in this capacity that she has the pride of place in her personal pantheon, as highlighted by the title of the book.

Osmosis with Heine: Germany 1975, a New Winter's Tale?

These first two beacons are joined by a third, whose founding and "integrative" role is no less significant: Heinrich Heine. This other Jewish poet who came earlier historically and who had been subject to exclusion, persecution, and exile only appears as a model later in the chronology of the Özdamarian *Bildungsroman*. Unlike Brecht, who was already a reference – collective and supranational – for the narrator prior to her departure from Turkey, and Lasker-Schüler, whose poetry she discovered in a context of romantic intimacy shortly after her arrival in (West) Berlin, Heine is the object of a solitary and relatively late discovery. His name is not mentioned once in the first part of the volume. It is within the context of her second assignment at the Volksbühne, when the "dream" she had in Turkey of joining the troupe led by Besson to "learn the theater of Brecht" is coming true (a sequence reported in the volume in diaristic form) that the young foreign intern starts to read Heine at her own initiative, which deepens her knowledge of German literature in a targeted manner, and this time directly in German. This event is recorded without comment in a note from the journal dated 5 May 1976. It provides an enumerative description of her progressive integration within the troupe and in its new socio-cultural environment:

---

55 In Özdamar, the drawings in the margins mainly serve to spatially situate moving and objects and figures. Produced simultaneously with the text, they aspire to nothing more than mere sketches, visual evidence of her work as an assistant director and of her various encounters. Thus, they divert the attention of the author's personality, decentering the autofictional narrative and deconstructing the very principle of modern literature of the 'I' as a self-referential and self-reflexive document.

> Everyone's gotten used to me. I've gotten used to them. The trains took me to the theater and I got in and out. I got tea at the theater canteen for fifty pfennig, now I love Mozart, rehearsal from nine to three in the afternoon, Fritz laughs at me, every day I draw the rehearsals, I'm understanding more and more German, I'm reading Heine.[56]

Scarcely a page later, still in the same journal entry, the impact of this reading can already be felt when, at the turn of a sentence evoking the beauty of the snowy nights in Berlin, there is an incidental reference to the cold that, instead of being biting, would be "a winter's tale" for the children of Berlin.[57] In these pages imbued with a new, almost exalted serenity, the allusion to the poetic cycle *Deutschland, ein Wintermärchen* ("Germany, a Winter's Tale") emerges unexpectedly, and in such a discreet manner that it could very well go unnoticed if the text did not contain a number of further indications making it possible to substantiate the argument that Özdamar's writing actively engages with Heine's.

However, it so happens that this quote from one of Heine's titles, buried in a descriptive passage on the winter atmosphere in Berlin, constitutes the only concrete evocation of a text by this author throughout the volume. The diarist is reading "Heine," without any additional details as to the nature of the writings in question. Yet the importance of this reading for her initiatory journey is confirmed at various levels. First and foremost, by its strategic occurrence at this pivotal moment when the young woman, nearing the goal she had set for herself in Turkey, looks back at the path she has taken and makes the decision to "become an adult" by accepting solitude and supporting her political commitment by studying history (SSE 104–105). It is in this state of mind, at once grave and optimistic, under the effects of a new readiness to accept the game of life with its joys and its risks, that her reading of Heine takes place. This author's effect on her is so powerful that she decides six months later, as recorded in the entry dated 29 November 1976, to buy no less than seven copies of his complete works to give one to each of the roommates at "her shared flat" in Wedding. No sooner has she arrived than she shares her enthusiasm with them by organizing improvised sessions reading "Heinrich Heine" (again without additional

---

[56] "Alle haben sich an mich gewöhnt. Ich habe mich an sie gewöhnt. Die Züge haben mich zum Theater getragen, ich bin ein- und ausgestiegen, die Theaterkantine hat mir Tee gegeben, für fünfzig Pfennige, ich liebe jetzt Mozart, von neun bis fünfzehn Uhr Probe, Fritz lacht mich an, ich zeichne jeden Tag die Proben, ich verstehe mehr und mehr Deutsch, ich lese Heine" (SSE 102).

[57] "Wie schön sind die Nächte in Berlin, wenn es schneit. Es hat ein weiches Herz, Berlin, die Kinder frieren nicht, die Kälte ist für sie ein Wintermärchen" (SSE 104).

details) aloud.⁵⁸ Inverting the dynamics of cultural mediation, this time it is the foreigner who is the one to introduce her German friends to one of the greatest authors of their national literature. This reversal of roles accounts for the ambivalent status of Heine, particularly in this context of the Cold War. Praised to the skies by the authorities of the GDR who instrumentalized him as a revolutionary thinker, the legendary *provocateur* still did not enjoy great esteem in the West-German academic world, which persisted in reproaching him, in the best of cases, for his "frivolity" and lack of political and aesthetic coherence. This was so persistent that attempts to attach his name to the university in Düsseldorf, his city of origin, were met for a quarter of a century with relentless resistance by the leaders of the institution and were not successful until 1988.

The reference to Heine slipped into the description of the Berlin winter, as discreet as it may be, fractures the idyll that is sketched there. The reminiscence of Heine's violently satirical poem introduces a grating tone that robs it of all its complacency – and serves as a reminder of the "contraband" in his head that the author of *Deutschland, ein Wintermärchen* prides himself on smuggling through customs, where he was subject to search.⁵⁹ Heine wrote this "travel picture" on the occasion of his penultimate return to Germany in the autumn of 1843, following an absence of twelve years. Combining first-person narrative and satirical epic, the work paints a brutal picture of Vormärz Germany, asphyxiated by absolute monarchy, clericalism, and the opportunism of the middle class. *Deutschland, ein Wintermärchen* is in the same parodic vein as *Atta Troll*, which was, as previously discussed, important for Özdamar's *Keloglan in Alamania*, yet it is in a darker register. It draws up a critical survey of a reactionary Germany as seen by a free spirit breathing the more invigorating and "summery" air of France. Satire in *Atta Troll*, with references to the dreamlike metamorphoses of *A Midsummer Night's Dream*, was based on a joyously whimsical and caricatured revival of the tradition of medieval legends and animal fables, whereas it is the tale, a Romantic genre par excellence, that serves as a generic anchor for ridiculing the German "winter," a metaphor for political and social lethargy as well as the intellectual regression the country had been sinking into since the Congress of Vienna. Indeed, elements of the marvelous abound in the twenty-seven sections (or "caputs") of this poem, which is one of the most caustic and disillusioned writings that Heine produced about Germany.

---

58 "Wir setzten uns wieder zu viert in die dreibeinige Badewanne und lasen uns laut Heinrich Heine vor" (SS3: 179).
59 "Ihr Toren, die ihr im Koffer sucht! / Hier werdet ihr nichts entdecken! / Die Contrebande, die mit mir reist, / Die hab ich im Kopfe stecken" (Heine 1976, Vol. 7: 579). On this specific aspect of Özdamar's relationship to Heine, see B. Venkat Mani (2006).

In her text, Özdamar does not reproduce either Heine's style or his scathing irony. Indeed, she does not have – or at least no longer has – the same targets. She was "exiled" in Germany a bit like Heine was in France: she had not been formally expelled from her country of origin, and had freely chosen her host country. She therefore has no reason in this book to attack Germany or the Germans. The virulence and pessimism of *Keloglan in Alamania*, which arose as a reaction to a disturbing rehabilitation of nationalist and xenophobic rhetoric at the time of reunification, seem to have been left behind. In addition, this time it is a matter of retracing a personal itinerary and setting up beacons for a positioning that is simultaneously intellectual, social, political, cultural, and artistic. While in the 1970s German society as a whole (whether in the East or the West) was not a model of openness, it certainly offered an environment much more conducive to personal fulfillment than Turkish society, at that time suffocated by repression, and the milieus that welcomed the young actress on both sides of the Wall were especially stimulating.

Özdamar also has no reason to dwell on her complaints about the military regime then raging in Turkey or to scorn the past or present political maturity of the Turkish people, for a German audience. Nevertheless, her concerns coincide with Heine's on several points. The fight against a regime of lawlessness that imposes censorship and brutality, the emancipation of the people, and cosmopolitanism are causes she defends with as much determination as Heine. A rereading of the first part of *Seltsame Sterne* in the light of the later references, intermittent but unambiguous, to her esteem for the German *satirical* poet, makes it possible to see that the two elements that make up the metaphor of the "winter's tale" are omnipresent. Winter (referring to stagnation, torpor, and political paralysis) and the tale (representing childishness, immaturity, the propensity to escape reality and take refuge in dreams) are recurring structural elements that the author offers at various levels, extending this metaphor, which Heine, drawing on Shakespeare himself, used for the title of his fierce epic. The tale in particular provides her with the major generic reference for her narrative – the very process of her narrative approach.

References to tales of the marvelous pervade all of Özdamar's work. *Das Leben ist eine Karawanserai* ("Life is a Caravanserai"), a story of childhood, gets its originality from a narrative technique that is imbued with the imagination and style of traditional Turkish tales that the narrator hears from her grandmother. The play with symbols, narrative devices (repetitions, digressions, embedded narratives), and discursive devices (the erasure of causal links), and magical formulas and proverbs from the popular Arab-Muslim tradition is at the core of the particular form of "magical realism" that made her famous.⁶⁰ The resulting generic diversity is coupled with cultural diversity when, as in *Keloglan in Alamania*, the author brings traditional Turkish characters and motifs together with emblematic figures from European fairy tales like Little Red Riding Hood. This time, however, in the third (and most directly "autobiographical") part of her autofictional cycle, the European repertoire takes precedence over the universe of *The Thousand and One Nights*. The "realistic" craftsmanship of the autofictional narrative is thwarted by a recurrent process of phantasmatic transfiguration that this time draws support from motifs primarily derived from the Grimms' tales. Yet as we shall see, this reference is handled in a much more ambivalent and polysemic way than in *Keloglan in Alamania*.

Refraction of Popular Mythology: Like in One of Grimms' Fairy tales

Of the tales underlying the storyline in *Seltsame Sterne*, the most visible is *Schneewittchen* ("Snow White"), which provides the frame of reference for the entire sequence set in the Wedding community. Özdamar compares her arrival there to Snow White's initial encounter with the dwarves. After finding her way to this temporary asylum for the time needed to obtain her visa for the GDR, a loft nestled on the top floor of a building housing a sewing studio and a brothel, located in a former working-class district of West Berlin, seven young men and women greet her with spontaneous warmth and invite her to share their breakfast. While greedily swallowing buttered toast with jam, eggs, muesli, and milk, her hosts stare at her "like the children at a nursery school stare at a new kid."⁶¹

At first discreet, the allusion to the tale becomes more insistent as the description of this comfortably non-conformist household acquires new details about its friendliness and the daily routine, which is surprisingly well-regulated. The allusion becomes entirely explicit when one of the seven housemates discovers that their new friend did the dishes while they were gone and exclaims, "clearly we are the seven dwarves and she is Snow White." He continues, "personally I'd like you to move in right away, but not because you do the dishes.

---

60 See for example Meral Oraliş (2004).
61 "[...] alle schauten mich an, wie die Kinder im Kindergarten ein neues Kind anschauen" (SSE 49).

Because you smoke unfiltered Gauloises."⁶² Even though the metaphor is formulated in a self-ironizing way by a member of the community, it is clearly attributable to the heroine's half-dazzled, half-amused gaze, and her cultural exteriority. The trials she has endured inspire this perception that she is somewhat displaced in her new environment. A survivor of military jails and the terror then raging in Turkey, in this household that is as welcoming as it is unusual, following a rhythm of collective bathing and the joyful jumping of slices of toast ejected from three continuously-operating toasters, she has the experience of being immersed in the nostalgic childhood paradise of Grimms' tales: "In the apartment there was always coffee on the table, cheese, bread, macaroni, jam, orange juice, the door was always open, like in the brothel below you could walk in and out, walk around naked. We had breakfast naked. Our breasts were beautiful. The bread machine kept time. Somebody was always taking a bath."⁶³

As clear as it may appear to be, the reference to Snow White is more difficult to assess than it may seem. While it may be easy to understand the allusion that it contains to the heroine's plight at the time of her arrival and to the painful circumstances that forced her to leave her country (like Snow White fleeing her father's castle to escape her stepmother's murderous hatred), it is more challenging to decipher the parallel between the seven roommates and the dwarves of the tale. Indeed, it is difficult not to perceive, behind the homage to the warm welcome the young refugee receives in the alternative milieus of West Berlin, a malicious allusion to the blind spot of the counter-culture resulting from 1968, this nostalgia for the green paradise of childhood that underpinned (especially in Germany?) the libertarian and anarchist utopias of that era. Yet the irony is not exactly slight in making a comparison between the rebellious, anti-bourgeois, and revolutionary youth and the quiet, poor, and industrious dwarves of Snow White, these friendly, asexual beings toiling in underground mines, whose zeal and attachment to their household made them the paradigmatic representatives of petty-bourgeois conservatism.

Should this reference then be seen as a form of serious critique, and in this case quite caustic, of the specifically German forms of international counter-cul-

---

62 "Es ist klar, wir sind die sieben Zwerge, und sie ist Schneewittchen. Von mir aus kannst du sofort hier wohnen, aber nicht, weil du abgewaschen hast, sondern weil du Gauloises ohne Filter rauchst" (SSE 53).
63 "In der WG gab es immer Kaffee auf dem Tisch, Käse, Brot, Makkaroni, Marmelade, Orangensaft, die Tür war immer offen, man konnte wie unten im Puff rein- und rausgehen, nackt herumlaufen, wir frühstückten nackt, unsere Brüste waren schön, die Brotmaschine arbeitete im Takt, immer badete jemand" (SSE 59–60).

ture in the years following 1968? Such an interpretation would be at odds with the overall positive assessment of this group in the narrative. However, the irony of the metaphor enables a penetrating look at the milieu in question. A subdued but nonetheless insistent palimpsest, the tale functions at least in part to reveal the paradoxes of West German counter-culture, highlighting certain "childish" and even regressive aspects: the family spirit (transposed to the "alternative" family as represented by the community), attachment to security and ritual, and a certain appreciation of innocence and naïveté (concealed by the pretext of rejecting prudishness and sexual exploitation). There is a way for the writer to show that, despite all her affection, she is not fooled by the transgressive posture that characterizes the alternative movement of the 1970s. The picture that she paints reflects both her fundamental solidarity and her reluctance to give in to the temptation of ingenuous idealization. Moreover, the touch of malice contained in this superimposition of the Grimmian patterns and motifs over the heroic saga of the protest movement is addressed just as much to the conservative and self-righteous majority (past and present), in order to counter the demonization of the movement in question: no, this scandalously emancipated and amoral youth was decidedly not comprised of misfits, provocateurs, and potential terrorists. It consisted, above all, of easygoing kids who were avatars of Snow White's dwarves.

In Heine's story, the metaphor of the tale referred to the honeyed hypocrisy of monarchism as well as to the childishness of the German people incapable of freeing themselves from its yoke. The signified of immaturity is preserved, but the perspective for the rest is reversed. The childhood paradise is located in a democracy, the FRG, and the narrator, who arrives there as a foreign refugee from a military dictatorship, has a distant but far less critical view of it than Heine did of the Germany he rediscovered after twelve years of exile. However, the metaphor of the tale is not limited to the narrative about the Wedding community, nor the individual hypotext of *Snow White*, but extends in other forms to all the milieus the heroine explores. Thus, Turkey plunged into the nightmare of the military coup is described as a subjugation, a spell that causes lethargy and derealization. As if someone had cast a spell on them, fruits and vegetables start to look like human beings (pomegranates fall from stalls like men mowed down by bullets, zucchinis in the garden make sounds while growing at night, and eggplants look like swaddled babies).[64] Humans, on the other hand, turn into

---

64 "Dort im Garten hörte ich die Zucchini wachsen. Sie machten Tschttscht in der Nacht. Die Auberginen sahen aus wie Babies, denen man lilafarbene Windeln aus Samt angezogen hatte" (SSE 24).

stones when they do not just purely and simply vanish into nature to "become photos."⁶⁵ Here, the image of the "winter's tale" imposes itself again, this time in the political sense that Heine provided it with for his depiction of Vormärz Germany: Turkey sinks into the winter of the military regime, just like Germany, following the Congress of Vienna, sank into the regime of the police State established in the German Confederation under the aegis of Metternich.

But the Cold War also produced situations of an unreality that evoked the phantasmagorical and ritualized universe of tales. Apprehended by Özdamar in a more detached manner than the terror that prevailed in Turkey, the GDR's bureaucratic totalitarianism generated – especially around the border separating it from the Western world – an infinity of material and immaterial obstacles, formalities, prescriptions, taboos, and ceremonials that she describes in the narrative as characteristic elements of the tale: a prohibition against bringing newspapers or jeans to the East, a prohibition against bringing out local currency or food products, an obligation to reach the checkpoint before precisely midnight so as to be able to return to the West, and so on. Some places seem plunged into a long slumber, like Sleeping Beauty's castle, such as the "ghost stations" (SSE 155, 158) of the East Berlin underground, closed to traffic because they were traversed by the western sector's network.

As for the narrator, freshly arrived from a country battered by the evil of military repression, she approaches the opaque and absurd laws that reign in this city with the disarming flexibility of an authentic fairy tale hero, showing little astonishment at these peculiarities. She has seen worse before and does not allow herself to be intimidated. She adapts, observing with interest these ghost stations where the underground train never stops, having fun breaking the rules (swallowing the pfennig left in her pocket to retrieve it later in the toilet, for example) and circumventing the imperative to return to the West within 24 hours by presenting herself at the checkpoint a few minutes before midnight to then immediately cross back through it in the opposite direction. The metaphor of Cinderella, which shows through in the series of narratives about this notorious midnight rule, is extended with a certain consistency until the narrator herself discloses her kinship with the Grimm character – this time in a completely different context since the scene is located in East Berlin where she now resides, and the midnight rule therefore no longer applies to her:

> I came home and was fixing my skirt until midnight. I've never been so patient with sewing before. Maybe working in the theater has taught me patience. I sat in my pajamas, sewed,

---

65 "Menschen verschwanden ganz plötzlich und wurden zu Fotos. Die Eltern liefen mit Fotos in den Händen herum und fragten: 'Wo sind unsere Kinder?'" (SSE 26).

boiled cauliflower, Katrin came out of her room, and her eyes were puffy from reading a lot. "I feel like Cinderella," I said. Katrin said, "Yes, somebody is going to come ring the doorbell soon and ask, "Is this your shoe?" Katrin held her hands out like for an eighty-centimer shoe, I laughed.[66]

The reference here has its origins in self-ironization. It is by becoming aware, with amused astonishment, of her new "patience," and more generally of her docility and the application she puts into performing household tasks, that the narrator discovers a resemblance – unexpected and incongruous for her – to Cinderella. If this "revelation" makes her laugh, it is because she is certainly not a model of sweetness and submission, nor the scapegoat of a wicked stepmother, and she is not spending her life waiting for a prince charming to come and free her. She freely accepts her current constraints, and she voluntarily devotes herself – quite occasionally – to domestic tasks. After having rebelled against the yoke of marriage and celebrated her emancipation in all possible ways, she finally discovers true freedom, which consists of being able to do of her own free will what she would not have done as long as it was imposed on her. The reference in this context to the German tale, rather than a traditional tale from her childhood, is an incidental indicator, again with self-irony, of her acculturation. She has acclimatized so well to Germany that her cultural references are now German. One reason for this is they make it possible for her to connect with the people around her, as demonstrated by the quote above.

If the narrator occasionally identifies some points she has in common with Snow White or Cinderella, she likewise recognizes herself – in a manner that is certainly more insightful – in the malicious goblin Rumpelstiltskin, who rejoices at the idea of keeping his identity secret: "Wie schön, daß keiner weiß, daß ich Rumpelstilzchen heiß" ("How nice it is that nobody knows that my name is Rumpelstiltskin," SSE 173). This approximate quote from the famous refrain ("Ach, wie gut ist, daß niemand weiß, daß ich Rumpelstilzchen heiß") spoken by an evil dwarf of Germanic folklore[67] serves as a self-ironic comment on the bizarre

---

[66] "Ich kam nach Hause und reparierte bis Mitternacht meinen Rock. Ich habe noch nie soviel Geduld mit Nähen gehabt. Vielleicht hat mir die Theaterarbeit die Geduld beigebracht. Ich saß im Pyjama, nähte, kochte Blumenkohl, Katrin kam aus ihrem Zimmer, vom vielen Lesen hatte sie ganz dicke Augen. ‚Ich fühle mich wie Aschenputtel', sagte ich. Katrin sagte: ‚Ja, gleich wird jemand an der Tür klingeln und fragen: ‚Ist das Ihr Schuh?' Katrin zeigte mit ihren Händen einen Schuh von achtzig Zentimetern, ich lachte" (SSE 118).

[67] In the tale, Rumpelstiltskin, who is a crippled and "very ridiculous" dwarf, plays a dirty trick on a young miller's daughter by saving her life in exchange for the promise that she will give her first child away to him. Once the child is born, he consents to renounce his reward if she can guess his name within three days. On the final night, she goes into the woods in search of

wandering the young woman experienced for a while in East Berlin. Despite her employment contract and the renewal of her visa for the GDR, she is not in good standing because she no longer has official accommodations there and is therefore forced to stay with one person after the next, whoever is available to accommodate her, when she is not hiding in the sauna at the theater. Isolated from the primary literary context and presented in the form of an internal monologue, the evocation of Rumpelstiltskin is all the more revealing, both in terms of the degree of the heroine-narrator's acquisition of German culture and of the paradigmatic posture consisting of provocation, ingenuity, and nonchalance, that she adopts throughout the narrative in the face of the obstacles she encounters. At the same time, the formula is emblematic of Özdamar's roleplaying. Thumbing her nose at all those who would like to assign her a stable and homogeneous identity (preferably pinned to a well-identified cultural "community"), Rumpelstiltskin's motto is in a way the encoded formula of her constant game of hide-and-seek with readers.

Therefore, despite its recurring, emphatic presence in this narrative, the reference to Grimms' tales is not a serious homage. Even if the hypotexts mentioned are not explicitly mocked, the identification of the characters, especially the heroine-narrator herself, with one character or another from the Grimms' tales is a deliberate and ironic game with Germanic folklore. For the author, the usage of the mythological material of the tale is a way of introducing the distance needed to check sentimentalism. By giving a twist that is simultaneously poetic and parodic to her adventures, she executes a rhetorical spin that is part of her strategy of distancing and self-mockery.

All the same, the consideration here of Grimms' tales is undeniably less caustic than in *Keloglan in Alamania*. By developing a feedback loop between the autofictional narrative and the repertoire of marvelous tales, Özdamar thwarts expectations and to some extent invalidates hastily-drawn conclusions. This system of echoes blurs significations and makes the narrative ambiguous. The discourses brought into play are refracted on all sides, making it uncertain what meaning to attribute to them. Who are we laughing at? Is Özdamar making fun of the student protest and West German alternative movements by comparing her roommates in Wedding to the dwarves of *Snow White?* Or does she imply, in opposition to the frame of reference introduced (and ratified by posterity) by the Brothers Grimm, that these courageous dwarves had a revolutionary side?

---

him, and comes across his remote cottage. There she watches, unseen, as he hops about his fire and sings: "Heute back ich, morgen brau ich, / übermorgen hol ich der Frau Königin ihr Kind; / ach, wie gut ist daß niemand weiß / daß ich Rumpelstilzchen heiß!" (Grimm 1857: 283).

Once established that it is possible to detect similarities between the libertarian ideals borne by the student movement and the qualities attributed to the dwarves – disinterested generosity towards a fugitive foreigner, community and autarkic social organization, proximity to nature, indifference to power and to wealth, non-acceptance of gender as a binary system of domination – what conclusion should be drawn from this? By drawing the dwarves (as well as all the other fairy tale characters evoked throughout the story such as Snow White, Cinderella, and Rumpelstiltskin) into a value system with connotations strictly opposed to their canonical frame of reference, the author casts suspicions of anarchy on them, the whole point being to destabilize certainties. For it is ultimately the very way we look at people and things that is called into question in this game of mirrors and counter-mirrors.

Seltsame Sterne starren zur Erde therefore lives up to its title. The inversion of perspective is decidedly programmatic in this text, which is deeply informed by a movement of internal protest that never ceases to highlight its own relativity. All the discourses and the hypotexts that feed the initiatory narrative are affected by this game of subjectivity.

Conclusion – and Return to Heine

Through the lens of Grimms' tales to which the text of Özdamar constantly refers, the nocturnal barking that opens the narrative and that the narrator tries to conjure by "barking" in return the poems of Lasker-Schüler cannot fail to retrospectively evoke the mythical wolf of European folklore – this wolf that the author, inspired by the figure of the Swabian poet "pugged" by Heine in *Atta Troll*, had maliciously transformed into a domestic dog in *Keloglan in Alamania*. However, the scene also recalls a central episode in *Deutschland, ein Wintermärchen*. The narrator-traveler, who is stranded in a German forest in the middle of the night, suddenly finds himself surrounded by a pack of wolves. He thwarts the attack of wild beasts, whose presence he perceives only by a "choir" of howls, by boldly countering this choir with an improvised rant in which he declares himself "still a wolf," who "always [will howl] with wolves" (Heine 1976: VI, 603–604). Where does the strange threat of terror embodied by the figure of the dog howling in the night come from in *Seltsame Sterne*, as if echoing the mythical predator of tales, creating a feeling of helplessness and confusion in the narrator? Of course, it is conceivable that it comes from the trauma suffered in Turkey, more than in the Germany where she took refuge. Yet, in the intertextual configuration that the narrative creates, these images of violence and persecution inevitably collide with the Heinean satire of Vormärz Germany.

In her analysis of this incipit, writer Katja Lange-Müller (2016) underscores the connection between the inaugural scenario that depicts the narrator entering into a "new language" in the Berlin of the Cold War era. An intertextual configuration brings these different spaces and levels of experience into relation with one another, with the main and all-encompassing reference provided by Heine's *Wintermärchen*, notably through the titular metaphor that condenses its different signifieds. For the narrator taking refuge there, Berlin in the 1970s is a fairy tale from the Brothers Grimm. Turkey is (henceforth) a "winter's tale" in Heine's sense, meaning that it is a distorted reflection of Vormärz Germany. However, the "Cold War" into which Europe is then plunged also traces the backdrop against which the narrator's experience of Berlin detaches itself, like an enchanted digression. It is this oppressive political context that gives this initiation, in counterpoint, the unreal appearance of a Grimm tale.

It is thus as if Özdamar had drawn from Heine, and in particular from *Deutschland, ein Wintermärchen*, the founding metaphor that enabled her to find the specific tone for this initiatory narrative, the poetic and rhetorical "cipher" of her project. As if, in short, she had taken Heine at his word, relying on his intertextual metaphor to recount the journey she had taken herself, though in reverse: from despotism to freedom. The subjectivity that she showcases has a trapdoor. In this *Bildungsroman*, she bares all while hiding, and reflected in this subjectivity is a narrative attitude very close to the poet-satirist Heine, whose lyrical subject *almost* becomes conflated with the person of the author, without ever merging with it. With the tale as the common frame of reference, what Özdamar also evokes is Heine's quest for a synthesis (always precarious) between poetry and politics, as well as the flexibility of thought and style, the ability to pass seamlessly from gravitas to euphoria, from pathos to playful irony. All these thematic and discursive connections make Heine a "mirror" of preference for Özdamar,[68] and perhaps even, despite the very discreet references to his work, the most radiant star of the constellation described here of authors who have delineated the quest for a "new language" allowing for the subject's self-reconstruction.

---

[68] I borrow this metaphor from Ottmar Ette (2005: 192), who used the mirror motif to describe the status of German literature, especially by exiled and diasporic authors as a "projection surface for desire", in Özdamar's work.

Chapter 6
Claiming Access to the German Canon: Zaimoglu's Conquering Down-Top Approach

The Life and Battles of an *Enfant Terrible*

In order to place himself front and center in the German literary scene, Feridun Zaimoglu had to overcome a double handicap. Not only did his ethnocultural origins predestine him to inclusion among the ranks of authors of "migration" or "intercultural" literature, but what's more, he comes from the underclass of economic migrants, to which his seniors Schami and Özdamar never truly belonged except by accident. Let us recall that they, like their juniors Navid Kermani, Zafer Şenocak, and Yoko Tawada, all came from cultured bourgeois families, and they found themselves in the working class only temporarily, on the threshold of adulthood, when they arrived in a country they fled to for different (political and artistic) reasons where they did not know the language sufficiently at first to perform anything but manual labor.

Zaimoglu, in contrast, is truly a child of the "ghetto" where the second generation of 1960s economic immigrants came of age. Born in 1964 in Bolu in Anatolia and arriving in the FRG with his parents' luggage, he never knew, as he likes to emphasize, any "homeland" other than Germany.[1] After a childhood spent between Bonn, Berlin, and Munich, he passed his *Abitur* with flying colors and began studying medicine and plastic arts in Kiel before launching first into journalism, then literature. He settled in Kiel, a municipality which today vaunts having an internationally renowned author among its residents, the more so since Zaimoglu shouts his rootedness in this northern German town from the rooftops. Laureate of numerous literary honors (he has obtained, among others, the Chamisso, Grimmelshausen, and Jakob Wassermann Prizes, and a stipend from the Villa Massimo in Rome), Zaimoglu receives requests to lecture on poetics and host writing workshops. He has written with success for the stage in collaboration with his friend Günter Senkel, adapting the repertoire[2] and delivering original works staged in prestigious venues and regularly publishes opinion col-

---

[1] "Ich hatte immer nur eine Heimat. Es kann für mich nur eine Heimat geben, und das ist Deutschland" ["I always had only one homeland. For me there can be only one homeland, and that is Germany]" (Zaimoglu 2017c).
[2] They adapted, among others, plays by Shakespeare (*Romeo and Juliet*, *Othello*, *Hamlet*), Molière (*The Misanthrope*, *Dom Juan*, *Tartuffe*, *The Miser*), Lessing (*Nathan*), and Wedekind (*Lulu*).

umns in periodicals and cultural reviews (*Freitext*). Well-connected within the literary network, he was also, starting in 2005, among the writers invited to the annual Lübecker Literaturtreffen ("Literature Meetings") organized by Günter Grass.

This brilliant career has not been without its clashes and conflicts. The son of Kurdish peasants turned *Gastarbeiter*,[3] Zaimoglu could not count on the "exotic bonus" (double-edged though it be) that gave foreign-born authors their double cultural belonging. For his generation, the discourse around uprooting and identity cleavage was outmoded although it continued to prosper in the public arena, feeding the 1980s ideal of a "multicultural" society, pluralistic and tolerant, where everyone would have the right to prosper according to their own "culture." The children of immigrants growing up or reaching adulthood in this period – whether they be writers like Zaimoglu, Yadé Kara, Zehra Çırak, or Selim Özdoğan; directors like Fatih Akın, producers like Neco Çelik, or politicians like Cem Özdemir (Alliance 90/The Greens), Mehmet Daimagüler (FDP), Aygül Özkan (CDU), or Aydan Özoğuz (SPD); or even journalists like Özlem Topcu (*Die Zeit*) – did not recognize themselves in this discourse reducing them to an ethnocultural minority. Many among them, like Zaimoglu, would not stop voicing their refusal of any identity assignment, particularly in the name of a "multiculturalism" that, behind the pretext of valorizing diversity, was often no more than a screen to perpetuate discrimination.

It is in the context of this fight for recognition, not of difference but of the full legitimacy of immigrants' children to occupy the social commons, that Zaimoglu made his entrance on the literary scene in 1995. With *Kanak Sprak: 24 Mißtöne vom Rande der Gesellschaft* ("Kanak Speak: 24 Discordant Notes from the Margins of Society"), he gave literary visibility for the first time to a youth on the "margins" that majority society ethnically and socially stigmatized while simultaneously denying it the right to make political demands. Consisting of twenty-four monologues presented in the preface as authentic transcripts, the book clamorously celebrates the power of a language, the hybrid sociolect of a generation that called itself *Kanak*, wherein a creativity, a critical intelligence, and a self-regard no one would have previously ascribed to this population relegated to a social non-space all express themselves. The antipode of the still-widespread caricatured vision of a simplistic and simple-minded *Gastarbeiterdeutsch*, the language of the *Kanaks* (or *Kanaksta*), as (re)produced by Zaimoglu, unveils – in the sheer virulence of its invective and obscenity – an opulence, a

---

[3] Zaimoglu mentions his mother's work as a charwoman and his father's as an unskilled laborer for BASF and in the metalworking industry (Zaimoglu 2006d).

virtuosity, and an expressivity unexpected at the time from a youth as disdained as they were feared and ignored, not just by political representatives on all sides, but also by well-intentioned intellectuals.

"Kanak," the self-designation term for the subcultural movement Zaimoglu popularized, was created on the "inversion of stigma"[4] model by appropriating a term originally used in the French colonial context to disparage the natives of New Caledonia with a word from their own language. With the undifferentiated use of this racist epithet being widespread in German far-right circles since the 1970s to label non-natives regardless of origin, second-generation immigrants appropriated it as a rallying cry in the context of rising xenophobic violence. The derivation "Kanaksta," according to Zaimoglu (1997b), was formed as a contraction of "Kanak" and "youngster" as well as "Kanak" and "gangster." Thus, the *Kanak* identity, understood as a counter-culture that is like a slap in the face to a well-intentioned society refusing to recognize the violence dwelling within it, was forged in a spirit of struggle. As Zaimoglu explained during his public appearances when the book came out, the *Kanak* movement was born in reaction to the state's abandonment of youth exposed in the street to repeated aggressions by bands of skinheads connected to neo-Nazi groups. Because they received no institutional support from the police or courts, these youths from the "ghetto" organized into networks of self-defense (Zaimoglu 1998b). In its very haziness (and its misapplication in the German context), the choice of the term "Kanak" reflects the nature of the solidarity then forming as clearly as possible. In effect, it indicated that a movement bearing such a name based itself, not on claiming an identity but the struggle for the recognition of a social stigmatization – according to the logic that, if people perceived them as undifferentiated "Kanaks," i.e. as ethnic "Others" irrespective of their individual cultural origins or where they grew up, then so be it. It was this totalizing anathema that ultimately best defined them, beyond and much more powerfully than the cultural references transmitted to each of them by their parents.

The meaning of this semantic appropriation of an exclusionary term as a pragmatic act of self-legitimization has largely escaped the media wherein *Kanake* was merely received (and amply relayed) as a "trendier" synonym for "Turkish-German" – when not, at first, for simply "Turkish." Failing to recognize that the term did not designate an (ethnocultural) "identity" but a social (non-)space, journalists upheld precisely the misconception and stereotypes which the members of the group in question were rising up against alongside their literary figurehead, this young man himself from "the margins," propelled overnight by his

---

[4] Regarding this concept, see especially Goffman (1963) and Butler (1997).

book-manifesto into primetime on public network television channels. Received like a bolt from the blue by a public that, despite the wave of racist attacks at the beginning of the 1990s, was still drunk on the euphoria of reunification and the hope of watching a pacified pluralistic society enriched by its diversity emerge, *Kanak Sprak* earned its young author a notoriety seasoned with scandal.

The reactions were all the more violent because Zaimoglu demonstrated an undeniable talent in his first effort. A reading of extracts from his book performed by young actors on a talk show where the author had been invited alongside figures from the world of politics (Norbert Blüm, Heide Simonis) and culture (Wolf Biermann, Harald Juhnke) touched off *ad hominem* attacks of a rare virulence not just from the public and political ranks but also, to a surprising degree from among his own colleagues (Zaimoglu 1998c). Notably, in his perplexity, the poet and singer Wolf Biermann was driven to the point of ordering the newcomer, who calmly attempted to defend a work of art – which none of those present considered as such – to "shed his mask." Pointing to the disparity between the sanctimoniousness ("pfäffische Art") he claimed Zaimoglu was affecting in the debate and the raw aggressivity in his book, he lobbed the question: "Just tell us, who are you really? What's real about you?"[5] Despite this scandal and in part because of it, Zaimoglu's first book proved essential to bringing the generation born of immigration into the public sphere, to valorizing its culture and its modes of life – and so, in the medium term, to reconfiguring the German nation's collective imaginary after the attacks in Hoyerswerda, Rostock, Mölln, and Solingen.

Following on the heels of this clamorous entry onto the scene in the posture of a militant writer, Zaimoglu published *Abschaum: Die wahre Geschichte des Ertan Ongun* ("Scum: The True Story of Ertan Ongun," 1997), adapted for the screen in 2000 by Lars Becker as *Kanak Attack*, then *Koppstoff: Kanaka Sprak vom Rande der Gesellschaft* ("Head Scarf: Kanaka Speak from the Margins of Society," 1999), which revisits the proven formula of monologues where social documentary and political-cultural provocation meet in order to apply it to women this time (the speakers in *Kanak Sprak* were all men). Read as authentic documents, these first three books built a solid reputation for the author as a spokesperson for second-generation immigrants, even as a standard bearer for the *Kanak* subculture – largely (mis)understood as a movement for claiming identity. Little by little, scholarly critique brought to light the part that literary elaboration and fictionalization played in the composition of his speakers' inimitable "gift of the gab" and concluded he had constructed "performative" iden-

---

[5] "Sagen Sie mal, wer sind Sie eigentlich? Was ist an Ihnen echt?" (Zaimoglu 1998c).

tities meant to deconstruct the dichotomies erected by the institution in order to find a place in the literary field for this "Germanophone but 'not exactly German'" literature that immigrant authors are supposed to represent.[6]

This first phase reached its high point with two novels, *Liebesmale, scharlachrot* ("Love Marks, Scarlet Red," 2000), an epistolary novel, and *German Amok* (2002), which mark in different ways the development of Zaimoglu's linguistic performativity toward other discursive postures. This chapter will devote its analysis solely to the former of these transitional works. If the turn initiated in *German Amok* truly takes place on the level of the social milieu described and the targets of rebellious discourse presented (the narrator-protagonist is an unsuccessful painter who has cut ties with the cultural establishment), *Liebesmale, scharlachrot* effectuates a repositioning essentially onto the level of work on the canon. Here, Zaimoglu reconfigures his initial writing project in relation to a central reference in national literary history: *Sturm und Drang*. While this pre-Romantic reference is handled here in a mode one might still understand as largely ironic, the later evolution of this writer's work confirms the hypothesis that the reader is in the presence of a true turning point in his œuvre. Let us follow this lead by examining how he appropriates the pre-Romantic canon, specifically in re-adopting of narrative, thematic, and stylistic elements from Goethe's *Die Leiden des jungen Werthers*. This appropriation, which can be read as a form of response – or alternative proposition – to the rewriting of the same hypotext by the East German writer Ulrich Plenzdorf in 1973, marks the entrance onto the scene of a "new" Zaimoglu applying for admission into the center of the literary field by now publishing "serious" literature.

This literary and cultural repositioning goes hand in hand with the evolution of his social situation. The notoriety of his first three books and the institutional recognition that they ultimately brought him liberated Zaimoglu from financial concerns. The Ingeborg Bachmann Prize he won in 2003 for a short story from the then still-unreleased collection *Zwölf Gramm Glück* ("Twelve Grams of Happiness," 2004) marks the beginning of his career as an independent author. Now, his novels are no longer edited by the small publishing house Rotbuch with its leftist brand but by the large, general-interest publisher Kiepenheuer & Witsch, where Zaimoglu was admitted thanks to the support of Emine Sevgi Özdamar. More classical in its craftsmanship than his first works, *Zwölf Gramm Glück* opens the series of fictional works that narrate personal stories. With *Leyla* (2006), which has its place in the tradition of biographic tales of immigration, Zaimoglu achieved his first commercial success and strengthened his position

---

6 See in particular Bodenburg (2006), Abel (2006), and Schmidt (2008).

as a "respectable" author of migration literature. The polemic provoked by the suspicion of plagiarism and "matricide" against Özdamar[7] did not make a dent in his newfound popularity with the public at large, but this first novel centered on immigration was also the last – to this day – Zaimoglu has dedicated to the subject. His subsequent novels, *Liebesbrand* ("Blazing Love," 2008) and *Hinterland* (2009), tell stories in which the ethno-cultural origins of their protagonists, even though they still have a Turkish or Kurdish "immigration background," hardly play a role in the plot's progression. Socially well integrated and lacking financial difficulties, they develop naturally in milieus that are not majority "Turkish," much less "Kanak."

With *Ruß* ("Soot," 2011), Zaimoglu seems to have reached the end of his path of literary "assimilation." Situated in the social context of the proletariat of the industrial Ruhr valley "who could not be any more German" according to the publisher (per the back cover), the novel depicts characters who no longer have a history of migration. Yet Zaimoglu chooses this time to place the focus on the very bottom of the social ladder, something that represents in certain respects a return to his old position as the spokesman for the disadvantaged. In addition, the fashion in which he describes this setting of social outcasts, his empathy for taciturn characters on the brink of poverty (alcoholics, the homeless, dropouts), and the crude nature of the connections that knit their community of *Kumpel* ("buddies") together all recall his solidarity with the *Kanak* movement at his debut. Here the reader is also in the presence of characters relegated to the "margins" who cannot count on support from institutions and are reduced, when necessary, to taking justice into their own hands. Thus, the main character whose wife is brutally murdered undertakes, with the help of his friends, to find the perpetrator in order to kill him. According to Julia Abel (2011: 53), there is in this depiction of an "archaic" (to which she adds: "one is almost tempted to say: Oriental") microcosm a resurgence of motifs – loss of reference points, networks of masculine solidarity, eye-for-an-eye justice, "crimes of honor" – that crystalize in a quasi-obsessional manner the anxieties in the public arena regarding Islam and "parallel societies" created on the German soil by immigrants. Abel wonders what the significance is of transposing these *topoi* of culturalist discourse on immigration into a milieu "that could not be more German?" "Is Zaimoglu then flipping things on their head and telling the immigration story expected from him but this time with a German cast?"[8] Assuredly this hypothesis bears looking

---

[7] See chapter 4 for details.
[8] "Dreht Zaimoglu also hier einmal den Spieß um und erzählt die von ihm erwartete Migrationsgeschichte, nun aber mit deutschem Personal?" (Abel 2011: 53).

into. For the moment, however, this chapter merely maintains that while Zaimoglu has kept his distance from the overtly militant writing of his debut and has moved, in his thematic choices as in his attitude, toward the center of the literary field, he nevertheless continues to adopt, in *Ruß* and beyond, transgressive positions.[9]

There is, perhaps, in this observation the beginnings of a response to the question of knowing if Zaimoglu's literary evolution, which goes hand in hand with a modification of his authorial posture, equally reflects a transformation of his ethos. Journalistic critique, at least, has found a handy means of evading the problem by labeling this author who never ceases to reinvent himself as an *enfant terrible* on the German literary scene. It is taken for granted that the sole constant in his career resides in his love for paradox and provocation. In this interpretation, the antiracist activist he started as, the "Malcolm X of German Turks" (Lottmann 1997), would come to play the misanthropic part of a "German Houellebecq," pitilessly mocking the *intelligentsia* on the left and the "politically correct" before assuming the role of the old-fashioned "great writer" (Granzin 2011), bourgeois and humanist. The comparison to Houellebecq, which has become a leitmotif in portraits of the author, seems to rest on a statement Zaimoglu himself made one day in the course of an interview conducted upon the release of *German Amok* – a novel for which it has a certain pertinence since its narrator shows disdain for and resentment towards the humanist, progressive, ecological, and "alternative" ideas upheld by the bourgeois intellectuals on the left. However, this self-definition should not be taken at face value, particularly as the interviewer seems to have extrapolated somewhat the author's words in attributing it to him (see Zaimoglu 2002b). On the contrary, in other circumstances, Zaimoglu has clearly distanced himself from the famous French author's cynicism, grouping Houellebecq's admirers into the category of those "modernists" exhibiting the petit-bourgeois snobbishness he abhors (Cheesman and Yeşilada 2012: 58). In the same interview, Zaimoglu conversely describes himself as an "old-fashioned social democrat" or even a "socialist humanist," someone who "can't stand lies."[10] However, as Zaimoglu's numerous public declarations abound with self-definitions supporting any sort of claim and its opposite, it would be better to rely on the actual stances he takes (understood as tangible manifesta-

---

[9] See especially: *Evangelio. Ein Luther-Roman* (2017), reworked for the theater in the same year as *Luther* and produced in Kiel (directed by Annette Pullen); *Siegfried*, a farcical adaptation of the Nibelungen saga (directed by Christian Stückl, Münchner Volkstheater, 2015); and *Siegfrieds Erben* (directed by Roger Vontobel, Worms, Nibelungen-Festspiele, 2018).

[10] "Ich bin ein altmodischer Sozialdemokrat, ein sozialistischer Humanist, aber als so einer kann ich Lügen nicht ab" (Cheesman and Yeşilada 2012: 58).

tions of his discursive ethos in the political field) rather than these cookie-cutter formulas generously dispensed to media outlets hungry for them.

From the beginning of his career, precisely because of his inflammatory reputation as the representative of the *Kanak* generation, Zaimoglu has been asked again and again to participate in public debates. He has often gone along with the exercise, seizing the opportunity to make his opinions known, which, though not mainstream, cannot be reduced to simple provocations. Invited to participate in the second German Conference on Islam, organized by the Minister of the Interior Thomas de Maizière in 2006, as a representative of civil society, he made a scene denouncing the overrepresentation of women hostile to Islam (like Necla Kelek) or at least to its traditional practices (like Seyran Ateş) while the defenders of orthodox positions were all men. Demanding an assembly composed to more aptly reflect the existing diversity within the female portion of the Muslim population in Germany, he offered to give his place to a woman proud to wear the hijab.[11] This withdrawal was interpreted as a communitarian gesture, and the accusation of hysteria that Zaimoglu leveled on that occasion against the "so-called enlightened minds" (2007c) provoked incomprehension and indignation.

Tempers did not run any cooler when, ten years later, the writer reacted to the massive instances of sexual assaults in Cologne on New Year's Eve by stating: "We're experiencing a crisis of Muslim men" (Zaimoglu 2016). He backed up this assertion with an analysis of traditional popular Islam as a "culture of violence" that agreed in substance with what led the Algerian journalist and writer Kamel Daoud to decry, in the same circumstances, the sexism of the Muslim world in terms that drew very sharp critiques from numerous French intellectuals – some culturally Muslim – steeped in postcolonial ideas (Daoud 2016). Like Daoud, Zaimoglu refused to defend the assaulters just because a large number of them happened to be refugees. Concluding that it was necessary for Muslim men to question their value system and their relationship to women, he called for an evolution in mentalities within Islam itself. Once again, his position was understood by many as a provocation, this time against the politics of welcoming implemented by Angela Merkel with regard to Syrian refugees – a move, however, Zaimoglu had explicitly saluted not long before.

These differing stances are only contradictory in appearance and in terms of the dichotomies that structure public debate in Germany. For Zaimoglu, there is no contradiction in calling himself "an enthusiastic" German[12] (and German au-

---

11 See Zaimoglu (2007c) and Bahners (2007: 40).
12 "Ich bin ein begeisterter Deutscher" (Zaimoglu 2008b).

thor) – something that amounts to refusing to be assigned to a subfield of minority literature, whatever it is called – and Muslim at the same time. Nor is there a contradiction in being comfortable with his devotion to Islam while calling for a revision in gender relations within the Muslim world – and demanding, on the other hand, the same respect for practicing Muslim women as for secular feminists.[13] It seems that a number of the (necessarily contradictory) myths that have developed around this author thus come from a somewhat overly literal, superficial, and cursory reading of his literary texts as well as his contributions to public debates. Particularly on the question of gender Zaimoglu's position is much more nuanced than it is usually perceived when one reduces his conception of maleness to the belligerent masculinity of some of his protagonists, particularly those in the *Kanak* cycle. Yet this chapter's analysis of the novel *Liebesmale, scharlachrot* will, in part, demonstrate that even these seemingly caricatured male characters convey an image of masculinity and male / female relations more complex than one might think.

Ultimately, the dominant ideology of the Zaimogluan ethos, the discursive motivation that spans his body of works from beginning to end and that equally defines his engagement in the political field, seems to reside in a committed stance against any form of institutionalized power sure of itself and its legitimacy. This struggle has its origin in Zaimoglu's own positioning at the "bottom" of the social ladder and his revolt against the domination of the "top." This sociopolitical engagement has taken (and likely might still take) very diverse and sometimes unexpected forms, more according to the relations of power between participating parties than to the nature of the stakes. However, beyond the apparent diversity of roles that this positioning leads Zaimoglu to assume over time, a constant emerges: his refusal to bend to authority whether it be that of the ruling classes, that of the dominant pressure group in a field (especially an intellectual one), or more generally, that of discourses that shape opinion by using self-validating rhetoric based on effects of evidence to impose apodictic certitudes. A number of Zaimoglu's polemical stances can thus be read as instinctual defensive reactions against a *doxa* ossified within stereotypes and clean consciences. If called upon to summarize in one word the thousand-headed hydra against which he never ceases to rise up – albeit sometimes in a quixotic posture – one could say alongside Julia Abel (2011) that it is "das Bürgerliche" (the *bourgeoisie* as social institution and ideology).

---

13 Zaimoglu calls himself a believer, and he often participates in forums and events addressing theological, spiritual, and social issues related to Muslim life in Germany such as *Das muslimische Quartett*, a discussion group created by the alternative Muslim organization Alhambra-Gesellschaft.

Despite the moments of incoherence to which this systematic stance of insubordination sometimes leads, it seems difficult to cast doubt on his sincerity. Certainly, Zaimoglu, with a certain relish for provocation, takes it upon himself to fight hammer and tongs against those with whom he essentially shares political struggles, often to the point of delighting in being considered "reactionary." Thus, he can vituperate against modernism, rationalism, the *Aufklärung*, postcolonial thought, and the discourse of tolerance mobilized in the context of the "dialogue of cultures" (Zaimoglu 2006d) while simultaneously waving the banner of cultural assimilation and love of (German) country, declaring himself an "old-fashioned humanist," and asserting his "cultural conservatism" (see Mangold 2018). Beyond the deconstructive game with "politically correct" reflexes and the dictates of good taste,[14] there is in this fashion of defining himself as "anti-modern" a tenacious will to unmask hypocrisy and escape instrumentalization. The question of authenticity that every critical reflection never tires of wrestling with (recall Wolf Biermann's piqued incomprehension in the face of the disparity between the coarseness of *Kanak Sprak* and its young author's thoughtful argumentation) perhaps finds a response here. What Zaimoglu never ceases to emphasize across the perpetual reinvention of his authorial identity is a profound skepticism regarding all certitude.[15] Even having "arrived" (at the center of the literary field and topping the bestseller lists), Zaimoglu remains an author who thinks from the "margins."

To conclude this overview of the Zaimogluan ethos and postures, here is an excerpt from an interview wherein the author defines his own position very explicitly (2006b). To the question of what effect he envisions for his books, Zaimoglu responds:

---

14 Zaimoglu notably decorated the walls of his home with about 200 terracotta figurines representing emblematic characters of German folklore that he likes to call "sprites" (*Wichtel*) rather than "garden gnomes" (*Gartenzwerge*).

15 "Mein Glaube an die Aufklärung ist nicht so groß. Jede aufklärerische Pose ist mir suspekt. Ich bin mit der Aufklärung, wenn es darum geht, den religiösen Wahnsinn einzudämmen. Aber ich weiß, dass die Aufklärung die Konzentrationslager nicht verhindert hat. Wie kann ich da ein Freund der Aufklärung sein? [...] Andererseits kann ich auch nicht Partei ergreifen für den Irrationalismus. Sie sehen, ich habe keine klare Haltung. Ich bin da hin- und hergerissen" (Zaimoglu 2006d). ("I do not have great faith in the Enlightenment, and I am suspicious of any Enlightenment posture. I'm with the Enlightenment when it comes to curtailing religious lunacy. But I know that the Enlightenment did not prevent the concentration camps. How, then, can I be a friend of the Enlightenment? On the other hand, I can't side with irrationalism either. You see, I have no clear position. I'm torn between the two.")

I don't have a pessimistic, more of a realistic, view of my role as a writer. The engaged author who makes the big catches, so to speak, is a legend. But that doesn't mean I sit on the fence. I've seen the rat race for jobs and training positions in "real life." And once I stepped into the bourgeois discipline of literature and culture, I discovered that it's not any different there. It's a battle for the dominant opinion, a battle over who'll write the frontpage article in *Die Zeit*, a battle over microphones and dictaphones, a battle for key positions. It's not about power but the possibility to maybe set a few things right. If I succeed in touching and not demagoguing people with my stories, then that's nice. But I certainly don't get up there thinking that, just because I have the microphone, I'm making big changes. I'm one of many, but I believe you shouldn't forget where you come from – and I don't forget. But you also shouldn't let things get to you and act as if it's only about culture. Because culture is sometimes the protective cover for ideological beliefs.[16]

Liebesmale, scharlachrot: Reconfiguring Pre-Romantic Heritage in "Kanak" Literature

A Coming-of-Age Novel and Its Canonical References

After his three novel-manifestos, *Kanak Sprak* (1995), *Abschaum* (1997), and *Koppstoff* (1999) – which earned him, as already alluded to, a reputation as the "Malcolm X of German Turks" – Zaimoglu published a novel in 2000 that, while situating itself in the linguistic and thematic continuity of the *Kanak* vein, communicates for the first time his desire to enter straightaway into "great" literature. The protagonists – two young, second-generation Turkish immigrants – resemble the marginalized (anti)heroes of his first books in that, at first glance, they embody their prototypical roles: that of the "hardboiled Kanak-

---

16 "Ich habe über meine Rolle als Schreiber nicht eine pessimistische, eher eine realistische Ansicht. Der engagierte Schriftsteller, der sozusagen große Fänge macht, ist eine Legende. Aber es bedeutet nicht, dass ich mich heraushalte. Ich habe im "wirklichen Leben" das Rattenrennen um Jobs und Ausbildungsplätze gesehen. Und als ich dann eingestiegen bin in die bürgerliche Disziplin der Literatur und Kultur, habe ich entdeckt, dass es sich dort nicht anders verhält. Es ist ein Kampf um Meinungsherrschaft, ein Kampf darum, wer den Leitartikel in der *Zeit* schreibt, ein Kampf um Mikrofone und Diktafone, ein Kampf um Schlüsselpositionen. Es geht [mir] nicht um Macht, aber um die Möglichkeit, manche Dinge vielleicht richtig zu stellen. Wenn es mir gelingt, mit den Geschichten, die ich erzähle, die Menschen zu berühren und nicht zu ideologisieren, dann finde ich das schön. Aber ich hebe ganz sicher nicht ab und denke, dass ich bloß, weil ich am Mikrofon bin, für große Veränderungen sorge. Ich bin einer von vielen, aber ich glaube, man sollte nie vergessen, woher man kommt – und ich vergesse das nicht. Aber man sollte sich auch die gute Laune nicht verderben lassen und so tun, als ginge es nur um Kultur. Denn Kultur ist manchmal das Schondeckchen für Gesinnungen" (Zaimoglu 2006b).

sta"[17] scraping by on the margins of society without a thought for the future (Hakan) and that of the "Abi-Türke" (a Turkish high school graduate) or "Assimil-Ali" (an "overly" assimilated immigrant), nursing intellectual ambitions and seeking to integrate into the cultured middle class (Serdar).

However, the narrative is more developed, and the action takes place on a broader canvas. The novel opens with Serdar's arrival in Turkey at a seaside locale on the Aegean where he is spending the summer at his retired parents' home while his friend Hakan remains in Kiel, where both of them grew up and began (but broke off) their higher education. Serdar has seized on this pretext to distance himself from two women with whom he has been pursuing romantic relationships at the same time, his ex-girlfriend Anke and his mistress Dina, a Jewish intellectual older than him teaching at the university. By putting the turbulence of his daily life on hold, he hopes to find his inner equilibrium and devote himself to writing poetry.

He does not have to wait long for the beneficial effects of rest and relaxation. He has barely arrived "heil und ohne Gram" ("safe and sorrowless," LS 9) and is already savoring the relaxation brought by the break from routine and the absence of material concern, even noting the quasi-miraculous disappearance of his chronic back pain. His physical and mental wellbeing, though, are accompanied by a new lethargy that manifests itself particularly in a lack of inspiration and, moreover, erectile dysfunction.[18] Although this temporary infirmity does not bother him too much at first, it becomes the subject of growing preoccupation the more time passes without any relief – not from the mixtures sold by the merchants at the bazaar, nor the attempts at erotic flings on the beach, nor even love at first sight of a cute young local girl. It is only at the end of his stay, on the airplane taking him back to Germany, that he is "miraculously" able to have a satisfying erection (LS 292–293).

In the meantime, he experiences the joys and torments of frustrated love, for his attraction to the beautiful Rena whom he falls for "body and soul"[19] and who is willing to reciprocate arouses the jealousy of a local big shot he has more or less befriended and who transforms into a dangerous rival. The affair ends with a razorblade attack, which Serdar only escapes with his life thanks to the interven-

---

17 Zaimoglu, *Liebesmale, scharlachrot* [2000] (Cologne: KiWi), 110. All subsequent references are to this edition and will be cited as LS plus page number.
18 "[...] ich jedenfalls wundere mich nicht schlecht über meinen geraden Rücken, muss jedoch über ein anderes, mir teures Organ Beschwerde einlegen [...] Ich habe nämlich, Trauer über mein Haupt, eine tatsächliche Vollgliedlähmung, ich fühle meinen Penis nicht mehr, wie soll ich sagen, er hat sich, Gott sei's geklagt, vom Rest des Körpers verabschiedet" (LS 10–11).
19 "Abgesehen davon bin ich Rena mit Haut und Haaren verfallen" (LS 244).

tion of Hakan, who had come at his request from Kiel to protect him from the attentions of his ex-partner Anke – who, for her part, had arrived spontaneously after he had inconsiderately encouraged, long-distance, her desire to renew their relationship. So, it is with relief that Serdar embarks after leaving the hospital for his "cold homeland"[20] in northern Germany. Even if it is with regret that he leaves his "Eastern Light,"[21] to whom he implies in an impassioned letter that he will be awaiting her in Germany, he has overcome the crisis that had prompted his expedition. Liberated from his existential questioning, finally recognizing and accepting his limitations, he gives up his writing projects and returns disillusioned but "wie neugeboren" ("like newborn," LS 293) to an existence in which the prospects for the future remain uncertain.

The removal from his familiar setting, triggered by a crisis that necessitates making some space and taking stock of what he "actually wants,"[22] functions as a catalyst both on the pragmatic level (during his retreat Serdar willingly undertakes new experiences and new encounters) and on the reflexive and discursive level (what he sees inspires observations and analyses he shares with his friend who stayed in Germany). The whole point of this trivial and burlesque story of young men lacking cultural, social, affective, and sexual reference points resides in Zaimoglu's choice of the narrative device of the epistolary novel for this book. This allows Serdar, the budding poet, to recount to Hakan in minute detail – in a picturesque style blending the obscenity of the contents with a stylistic sophistication (and vice-versa) – everything that happens to him in this singularly strange *Heimat* and the latter to respond with letters no less delightful and prolix that comment, most often sarcastically, on his far-off friend's adventures, offering in return tales of his own tribulations in Kiel's "ghetto."

By resorting to this codified technique, traditionally dedicated to the expression of subjectivity and sentiments, Zaimoglu draws an untimely and overtly parodic parallel with the sentimental novels of the eighteenth century, which had a predilection for the epistolary narrative. With this generic reference established, two hypotexts in particular stand out in connection with *Liebesmale, scharlachrot*: first, Goethe's *Leiden des jungen Werthers* and, less emphatically, Friedrich Hölderlin's *Hyperion*. The initial configuration and psychological portrait of the protagonist more or less recalls the young Goethe's famous novel, the para-

---

20 "Ich habe beschlossen, wieder in die kalte Heimat zurückzukehren, mein lieber Kumpel" (LS 290).
21 "Rena ist mein Licht aus dem Osten, sie hat sich mir versprochen unter der Palme und angesichts des mondgeleckten Wassers" (LS 253).
22 "[...] ich bin [...] zu meinen Eltern an die Ägäis geflogen, um mir mal darüber klar zu werden, was ich nun eigentlich will" (LS 9).

digmatic work of *Sturm und Drang* to which, moreover, it expressly alludes in the text's first pages when Hakan tells his friend to stop posing and give up his stylized "act," which he identifies as a pastiche of Goethe: "Quit your Goethe act; forget it and just watch the clouds go by."[23] This explicit allusion makes it difficult to credit the author's protestations that he did not intend to parody the celebrated opuscule – going so far as to claim not to have read it at the time of composition (Zaimoglu 2007a: 450).

In reality, there is no lack of elements encouraging the reading of *Liebesmale, scharlachrot* as at least a partial parodic rewriting of *Werther:* the introspective language, the distance from familiar settings envisioned as a retreat far from the constraints of urban life, the triggering moment of flight in the face of romantic entanglement and the quest for personal development in a more "natural" environment, the plunging into a beatific state to the point of paralysis, and finally the blooming of passion and its hold on the spirit of the unhappy lover. A bundle of shared motifs likewise emerges with *Hyperion*, another text by a legendary writer: the organization of space around an Orient/Occident dichotomy doubled by a South/North opposition, the friendship between an enthusiastic dreamer with melancholy tendencies and an adventurer of heroic prowess, the quest for the purity of the ideal, the hymn to youth and love, and Rousseauian nostalgia for a natural state uncorrupted by civilization. Moreover, certain motifs borrow more or less equally from these two hypotexts, such as the exaltation of affect, the idealization of the female beloved, the rejection of economic and social constraints, the refusal of an existence dedicated to work (as opposed to the life of the artist and/or adventurer), and an intellectual and emotional elitism leading to a disdain for "ordinary" people who lack access to the elevation of the soul.

Certainly, as previously mentioned, the text's perspective on all of these points is parodic. The themes and motifs characteristic of pre-Romantic thought are most often evoked in a derisive mode. All of the stylistic virtuosity deployed in the letters exchanged between Serdar and Hakan aims to demonstrate again and again that these two protagonists are precisely not tragic heroes, that they are not capable of experiencing an exclusive, infinite, and sacred love, and

---

[23] "Hör auf mit der Goethe-Nummer, pfeif drauf und lass einfach die Wolken ziehn" (LS 18). The image of the clouds moving across the sky is in itself a nod to Goethe, who repeatedly uses this metaphor in *Werther*. At the very end of Goethe's novel, the "lovely clouds" of the first chapter (W 393) have turned dark and stormy, thus announcing the imminent suicide of the protagonist. See Werther's letter from 20 December in *Die Leiden des jungen Werthers*, second version (Goethe 2006, part 2, vol. 2, 349–465), part II: 463. All subsequent references to this work are to this edition and will appear as W plus page number in the text.

that the objectives of their quest and the reasons for their suffering are not metaphysical. So, what is the point of this elaborate intertextual work beyond the simple stylistic exercise? It assuredly resides in good measure in the fact that the characters themselves (and precisely these characters: *Kanaks*, second-generation Turkish immigrants in Germany) make, explicitly or not, reference to "classic" texts, using the style and clichés of the masterpieces of the German literary pantheon to mock *themselves*. In that, and that alone, they can well and truly sustain comparison with Goethe and Hölderlin's heroes. Their magisterial capacity to manipulate the (German) language across all its registers, which implies at once mastery of multiple social and group codes and that of the most noble literary language, now perceived as archaic and grandiloquent, is a very real mark of distinction that elevates them above their mediocre condition and draws, despite all the vulgarity they complacently make a show of, the reader's amused sympathy and often admiration. Beyond the purely technical mastery of styles, codes, and discourses, the demonstration of which has a value in itself as a provocation in a society that devalues individuals afflicted with an "immigration background," it is the relationship they enjoy with language that turns these young anti-heroes into worthy descendants of Werther and Hyperion: a ludic, intimate, and sensual relationship, even "libidinous" (Rüdenauer 2003) and strongly narcissistic, impelling them to describe in a hyperbolic mode and with self-deprecating emphasis, with a jubilatory verve, the merest setbacks and worries of their existence. The book's most powerful comic device resides in the discrepancy between the insignificance of the contents and the rhetorical prowess deployed throughout this self-reflexive outpouring – in the constant, implicit reference to the canonical precedents constituted by texts like *Werther* and *Hyperion*.

It is nevertheless necessary to consider the purpose of this double intertext in Zaimoglu's novel. Ultimately, what is the meaning of the discursive reappropriation operated on these works and what, beyond provocation and a stylistic exercise, are the literary and ideological stakes? Upon publication of the novel, the critics had a penchant for seizing on the Goethean references most often to salute the rather successful "poaching" Zaimoglu had undertaken in this piece of "arabesque rap" (Bartmann 2000), the narrative hybridity of which reflects the cultural hybridity of the protagonists "to give a voice to the 'storm and stress' ["Sturm und Drang"] of immigrant children" (Grumbach 2000). These critics agree in saying that the work at the very least demonstrates that Zaimoglu "knows his Goethe" (Hüfner 2000) and that he managed to breathe new life into the epistolary genre by transposing the sentimental novel into the contemporary *Kanak* milieu (Killert 2001). Others have used the reference to Goethe, on the contrary, to denounce the poverty of Zaimoglu's text in comparison to the semantic richness of his illustrious model. In *Die Zeit*, for example, Katharina Döbler (2011) critiqued the lack of "authenticity" as much in terms of style as of characters, noting that the attitude of the subcultural rebel attributed by the author to his anti-hero Serdar is hardly convincing.

Afterwards, since Zaimoglu has published new novels in the meantime ploughing the intertextual furrow from *Empfindsamkeit* to late Romanticism, researchers have taken an interest in the place of this persistent reference in his work, discerning in *Liebesmale, scharlachrot* the first indicators of a serious rehabilitation of Romantic thought. For Michael Hofmann, the novel is a transitional text between the social rebellion articulated in Zaimoglu's early militant writing and the "Romantic rebellion" that announces itself increasingly in the novels that followed, *Liebesbrand* ("Blazing Love," 2008) and *Hinterland* (2009). He concludes: "*Liebesmale, scharlachrot* sublimates the Romantic rebellion as presented in *Kanak Sprak*, almost substituting rebellion for a purely private, inward experience" (Hofmann 2012b: 249). This chapter generally supports this reading but will attempt to push a bit farther the analysis of the intertextual labor that produced this work.

As for the references to Hölderlin, they have only been sprinkled throughout to point out the ironic pastiche of tone and style characteristic of Hölderlin's prose. It is true that the parallels to *Hyperion* appear more as what Genette terms in a rather hazy manner as "architextuality," to wit: "the entire set of general or transcendent categories – types of discourse, modes of enunciation, literary genres, – from which emerges each singular text" (1997: 1). Once again, only Michael Hoffmann (2013c) has made the comparison with *Hyperion* the object of an "intercultural" thematic study centered on the Orientalist motif, in which it appears that the author of Turkish origin borrows from Hölderlin's "Romantic classicism" to describe the ambivalent positioning of his protagonist with regard to the country of his fathers, the "Asia minor" that, for him, is at once a space of origins and radically foreign. However well-founded, this assertion does not truly permit a response, once again, to the question of semantic contents put into play in this transposition.

By examining more closely the work undertaken by Zaimoglu on the Goethean hypotext, I will show the ways in which the discursive reappropriation of this work – not just in opening the way to a serious appropriation of the ideas, themes, and motifs developed in the eighteenth century by the *Sturm und Drang* and later German Romantic writers, but in situating itself in a contemporary context of rewriting the classics – helps Zaimoglu craft his own distinct posture as a Germanophone writer.

Pragmatic and Semantic Transformations: On the Importance of Social Ties

In terms of technique, the most obvious difference between the two novels is a quantitative one. To develop a somewhat meager plot, which only partially borrows its framework from *Werther* (without adding anything fundamentally new to it), Zaimoglu stretches his book to nearly three hundred pages, a bit more than double Goethe's novel. This considerable amplification combined with a reduction in action – a paradox that in part serves as the basis for the recurring reproach addressed to the author of having indulged in an ultimately tedious logorrhea – goes hand in hand with a transformation in the narrative schema. Abandoning Goethe's model of a one-way epistolary outpouring, Zaimoglu took inspiration from "classical" novels of letters based on reciprocity. Consisting of forty-three "pieces" total (forty-two numbered letters + an "epilogue" addressed to Hakan from Serdar and inserted between letters 41 and 42), *Liebesmale, scharlachrot* not only consists of Serdar's (twelve + the epilogue in question) letters to Hakan but also his (twelve) responses as well as a certain number of letters exchanged between Serdar and his two lovers in Germany: six with Anke (three in each direction), eleven with Dina (seven from Dina to Serdar, four from Serdar to Dina), added to which is a single letter from Serdar to Rena. This expansion of the communication network involves a multiplication of points of view and, as such, a certain distancing from the subjectivity of the central character.

This compositional schema equally affects the configuration of characters. If one can really say that Serdar occupies the central position to the extent that he is the one who, by leaving for Turkey, sets off these exchanges and remains the hub, the role that falls to Hakan is no less substantial. In contrast to Wilhelm, whose reactions to Werther's letters, mostly appeals to reason, can only be indirectly deduced from the allusions the latter makes to them, Hakan is not only given a "voice" (and a style), but also a personality and his own story. Far from contenting himself with commenting on his friend's confidences, he gives him the "recap" of his own adventures in Kiel. By establishing a sort of balance between the two main correspondents, the author creates two narrative threads that develop in parallel in two distinct places, Kiel and the Aegean coast, and then meet up again at the end.

This narrative structure leads to a mirrored doubling of the principal role, split between two protagonists presented as antagonistic at the start but who seem increasingly similar over the course of the novel. Contrary to the image each likes to present to himself and the other, Serdar and Hakan are in reality not at all as opposed in their existential setbacks as the reader might at first think. As the story progresses, the reader realizes that the stereotyped roles of the *Kanaksta* and *Abi-Türke* the two embody with the panache of actors well-versed in the genre actually represent two facets of the same reality, the two choices imposed by society on youths in their situation. Hakan, who cultivates his "tough guy" image with plebian swagger, is no less adept with language, nor less sentimental than Serdar. Moreover, he, too, attended university, even if he seems to have spent much less time there and only mixed with other marginalized youngsters born like him from immigration and living by uncertain expedients. Serdar, likewise, does not prove to be any more "delicate" than his friend in many respects, despite the bourgeois company he keeps and his ironically elevated and florid style.

As a counterpoint to these close friends, Baba, an uncouth, proletarian Turk whose psychological profile represents a third sociological and cultural variant of the "sorrowful" masculine subject, steps into the picture. Without authoring any letter, Baba, too, occasionally becomes the source of his own eloquent discourse. On a pragmatic level, he assumes a function reminiscent of the role that fell to Albert in *Werther:* that of amorous rival and antagonist to the hero. However, from a semantic point of view, he resides in the same sphere as the two other male protagonists, embodying in his fashion the drama of unhappy masculinity, characterized by frustration, a love-hate relationship with himself, and the specter of impotence.

While Hakan's role is markedly amplified with regard to the inconstancy that characterizes Wilhelm as Werther's confidant, Rena's is, inversely, far more tenuous than Charlotte's in Goethe's novel. Not appearing until the second half of the novel, she also has less of a presence than *Werther*'s female lead. Like Baba, she is not the source of any letter, but nor is she portrayed with any psychological or intellectual depth in indirect accounts. Reduced to an object of desire for Serdar – even if she is the one to initiate romantic relations – she occupies a marginal position that contrasts with the "immeasurable" value she acquires in record time in her lover's eyes. This position corresponds to her relative importance in the general economy of the novel since she shares the main female role, as far as Serdar is concerned, with two characters much more present than she is, the intellectual Dina and the impetuous Anke.

The major variable with reference to the schema of Goethe's novel rests in its multifocality. The reader is no longer amongst soliloquies but in a structure that brings the preeminence of social connections to the fore in the existential problems of the individual. Added to this multiplication of exchanges and disassociation of the main character into two (even three) complementary protagonists is the decisive role that the solidarity of friendship plays in the denouement. It is Hakan who, in – literally – flying to his friend's aid, originally just to save him from Anke's attentions and clear the path for his romance with Rena, ends up saving his life. This happy ending, which seals a tumultuous friendship, reflects the overall rather optimistic vision the text presents of human relations. Zaimoglu portrays two young men grappling with the problems connected to entry into adulthood and the necessity of social integration who finally come out the other end thanks to friendly solidarity. This solidarity that blossoms on the margin of majoritarian society is not based on community connections: Hakan and Serdar accuse each other often enough that they are not (or not any more) part of the same world. It unites two suffering, isolated individuals in conflict with their contemporaries who do not have the same personal aspirations and only agree on one thing: the rejection of common values and an anachronistic and unconditional faith in sensitivity and affect.

The Parody of *Werther:* An Intertext with a False Bottom

For the moment, let us return to the manifest parallels between *Liebesmale, scharlachrot* and *Die Leiden des jungen Werthers*. The two protagonists are about the same age (mid-twenties), are on the threshold of adult life, and have studied subjects (law for Werther, medicine for Serdar) that seem to destine them for a respectable social position. Their families expect them to embrace a profession that allows them to make a living and start a family, but they are loath to take that prosaic road and dream of a freer existence equal to their intellectual and artistic ambitions. If Serdar has broken off his studies while Werther finished his, they are both equally disinclined to meet the expectations placed on them and bow to social conventions. Enemies of conformism, they adopt a provocative and rebellious posture that expresses their disagreement with established norms[24] and their determination to embrace a form of "foolishness" admonished by those around them.[25]

---

[24] Serdar defends himself against the intolerance of his petty bourgeois environment by exhibiting the distinctive signs of rebellious youth such as long hair and a ponytail: "Die Leute reißen sich hier den Arsch auf, um Uniformität zu wahren, und jeden, der irgendwie aus der Reihe tanzt, verdächtigen sie der Perversion, egal ob derjenige eine Rockermatte trägt oder Kinder fickt. Daher der Pferdeschwanz" (LS 61).
[25] With Serdar, even a blatantly conventional way of acting can be asserted as a form of reverse provocation to the contempt of a brainwashed youth for "uncool" behavior. A case in point is when he explains to Anke that by ordering from the local pizzeria a pizza so common the waiters refer to it as the "conformist pizza" ("Spießer-Pizza"), he in reality demonstrated a freedom of mind and the "courage to be foolish" ("eine Art Mut zum Wahnsinn") in the face of an omnipresent need to "differentiate" at all costs, such as through "pogo punk" styling (LS 151).

The two novels begin with their protagonists distancing themselves from their urban life and suspending their routines under pretext. Werther accepts a mission given to him by his mother to manage an inheritance, whereas Serdar takes advantage of an opportunity to spend the summer at his parents' place on the coast of the Aegean Sea. In both cases, the *primum mobile* from the start is the need for distraction from a sentimental entanglement. Without meaning to, Werther had encouraged the attentions of a young girl whose sister he had halfheartedly courted (LS 350). Serdar takes flight under pressure from two intrusive lovers: "[T]he women were breathing down my neck" (LS 9), he reminds his friend. Retreating to a distant locale where they can temporarily live as they please far from daily constraints allows them to give free rein to their penchant for introspection, solitary meditation, and search for artistic inspiration. Let us recall the words with which Werther, already having arrived, expresses his ravishment to Wilhelm:

> How glad I am to have come away! [...] Otherwise I am quite happy here, the solitude in this paradisiacal region is a precious balm to my heart, and the youthful season in all its fullness warms my often shivering heart. Every tree, every hedge, is a bouquet of blossoms, and one would like to be a mayfly drifting about in the sea of heady aromas, able to find in it all one's nourishment.[26]

Then, on 10 May: "A wonderful serenity has taken possession of my entire soul, like these sweet mornings of spring which I enjoy with my whole heart."[27] The first of Serdar's letters reports the same mix of jubilation and relaxation kindled by a sensation of growing warmth, which is not merely metaphorical: "I'm healthy and feel every sort of vivacity, and I arrived safe and sorrowless, without losing an ounce of that transcendence that my highly physical being radiated in my cold homeland, on the west coast of the Turkish shelf."[28] The theme of regen-

---

26 "Wie froh bin ich, daß ich weg bin! [...] Übrigens befinde ich mich hier gar wohl, die Einsamkeit ist meinem Herzen köstlicher Balsam in dieser paradiesischen Gegend, und diese Jahrszeit der Jugend wärmt mit aller Fülle mein oft schauderndes Herz. Jeder Baum, jede Hecke ist ein Strauß von Blüten, und man möchte zum Maienkäfer werden, um in dem Meer von Wohlgerüchen herumschweben und alle seine Nahrung darin finden zu können" (W I, 350–351, letter of 4 May). Translation: *The Sorrows of Young Werther* (2005: 7–8). Subsequent references to this work will be from this translation, with the pagination added within brackets when following the German edition.
27 "Eine wunderbare Heiterkeit hat meine ganze Seele eingenommen, gleich den süßen Frühlingsmorgen, die ich mit ganzem Herzen genieße" (W I, 351, letter of 10 May [2005: 8]).
28 "Ich bin gesund und verspüre allerlei Munterkeiten, und ich bin heil und ohne Gram, ohne ein Gramm Verlust jener Transzendenz, die mein hoch körperliches Wesen in meiner kalten Heimat ausstrahlte, an der Westküste des türkischen Festlandsockels angekommen" (LS 9).

eration both spiritual and physical runs throughout the subsequent pages. Serdar feels "rather good here"[29] and decides to take advantage of the situation to retreat provisionally from the social and especially the romantic game: "At the moment I'm pretty tired of puzzling over women [...] and it seems to me, I don't want to go on the prowl for love. When I take a look at the honeys around here, I'd rather just mothball all my feelings."[30]

Thus contented, the two protagonists lapse into an analogous state of beatitude, hardly troubled at first by the fact that this brings with it a form of psychic ataraxia that renders them, to different degrees, incapable of realizing or sublimating their desires. The blossoming of a new passion is experienced in this context as an interior cataclysm, a transformation of their whole being. The coveted object is, in both cases, a woman of rather discreet charms but perceived at first glance as superior to all others by her "purity" and "authenticity." Werther's ravishment at watching Charlotte serve dinner to her orphaned little brothers and sisters is matched by Serdar's transport at smelling a perfume of Nivea cream wafting around Rena, a scent he associates with a maternal figure in opposition to the artifices of refined seduction.[31] The young woman thus endowed with qualities evoking the lost plenitude of childhood responds at first to the advances of her suitor, but ultimately remains inaccessible to him.

There the parallels on the level of action end since Werther, incapable of renunciation, goes on to succumb to his love for Charlotte to the point of suicide, whereas Serdar renounces a union with young Rena without too many qualms. Not only does he not consider killing himself, but despite the emphatic lyricism of the letter he writes from Germany (and with which the novel ends), there is no question of an exclusive and eternal passion in his case. He has continued since they met to nourish ongoing amorous relationships through letters with other women and leaves no doubt about the fact that he will resume this libertine way of life when he returns. He renounces his literary ambitions with a similar pragmatism. Taking sober stock of his unconvincing artistic experience,[32] he sol-

---

29 "Mir geht's ziemlich korrekt hier" (LS 11).
30 "Im Moment bin ich es relativ leid, mir den Kopf zu zerbrechen über die Frauen [...] und mich deucht, ich will in Liebesdingen nicht auf Sendung gehen. Wenn ich mir die hiesigen Schatzimausis so angucke, möchte ich stattdessen gleich alle Gefühle einmotten" (LS 11).
31 "[...] da roch ich den altvertrauten Duft, der mich bei Frauen um den Verstand bringt, Nivea-Handcreme und sonst nichts, die Creme der ersten Stunde, die Creme unserer Mütter und Schwestern, bevor sie auf das teure Zeug umstiegen" (LS 159).
32 "Ein kompletter Künstler wollte ich werden, ich verließ meinen vertrauten Hort, ich kam aus der Kälte und wollte heißlaufen. Auf die Gretchenfrage 'Kunst oder Geschlecht' weiß ich keine Antwort. [...] Die praktikabelste Lösung ist nicht immer die richtige, aber man lernt dadurch immerhin, in Augenhöhe mit den Gegenständen zu leben" (LS 293).

emnly announces to Hakan that he is resigning "from the club of haiku poets," even if he does not seem to have other projects lined up for the moment (LS 293).

At this stage, everything seems to indicate that Zaimoglu merely relied on Goethe's text the better to underline the points where he departs from it. Thus, Serdar becomes defined as an anti-Werther whose story, starting from similar conditions, takes a deliberately burlesque turn to end in farce, the opposite of Goethe's tragedy. Yet, what is the point of such a parody? Evidently, it is not about demonstrating the outmodedness of Goethe's text (which would not be of much interest anyway) nor poking fun at these immigrant youths whose subjective difficulties are quite real, even if they are a thousand miles from the preoccupations of a young bourgeois of the *ancien régime* rebelling against social hierarchy and the spirit of his age. One of the targets of parody seems to be, by contrast, contemporary society with its downsides that engender new forms of civilizational malaise. This applies to the relationship with nature, for example. Absent from Zaimoglu's novel, Werther's mythic communion with an apotheosized nature is implicitly evoked by its absence, which makes its loss feel all the more grievous. If Serdar has no intimate affinity with nature[33] and is relieved to return at the novel's end to his urban *biotope*, it means he lives in a world where elsewhere no longer exists. In this sense, his retreat does not have a setting in a "terrestrial paradise" (W 351) propitious to the elevation of the soul but in a bustling seaside resort, scorching and dedicated to frivolous pastimes, that form of modern tourist's "paradise," which seems more nightmarish than promising for the rejuvenation of the body and spirits. The inversion of Goethe's schema has the effect in this case of highlighting the curse of post-industrial civilization, which, by destroying mankind's natural environment, has denied it any possibility of escape. Urbanization, the tourism industry, and the global expansion of capitalism have led to a uniformity that extends from sartorial trends to canons of beauty to morals and to cultural references.[34]

---

[33] Even when Serdar seems to look for a source of poetic inspiration in his cookie-cutter surroundings (watching the glittering play of the waves, feeling the wind and sun on his skin, admiring the night starry sky, etc.), the picturesque description systematically comes to an abrupt end. For instance, as he describes an excursion to "the charming small town of Edremit" as one of the key moments that inspired one of his rare haikus, the aesthetic "shock" he reports ("Ich war wie vom Donner gerührt!", "Ich war sofort Feuer und Flamme") proves to originate each time from a purely cultural observation that is also based on a verbal production: an inscription on the bumper sticker of a truck, the crude "eloquence" ("Wortgewalt") of a mother yelling at her child on the beach (LS 33–34).

[34] The following statement is just one of many examples: "Was ist das bloß für eine Welt, das Gegenlicht muss her, in dem die Schönen und Arschbackigen, die Lustpavillon-Flittchen, fünfzehnjährige Slumgewächse und wahre Orient-Weibungetüme an ihrer Pop-Silhouette arbeiten.

The geographic and cultural uprooting specific to the post-migration generation adds to the denunciation of that general loss of reference points and authenticity, which constitutes one of the recurring motifs of the novel. It is significant in this respect that Serdar does not seek refuge far from his family in a place freely chosen as the aptly named "Wahlheim" ("Chosen Home") was for Werther. Instead, his journey specifically brings him near to his parents in a lodge with no privacy tucked into a subdivision closed to outsiders.[35] Confined to this inauspicious place, his parental abode even if he is in no way "at home," there he finds the relative reassurance of a regression into the position of a minor "stuffed" to the point of indigestion with his mom's home cooking (LS 34). His experience of Turkey, his "homeland," reduces itself to this anonymous locality straight out of a postcard[36] that he is neither tied to by memory nor family history. On this level, too, Goethe's novel functions as a contrasting matrix that makes it possible to measure the blurring of traditional standards that confronts today's *Kanaks*. Where Werther only had to leave the city of W. to find, in the verdant countryside at some distance from there, a bucolic place where he could take up residence and discover himself by contemplating nature and spending time with rural people with simple morals and upright hearts, the uprooted Serdar leaves his "ghetto" only to find himself thousands of kilometers away in another globalized heterotopic space: the vacation resort.[37]

The irony of this paradoxical reversal, induced by a double movement of historical transposition and cultural translation, is not, however, absolutely unidirectional. Did not Werther already find something in little Wahlheim to feed his own fantasies of nostalgic regression? The description he gives at the beginning

---

Das Fleisch ist alles, Silikon die halbe Miete, Anatolya steht auf Superperoxyd, ne gebleichte Matte und das Gesicht in mehreren Schichten aufgeschminkt [...]. Ich staune nur, zum Beispiel rase ich mit dem Auto an einer Werbefläche auf zwei Stelzen vorbei, und mir wird verkündet: 'Big chicken – touch your taste!'" (LS 52).

35 Serdar describes his parents' bungalow as just "a small part of a larger building complex fenced and shielded against the lousy peasant scum of the surrounding area", those "goat drivers out in the world" who "certainly know that there are plenty of bikini bottoms romping about on this side of the gate, but that on-site viewing is excluded", even less so since "night watchmen patrol the holiday village, communicating through their whistles", thus also disturbing the sleep of holidaymakers (LS 13).
36 "Du musst dir das mal vorstellen, mein phantasieloser Knecht der niederen Triebe, es ist ein Sommerabend wie aus dem Bilderbuch, das Meer ein ausgespanntes blaues Laken, der Mond hat sich in Schräglage aufgehängt" (LS 59).
37 Heterotopias, as defined by Foucault (1984, 2001), refers to certain cultural, institutional, and discursive sites that are embedded in our lives though being somehow "other," i.e. mirroring and at the same time distorting, unsettling or inverting other spaces.

of his adventure of this place preserving the appearance of a terrestrial paradise is not without its own allusions to the comfort of a return to the maternal bosom:

> Its situation on a hill is quite interesting, and when, taking the footpath up, you come out into the village, you suddenly look out over the whole valley. A good innkeeper, obliging and cheerful in her old age, dispenses wine, beer, coffee; and best of all are two linden trees, covering with their outstretched branches the small square in front of the church that is closed in by peasants' houses, barns, and yards. I could not easily have found so secluded, so inviting a place, and I have my little table brought out from the inn with my chair, drink my coffee there, and read my Homer. (Goethe 2005: 15)[38]

Rereading these lines in light of Zaimoglu's text, it becomes clear that the irony of the rewriting splashes back, to a certain extent, onto the model. There was, it seems, already a bit of Serdar in Werther. The point of this intertextual comparison is to uncover a rapport that, all appearances to the contrary, is not merely antithetical. Serdar holds our interest precisely because, at the end of the day, he is not simply an anti-Werther. In fact, to a certain extent and without the objective necessarily being to pick apart the model (that is clearly not the case here), every parody functions as a kind of developer for the older text. Hence, the situation of the immigrants' son torn between Germany and Turkey, between the multicultural exurban proletariat and the cultured German bourgeoisie of the city centers, of this young man who in his friend's words is "neither fish nor flesh"[39] (thus placing him under suspicion of treason against the community Hakan acts as a spokesperson for)[40] and never manages to find acceptance for just being what he is anywhere, recalls, all in all, that of Goethe's protagonist. Werther, too, was sidelined in his time, incapable of finding his place in the in-

---

38 "Die Lage an einem Hügel ist sehr interessant, und wenn man oben auf dem Fußpfade zum Dorf herausgeht, übersieht man auf einmal das ganze Tal. Eine gute Wirtin, die gefällig und munter in ihrem Alter ist, schenkt Wein, Bier, Kaffee; und was über alles geht, sind zwei Linden, die mit ihren ausgebreiteten Ästen, den kleinen Platz vor der Kirche bedecken, der ringsum mit Bauernhäusern, Scheuern und Höfen eingeschlossen ist. So vertraulich, so heimlich hab' ich nicht leicht ein Plätzchen gefunden, und dahin laß ich mein Tischchen aus dem Wirtshause bringen und meinen Stuhl, trinke meinen Kaffee da, und lese meinen Homer" (W I, 357, letter of 26 May).
39 "Manchmal frag ich mich, Alter, was wir eigentlich in Almanya suchen, wir sind Anatolier mit schiefem Herzen und haben es zu einigem Ruhm innere Krimibranche gebracht, dann gibt's noch Studierte wie dich, die weder Fisch noch Fleisch sind [...]" (LS 69).
40 As a result, Hakan calls his friend an "Uncle Tom," one of those cowards who are afraid to make fools of themselves if they don't behave as the Germans expect them to ("Alles, was aus der Reihe tanzt, wird von solchen Onkel Toms wie dir angemotzt, weil sie sich ja so schlecht benehmen und wir uns bloß nicht vor den Alemannen blamieren dürfen" [LS 225]).

sipid bourgeoisie of his origins but also brushed aside by an arrogant aristocracy that only tolerates his company temporarily without a thought to welcome him otherwise than as an exotic element. Humiliated by this rejection, the "wanderer" in search of a place and a destiny equal to him understands that he is condemned to remain a "pilgrim" without ties – and that this solitude of the marginal is at once that of the modern subject overall.[41] The parallel with Werther suggests that in today's world Serdar is not as isolated a case as one might think but rather that his experience as a minority subject is indicative of a condition with which society as a whole has not yet fully reckoned.

This precarious social position places Serdar, much like Werther, in a situation of potential exclusion. Incapable of adhering to the values of his original community (from which his parents have already distanced themselves by leaving their Anatolian countryside for Germany) and wanting to escape the unenviable living conditions of the immigrant "ghetto," he remains at the threshold of a *Bildungsbürgertum* that will only tolerate him as foreign element. His ideological positioning stems from this situation. Serdar is responding to the threat of exclusion by fleeing forward and provocation, proudly claiming his marginal status rather than seeing himself refused integration into majoritarian German society. The reader can identify this posture in the presentation he makes of himself as a poet who *shocks the bourgeoisie*:

> The barbarian invasion is as certain as the amen in the mosque. At least that's what they want us to believe in *Almanya*. So, I'm the raucous hatchet man who plies them with haikus, who coddles them with herpetic prose. In times of hostile take overs, learned idleness is obligatory, and the highest commandment should read: Make space and make way for the sensitive![42]

Resulting from his social marginality, the sentimental and solitary rebel persona Serdar adopts echoes the disdain Werther professes for norms and conventions, his refusal to subordinate himself, and his idealization of the "common people." Like him, Zaimoglu's protagonist cultivates a distance with respect to the community based on his intellectual superiority and his personal singularity, seeking to escape from economic imperatives, social convention, and common morality.

---

[41] "Ja wohl bin ich nur ein Wandrer, ein Waller auf der Erde! Seid ihr denn mehr?" (W II, 416, letter of 16 June) ("Yes, I am surely a wanderer, a pilgrim on earth. Are any of you more?" [89]).
[42] "Die Invasion der Barbaren ist so sicher wie das Amen in der Moschee. Zumindest wollen sie es uns in Almanya weismachen. Also bin ich der ungestüme Machetenmann, der es ihnen mit Haikus besorgt, der sie mit Feigwarzenprosa verhätschelt. In Zeiten feindlicher Übernahmen ist gelehrter Müßiggang obligatorisch, und die oberste Forderung sollte lauten: Gebet den Empfindsamen Raum und Weg!" (LS 32).

His need for distinction leads him to oscillate between bragging,[43] self-pity, and self-deprecation. Torn between rejection and the desire for integration, he suffers the *sorrows* that result in part from objective constraints: society's restrictions imposed on individual subjectivity.

His psychological profile accords well with this trajectory. Tormented, egocentric, and narcissistic, he succumbs to affect and cultivates melancholic tendencies.[44] Betting that his sensitivity predestines him to artistic creativity, he devotes himself to writing poems after trying his hand at painting (LS 217), but he shows himself incapable of real productivity. His need for recognition condemns him to remain a dilettante in art as in love. This problem of dilettantism, already central in Goethe's novel, appears in *Liebesmale, scharlachrot* in a doubly aggravated form. The disparity between pretension and reality manifests itself in part in the very nature of Serdar's poetic productions, the minimalist aesthetic of which seems difficult to reconcile with an overflowing subjectivity.[45] At the same time, his artistic sterility is coupled with sexual dysfunction, which clearly appears as another symptom of his identity crisis. This doubling, which produces a demystifying imbalance in relation to the hypotext, does not itself constitute a radical subversion of the Wertherian schema. By transposing, at least partially, the motif of creative impotence onto the psychological plane, Zaimoglu only expanded on a trait already present in *Werther:* the protagonist's inability to be-

---

[43] Writing to Anke, he reminds her of their shared feeling of being exceptional beings, ostracized because of their very superiority: "Waren wir uns nicht einig darin, dass man uns auf Partys links liegen ließ, weil man nichts mit unserer Art anzufangen wusste, weil wir keine wandelnden Ähnlichkeitsplätze waren?" (LS 140).

[44] The following passage, featuring Serdar "running through the ruins of [his] shadowy existence," is a good example of the parodistic variation on the motif of *Sehnsucht:* "Ich verzehre mich, wonach, ist mir wahrlich ein Rätsel, wie ein Wiedergänger laufe ich durch die Ruinen meiner Schattenexistenz und habe Hunger nach echtem Fleisch und nach echten Sehnen, obwohl meine Sehnenstränge wie irre Ausfluss in meine sensibelste Extremität pumpen und mein Zammazingo weiterhin eine traurige Gestalt abgibt" (LS 75).

[45] Serdar predominantly writes haikus, a type of poem he himself defines as "useless," "something that doesn't need to work, a little music in the ears," something volatile and unassuming that "only the eye of the connoisseur can recognize" ("Ein Haiku […] ist ein unbrauchbar Ding, etwas, was nicht zu funktionieren hat, eine kleine Musik in den Ohren. Ein Haiku streift dich kurz und scheut die Berührung, es will sich kurz auffalten, es will ein Streifen Leinwand sein, auf dem sich das Tageslicht in seine geheimen Nuancen zerstreut. Nur das Auge des Kenners kann erkennen," LS 130). After meeting Rena, however, he relies on his amorous transport to find inspiration for "a substantial love poem" (LS 163). Later on, he intends to "scrap the pale haikus and write hymns of praise of her" ("Ich werde die blassen Haikus fallen lassen und Lobeshymnen auf sie verfassen," LS 253).

come "a man"[46] by overcoming his disappointments and sublimating his desires. Werther is paralyzed, in his desire for artistic creation as in his amorous feelings, by his need to prove to the world what he is capable of. Serdar is, temporarily, stricken with impotence for the same reasons. He dreams of achieving a "Kraftakt" ("feat") that would reveal his genius to the world as soon as he could figure out how to "popularize his boo-boos" but is brutally reminded of his limits "as much in the domain of *agape* as in artistic activity."[47] His infirmity thus seems to be the metaphorical translation of the ill that afflicts Werther. However, it is also a metaphor for the generational malaise of post-migration youths. According to Zaimoglu, the *Kanaks* suffer from constant threats to their personal integrity and thus also from a chronic inferiority complex that makes them afraid to make mistakes and forget themselves. For this reason, he notes in the preface to *Kanak Sprak*, more than one has ended up in the psychiatric hospital. Their impotence ("Impotenz") can take forms as diverse as self-mutilation, depression, or schizophrenia. Serdar's sexual dysfunction is the most direct expression of this anxiety, the literal psychological translation of a problem that concerns, according to Zaimoglu, the entire second-generation of immigrants in Germany.[48]

This metaphorical translation stems from the effects of trivialization that suffuse every level of the novel. In the same register of introspective contemplation, Zaimoglu reproduces in part the narcissistic indulgence Werther devotes to the movements of his soul, in his letters to Wilhelm describing the echoes triggered in him by the most insignificant events of his daily life. Hence, Serdar asks himself existential questions:

> And, man, I've been giving thought to this skin I'm in. Am I the little flower in the pot, or am I the humus that fills the pot and gives nourishment to the tender, little plant? Am I the knitting needle in the hand of an old hag fading toward her *exitus* in a seniors' home, or am I just the dead possum? Am I the cold cigarette butt or the Prince from the Orient, or the Apache I mentioned before? Have I been laid in the cradle of depravity, or am I the savior

---

[46] This is what Charlotte demands of Werther during one of their last meetings: to be a man ("Ich bitte Sie, fuhr sie fort, indem sie ihn bei der Hand nahm, mäßigen Sie sich ! [...] Sein Sie ein Mann! wenden Sie diese traurige Anhänglichkeit von einem Geschöpf, das nichts tun kann als Sie bedauern," W II, 443–444).
[47] "Ich träume von einem genialen Kraftakt, einer regelrechten Erweckung von dem Tag, an dem ich endlich meine Wehwehchen popularisieren kann. Denn das wird ja da draußen erwartet, der Künstler soll bis zum letzten Blutplasmaklumpen ausbluten, und dann schauen wir uns mal diesen blassen Körper am Boden an!" (LS 176).
[48] "Als selbstbewußtes Individuum aber existiert der Kanake auch nur auf dem Paßfoto. Er lebt in dem Gefühl, minderwertig zu sein, fehlzugehen oder auf Abwege zu geraten. Manch einer wandert als krankes Exotikum in die geschlossene Abteilung: Impotenz als freiwillige Selbstverstümmelung, Depressionen, Schizophrenie" (Zaimoglu 1995: 11).

who disentangles the subtext of the scriptures for the masses? Am I the court lackey they throw monstrous mollusks at because he, forgetful as he is, has committed the offense of turning his back to a duke?[49]

Yet, this mania of self-observation extends in Serdar's case to the quasi-clinical itemization of his physical ailments – beginning with the back pain he miraculously recovers from upon arrival in Turkey, an affliction of his vertebral column easily recognizable as another symptom of his existential crisis, no less telling than the impotence that soon takes its place. Serdar also informs his friend (and the reader at the same time), not sparing the gory details, of his digestive and eliminative troubles (LS 34). With the same morbid fascination, he reports his fluctuations in weight, the appearance of pimples on his face, and his skin's reaction to the sun and insect bites.

By and large, such are the sort of "sorrows" that obsess Zaimoglu's protagonist: "boo-boos" of the soul and especially the body that seem rather risible compared to the ills that once plagued Werther but which he explores with no less delight. Moreover, it is clearly in the domain of love, where in Goethe the link between pain and passion, "Leiden" and "Leidenschaft," were most significant, that this trivialization expresses itself most intensely. The two protagonists of *Liebesmale, scharlachrot* are literally obsessed with sexuality, to which amorous relations seem to be reduced for them. Erotic descriptions play a major role in their exchanges, both of them taking delight in pages-long scenes of torrid coupling, more often fantasized than real, substituted sometimes with tales of solitary pleasure – incidentally, not always any easier to attain. Thus, Serdar mobilizes his imagination in an attempt to restore his defective manhood at all costs, passing from "classic" masturbation to various expedients including the voyeuristic, fetishistic, etc. In love with Rena, he is haunted by the fear of not being able to satisfy her, but he consoles himself in the meantime with his ex's panties sent by mail from Germany (LS 243–244). As for Hakan, who is not impotent but whose attempts to seduce his upstairs neighbor have long been unsuccessful, he refuses to air out his apartment after the object of his af-

---

[49] "Und, Alter, ich mache mir Gedanken über die Haut, in der ich stecke. Bin ich das Blümchen im Topf, oder bin ich die Humuserde, die den Topf füllt und dem zarten Pflänzchen Nahrung zuführt? Bin ich die Stricknadel in der Hand einer alten Schabracke, die in einem Seniorendomizil ihrem Exitus entgegendämmert, oder bin ich gar das tote Opossum? Bin ich die kalte Kippe oder der Prinz aus dem Morgenland, oder oben erwähnter Apache? Hat man mich in die Wiege der Verdorbenheiten gelegt, oder bin ich der Erlöser, der den Volksmassen den Subtext der Schriften entheddert? Bin ich der Hoflakai, den man den Monstermollusken vorwirft, weil er sich des Vergehens schuldig gemacht hat, vergesslich, wie er ist, einem Herzog den Rücken zu kehren?" (LS 12).

fection stops by in order to preserve the olfactory traces of her presence as long as possible.

By making such a show of their lubricity, the two young men seem to position themselves in rigorous opposition to the "ideal" lover the reader may be tempted to see in Werther. Although founded on a mystical idea of the communion of souls, the Goethean hero's discourse on love is nonetheless propelled by a powerful sensuality. Goethe insists throughout the novel on the elementary force of desire, portraying his protagonist transported by the exquisite pleasure of contact with a hand or foot,[50] only resisting with great effort the sudden desire to embrace Charlotte, to throw himself at her feet, to cover her with kisses, etc. The impossibility Werther finds himself in of satisfying this impulse to seize her, which he justifies to himself in terms of his primal and "natural" character (in the end, does he not conduct himself like a child who needs to touch anything that attracts him?),[51] leads him to make do with objects of substitution. Unable to kiss Charlotte's lips, he touches the notes she sends him to his own lips – and shows no compunction about telling her, going so far as to ask her not to use sand to dry the ink in order to spare him the disagreeable feeling of the grains against his teeth (W I, 383 [46]). Another time, realizing that he will not get the chance to see her that day, he sends his servant to her "just to have a person around [him] who will have been near her today," then waits on pins and needles for the return of his emissary, whom he must restrain himself from covering in kisses and caresses (W I, 381 [44]). So it goes with the ribbon Charlotte gives him for his birthday that he asks to be buried with and so on to the pistols he borrows from Albert to kill himself, which he kisses "a thousand times" because they "have been in [her] hands." The displacement of desire onto fetish objects is

---

[50] "Ach, was mir das durch alle Adern läuft, wenn mein Finger unversehens den ihrigen berührt, wenn unsere Füße sich unter dem Tisch begegnen; Ich ziehe zurück wie vom Feuer, und eine geheime Kraft zieht mich wieder vorwärts – mir wird's so schwindlich vor allen Sinnen [...]" (W I, 380, letter of 16 July) ("Oh, how it runs through all my veins if my fingers inadvertently touch hers, if our feet touch under the table! I pull back as if from fire, but a secret power draws me forward again – all my senses make me giddy" [43]).

[51] "Wenn ich nicht schon hundertmal auf dem Punkte gestanden bin, ihr um den Hals zu fallen! Weiß der große Gott, wie einem das tut, so viel Liebenswürdigkeiten vor einem herumkreuzen zu sehen und nicht zugreifen zu dürfen; und das Zugreifen ist doch der natürlichste Trieb der Menschheit; Greifen die Kinder nicht nach allem was ihnen in den Sinn fällt? – Und ich?" (W II, 425, letter of 30 October) ("If I haven't a hundred times been on the point of falling on her breast! God knows how one feels seeing so much amiability displayed in front of one and not being allowed to reach out for it; yet reaching out is the most natural drive of mankind. Don't children reach out for everything that catches their attention? – And I?" [100]).

recurrent and quasi paradigmatic of Goethe's novel, and its sexual connotations are obvious.[52]

One of the most suggestive passages from this point of view is the episode of the canary inserted into the second edition between Charlotte's marriage and Werther's departure. The young woman marvels under her unhappy lover's gaze at the delicacy with which the tame bird has just been pecking breadcrumbs directly from her hand and giving her "kisses" on her lips. Calling Werther to witness this game, she gives him the animal for his turn to be "kissed" on the lips by the bird, which thus flits from one to the other, to Werther's great pleasure – and also to his great torment since he does not fail to read in the canary's behavior the impulsive satisfaction denied to him and in Charlotte's at least an unconscious provocation.[53] In the context of German literature of the era, such scenes went as far as possible in representing erotic experience, especially considering the illicit character of the relations between Werther and Charlotte.[54] However, as we have seen, Zaimoglu's novel contains numerous scenes that can

---

[52] According to Paul-Laurent Assoun, this feature of the novel shows Goethe's early intuition of the link later established by Freud between fetishism and the overestimation of the "object" of passion (Assoun 2006: 103–111).

[53] "Als sie dem Tierchen den Mund hinhielt, drückte es sich so lieblich in die süßen Lippen als wenn es die Seligkeit hätte fühlen können die es genoß. Er soll sie auch küssen, sagte sie, und reichte den Vogel herüber. Das Schnäbelchen machte den Weg von ihrem Munde zu dem meinigen, und die pickende Berührung war wie ein Hauch, eine Ahndung liebevollen Genusses. Sein Kuß sagte ich, ist nicht ganz ohne Begierde, er sucht Nahrung und kehrt unbefriedigt von der leeren Liebkosung zurück. Er ißt mir auch aus dem Munde, sagte sie. Sie reichte ihm einige Brosamen mit ihren Lippen, aus denen die Freuden unschuldig teilnehmender Liebe in aller Wonne lächelten. Ich kehrte das Gesicht weg. Sie sollte es nicht tun! sollte nicht meine Einbildungskraft mit diesen Bildern himmlischer Unschuld und Seligkeit reizen und mein Herz aus dem Schlafe, in den es manchmal die Gleichgültigkeit des Lebens wiegt, nicht wecken!" (W II, 421, letter of 12 September) ("As she held the small creature to her mouth, it pressed itself so captivatingly on those sweet lips, as if it could have felt the happiness it was enjoying. 'He shall kiss you too,' she said, and handed the bird over to me. The little beak made its way from her lips to mine, and the pecking touch was like a breath, an intimation, of loving enjoyment. Its kiss, I said, is not entirely without desire, it is seeking food and withdrawn dissatisfied from the empty caress. 'He eats from my mouth,' too, she said. She offered it a few crumbs with her lips, from which the joys of innocently devoted love smiled in complete bliss. I turned my face away. She should not do this! Not fire up my imagination with these images of divine innocence and happiness, not wake my heart from the sleep in which it is sometimes cradled by the indifference of life!" [95]).

[54] On the "disturbing crudeness" of this passage, see Barthes (2007: 139–140). Béatrice Dumiche pointed to the parallels between the allegedly innocent eroticism of this scene and the latent erotic connotations of Charlotte's first apparition as a surrogate mother feeding her siblings (2002: 24).

be read as variations on this same metonymic logic, figuring desire that is displaced onto objects of substitution. This form of "deviant" enjoyment, which is nonetheless not necessarily perverse (the two young men only satisfy themselves with a fetishistic sexuality for want of an alternative), takes on the appearance of grotesquely exaggerated version of a sensuality already present in Goethe's text.

Granted, it is true that the passages dedicated to sexuality are not only cruder in Zaimoglu's novel but also proportionately more numerous, particularly as the narrative framework establishes a form of competition between the two protagonists in terms of bawdy eloquence and naughty fantasizing. If, however, this vulgar one-upmanship cannot help fostering a feeling of lassitude in the reader, this saturation effect does not in any way, as some critics have over-hastily concluded, stem from the bravado their descriptions contain.[55] Upon closer inspection, the two young men compete rather in their readiness to exhibit their weaknesses. Unhesitant in admitting their disappointments to each other, they relate one anecdote after another whence they do not emerge looking better, proving themselves to be at heart – here, too, like Werther – desirous subjects eternally disappointed and frustrated. Serdar might present himself in some regards as a seducer, and with some credibility – since this image is corroborated at once by Hakan's letters (envious of his success with women) and by the proof the three women (Anke, Dina, and Rena) with whom he maintains romantic relations present in their attachment to him – however his current impotence, which condemns him to sexual inactivity, represents a source of humiliation and numerous concerns. Even in this portrait of a Don Juan who becomes unhappy the day he falls in love with a woman whom he cannot or must not love, something of Werther's profile can be gleaned.[56] Hakan offers the reverse image, as a man in a state of constant sexual excitation whose attempts at seduction come up short. When, by chance, he achieves his ends with the woman he desires, he gives himself without holding back but falls into a deep sadness if the longed-for union reveals itself to be nothing but a passing caprice for the object of his desire.

In any case, the experience of love perpetually ends painfully for both characters, and they do not try to hide this from one another, or themselves. As Ser-

---

[55] See for example Steuten (2001): "What is more annoying, though, is the excess of sexual peacocking" ("Nerviger sind dagegen die in Überdosis verabreichten Sexprotzereien").
[56] Werther is himself a kind of "womanizer", a repentant socialite who sometimes wonders – not without vanity – about the attraction he exerts on others (see the letter of 17 May [11–12]).

dar phrases it, they resemble two defeated men, living "in some ways the same traumatic horror" consisting of "stumbling from one bombed-out trench to another."[57] Hence, neither really boasts of his amorous conquests. The bravado is located much more in the letters' tone than in their contents – and yet, to reduce their light-hearted bawdiness to a form of posturing is to pay little mind to the irony they contain. In fact, it is in this capacity to laugh at themselves that the point of divergence between these two characters and Goethe's protagonist resides. The aptitude for self-irony is also what finally puts Serdar in a position to overcome the crisis he is going through, to accept the limits placed on his desire, and to move forward.

Anyhow, even if love for them is inextricable from carnal desire, Zaimoglu's protagonists are nonetheless passionate lovers. In fact, their blasé attitudes even seem to make Serdar and Hakan all the more susceptible to love's call – likewise particularly vulnerable to the wounds it can inflict. So, if they pass easily enough from one woman to the next, they nonetheless feel the shock, at once physical and mental, of love with a capital L at each new encounter – at least to hear them tell it. After meeting Rena, Serdar writes to Hakan: "My dear rogue, something wonderful has happened, and I'm truly at a loss for words. My heart is bursting out of rightful place between two organ walls; it bounds like a little lamb's tail in the spring rain, my heart my heart my heart!"[58] And later:

> I don't know how it is with you, but when love throws the book at me, a shiver goes through my chest hair, every individual follicle stands up and becomes a highly sensitive tentacle. Does this sensitivity of mine come together with the increased pigment production? Well, I still haven't figured that out, but it stirs something in me. The old coziness is gone, and old Asia, the Asia of bulges and lusts, of the virtuosos in the *ashk* profession, of the cutthroats and the lords of the *hashashins* rise up in my chest [...][59]

---

[57] "Ich weiß, du fühlst dich wie ein Kriegsgott, dem die Spangen und Achselstücke abgerupft wurden, und in gewisser Weise durchleben wir beide dasselbe Horrortrauma und taumeln von einem zerbombten Schützengraben zum nächsten" (LS 268).

[58] "Mein lieber Schlingel, es ist etwas Wunderbares passiert, und mir fehlen wahrlich die Worte, mein Herz sprengt seinen angestammten Platz zwischen zwei Organhäuten, es hüpft wie ein Lämmerschwänzchen im Frühlingsregen, mein Herz mein Herz mein Herz!" (LS 188).

[59] "Ich weiß nicht, wie es sich bei dir verhält, aber wenn ich nach allen Regeln der Liebeskunst verschossen bin, gehen Schauer über meinen Brustpelz, jedes einzelne Haar richtet sich auf und wird zum hoch sensiblen Tentakel. Ob diese meine Empfindsamkeit mit einer erhöhten Pigmentproduktion einhergeht, nun ja, das habe ich noch nicht herausbekommen, aber es tut sich etwas in mir, die alte Gemütlichkeit ist dahin, und das alte Asien, das der Wülste und Wollüste, der Virtuosen im 'aschk'-Metier, der Messermeuchler und Hashischordens-herren regt sich nun in meinem Leib [...]" (LS 252).

This enamored state is presented here as a ravishment in the literal sense of the term,[60] ineffable and only capable of description by the physical effects it produces in the amorous subject, effects themselves expressed in metaphors. It is the same for Hakan who, when he finally receives a postcard from the neighbor he has been courting for weeks asking him to come get her from the train station, describes his feelings thusly:

> For me, it was as if confetti were falling, as if a polka band were belting out a smooth rendition of Whitney Houston's "best of" from the last five years, as if someone had pumped two vials of morphine and a full IV bag of sweet liqueur into my veins. Man, I swear this heaven-sent postcard was a pop song, and I was knocked on my ass. It was like all the shit of the last few days was blown away, and I was so gripped by that *ashk*, that absolute love *à la turca*, that I threw my arms up and danced in a circle snapping my fingers and stomping my feet.[61]

This superlative mad love that causes them to forget themselves and that both label *alla turca* with the word "aschk" (the Germanized form of the Turkish "aşk") is a feeling at once sensual and spiritual, a mystical experience promising the greatest joys but also the most profound affliction. Without ever lifting the characters beyond the carnal sphere to grant them access to an ethereal, idealized form of love, it nevertheless occasionally permits them to transcend the limits of their social ego. Hence Serdar's love at first sight for Rena inspires exalted reflections in him regarding the mysterious harmony uniting all the elements of the universe. Enraptured by the "immeasurable happiness" that comes to him, he invokes cosmic connections and intergalactic signals (LS 188), affirming: "He who I was a short time ago, a player strutting with his paltry props, trapped behind a mardi gras mask, wrestling with the merciless haiku spirits, now, that man is history; he simply doesn't exist anymore; he's vanished into thin air."[62]

---

[60] See the entry "Ravishment" in Barthes' catalogue of "figures" of amorous discourse (2007: 67).
[61] "Es war mir, als würden Konfettischnipsel niederregnen, als würd ne Polka-Kapelle Whitney Houstons 'Best of' der letzten fünf Jahre einschmeichelnd runterorgeln, als hätt man mir zwei Ampullen Morphium und ne volle Infusionsflasche Zuckerlikör inne Adern gejagt. Alter, diese gottgesegnete Postkarte war ganz sicher n Popsong, und ich war richtig vonnen Socken, der ganze Scheiß-Verdruss der letzten Tage war wie weggeblasen, und ich war so von 'aschk', der absoluten Liebe à la turca, eingefangen, dass ich die Arme aufwarf und fingerschnackelnd und schuhsohlenknallend n Rundtanz hingelegt hab" (LS 227).
[62] "Der, der ich bis vor kurzem war, ein mit seinen wenigen Beständen protzender Mime, in einer Blechlarve gefangen, mit den ungnädigen Haikugeistern ringend, nun, dieser jener ist Geschichte, ihn gibt es einfach nicht mehr, er hat sich in Luft aufgelöst" (LS 189).

Even if, here again, the self-ironic emphasis needs to be taken into consideration, there is no doubt that Zaimoglu's protagonists worship the rush of love, to which they devote themselves without compunction or reserve, exulting in the surrender of their liberty to the benefit of the woman they desire. The motif of dependence on the beloved, fundamental for Werther,[63] is taken up again with gusto by Zaimoglu's characters, employing the whole range of courtly love, from the adoration of the beloved woman elevated to the level of divinity[64] to the various forms of ostentatious self-castration that open the intertextual field to Lenz – as when Hakan shaves his eyebrows entirely in an act of radical mutilation (LS 207). In a manner similar to that in *Werther* but much more explicit, the object of veneration for the subject in love is not so much the individual desired (the women are ultimately interchangeable)[65] as love itself – or more precisely desire since both become confused in such an excited fervor seated in the lover's "heart." It is not by chance that this word, "Herz," flows almost as often, with multiple variations, from Zaimoglu's protagonists' pens as from Werther's.[66] The reader does find again something of Werther's absolute passion, wherein Barthes recognized "the game of idealism and materialism itself, of extreme idealism bordering on extreme materialism" (2007: 237). With regard to this central theme, the shift from Goethe to Zaimoglu appears to be a fall, a collapse corresponding the very character of burlesque: the components are the same, but they are handled on an inferior ethical and aesthetic level.

The novel's title seems to have been quite expressly chosen to underline this shift. It announces right away that this story does not deal with the (subjective, interior) "sorrows," but the "marks" or "traces" of love: "Liebesmale" designates in metaphorical fashion the little superficial bruises called "hickeys," or "love bites." Zaimoglu thus indicates precisely where he is situating the focal point of his transposition. The reader passes from the sorrows engendered by amorous passion to banal hematoma, the simple, material traces of an erotic game. By opting for this poetic term, which adjoins the outdated "Mal" to the word

---

[63] "Bester, ich bin dahin! Sie kann mit mir machen, was sie will" (W II, 427, letter of 8 November) ("Dear friend! I am lost! She can do with me what she will" [102]).

[64] In a blasphemous "ritual," Hakan gets up at five o'clock every morning to bow down in front of the apartment door of his beloved and kiss the threshold (LS 258).

[65] Barthes (2007: 97) has pointed out the "insipidity" of Charlotte ("Charlotte est insignifiante, fade. Elle est écrasée par l'amour de Werther: c'est la mise en scène, en énonciation, d'un amour – d'une structure –, non d'une relation. C'est le sentiment – non l'objet – qui est en quelque sorte fétichisé: 'perversion amoureuse'").

[66] See for example LS 9, 75, 78, 105, 109, 112, 126, 130, 136, 142, 144, 176, 188, 198, 238, 244, 246 ff, 252, 258, 267, 269, 270, 279, 292, 296.

"Liebe" – preferable to the more prosaic and unambiguous "Knutschfleck", which connotes a pubescent eroticism – Zaimoglu inscribes his text in a deliberately open semantic field. In the context of the novel, the word *Liebesmale* has at least two, perhaps three, meanings. It might as easily conjure the traces the torments of disappointed love leave on the soul, as the stigmata with which it (socially?) afflicts the amorous subject – a reading which could return the reader to Hakan's acts of self-mutilation or the scars on Serdar's body from the razorblade cuts he suffers for love of Rena at the hand of his rival, Baba. In any case, even if the first sense, the carnal, remains predominant, the book bears a title that reconnects implicitly with the Wertherian character of passion as synonym for sorrow. It is likewise significant that the word only appears twice in the body of the novel, at the very beginning and at the very end – and always in the subjunctive mood.[67]

This title seems to indicate that semantic gap in relation to *Die Leiden des jungen Werthers* is intentional, that the trivialization has programmatic value. In Zaimoglu, it is a matter of protagonists who are not only inferior (ethically and intellectually) to Werther, but who know it and play off of it. In fact, perhaps this knowledge and this game are precisely what enables them to confront the real, incidentally even making them thus less pathetic than they seem and than they think themselves. That, at least, is suggested by the letters from Dina, the older woman with whom Serdar maintains a simultaneously erotic and intellectual relationship. Independent and mature (she is a university instructor and mother of a little girl), cultured and realistic, she does not seem blinded by love to the point of being under any illusions about her young lover, to whom, however, she shows signs in her letters not just of unequivocal romantic attachment but, above all, of esteem and even admiration. Aware of her own marginality (due to her Jewishness) in German society, she feels close to him by way of her experience of being uprooted and of the weight of history, appreciates his poems, and believes in his talent. The only person in the novel to really command respect, she is also the one to formulate an idea that strongly resembles a profession of the author's poetological faith: "What an unbelievable freedom resides in our being able to choose between magic and Maggi Fix, be-

---

[67] In the opening letter of the novel, Serdar writes to Hakan: "Ich würde so gerne mit einem Knutschfleck am Hals herumlaufen, ein schönes, großes violettes Liebesmal, dass mich die anderen Hähne um mein erfülltes Liebesleben beneiden und ihre verdammten Kämme abschwellen" (LS 15–16). And at the very end, he tells Rena in his farewell letter what he longs to do when they meet again: "Ich drückte meine Lippen auf die Deinen, ich küsste dein göttliches Plebejerkinn, ich zöge am Haar deinen Kopf in den Nacken und bisse in den entblößten Hals ein Liebesmal, scharlachrot, ein Liebesmal, scharlachrot" (LS 296).

tween the comic and cosmic! Imagine there was no such choice. Of course, I wish for cosmic magic; with all the arrogance I'm due, anything else would be uninteresting, but I know how to season it with a little comical Maggi."[68] It is significant that it is precisely this woman who relativizes the hardly flattering image of Serdar projected in Hakan's and his own letters. Also, the reader will note in passing, as a supplementary guarantee of her testimony, that the letters she sends to him, with their biblical subtext and Judeo-Oriental imaginary, evoke the poems Else Lasker-Schüler dedicated to the young Gottfried Benn after their break: a secondary intertext that suggests, however discreetly, the possibility of a considerable revalorization of Serdar's character.[69]

Zaimoglu thus surreptitiously introduces several cracks into the otherwise sufficiently pathetic portrait he paints of his protagonists. These cracks invite us to call back into question the radicality of the shift alluded to above and recall that already in Goethe the sorrows attributed to Werther were the fruit of a desacralization that, in his day, represented a mighty provocation: the secularization of the biblical motif of Christ's passion.[70] The parallels Werther draws between his own destiny and that of God's son, between the sacrilegious gesture of a young man who sacrifices his life to liberate the woman he loves and Christ's sacrifice destined to save humanity, are brought to the fore in a fashion that could only shock Goethe's contemporaries. In using the word *Leiden* in his novel's title, Goethe not only seems to absolve his protagonist of the crime his suicide represented in the eyes of believers but embraces the biblical analogy Werther posits instead of placing all the blame on his character whose youth and confusion might have, *in extremis*, excused him. As emphasized by Matthias Luserke (1997: 130), this clearly amounts to putting the passion of Christ ("Leidensgeschichte", *passio*) and the sorrows of a worldly young bourgeois enamored of a married woman, the crucifixion and the impious act of suicide, on the same plane.

---

[68] "Was für eine unglaubliche Freiheit steckt darin, dass wir wählen können zwischen Magie und Maggi fix, zwischen komisch und kosmisch! Stell dir vor, es gäbe keine solche Wahl. Natürlich wünsche ich mir die kosmische Magie, anderes wäre bei aller mir gebotenen Arroganz uninteressant, aber ich kann sie gut mit dem komischen Maggi würzen" (LS 197).

[69] Rena's letter of 19 July (LS 87) in particular recalls the enunciative mode and characteristic lyricism of the poetic cycle Lasker-Schüler dedicated to her ex-lover, the man she called "the Barbarian" or "Giselheer," particularly "Das Lied des Spielprinzen (G.B. in Liebe)" (Lasker-Schüler 1917: 209).

[70] This reference has been weakened (if not erased) in all English and French translations of the novel's title, except for the new French translation by Philippe Forget, *Les Passions du jeune Werther* (1994).

By in turn "desacralizing" Werther's sorrows, Zaimoglu is only following a path Goethe had already trod. Christian iconography moreover appears in little touches in the writing of his novel's characters. Hence, after having imbibed a massive dose of an aphrodisiac he bought in a sex shop, which he intends to administer to Jacqueline out of desperation, Hakan labels himself a "martyr for love" because he is risking his life to test the potential dangerousness of the potion. Not long after, he learns that Jacqueline, after finally succumbing to his advances, not only will not renounce relations with other men but also practices tantric massage. He, who was ready for any sacrifice for her, then thinks he has hit rock bottom. Already reduced to the level of a sexual object by his new conquest, he sees himself turned in a way into her "lockiges Püdelchen" ("curly little poodle," LS 259–260) and confides in his friend:

> I've had it up to here, man. I'm not some fucking liberal namby-pamby, you know, I sucked up that business with the next-door paramours but now some nice rub-a-dub with a mantra? That's the end of the line. Next thing, she'll give me a crown of thorns and red pumps and take me as a maso-maniac with her to an S&M party. I'm at the end of my rope, shit, I wonder what kind of future it will be, having no more worth than a broken vial.[71]

The double intertext outlined through these occasional allusions to biblical history *and* Goethe's novel ("martyr for love," "crown of thorns") certainly situates itself in the profanest context of pornographic and sadomasochistic scenarios. Yet this is an instance of the process, already brought to light, that consists of seizing on the Goethean motifs in order to submit them to a systematic exaggeration. The Christian references that the reader might interpret here as an intertextual signal more generally reflect mainstream Western culture, suffused down to its most decadent forms by Christianity. In a personal capacity, Zaimoglu's protagonists refer more willingly to the Islamic tradition – which, however, they submit to the same secularization. Thus Hakan rails to his friend in jeremiads on the subject of his impotence, advising him to announce his affliction in the streets in the manner of those "drummers of the dawn" (*sahur davulsuhu*) of yore charged with waking the faithful for the day's first prayer during Ramadan. In this way, he could reveal the truth about his "beschissenen Leiden" ("shitty sorrows") to his heart's content ("nach Herzenslust") in the guise of the good

---

[71] "[I]ch hab die Schnauze gestrichen voll, Alter, ich bin doch hier keine scheiß-liberale Kuschelmuschel, die Sache mit den Nebenbuhlern hab ich noch geschluckt, aber jetzt auch noch Schöner Rubbeln mit ner Keimsilbe, da hört der Spaß auf, als nächstes verpasst die mir ne Dornenkrone und rote Pumps und nimmt mich als Masomaniac mit zu ner SM-Party. Ich bin am Ende meiner Kräfte, Scheiße, ich frag mich, was soll ich inner Zukunft, in der ich weniger wert bin als ne kaputte Ampulle" (LS 265).

word – since it is true, he adds, that "the complaint belongs to the Orient like my balls to my dick" (LS 65–66).

In this misappropriation of religion, namely Islam, the reader once again finds the blasphemous premise of an equivalence between the mystic asceticism of the believer and the masochistic complaisance of the lover (or more precisely, of the erotomaniac) blended with the idea that religious discourse, by exalting suffering, provides a privileged model for the articulation of complaint and self-pity. Rather than a demolition (or refutation) of Goethe's text, our contemporary author is playing a game of one-upmanship in provocation, pushing the transgressive logic of *Sturm und Drang* to its ultimate conclusion. It is a means of changing the game, as if to say: this is what a man would say and do today if animated by the irreverent and impassioned spirit of the young Goethe, a writer who would not hesitate to run against the dominant ideology of the self-righteous and forcefully call for the emancipation of the subject from the chains of reason and orthodoxy. In order the better to capture everything at stake for Zaimoglu's project in referencing *Sturm und Drang*, it is worth taking a closer look at the call for emancipation articulated in this text.

The *Kanak* Generation's *Sturm und Drang:* Male Trouble and Re-Narcissization through Language

The insolently reclaimed (or proclaimed) emancipation in *Liebesmale, scharlachrot* at once concerns the individual, considered as a prisoner in fetters of injunctions and prohibitions hindering personal achievements, and language, which allows for the articulation of this liberated relationship to the real. The generation whose "sorrows" Zaimoglu depicts here is squeezed between several value systems: on one side, by that of the mainstream society in which they develop in Germany (efficiency, viability, profit, social success, self-control, sexual freedom but control of feelings), on another, by that handed down from their family circle (petit-bourgeois respectability, patriarchal order, the restriction of sexuality to the institution of marriage, endogamy), but also by that which developed within the "ghetto" among youths of their generation as a reaction to the combined pressures of the other two and of marginalization (a cult of fraternity, of autonomy, and of honor, rebellion against any form of indoctrination and conformism, the claiming of a reinvented "Oriental" identity) – and finally, if they ever manage to integrate into the cultured middle class, by the values extolled in the progressive intellectual milieus (tolerance, sharing, dialogue, respect for the environment, women, and minorities, etc.). The collision of these different normative systems, which makes it difficult for young people to construct a life project they can stick to, crystalizes most clearly in gender relations and gender identities.

Confronted by antagonistic models, the protagonists cannot prosper either in the traditional role of the dominant male (disqualified in the public discourse of the society they are trying to integrate into) or in that of the "emancipated" man who approaches women as equals – because positioning themselves as such on the plane of sex and sentiment would, in reality, mean accepting being inferior to them, given their social subalternity. They thus live with a particular intensity, an experience that must probably be interpreted as a general crisis of masculinity from Zaimoglu's perspective.[72]

Let us recall that, since *Kanak Sprak*, Zaimoglu's masculine characters have largely been perceived by critics, whether journalists or academics, as stereotypical chauvinists whose subversive capacity lies solely in the domain of their ethnicity, their aptitude to deconstruct the essentialist cleavages in the racialist vein going hand in hand with a propensity no less characteristic to rehabilitate sexism.[73] Wanting to denaturalize ethnic categories, they renaturalize "sex," leaving themselves wide open – paradoxically – to an ideology that racializes sexism. In examining the treatment of male / female relations in *Liebesmale* in light of the Goethean model, I intend to complicate this interpretive framework, which fails to recognize possible intersectional analyses (e.g. ethnic / socio-economic / gendered domination).

Serdar and Hakan's tribulations can, in effect, be read as variations on their difficulties in positioning themselves in life as men according to the traditional criteria of masculinity. If they cut pretty pitiful figures in amorous relations, it is not, or at least not merely, because of their personal insufficiency but also be-

---

[72] The "masculinity-crisis" discourse, originally promoted by right-wing intellectuals and popularized by the media since the 1990s, has become a widely-used cliché even among feminists. In contrast to this notion of "crisis," according to which men today suffer from a loss of manhood and self-esteem because of the "undue influence of women in general and of feminists in particular" (Dupuis-Déri 2012), a structural approach to masculinity, most influentially articulated by Connell (1995), highlights the intimate links between gender and power as well as patriarchal and economic domination. This intersectional approach challenges normative framings of gender and makes it necessary to rethink "masculinity" as fluid, performative, and plural. Connell posits four types of masculinities: hegemonic, complicit, subordinated, and marginalized. Many scholars have used these categories to expand the analysis of masculinity as a social construct and consider alternative models of male identity. See for example Meuser (2006, 2008, 2009), Bauer and Luedtke (2008), Hazan (2009), Corbin, Courtine, and Vigarello (2011, especially vol. 3).

[73] See for example the chapter on Zaimoglu in Ernst (2013: 279–393) and, above all, its conclusion (389–393).

cause the women they are dealing with are not easy-to-conquer "objects" – particularly not for them who, as immigrants from a Muslim culture, are a priori suspected of retrograde behavior. Economically and intellectually autonomous, these women make use of their bodies with a liberty that prohibits them from being approached in a paternalistic mode of machismo. For a young *Kanak* wanting to seduce them, the first objective is thus to assure them of his respect by yielding to the rules they establish. Even if this strategy promises the possibility of assuaging his desire in the short or medium term, since these women no longer deny themselves out of respect for social conventions, they place young men under the obligation to fight relentlessly to make the "conquest," which brings them some narcissistic satisfaction, last. Whether they manage to attract the woman they covet into their bed or not, sexual success in no way guarantees they have reached the end of their efforts, for they must still do their utmost to attain then conserve a position that, in any case, remains precarious. As such, they feel themselves confined within an affective insecurity that only adds to their social vulnerability.

Zaimoglu does not cease to push this problematic to the fore by making the incompatibility of his female characters with the traditional soft and submissive image of women a recurrent source of comedy. When Hakan, transfixed with desire for his beautiful neighbor, is invited to cross the threshold of her apartment for the first time, a pornographic photo of his hostess exposed to everyone's view catches his eye. At once excited and shocked, he forbids himself from showing any of his unease and feigns detachment nevertheless without managing to affect the nonchalance he thinks the situation calls for. Even Rena, whose youth and perception by Serdar as "native" might let him suppose her to be less brazen than emancipated German women like Jacqueline, Anke, or Dina, proves from their first encounter more forward than her beau. In proposing to him that he come away from the group to swim with her, she lets him understand unambiguously that she has noticed his attraction and is inclined to respond. In fact, instead of leaping at the chance, Serdar (embarrassed, true, by his impotence problem) beats a pitiful retreat, under a pretext as fallacious as it is infantile that his mother expects him at home.

The gap between the unease the protagonists feel and the braggadocio they otherwise affect offers the reader a glimpse of the impasse in which they find themselves. There can be no return to patriarchal norms (i.e. to a hierarchical rapport between the sexes), but the path to constructing a new masculinity, one free of the obligation to impose oneself by force and the subordination of women, remains to be invented. Hence, Charlotte's exhortation to Werther to "Be a man" proves no less difficult for these young men to accomplish than for Goethe's hero. The confusion they experience expresses itself in ways including the perception of an absence (real or supposed) of positive masculine role models in mainstream German society. For this reason, Hakan incriminates advertising discourse, which according to him reduces men to the role of foils for women who are invariably presented as radiant and triumphant, enjoying a limitless power at once economic, social, and affective.[74] In a world where the media demagogically conveys a degrading image of men, there is no place, he laments, for "Kümmel" ("wogs")[75] of his ilk. The sole means for a son of immigrants to be "accepted by female society" would be to play, like his friend, the "sanften Exot-Kanaken" ("soft exoti-Kanak") who has surrendered all masculinity and wheedles women with the sentimentalism of a "button-eyed teddy bear."[76]

Despite this severe critique, Hakan, as has been seen, willingly wallows in self-abasing romantic behavior himself. Nevertheless, he justifies this conduct by claiming another tradition present in his home culture, itself non-patriarchal: the Eastern mystic tradition of amorous delirium (*açk*) as it has been celebrated for centuries by Arab-Persian poets. The reference to this pre-Islamic tradition allows him to adopt, without too much damage to his self-esteem, a masculine position understood as degrading *a priori*. By symbolically reconnecting with the archaic schema of courtly love, he is not really doing anything different than Serdar imitating Werther, i.e. compensating for his feeling of masculine deficiency by exalting tragic passion and the feminine eternal. In brief, the social and historic situation in which the two young men find themselves, as depicted in the novel, leaves them no other way out than to rely on literary models that offer them an alternative image of masculinity. By adopting the anachronistic poses of the devoted knight or romantic lover, they manage to surmount their feelings of insufficiency and take pride in their own abasement, claimed as a choice. By making a point of honor of "serving" (sexually and socially) the women they desire, they make themselves feel better about possible reversals and cloak themselves in the aura of a man who places love above all else.

---

[74] By way of illustration, he describes at length and with great exasperation, a Visa advertisement from 1991 that featured an athletic young woman turning up in a swim gear shop "like Venus rising out of the foam" and asking a baffled, stupid-looking clerk for a snorkel before triumphantly pulling a credit card out of her bikini and returning to her luxury yacht (LS 170–171).
[75] "Wir Kümmel haben da ja ausgeschissen" (LS 171).
[76] "Vielleicht du nicht, denn du wirst inner Frauengemeinde aufgenommen, weil du n sanften Exot-Kanaken mimst und echt alles vermasselst, deshalb lieben sie dich wien Teddybär mitn Knopfaugen" (LS 171).

If Goethe's novel has a privileged status in this respect, it is to the extent that, contrary to the other canonical works cited by the two correspondents (whether drawn from the Western patrimony, like *Romeo and Juliet*, or the Eastern, like the legend of Layla and Majnun),[77] it presents the paradigmatic model of a hero *already* in crisis. Hysterical and rebellious, in conflict with his era's social hierarchy and code of values, Werther is an (anti)hero who affirms with insolent aplomb a "sensitive masculinity" (Gutermann 2007: 71) already not very "manly" according to the standards of the time.[78] Refusing to have his conduct and his masculine ideal dictated to him by any outside authority, he claims not to obey anything but "his heart," that is, the inner law of his desire. The call for an emancipation of affect (of "passion"), of which he is simultaneously the illustration and the spokesman, the main objective of the *Sturm und Drang* generation and of the young Goethe in particular, has its echo in Zaimoglu's protagonists' need for freedom in relation to the repressive discourse they themselves have to confront. If Werther (and through him Goethe) elevates himself by brandishing the irrational power of the affective against the rationalist discourse imposed in the wake of the *Aufklärung*, the discourse from which Zaimoglu's protagonists (and their author with them) seek to free themselves is that of contemporary rationalism whether in its (positivistic, pragmatic, neoliberal) conservative variation or its progressive version (with its well-meaning dogma on the left, its supposed "political correctness").

Hence it seems impossible to maintain, as do the authors of *Transkulturalität. Türkisch-deutsche Konstellationen in Literatur und Film*, for example, that Zaimoglu's novel is a "defense of the *Kanak* posture against a position of in-betweenness, here associated with loss of masculinity and power."[79] If one understands "*Kanak* posture" to mean the mix of ostentatious, macho hypersexuality and contempt for the decorum that Hakan makes himself the paradigmatic herald of from his first letter,[80] it would appear that, in glaringly contrary fash-

---

[77] Hakan twice mentions both works together in a single letter, once to mock his friend's sentimental rhetoric (LS 62) and again in relation to his own amorous transport after meeting Jacqueline (LS 66).
[78] See the chapter "Wertherfieber" in Forster (1989: 332–351).
[79] "Insofern ließe sich der Text als Plädoyer für die kanakische Pose und gegen eine – hier mit Männlichkeits- und Machtverlust einhergehende – Position des Dazwischen lesen" (Blumentrath et al. 2007: 78).
[80] "Serdars Adressat Hakan dagegen inszeniert sich als prolliger Kanake, der keinerlei Erektionsprobleme hat, aber dennoch keine Frau findet. Anhand dieser 'potenten', alle Klischees vom 'Ghettokollega' ausstellenden Figur wird Differenz gesetzt: Hakan will auf keinen Fall so 'scheißzivilisiert wie'n Aleman-Bub' sondern lieber der 'Macho-Stecher' (Ls 118) sein" (Blumentrath et al. 2007: 78).

ion, on the pragmatic level, the novel never stops contradicting this stereotypical discourse's claim. What Zaimoglu demonstrates through his protagonists is precisely that the *Kanak* rhetoric in its simplest form is a war machine stuck spinning its wheels, an untenable posture riddled with cracks and contradictions. If, despite everything, Hakan is a more endearing – and also more dynamic – character than Serdar, it is not because his more assertive cultural and social identity spares him the pangs of "in-betweenness" but rather because his façade of proletarian machismo is constantly stymied (if not neutralized) by a discourse *a priori* incompatible with the self-confidence he projects, a discourse of softness and non-violence, of asceticism, of fervor, and of abnegation wherein love takes center stage.

Furthermore, perhaps claiming this discourse inherited in part from the (pre-Islamic) Arab-Persian poetic tradition, in part from Sufism (a sect dissenting from orthodox Islam), which places love among the highest spiritual values and makes it the ultimate stage in wisdom, is not as opposed to *Kanak* orthodoxy as is thought within a Western reading framework. As a product of heterogeneous influences (ethnic as well as linguistic, religious, and national), "Kanakism" itself represents in effect an in-between position; it is assuredly not exempt from halftones and disparities. At any rate, since they refer explicitly and exclusively to the most caricatured version of the "*Kanak* posture," the authors of *Transkulturalität* do not call for a nuanced reading of the phenomenon when they affirm that Zaimoglu is writing an apologia for it in his novel.

The reader may note that the references to Sufism in Zaimoglu seem to fill a similar function as that reflected in the Pietist references in Goethe's novel. Pietism offered young writers of Goethe's generation arguments to raise at once against religious orthodoxy and against rationalist excess. Attracted to the mysticism of the Pietists, to their simultaneously sensual and occult approach to the divine and the importance they accorded to devotion and love, the young Goethe drew from this source to create the enthusiastic and rebellious character of Werther. To an extent, in *Liebesmale, scharlachrot*, Zaimoglu transposes these Pietist references into the Muslim context. By placing alongside his pseudo-Werther Serdar (the over-assimilated Turk), a character who combines the hard-boiled macho Turk with Sufism, Zaimoglu adds complexity to the Wertherian intertext by inserting an intra-Islamic dimension. Just as Werther is influenced by Pietism when he claims submission to love as the supreme form of autonomy, Hakan makes reference to Sufism when he extols amorous devotion as the *summa* of masculinity. The paradox is of the same nature: the love of a woman is magnified by its assimilation into the love of God, and the lover attains the greatest glory in the very abdication of his masculine prerogatives. Mystic thought thus serves as base of legitimacy for claiming an emancipation of the individual (and of men in particular) from the repression of feelings.

This emancipation of affects, which Zaimoglu reclaims following Goethe, essentially takes place through a conquest of language. The re-narcissization provided by the protagonists of *Liebesmale*'s posture as passionate lovers develops within a discourse. It is in recounting, by narrativizing their joys and pains, their disappointments and passing triumphs, and in sharing this discursive elaboration with a confidant who serves at once as an antagonist and a mirror that they manage to regain some self-respect. On the grounds of eloquence, and only there, Serdar and Hakan can rival Werther, that character who is "worth" considerably more than they are otherwise.[81] Their discourse is certainly more constructed than his, which is characterized by an aesthetic of asymmetry, irregularity, and disorder. Yet, the "language of the heart," of which they too make, beneath a nonchalant exterior, inflated and unbridled use, has one feature in common with the Wertherian discourse: it is equally performative and weighted with existential concern. For them, it is simultaneously a means of being in the world and of affirming their difference in relation to other forms of language perceived as artificial and ossified, alienating and sterile.

According to Matthias Luserke, Werther's superiority, the specific "value" ("Wert") that lifts him above rational spirits like Albert, resides entirely in his tooth-and-nail combat for the emancipation of affects.[82] For his part, Roland Barthes sees in Werther's amorous discourse "something like the *language* of narcissism": a form of language that defies the laws of moderation and rationality and for that very reason is considered "sincere" in opposition to all other constructed languages, reduced to sociolects felt as intolerable because of their facticity – put another way, a language that does not so much say some-

---

[81] Werther's family name (for he is notably the only character in the novel who doesn't bear a first name) can be interpreted as the comparative form of the adjectival locution *wert sein*. "Werther is worth more" ("Werther ist 'mehr wert'") (Luserke 1997: 86). See also Simpson (2012). This reading should be kept in mind with regard to the anguished self-doubts that Zaimoglu's protagonists have as they question, as Hakan puts it, "what [they are] supposed to do in a future where [they are] worth less than a broken vial" ("was soll ich inner Zukunft, in der ich weniger wert bin als ne kaputte Ampulle?" [LS 265]). It is also noteworthy that Serdar, too, has a name that communicates prestige and authority: "Serdar" is the Turkish spelling of the Persian name Sardar, which means Field Marshal, a military rank in the Ottoman Empire. Serdars served at the borders of the Empire and were responsible for the security of the land.

[82] This analysis is in keeping with the previous quotation: "In other words: Werther's attempt to emancipate the passions is worth more than Albert's capacity to keep them under control" ("Oder anders formuliert: Der Versuch einer Emanzipation von Leidenschaften durch Werther ist mehr wert als deren Bändigung durch Albert") (Luserke 1997: 86).

thing "about" the real as it constructs the very reality of its speaker (writer), a language in which the posture of enunciation takes precedence over the enunciated content.

For Zaimoglu's characters, a similar discursive production is largely second degree: firstly, because it is interwoven with borrowings, allusions, and citations (recycling, sampling), secondly because the characters make use of it in an ostensibly detached, self-ironic, and schoolboyish manner, and finally, because most of the time it is out of step with its object. There is a flagrant, and comical, disparity between the exalted lyricism that the women they sigh for inspire in the two protagonists and the image the reader might develop of these same women from their stories. Rena, most of all, embodies total vapidity. Nothing leads the reader to suppose that her adolescent freshness, smelling sweetly of Nivea cream, is concealing any peculiar intellectual, spiritual, or moral qualities. This impression of vapidity is supported by the poverty of her participation in the flow of several dialogues reported by her suitor. In relationship to the Goethean hypotext, this comic tension has demonstrative value. Here again it is a matter of exaggerating the trait owing to the preeminence of the sentiment (of desire) toward the beloved object. If Charlotte was already, according to Barthes, "flattened" or "crushed" ("écrasée") by Werther's love, Rena is nothing but a springboard for Serdar's amorous imagination. Her bland image unequivocally signals that what enthralls Zaimoglu's protagonist has less to do with the woman he meets than with the transports of his own "heart" ("mein Herz mein Herz mein Herz!"), the leitmotif of the long letter in which he depicts the interior revolution this love at first sight has sparked within him (LS 187–196). It goes much the same for Hakan with regards to Jacqueline, even if in this case the idealization of the beloved, which justifies in the eyes of the amorous subject the failures sustained, is jeopardized not by stupidity but by a libertinage difficult to reconcile with the amorous discourse called upon. It is when the incompatibility between the object of desire and the feeling she inspires is complete that the narcissistic nature of desire bursts into the open.

Evidently, such a demonstration might turn back on the amorous subject – under the condition that the subject is the dupe of their own discourse. That is not, in fact, the case here. Despite his amorous enthusiasm, Serdar has enough common sense to register that Rena is not at all "worth" the emotional investment he makes in her, and Hakan soon knows enough about his neighbor to suspect that the resistance she shows him has less to do with an excess of chastity and more to do with a merely moderate interest in his person. Their love frenzy is thus not exactly out of blindness but rather a pugnacious and obstinate affirmation of their romantic credo. This stubbornness in claiming to be head over heels for a run-of-the-mill girl encountered at the beach or a libertine only willing to confer the status of "harem boy"[83] participates in the subject seizing power over the real. It is a manner of magnifying the adventure, that is, of enlarging oneself in one's own eyes and affirming the autonomy of the ego, all the while giving into the thrill of letting go.

However, if there is some mystification in the exaltation of Zaimoglu's protagonists, the detachment they otherwise affect is not entirely credible either. The "posture of sincerity" they adopt in moments of paroxysmal emotion forms a counterpart to a "posture of imposture" with which it is inextricably blended. Beneath the sarcasm of their invective and provocations, their parody and pastiche, a real vehemence of feelings breaks through, an obstinate claim of authentic sensitivity, a "truth in the lie." In this game of potentially infinite masks, the affective overinvestment is in no way in contradiction with ironic detachment, for it is precisely thanks to the large helping of self-deprecation displayed by the two correspondents (an attitude symptomatic of postmodernity) that they manage to recover a form of emotional freshness that definitively allows them to be comfortable with the discourse they produce. Werther, by contrast, does not know the second degree. Indeed, it is by way of an ironic rapport with the prefabricated forms of language hindering them (economic, political, advertising, media, "alternative," esoteric, etc. phraseologies) that Zaimoglu's characters paradoxically manage to establish themselves as subjects of their own discourse by reappropriating against all odds a pathos that would otherwise condemn them to grandiloquence, kitsch, and affectation, for they are moving through a minefield. What can one say today that is new or true about desire, sorrow, solitude, abandonment, or loss? What was already a challenge for Werther's generation, which had hardly entered modernity's "era of suspicion,"[84] could only, at the dawn of the twenty-first century, be an untenable wager. The ironic distance cultivated by Serdar and Hakan thus saves them from alienation by paradoxically putting them in a position to surmount the impossibility of articulating an "authentic" discourse. Access to a "revisited" pathos preserves them, in another light, from rank vulgarity – and also from the cynicism in which other characters of Zaimoglu's would later wallow (*German Amok*).

This seizing of power over and through language is not unrelated to what developed starting in the 1980s in the popular music coming from cultural inter-

---

[83] Hakan to Serdar: "Tja, Alter, so wie's aussieht, bin ich innen lackierten Fängen der Frauenmafia gelandet und ausgezeichnet als ne Art Haremslover" (LS 235).

[84] For Barthes (2007: 157), the Romantic era was "the beginning of the era of suspicion, the beginning of the suspicion of language, the first cultural censoring of amorous expression" ("Époque romantique: début de l'ère du soupçon, début de la suspicion du langage, première censure culturelle de l'expression amoureuse").

mixing as a form of empowerment, of resistance to mainstream codes by provocative reclaiming of devalued or anachronistic modes of expression. The parallel between the logorrheic "gift of the gab" of Zaimoglu's characters and the subversive phrasing of rap has already been brought up repeatedly apropos of *Kanak Sprak* (ritual insults, etc.). This reference is likewise valid for *Liebesmale, scharlachrot*, particularly in Hakan's letters throughout, but here it vies with another musical reference, one equally popular and hybrid as a movement but specific to the Turkish context: Arabesk. Contrary to the urban music styles born in the West like jazz, rock, or hip-hop that are originally products of the underground counter-culture, this style (like the blues) came from the proletarian masses. Birthed in the slums over the course of the 1960s in a context of massive rural exodus, it was banned from Turkish public radio and television channels because it ran counter to the desire for Westernization the republic had been promoting since Atatürk. Regarded as the "music of the exodus," it sparked a resurgence of the Ottoman past the authorities had wanted to forget and drew much more contempt from the local elites than Western hip-hop in spite and because of its immense popular success (Bengi 2009: 102). A sentimental genre issuing from the meeting of native regional folk forms and elements borrowed from neighboring cultures as well as Western pop, it became the "soundtrack of the new social dynamics" (Hür 2011)[85] in 1990s Turkey before diversifying upon contact with commercial pop, which consequently "arabesked" massively (up to the 2003 victory of the singer Sertab Erener in the Eurovision contest). According to the ethnomusicologist Martin Stokes, Arabesk, which rehabilitated Turkey's "Oriental" roots in the eyes of the public at large, is "an entire anti-culture, a way of life whose influence, it is often said, can be detected as an aura of chaos and confusion surrounding every aspect of urban existence, from traffic to language, from politics to kitsch" (1992: 1). For psychoanalyst Fatih Karaman, Arabesk nonetheless represents "a sort of masochistic social regression" because the plaintive ballads, dedicated to the expression of despair and sorrow, stage, through a seesawing game between two opposed systems of representation, the metamorphosis of the "bad lot" ("mauvais sujet") into a sublimated incarnation of scorned masculinity: "The good subject emerges from the bad one. From the expulsed, rejected, and devalued subject arises, as if by illusion or a magic trick, a worthy subject, noble and sure of itself!"[86]

---

[85] See also Özbek (1997).
[86] "Du mauvais sujet découle le bon. Du sujet expulsé, rejeté, dévalorisé se fait jour, comme un jeu d'illusion et de magie, un sujet digne, noble et sûr de lui-même!" (Karaman 2010).

In the novel, this music of social outcasts finds its representative in the character of Baba. In addition to being leader of a gang, the young man whom Serdar describes as a representative specimen of the autochthonous primitive Turk is likewise presented as a diehard fan of singer Müslüm Gürses (LS 104 ff). [87] The success of Gürses (1953–2013), a star with provincial and underclass origins, was founded on songs glorifying exclusion, melancholy, and romantic hard luck to the point of masochism. Baba, whose *nom de guerre* is in all probability inspired by his idol, "Müslüm Baba" ("Father Müslüm") to his fans, undergoes a rite of initiation at one of the star's concerts, an experience he recounts to Serdar with an unexpected eloquence:

> The hall was full, and a pin, which you sometimes inattentively drop, wouldn't have found its way to the ground, and he made out hearts accustomed to aches bleed; he was Azrael, the Angel of Death, tearing our souls from our bodies with songs; his voice was like freshly squeezed limonata and poison in one, and we drank from this hemlock cup; we emptied it to the last, bitter drop, and then it happened, then I was done for; the master had hardly stepped onto the stage, and after the second song – may it be a hymn to all those who had rolled around in the dirt and bathed in mud – the jinn rose into my head, and I was, like I said, done for...[88]

Stupefied, Serdar witnesses the metamorphosis of the uncouth young man into an inspired poet and then into a mystic martyr:

> I didn't recognize Baba anymore. This guy, who otherwise kept his tongue tied, out of whose mouth you had to pluck words with a tweezer, was overcome with ecstasy, and he spoke like a berserker raging in a dollhouse with a fire poker. There was no end to my amazement, least of all after he suddenly ripped open his shirt so that one or two buttons went flying.

---

87 This assessment should, however, be put in perspective. Although his German is far from perfect ("Sonderdeutsch"), he is able to communicate in this language since he has also spent time in Germany. Having loitered "for four months in Heidelberg", he has acquired some cultural varnish which even in Serdar's opinion raises him above the "beach populace" (LS 51).

88 "Der Saal war voll, und eine Stecknadel, die man manchmal unachtsamerweise fallen lässt, hätte den Weg zum Boden nicht gefunden, und er hat unsere kummergewöhnten Herzen bluten lassen, er war Asrael, der Todesengel, der uns die Seelen aus dem Leib riss mit Gesängen, seine Stimme war wie frisch gepresste Zitronenlimonata und Gift in einem, und wir tranken aus diesem Schierlingsbecher, wir leerten ihn bis zum bitteren letzten Tropfen, und da ist es passiert, denn es war um mich geschehen, kaum hatte der Meister die Bühne betreten, und nach dem zweiten Lied, das allen in den Staub Gepurzelten und in Schlick Badenden eine Hymne sei, stieg mir der Dschinn in den Kopf, und da ist es, wie gesagt, um mich geschehen..." (LS 105).

"Do you see these gashes? My blood became thicker and thicker and so I took a razorblade and cut myself..."[89]

Transgressive and ecstatic, the stagecraft of "Müslüm Baba" gave rise to a veritable cult. His most fervent admirers would attend his concerts equipped with razors, which they would use to cut their own arms and torsos while singing and dancing in unison with their idol. Wounding their own flesh, the *müslümcüler* ("children of Müslüm"), as they called themselves, would intensify their sense of communion with the singer by inflicting themselves with substitutes for the sufferings endured by Gürses himself. For this reason, they are also called *jiletçi*, or razor-wielders.[90] The Baba of Zaimoglu's novel also engages in this practice, proudly exhibiting his stigmata to his antagonist, this "Deutschländer" ("Germanian")[91] whom he views as effeminate and degenerate.[92] To some extent, this conspicuously self-destructive behavior is linked to the mutilations Hakan inflicts on himself out of love for Jacqueline. In both cases, it is a matter of expressing emotion while also asserting a form of masculinity.

Müslüm Gürses's wildly heroic-sentimental art thus occupies a position in the symbolic economy of the novel that is comparable to that of Ossianic poetry in *Werther*. Those poems published in 1760 by Scottish writer James Macpherson, who presented them as English translations from third-century Gaelic originals, were also "popular" in both senses of the term insofar as they drew from a reworked ancient cultural source and generated massive enthusiasm in their day. Goethe himself translated excerpts, attributing his translations to his hero

---

[89] "Ich erkannte Baba nicht wieder, er, der sich sonst in Maulfaulheit übte, er, aus dessen Mund man mit einer Pinzette die Worte picken muss, war geradezu ekstatisch angewandelt, und er sprach wie ein Berserker, der mit dem Feuerstocher im Puppenhäuschen wütet. Ich kam aus dem Staunen nicht heraus, vor allem nicht, als er sich plötzlich das Hemd aufriss und ein, zwei Knöpfe davonflogen. "Siehst du die Schmisse, mein Blut wurde dicker und immer dicker, und da nahm ich eine Rasierklinge und ritzte mich auf..." (LS 105–106).
[90] The term refers to the blades of the American brand of razors, Gillette (Bengi 2009: 107).
[91] The term "Deutschländer" is the translation of the Turkish expression "Almancılar" and means "those from Germany". It was used in Turkey to describe Turkish migrants or German citizens with ancestors from Turkey who lived and worked in Germany or were born there as the children of labour migrants.
[92] "Deutschländer, wir sprechen jetzt nicht wieder über dein welkes Tüpferchen, hier geht es um eine hoch männliche Angelegenheit, um Wohl und Wehe, um Kampf und Schicksal. Bevor ich mich aber weiter ausbreite, eine Frage: Kennt man bei euch drüben den Gottvater des Arabesk, Müslüm Gürses? [...] Müslüm ist unser aller preisgekrönter Padischah, das lass dir mal gesagt sein [...]" (LS 104–105).

Werther, thus further accentuating the passionate and tragic character of his first translation.⁹³ The dark vision of these ballads, which treat only of star-crossed lovers and warriors who die in combat, is posed as the opposite of the luminous epics of Homer, the novel's other legendary (and blind) poet. Its increasing grip on Werther's troubled mind represents his descent into hell while also assisting and precipitating it.

Although far from having a comparable status in terms of the characters' psychology in *Liebesmale* (with "Baba" eliciting readers' sympathies even less than Serdar and Hakan), the evocation of the music of Müslüm Gürses, the proletarian singer who draws inspiration for his heartbreaking ballads from an eclectic heritage, still gestures to the figure of the fictional Gaelic bard who captivated European intellectuals in the second half of the eighteenth century. With the evocation of Gürses and the hysteria triggered by his public appearances, it is the Arabesk culture – a culture of mass consumption decried for its sentimentality and affectation, its popularity and irrationalism – that enters into a *mise-en-abyme* by returning indirectly to the "Gothic" fever that helped found European Romanticism by rehabilitating a medieval fantasy woven from mythological and biblical elements. If there is an intertextual game here, it certainly does not consist of playing East and West, tradition and modernity, literary culture and mass culture off against each other, but rather of deconstructing the very notions of originality, of value, and of authenticity by pointing out fundamentally dialectical dynamics on both sides.

As is the case for the real fans of Müslüm Gürses, the self-destructive behaviors of Zaimoglu's characters have a prominent model in the Islamic context: the mortification practices performed by penitents of certain Shiite sects during the celebrations for Ashura, which commemorates the martyrdom of their third imam, Hussein (see Mervin 2006). Whether the aim is disfigurement, as in Hakan's case, or scarification, as in Baba's, the profane self-mutilations of Zaimoglu's characters resemble these ritual practices in that they likewise seem to be forms of marking the body intended to express (or restore) self-esteem and lost wholeness while conjuring an illusion of self-assertion or self-control through self-castration. Psychoanalyst Guy Lérès offers an interesting insight into the role of scarification in traditional societies:

> The signifying marks from scarification offer the subject symbolic aid in making One this diffluent body while rendering the subject cohesive with the group to which it belongs. It is then society as a whole that acts as the Name-of-the-Father and affirms this through the

---

93 At the end of the novel, Lotte asks Werther to read out his translation of some Ossian songs. This reading, presented by the editor in full, makes up more than 5 percent of the whole work.

actual marks on the body to symbolize the unity of its image, thereby allowing the subject to separate this image of the body from all vestiges of uncivil enjoyment [*jouissance*], and it does so in a manner evocative of castration. The subject pays for this separation in flesh, as if the symbolism of the act, to mark and to count, had to operate upon the real of the body.[94]

As Lérès emphasizes, there is an evident connection between scarification and writing:

> The marks, traces, incisions, and burns attest, to say the least, to their relationship to writing, to their proximity to a letter. As such, they relate to the logic of language, accentuated by the fact that they add materiality to it. Like scarification, the letter crosses the symbolic and the real, yet it alone, by not making reference to any meaning, can accommodate the dimension of semblance. It can be operative in relation to enjoyment [*jouissance*] without the meager offering of flesh and renders the metonymic relation to the phallus more discretionary.[95]

In Zaimoglu's epistolary novel, which contains the word "Male" in the title, it is difficult not to see variations on several levels of this "logic of accentuated language" that serves, according to Lérès, an initiatory and integrative role. Although Zaimoglu's protagonists, unlike most of the young people of their generation whose codes Lérès discusses in his article, do not seek to assert themselves in the group by "wearing brands" in the commercial sense of the term, they are just as constantly leaving marks, on paper or their own flesh, that possess value as signs.[96] Their predilection for distinctive markings is therefore a way of physi-

---

[94] "Les traces signifiantes de la scarification offrent au sujet une aide symbolique à faire Un de ce corps diffluent tout en se rendant cohérent avec son groupe d'appartenance. C'est alors la société tout entière qui fait office de Nom-du-père et en atteste par le marquage réel du corps pour symboliser l'unité de son image. Elle permet donc au sujet de disjoindre cette image du corps de tout reste de jouissance incivile, et elle l'a fait d'une manière qui n'est pas sans évoquer une castration. Le sujet paie cette séparation de quelque part de sa chair, comme si le symbolique de l'acte, pour marquer, pour compter, devait opérer dans le réel du corps" (Lérès 2005: 224).

[95] "Les marques, traces, incisions, brûlures attestent pour le moins de leur relation à l'écriture, de leur proximité à une lettre. Comme telles, elles participent de la logique du langage accentué de ceci qu'elles y ajoutent une matérialité. Comme la scarification, la lettre croise symbolique et réel, mais elle seule, de ne se référer à aucune signification, peut supporter la dimension du semblant. Elle peut être opérante par rapport à la jouissance sans l'obole de chair et rend plus facultative la relation métonymique au phallus" (Lérès 2005: 224).

[96] Zaimoglu's characters look with ostentatious nonchalance at the codes of mainstream society. Though very concerned by their physical appearance, they display utter disregard for brands, differentiating themselves from their peers who submit to the dictates of fashion. Even when Serdar wears a "trendy" garment capable of garnering the admiration of wealthy tou-

cally realizing what they also do by means of verbal expression: manifesting their individuality, containing pleasure within the limits of their body, and (re)establishing a hold on reality. At the same time, these behaviors reproduce, by way of the Arabesk culture and the bloody rituals of the "Müslüm Baba" concerts, the cathartic scarifications of the Shiite devotees, while also echoing Wertherian masochism, itself inspired by Christ's martyrdom.

The reference to Turkish pop's "man of sorrows" (another one of Müslüm Gürses's nicknames) thus amplifies at another level, and in relation to another cultural context, the reference to *Die Leiden des jungen Werthers*. Additionally, it is merged with remarks made by Serdar, who makes this reference in particular in his last letter to Rena:

> My beautiful lady, your right cheek tastes like Turkish sherbet, your left is like a full moon when, in the outskirts of Istanbul, the coal dust shimmers in the air like divine black powder. And if the charcoal burner saw you, he would start to hum an Arabesk song: Go blind, oh fate, for you have intended only unripe melons for me![97]

The relationship Zaimoglu's characters have with language(s) thus participates in the same empowerment strategy as the incantation practiced in popular music such as hip hop or, in a completely different way, Arabesk. Their verbal frenzy serves simultaneously as an expression of pain endured, revenge for the stresses they have undergone, and paradoxical self-assertion. Like the discourse that Werther produces "about" love, the expression of the amorous subject in *Liebesmale, scharlachrot* "is not a metalanguage" (Barthes 2007: 282) but a performative discourse.

The performativity of discourse in *Liebesmale, scharlachrot*, however, differs on one essential point from that which characterizes the Wertherian discourse: it is not autarkic but subsists on interpersonal relationships. Even though the characters are highly egocentric, it is worth recalling that the power of their writing is deployed within the dynamics of the exchange. Unlike Goethe, who stages a solipsistic address pronounced in an effusive mode, Zaimoglu portrays characters caught in a verbal game to which the relational dimension is fundamental.

---

rists, he recounts this critical success with typically dry self-irony: "Mein taubengraues Tunnelzug-Zupfpantalon aus Fallschirmseide macht hierzulande fett Eindruck [...]. Ein braun gebranntes Girl hier aus diesem Luxus-Ghetto hat mir gestern den Bescheid gestoßen: 'Dein Gesicht ist zwar Sonderdeponie, aber mit dieser Hose bist du mega-in'" (LS 13–14).

[97] "Meine schöne Frau, deine rechte Wange schmeckt wie türkische Limonade, deine Linke ist wie ein Vollmond, wenn in Istanbul-Vorstadt die Kohlenlösche wie ein schwarzer Staub Gottes in der Luft flirrt. Und wenn der Köhler dich sähe, würde er ein summiges Arabesk-Lied anstimmen: Erblinde, o Schicksal, denn du hast für mich nur unreife Melonen vorgesehen!" (LS 295).

Their words, less exhibitionist and confidential than interjective and declamatory, derive their therapeutic effect from confrontation with the other. This interactivity becomes more obvious when examining the dialogue that is created, by way of common references to *Werther*, between Zaimoglu's novel and Ulrich Plenzdorf's *Die neuen Leiden des jungen W.*

The "New Sorrows of Young Ali," or Zaimoglu's Response to Plenzdorf

Zaimoglu's reference to *Werther* is coupled with the more historically proximal reference to East German literature of the 1970s, which Zaimoglu appears to lay claim to and evokes by way of his illustrious precedent in Plenzdorf's text. In ironically designating his own novel as the "New Sorrows of young Ali," Zaimoglu is alluding to Plenzdorf's *Die neuen Leiden des jungen W.* ("The New Sorrows of Young W."),[98] which enjoyed resounding success in the form of a play (1972) before being published as a novel (1973) and then adapted to the screen by Eberhard Itzenplitz (Artus Film, FRG, 1976). As in Özdamar's *Karriere einer Putzfrau*, a second reference thus looms behind the reference to the traditional canon that situates the text within a tradition of intracultural rewriting. Zaimoglu differentiates himself from his East German predecessor by inserting his own rewriting into the cultural context of immigration: the generic name *Ali*, which does not designate any character in the novel, refers expressly to the stereotypical figure of the immigrant in Germany, where, as stated in the initial title of Rainer Werner Fassbinder's film *Angst essen Seele auf* ("Fear Eats the Soul," 1974), "Alle Türken heißen Ali" ("All Turks Are Named Ali").[99]

It is worth noting at the outset that Zaimoglu may have drawn inspiration for this project from *Tränen sind immer das Ende* ("It Always Ends in Tears," 1980), an earlier effort by a writer of Turkish origin to appropriate Plenzdorf's reworking of the Wertherian material. Given the relevance that this first "intercultural" variation of the Goethe/Plenzdorf double hypotext has for an assessment of the project taken on thirty years later by the author of *Kanak Sprak*, a discussion later in this chapter of Pirinçci's work will follow the comparative analysis of the novels by Zaimoglu and Plenzdorf.

Die neuen Leiden des jungen W. is one of Ulrich Plenzdorf's two major works, along with the screenplay *Die Legende von Paul und Paula* ("The Legend of Paul

---

[98] This information is derived from a laudatory review of the novel published in *Frankfurter Rundschau* (Hückstädt 2000).
[99] Significantly enough, the character named Ali in Fassbinder's film is from Morocco.

and Paula," 1973), which he wrote at the same time as *Die neuen Leiden* and which was no less popular. Edgar Wibeau, the "Young W.," is abandoned by his father at the age of five and grows up in his mother's care in the (fictional) small town of Mittenberg. At the age of sixteen, he has begun occupational training and so far met all the expectations for socialization placed on him: he is a good student, a model son, and an exemplary apprentice. Nonetheless, he aspires to a more exciting fate than simply being a diligent worker and family man, and he surprises those close to him by abruptly breaking ties after a fight with his supervisor. Dreaming of pursuing a career as a painter (like his father), he secretly goes to Berlin with his friend Willi to apply to study at the academy of fine arts. Though he is not admitted, he decides to stay in the capital city (the direction of escape is the opposite of Werther's, who left the city for the countryside), but he settles there alone, unbeknownst to anyone, in the shed of a garden allotment located on land that is slated for demolition. Exhilarated by the newfound freedom he enjoys in this secret retreat, he devotes himself to his favorite activities: listening to jazz cassettes, daydreaming, and painting. In this refuge, he meets a twenty year-old nursery school teacher and falls in love with her, though she is already engaged. The bonds that form between Edgar, the young teacher he jokingly calls "Charlie," and her fiancé Dieter, who will soon return from the army to commit to conjugal and civilian life, recall at every turn the triangular relationship between Werther, Charlotte, and Albert. Seduced by this boy who looks like a beatnik and about whom everything is "confused" and "unkempt," the poised young woman lets herself be drawn into a fleeting escapade before she returns to her austere fiancé and her plans for conjugal life.

Edgar is devastated when she abandons him, and he takes refuge in work by joining a brigade of house painters. He dies at the age of seventeen, one year after fleeing his small town, with the circumstances of his death remaining murky. He is electrocuted while working on a machine intended to revolutionize house painting, and it is not clear whether he committed a desperate act or made a heroic sacrifice. The story begins after this fatal outcome, with Edgar Wibeau addressing the reader from beyond the grave, in a retrospective and analytical mode unfolding on two different levels. There is, on the one hand, the investigation conducted by Edgar's father to get to the bottom of the cause for his son's death; on the other, the post mortem comments Edgar himself makes regarding the answers his father receives from all those who had contact with him during the last months of his life: Willi, the faithful confidant to whom he sent cassettes with recorded messages from Berlin, "Charlie" herself, his supervisor Fleming, his team leader Addi, and the old worker Zaremba who inculcated in him a sense of solidarity and proletarian ethics. The reader reconstructs the framework of events leading to his death based on the posthumous comments the hero addresses to an anonymous and collective audience – "Leute" ("folks") –, interspersed with snatches of dialogue between his father and the various individuals involved in his brief life.

The psychological profile of Edgar Wibeau is that of a sensitive, outspoken boy endowed with imagination and a critical mind and who, in spite of his intellectual and moral qualities, fails to transform his dreams into a positive life project. Driven by a legitimate (and ultimately commonplace) aspiration for personal fulfilment, he collides with the rigidity of a society that has, hiding behind its superficial ideology, an oppressive, petit-bourgeois mindset leaving no room for individuality. To free himself of these strictures and strive for distinction, Edgar – who idealizes his father's (noble and romanticized) Huguenot origins – cultivates a subversive pose inspired by the American counter-culture of the 1950s and 1960s (still repressed by his country's authorities), imagines himself as a modern Robinson Crusoe, and devotes himself to abstract painting. In the bathroom of his refuge, Edgar chances upon a worn paperback copy of Goethe's early novel, which in this context works as a kind of photographic developer: at first, he is annoyed by the grandiloquence and archaism of this language that he cannot place (having torn up the cover page to use as toilet paper, he is unaware of the work's title and author and thus its canonical status), but soon he is seduced in spite of himself by the Wertherian eloquence, in which he finds the perfect expression of his own aspirations – as well as, subsequently, his personal torments. It is because of his identification with Goethe's character that he calls the first woman he falls in love with (the "first serious woman"[100] in his life) by the nickname "Charlie," a nod to Werther's love interest Charlotte, and it is because of his spontaneous adherence to Wertherian lyricism that he addresses her in Werther's very words, just as he "confides" in his friend Willi (sic) with cassette-tape recordings of excerpts from Werther's letters to Wilhelm.

Although the recipients do not know what to make of these fragmentary excerpts, they arrive at just the right moment of his development, communicating at each stage more about his states of mind than any "authentic" statement would; this is because the spirit of the times is not favorable to the expression of feelings. The phraseology of "real socialism," the cold rhetoric of petty bourgeois self-righteousness (which forces one to choose a "respectable profession" and stigmatizes those who have the misfortune of breaking rank), and the irrev-

---

[100] "Charlie war die erste ernsthafte Frau, mit der ich zu tun hatte." Plenzdorf, *Die neuen Leiden des jungen W.* [1973] (1981: 72). Subsequent references to this work will appear as NL plus page number.

erent and jaded prattle of his own generation (which Edgar nevertheless masters brilliantly, to his readership's delight) are all unable to express the states of mind of a young man grappling with the cold rationality and utilitarianism of his time. This case, as presented by Plenzdorf, shows that the tribulations of the self are both individual and universal, and as such young Wibeau, a fan of American subculture who has contempt for institutional models, discipline, and any "rules" imposed on his socialization, paradoxically comes to behave, to use Genette's words, "both as a new Werther and as an anti-Werther" (1982: 435; 1997: 306).

The fact that this work elicited such controversial enthusiasm in the GDR demonstrates to what extent the parallel touched a nerve, at a time marked by political thaw and demands for freedom – demands inspired by youth revolts in the West but aimed at reforming East German society from within. In portraying a subject's aborted attempt at self-formation in the supposedly "open" and "appeased" GDR of Erich Honecker, Plenzdorf was denouncing the oppressive character of the demand for socialization supported by the institutions of his country. At the same time, he joined in the vogue for literary reappropriations launched by the *Erbedebatte* ("heritage debate") which had been raging in the cultural circles of the GDR since the foundation of the young Republic. The issue was determining which tradition(s) East German writers should build on, beyond the anti-fascist and proletarian literature of the twentieth century (Weimar Republic, resistance to Nazism). Initially, founding fathers Wilhelm Pieck and Anton Ackermann had urged writers to draw inspiration from classical models to anchor the literature of the workers' and farmers' state in the "humanist" cultural heritage of the German nation, preferably choosing authors who, despite being bourgeois themselves, were likely to be recovered for the "progressive" ideals of democracy, equality, and freedom such as Lessing, Goethe, Schiller, and Heine. There were some ideological contortions to the reactionary aesthetic underlying this position, which was explained by the desire to thwart the tendencies towards "modernism," "cosmopolitanism," and "nihilism" (and thus in particular to formalism), with all radical innovation on principle being suspect of manipulation by US imperialist propaganda. The precept of imitating classics was, however, undermined by the Socialist Unity Party's decision to follow the "Bitterfeld Path" (1959), which encouraged writers to anchor their works in the world of workers. The limits of the desired rapprochement between cultural circles and the working class were quickly revealed, and this partial failure had the effect of relaunching the "heritage debate," which then entered a new phase: instead of slavishly conforming to classical models, it was better to use a selective approach with the aim of "critical reappropriation."[101] Writers like Peter Hacks eagerly seized on the great works of the Western canon (Shakespeare, Aristophanes, etc.), subjecting them to modern and parodic readings while using this approach to point – within certain limits – to the shortcomings of contemporary society.

With his *Neue Leiden*, Plenzdorf fits into this movement, which was made possible by the political context of "détente" and "normalization" the GDR had entered into in the early 1970s. Using *Werther* to describe his generation's lifestyle and the form that the conflict between the individual and society had assumed at the start of the Honecker era, he situated the Goethean heritage at the heart of "real socialism." He thus emphasized both the subversive character of young Goethe's work (and the legitimacy of the German Democratic Republic honoring him in this regard), and its relevance to the emancipatory struggle in East German society: the young *ancien régime* bourgeois in conflict with his milieu and rejected by the aristocracy finds his East German counterpart not in a young heir raised on classical culture, but rather a prototypical representative of the middle class, an all-around good boy who is marginalized for asserting his right to wear jeans, listen to jazz, and live his life as he sees fit. While Werther worships Homer and Ossian, Wibeau is a fan of "Satchmo" (Louis Armstrong), Defoe, and especially Salinger. Rejecting the models imposed upon him and aspiring only to become himself,[102] he fails to find his place in a socialist society.

The criticism was harsh, but it did not dispute the ideological foundations of the State. On the contrary, Plenzdorf's novel can be read as a call to reconnect with the fundamental ("humanist") objectives of communism: to build a non-repressive society that allows individuals to flourish and make use of their talents for the greater common good. In this respect, the circumstances of Edgar Wibeau's death are significant. Whether his unfortunate initiative can be equated with a form of suicide or not, it is in developing a machine capable of facilitating workers' labor and increasing collective productivity that he dies. Unlike Werther's melodramatic and narcissistic gesture of killing himself with the pistols he received from the woman he loved, Edgar's is an act of "positive rebellion"[103]

---

[101] Kurt Hager, "Zu Fragen der Kulturpolitik der SED: Referat auf der 6. Tagung des ZK der SED," 6 July 1972 (Brenner 1982: 24–25).
[102] "Alle forzlang kommt doch einer und will hören, ob man ein Vorbild hat und welches, oder man muß in der Woche drei Aufsätze darüber schreiben. Kann schon sein, ich hab eins, aber ich stell mich doch nicht auf den Markt damit. Einmal hab ich geschrieben: Mein größtes Vorbild ist Edgar Wibeau. Ich möchte so werden, wie er mal wird" (NL 15).
[103] Wolfgang Werth, "Rebell mit positiver Haltung: Plenzdorfs neuer Werther," *Deutsche Zeitung / Christ und Welt* 22.6.1973 (Brenner 1982: 284 ff.).

against a rigid social order and an imposed ideology, in the name of the very ideals on which the socialist state had been built – the tragic end of a career that, under other circumstances, could have led to an altruistic existence in the service of his community. Though this conclusion, which is optimistic overall (from a socialist perspective), could have been interpreted as a simple concession to censorship – as the novel was initially meant to end in suicide – this does not change the fact that Edgar Wibeau's revolt, from beginning to end, is turned not against socialist ideals themselves but against their distortion.

It is therefore not surprising that the text had a more mixed reception in the FRG, where a number of voices spoke out at the time to deplore the lack of "radicality" and "courage" in denouncing the regime.[104] The novel nonetheless quickly received an enduring place in school curricula, with educators seeing in this irreverent and joyfully parodic take on *Werther* an interesting way to invigorate the study of the classics, while giving young people a glimpse of East German literature and society. The play has also continued to be staged regularly in German theaters, both before and after reunification. Zaimoglu thus wrote for a readership largely comprised of readers who, like himself, may have read, studied, or seen a production of Plenzdorf's work during their studies.

Producing his own "Wertheriad" approximately thirty years later, Zaimoglu could not have more clearly placed his rewriting in line with Plenzdorf's project. If alluding to his novel as "The New Sorrows of Young Ali" does not provide direct confirmation, the very choice of Serdar as the protagonist's first name functions as a hypertextual signal. While Plenzdorf had imitated Goethe's title and borrowed the first initial of the protagonist's last name ("W.": Wibeau/Werther), Zaimoglu does not reveal the hero's last name but the first name Serdar resonates as an Anatolian replica of the Germanic *Edgar* (with the open E of the first syllable and the perfect rhyme of the second syllable), as if to signify that his character is indeed a Turkish-German variation of the 1973 East German "Werther" with Prussian and Huguenot roots.

As suggested by this more discreet reference to the Wertherian intertext (consisting of the founding text augmented by its recent rewriting), Zaimoglu certainly pushes emancipation from the Goethean model farther than Plenzdorf in certain respects. In particular, he drops the love triangle as a structuring element of the plot, unlike his predecessor, who had strictly followed the pattern of the hypotext by reproducing the Werther / Charlotte / Albert relationship as the Wibeau / Charlie / Dieter trio, going so far as to pastiche the scene of the meeting between Werther and Charlotte with the touching portrayal of a "Charlie" simi-

---

[104] See for example the review by Wolfram Schütte (Brenner 1982: 278).

larly surrounded by the children she cares for like a mother. By dispensing with this type of palimpsest (understood as a direct translation from text to text on the pragmatic level), Zaimoglu removes the romantic dimension from the story, and this inevitably leads to a far less melodramatic outcome.

The trivial discrepancy thus created was, however, already an essential feature of Plenzdorf's *Neue Leiden* in other ways. It is worth recalling how provocative the image was in Plenzdorf's time of the young Wibeau tearing out the first page of Goethe's novel to wipe his buttocks in the bathroom before abandoning himself, incredulous and laughing, to the text that has been sanctified in the history of literature – only to inadvertently find an interest, first amused and then increasingly sincere, in the tormented and lyrical outpourings of "Old Werther," as he calls him in English. The blasphemous deviation from the model was not limited to this scatological anecdote, which here serves as a sign. Rather than spiritual elevation, Edgar Wibeau dreams of personal emancipation, fundamentally desiring no more than to "enjoy without hindrances" ("jouir sans entraves"), to use a French slogan expressing the global movement of his generation. By replacing Werther's metaphysical quest – the "abyssal questioning" that he opposed to "eighteenth-century rationality in decline"[105] – with a much more down-to-earth demand for individual freedom and personal fulfillment, Plenzdorf ignored the grandiose and sublime dimension that can be attributed to Werther's struggle. Many commentators, even those who had a favorable opinion of parodying the canon and satirizing the system, interpreted this trivialization as a weakness of the novel. Such is the case, for instance, for Pierre Vaydat (2002: 98) who, thirty years after the publication of *Die neuen Leiden des jungen W.*, finds it to the author's discredit that his hero "confuses authentic freedom with leisure adrift in a (meagerly) aesthetic existence" and that the "anti-establishment negation" boils down, in his case, to "a sulky anarchism" and a "hedonistic narcissism."

This is quite possibly a misinterpretation of Plenzdorf's intentions. Perhaps the author never wanted to follow Goethe down the path of this "abyssal questioning" because he did not detect an equivalent preoccupation among the young people of his time. Anyhow, it seems as if Zaimoglu, in turn attacking this treasure of German literature, were set on cutting short any ambiguity by going straight in for vulgarity. As discussed above, the focus on material and physical concerns here far surpasses, both thematically and quantitatively, the

---

105 "Werther, sans parvenir à être un créateur, a une personnalité suffisamment forte et originale pour opposer à la plate rationalité du XVIIIe siècle déclinant un questionnement abyssal" (Vaydat 2002: 98).

scatological domain. Like Hakan, Serdar is constantly preoccupied by his body, just as much on a subjective and intimate level (various pains, dietary concerns, disruption of digestion and elimination functions, ability to be satisfied sexually) as from an interpersonal and social perspective (weight and skin problems, fear of not performing well enough in sexual intercourse).

Zaimoglu is also much more explicit about these subjects than his predecessor, and the attention that his two heroes give to their "base" bodily concerns maintains a relationship with the source text not just of contrast but also of analogy, with their intimate misadventures giving rise to rants that are every bit as extravagant and intense as Werther's meditations. The combination of the two – contrast and analogy – produces the distorting mirror effect that adds a surprising element for readers familiar with Goethe's text. In other words, the scandal is not so much the (one-time) displacement of the iconic text into the lavatory and its blasphemous misuse (also one-time) – the foundational moment of Plenzdorf's parody – as it is the systematic and extensive reproduction of Werther's introspective discourse in this realm of preoccupation. It is as if Zaimoglu had taken up Plenzdorf's idea of taking an unseemly approach to Goethe, but interpreting his sorrows literally, giving them a concrete form as physical symptoms, and applying this systematically throughout the novel. Between Wibeau's pithy catchphrase, "Das war ein echtes Leiden von mir" ("That was always the trouble with me," NL 35) which serves Plenzdorf as a recurring nod to Goethe,[106] and the abundance of details, the intensity, and the variety of nuance used to treat the same theme in *Liebesmale, scharlachrot*, there exists more than a simple difference of degree. By opting for the hyperbolic rather than the allusive and elliptic, Zaimoglu takes the body – and its relation to the "heart" and mind – as the object of introspective investigation, thus placing it at the center of the portrait he creates of this generation.

The parodic force of the novel largely comes from the fact that the transfer of the introspective dynamic to the somatic level is psychologically motivated. Serdar and Hakan's sufferings may primarily just be common scrapes compared to the metaphysical torments that trouble Werther, yet they incontestably express genuine malaise. This complex and disturbed relation of the subject to the body has no equivalent in Wibeau, whose complacent evocation of "Leiden" ("sufferings") stems by and large from the exaggerated language characteristic of young people. In his case, he uses this clichéd term to refer to discomforts

---

[106] See also: "Das war ein wirkliches Leiden von mir" (NL 56); "Ich weiß nicht, ob sich einer vorstellen kann, was das für ein Leiden war" (NL 61); "Das war lange Zeit ein echtes Leiden von mir" (NL 63).

that are minor overall and that do not grow worse over the course of the story but are instead replaced by real suffering – romantic disappointment and a feeling of abandonment – expressed solely through quotes from Goethe. Given the unseemly details he provides at the beginning of the novel about his activities in the lavatory, Edgar Wibeau, contrary to his own assertions, obviously has no body image issues. He is a young man who is "comfortable in his own skin" and whose worries stem primarily from a difficult relationship with the outside world.

Thus, Serdar's sexual impotence, which is arguably an extension and physical manifestation of Werther's inability to act and to create, can also be seen as a response to Plenzdorf, whose hero portrays himself smugly as "someone who's never had any sexual problems."[107] Representative of a generation that freed itself from the repressive sexual morals of the 1950s, Wibeau is aware of the advantage that the more permissive mores give him in this respect over the literary figures with whom he most closely identifies. Though just sixteen years old, he looks with pity on the erotic misadventures of Holden Caulfield, the teenage runaway from Salinger's *The Catcher in the Rye*, as well as Werther's romantic shyness. His incomprehension finds a certain echo in Hakan's mocking reaction to Serdar when he tells him about the problems he has with his libido. Wibeau, like Hakan, will then learn that it is not enough to be daring, uninhibited, and in full possession of his physical resources to achieve fulfillment in love. Yet for Wibeau, the problem is not in the sexual realm (this matter seems to be resolved): the painful discovery that awaits him essentially concerns the distinction between eroticism and love. For Hakan as well as his friend with the opposite diagnosis, sexuality remains a serious problem, distinct from love and yet inseparable from it, deeply affecting the integrity of the (masculine) individual in terms of self-perception and interactions with others (especially the opposite sex) along with the ability to act upon reality. With Serdar, Zaimoglu revisits and amplifies the motif of impotence, which Goethe hinted at in connection with the artist's challenges, carrying forward this pattern in both realms – that of sex and that of the aesthetic act.

The artistic theme is indeed likewise an element of the hypotext, but the lines that Plenzdorf and Zaimoglu follow in this regard diverge significantly. Serdar and Wibeau are weak-willed painters and poets whose dreams of creation are short-lived. They are both failed artists, just like Werther, but even more radically so. Wibeau's ambition seems to relate largely to the posturing: he takes pleasure in using the role of the "misunderstood genius" to establish and mag-

---

[107] "Das sagt sich vielleicht leicht für einen, der nie sexuelle Probleme hatte" (NL 34).

nify his marginality while almost everyone – himself included – agrees that he "doesn't know how to draw" and doesn't have one iota of talent or inspiration. Whether or not he has an aptitude for painting (the polyphonic organization of the narrative makes it impossible to decide), his desire to create remains outside the scope of his intimate life and centers on the social status and aura of freedom assigned to the particular position, both overexposed and extremely precarious, of the artist in the GDR.

Here again, the situation seems more complex in Zaimoglu's work. Even if it is difficult to determine precisely to what extent his confidences are sincere because of the game that arises in the exchange of letters, there is reason to think that even though he admits he has no poetic inspiration or aptitude for painting and the haikus he sends to his friend are woefully lacking, Serdar is still a smooth talker who doesn't just have "the gift of gab" but also a need for expression he attempts to realize artistically. The most obvious proof in this regard, beyond the correlation between his lack of creativity and his sexual impotence (which suggests that the problems he experiences with his libido are a somatic manifestation of his difficulty in achieving his desires and thus contribute to the parody of the Wertherian hypotext), resides in his impressive mastery of language. Any page could serve to persuade the reader of a discursive ability that denotes real creativity and a truly sensual relationship to language that situates him much more in the line of Werther than of Wibeau. In fact, the expression of the latter is discursively reduced to its simplest form. The recurring phrase "I quickly analyzed myself" ("ich analysierte mich kurz"), by shortcutting Werther's poetic and analytical introspections, uses allusion and ellipsis to leave to the imagination that which Goethe made plain to see: a surrender to the sensuality of expression. Zaimoglu fills this void with characters who become intoxicated with words and who create their own language, rediscovering what was lost in the transition from pre-Romantic eloquence to the hard-boiled style of a generation playing at blasé brevity.

However, form is not secondary in Plenzdorf's work. Rather, *Die neuen Leiden des jungen W.* paints the portrait of a generation through its language, as had been the case with *The Catcher in the Rye* in the United States twenty years before. While Wibeau's language, which was a major reason for the success of both the novel and play, still comes across as impoverished in comparison with what Zaimoglu creates for his two heroes (not to mention Werther), this is largely due to his situation and mode of enunciation. Whereas Plenzdorf, resolutely deviating from the Goethean model, had opted for the oral form (monologue, dialogues, quotes recorded on cassettes) as the most flagrant element of modernization, Zaimoglu does not shy from returning to the epistolary narrative, a dated form that provides him with a justification for his characters' recourse to the most formal registers of the written code (epic, lyric, irony, pathos). By renouncing the oralization that established the "modernity" of Wibeau's language (characterized in particular, in keeping with Salinger's model, by hyperbole, digressions, verbal tics, and Americanisms), he also returns to a device that combines the completed aspect of the delayed narrative and the procedural aspect of "in the moment" narrative.

The written / oral difference therefore coincides with a difference in point of view, temporal perspective, and – in terms of linguistic categories – aspect. If Wibeau develops neither his introspective analyses nor the presentation of his "sorrows" but contents himself with allusion, this is partially because his perspective is one of reviewing reported events. As spontaneous and colorful as his words may be from a formal point of view, they relate to a bygone past and are literally situated in the "beyond." A posthumous narrative establishes a theatrical monologue, and in opting for this as a narrative device, Plenzdorf retains and amplifies the monological aspect that already characterized Werther's one-way epistolary discourse. Instead, Serdar and Hakan's conversations relate to very recent events and ongoing processes. In referring to reflections and affects that are, for them, of burning topicality, they allow Zaimoglu to develop this (written) "language of the heart," full of ardor and zeal, with a tradition dating back to Christian mysticism that formed the basis for the *Sturm und Drang* movement.

The difference between the narrative strategies of the two rewritings can, by way of an extreme simplification, be compared to the formal opposition between parody and pastiche. Plenzdorf would thus, in the words of Genette, recount "the same story in another way" (parody), while Zaimoglu would tell "another story in the same way" (pastiche). This distinction is obviously too schematic, for Zaimoglu's novel is only partially characterized by the reproduction of Goethe's "manner," just as *Die neuen Leiden* cannot be reduced solely to the parodic dimension. However, the application of these categories makes it possible to ascertain what the stakes of Zaimoglu's rewriting are. If he intends, as Plenzdorf does, to give his young, contemporary characters some of Werther's dignity and romantic consistency, this is not revealed in the paths that their lives take but rather at the formal level – more precisely, in the status and the quality of their language.

Like Goethe, Plenzdorf intended to create a novel about the struggles a generation had flourishing in a repressive society, emphasizing his character's points of friction with established authorities and institutions, with *Werther* serving as a touchstone (and *Catcher in the Rye* providing a stylistic model). Zaimoglu's aim is quite different: although he also shows young people facing massive difficulties with integration, he forgoes blaming social structures (though nothing less would be expected from the figurehead of the *Kanak Attak* movement) to instead focus on a more general critique of "civilization," on the one hand, and on the interiority of his characters, whom he provides with a form (a *voice*) powerful enough to transcend the baseness of their concerns, on the other. It is by inventing this language with which he endows his heroes, or rather by the very capacity with which he endows them to forge a language of their own in a world where all discourse is a trap, that Zaimoglu invites comparison with the author of *Werther*. Here, the canonical text functions less as a touchstone (for the degree of a society's sclerosis) than a stylistic archetype, taken as the yardstick for depicting a generation through its language and through its ability to develop itself in language.

The fact that the modern take on this model assumes the form of a half-ironic, half-playful pastiche does not detract from the homage paid to the "prince of poets," nor from the audacity of the writer who claims his legacy. By imitating the *manner* of the young Goethe exposing the "sorrows" of the bourgeois youth of his time, the spokesperson of the post-migratory generation, whose reputation as a writer was based at the time solely on the ambivalent success of *Kanak Sprak*, quite patently seeks his own admission into the center of the national literary field. This includes his claim to reproduce and even surpass the feat of his East German predecessor whose modern Wertheriad is now part of the academic and university canon. In response to Plenzdorf's "serious parody," which limited itself to reproducing elements of the plot by pouring them into an ostensibly "modern" generic and stylistic mold, ignoring any tribute to the language (in its formal register) and to interiority, Zaimoglu offers a transposition in which, on the contrary, form prevails over content and the inanity of the statements, oscillating between trivial pathos and self-derision, is, to use the words used by Paul Aron in another context, "absorbed by a language that evolves into a perfectly mastered spiral."[108] He thus exploits the whole range of potentialities of the pastiche: it is indeed in itself, as Aron points out, "a neutral technique" which "thus combines perfectly with the parodic, satirical, and playful registers, since it can also differentiate itself from them when it targets plagiarism or falsification."[109] Taking the exact opposite approach of Plenzdorf, whose plot evokes the model as commandingly as his style puts it at a remove (in particular, through the use of duly-framed quotes that contrast with the

---

[108] "Le propos, en soi un peu ridicule, est aspiré par un verbe qui évolue en une spirale parfaitement maîtrisée" (Aron 2013).

[109] "C'est pourquoi je crois qu'il faut [...] considérer [le pastiche] davantage comme une technique neutre (le fait d'imiter un style). Dans ses usages, il se combine donc parfaitement avec les registres parodique, satirique ou ludique, comme il peut aussi s'en différencier lorsqu'il vise au plagiat ou à la falsification" (Aron 2013).

hero-narrator's careless language), Zaimoglu offers a virtuoso performance that is all the more striking because his project was such a challenge. Having young *Kanak* underdogs *convincingly* speak, or rather write, with as much eloquence, impetuosity, and searing intensity as Werther. In order for this to be effective, it was not only possible but presumably necessary for the subjects that fire his heroes up to be objectively not worth the fuss so as to motivate the ironic distancing that alone could justify, in the historical context of the first decade of the twenty-first century, such a discursive investment.

By contrast, it almost seems as if Plenzdorf used the iconic work only as a pretext (clever but bordering on the flashy) to denounce a sclerotic political system.[110] While this reading may be reductive, if only because it undervalues the political dimension already present in Goethe, it is important not to dismiss the hypothesis that, for Zaimoglu, such an undervaluing of the political was accordingly part of the plan for his response to Plenzdorf. Did the latter denounce the flaws of "real socialism" in his novel, with implicit pleas for us to return to the true socialist ideal? Zaimoglu refrains from delivering any messages of this kind. He provides neither a critique of institutions nor a defense of an alternative social model. The end of *Die neuen Leiden des jungen W.* implies – even when making allowances here for self-censorship – that if Wibeau had not been the victim of a tragic and needless accident, he might have been able to cope, rediscovering a sense of collectivity and working for the common good: in other words, that individual rebellion has a chance for success only if it leads to reintegration into the social body and that society can only change if individuals become actively involved in its (re)construction. As for *Liebesmale*, its conclusion does not make it possible to infer any fixed creed – at most, that the values of compassion and mutual assistance can flourish thanks to the connections forged between autonomous individuals outside the established structures both within mainstream society as well as within the "ghetto." If there is indeed a (provisional) "salvation" for Serdar, it is not thanks to his integration into the collective but to a personal intervention based on friendship. He merely reaps the fruits of an intimate relationship that has deepened and strengthened throughout the novel, precisely by way of the letters exchanged between the two outsiders. Here again, the driving force is language, through which the subject is constructed and builds a relationship to the other.

---

110 For Reich-Ranicki (1973), the Wertherian intertext in Plenzdorf's novel (which he considered "anyway important", that is to say: on a political level) is nothing more than a lucky find, a "striking gag", an "amusing trick" (Brenner 1982: 264).

However, it would be wrong to accuse such a project of being apolitical. In Zaimoglu's work, it is less a matter of social criticism than empowerment through language and individual passions, with the characters realizing this power along with, on another level, the author himself (the idea of genius is not far off), which is tantamount to saying that his novel has symbolic stakes that are eminently political. It is highly political indeed, at the dawn of the twenty-first century, to attribute such power to language, just as it is subversive for an author from the most disadvantaged and marginalized fringes of German society to assert that he is ascending to the level of the young Goethe.

Reading *Liebesmale, scharlachrot* as a response to Plenzdorf also allows for a better appreciation of the role that falls to intermedial and intercultural elements of this text. By replacing jazz, Wibeau's musical reference, with Arabesk (preferred over hip hop) and "Satchmo" with "Müslüm Baba," Zaimoglu makes the case that Germany is no longer under the exclusive control of American cultural hegemony but rather shaped by new intermixtures, particularly with Turkish (popular, religious, and literary) culture. Likewise, it shifts the center of gravity of the national literary imagination from the Christian West to the Muslim East by contrasting *Kanaks* descended from immigrant and proletarian Turkish peasantry with the young, provincial descendant of (noble) Huguenot refugees, and by fusing Pietism and Sufism into the same "revived" heterodox spirituality. Seen from this angle, the novel perhaps serves an ambition that is even greater than it seems at first glance: that of being not only the *Werther* of the first Turkish-German generation – a significant minority among the youth population in (West) Germany in the first decade of the twenty-first century – but *the* youth novel of post-reunification Germany, period.

In this case, *Liebesmale, scharlachrot* would thus constitute a key text, almost a manifesto of the "Turkish turn" in German literature that Adelson highlighted in her important study: a text that is not limited to showing what contributions immigrant populations have made to German culture (by enriching it with "foreign" elements) but which in itself contributes to the reconfiguration of the national imagination, in particular by weaving a dialectical relationship between old and new, self and other, local and global. Zaimoglu's novel, pleading ardently and irreverently for Germany to reconcile with its own cultural and spiritual roots – and with a literary heritage it has cut itself off from despite it being the source of its global reach – offers an emblematic illustration of what Adelson means by "touching tales," i.e.: literary narratives that decenter the gaze on national culture insofar as they "commingle cultural developments and historical references generally not thought to belong together in any proper sense" (2005: 20). Far from the culturalist pathos of the "in-between" and uprootedness, Zaimoglu portrays a generation that, by shaking up preconceived ideas about the relationships of young people (especially those from immigrant backgrounds) to culture (especially national), carries the key to the rebuilding of German society. In this sense, it is indeed a novel of the "Turn," in the sense of the *Wende:* a novel that, at the time of political "reunification" between East Germany and West Germany, calls for Germany to come to a cultural reconciliation with itself and with its history through the eyes of its "Others."

This book thus inaugurates a new phase in Zaimoglu's career. On the one hand, he shifts settings from the subcultural "ghetto" to the "gray areas" of socio-ethnic diversity, and on the other hand he revisits his approach to literary codes and references, while remaining iconoclastic throughout. If the subversive potential of *Kanak Sprak* resides in an ambiguous play on the authenticity of the parlance represented and on the "discordance" that loans itself to the deconstruction of assigned ethnic (if not gendered) identities, *Liebesmale*'s subversiveness consists in fully assuming the artefactual character of the text and its intertextual dimension, paving the way for a profound reappropriation of literary heritage. Thus, in a single motion Zaimoglu explores new ways of inscribing the Turkish presence into German society, a new relationship with tradition, and new means of establishing himself in the literary field. In order to fully appreciate this challenge, it makes sense to revisit the missing link in the novel's intertextual genealogy: Akif Pirinçci's literary début entitled *Tränen sind immer das Ende* ("It Always Ends in Tears").

The Pirinçci Precedent: Developments and Limits of a Post-Ethnic Variation on the Wertherian Theme

Akif Pirinçci was born in Istanbul in 1959 and, like Zaimoglu, was raised in Germany by *Gastarbeiter* parents who ultimately left to retire on the Aegean coast. A prolific writer, he had a dazzling career writing crime fiction when in 1989 he created the character of Francis, a detective cat and the hero of what now constitutes a series of eight novels, which have been translated into 17 languages. The first book in the series was adapted, first for film and then comics.[111] Despite this success, which has made him one of the most widely-read living German authors in the world, Pirinçci is completely isolated in the national literary field. This unique position is partly due to the stigmatization that generally results

---

[111] *Felidae* (directed by Michael Schaack after a script co-written by Pirinçci, Trickompany 1994) was the most expensive animated film produced in Germany. In the same year the comic *Felidae – Katzencomic*, with graphics by Rob Koo, was published (Munich: Goldmann).

from writing genre fiction, but it can also be explained by the doggedness with which the author endeavored to eradicate all traces of his ethnicity from his work. He did this so effectively that his texts were not classified by critics as immigration literature, though neither were they admitted into the corpus of mainstream German literature. Thus, as Petra Fachinger (2001: 10) pointed out, his tenacious desire to be recognized as a full-fledged German author has paradoxically caused Pirinçci to fall into the no-man's land of overlooked authors. As if to further amplify his pariah status, the author of *Felidae* has, in recent years, thrown himself into unbridled political activism, voicing his support on far-right social networks and in polemical, high-circulation works for Islamophobic, racist, misogynistic, and homophobic positions of unprecedented violence.[112] In hindsight, it would seem that this move towards national populism, far from being an epiphenomenon of his career, finds its origin in a positioning that serves as the basis of his aesthetic and discursive project.

Before finding his niche by inventing the "cat thriller" formula, Pirinçci had attempted an initial breakthrough when he was just twenty-one with an intercultural variant of Plenzdorf's rewriting. The author published this first "novel" (according to the generic designation on the front cover) at his own expense before Goldmann printed 20,000 copies following an effective campaign of televised self-promotion (Pokatsky 1982). He had adapted the framework of Plenzdorf's *Neue Leiden* to West German society with a first-person account of an unhappy love story between an eighteen-year-old Turkish immigrant and a German girl from a good family with the evocative name of Christa Born.[113] Openly autobiographical (the hero is called Akif Pirinçci), the narrative mines the vein of the Goethean generational novel à la Plenzdorf by portraying two ill-matched lovers whose misfortune, however, is attributable to the lovers themselves (the character of the rival has disappeared), their respective social situations, and especially their opposing views on life.

Equipped with just a primary school certificate, Akif leaves the small town near Koblenz where he grew up with his immigrant worker parents to become

---

[112] See especially Pirinçci 2014, 2015, and 2016. Yet it is primarily through his interventions in the far-right blogosphere and on his own website that Pirinçci has sharpened a discourse of hatred capable of polarizing even PEGIDA-participants, as the address with Neo-Nazi overtones he delivered in Dresden on 20 October 2015 has shown.

[113] The patronym Christa Born may be deciphered either as "the native Christian" or as "the well-born Christian," if *born* is understood as an Anglicism. However, this does not exclude the possibility of a reference to the old German word *Born* ("spring"), which would in turn imply a nod to the *Lebensborn* ("fount of life") project, the SS eugenics program devised to propagate Aryan traits.

a writer and filmmaker in Cologne. He has no experience of life in general or of women in particular and scrapes by on odd jobs while waiting for a chance to fulfill his ambitions. He meets his sweetheart, who is a few years older than he is and from a wealthy family, while out at a nightclub. She is studying law – the pinnacle of respectability – and she already has some experience in sex and romance, meaning she is the one to initiate Akif into the ways of love, though she is sidelined by the young man's raw spontaneity that moves between domination and supplication. Although she has recently arrived from her small town as well, Christa is also well-integrated socially: she has housemates and spends time with, much to her lover's despair, a group of intellectuals who flaunt a lifestyle and ideas inspired by the protest movements of the 1970s.

The story portrays the hero-narrator, the author's alter ego, as a boy riddled with anxiety and inhibitions as well as a resentment that is vague – but all the more pronounced – and that is focused on this specific environment, a sphere he perceives as being monolithic and dominant: a mainstream cultural establishment that asserts values (tolerance, emancipation, critical thinking, pacifism, respect for others) which he believes only serve to cover up hypocrisy, arrogance, and latent aggression. Refusing to make any compromises with this insidious ideology, Akif cultivates a solitary and asocial ethos resulting from emotional hypertrophy, romantic possessiveness, and megalomania. This fiercely apolitical non-conformity manifests itself as a penchant for provocation and excesses of all kinds. As his relationship with Christa deteriorates, he succumbs to alcohol, which precipitates the dreaded outcome. In short, Pirinçci's version of the melancholy rebel is a tormented soul, an instinctive anarchist in the same raging and dilapidated vein as Charles Bukowski, whom he explicitly claims as a model.

Among the novel's innumerable intertextual references, this one is strategically placed at the start of the story as a part of the first dialogue between the future lovers. The autodidact Akif declares himself a passionate reader of Bukowski, who is "obviously" his "favorite author"[114] whereas Christa, who has received a classical education, confesses her predilection for "the German ballads," particularly *Lenore* (1774) by Gottfried August Bürger. Serving as a counterpoint to the reference to underground American literature, the evocation of this *Sturm und Drang* masterpiece that inspired both Walter Scott and Edgar Allan Poe opens up a space that allows the socio-cultural abyss dividing the two protagonists to disappear temporarily. By briefly summarizing the plot of

---

114 "Danach fragte sie, was ich denn so lese. Bukowski! Natürlich Charles Bukowski. Er ist wirklich mein Lieblingsautor." Akif Pirinçci, *Tränen sind immer das Ende* (1980: 12). Subsequent references to this work will appear as T plus page number.

this fantastic ballad to Akif, who is unfamiliar with the text, the girl immediately elicits in him surprise mixed with delight:

> I really hadn't expected that of her. What I mean is that girls who get excited about ancient stuff like that have, in my experience, been either weird or uptight, or too ugly to bother. However, I should add that I go crazy for old ballads, sagas, poems or folk songs like that, too. [...] I can actually have an orgasm when I hear about the dead coming back to life, languishing virgins, painful love affairs, wars that tear people apart, family downfalls, dramatic encounters after a thousand years, and so on. That's why I've gone to see *Dr. Zhivago* exactly nine times. I gushed about how much she surprised me and the usual nonsense.[115]

Over the course of the romantic relationship built on the basis of this shared receptivity to the melodramatic register, Bürger's ballad gradually acquires in Akif's eyes the status of their story's foundational and fetish text. Even though Christa, who is also passionate about E. T. A. Hoffmann's *Die Elixiere des Teufels* ("The Devil's Elixirs") and *Der Sandmann* ("The Sandman"), soon begins to distance herself from him, Akif appropriates the reference to Bürger and later sees the foreshadowing of their demise in this long, macabre poem. From his first reading of *Lenore*, which takes place in Christa's apartment just before their first night of passion, the "unusually cruel and at the same time sad" words that the ghost addresses to his fiancée as he carries her towards death ("Is my darling frightened? The moon is bright ... Hooray! The dead travel fast. Is she scared of the dead?") provoke a premonitory melancholy in him.[116] By immediately locating the relationship forming between the two in a universe of poetic fiction considered "Gothic" and rooted in the German canon, Pirinçci gives *Lenore* a role comparable to the one that Klopstock's ode *Die Frühlingsfeier*

---

[115] "Das hatte ich von ihr wirklich nicht erwartet. Ich meine damit, die Mädchen, die sich für derart vergreistes Zeug begeistern, waren nach meinen Erfahrungen entweder abnormal oder verklemmt oder zum Aufgeben häßlich. Allerdings muß ich noch hinzufügen, daß ich bei solchen alten Balladen, Sagen, Gedichten oder Volksliedern gleichfalls überschnappe. [...] Ich kann tatsächlich einen Orgasmus kriegen, wenn ich von auferstandenen Toten, schmachtenden Jungfrauen, schmerzlichen Liebeleien, von Kriegen, die die Menschen auseinanderreißen, Familienuntergängen, dramatischen Begegnungen nach tausend Jahren und so fort etwas höre. Deswegen bin ich auch genau neunmal in 'Dr. Schiwago' hineingegangen. Ich erzählte ihr total überspannt, wie überrascht ich von ihr sei, und den übrigen alten Käse" (T 12).

[116] "Unerwartet erfaßte mich ein seltsames Gefühl. Das Ganze hörte sich zwar wie ein lustiger Dracula-Film an, doch wenn ich es leise vor mich hin murmelte, machte es mich richtig traurig. Ich schmiß das Buch in irgendeine Ecke, schloß die Augen, versuchte darüber nicht nachzudenken [...]. Aber diese Sätze kamen mir immer wieder in den Sinn. Graut Liebchen auch?... Graut Liebchen auch?... Graut Liebchen auch?... Unvermittelt tauchten dann auch noch Bilder auf. Vorstellungen, Visionen – oder Vorahnungen?" (T 77–78).

("The Celebration of Spring") – associated with the poetry of Ossian, which served as inspiration for the former – has for Werther and Charlotte: to anchor their romantic relationship in a shared poetic sensibility by way of a catalyzing hypotext that seals their sentimental pact in the manner of a communion of soul mates.

The reference to pre-Romanticism thus enters, from the "Gothic" side, into the world of imagination that will serve as creative inspiration for the hero. For if there is one thing that Akif never doubts, it is his talent: he *is* a writer, he has no hesitation about this nor any problems producing. His only concern is to secure the means of subsistence necessary to write the works – detective novels – that will make his name known. This ambition forces him to lead a very constricted lifestyle, which is hardly compatible with his amorous projects. This is why he resolves to apply for a job as a laborer, which he finds as if by chance in the holy of holies of institutional culture, the opera. This detail makes it possible to give credence to the image of a society in which the proletarians, whom Akif spends time with in this context, are exploited not by capital but by subsidized culture. After the inevitable break-up and a failed suicide attempt (on a stormy night),[117] the young man finally gets back to work and in the space of twenty-one days he writes... the 256-page book the reader is holding. This is a record in itself since it is even less time than it took Goethe to write the first version of *Werther*.

Pirinçci dispenses with the love triangle as well as an enunciative device that aims, as Plenzdorf's did with the hero recording audio cassettes that he sent to his friend, to adapt the epistolary model to the current stage of communication technologies: his story makes no secret of being a literary creation. On the other hand, unlike Plenzdorf's text and the one Zaimoglu would later write, it inscribes itself in the continuity of the Goethean novel with its character of a strongly autobiographical work for young adults that the author dashed off. This work is indeed the impetuous début of a highly gifted writer who used the material from his own life, as young as he may have been, without – or almost without – any filter.

---

117 This is itself a pronounced nod to Werther, whose name has been mentioned for the first and only time earlier that night. During this breakup scene, which took place in a pizzeria, Akif made final efforts, if not to save their relationship, then at least to give their separation a dramatic dimension. But to his disappointment, Christa remained distant and ordered a soft drink: "Herr im Himmel, Limo ist so ein undramatisches Getränk! Wie soll man da tragische Sätze aufsagen! Immer wenn ich dieses Scheißglas mit der Pißgelben Flüssigkeit drin vor mir sah, verging mir die Lust am 'Werther'-spielen" (T 232).

It is all the more remarkable to see to what extent the product of this creation resists socio-ethnic interpretation. There is no narrative or discursive elaboration of the conflict between the protagonists' respective positions in this regard, even though the hero is a Turkish immigrant and the failed romance he relates is of a love that is presented from the outset as intercultural. Akif stoically assumes his identity as a "Turk" in relation to others (there being no foreseeable naturalization in this era), and if this title earns him some stereotypical reactions that he finds tiresome,[118] the position designated as such has no impact either on his perception of German society (and vice-versa) nor on the course of his romance with Christa, the well-bred German. While this relationship quickly takes a catastrophic turn, the story is told in such a way that it never occurs to the reader that their difficulties are due to prejudice or mutual misunderstanding, much less a relationship of unequal power between these two groups within German society. No, the young lovers only have themselves to blame: she – by her own admission – because she is "independent," even "selfish" (i.e. emancipated, modern) and he because he suffers from exaggerated sensitivity and indomitable pride, combined with an unhealthy possessiveness and an excessive sexual appetite – characteristics that he takes as being completely out of step with the spirit of the times and in keeping with the model of the lone wolf in legendary Hollywood movies.

Tom Cheesman has provided a subtle analysis of the paradox of the "cosmopolitan and post-ethnic" imagination that Pirinçci, a future master of suspense, inaugurated with a lively pen several decades before other writers of the same origin, such as Zaimoglu, took on the difficult task of extracting their writing from the ghetto of "migrant" and "intercultural" literature.[119] The success – at least intratextual – of this enterprise is due to the fact that this creation confirms the unwavering devotion to a national collective perceived as a monolithic block anchored within the frontiers of the Western world. Such an allegiance requires the contender to completely recant all previous ties and points of reference: this is the price to pay for acculturation. By all appearances, the elements of ethnicity strewn throughout the novel are indeed provided for the sole reason that they

---

[118] "'Ich heiße Akif. Bin Türke, weißt du', antwortete ich ungeheuer natürlich. Ich wartete nur auf das 'Du kannst aber sehr gut Deutsch'. Und es kam prompt. Ja, ich bin Türke. Ich kam mit meinen Eltern und meiner Schwester vor zehn Jahren nach Deutschland. Und es ist wirklich nicht mehr originell, wenn man nach so langer Zeit andauernd das 'Kannst gut Deutsch' vorgesetzt bekommt" (T 8–9).

[119] "Pirinçci composes a postethnic, cosmopolitan narrative that resists ethnicization or radicalization through declarations and demonstrations of belonging to the culture where one is settled and denials of all interest in the culture of origin" (Cheesman 2007: 85).

are authentic and that the author, writing the novel straight through with all the raw candor of a *Stürmer und Dränger* of the Beatnik generation, did not make an effort to erase the traces of his subjectivity. Yet the paradox (and interest) of this explanation is that it only makes the very insignificance of these same elements all the more obvious in comparison with the author's remarkable mastery of national – and, more broadly, Western – linguistic and cultural codes, of which the book provides evidence as a whole. The novel thus demonstrates and simultaneously effects the transformation of the young Akif, son of Turkish immigrants, into a full and equal member of the national community.

Thus, in the rare instances that Akif, more or less in spite of himself, comes into contact with the Turkish immigrant community in Cologne, there is an opportunity for the narrator – and for Pirinçci – to show how much distance there is separating him from this world. Because of his opera job, he crosses paths with an old Turkish worker, Hassan, who takes him under his wing. This ultimately sympathetic paternal character (a variation of Plenzdorf's Zaremba) can find nothing to console him apart from offering him his three goats and the hand of his fifteen year-old daughter still in Turkey if he would agree to return and settle down there (T 184). This proposal is so far removed from Akif's mental universe with his dreams of glory and love that the very suggestion of it is enough to demonstrate how odd it would be for there to be any point of comparison between this outcast, solitary young man and such "compatriots," however well-intentioned they may be, because at best they can offer a primitive vision of the world and degenerate customs. It is clear that he no longer has anything in common with the backwardness of provincial Turkey. His detachment from this world is such that he does not even need to turn his back on it. When he is wandering at night and randomly comes across a "Türkenlokal" ("hole-in-the-wall owned by Turks"), the idea that this establishment "was constantly striving to exude an exotic flair and always cooked these Turkish dishes that even Turks didn't want to stuff themselves with" (T 181) could have deterred him. But, recalling at the last second (!) his own Turkish origins ("daß ich ja ebenfalls ein gebürtiger Türke war"), he understands that he will be more at peace there than elsewhere "since this world does not show much interest in sickly love stories." Akif can remain among these Turkish immigrants *because* he is not part of their world, because for him this tavern is not a home base or a place of nostalgia, but a place where he will feel just as foreign, if not more so, than in any anonymous bar in the city.

In this way, the novel accomplishes a subtle operation of ethnic neutralization. At the end of a coming-of-age story constructed as a mise-en-abyme, the uprooted Turk, freed of his attachments, becomes a full-fledged German, and the very proof of this is right before the reader's eyes.[120] He who at the outset considered himself "fundamentally not at all a Turk, but not a German either," unable to even say that he oscillated vaguely "between the two,"[121] ultimately emerges from the limbo of inexistence as something *better* than the average German: a German writer. Upon closer examination, this neutralization (or denaturalization) is not without some inconsistencies. For example, one of the few letters inserted into the story, written by Akif to his mother, raises a certain number of questions: Why does Akif write to his mother in German? Does she even know how to read this language, assuming she understands it well enough to follow her son's elaborate syntax? Why does the letter not contain the slightest reference to what one might imagine to be the cultural universe of a woman of her origins and socio-cultural background? These inconsistencies, however, are balanced by the panache with which Pirinçci achieves his linguistic and stylistic prowess. While his lively and bold writing, characterized by a studied carelessness, contains many clichés (notably in the sexual domain and the description of the female body, where lewd terms stand alongside the most hackneyed euphemisms), it is nonetheless surprisingly powerful for a first novel. A self-taught writer, Pirinçci not only flaunts his cultural breadth (which he attributes to his hero, a cinephile and, like Werther, a passionate reader) but also demonstrates his ability to compete with his models on the technical level, using a language that is authentically German in its cultural resonances and its idioms[122] while being attuned to a world in flux (Americanisms, references to a globalized culture).

In his own way, Pirinçci's writing is therefore also performative. His story actually accomplishes exactly what he describes his hero-narrator doing, namely rallying behind a "Germanness" that only has room for a voice of cosmopolitanism firmly anchored in the national cultural landscape. The most obvious marker of the totalitarian character (in all senses of the term) of this vision is the recurrence of the allusions made by the hero-narrator to the Nazi past and, more specifically, the extermination of the Jews. These evocations are few in number but strategically placed, all the more incongruous – and therefore chilling – because

---

120 This provides the paradoxical form of mise-en-abyme Dällenbach described as "aporetic duplication": "a sequence that is supposed to be enclosed within the work also encloses it" (Dällenbach 1977: 51). This structure conforms less to the model of *Werther* and more to that of Proust's *À la recherche du temps perdu*.
121 "Im Grunde fühle ich mich gar nicht als Türke, aber auch nicht als Deutscher. Ich schwanke nicht einmal so in der Mitte. Wahrscheinlich bin ich gar nichts" (T 9).
122 To cite just one example: "Man wollte mich einfach sterben sehen, das war klar wie Kloßbrühe!" (T 239).

they emerge without any contextual reference to this chapter of history, thus coming across as entirely gratuitous. For example, the first lines of the first chapter describe the nightclub where Akif and Christa meet that evening as being "überfüllt wie Dachau" ("crowded like Dachau," T 5), and there is nothing that allows the reader to understand, either at this time or later, what may have motivated the use of such a truly obscene image – nothing apart from Pirinçci's need from the beginning to establish, beyond all shadow of a doubt, how acculturated his hero is to the German context. To so effortlessly adopt the provocative formulas a certain fringe of young people favored during this period in reaction to a process of *Vergangenheitsbewältigung* ("coping with the past") they perceived as being oppressive and doctrinaire, it was indeed necessary to have internalized the Germans' way of thinking to its darkest recesses.

Even when they occur in a more poignant and darker context, as when Akif slides into an aggressive and self-destructive asociality that Christa can only respond to with powerless anger, the concentration camp metaphors used to describe the reproach the narrator sees in his girlfriend's eyes ("Auschwitz-like gaze," "my merciless Nazi gauleiter"[123]) do not suggest that their relationship has failed due to ethnic polarization. Purely circumstantial, they neither manifest nor signal any deterioration of Akif's feelings for his "kind, gentle, beautiful Christa," but at most denote a self-depreciation proportional to his increasing discouragement and his sentimental resignation. Similarly, Akif feels able use the term *Endlösung* ("final solution") to refer to the last step he takes with Christa before resolving to commit suicide.[124] All these references to National Socialism do not create a political subtext. Deployed merely as abuses of language, they come across as so disproportionate that it is impossible to read into them anything apart from an extreme form of exaggeration characteristic of the youthful parlance that in Plenzdorf would manifest itself with the inflationary use of the word "sorrows." Applied to the semantic field of extermination, this rhetorical inflation – which mechanically induces a devaluation of meaning – trivializes the crimes of the memory it invokes.

---

123 "Daraufhin erschien Christa mit einer Cognacflasche an der Tür und warf mir einen auschwitzähnlichen Blick zu. (Christa, meine unbarmherzige Gauleiterin!)" (T 164–165).
124 "Da ging mir ein Licht auf! Urplötzlich sah ich die 'Endlösung': Also ich war ganz schön kaputt, hatte den tiefsten Punkt meines Lebens erreicht; schlimmer konnte es nur noch kommen, wenn ich auf einmal eine Schwangerschaftspsychose gekriegt hätte oder so. Christa hatte mich aufgegeben – fast aufgegeben! [...] Kurzum, ich war sozusagen fast tot. Der einzige Mensch, der mich wieder zum Leben erwecken konnte, der mir neuen Lebensmut zu spenden vermochte, dieser Mensch war einzig und allein meine liebe, süße, schöne Christa" (T 188).

According to Fachinger's benevolent reading, the hero's use of these expressions is "apparently innocent" and thus indicates Pirinçci's desire to demonstrate "how language can be abused and to what extent the German past is still haunting its language" (2001: 11). This hypothesis appears to be unfounded. In this regard, Cheesman's interpretation is far more convincing, insofar as it refutes the premise that Pirinçci's aims are emancipatory and critical:

> Pirinçci's Akif is deliberately not positioning himself in ethnic terms as a minority, or marginal, or different. Nor is he allying himself with Jews as a victim of German racism. Instead, he speaks as a rebellious, postnational, postethnic German of his generation. [...] Both Akif and the author are surely fully conscious of the origins, and of the effect. They are not mimicking, in postcolonial fashion, but straightforwardly using German slang expressions to linguistically assert unquestionable membership in a bohemian, antiestablishment, cosmopolitan subculture within the nations. (2007: 87)

All in all, though Pirinçci wanted his first draft to appear spontaneous, he seems to have calculated its effects so as to ensure that the work, provided it was successful, received direct recognition on the national literary scene without finding a place in the "foreign literature" box. Goethe's worldwide bestseller, transposed successfully by Plenzdorf into a contemporary context several years prior, provided him with the ideal framework for his project. The enthusiastic reception of *Die neuen Leiden des jungen W.* proved that the concept was still a fertile one, even if the spirit of the times and his personal inclinations dictated other references – precisely those he attributes to his hero, such as Bukowski and Ginsberg.[125] In addition, *Werther* harbors resources that Plenzdorf did not mine, such as the pre-Romantic exaltation of sensitivity. He taps into this underexploited vein by injecting a dose of *Sturm und Drang* into the neo-Romantic American writing from the counter-culture: love is total and tyrannical, sorrow is (almost) deadly, and melancholy is eloquent – and tears (as the title announces) flow freely.

Why did Pirinçci not achieve his goal? The reason is that while the novel that was to grant him access to the literary field through the front door, rather than one of the "rear courtyards" (Tantow 1984) foreign authors were only just being granted access to, certainly brought him both commercial[126] and critical[127] suc-

---

[125] The homage to Ginsberg appears to be already expressed in the title, as suggested by the narrator's claim that "Tränen sind immer das Ende" is a quote from the tutelary figure of the Beat Generation ("mußte plötzlich an diesen einen Satz von Ginsberg denken: Tränen sind immer das Ende" [T 228]).

[126] According to Pokatsky (1982), the book had reached a circulation of 24,000 copies in only two years.

cess, it did not, in the long term, propel him to the heights he had had in mind. Republished several times between 1980 and 1997, today it can only be procured on the second-hand book market. There are several possible explanations for this, starting with the immaturity of the story and its unfinished nature: though it attests to an undeniable talent, *Tränen sind immer das Ende* remains mired in certain platitudes. The narrative investment is disproportionate to the thinness of the plot, which often makes the reading tedious. Moreover, the hero-narrator's emotional credibility is weighed down by cheap eroticism, constantly wavering between trashy obscenity and cloying metaphor with sexist overtones. Ultimately, Pirinçci fails to construct a fictional orality leading to the emergence of a coherent and complex "voice."

However, another possibility is that the author made his move too early and that the moment was not ripe. Had Pirinçci written a novel that was equal in quality to Plenzdorf's, would he have received the same welcome as the East German writer? Setting aside the fact that this was the début novel of a twenty-one year-old, how conceivable is it that, in the context of the time, the literary world would have gauged his book by the same yardstick as any other German-speaking author? The literature of foreign-born authors did not enjoy any recognition and it was not even niche literature (the Chamisso Prize was not created until five years later), but an almost confidential production confined to a socio-documentary approach to the real. The fact that this text, under these circumstances, opened the doors of publishing houses to the young author and attracted numerous readers and the esteem of avant-garde critiques is remarkable in and of itself.

In any event, even though it remains isolated among its author's literary works and, most importantly, had no direct descendants in the works of literature written by foreign-born authors, *Tränen sind immer das Ende* was undeniably a work that served as a predecessor to others. It was only 1980 when Pirinçci broke from the themes of first-phase immigration literature (exploitation, exclusion, quest for identity, etc.) and its narrative codes (social testimony, confession) and gave German literature, as Cheesman argues, its first "post-ethnic" work: a text which, while featuring immigrant characters, effectively avoids any assigned socio-ethnic, confessional, or cultural identities by placing these characters in a simultaneously narrower (national) and broader (transnational) mental universe that transcends the confrontation between Germans and immigrants. Twenty

---

127 Particularly noteworthy is an ecstatic review published in *Sounds* magazine that placed Pirinçci's novel at the same level as both Goethe's *Werther* and Christiane F.'s *We Children from Zoo Station* (Berger 1981: 59). There were plans to adapt the book into a film, but the project was not completed.

years later, when Zaimoglu in turn set out to adapt the *New Sorrows* formula to young Turkish-Germans, he in part adopted the same approaches as his predecessor, but re-semanticized them in relation to a trans- or supranational frame of references that extended to the Arab-Islamic and more specifically Turkish culture. He thus appears to have built on Pirinçci's experience, partly to do better than him (by going in the same direction but without repeating his mistakes), partly to provide a sort of corrective to his pioneering work.

In contrast to Plenzdorf, the author of *Liebesmale, scharlachrot* actually adopts a position very similar to Pirinçci's by returning to a revindication of emotions modeled on the pre-Romantic tradition. Challenging the "modern" affective restraint and stylistic laconism that Plenzdorf had, deviating from the Goethean model, propagated in creating the character of Wibeau, he endows his characters with an unapologetic inclination to dissect feelings, analyze suffering, and lay bare the wounded heart. This restoration of the passions, running contrary to a mainstream perception viewed as normative, goes hand in hand with a redefinition of rebellious masculinity that does not exclude sentimentalism but instead takes pride in it. Nevertheless, Zaimoglu deviates dramatically from the path Pirinçci paved by providing this posture with an ethnocultural dimension the latter had worked to free it from. Far from presenting the return to interiority as an individual, singular, and solitary endeavor, he recontextualizes it by incorporating his characters into an ethnically hybrid perspective. Serdar and Hakan expressly define themselves and each other from their ethnic and social positioning within a community that is sometimes considered national (Germany as well as, more marginally, Turkey), sometimes local (the city, the "ghetto," the heterotopic holiday resort), sometimes transnational (the Turkish community, deterritorialized or not), and this plainly inexhaustible subject provides them with abundant material for commentary, witticisms, and teasing. This playful sparring on issues of cultural "identity" operates according to the dialectical principle of *antiperistasis*, the rhetorical trope forming the very basis of what psychologists and sociologists have referred to as the "appropriation of the stigma" (Goffman 1963). When Serdar wonders if he is "the cold cigarette butt or the prince of the Orient" or designates his friend as a "pitiful suburban wog" ("elender Vorstadtkanake"), or when Hakan defines himself as a "Kümmeltürke" and in turn calls him "Assimil-Ali," these are ways of subverting the racially or ethnically-tinged stigmas they are subjected to by society.

This bantering implicitly highlights the multiple facets of xenophobia that persist in society at the turn of the twenty-first century, from outright hostility to more insidious forms of exoticization of the other (xenophilia, idealization). For the characters (as well as, indirectly, the author), these verbal jousts are a way of refusing the subjugation implied by the rhetoric of otherness used by the dominant group for the dominated. By coming to terms with himself as "someone one can say this or that about [...], who is the object of looks and of discourse and who is stigmatized by these looks and this discourse" (Éribon 1999: 30), the speaker-writer signals that he is aware of the asymmetry established by reifying discourse, on the one hand, and demonstrates that it does not have power over him, on the other, because he has gone from being an object to becoming a subject by the very effect of the speech act. By taking over the heterodefinition that aims to pin him down, he reappropriates the power that is denied him and recovers part of his agency. This operation, already featured in Zaimoglu's previous books and repeated here in multiple forms, is closely linked in the novel to the references to Werther, and more broadly to *Sturm und Drang*. Just like Goethe's character, the protagonists of *Liebesmale, scharlachrot* are at war with the normative values of "reasonable people," but their solitary battle against the philistines – unlike that of Pirinçci's autobiographical narrator – is deeply rooted in their ethnocultural condition.

Compared with Pirinçci's "post-ethnic" rewriting of *Werther*, Zaimoglu's resemantization is anything but incidental. By relating the rebellious posture of his characters, their emancipatory rhetoric, and their love of pathos to their dominated position, Zaimoglu makes diametrically opposed use of something that Pirinçci, due to the logic of his own aesthetic and personal project, could not give full measure to: the idea of applying Werther's profile in its complete psychopathological dimension – not just the politico-cultural aspect – to young men from immigrant backgrounds. Indeed, Zaimoglu gives entirely new meaning to the gulf thus created compared to Plenzdorf's interpretation of the same archetype. The same "neo-Wertherian" traits that the author of *Tränen sind immer das Ende* had endowed his alter ego with are no longer attributed to the "temperament" of individuals evolving like free electrons in a sterile social place (i.e., to their radical subjectivity). But they are also not simply related, in an ethnographic fashion, to a shared "mentality" that could be credibly designated as "Turkish" or "Eastern." This essentialist reading is certainly offered and even underscored again and again in Zaimoglu's novel, but it becomes inadmissible by the very fact of its overexposure, and even more, by the argumentative context in which the characters use it. By themselves advancing culturalist interpretations of their idiosyncrasies, the protagonists pull the rug out from under any attempt to reduce them to this interpretative framework. For example, when Serdar, to justify his romantic disenchantment with Anke, invokes an incapacity for the commitment that would result from an excess of emotional investment on his part, and does not hesitate to blame these shortcomings on a cultural deformity, the obvious bad faith of the argument makes it impossible for the reader to agree with it:

> Here, with your permission, I would like to vent about the problem with the "Anatolian visual defect," which consists primarily in primping and preening any worthwhile circumstance. There can be no simple, easy love under these conditions. It gets majestized, it gets put in a cage of superlatives like an exotic animal you can't even pet. Even if the man is stupid as a shoe and the woman as dumb as gravy, when the two find each other, the invocation of super-sized feelings begins. The man excels in it especially, and so he wants to pick out whatever notes from simple words or nothing at all. I didn't understand you because we were broadcasting on different frequencies and I was just looking at your head instead of taking the occasional look at your feet.[128]

Used to support or parry expectations from the outside, this seemingly ethnographic defense is no sooner advanced than it is called into question, if not completely destroyed, by its strategic use in an apologetic context. Cultural permeation is therefore neither renounced, as in Pirinçci, nor provided to the reader as a plausible explanation for behavior and values. Upheld as a banner by the interested parties themselves, culturalist discourse is held at a remove, in the same way as rude xenophobic remarks, by its distortion in service to a culture of riposte.

However, Zaimoglu's treatment of ethnicity does not limit itself to this multilayered ironic game. Although the characters themselves and the textual device that undermines the credibility of their discourse heartily mocks culturalist logic in its essentialist and deterministic dimension, the importance of the ethnic factor in the construction of identity is nevertheless highlighted on another level: that of the appropriation – conscious and active – of the cultural heritage specific to a community. As previously observed, the ethnic mix of the two protagonists correlates with their ability to easily evolve mentally in a transnational frame of references expanded beyond the Germany / United States axis posed by Pirinçci. The syncretic imagination that their exchanges trace does not flatly deny depreciated origins (because they are "primitive" and therefore in reality a-cultural), but encompasses the literary and spiritual heritage of the Arab-Muslim

---

128 "Wenn du mir an dieser Stelle erlaubst, will ich mich über den 'anatolischen Sehfehler' auslassen, der nämlich vor allem darin besteht, dass man würdige Gegebenheiten aufrüscht und aufplüscht. Eine einfache bloße Liebe kann es dabei nicht geben, sie wird verhoheitlicht, sie wird in einen Käfig der Superlative gesteckt wie ein exotisches Tierchen, das man nicht mal streicheln darf. Auch wenn der Mann dumm wie Schuh ist und die Frau dämlich wie Soße, wenn die beiden zueinander finden, setzt die Anrufung der Übergrößen ein. Vor allem der Mann tut sich darin hervor, und also will er aus einfachen Worten irgendwelche Winde heraushören oder gar nichts. Ich habe dich nicht verstanden, weil wir beide auf unterschiedlichen Frequenzen gesendet haben und ich nur deinen Kopf ansah, anstatt auch mal deine Füße zu besehen" (LS 219–220).

world. Werther's desperate love is a natural neighbor to the *aşk* of Persian poets, just as the story of Romeo and Juliet overlaps with that of Majnun and Layla, the Pietist tradition with Sufi mysticism, and the Christian exaltation of suffering with traditional Islam's rituals of penance, as well as the cathartic experiences of Arabesk music concerts.

The reference to *Werther*, and more broadly to the German literary tradition as a whole, falls within this expanded framework. Unlike Pirinçci, Zaimoglu does not pit Western culture – understood as the only one worthy of the name – against what would be the non-culture of rural Turkey, coarse and backward. On the contrary, he proclaims the rise of a post-migration generation that, rich in its double culture, has absorbed national references to the point of wielding them with just as much – if not greater – dexterity than "authentic" Germans, even without breaking from its culture of origin's heritage. Moreover, he portrays characters whose relationship to native German traditions is all the freer (and more creative) because they are burdened neither by a violent break with their origins nor by a legacy of distrusting emotion like their contemporaries in mainstream society, marked by the silences and taboos of the German post-war generation. Hence, they can carry the torch of *Sturm und Drang* with greater credibility and legitimacy than Pirinçci's impeccably acculturated immigrant, who claims the distant legacy of Werther while also striving to align his mode of thought and expression with the majority. Unlike Akif, Hakan and Serdar did not internalize the fetishes or the taboos weighing on the "ethnic" Germans of their generation. When they reengage with the aesthetic and spiritual impulses of German pre- Romanticism, they do so by combining with perfect nonchalance elements of *Sturm und Drang* and *Empfindsamkeit* (such as impetuosity, proclivity for introspection, the roiling of violent passions, stylistic expressiveness) with eclectic references to a globalized culture (Sufism, rap, haikus, Arabesk). These letters constantly foreground the advantage they derive from their in-between position, where a feeling of superiority over mainstream society partially compensates for a civilizational malaise. Additionally, their non-conformist posture is less gratuitous and more caustic than in Pirinçci, whose only target was a largely fantasmatic establishment confusedly characterized as "hippie" and "leftist" – even if the narrator occasionally has an ironic distance regarding his own condemnation of intellectuals.

The real question is whether Zaimoglu, by renouncing the cultural denial that his predecessor's experimentation included, opposes Pirinçci's post-ethnic approach or if he only gives an updated version that is less homogenizing, more playful, and thus more acceptable in a context of ethnic diversification and openness to a globalized culture no longer merely Western. Certainly, Pirinçci's cultural patriotism, fashioned in the Federal Republic of Germany during the

Cold War, had become obsolete in a Germany which was "reuniting" at the very moment when the nation as a reference value is undergoing mounting depreciation. However, the ethical and aesthetic project outlined by Zaimoglu's novel cannot be assimilated to any particularist claim. The evolution of his writing since 2000, with an increasing concentration on universal themes instead of socio-ethnic concerns and a confirmed interest in the canonical origins of the national culture (which he ticks through book after book, from late Romanticism to the inaugural Lutheran moment via predominantly regional proletarian neo-Romanticism) makes it obvious that his approach also proceeds from a form of universalism centered around a mythical Germany. Zaimoglu undoubtedly has more than one point in common with Pirinçci, from the passionate attachment to the great German literary tradition and the refusal to allow himself to be ranked among the representatives of a minority literature, to an attraction for the transgressive posture of one who breaks taboos and holds "political correctness" in contempt. The fact remains that, if this epitextual data is not taken into account, the novel itself makes it impossible to draw any definitive conclusions, and this is its true strength. A pivotal work, it gives shape *simultaneously* to an unprecedented form of inscribing ethnicity within national culture – which amounts to profoundly redefining these cultural contours according to the model of the "touching tales" that established, according to Leslie Adelson, the Turkish turn in German literature – and to an improved and updated version of the cosmopolitan "Germanness" imagined by Pirinçci.

However, Zaimoglu's reorientation of the totalizing (even in some respects totalitarian) approach of his predecessor with his reconfiguration of the West-East axis is not attributable solely to modernization. By asserting the legitimacy of the children of the "ghetto" to claim ownership of German "classics" in the face of a mass culture drawn from American subculture, Zaimoglu adopts a very particular positioning within the literary field. From a socially marginal position, he builds an aesthetic project that, through its intertextual references as well as the sophistication of his writing, presents itself as "central." Situating himself simultaneously on the "outside" and "inside," Zaimoglu distinguishes himself from a very popular contemporary literary current that one might be tempted to associate him with, one that Pirinçci entered into seamlessly: pop literature.

By Way of Conclusion: *Sturm und Drang* Revisited, or Zaimoglu Versus *Popliteratur*

Zaimoglu, by supplying his double reference to *Sturm und Drang* and to the politicized literature of the GDR with two incontestable literary guarantors, confirms his participation in a generic context that in the twentieth century took the form of "pop" literature: that of the generational narrative. Birthed in the United States during the 1940s–1950s from the pens of key players of the Beat Generation like Kerouac, Burroughs, and Ginsberg, pop literature advocates full-fledged anti-conformism, which is expressed through the celebration of a lifestyle free of constraints, frequently characterized by risky behavior and excessive consumption of psychotropic drugs, and an aesthetic eclecticism encompassing techniques of collage, montage, and generic and formal hybridization, with a central place given to music (jazz, rock, pop) in particular. Though he could not be classified as a member of this movement, J. D. Salinger provided it with what would become one of its flagship works: *Catcher in the Rye* (1951).

In the 1960s, the pop current was established in the German-speaking world by young writers who challenged the moral authority and political austerity of the previous generation: Rolf Dieter Brinkmann in West Germany against the Group 47, Peter Handke in Austria, and Ulrich Plenzdorf in the GDR. In the 1980s, a second generation took over with authors from the underground punk scene (Rainer Götz, Max Goldt, Wiglaf Droste) before the collapse of the Soviet bloc and German reunification gave new life to this trend with the commercial and media success of far less subversive novels. The authors of this third generation, who began to write in the 1990s – Christian Kracht, Thomas Brussig, Benjamin Lebert, Benjamin von Stuckrad-Barre, etc. – returned to the codes of the counter-cultural movements from the United States but distinguished themselves from their predecessors through a jaded hedonism without the ethical or socio-political pretension bordering on snobbery (Strasser 2011).

It is with them that Zaimoglu was in direct competition both on the book market and on the media stage, with his texts likewise celebrating a lifestyle and mode of expression portrayed as representative of contemporary youth, and his media presence no less savvy. However, he feels no sense of commonality with these postmodern dandies, characterized by their calculated insolence and oversized egos, whom critics have tended to associate him with since *Kanak Sprak*. Anxious to differentiate himself from Kracht, Stuckrad-Barre, and others, he readily denounces the political and literary immaturity of their bestsellers, which in his eyes amount to nothing but cheap "Schulbubenreporte" ("schoolboy reports").[129] He contrasts the transgressiveness of his own books, at the intersection of social documentary, political manifesto, satirical provocation, and inspired lyricism with the "Knabenwindelprosa" ("boy diaper prose")[130] that he characterizes as "reaktionäres Kunsthandwerk" ("reactionary art and crafts") (Zaimoglu 1999).

In this context, the double reference to Goethe and Plenzdorf is a way for him to mark his difference and to lay claim to a more prestigious lineage. Placing his new novel under the sign of *Werther* serves as a reminder that the modern coming-of-age narrative has a distant German predecessor and that it is possible to draw from this source in order to revivify the genre, to restore its nerve and substance. Moreover, by invoking Plenzdorf's precedent, he challenges the *Popliteratur* authors, also great admirers of Salinger, on their own turf: the lucid challenger of the East German writer does not overlook that what had "cult" status in the GDR for disrupting the dominant ideology was no longer subversive in the reunified Germany of Chancellor Helmut Kohl. He therefore abandons Americanisms (clothing, music, and language), new technologies, and above all Salinger, Plenzdorf's second major intertext, to return to the epistolary novel and an old school eloquence, with a lyricism steeped in the young Goethe's Pietism piercing through the *Kanak*-style loquacity.

Zaimoglu no doubt draws in this respect as well on lessons from the experiment Pirinçci conducted with his rewriting of *Werther*. One of the reasons that this first attempt to draw a parallel between the literature of "the other Germany" (GDR) and that of the "Others" of the FRG (and simultaneously to attempt, in his capacity as a representative of the latter, to enter the national canon by playing the "Werther" card) did not find the response that the initial idea certainly deserved is perhaps his epigonic treatment of American models. Emerging from the same matrix as Pirinçci's novel (Goethe / Plenzdorf), *Liebesmale, scharlachrot* stands out in another fundamental point beyond the question of ethnicity: while Pirinçci plodded in the footsteps of the American generational novel without finding much to contribute and thus condemning himself to remain in the shadow of his direct model, Zaimoglu manages to blur the lines (of East and West, self and other, old and new, true and false, masculine and feminine) by undermining the reader's position through parody, hyperbole, sampling, code switching, and strategic exoticization. In this, he reveals himself as a much more subtle emulator of Plenzdorf, whom he even succeeds in surpassing in certain

---

129 Quoted in Minnaard (2008: 277), footnote 31.
130 It is worth noting that the invented compound word "Knabenwindelprosa" contains yet another nod to the master of *Sturm und Drang*, for it echoes the famous neologism "Knabenblütenträume" of Goethe's ballad *Prometheus*.

respects, notably when he draws directly from elements of their shared hypotext that Pirinçci had preferred to leave out, such as the combination of a rebellious posture and sociocultural marginality. By making this theme a major axis of his novel, Zaimoglu makes his text representative in a way that Pirinçci's is not. It is precisely at the point where he deviates from the trail blazed by the latter, choosing not to retrace the individual trajectory of a solitary figure in order instead to embark on an epistolary novel and thus escape the categories of pop fiction, that his work acquires historical relevance. This was doubtless his intention, if the reader believes his alleged description of the book as "The New Sorrows of Young Ali." Where Pirinçci only claimed to relate "the sorrows of young Akif," an underdog and aspiring writer disconnected from his roots and the social collective, Zaimoglu does not merely relate "the sorrows of young Feridun," or even "of young Serdar" or "Hakan," but appropriates a framework intended to raise him to the level of his models, Goethe and Plenzdorf.

By situating his *Neue Leiden* under the star of Salinger, Plenzdorf had drawn a line leading from the *Sturm und Drang* to the young literature of the GDR by way of contemporary US pop culture. Paradoxically, Zaimoglu appears in keeping with this line when he abandons the cult of Salinger and the counter-cultural codes to his epigones so as to give better credence to his own line of descent (in spirit, not in style) from the angry young men of America – the writers who were able to renew the genre by daring to radically reshape language and motifs. Going back to the source proved to foster innovation, while artifice served as a sign of authenticity. In the face of a literature of exhaustion, or what another *enfant terrible* of the German cultural scene called "Schlappschwanzliteratur" ("limp-dick literature") (Biller 2000: 49), Zaimoglu mischievously offers a novel about impotence that simultaneously serves as a manifesto of empowerment, an appeal for a renewed relationship to tradition, and a strategic advance into the center of the national literary field.

If this attempt seems rather successful on the literary level, it must be said that it, too, enjoyed only moderate success – far less, in any case, than *Kanak Sprak* before it. No more than Pirinçci, Zaimoglu managed to force his way through the doors of the closed circle of internationally-renowned German authors with his Wertheriad. It was only subsequently that he was to obtain his most prestigious literary awards, and for other works: the Grimmelshausen Prize in 2007 for *Leyla*, a novel located in Turkey retracing the path of a Turkish woman who ended up emigrating to Germany, the Jakob-Wassermann Prize in 2010 for his "commitment to the excluded" and his role as "mediator in the Turkish-German dialogue," and the Berlin Literary Prize in 2016 for all of his works and in particular for his "mastery of the entire repertoire of German literature."

Conclusion

The purpose of this study has been to investigate the texts of the corpus in terms of the relationship they establish with the international (i.e., Western) as well as the specifically German literary canon. Analyzing the strategies by which authors of migration literature locate their literary project within a shared cultural memory has helped to identify the main features of a canon-related discourse that covers a relatively broad spectrum, ranging from appropriation to repudiation, mimicry to resistance, and grafting to rejection. This inquiry has built on the numerous postcolonial studies of the past thirty years, primarily focused on Anglophone and Francophone corpora, and the textual "counter-attacks" aimed at deconstructing the typologies and dichotomies of colonial discourses that constitute the "canon," or the body of works that are authoritative at the level of individual nations and former empires and often, as a consequence, also on a global scale. I conjectured that German minority literature, this subfield of contemporary German literature that academic criticism still struggles to grasp beyond the opposition between identity and otherness, might contain something analogous to the renegotiation of the relationship to the colonizer's culture identified by writers in post-colonial regions.

With the hypothesis that in contemporary migration literature there exist forms of counter-writing comparable to the "writing back" among postcolonial authors, it was expected that there would be both parallels and differences with what has been identified in Francophone and Anglophone postcolonial literature. I anticipated the discourse of German-speaking writers about the canon would probably reveal itself to be on the whole more "approving" than deconstructive, dissenting, or critical. On the one hand, this is due to the very nature of the discourse conveyed by the works considered canonical in Germany, as this discourse was not built on the expansionist and missionary model of French or British cultural imperialism, but focused on a notion of a "cultural nation" determined by ethnic and linguistic homogeneity. For this reason, it was conceivable that it would probably not provoke reactions of protest or disavowal as vehement as a more direct and more intrusive discourse of domination would. On the other hand, Germany's colonial empire was younger than those of other European powers and it was dismantled as early as 1918 for the benefit of those latter powers, and as such its history is less entangled today with the memory of previously colonized peoples to the same degree as is the case with these other empires, which implanted their cultural systems profoundly and durably in the regions they conquered – regions that remain partly in their spheres of economic and political influence to this day, after the processes of decolonization. Thus, there is currently not, at least not to a significant degree, any German-language "postcolonial literature" in the sense that one can speak of one or more postcolonial literature(s) in the French, English, Portuguese, Spanish, Italian, or even Dutch language. Finally, although German society eventually became, despite its best efforts, a "country of immigration," the vast majority of non-natives who have settled since 1945 are not former subjects of the German Empire.[1]

For all of these reasons, the conclusion could be drawn that the relationship of these ethnocultural minorities toward the dominant culture of their host country would be fraught with less tension and resentment than that of a population previously subjected to the colonial yoke toward the same nation that once placed the yoke upon it. Between the German immigrant minorities and the mainstream society, there is certainly not the same history of both overt and concealed violence, nor the paternalistic domination and subjugation that exists, for example, between the Maghrebian and African minorities and the mainstream society in France, or between British Indian and Pakistani minorities and British mainstream society – and therefore not the same equivocal legacy of dependence, fascination, imitation, and envy. To date, a relationship comparable to the colonial dialectic has existed in Germany only between the dominant population and the Jews, who were acculturated and assimilated before being brutally rejected and exterminated.

If all of these factors should prompt us to think that German immigrants and their descendants would not enter into a relationship of the dominated / dominant type with Germany and its distinctive "culture," there are other factors, however, that would suggest that the particular configuration of the German social space could nevertheless give rise to adversarial positions towards the dominant culture on the part of immigrant populations. On the one hand, German colonialism did in fact exist, and it was by no means less aggressive than others, quite the contrary (one need only think of the Herero and Nama genocide in Namibia). It would be foolish to think that this colonial violence did not leave significant traces in the mindsets of those who perpetrated it. The memory of colonialism has only been repressed in Germany, covered by the more recent and even more violent trauma of Nazism. However, since the first decade of the twenty-first century, the survival of that past has started to become perceptible in the collective memory, with traces detected in mindsets and its resurgence noticed in political discourse from the 1960s, when the figure of the foreigner reappeared in

---

[1] Waves of immigration from Eastern European countries like Poland, Russia, Rumania, former Yugoslavia, etc. have not been included in this study because they are rooted within different historical configurations.

the public space, specifically in the form of the immigrant (*Gastarbeiter*, "Turk," "migrant," and more recently "Muslim" and "refugee").[2]

The other aspect of the question resides in the fact that today there is no de facto or legal equality – indeed, far from it – between a native majority that perceives itself as being quintessentially monocultural, static, and primordial, and the minorities who have been settling in German territory since the mid-1950s. While the oppressions and humiliations inflicted on the first wave of immigrant workers[3] were partly overshadowed by the patent social success of some of their descendants, the memory of this first generation is still alive – if not in the majority society, at least among those from the second generation.[4] This is evidenced by the perpetual and heated debate about the "integration" of foreigners in Germany, as well as by the very violent backlash against them from the political and even the intellectual world.[5]

It is also important to recall that, although most of the non-natives living in Germany today are not former subjects of the German Empire, many of them nonetheless come from formerly colonized countries, and that it is precisely these, along with their descendants, who are the most stigmatized because they are perceived as "culturally" different (the term culture being very often used in the same sense as race was previously). Even the population of Turkish origin, the largest ethnocultural minority in Germany, despite never having undergone colonial domination, nevertheless inherits a situation of dependence on the West, and especially Germany. This dates back to the nineteenth century, when the Ottoman Empire saw its power decline, making Turkey "the sick man of Europe."

---

[2] See for example: Ha (1999/2004); Ha, Lauré as-Samarai, and Mysorekar (2007); Dhawan (2007); Steyerl and Gutiérrez Rodríguez (2012).

[3] Regarding this matter, it is worth recalling Wallraff's famous enquiry *Ganz unten* ("At the Bottom," 1985; Engl. trans. *Lowest of the Low*).

[4] By way of illustration, see Mehmet Daimagüler's critical testimony *Kein schönes Land in dieser Zeit: Das Märchen von der gescheiterten Integration* ("No Fair Land at this Time: the Fairy Tale of Failed Integration", 2011). Daimagüler, a Berlin attorney-at-law, was among the first people of Turkish origin (before Cem Özdemir of the Green Party) to access the governing body of a political party; in his case, it was the Free Democratic Party (FDP), which he eventually left in 2007. The book gives a blunt account of the discrimination that second-generation immigrants suffered in Germany and denounces the hypocrisy of public discourse on this matter. The testimonial evidence provided is all the more significant for stemming from a man who cannot be labelled as leftist but fully embraces the liberal ethos of capitalist ideology.

[5] It is worth again recalling Thilo Sarrazin, whose anti-immigration bestseller (2010) greatly contributed to the rehabilitation of racist ideas within mainstream political and media discourse, thus paving the way for a full range of polemists who have been promoting the same nationalistic and xenophobic ideas with varying degrees of skill and efficiency.

Even if in reality things are not as bad as suggested by alarmist discourse both on the left and right (the nationality code was modified in 2005, and the intermixing of populations has ended up taking hold: social advancement, access to education, to cultural and political fields, to the liberal professions), media and political rhetoric remains largely closed to these changes. The call to "integration" is thus most often formulated only as a unilateral injunction by the majority society towards the "foreigner," who is told to adapt to local mores (subsumed under the term "Leitkultur") and in no way as a commitment by the nation to open up and to facilitate reciprocal rapprochement (see Ha 2007 and Terkessidis 2010: 39 – 76). Thus it is undeniable that in Germany, where there is a majority that views itself as culturally homogeneous and holding indisputable cultural authority and minorities that must still fight to obtain their legitimacy or have it recognized, the structure is, if not postcolonial or even neocolonial, at least highly hegemonic. The institutional recognition enjoyed today by authors who have "made it" such as Schami, Özdamar, Zaimoglu, Kermani, Şenocak, and Tawada should not make us forget that the field of cultural popularization is regularly dominated by some such as Peter Sloterdijk, Rüdiger Safranski, and Thea Dorn. The latter, a prominent playwright, literary critic, and television host, for example, explained in an interview for her latest book, *Deutsch, nicht dumpf. Ein Leitfaden für aufgeklärte Patrioten* ("German, Not Dumb. A Guide for Enlightened Patriots"),[6] – that she takes it for granted that it is "more appropriate to stage Goethe's *Faust* than a refugee performance."[7]

There would therefore be compelling reasons to believe that the work on the literary canon performed by the authors in my corpus would not be free of ambivalence. The analyses in this book of the texts by Schami, Özdamar, and Zaimoglu have indeed revealed a double dynamic. On its positive side, the discourse on the canon is constructed according to a logic of appropriation that is based on adhesion to shared values and and recalls the processes of derivation (of reception, transmission, and adaptation) identified as cultural transfers (Espagne and Werner 1988). The authors, in making references to selected canonical works they blend with their own texts according to different hypertextual procedures,

---

[6] *Deutsch, nicht dumpf. Ein Leitfaden für aufgeklärte Patrioten* (2018) has been described by its author (whose real name is Christiane Scherer and who drew inspiration for her pen name from the philosopher Theodor Adorno) as a balanced plea, "neither left nor right," for a "new," healthy cultural patriotism capable of counteracting the racist, antisemitic, and anti-feminist rhetoric of the extreme right. In reality, the book defends a narrowly patriarchal and hegemonic vision of the German "Leitkultur."

[7] "Ich halte es beispielsweise für richtiger, wenn im Theater Goethes *Faust* als wenn eine Flüchtlingsperformance gegeben wird" (Dorn, Radisch, and Soboczynski 2018).

integrate these objects into their system of references and thus assume a position both ethical and strategic vis-à-vis the context of production as well as the context of reception. In the configuration of migration literature, this operation always amounts in one way or another to the "denaturalization" or "de-ethnicization" of texts fetishized by the canonizing bodies, so as to emphasize the aspects that do not fit with the ideology of the *Kulturnation*. To this end, authors like Chamisso, Heine, Lasker-Schüler, and even Goethe (for his openness to the dialogue of cultures, his appreciation of the Orient, and his ideal of *Weltliteratur*) are reread in the "minor" mode and recontextualized in a contemporary, decentered space. As such, they serve as precious aids in questioning the dichotomies erected by literary historiography between identity and otherness, East and West, center and periphery. Refuting the myth of cultural homogeneity intrinsic to national ideology, those canonical writers resist being exploited for nationalist ends by institutions and can be called upon by the authors of migration literature seeking to support their own ethos and promoting the idea that they, too, are by no means "eccentric" (in every sense of the term) in the national intellectual landscape.

In addition to its legitimizing function for the receiving authors, such appropriation has a hermeneutical value. By making canonical authors appear retrospectively as having cleared terrain that, while still not yet (fully) appreciated, can still lay claim to an "equal dignity" (Espagne 1999: 20) as the original terrain, and by drawing them into their own system of reference, non-native authors impose a change in outlook on these fetishized writers and their works. Thus, for example, behind the singular figure of poet Else Lasker-Schüler takes shape the image of an "Oriental" woman that is not simply a fake, since her extravagant and transgressive play of personae paved the way for German writers who, like Özdamar, really come from the East. Instead, she emerges as a pioneer of playful self-Orientalization whose travesties – both masks and emblems of her very real social marginality – opened up a vast field of potential for the creation of a literature that could legitimately claim to be both "German" (in the sense of the cultural nation) and "hybrid" (in the postcolonial sense). Such recontextualization is no less fruitful when applied to Goethe, as when Schami outlines the contours, behind the hieratic figure of the privy counselor at the court of Weimar, author of *Faust* and *Wilhelm Meister*, of a Goethe who was "Oriental" (rather than Orientalist), or at least sufficiently close enough in his thinking and his work to the original culture (pre-colonial) of the Middle East to be able to rightly claim admission, at the end of a very selective examination, to the transnational canon created by an imaginary Arab jury free of any Western influence.

Even more disruptive to the Olympian aura of the representative *par excellence* of the German nation is the image of Goethe serving as a forerunner to the multiracial cross-culture that invaded the public sphere in the 1990s, borne by young people subjected to discrimination who claimed their rightful place by upsetting the codes of artistic and cultural expression. It is precisely this argument that Zaimoglu upholds with the epistolary novel *Liebesmale, scharlachrot* by drawing a parallel between the young creators of the *Kanak* generation (rejection of rules and conventions, exaltation of subjectivity and affects, invention of a new poetic language and a new form of masculinity) and the literary movement that Goethe's *Werther* provided the founding text for: *Sturm und Drang*. The originator of the first current in literary history brought about by an insolent and iconoclastic youth, Goethe thus paved the way two centuries ahead of time for the exuberant talents of the *Kanak* movement such as Zaimoglu and Fatih Akın (*Gegen die Wand*, "Against the Wall," 2004; English trans. *Head On*).[8] The assertion that there is a direct line of descent from *Sturm und Drang* to the *Kanak* cultural revolution has an obvious political dimension, and as such constitutes a provocation for the sites of cultural legitimization. To say that the children of immigrants can claim the legacy of German pre-Romanticism is to say that the group of students who gathered around Goethe and Herder in Strasbourg in the 1770s and the hotheads of the *Kanak Attak* movement do not differ in nature and are possibly even at the same level, sharing a spiritual affinity that transcends ethnocultural boundaries. And, even more daring still: that such spiritual kinship, based on similar social and political aspirations motivated by comparable historical conditions, is the preserve of this justifiably rebellious youth in the contemporary social space. In claiming this filiation for himself and others like him "on the margins of society," Zaimoglu indeed simultaneously denies it to contemporary representatives of the "dominant" line. At the very least, by engaging in a kind of intertextual competition with Plenzdorf, whose rewriting of *Werther* became a cult work of GDR literature in the 1970s and 1980s (anointed by the institutions overseeing canonization in both of the German States), he suggests that his own reading of the *Sturm und Drang* is as legitimate as the East German writer's. He also suggests that this rich heritage was abandoned by contemporary mainstream writers who were more concerned with mimicking American subcultural codes than delineating a territory of expression of their own.

While a strong tendency towards "positive" appropriation of the canon has been observed in the discourse of minority writers, this dynamic of appropriation

---

[8] In his highly enthusiastic review of *Gegen die Wand* (*Head-On*), Zaimoglu confirmed his theory of a structural affinity between German pre-Romanticism and the countercultural movement initiated by second-generation immigrants in Germany, especially those of "oriental" (i.e. Turkish) origin (Zaimoglu 2004b).

has turned out always to *also* have a counter-discursive dimension. The receiving authors lay claim to a tradition so as to better challenge another or others and/or to invalidate the academic discourse focused on this tradition (in principle, a discourse of sacralization), on the one hand, and on their own restricted field of production (in principle, a discourse of more or less condescending benevolence), on the other. Whether presenting Werther as the archetype of today's *Kanak*s or reframing Hamlet – the Shakespearean hero who has, from Freiligrath onwards, served as the embodiment of the German national character[9] – as the prototype of the bourgeois Turkish intellectual (as Özdamar suggests), what is at stake for the authors is the unpacking of the national mythology constructed by literary historiography in order to delimit a territory for themselves where their expression reaches full legitimacy. The shift they effect is itself subversive in character, even when, as with Schami (at least in his mature writings), it assumes a reverent and polished appearance.

In addition to this structure of appropriation, the texts also reveal, though to a lesser extent, an oppositional structure similar to that which founded the "writing back" paradigm in the postcolonial context, as a "counter-attack" of the subjugated and marginalized populations writing against a hegemonic power. This dynamic of head-on counter-writing, which functions by redistributing roles and reversing perspectives, is exercised mainly against texts and authors having served – or serving still – to support the claim of the "cultural nation" in order to endorse, disqualify, or even altogether eliminate all those who can be perceived as a threat to the integrity of the national collective. The main target of this protest discourse was the folkloric corpus inherited from Romanticism, consisting mainly of the collection of the Grimms' folk tales and the repertoire of *Volkslieder* established by Brentano and Arnim in *Des Knaben Wunderhorn* ("The Youth's Magic Horn"). Helping to cement the mythical base of German cultural identity, countless poets, playwrights, and composers have drawn from this cultural resource, which continues to this day to convey a Romantic exaltation of the concept (originally polysemic) of "Volk" as the founding organic unit of the nation. Developed in the context of the wars of liberation against Napoleon and the struggle for the unification of the German states, this corpus was instrumentalized so aggressively, notably under Nazism, that it provided the authors of migration literature a textbook case for the renegotiation of their relationship to the German nation as it defines itself through its favorite texts. The Grimms' tales lend themselves particularly well to this critical reflection insofar as they present

---

[9] Freiligrath famously began his polemical poem *Hamlet* (1844) with this simple equation: "Deutschland ist Hamlet!" ("Germany is Hamlet!").

the fairly rare case of a work that has always been situated (this was even one of the main objectives of the utopian project from which it originated)[10] at the intersection of several a priori distant, if not incompatible, fields of production: "elite culture" and "mass culture," adult and children's literature, scholarly and commercial literature, "authentic" popular literature and poetic re-creation. This categorical hybridization makes them choice objects for parodic distortion, both because they represent the entire social spectrum (the whole of Germany "is" a Grimms' tale, as Heine had already speculated and Özdamar would subsequently observe), and because the parody requires that the target audience have a good knowledge of the source texts. Thus we find, both in Schami's early work and in several texts by Özdamar, satirical hypertextual transformations of this corpus that aim to expose a highly deadly and reactionary ideological subtext – nationalist, phallocratic, and xenophobic – behind the benign appearances that have often been ascribed to this folklore.

The controversial rereading of this cultural heritage resulting from political Romanticism follows, in Schami as in Özdamar, an approach that joins a critique of nationalism to that of capitalism and colonialism. Works like Schami's *Die Wahrheit über Vampire und Knoblauch* ("The Truth about Vampires and Garlic") and Özdamar's *Keloglan in Alamania* thus shape an intertextual space in which the national paradigm is placed in the broader context of the exploitation of capital, of the colonial conquest, and the West's construction of a reified and stereotyped East. The spectrum of works received in this regard extends, in the texts we have studied, from operas by Mozart (*Die Zauberflöte*), Smetana (*Prodaná nevěsta*) and Puccini (*Madama Butterfly*) to the fantastic literature that has developed from Bram Stoker onwards about the character of Dracula. This anti-nationalist and postcolonial approach challenges the popular belief that Germany has in some ways been spared a colonial ideology in its normative and cultural dimension.[11] From the perspective of the texts under discussion in this study, German nationalism specifically appears, on the contrary, to be closely intertwined with Orientalism in *all* its forms.

The main target of the counter-discourse produced by the authors of this corpus is the nationalist ideology sedimented in the canon (mainly Romantic and post-Romantic), understood as a predatory and totalitarian structure of thought

---

10 See Weinmann (2010).
11 It is worth recalling that Edward Said himself more or less exempted Germany from the responsibility of having participated in developing the domineering, normative discourse he called Orientalism, on the grounds that "at no time in German scholarship during the first two thirds of the nineteenth century could a close partnership have developed between Orientalists and a protracted, sustained *national* interest in the Orient" (1979: 19).

connected to the structure of colonial domination. Particularly with Özdamar, this creative counter-writing fits into the context of the resurgence of a nationalist rhetoric popular at the turn of the 1990s during the process of German political reunification. However, the dynamic of rejection it expresses is itself firmly tied to a dynamic of adherence. In *Keloglan in Alamania*, the dismantling of the patriotic popular canon is placed under the explicit auspices of a few authors who not only never allowed themselves to be won over by nationalist thought but whose entire work can be considered as a form of resistance to this ideology: Shakespeare, Heine, and Brecht. These authors, claimed as models and beacons, are invoked for support in the author's struggle against both cultural and political nationalism. Schami, in his texts from the 1980s, may attack the "Grimm Bros." at the ideological and political level, but he rehabilitates them from a philosophical and aesthetic point of view in his mature work, linking their pioneering efforts to promote a popular and oral culture to the preservation and revitalization – in his eyes all the more crucial in the post-colonial and post-industrial context – of the cultural heritages of all peoples, at the local as well as the global level. In this sense, he sees himself to a certain degree as continuing the philologists' work, in keeping with a critical analysis of the culture for which he aligns himself with (at least) one other German author: Walter Benjamin.

Hence it appears that the two sides of our authors' discourse about the canon are complementary and closely connected. Grafting and rejection, adherence and repudiation are interdependent. Authors lay claim to one part of the national heritage because they are challenging another, and it is only because they adhere to one tradition that they can afford to oppose another or the dominant social discourse about any issue at all. In Germany, authors of foreign origins need all the more to rely on the words of canonized authors insofar as they do not overtly represent – at least not to the same extent as the "postcolonials" or, in another way, the Black Americans descended from the slave trade – a population long subjugated, denied, and alienated by the "center" on which they depend today. Whatever their primary motives for settling on German soil (economic insecurity, political persecution, independent choice for professional or personal reasons) and whatever their grievances with the country which, after having received them, may have subjected them or their loved ones to humiliations and discriminations of all kinds, they do not allow themselves to directly challenge the hegemonic "center" in constructing a point of view of frontal opposition to its emblematic creators, and would not even have reasons to do so.

It is thus arguable that their approach to the canon is defined rather – as the case is for many authors writing in postcolonial configurations as well, but perhaps more so – as a "writing in" or "writing with" approach than "writing back." In any event, even and especially when it comes to prosecuting the case of the mainstream society or the ruling class, they place themselves under the protection of canonized authors. Thus Özdamar, in a manner of speaking, put all of her work under the auspices of Brecht. In some cases, the authors of the national canon are even directly cited as witnesses for the prosecution in the inquiry, as we have seen for certain metafictional texts constructed on the model of the "dialogue with the dead". Heine can thus be invited to comment post-mortem on current events (German reunification, the revival of a "national sentiment," discrimination against minorities), hence taking responsibility for an accusatory speech that the author (Schami) does not want or cannot formulate with the same causticity in his own name.

Although Goethe or Chamisso may also be the subject of occasionally virulent interrogations about political positions deemed inappropriate (counter-revolutionary and/or nationalist), as observed in Schami and SAID, they are at least partially redeemed by other positions that demonstrate an ambitious vision not only exceptional for their time, but also in comparison with the mediocrity of the contemporary mainstream. It is by noting the arrogance and the intellectual poverty of current opinion makers, who are the media icons of the nation's cultural apparatus, that Schami suddenly discovers sympathies for Goethe; at least this is how he justifies his polemical intervention on the subject, supporting his interference in the public debate by claiming the humility of an exile who has recognized in "Mister Goethe," belatedly and "despite everything," an ally in his resistance to the hegemony of mediocrity embodied by "Mister Tröte" ("Mister Average Citizen") (1999a).

Of course, this analysis should be extended to other texts. The field of works that lend themselves to it is vast. For the three authors of my main corpus alone, it would be necessary to examine from this angle Zaimoglu's entire body of fictional works as well as his theatrical adaptations, Özdamar's rewriting of the *Odyssey* in the play *Perikızı. Ein Traumspiel*, and Schami's novels. However, the analysis conducted on a more restricted corpus already makes it possible to state that, under the conditions of production for migration literature, the discourse on the canon, irrespective of its dominant tone, always has an eminently political dimension. On the one hand, such discourse implies a strategy of legitimizing authors in view of the marginal position they occupy in the literary field as producers of minority literature. On the other hand, their subjective approach to the canon is part of a social and cultural context in which any positioning on their part on this issue assumes an ideological dimension (whether as provocation or allegiance) in terms of the German nation's projections of identity as well as in terms of public discourse on Islam, integration, and the East / West relationship. At both the strategic and ideological levels, nothing they say about the literary canon is free of political implications.

Bibliography

[Anonymous] (2000) "Feridun Zaimoglu: *Liebesmale, scharlachrot,*" *INTRO* [online], 25 October, <https://www.intro.de/popmusik/feridun-zaimoglu-1> (accessed 23 April 2020).
[Anonymous] (2015) "Berliner Literaturpreis für Feridun Zaimoglu," Rowohlt Theater Verlag [online]: <http://www.rowohlt-theaterverlag.de/artikel/Berliner_Literaturpreis_fuer_Feridun_Zaimoglu.3301022.html> (accessed 23 April 2020).
[Anonymous] (2016) "Hamburger Händler verkauft kein Schweinefleisch – nun nimmt Edeka ihm die Körbe weg," *Focus*, 30 April.
Abel, Julia (2006) "Konstruktionen 'authentischer Stimmen.' Zum Verhältnis von 'Stimme' und Identität in Feridun Zaimoglus 'Kanak Sprak,'" in *Stimme(n) im Text. Narratologische Positionsbestimmungen*, ed. Andreas Blödorn, Daniela Langer, and Michael Steffel (Berlin and Boston: De Gruyter), 297–320.
Abel, Julia (2011) "'Ansichten vom Nicht-Bürgerlichen.' Modelle von Autorschaft und Schreiben bei Feridun Zaimoglu," in *Feridun Zaimoglu in Schrift und Bild*, ed. Rüdiger Schütt (Kiel: Edition Fliehkraft), 47–56.
Ackermann, Irmgard and Harald Weinrich (eds) (1986) *Eine nicht nur deutsche Literatur: Zur Standortbestimmung der 'Ausländerliteratur'* (Munich: Piper).
Ackermann, Irmgard (2009) "Der Chamisso-Preis und der Literaturkanon," in *Von der nationalen zur internationalen Literatur: Transkulturelle deutschsprachige Literatur und Kultur im Zeitalter globaler Migration*, ed. Helmut Schmitz (Amsterdam: Rodopi), 47–52.
Adelson, Leslie A. (2005) *The Turkish Turn in Contemporary German Literature. Toward a New Critical Grammar of Migration* (New York: Palgrave Macmillan).
Adelson, Leslie A. (2006) "Against Between – Ein Manifest gegen das Dazwischen," in *Literatur und Migration*, ed. Heinz-Ludwig Arnold (Munich: text + kritik), 36–46.
Adorno, Theodor W. (1998) *Prismen. Kulturkritik und Gesellschaft* [1951], in *Kulturkritik und Gesellschaft I. Gesammelte Schriften*, vol. 10.1, ed. Rolf Tiedemann (Darmstadt: Wissenschaftliche Buchgesellschaft), 11–30. English edition: *Prisms*, trans. Samuel and Shierry Weber (Cambridge: MIT Press), 1997.
Aifan, Uta (2003) *Araberbilder. Zum Werk deutsch-arabischer Grenzgängerautoren der Gegenwart* (Aachen: Shaker).
Al-Dabbagh, Abdulla (2010) *Literary Orientalism, Postcolonialism, and Universalism* (New York etc.: Peter Lang).
Algeriani, Adel Abdul-Aziz, and Mawloud Mohadi (2017) "The House of Wisdom (Bayt al-Hikmah) and Its Civilizational Impact on Islamic libraries: A Historical Perspective," *Mediterranean Journal of Social Sciences* 8, 5 (September), 179–187.
Alsarras, Nader (2010) *Die Orientbilder im Werk Rafik Schamis. Eine literaturwissenschaftliche Untersuchung am Beispiel seines Romans* Die Dunkle Seite der Liebe," PhD Diss., Ruprecht-Karls-Universität Heidelberg. Online at: <http://archiv.ub.uni-heidelberg.de/volltextserver/11662/1/Dissertation_final.pdf> (accessed 21 April 2020).
Améry, Jean (2002) *Jenseits von Schuld und Sühne* [1966], in *Werke*, ed. Irene Heidelberger-Leonhard, Vol. II (Stuttgart: Klett-Cotta).
Ames, Eric (ed.) (2005) *Germany's Colonial Pasts* (Lincoln, Neb., and London: University of Nebraska Press).
Amodeo, Immacolata (1996) *'Die Heimat heißt Babylon.' Zur Literatur ausländischer Autoren in der Bundesrepublik Deutschland* (Opladen: Westdeutscher Verlag).

Amodeo, Immacolata (2009) "Betroffenheit und Rhizom: Literatur und Literaturwissenschaft," *Migrationsliteratur. Eine neue deutsche Literatur?* (Berlin: Heinrich Böll Stiftung), 6–8.
Amossy, Ruth (ed.) (1999) *Images de soi dans le discours: La construction de l'ethos* (Lausanne and Paris: Delachaux Niestlé).
Amossy, Ruth (2010) *La Présentation de soi: Ethos et identité verbale* (Paris: PUF).
Anderson, Benedict (1991) *Imagined Communities. Reflections on the Origin and Spread of Nationalism* [1983], revised edition (London and New York: Verso).
Andries, Lise (2013) "Querelles et dialogues des morts au XVIIIe siècle," *Littératures classiques*, 81, 2, 131–146.
Apitzsch, Ursula (ed.) (1999) *Migration und Traditionsbildung* (Opladen: Westdeutscher Verlag).
Appadurai, Arjun (1996) *Modernity at Large: Cultural Dimensions of Globalization* (London and Minneapolis: University of Minnesota Press).
Arens, Hiltrud (2000a) *'Kulturelle Hybridität' in der deutschen Minoritätenliteratur der achtziger Jahre* (Tübingen: Stauffenburg).
Arens, Hiltrud (2000b) "Rafik Schami: Eine phantastische Erzählkunst für eine andere Gesellschaft," in *'Kulturelle Hybridität' in der deutschen Minoritätenliteratur der achtziger Jahre*, ed. Hitrud Arend (Tübingen: Stauffenburg), 87–246.
Arnds, Peter (2005) "Orientalizing Germany in Rafik Schami's *Die Sehnsucht der Schwalbe* and *Sieben Doppelgänger*," *Seminar – A Journal of Germanic Studies* 41, 3, 275–288.
Arnold, Heinz Ludwig (ed.) (2002) *Literarische Kanonbildung, Text + Kritik* Sonderband IX (Munich: text + kritik).
Arnold, Heinz-Ludwig (ed.) (2006) *Literatur und Migration, Text + Kritik* Sonderband IX (Munich: text + kritik).
Arnold, Heinz-Ludwig (ed.) (2016) *Emine Sevgi Özdamar, Text + Kritik* 211 (Munich: text + kritik).
Aron, Paul (2013) "Le pastiche et la parodie, instruments de mesure des échanges littéraires internationaux," in *Littératures francophones: Parodies, pastiches, réécritures*, ed. Lise Gauvin, Cécile Van den Avenne, Véronique Corinus, and Ching Selao (Lyon: ENS Éditions), 23–42.
Ashcroft, Bill, Gareth Griffiths, and Helen Tiffin (eds) (1989) *The Empire Writes Back: Theory and Practice in Post-Colonial Literatures* (London: Routledge).
Ashcroft, Bill, Gareth Griffiths, and Helen Tiffin (eds) (2001) *Post-Colonial Studies: The Key Concepts* (London: Routledge).
Assmann, Aleida (1998) "Kanonforschung als Provokation der Literaturwissenschaft," in *Kanon Macht Kultur: theoretische, historische und soziale Aspekte ästhetischer Kanonbildung*, ed. Renate von Heydebrand (Stuttgart: Metzler), 47–59.
Assmann, Aleida and Jan Assmann (eds) (1987) *Kanon und Zensur: Beiträge zur Archäologie der literarischen Kommunikation*, II (Munich: Fink).
Assmann, Jan (2006) "Die Zauberflöte – Märchen oder Mysterium?," in *Mozart. Experiment Aufklärung im Wien des ausgehenden 18. Jahrhunderts*, ed. Herbert Lachmeyer (Ostfildern: Hatje Cantz), 761–769.
Assoun, Paul-Laurent (2006) *Le Fétichisme* (Paris: Presses Universitaires de France, coll. "Que sais-je?").

Ateş, Seyran (2004) "Religionsfreiheit nicht auf Kosten von Frauen und Mädchen – Durchsetzung der Grundrechte auf Gleichberechtigung und Selbstbestimmung," *Streit – feministische Rechtszeitschrift* 22, 99–103.

Ateş, Seyran (2009) *Der Islam braucht eine sexuelle Revolution. Eine Streitschrift* (Berlin: Ullstein).

Augstein, Rudolf et al. (1987) *"Historikerstreit." Die Dokumentation der Kontroverse um die Einzigartigkeit der nationalsozialistischen Judenvernichtung* (Munich and Zurich: Piper).

Auer, Michaela and Ulrich Müller (eds) (2001) *Kanon und Text in interkulturellen Perspektiven: "andere Texte anders lesen"* (Stuttgart: Heinz).

Babka, Anna (2006) "'In-side-out' the Canon. Zur Verortung und Perspektivierung von postkolonialen Theorien & Gendertheorien in der germanistischen Literaturwissenschaft," in *A Canon of Our Own: Kanonkritik und Kanonbildung in den Gender Studies*, ed. Marlen Bidwell-Steiner and Karin Wozonig (Innsbruck: StudienVerlag), 117–132.

Bach, Bernard (ed.) (2012) *La Littérature interculturelle de langue allemande: Un vent nouveau venu de l'Est et du Sud-Est de l'Europe, Germanica* 51.

Bachmann-Medick, Doris (2001) "Is There a Literary History of World Literature?," in *Literary History / Cultural History: Force-Fields and Tensions* (= REAL: Yearbook of Research in English and American Literature, vol. 17), ed. Herbert Grabes (Tübingen: Narr), 359–372.

Bachmann-Medick, Doris (ed.) (2004) *Kultur als Text: Die anthropologische Wende in der Literaturwissenschaft* [1996], 2. aktualisierte Aufl. mit neuer "Bilanz" (Tübingen and Basel: Francke).

Bachmann-Medick, Doris (2006) *Cultural Turns: Neuorientierungen in den Kulturwissenschaften* (Reinbek bei Hamburg: Rowohlt).

Bachmann-Medick, Doris (2007) "Literary Texts between Cultures. An Excursion into Postcolonial Mappings," in *World Literature: Contemporary Postcolonial and Post-Imperial Literatures*, ed. Nilufer E. Bharucha (New Delhi: Prestige Books), 40–51.

Bacqué, Marie-Hélène (2006) "Empowerment et politiques urbaines aux États-Unis," *Géographie, économie, société* 1, 8, 107–124.

Bahners, Patrick (2007) "Kritiker der Islamkritikerinnen," *Frankfurter Allgemeine Zeitung*, 26 April.

Baillet, Florence (2004) *L'Utopie en jeu: Critique de l'utopie dans le théâtre allemand contemporain* (Paris: CNRS éditions).

Baneth-Nouailhetas, Emilienne (2009) "Énigmes postcoloniales: des disciplines aux institutions," *Littérature* 154, 2, 24–35.

Bänsch, Dieter (1971) *Else Lasker-Schüler: Zur Kritik eines etablierten Bildes* (Stuttgart: Metzler).

Bardolph, Jacqueline (2002) *Études postcoloniales et littérature* (Paris: Champion).

Barthes, Roland (2007) *Le Discours amoureux: séminaire à l'École pratique des hautes études, 1974–1976; suivi de Fragments d'un discours amoureux: pages inédites* (Paris: Seuil).

Bartmann, Christoph (2000) "In Liebesdingen ging der Platzhirsch nicht auf Sendung: Der Meister aller hybriden Formate: Feridun Zaimoglu wildert," *Frankfurter Allgemeine Zeitung*, 12 December.

Baur, Nina and Jens Luedtke (eds) (2008) *Die soziale Konstruktion von Männlichkeit. Hegemoniale und marginalisierte Männlichkeiten in Deutschland* (Leverkusen: Budrich).

Bavar, Amir Mansour (2004) *Aspekte der deutschsprachigen Migrationsliteratur. Die Darstellung der Einheimischen bei Alev Tekinay und Rafik Schami* (Munich: Iudicium).
Beck, Laura (2011) *Kolonialgeschichte(n) neu schreiben: Postkoloniales Rewriting in Christof Hamanns 'Usambara'* (Marburg: Tetum).
Bein, Alexander (1965) "Der jüdische Parasit: Bemerkungen zur Semantik der Judenfrage," *Vierteljahrshefte für Zeitgeschichte*, 18, 2, 121–149.
Bein, Alex (1980) *Die Judenfrage. Biographie eines Weltproblems*, 2 Bde (Stuttgart: Deutsche Verlagsanstalt).
Bengi, Derya (2009) "Abécédaire musical, ou comment feuilleter les meilleures pages du grand album sonore d'Istanbul," *La Pensée de midi*, 29, 3, 102–114.
Benjamin, Walter (1972–1989) *Gesammelte Schriften*, ed. Rolf Tiedemann and Hermann Schweppenhäuser (Frankfurt/M.: Suhrkamp).
Berger, Inge (1981) [Review of Pirinçci's *Tränen sind immer das Ende*], *Sounds* 51, 59.
Berman, Nina (1997) *Orientalismus, Kolonialismus und Moderne: Zum Bild des Orients in der deutschsprachigen Kultur um 1900* (Stuttgart etc.: M & P Verl. für Wiss. und Forschung).
Bhabha, Homi K. (1994) *The Location of Culture* (London and New York: Routledge).
Bharucha, Nilufer E. (ed.) (2007) *World Literature: Contemporary Postcolonial and Post-Imperial Literatures* (New Delhi: Prestige Books).
Bhatti, Anil (1998) "Aspekte der Grenzziehung: Postkolonial," in *Kulturelle Grenzziehungen im Spiegel der Literaturen, Nationalismus, Regionalismus und Fundamentalismus*, ed. Horst Turk, Philipp Löser u. a. (Göttingen, Wallstein), 339–356.
Bhatti, Anil (2004) "Im Kielwasser des Kolonialismus: Ambivalenzen im deutschen Orientalismus des 19. Jahrhunderts," in *Das verschlafene 19. Jahrhundert. Die deutsche Literatur zwischen Klassik und Moderne*, ed. Hans-Jörg Knobloch (Tübingen: Niemeyer), 175–189.
Bhatti, Anil (2007) "'…zwischen zwei Welten schwebend…' Zu Goethes Fremdheitsexperiment im West-östlichen Divan," in *Goethe. Neue Ansichten-Neue Einsichten*, ed. Hans-Jörg Knobloch and Helmut Koopmann (Würzburg: Königshausen & Neumann), 103–122.
Bhatti, Anil (2009) "Der Orient als Experimentierfeld. Goethes *Divan* und der Aneignungsprozess kolonialen Wissens," *Goethe-Jahrbuch* 126, 115–128.
Bidwell-Steiner, Marlen and Karin Wozonig (eds) (2006) *A Canon of Our Own: Kanonkritik und Kanonbildung in den Gender Studies* (Innsbruck: StudienVerlag).
Biller, Maxim (2000) "Feige das Land, schlapp die Literatur. Über die Schwierigkeiten beim Sagen der Wahrheit," *Die Zeit*, 13 April, 47–49
Biller, Maxim (2014) "Letzte Ausfahrt Uckermark," *Die Zeit*, 2 February.
Bird, Stephanie (2003) *Women Writers and National Identity: Bachmann, Duden, Özdamar* (New York: Cambridge University Press).
Bloom, Harold (1994) *The Western Canon: The Books and School of The Ages* (New York: Harcourt Brace).
Blum-Barth, Natalia (2013) *"Chamisso-Literatur." Einige Anmerkungen zu ihrer Definition, Provenienz und Erforschung, literaturkritik.de* [online]; <http://www.literaturkritik.de/public/rezension.php?rez_id=18242> (accessed 20 April 2020).
Blumentrath, Hendrik, Julia Bodenburg, Roger Hillman, and Martina Wagner-Egelhaaf (eds) (2007), *Transkulturalität: Türkisch-deutsche Konstellationen in Literatur und Film* (Münster: Aschendorff).

Bodenburg, Julia (2006) "Kanaken und andere Schauspieler: Performative Identitäten bei Feridun Zaimoğlu und Yadé Kara," *Germanica* 38, 129–140.
Bogdal, Klaus-Michael (ed.) (2007), *Orientdiskurse in der deutschen Literatur* (Bielefeld: Aisthesis).
Bollack, Jean (2001) *Poésie contre poésie. Celan et la littérature* (Paris: PUF).
Bonn, Charles (ed.) (1995) *Littératures des immigrations*, 2 volumes (Paris: L'Harmattan).
Boran, Erol M. (2004) *Eine Geschichte des deutsch-türkischen Theaters und Kabaretts*, PhD Diss. (Ohio State University: *OhioLINK Electronic Theses and Dissertations Center*).
Boratav, Pertev Naili and Wolfram Eberhard (1953) *Typen türkischer Volksmärchen*, (Wiesbaden: Steiner).
Borsò, Vittoria (2003) "Europäische Literaturen versus Weltliteratur – Zur Zukunft von Nationalliteratur," *Jahrbuch der Heinrich-Heine-Universität Düsseldorf 2003*, 233–250.
Boschetti, Anna (ed.) (2010) *L'Espace culturel transnational* (Paris: Nouveau Monde).
Bourdieu, Pierre (1998) *Les Règles de l'art: Genèse et structure du champ littéraire* [1992], nouvelle édition revue et corrigée (Paris: Seuil).
Brecht, Bertolt (1999) *Das Verhör des Lukullus. Hörspiel* [1940] (Frankfurt/M.: Edition Suhrkamp).
Brecht, Bertolt (2001–2003) *Brecht-Handbuch in fünf Bänden*, ed. Jan Knopf (Stuttgart and Weimar: Metzler).
Breitfeld, Arndt (2006) "Plagiatsvorwurf gegen Zaimoglu: Zwei Romane mit derselben Matrix?," *Der Spiegel*, 8 June.
Brenner, Peter J. (1982) *Plenzdorfs. "Neue Leiden des jungen W."* (Frankfurt/M.: Suhrkamp Taschenbuch Materialien).
Brentano, Clemens and Achim von Arnim (1987) *Des Knaben Wunderhorn* [1805] (Stuttgart: Reclam).
Briegleb, Klaus (1997a) *Bei den Wassern Babels: Heinrich Heine, jüdischer Schriftsteller in der Moderne* (Munich: DTV).
Briegleb, Klaus (1997b) "Ingeborg Bachmann, Paul Celan. Ihr (Nicht-) Ort in der Gruppe 47," in *Ingeborg Bachmann und Paul Celan. Poetische Korrespondenzen*, ed. Bernhard Böschenstein and Sigrid Weigel (Frankfurt/M.: Suhrkamp), 29–82.
Briegleb, Klaus (2003) *Missachtung und Tabu. Eine Streitschrift zur Frage: "Wie antisemitisch war die Gruppe 47?,"* (Berlin: Philo).
Broch, Hermann (1955) *Gesammelte Werke 6: Dichten und Erkennen*, ed. Hannah Ahrendt (Zurich: Rhein-Verlag).
Büchner, Georg (2002) *Dichtungen, Schriften, Briefe und Dokumente*, 2 Teilbände, ed. Henri Poschmann unter Mitarbeit von Rosemarie Poschmann (Frankfurt/M.: Suhrkamp [Insel]).
Büchner, Georg (2012) *Woyzeck* [1837], Studienausgabe (Stuttgart: Reclam).
Buchner, Wilhelm (1882) *Ferdinand Freiligrath: Ein Dichterleben in Briefen* (Lahr: Schauenburg).
Bürger, Gottfried August (1778), *Lenore* [1773], in *Gedichte* (Göttingen: Dieterich), 81–96.
Butler, Judith (1997) *Excitable Speech: A Politics of the Performative* (New York and London: Routledge).
Cahen, Michel (2011) "À propos d'un débat contemporain: du postcolonial et du post-colonial," *Revue historique* 660, 4, 899–913.
Calero Valera, Ana R. (2015) "Glokalisierungsprozesse auf der Bühne: Emine Sevgi Özdamars *Karagöz*, *Keloglan* und *Perikızı*," *Lendemains* 160, 54–63.

Canetti, Elias (1994) *Das Augenspiel. Lebensgeschichte 1931–1937* [1985], *Gesammelte Werke*, Vol. 9 (Munich: Hanser).
Casanova, Pascale (2008) *La République mondiale des lettres* (Paris: Seuil).
Castein, Hanne (ed.) (1988) *Es wird einmal. Märchen für morgen. Moderne Märchen aus der DDR*, (Frankfurt/M.: Suhrkamp).
Castein, Hanne and Alexander Stillmark (eds) (1986) "Arbeiten mit der Romantik heute: Zur Romantikrezeption der DDR, unter besonderer Berücksichtigung des Märchens," in *Deutsche Romantik und das 20. Jahrhundert. Londoner Symposium 1985* (= Stuttgarter Arbeiten zur Germanistik 177), 5–23.
Cattani, Francesco and Amanda Nadalini (eds) (2006) *The Representation and Transformation of Literary Landscapes* (Venezia: Cafoscarina).
Cazanave, Claire (2007) *Le Dialogue à l'âge classique* (Paris: Champion).
Celan, Paul (1999) *Der Meridian – Endfassung, Entwürfe, Materialien, Werke. Tübinger Ausgabe*, ed. Bernhard Böschenstein and Heino Schmull (Frankfurt/M.: Suhrkamp).
Celan, Paul (2004) *Mohn und Gedächtnis – Vorstufen, Textexegese, Endfassung, Werke. Tübinger Ausgabe*, ed. Jürgen Wertheimer (Frankfurt/M.: Suhrkamp).
Chakrabarty, Dipesh (2007) *Provincializing Europe: Postcolonial Thought and Historical Difference*, new edition (Princeton, NJ: Princeton University Press).
Chamisso, Adelbert von (1975) *Sämtliche Werke in zwei Bänden*, nach dem Text der Ausgaben letzter Hand und den Handschriften, Textredaktion Jost Perfahl, Bibliographie und Anmerkungen Volker Hoffmann (Munich: Winkler).
Cheesman, Tom (2007) *Novels of Turkish German Settlement: Cosmopolite Fictions* (Rochester, NY: Camden House).
Cheesman, Tom (2013) "Incriminating texts. With reflections on the justiciability of Esra and Leyla," in *German Text Crimes. Writers Accused, from the 1950s to the 2000s*, ed. Tom Cheesman (Amsterdam and New York: Rodopi), 1–22.
Cheesman, Tom and Deniz Göktürk (1999) "Türkische Namen, deutsche Texte: Ein Literaturüberblick Ende 1999," aus dem Englischen von Alexander Schlutz, *parapluie*, 6, Summer 1999, <http://parapluie.de/archiv/generation/texte/> (accessed 18 August 2018).
Cheesman, Tom and Karin E. Yeşilada (eds) (2012) *Feridun Zaimoglu* (Oxford, Bern, Berlin: Peter Lang).
Chevalier, Karine (2008) *La Mémoire et l'Absent. Nabil Farès et Juan Rulfo, de la trace au palimpseste* (Paris: L'Harmattan).
Chiellino, Carmine (2007) *Interkulturelle Literatur in Deutschland: Ein Handbuch* (Stuttgart: Metzler).
Connell, Raewyn (1995) *Masculinities* (Sidney: Allen & Unwin).
Corbin, Alain, Jean-Jacques Courtine, and Georges Vigarello (eds) (2011) *Histoire de la virilité*, 3 vol. (Paris: Seuil).
Corngold, Stanley (2004) "Kafka and the Dialect of Minor Literature," in *Debating World Literature*, ed. Christopher Prendergast (London: Verso), 272–290.
Daimagüler, Mehmet (2011) *Kein schönes Land in dieser Zeit: Das Märchen von der gescheiterten Integration* (Gütersloh: Gütersloher Verlagshaus).
Dällenbach, Lucien (1977) *Le Récit spéculaire: Essai sur la mise en abyme* (Paris: Seuil).
Daoud, Kamel (2016) "Cologne, lieu de fantasmes," *Le Monde*, 31 January.

Dayıoğlu-Yücel, Yasemin (2005) *Von der Gastarbeit zur Identitätsarbeit: Integritätsverhandlungen in türkisch-deutschen Texten von Şenocak, Özdamar, Ağaoğlu und der Online-Community vaybee!* (Göttingen: Universitätsverlag Göttingen).
Dayıoğlu-Yücel, Yasemin (2012) "Authorship and Authenticity in Migrant Writing: The Plagiarism Debate on *Leyla*," in *Feridun Zaimoglu*, ed. Tom Cheesman et Karin E. Yeşilada (Oxford, Bern, Berlin: Peter Lang), 183–199.
Deeken, Annette (1995) "Der listige Hakawati: Über den orientalischen Märchenerzähler Rafik Schami," *Deutschunterricht*, 48. Jg., 7–8, 363–370.
Deleuze, Gilles and Félix Guattari (1972) *L'Anti-Œdipe* (Paris: Minuit).
Deleuze, Gilles and Félix Guattari (1975) *Kafka. Pour une littérature mineure* (Paris: Minuit).
Deleuze, Gilles and Félix Guattari (1980) *Mille plateaux. Capitalisme et schizophrénie* (Paris, Minuit).
Detue, Frédérik (2012) "À l'heure fatale de l'art – La critique du kitsch au XXe siècle," *Texto! Textes & Cultures*, XVII, 1–2, <http://www.revue-texto.net/docannexe/file/2992/detue_kitsch.pdf> (accessed 21 April 2020).
Deutsche Armeemärsche, vol. II: Parademärsche für Fußtruppen (1970) (Berlin: Bote & Bock).
Deutscher Liederhort (1893–1894), ed. Ludwig Erk and Franz-Magnus Böhme, 3 Bde (Leipzig: Breitkopf und Härtel).
Dhawan, Nikita (2007) "Can the Subaltern Speak German? And Other Risky Questions. Migrant Hybridism versus Subalternity," *Translate*, 25 April [electronic version]: <http://translate.eipcp.net/strands/03/dhawan-strands01en> (accessed 11 June 2018).
Diallo, Moustapha and Dirk Göttsche (eds) (2003) *Interkulturelle Texturen. Afrika und Deutschland im Reflexionsmedium der Literatur* (Bielefeld: Aisthesis).
Diner, Dan (1986) "Über Rafik Schami," in *Chamissos Enkel: Zur Literatur von Ausländern in Deutschland*, ed. Heinz Friedrich (Munich: DTV), 63–67.
Dionne, Graig and Parmita Kapadia (eds) (2008) *Native Shakespeares: Indigenous Appropriations on a Global Stage* (Aldershot: Ashgate).
Do Paço, David, (2010) "La 'Phantasie' orientaliste dans les opéras allemands de Mozart. Un regard sur la 'théorie du jeu et du fantasme' de Gregory Bateson," *Hypothèses* 13, 1, 267–275. Online at: <https://doi.org/10.3917/hyp.091.0267> (accessed 3 June 2020).
Döbler, Katharina (2001) "Kunst oder Liebe, Dunst oder Triebe: Feridun Zaimoglu schickt seinen Jüngling an den Strand. Dort wird er ein Mann," *Die Zeit*, 10 May.
Doğan, Şerife (1995) "Komparatistischer Blick auf die alten ausgewählten Keloğlanmärchen und die neuen deutschen Versionen 'Keloğlan in der Bundesrepublik,'" *Studien zur deutschen Sprache und Literatur / Alman Dili ve Edebiyatı Dergisi* 10, 35–66.
Dorn, Thea [aka Christiane Scherer] (2018) *Deutsch, nicht dumpf. Ein Leitfaden für aufgeklärte Patrioten* (Munich: Knaus).
Dorn, Thea, Iris Radisch, and Adam Soboczynski (2018) "Lieber 'Faust' als Flüchtlingsperformance: Ein Gespräch mit der Autorin Thea Dorn über die Notwendigkeit eines neuen Kulturpatriotismus und die Bereitschaft, für seine Werte zu sterben?," *Die Zeit*, 1 January.
Dubiel, Jochen (2007) *Dialektik der postkolonialen Hybridität: Die intrakulturelle Überwindung des postkolonialen Blicks in der Literatur* (Bielefeld: Aisthesis).
Dufresne, Marion (2006) "Emine Sevgi Özdamar *Mutter(s)zunge:* Der Weg zum eigenen Ich," *Germanica* 38, <http://germanica.revues.org/373> (accessed 22 April 2020).

Dumiche, Béatrice (2002) *Weiblichkeit im Jugendwerk Goethes. Die Sprachwerdung der Frau als dichterische Herausforderung* (Würzburg: Königshausen & Neumann).
Dunker, Axel (2008) *Kontrapunktische Lektüren. Koloniale Strukturen in der deutschsprachigen Literatur des 19. Jahrhunderts* (Munich: Fink).
Dunker, Axel (ed.) (2005) *(Post-)Kolonialismus und Deutsche Literatur. Impulse der anglo-amerikanischen Literatur- und Kulturtheorie* (Bielefeld: Aisthesis).
Dunker, Axel, Dirk Göttsche, and Gabriele Dürbeck (eds) (2017) *Handbuch Postkolonialismus und Literatur* (Stuttgart: Metzler).
Dunphy, Graeme (2000) "Rafik Schami," in *Encyclopedia of German Literature*, ed. Matthias Konzett (Chicago: Fitzroy-Dearborn Publishers), 874–951.
Dupuis-Déri, Francis (2012) "Le discours de la 'crise de la masculinité' comme refus de l'égalité entre les sexes: histoire d'une rhétorique antiféministe," *Cahiers du Genre* 52, 1, 119–143.
Ecker, Gisela (2012) "Schaltstellen des Kategorienwechsels: Putzfrauen in Literatur und Film," *Zeitschrift für Germanistik* 22, Neue Folge, 1, 101–114.
El Hissy, Maha (2012a) *Getürkte Türken: Karnavaleske Stilmittel im Theater, Kabarett und Film deutsch-türkischer Künstlerinnen und Künstler* (Bielefeld: Transcript).
El Hissy, Maha (2012b) "Krise der Fiktion, Fiktion der Krise: Emine Sevgi Özdamars *Keloğlan in Alamania* (1991)," in *Getürkte Türken: karnavaleske Stilmittel im Theater, Kabarett und Film deutsch-türkischer Künstlerinnen und Künstler* (Bielefeld: Transcript), 88–110.
El Wardy, Haimaa (2007) *Das Märchen und das Märchenhafte in den politisch engagierten Werken von Günter Grass und Rafik Schami* (Frankfurt/M.: Peter Lang).
Elias, Norbert (1990) *Über den Prozeß der Zivilisation: Soziogenetische und psychogenetische Untersuchungen, 1. Bd : Wandlungen des Verhaltens in den weltlichen Oberschichten des Abendlandes* [1939] (Frankfurt/M.: Suhrkamp Taschenbuch Wissenschaft].
Ellerbach, Benoît (2018) *L'Arabie contée aux Allemands. Fictions interculturelles chez Rafik Schami* (Würzburg: Königshausen & Neumann).
Emmerich, Wolfgang (1994) *Die andere deutsche Literatur. Aufsätze zur Literatur aus der DDR* (Opladen: Westdeutscher Verlag).
Engel, Manfred and Dieter Lamping (eds) (2006) *Franz Kafka und die Weltliteratur* (Göttingen: Vandenhoeck & Ruprecht).
Engélibert, Jean-Paul (2007) "Portrait de l'artiste en vieux singe: J. M. Coetzee, Kafka et le problème du réalisme," in *Sillage de Kafka*, ed. Philippe Zard (Paris: Le Manuscrit), 147–162.
Enzensberger, Hans Magnus (1999) *Ohne uns. Ein Totengespräch* (Hamburg: Raamin-Presse).
Éribon, Didier (1999) *Réflexions sur la question gay* (Paris: Fayard).
Erk, Ludwig and Wilhelm Irmer (eds) (1838) *Die deutschen Volkslieder mit ihren Singweisen. Gesammelt und hrsg. von Ludwig Erk und Wilhelm Irmer*, 1. Heft (Berlin: Plahn'sche Buchhandlung [Louis Ritze]).
Ernst, Thomas (2013) *Literatur und Subversion. Politisches Schreiben in der Gegenwart*, (Bielefeld: Transcript).
Espagne, Michel (1996) *Les Juifs allemands de Paris à l'époque de Heine: La translation ashkénaze* (Paris: PUF).
Espagne, Michel (1999) *Les Transferts culturels franco-allemands* (Paris: PUF).
Espagne, Michel (2013) "La notion de transfert culturel," *Revue Sciences/Lettres*, 1. Online at: <http://rsl.revues.org/219> (accessed 21 April 2020).

Espagne, Michel (2014) "Heine et la littérature populaire," in *Heine à Paris – Témoin et critique de la vie culturelle française*, ed. Marie-Ange Maillet and Norbert Waszek (Paris: L'éclat), 17–31.

Espagne, Michel and Michael Werner (1988) *Transferts. Les Relations interculturelles dans l'espace franco-allemand (XVIIIe-XIXe siècles)* (Paris: éd. Recherche sur les civilisations).

Espagne, Michel and Michael Werner (eds) (1994) *Philologiques III, Qu'est-ce qu'une littérature nationale? Approches pour une théorie interculturelle du champ littéraire* (Paris: MSH).

Espagne, Michel et al. (eds) (2004) *L'Horizon anthropologique des transferts culturels / Der anthropologische Horizont von Kulturtransfers / The anthropological Horizon of Cultural Transfers, Revue germanique internationale* 21 (Paris: PUF).

Esselborn, Karl (2004) "Deutschsprachige Minderheitenliteraturen als Gegenstand einer kulturwissenschaftlich orientierten 'interkulturellen Literaturwissenschaft,'" in *Die 'andere' Deutsche Literatur: Istanbuler Vorträge*, ed. Manfred Durzak and Nilüfer Kuruyazıcı (Würzburg: Königshausen & Neumann), 11–22.

Ette, Ottmar (2005) *ZwischenWeltenSchreiben: Literaturen ohne festen Wohnsitz* (Berlin: Kulturverlag Kadmos).

Ewers, Hans-Heino (2000) "Ein orientalischer Märchenerzähler, ein moderner Schriftsteller? Überlegungen zur Autorschaft Rafik Schamis," in *Konfiguration des Fremden in der Kinder- und Jugendliteratur nach 1945*, ed. Ulrich Nassen and Gina Weinkauff (Munich: Iudicium), 155–167.

Ezli, Özkan (2006), "Von der Identitätskrise zu einer ethnographischen Poetik. Migration in der deutsch-türkischen Literatur," in *Literatur und Migration*, ed. Heinz-Ludwig Arnold (Munich: text + kritik), 61–73.

Ezli, Özkan, Dorothee Kimmich, and Annette Werberger (eds) (2009) *Wider den Kulturenzwang: Migration, Kulturalisierung und Weltliteratur* (Bielefeld:Transcript).

Fachinger, Petra (2001) *Rewriting Germany from the Margins: "Other" German Literature of the 1980s and 1990s* (Montreal: McGill-Queen's University Press).

Fanon, Frantz (1995) *Peau noire, masques blancs* [1952] (Paris: Seuil).

Fanon, Frantz (2002) *Les Damnés de la terre* [1961] (Paris: La Découverte).

Federmair, Leopold (2012) "Der neue Diamant. Verfremdungseffekte bei E.S. Özdamar," *Arcadia* 47, 1, 153–172.

Félix, Brigitte and Marie-Claude Perrin-Chenour (eds) (2006) *Qui a peur des nouveaux canons?, Revue française d'études américaines* 110, 4.

Feyzioğlu, Yücel (1984) *Keloğlan in der Bundesrepublik* (Oberhausen: Ortadoğu).

Feyzioğlu, Yücel (1992a) *Keloğlan Glatzbub und die Gazellen* (Hückelhoven: Anadolu).

Feyzioğlu, Yücel (1992b) *Keloğlan in Deutschland* (Hückelhoven: Anadolu).

Feyzioğlu, Yücel (2017) *Keloğlan und der magische Donut* (Hückelhoven: Anadolu).

Finlay, Frank and Stuart Taberner (eds) (2002) *Recasting German Identity: Culture, Politics, and Literature in the Berlin Republic* (Rochester, New York, etc.: Camden House).

Fischer, Alexander M. (2014) "'Brecht hätte gerne eine Mitarbeiterin wie dich gehabt.' Zur Inszenierung von transkultureller Autorschaft und auktorialem Traditionsverhalten bei Emine Sevgi Özdamar," in *Subjektform Autor: Autorschaftsinszenierungen als Praktiken der Subjektivierung*, ed. Sabine Kyora (Bielefeld: Transcript), 247–266.

Fischer, Robert (1990) *Adelbert von Chamisso: Weltbürger, Naturforscher und Dichter*, mit einem Vorwort von Rafik Schami (Berlin: E. Klopp).

Fischer, Sabine and Moray McGowan (eds) (1997) *Denn du tanzt auf einem Seil: Positionen deutschsprachiger MigrantInnenliteratur* (Tübingen: Stauffenburg).
Forster, Edgar J. (1989) *Unmännliche Männlichkeit: Melancholie, "Geschlecht," Verausgabung* (Vienna, Cologne, Weimar: Böhlau).
Foucault, Michel (1984) "Des espaces autres," *Architecture, Mouvement, Continuité* 5, October, 46–49.
Foucault, Michel (2001) *Dits et écrits II, 1976–1988* (Paris: Gallimard, "Quarto").
Freiligrath, Ferdinand (1905) *Ferdinand Freiligraths Werke in neun Bänden*, ed. Eduard Schmidt-Weißenfels (Berlin and Leipzig: Th. Knaur Nachf.).
Friedrich, Heinz (ed.) (1986) *Chamissos Enkel. Zur Literatur von Ausländern in Deutschland*, (Munich: DTV).
Fröhlich, Holger (2016) "Lammfromm – Muslimischer Schlachthof," *Stuttgarter Zeitung*, 5 November 2010.
Fuchs-Sumiyoshi, Andrea (1984) *Orientalismus in der deutschen Literatur: Untersuchungen zu Werken des 19. und 20. Jahrhunderts, von Goethes West-östlichen Divan bis Thomas Manns Joseph-Trilogie* (Hildesheim: Olms).
Gauvin, Lise (2013) "Le palimpseste franocophone et la question des modèles," in *Littératures francophones: Parodies, pastiches, réécritures*, ed. Gauvin et al. (Lyon: ENS Éditions), 7–19.
Gauvin, Lise, Cécile Van den Avenne, Véronique Corinus, and Ching Selao (eds) (2013) *Littératures francophones: Parodies, pastiches, réécritures* (Lyon: ENS Éditions).
Geiser, Myriam (2014) *Der Ort transkultureller Literatur in Deutschland und in Frankreich: Deutsch-türkische und frankomaghrebinische Literatur der Postmigration* (Würzburg: Königshausen & Neumann).
Gendolla, Peter and Carsten Zelle (eds) (2000) *Der Siegener Kanon* (Frankfurt/M., Berlin, Bern, Bruxelles (New York: Peter Lang) (Forschungen zur Literatur- und Kulturgeschichte, vol. 70).
Genette, Gérard (1982) *Palimpsestes. La littérature au second degré* (Paris: Seuil). English edition: *Palimpsests: Literature in the Second Degree*, trans. Channa Newman and Claude Doubinsky (Lincoln: University of Nebraska Press), 1997.
Genette, Gérard (1987) *Seuils* (Paris: Seuil).
Gilleir, Anke (2011) "Melancholia, Migration, and Mise en Scène: Comparing Else Lasker-Schüler and Emine Sevgi Özdamar," *European Review* 19, 385–403.
Girardin, Cécile and Philip Whyte (eds) (2013) *Continuité, classicisme, conservatisme dans les littératures postcoloniales* (Rennes: Presses Universitaires de Rennes).
Goer, Charis and Michael Hofmann (eds) (2008) *Der Deutschen Morgenland: Bilder des Orients in der deutschen Literatur und Kultur von 1770 bis 1850* (Munich: Fink).
Goethe, Johann Wolfgang (2006) *Sämtliche Werke nach Epochen seines Schaffens*, Münchner Ausgabe, 21 Bde (in 33), ed. Karl Richter in Zusammenarbeit mit Herbert G. Göpfert, Norbert Miller, Gerhard Sauder und Edith Zehm (Munich: Hanser [btb]).
Goethe, Johann Wolfgang (1994) *Les Passions du jeune Werther*, trad. Philippe Forget, Paris, Imprimerie nationale.
Goethe, Johann Wolfgang (2005) *The Sorrows of Young Werther*, trans. Burton Pike (New York: The Modern Library).
Goffman, Erving (1963) *Stigma. Notes on the Management of Spoiled Identity* (London: Penguin).

Göktürk, Deniz, David Gramling, and Anton Kaes (eds) (2007) *Germany in Transit. Nation and Migration 1955–2005. A Sourcebook* (Berkeley: University of California Press).
Görbert, Johannes (2013) "Das literarische Feld auf Weltreisen. Eine kultursoziologische Annäherung an Chamissos Rurik-Expedition," in *Korrespondenzen und Transformationen: Neue Perspektiven auf Adelbert von Chamisso*, ed. Marie-Theres Federhofer and Jutta Weber (Göttingen: V & R Unipress), 33–50.
Görling, Reinholf (1997) *Heterotopia: Lektüren einer interkulturellen Literaturwissenschaft*, (Munich: Fink).
Granzin, Katharina (2011) "Da reimt sich Flittchen auf Igittchen: Kapitalismuskritik, jetzt auch gesungen: Feridun Zaimoglu und Günter Senkel machen erstmals Musiktheater," *Die Tageszeitung*, 21 March.
Grazin, Katharina (2010) "Ein Schelmenkonzert: Das Musiktheater Atze erzählt das Märchen 'Keloglan und die Räuberbande' nach dem Berliner Autor Kemal Kurt, mit Musik von Sinem Altan," *Die Tageszeitung*, 10 November.
Grimm, Jakob and Wilhelm Grimm (1857) *Kinder- und Hausmärchen Band 1*, 7. Auflage (Ausgabe letzter Hand) (Göttingen: Dieterich).
Grimm, Jakob and Wilhelm Grimm (2014) *Brüder Grimm, Kinder- und Hausmärchen. Ausgabe letzter Hand mit Originalanmerkungen der Brüder Grimm, mit einem Anhang sämtlicher, nicht in allen Auflagen veröffentlichter Märchen und Herkunftsnachweisen* herausgegeben von Heinz Rölleke, 3 Bde (Stuttgart: Reclam).
Grumbach, Detlef (2000) "Wieder schwelgt Feridun Zaimoglu in der Schönheit der Kanaksprak, vermischt mit Goethe: 'Ohne Geld gibts keine Schickness,'" *Berliner Zeitung*, 16 September.
Grumbach, Ernst and Renate Grumbach (eds) (1999) *Goethe. Begegnungen und Gespräche*, vol. VI (Berlin and New York: De Gruyter).
Grünberg, Serge (1994) *Le Roman de M. Butterfly* (Paris: Calmann-Lévy).
Guattari, Félix and Olivier Zahm (1994) "Félix Guattari et l'art contemporain," Interview, 28 April 1992, *Chimères* 23, 1–18.
Guillory, John (1993) *Cultural Capital: The Problem of Literary Canon Formation* (Chicago: The University of Chicago Press).
Günter, Petra (2002) "Die Kolonisierung der Migrantenliteratur," in *Räume der Hybridität. Postkoloniale Konzepte in Theorie und Literatur*, ed. Christof Hamann and Cornelia Sieber (Hildesheim, etc.: Olms).
Gutermann, Deborah (2007) "Le désir et l'entrave. L'impuissance dans la construction de l'identité masculine romantique: première moitié du XIXe siècle," in *Hommes et masculinités de 1789 à nos jours*, ed. Régis Revenin (Paris: Autrement), 55–73.
Gutjahr, Ortrud (2002) "Alterität und Interkulturalität. Neuere deutsche Literatur," in *Germanistik als Kulturwissenschaft*, ed. Claudia Benthien and Hans Rudolf Velthen (Reinbek bei Hamburg: Rowohlt), 345–369.
Gutjahr, Ortrud (ed.) (2000) *Westöstlicher und nordsüdlicher Divan. Goethe in interkultureller Perspektive* (Paderborn and Munich: Schöningh).
Gutjahr, Ortrud (ed.) (2012) *Transkulturalität und Intermedialität in der Germanistik des globalen Zeitalters*, Panel 2, *Akten des XII. internationalen Germanistenkongresses Warschau 2010. Vielheit und Einheit der Germanistik weltweit*, vol. 2: *Eröffnungsvorträge – Diskussionsforen*, ed. Franciszek Grucza (Frankfurt/M.: Peter Lang).

Gutjahr, Ortrud and Stefan Hermes (eds) (2011) *Maskeraden des (Post-)Kolonialismus. Verschattete Repräsentationen 'der Anderen' in der deutschsprachigen Literatur und im Film* (Würzburg: Könisghausen & Neumann).
Ha, Kien Nghi (2004) *Ethnizität und Migration Reloaded. Kulturelle Identität, Differenz und Hybridität im postkolonialen Diskurs* [1999], überarb. und erw. Neuauflage (Berlin: Wissenschaftlicher Verlag).
Ha, Kien Nghi (2007) "Deutsche Integrationspolitik als koloniale Praxis," in *re/visionen, Postkoloniale Perspektiven von People of Color auf Rassismus, Kulturpolitik und Widerstand in Deutschland,* ed. Kien Nghi Ha, Nicola Lauré al-Samarai, and Sheila Mysorekar (Münster: Unrast), 113–128.
Ha, Kien Nghi, Nicola Lauré al-Samarai, and Sheila Mysorekar (eds) (2007) *re/visionen, Postkoloniale Perspektiven von People of Color auf Rassismus, Kulturpolitik und Widerstand in Deutschland,* (Münster: Unrast).
Hall, Stuart (1993) "Culture, Community, Nation," *Cultural Studies* 7, 3, 349–363.
Hamann, Christof and Cornelia Sieber (eds) (2002) *Räume der Hybridität. Postkoloniale Konzepte in Theorie und Literatur* (Hildesheim, etc.: Olms).
Hamann, Christof and Michael Hofmann (eds) (2009) *Kanon heute: Literaturwissenschaftliche und fachdidaktische Perspektiven* (Baltmannsweiler: Schneider-Verl. Hohengehren).
Hamann, Christof and Klaus von Stosch (eds) (2012) *Islam in der deutschen und türkischen Literatur* (Paderborn, Munich: Schöningh).
Harnoncourt, Nikolaus (1987) "Ein Familiendrama," in *W.A. Mozart, Die Zauberflöte,* ed. Nikolaus Harnoncourt, 3 CD boxset, accompanying booklet (Opernhaus Zürich), 14–15.
Hazan, Marie (2009) "Y a-t-il une condition masculine? Le masculin aujourd'hui: crise ou continuité?," *Dialogue,* 1, 183, 81–93.
Heine, Heinrich (1976) *Sämtliche Schriften in zwölf Bänden,* ed. Klaus Briegleb (Munich: Hanser).
Heller, Hartmut (1998) "Flüche und andere unanständige Wörter. Über Sprachtabus," in *Zur Evolution von Kommunikation und Sprache – Ausdruck, Mitteilung, Darstellung,* ed. Max Liedtke (Graz: Austria Medien Service), 245–254.
Hellot, Marie-Christine (2009) "La tradaptation: quand traduire, c'est adapter Shakespeare," *Jeu: Revue de théâtre* 133, 78–82.
Helm, Barbara (1997) "Bertha von Suttner," in *Philosophinnen-Lexikon,* ed. Ursula I. Meyer and Heidemarie Bennent-Vahle (Leipzig: Reclam).
Heydebrand, Renate von (ed.) (1998) *Kanon Macht Kultur: theoretische, historische und soziale Aspekte ästhetischer Kanonbildung* (Stuttgart: Metzler).
Heydebrand, Renate von and Simone Winko (1996) *Einführung in die Wertung von Literatur. Systematik – Geschichte – Legitimation* (Paderborn: Schöningh).
Hobsbawm, Eric and Terence Ranger (eds) (1983) *The Invention of Tradition* (Cambridge: Cambridge University Press).
Hobsbawm, Eric J. (1990) *Nations and Nationalism since 1780: Programme, Myth, Reality* (Cambridge: Cambridge University Press).
Höfer, Simone (2007) *Interkulturelles Erzählverfahren: ein Vergleich zwischen der deutschsprachigen Migrantenliteratur und der englischsprachigen postkolonialen Literatur* (Saarbrücken: VDM).
Hofmann, Michael (2006) *Interkulturelle Literaturwissenschaft: Eine Einführung* (Paderborn: Fink).

Hofmann, Michael (2012) "Romantic Rebellion: Feridun Zaimoglu and Anti-Bourgeois Tradition," in *Feridun Zaimoglu*, ed. Tom Cheesman and Karin Yeşilada (Oxford, Bern, Berlin: Peter Lang), 239–257.

Hofmann, Michael (2013a) *Deutsch-türkische Literaturwissenschaft* (Würzburg: Königshausen & Neumann).

Hofmann, Michael (2013c) "Hölderlin und Zaimoglu, Hyperion und Serdar: Izmir, die Ägäis und Kleinasien in der deutschen Literatur," in *Von Generation zu Generation: Germanistik. Festschrift für Kasım Eğit zum 65. Geburtstag*, ed. Saniye Uysal Ünalan, Nilgin Tanış Polat, Mehmet Tahir Öncü (İzmir, Ege Üniversitesi Basımevi), 155–165.

Hofmann, Michael (ed.) (2012a) *Deutsch-afrikanische Diskurse in Geschichte und Gegenwart: Literatur- und Kulturwissenschaftliche Perspektiven* (Amsterdam: Rodopi).

Hofmann, Michael (ed.) (2013b) *Unbegrenzt: Literatur und interkulturelle Erfahrung*, (Frankfurt/M.: Peter Lang).

Höhn, Gerhard (1997) *Heine-Handbuch: Zeit – Person – Werk*. 2., aktualisierte und erw. Aufl. (Stuttgart and Weimar: Metzler).

Hölderlin, Friedrich (1957) *Sämtliche Werke*, vol. 3, ed. Friedrich Beissner (große Stuttgarter Ausgabe in 8 Bänden) (Stuttgart, Kohlhammer).

Honold, Alexander (ed.) (2011) *Ost-westliche Kulturtransfers: Orient-Amerika* (Bielefeld: Aisthesis).

Horst, Claire (2007) *Der weibliche Raum in der Migrationsliteratur. Irena Brezna – Emine Sevgi Özdamar – Libuše Moníková* (Berlin: Schiler).

Howard, Mary (ed.) (1997) *Interkulturelle Konfigurationen: Zur deutschsprachigen Erzählliteratur von Autoren nichtdeutscher Herkunft* (Munich: Iudicium).

Hückstädt, Hauke (2000) "Liebeswut in den Pulspumpen," *Frankfurter Rundschau*, 4 November.

Hüfner, Agnes (2000) "Werthers Ächter. Orient ne va plus: Feridun Zaimoglus wilder Briefroman 'Liebesmale, scharlachrot,'" *Süddeutsche Zeitung*, 17 November.

Huggan, Graham (2001) *The Postcolonial Exotic: Marketing the Margins* (London and New York: Routledge).

Hür, Ayse (2011) "L''arabesk', des bidonvilles à l'Eurovision," *Courrier International*, 1 June. Online at: <http://www.courrierinternational.com/article/2011/01/06/l-arabesk-des-bidonvilles-a-a-l-eurovision> (accessed 22 April 2020).

Hwang, David Henry (1988) *M. Butterfly* (New York: Penguin Books).

Ineichen, Stefan (2006) "Der Gefährte aus Damaskus," *WOZ*, 31, 3 August.

Jamison, Anne Elizabeth (2003) "Kafka and Czech: Away from 'minor literature,'" *Journal of the Kafka Society of America* (New International Series) 27, 1–2, 31–39.

Janosch (1983) *Janosch erzählt Grimm's Märchen. Fünfzig ausgewählte Märchen, neu erzählt für Kinder von heute*, 8. Aufl. (Weinheim and Basel: Beltz und Gelberg).

Janota, Johannes (ed.) (1993) *Germanistik, Deutschunterricht und Kulturpolitik* (Tübingen: Niemeyer).

Jeanneret, André (1969) "Le théâtre d'ombres en Orient," *Asiatische Studien* 23, 155–166.

Jelinek, Elfriede (2003) "Liebeserklärung an Else Lasker-Schüler" (Rede aus Anlass der Verleihung des ELS-Dramatikerpreises des Landes Rheinland-Pfalz am 20. November 2003 in Mainz an Elfriede). Online at: <http://www.exil-archiv.de/grafik/biografien/lasker-schueler/Elfriede_Jelinek.pdf> (accessed 3 June 2020).

Jens, Walter (2001) *Der Teufel lebt nicht mehr, mein Herr! Erdachte Monologe, imaginäre Gespräche* (Stuttgart: Radius).
Jessen, Jens (2014) "Feridun Zaimoglu, Isabel: 'Am Anfang war der Hass,'" *Die Zeit*, 13 March.
Joubert, Claire (2009) "Théorie en traduction: Homi Bhabha et l'intervention postcoloniale," *Littérature* 154, 2, 149–174.
Jung, Thomas (2010) "Ansprache von Oberbürgermeister Thomas Jung," in *Reden zur Preisverleihung 2010 an Feridun Zaimoglu*, Jakob-Wassermann-Literaturpreis, <http://www.fuerth.de/Portaldata/1/Resources/lebeninfuerth/dokumente/kultur/wassermannreden2010.pdf> (accessed 23 April 2020).
Kapadia, Parmita (2008) "Transnational Shakespeare: Salman Rushdie and Intertextual Appropriation," in *Borrowers and Lenders. The Journal of Shakespeare and Appropriation* III, 2, Spring/Summer.
Karaman, Fatih F. (2010) "La Musique Arabesque Turque: une expression masochiste dans la modernisation turque," *Parole sans frontière – Psychanalyse et exil*, 23 August. Online at: <http://www.parole-sans-frontiere.org/spip.php?article247> (accessed 3 June 2018).
Kassajep, Margaret (1980) *Deutsche Hausmärchen, frisch getrimmt* (Dachau: Baedeker & Lang).
Keil, Thomas (2003) *Die postkoloniale deutsche Literatur in Namibia (1920–2000)*, PhD Diss., Universität Stuttgart. Online at: <http://dx.doi.org/10.18419/opus-5230> (accessed 22 April 2020).
Kelek, Necla (2005) *Die fremde Braut: Ein Bericht aus dem Inneren des türkischen Lebens in Deutschland* (Cologne: Kiepenheuer & Witsch).
Kermani, Navid (2008) "Was ist deutsch an der deutschen Literatur?," in *Was eint uns? Verständigung der Gesellschaft über gemeinsame Grundlagen*, ed. Bernard Vogel and Konrad-Adenauer-Stiftung e.V. (Freiburg: Herder Verlag), 78–98.
Kermani, Navid (2011) *Dein Name*, Roman (Munich: Hanser).
Kermani, Navid (2012a) *Über den Zufall. Jean Paul, Hölderlin und der Roman, den ich schreibe. Frankfurter Poetikvorlesungen* (Munich: Hanser).
Kermani, Navid (2012b) *Vergesst Deutschland! Eine patriotische Rede. Zur Eröffnung der Hamburger Lessingtage 2012* (Berlin: Ullstein).
Khair, Tabish and Johan Höglund (eds) (2013) *Transnational and Postcolonial Vampires: Dark Blood* (Basingstoke and New York: Palgrave Macmillan).
Khalil, Iman Osman (1990) "Rafik Schami's Fantasy and Fairy Tales," *International Fiction Review*, 17, 2, 121–123.
Khalil, Iman Osman (1994a) "Narrative Strategies as Cultural Vehicles: On Rafik Schami's Novel *Erzähler der Nacht*," in *The German Mosaic. Cultural and Linguistic Diversity in Society*, ed. Carol Aisha Blackshire-Belay (Westport, CT: Greenwood), 217–224.
Khalil, Iman Osman (1994b) "Zum Konzept der Multikulturalität im Werk Rafik Schamis," *Monatshefte für deutschsprachige Literatur und Kultur*, 86, 2, 201–217.
Khalil, Iman Osman (1997) "Zur Rezeption arabischer Autoren in Deutschland," in *Denn Du tanzt auf einem Seil: Positionen deutschsprachiger MigrantInnenliteratur*, ed. Sabine Fischer and Moray McGowan (Tübingen: Stauffenburg), 115–131.
Khalil, Iman Osman (1998) "From the Margins to the Center. Arab-German Authors and Issues," in *Transforming the Center, Eroding the Margins: Essays on Ethnic and Cultural Boundaries in German-Speaking Countries*, ed. Dagmar Lorenz and Renate Posthofen (Columbia, SC: Camden House) 227–237.

Killert, Gabriele (2001) "Spätbarock und präpotent. Feridun Zaimoglu im Zeichen des Unterleibs," *Neue Zürcher Zeitung*, 17 April.
Kirschnick, Sylke (2007) *Tausend und ein Zeichen: Else Lasker-Schülers Orient und die Berliner Alltags- und Populärkultur um 1900* (Würzburg: Königshausen & Neumann).
Kobbé, Gustave (1997) *The New Kobbé's Opera Book*, ed. Earl of Harewood and Antony Peattie, 11th ed. (New York: Putnam).
Koiran, Linda (2009) *Écrire en langue étrangère: Études des œuvres allemandes des auteurs d'origine asiatique / Schreiben in fremder Sprache: Studien zu den deutschsprachigen Werken von Autoren asiatischer Herkunft* (Munich: Iudicium), 222–248.
Kontje, Todd Curtis (2004) *German Orientalisms* (Ann Arbor, Mich.: University of Michigan Press).
Konuk, Kader (2001) *Identitäten im Prozess: Literatur von Autorinnen aus und in der Türkei in deutscher, englischer und türkischer Sprache* (Essen: Die blaue Eule).
Kortländer, Bernd (1995) "Die Sphinx im Märchenwald," in: *Interpretationen. Gedichte von Heinrich Heine*, ed. B. Kortländer (Stuttgart, Reclam), 13–31.
Kraft, Helga (2011) "Das Theater als moralische Anstalt? Deutsche Identität und die Migrantenfrage auf der Bühne," in *GeschlechterSpielRäume: Dramatik, Theater, Performance und Gender*, ed. Gaby Pailer and Franziska Schößler (Amsterdam: Rodopi), 121–140.
Kreutzer, Eberhard (1995) "Theoretische Grundlagen postkolonialer Literaturkritik," in *Literaturwissenschaftliche Theorien, Modelle und Methoden: Eine Einführung*, ed. Ansgar Nünning (Trier: Wissenschaftlicher Verlag Trier), 199–213.
Kurt, Kemal (1998a) *Ja, sagt Molly*, Roman (Berlin: Hitit Verlag).
Kurt, Kemal (1998b) *Als das Kamel Bademeister war – Keloğlans lustige Streiche* (Berlin: Edition Orient).
Lamine, Anne-Sophie (2005) "L'ethnicité comme question sociologique," *Archives de sciences sociales des religions* 131–132, 189–197.
Lamping, Dieter (1998) *Von Kafka bis Celan: Jüdischer Diskurs in der deutschen Literatur des 20. Jahrhunderts* (Göttingen: Vandenhoeck & Ruprecht).
Lamping, Dieter (2011) "Deutsche Literatur von nicht-deutschen Autoren: Anmerkungen zum Begriff der 'Chamisso-Literatur,'" in *Chamisso. Viele Kulturen – eine Sprache*, Robert Bosch Stiftung, 5 March, 18–21.
Lange-Müller, Katja (2016) "Der Hund und die Kälte – Das ist doch mal ein Anfang!," *Emine Sevgi Özdamar, Text + Kritik* 211, ed. Heinz-Ludwig Arnold (Munich: text + kritik), 3–7.
Lasker-Schüler, Else (1902) *Styx. Gedichte* (Berlin: Axel Juncker).
Lasker-Schüler, Else (1917) *Gesammelte Gedichte* (Berlin: Verlag der Weißen Bücher).
Lasker-Schüler, Else (1920) *Hebräische Balladen* (Berlin: Cassirer).
Lauer, Gerhard (2006) "Die Erfindung einer kleinen Literatur: Kafka und die jiddische Literatur," in *Franz Kafka und die Weltliteratur*, ed. Manfred Engel and Dieter Lamping (Göttingen: Vandenhoeck & Ruprecht), 125–143.
Lauterwein, Andréa (2014) "Paul Celan: le rossignol bègue. Un changement de perspectives dans la poésie," *Revue d'Histoire de la Shoah* 201, 403–430.
Lawrence, Karen R. (ed.) (1992) *Decolonizing Tradition: New Views of Twentieth-Century 'British' Literary Canons* (Urbana: University of Illinois Press).
Lecercle, Jean-Jacques (2006) "Leçon du canon," *Revue française d'études américaines* 110, 4, 10–22.

Lehmann, Hans-Thies (1990) *Postdramatisches Theater* (Frankfurt/M.: Verlag der Autoren).
Lejeune, Philippe (1975) *Le Pacte autobiographique* (Paris: Seuil). English edition: "The Autobiographical Contract," trans. R. Carter, in *French Literary Theory Today*, ed. Tzetvan Todorov (Cambridge: Cambridge University Press), 1982.
Lérès, Guy (2005) "D'un usage singulier de la marque," in *Les Désarrois nouveaux du sujet*, ed. Jean-Pierre Lebrun (Paris: Érès), 219–225.
Littler, Margaret (2002) "Diasporic Identity in Emine Sevgi Özdamar's 'Mutterzunge,'" in *Recasting German Identity: Culture, Politics, and Literature in the Berlin Republic*, ed. Frank Finlay and Stuart Taberner (Rochester, NY: Camden House), 219–234.
Littler, Margaret (2009) "Profane und religiöse Identitäten: Die islamische Kultur im Werk von Emine Sevgi Özdamar und Feridun Zaimoğlu," in *Von der nationalen zur internationalen Literatur: Transkulturelle deutschsprachige Literatur und Kultur im Zeitalter globaler Migration*, ed. Helmut Schmitz (Amsterdam: Rodopi), 143–154.
Lohse, Rolf (2005) *Postkoloniale Traditionsbildung: Der frankokanadische Roman zwischen Autonomie und Bezugnahme auf die Literatur Frankreichs und der USA* (Frankfurt/M. and New York: Peter Lang).
Lorenz, Dagmar and Renate Posthofen (eds) (1998) *Transforming the Center, Eroding the Margins: Essays on Ethnic and Cultural Boundaries in German-Speaking Countries* (Columbia S.C.: Camden House).
Lornsen, Karin (2009) "The City as Stage of Transgression: Performance, Picaresque Reminiscences, and Linguistic Incongruity in Emine S. Özdamar's *The Bridge of the Golden Horn*," in *Gender and Laughter: Comic Affirmation and Subversion in Traditional and Modern Media*, ed. Gabi Pailer (Amsterdam: Rodopi), 201–218.
Lottmann, Joachim (1997) "Ein Wochenende in Kiel mit Feridun Zaimoglu, dem Malcolm X der deutschen Türken," *Die Zeit*, 14 November.
Lubrich, Oliver (2004) *Das Schwinden der Differenz. Postkoloniale Poetiken: Alexander von Humboldt, Bram Stoker, Ernst Jünger, Jean Genet* (Bielefeld: Aisthesis).
Luserke, Matthias (1997) "Die Leiden des jungen Werthers," in *Sturm und Drang. Autoren – Texte – Themen* (Stuttgart: Reclam), 125–157.
Luste Boulbina, Sélua (2008) *Le Singe de Kafka et autres propos sur la colonie* (Lyon: Parangon).
Lützeler, Paul Michael (1997) *Der postkoloniale Blick: Deutsche Schriftsteller berichten aus der Dritten Welt* (Frankfurt/M.: Suhrkamp).
Maar, Paul (1968) *Der tätowierte Hund* (Reinbek bei Hamburg: Rowohlt).
Maier-Schaeffer, Francine (1992) *Heiner Müller et le "Lehrstück"* (Bern: Peter Lang).
Maingueneau, Dominique (1993) *Le Contexte de l'œuvre littéraire. Énonciation, écrivain, société* (Paris: Dunod).
Maingueneau, Dominique (1999) "Ethos, scénographie, incorporation," in *Images de soi dans le discours. La construction de l'ethos*, ed. Ruth Amossy (Lausanne and Paris: Delachaux Niestlé), 75–100.
Malkani, Fabrice, Anne-Marie Saint-Gille, and Ralf Zschachlitz (eds) (2007) *Canon et mémoire culturelle: Œuvres canoniques et postérité*, *Études germaniques* 243, 3.
Malkani, Fabrice, Anne-Marie Saint-Gille, and Ralf Zschachlitz (eds) (2010) *Canon et identité culturelle: Élites, masses, manipulation* (Saint-Étienne: Publications de l'Université de Saint-Étienne).
Mandelkow, Karl Robert (ed.) (1977) *Goethe im Urteil seiner Kritiker*, 4 Bde (Munich: Beck).

Mangold, Ijoma (2010) "Vom 'Kümmel-Outlow' zum Kulturkonservativen: Eine Begegnung mit Feridun Zaimoglu," *Die Zeit*, 14 May.
Mani, B. Venkat (2016) "Weltliteratur als *bibliomigrancy*. Auf Emine Sevgi Özdamars 'Sprachzügen,'" *Emine Sevgi Özdamar, Text + Kritik* 211, ed. Heinz-Ludwig Arnold (Munich: text + kritik), 59–70
Marx, Karl (1867) *Das Kapital, Buch I: Der Produktionsprocess des Kapitals* (Hamburg: Meissner).
Massin, Brigitte and Jean Massin (1970) *Wolfgang Amadeus Mozart* (Paris: Fayard).
May, Manfred, Peter Goßens, and Jürgen Lehmann (eds) (2008) *Celan-Handbuch. Leben – Werk – Wirkung* (Stuttgart and Weimar: Metzler).
Mayer, Hans (1971) *Der Repräsentant und der Märtyrer: Konstellationen der Literatur*, (Frankfurt/M.: Suhrkamp).
McGowan, Moray (2010) "The Tash her Father Wore: World Literature, Joyce, Kafka and the Invisible in Kemal Kurt's *Ja, sagt Molly*," in *Crossing Frontiers. Cultural Exchange and Conflict. Papers in Honour of Malcolm Pender*, ed. Barbara Burns and Joy Charnley (Amsterdam and New York: Rodopi), 43–53.
Mecklenburg, Norbert (2004a) "Eingrenzung, Ausgrenzungn, Grenzüberschreitung," in *Die "andere" Deutsche Literatur. Istanbuler Vorträge*, ed. Manfred Durzak and Nilüfer Kuruyazıcı (Würzburg: Königshausen & Neumann).
Mecklenburg, Norbert (2004b) "Ein weiblicher Schelmenroman: Das Erzählprinzip der komischen Verfremdung in Emine Sevgi Özdamars *Brücke vom Goldenen Horn*," *Studien zur Deutschen Sprache und Literatur / Alman Dili ve Edebiyatı Dergisi* 16 (Istanbul: İ.Ü. Basımevi), 1–21.
Mecklenburg, Norbert (2006) "Leben und Erzählen als Migration: Intertextuelle Komik in *Mutterzunge* von Emine Sevgi Özdamar," in *Literatur und Migration*, ed. Heinz-Ludwig Arnold (Munich: text + kritik), 84–96.
Mecklenburg, Norbert (2008) *Das Mädchen aus der Fremde: Germanistik als interkulturelle Literaturwissenschaft* (Munich: Iudicium).
Meizoz, Jérôme (2007) *Postures littéraires. Mises en scène modernes de l'auteur* (Genève, Slatkine).
Meizoz, Jérôme (2011) "La fabrique d'une notion. Entretien avec Jérôme Meizoz au sujet du concept de 'posture,'" propos recueillis par David Martens, *Interférences littéraires/ Literaire interferenties*, nouvelle série, 6, May, 199–212.
Meizoz, Jérôme, Jean-Claude Mühlethaler, and Delphine Burghgraeve (eds) (2014) *Postures d'auteurs: du Moyen Âge à la modernité*, Actes du colloque tenu les 20 et 21 juin 2013 à Lausanne, *Fabula / Les colloques*, <https://www.fabula.org/colloques/sommaire2341.php> (accessed 22 April 2020).
Mervin, Sabrina (2006) "Les larmes et le sang des chiites: corps et pratiques rituelles lors des célébrations de 'Âshûrâ' (Liban, Syrie)," *Revue des mondes musulmans et de la Méditerranée* [online], November, 113–114: <http://journals.openedition.org/remmm/2973> (accessed 22 April 2020).
Meuser, Michael (2006) *Geschlecht und Männlichkeit. Soziologische Theorie und kulturelle Deutungsmuster* (Wiesbaden: Springer).
Meuser, Michael (2008) "Ernste Spiele: zur Konstruktion von Männlichkeit im Wettbewerb der Männer," in *Die Natur der Gesellschaft: Verhandlungen des 33. Kongresses der Deutschen Gesellschaft für Soziologie in Kassel 2006*, ed. Karl-Siegbert Rehberg and

Deutsche Gesellschaft für Soziologie (DGS), vol. 1–2. (Frankfurt/M.: Campus), 5171–5176.
Meuser, Michael (2009) "Hegemoniale Männlichkeit – Überlegungen zur Leitkategorie der men's studies," in *FrauenMännerGeschlechterforschung. State of the Art*, ed. Brigitte Aulenbacher (Münster: Westfälisches Dampfboot), 160–171.
Meyer, Christine (2013) "Istanbul, ville-personnage au cœur de l'Europe: les romans d'Orhan Pamuk, Emine Sevgi Özdamar et David Boratav," in *Europe du roman, romans de l'Europe*, ed. Carlo Arcuri (Paris: Garnier), 191–210.
Meyer, Christine (2014) "Feridun Zaimoglu adaptateur de Shakespeare," in *Interprétations postcoloniales et mondialisation. Littératures de langues allemande, anglaise, espagnole, française, italienne et portugaise*, ed. Françoise Aubès, Silvia Contarini, Jean-Marc Moura, and Idelette Muzar-Fonseca dos Santos (Bern: Peter Lang), 173–192.
Meyer, Christine (2016) "Guerres esthétiques et conflits communautaires: le roman d'artiste comme riposte au 'choc des civilisations' (Orhan Pamuk, Rafik Schami, Metin Arditi)," in *Orients et orientalisme dans la culture des pays de langue allemande au XXe siècle. Perceptions, appropriations, constructions et déconstructions*, ed. Philippe Alexandre (Nancy: PUN), 365–383.
Meyer, Christine (2017) "*Karriere einer Putzfrau* oder die Stimme der Subalternen: eine Relektüre *Hamlets* durch das Prisma von Heiner Müllers *Hamletmaschine*," in *La littérature interculturelle de langue allemande – Emine Sevgi Özdamar*, ed. Bernard Banoun, *Études germaniques 287*, July/September, 431–447.
Meyer, Christine (2019) "Titania zwischen Istanbul und Berlin. Zur Deterritorialisierung des westlichen Theaterkanons in E. S. Özdamars *Die Brücke vom Goldenen Horn*," in *Emine Sevgi Özdamar: une écriture contemporaine de l'interculturalité*, ed. Bernard Banoun, Frédéric Teinturier, and Dirk Weissmann (Paris: L'Harmattan), 53–73.
Meyer, Christine (ed.) (2012a) *Kosmopolitische "Germanophonie": Postnationale Perspektiven in der deutschsprachigen Gegenwartsliteratur* (Würzburg: Königshausen & Neumann = Saarbrücker Beiträge zur Vergleichenden Literatur- und Kulturwissenschaft, vol. 59).
Meyer, Christine (2012b) "Elias Canetti als Ahne?," in *Kosmopolitische "Germanophonie,"* ed. Christine Meyer (Würzburg: Königshausen & Neumann), 81–104.
Meyer, Christine (forthcoming) "Rafik Schami und seine deutsch-französischen 'Ahnen,'" in *L'Interculturalité à travers le prisme des migrations dans la sphère franco-allemande*, ed. Cécile Chamayou-Kuhn, Ingrid Lacheny, Romana Weiershausen, and Dirk Weissmann (Nancy, PUN).
Mieder, Wolfgang (ed.) (1986) *Grimmige Märchen. Prosatexte von Ilse Aichinger bis Martin Walser* (Frankfurt/M.: Fischer).
Milevska, Suzana (2003) "Resistance that Cannot Be Recognized as Such," Interview with Gayatri Chakravorty Spivak, 8 July, Skopje, *Journal for Politics, Gender, and Culture*, 11, 2, 27–45.
Milevska, Suzana, Swapan Chakravorty, and Tani E. Barlow (eds) (2006) *Conversations with Gayatri Chakravorty Spivak* (London: Seagull Books).
Minnaard, Liesbeth (2008) *New Germans, New Dutch: Literary Interventions* (Amsterdam: Amsterdam University Press).
Morrison, Toni (1992) *Playing in the Dark: Whiteness and the Literary Imagination* (Cambridge, MA: Harvard University Press).

Mousel Knott, Suzuko (2010) "Yoko Tawada und das 'F-Word:' Intertextuelle und intermediale Prozesse des Romans *Ein Gast* im feministischen Diskurs," *Études Germaniques* 259, 3, 569–580.

Müller, Heiner (1978) *Hamletmaschine*, in *Mauser* (Berlin: Rotbuch/Verlag der Autoren), 89–97. English edition: *Hamletmachine and Other Texts for the Stage*, trans. Carl Weber (New York: Performing Arts Journal Publications), 1984.

Müller, Heiner (1982) "Walls/Mauern. Interview mit Sylvère Lothringer," in *Rotwelsch* (Berlin: Merve).

Müller, Heiner (1992) *Krieg ohne Schlacht. Leben in zwei Diktaturen. Eine Autobiographie* (Cologne: Kiepenheuer & Witsch).

Nethersole, Reingard (1989) "Die deutschsprachige Literatur im südlichen Afrika," in *Deutschsprachige Literatur des Auslandes*, ed. Erwin Theodor Rosenthal (Bern, Frankfurt/M., New York, and Paris: Peter Lang), 25–46.

Nettesheim, Josefine (1969) "Ferdinand Freiligraths Neger- und Wüstenlieder und das Problem der Exotik," *Jahrbuch des Wiener Goethe-Vereins* 73, 93–106.

Nünning, Ansgar (2006) *Literature and Memory: Theoretical Paradigms, Genres, Functions* (Tübingen: Francke).

Nünning, Ansgar (ed.) (1995) *Literaturwissenschaftliche Theorien, Modelle und Methoden: Eine Einführung* (Trier: Wissenschaftlicher Verlag Trier).

Ogane, Atsuko (2011) "Parcours du mythe d'Hérodia: *Ysengrimus, Atta Troll, Trois contes, Salomé*," *Romantisme* 154, 4, 149–160.

Okay, Erman (1991) *Keloğlan und der Riese*, Märchen in deutscher und türkischer Sprache. Mit Begleitheft von P. Oberhuemer und M. Ulrich: "Zwischen Keloğlan und Rotkäppchen" (Weinheim and Basel: Beltz).

Okay, Erman (2004) *Keloğlan und Rotkäppchen / Keloglan ve Kirmizi Sapkali Kiz*, Märchen für Kinder, Hörspiel (Hückelhoven: Schulverlag Anadolu).

Oraliş, Meral (2004) "Der Spiegel als Wunschraum oder Das literarische Schreiben als 'Provinz des Fremden' bei E. Sevgi Özdamar," in *Interkulturelle Begegnungen. Festschrift für Şara Sayın*, ed. Manfred Durzak and Nilüfer Kuruyazıcı (Würzburg: Königshausen & Neumann), 49–60.

Osterhammel, Jürgen (2003) *Kolonialismus: Geschichte, Formen, Folgen*, 4th ed. (Munich: Beck).

Osthues, Julian (2017) *Literatur als Palimpsest. Postkoloniale Ästhetik im deutschsprachigen Roman der Gegenwart* (Bielefeld: Transcript).

Özbek, Meral (1997) "Arabesk Culture: A Case of Modernization and Popular Identity," in *Rethinking Modernity and National Identity in Turkey*, ed. Sibel Bozdoğan and Reşat Kasaba (Washington D.C.: University of Washington Press).

Özdamar, Emine Sevgi (1982) *Karagöz in Alamania: Ein türkisches Stück*. Dir. E. S. Özdamar. Stage manuscript (Frankfurt/M.: Verlag der Autoren).

Özdamar, Emine Sevgi (1990) *Mutterzunge*, Erzählungen (Berlin: Rotbuch). English edition: *Karagoz in Alamania / Blackeye in Germany*, in: *Mother-Tongue*, trans. Craig Thomas (Toronto: Coach House Press, 1994).

Özdamar, Emine Sevgi (1991) *Keloglan in Alamania oder die Versöhnung von Schwein und Lamm*. Stage manuscript (Frankfurt/M.: Verlag der Autoren).

Özdamar, Emine Sevgi (1992) *Das Leben ist eine Karawanserei, hat zwei Türen / aus einer kam ich rein / aus der anderen ging ich raus*, Roman (Cologne: Kiepenheuer & Witsch [KiWi]).
Özdamar, Emine Sevgi (1998) *Die Brücke vom Goldenen Horn*, Roman (Cologne: Kiepenheuer & Witsch [KiWi]).
Özdamar, Emine Sevgi (2001) *Der Hof im Spiegel*, Erzählungen (Cologne: Kiepenheuer & Witsch [KiWi]).
Özdamar, Emine Sevgi (2003) *Seltsame Sterne starren zur Erde. Berlin – Pankow 1976/77* (Cologne: Kiepenheuer & Witsch [KiWi]).
Özdamar, Emine Sevgi (2010) *Perikızı. Ein Traumspiel*, in *Odyssee Europa. Aktuelle Stücke 20/ 10*, ed. Uwe B. Carstensen and Stefanie von Lieben (Frankfurt/M.: Fischer Taschenbuch Verlag), 271–336.
Ozil, Şeyda, Michael Hofmann, and Yasemin Dayioğlu-Yücel (eds) (2011) *Türkisch-deutscher Kulturkontakt und Kulturtransfer. Kontroversen und Lernprozesse* (Göttingen: V & R Unipress).
Öztürk, Serdar (2006) "Karagöz Co-Opted: Turkish Shadow Theatre of the Early Republic (1923–1945)," *Asian Theatre Journal* 23, 2 (Fall), 292–313.
Parmentier, Sabine (2002) "Œuvre et vie d'Adelbert de Chamisso," *Figures de la psychanalyse* 7, 2, 167–185.
Patrut, Iulia Karin (2011) "Kafkas 'Poetik des Anderen:' Kolonialer Diskurs und postkolonialer Kanon in Europa," in *Postkolonialismus und Kanon: Relektüren, Revisionen und postkoloniale Ästhetik*, ed. Uerlings, Herbert and Iulia Karin Patrut (Bielefeld: Aisthesis), 261–288.
Pirinçci, Akif (1980) *Tränen sind immer das Ende* (Munich: Goldmann).
Pirinçci, Akif (2014) *Deutschland von Sinnen: Der irre Kult um Frauen, Homosexuelle und Zuwanderer* (Waltrop: Manuscriptum).
Pirinçci, Akif (2015) *Die große Verschwulung: Wenn aus Männern Frauen werden und aus Frauen keine Männer* (Waltrop: Manuscriptum).
Pirinçci, Akif (2016) *Umvolkung: Wie die Deutschen still und leise ausgetauscht werden* (Steigra: Antaios).
Pizer, John (2004), "The Transnationalization of the Double Motif: Rafik Schami's *Sieben Doppelgänger*," *Gegenwartsliteratur*, 3, 278–300.
Pizer, John (2005) "Moving the *Divan* Beyond Orientalism: Rafik Schami's Instrumentalization of Goethe," *Seminar – A Journal of Germanic Studies* 41, 3, 261–274.
Plenzdorf, Ulrich (1981) *Die neuen Leiden des jungen W.* [1973] (Frankfurt/M.: Suhrkamp Taschenbuch Verlag).
Pokatsky, Klaus (1982) "Ich bin ein Pressetürke: Akif Pirinçci und der deutsche Literaturbetrieb," *Die Zeit*, 28 May.
Polaschegg, Andrea (2005) *Der andere Orientalismus: Regeln deutsch-morgenländischer Imagination im 19. Jahrhundert* (Berlin: De Gruyter).
Poschmann, Gerda (2007) *Plädoyer für ein postdramatisches Drama* (Vienna: Passagen).
Pradeau, Christophe and Tiphaine Samoyault (eds) (2005) *Où est la littérature mondiale?* (Saint-Denis: PUV).
Pratt, Mary Louise (1991) "Arts of the Contact Zone," *Profession 91* (New York: MLA), 33–40.
Pratt, Mary Louise (1992) *Imperial Eyes: Travel Writing and Transculturation* (London: Routledge).

Propp, Vladimir (1965) *Morphologie du conte*, [1928] (Paris: Seuil).
Pujol, Stéphane (2005) *Le Dialogue d'idées au dix-huitième siècle* (Oxford: Voltaire Foundation).
Raddatz, Frank-Michael (1991) *Dämonen unterm Roten Stern. Zu Geschichtsphilosophie und Ästhetik Heiner Müllers* (Stuttgart: Metzler).
Regnauld, Hervé (2012) "Les concepts de Félix Guattari et Gilles Deleuze et l'espace des géographes," *Chimères* 76, 1, 195–204.
Reich-Ranicki, Marcel (1973) "Der Fänger im Roggen: Ulrich Plenzdorfs jedenfalls wichtiger Werther-Roman," *Die Zeit*, 4 May (also in Brenner 1982: 262–269).
Reich-Ranicki, Marcel (2005–2006) *Der Kanon*, 10 Bde (Frankfurt/M. and Leipzig: Insel).
Reif-Hülser, Monika (2006) *Fremde Texte als Spiegel des Eigenen. Postkoloniale Literaturen und ihre Auseinandersetzung mit dem kulturellen Kanon* (Munich: Fink).
Rich, Adrienne (1972) "When We Dead Awaken: Writing as Re-Vision," *College English* 34, 1 (October), 18–30.
Robertson, Roland (1995) "Glocalization: Time-Space and Homogeneity-Heterogeneity," in *Global Modernities*, ed. Mike Featherstone, Scott Lash, and Roland Robertson (London: Sage), 25–44.
Röther, Christian (2017) "Feridun Zaimoglu, Der Reformator als Romanheld," *Deutschlandfunk*, 17 September. Online at: <http://www.deutschlandfunk.de/feridun-zaimoglu-evangelio-ein-luther-roman-der-reformator.886.de.html?dram:article_id=386292> (accessed 22 April 2020).
Rouby, Francine (2006) "Said: Bewegung bis zur Ent-Fremdung. Ein Portrait," *Germanica* 38, 157–171.
Rüdenauer, Ulrich (2003) "Etwas weniger zerebralminimal vor sich hin dämmern: Feridun Zaimoglus Romane 'Liebesmal [sic], scharlachrot' und 'German Amok,'" *literaturkritik.de* [online], <https://literaturkritik.de/id/5584> (accessed 8 May 2020).
Rushdie, Salman (1991) *Imaginary Homelands: Essays and Criticism 1989–1991* (London: Granta Books).
Saalfeld, Lerke von (ed.) (1998) *Ich habe eine fremde Sprache gewählt: Ausländische Schriftsteller schreiben deutsch* (Gerlingen: Bleicher).
SAID (1999) "'Sehr geehrter Herr Geheimrat.' Zwischen Orient und Okzident: Zum Ende des Goethe-Jahres ein Brief an den Dichter," *Berliner Zeitung*, 30 December.
SAID (2002) *Friedrich Hölderlin empfängt niemanden mehr: Ein Hörspiel*, 1 CD (Munich: C.H. Beck) with booklet (16 p.).
Said, Edward W. (1994) *Culture and Imperialism* [1993] (New York: Vintage).
Said, Edward W. (1979) *Orientalism* [1978] (New York: Vintage).
Saint-Gelais, Richard (2011) *Fictions transfuges: La transfictionnalité et ses enjeux* (Paris: Seuil).
Saleh, Arig (2011) *Rezeption arabischer Migrationsliteratur in Deutschland: Eine Untersuchung am Beispiel der in Deutschland lebenden syrischen Autoren*, PhD Diss., FU Berlin. Online at: <https://refubium.fu-berlin.de/bitstream/handle/fub188/9718/Inauguraldissertation_____Arig_Saleh.pdf> (accessed 22 April 2020).
Sanna, Simonetta (ed.) (2009) *Der Kanon in der deutschen Sprach- und Litertaturwissenschaft*, Akten des IV. Kongresses der Italienischen Germanistenvereinigung Alghero, 27.-31.5.2007 (Bern: Peter Lang).

Sarrazin, Thilo (2010) *Deutschland schafft sich ab: Wie wir unser Land aufs Spiel setzen* (Munich: Deutsche Verlags-Anstalt).
Schader, Angela (2002) "Deutschland, (k)eine Heimat: Said spricht mit Hölderlin und zur Geliebten," *Neue Zürcher Zeitung*, 4 December.
Schami, Rafik (1983a) "Warten ist schlechter Rat in einer eilenden Zeit. Über Illusionäres und Revolutionäres in der Phantasie II," *Linkskurve* 3, 38–41.
Schami, Rafik (1983b) "Warum heiratet der Prinz die Pförtnerstochter nicht? Über Illusionäres und Revolutionäres in der Phantasie I," *Linkskurve*, 2, 19–21.
Schami, Rafik (1986a) "Dankrede zur Preisverleihung," in *Chamissos Enkel. Literatur von Ausländern in Deutschland*, ed. Heinz Friedrich (Munich: DTV), 71–76.
Schami, Rafik (1986b) "Eine Literatur zwischen Minderheit und Mehrheit," in *Eine nicht nur deutsche Literatur. Zur Standortbestimmung der 'Ausländerliteratur,'* ed. Irmgard Ackermann and Harald Weinrich (Munich: Piper), 55–58.
Schami, Rafik (1987a) *Eine Hand voller Sterne*, Roman (Weinheim and Basel: Beltz).
Schami, Rafik *(1987b) Malula: Märchen und Märchenhaftes aus meinem Dorf* (Kiel: Neuer Malik Verlag).
Schami, Rafik (1999a) "Ein Vierteljahrhundert Nachbarschaft mit den Herren Goethe und Tröte," *Die Gazette*, May/June 1999, 15–16.
Schami, Rafik (1999b) "Versuch's doch mal mit Goethe! Ein Interview mit Rafik Schami," *Bulletin Jugend & Literatur* 30, 9, 10.
Schami, Rafik and Uwe-Michael Gutzschhahn (2001) *Der geheime Bericht über den Dichter Goethe, der eine Prüfung auf einer arabischen Insel bestand* [1999] (Munich: DTV).
Schami, Rafik (2001) *Sieben Doppelgänger*, Roman [1999] (Munich: DTV).
Schami, Rafik (2005) *Al-Taqrîr al-sirrî'an al-Sha'ir Goethe [=Der Geheime Bericht über den Dichter Goethe]*, trans. Nura Forst (Cologne: Al-Kamel Verlag).
Schami, Rafik (2009) *Damaskus im Herzen und Deutschland im Blick* [2006] (Munich: DTV).
Schami, Rafik (2011a) *Das letzte Wort der Wanderratte* [1987] (Munich: DTV).
Schami, Rafik (2011b) *Die Sehnsucht fährt schwarz. Geschichten aus der Fremde* [1988] (Munich: DTV).
Schami, Rafik (2012) *Die Frau, die ihren Mann auf dem Flohmarkt verkaufte, Oder wie ich zum Erzähler wurde* [2011] (Munich: DTV).
Schami, Rafik (ed.) (2001) *Angst im eigenen Land. Israelische und palästinensische Schriftsteller im Gespräch* (Zurich: Nagel & Krimme).
Schami, Rafik and Franco Biondi (1981) "Literatur der Betroffenheit. Bemerkungen zur Gastarbeiterliteratur," (unter Mitarbeit von Jusuf Naoum und Suleman Taufiq), in *Zuhause in der Fremde. Ein bundesdeutsches Ausländer-Lesebuch*, ed. Christian Schaffernicht (Fischerhude: Verlag Atelier im Bauernhaus), 124–136.
Schmeling, Manfred (2001) "Der Schriftsteller als Anthropologe? Zur Dialektik von interkultureller und ästhetischer Vermittlung," in *Theory Studies? Konturen komparatistischer Theoriebildung zu Beginn des 21. Jahrhunderts*, ed. Beate Burtscher-Bechter and Martin Sexl (Innsbruck: StudienVerlag), 297–315.
Schmeling, Manfred (ed.) (1995) *Weltliteratur heute – Konzepte und Perspektiven* (Würzburg: Königshausen & Neumann).
Schmeling, Manfred, Monika Schmitz-Emans, and Kerst Walstra (eds) (2000) *Literatur im Zeitalter der Globalisierung* (Würzburg: Königshausen & Neumann).

Schmidt, Arno (1984) *Dichtergespräche im Elysium*, Transkription des handschriftlichen Originals [1941] und Nachwort von Alice Schmidt und Jan-Philipp Reemtsma (Zurich: Haffmanns).

Schmidt-Dengler, Wendelin, Johann Sonnleitner, and Klaus Zeyringer (eds) (1994) *Die einen raus – die anderen rein. Kanon und Literatur. Vorüberlegungen zu einer Literaturgeschichte Österreichs* (Berlin: Erich Schmidt).

Schmidt, Gary (2008) "Feridun Zaimoglu's Performance of Gender and Authorship," in *German Literature in a New Century: Trends, Traditions, Transitions, Transformations*, ed. Katharina Gerstenberger and Patricia Herminghouse (New York: Berghan Books), 196–213.

Schmitz, Helmut (ed.) (2009) *Von der nationalen zur internationalen Literatur: Transkulturelle deutschsprachige Literatur und Kultur im Zeitalter globaler Migration* (Amsterdam: Rodopi).

Schneider, Manfred (1986) *Die erkaltete Herzensschrift: Der autobiographische Text im 20. Jahrhundert* (Munich: Hanser).

Schneider, Manfred (1997) "Die Debatten um den deutschen Literaturkanon: Ein Offenbarungseid," *Die Zeit*, 13 June. Online at: <https://www.zeit.de/1997/25/kanonsch.txt.19970613.xml> (accessed 22 April 2020).

Schöning, Udo (ed.) (2000) *Internationalität nationaler Literaturen: Beiträge zum Ersten Symposion des Göttinger Sonderforschungsbereichs 529* (Göttingen, Wallstein).

Schröder, Gerhard (1998) *Regierungserklärung des Bundeskanzlers*, 3. Sitzung des 14. Deutschen Bundestags am 10. November 1998, in *Das Parlament* 48, 20 November. Online at: <http://dip21.bundestag.de/dip21/btp/14/14003.pdf> (accessed 10 June 2019).

Schütt, Rüdiger (ed.) (2011) *Feridun Zaimoglu in Schrift und Bild* (Kiel: Edition Fliehkraft).

Schwanitz, Dietrich (1999) *Bildung: Alles, was man wissen muss* (Frankfurt/M.: Eichborn).

Schwilk, Heimo and Ulrich Schacht (eds) (1994) *Die selbstbewußte Nation* (Frankfurt/M. and Berlin: Ullstein).

Seeba, Hinrich C. (1994), "'Germany: A Literary Concept.' The Myth of National Literature," *German Studies Review*, 17, 2, 353–369.

Sen, Amartya (2006) *Identity and Violence. The Illusion of Destiny* (New York and London: W.W. Norton & Co).

Şenocak, Zafer (1992) *Atlas des tropischen Deutschland* (Berlin: Babel).

Şenocak, Zafer (1994) *War Hitler Araber? IrreFührungen an den Rand Europas* (Berlin: Babel).

Şenocak, Zafer (1995) "Gegen die Verortung ins Reservat. Migrationsliteratur 2000 – Eingewanderte Autoren äußern sich zu Deutschland, ihrer Literatur und ihren Perspektiven. Drei Fragen, zehn unterschiedliche Antworten und Selbstbewertungen," *Die Tageszeitung*, 17 October.

Şenocak, Zafer (2006) *Das Land hinter den Buchstaben: Deutschland und der Islam im Umbruch* (Berlin: Babel).

Şenocak, Zafer (2011) *Deutschsein: Eine Aufklärungsschrift* (Hamburg: Editon Körber-Stiftung).

Seyhan, Azade (2001) *Writing outside the Nation* (Princeton: Princeton University Press).

Seyhan, Azade (2016) "Unübersetzbare Schicksale: Umschreibungen von Exil, Schweigen und sprachlichen Zielorten im Werk Özdamars," *Emine Sevgi Özdamar, Text + Kritik* 211, ed. Heinz-Ludwig Arnold (Munich: text + kritik), 19–25.

Shakespeare, William and August Wilhelm Schlegel (1797) *Ein Sommernachtstraum*, in *Shakspeare's dramatische Werke*, übersetzt von August Wilhelm von Schlegel, ergänzt und erläutert von Ludwig Tieck, 3. Theil (Berlin: J. F. Unger), 171–290.

Shakespeare, William (1997) *A Midsummer Night's Dream*, in *The Norton Shakespeare: Based on the Oxford Edition*, ed. Stephen Greenblatt et al. (New York and London: W. W. Norton & Company), I, 849–896.

Siebert, Hans (1952) *Was sind Märchen? Eine kurze Anleitung für Erzieher, Lehrer, Pionierleiter und Eltern* (Berlin: Kinderbuchverlag).

Sieg, Katrin (2002) *Ethnic Drag: Performing Race, Nation, Sexuality in West Germany* (Michigan: University of Michigan Press).

Simo, David (2002) *Die Erfahrungen des Imperiums kehren zurück: Inszenierungen des Fremden in der deutschen Literatur* (Leipzig: Leipziger Universitäts-Verlag).

Simpson, David (2012) "Because he's worth it" (on *The Sufferings of Young Werther*, trans. Stanley Corngold), *London Review of Books*, 34, 27, 13 September [online]: <https://www.lrb.co.uk/the-paper/v34/n17/david-simpson/because-he-s-worth-it> (accessed 11 May 2020).

Smith, James (2004) "Karagöz and Hacivat: Projections of subversion and conformance," *Asian Theatre Journal* 21, 2 (Autumn), 187–193.

Spencer, Robert (2011) *Cosmopolitan Criticism and Postcolonial Literature* (Basingstoke: Palgrave Macmillan).

Spivak, Gayatri Chakravorty (1988) "Can the Subaltern Speak?," in *Marxism and the Interpretation of Culture*, ed. Cary Nelson and Lawrence Grossberg (Urbana: University of Illinois Press), 271–313.

Spivak, Gayatri Chakravorty (1999) *A Critique of Postcolonial Reason: Toward a History of the Vanishing Present* (Cambridge, MA, and London: Harvard University Press).

Spivak, Gayatri Chakravorty and Ranajit Guha (eds) (1988) *Selected Subaltern Studies* (Oxford: Oxford University Press).

Spivak, Gayatri Chakravorty and Ranajit Guha (eds) (2010) *Nationalism and Imagination* (London, New York, and Calcutta: Seagull Books).

Starobinski, Jean (1978) "Pouvoir et Lumières dans *La Flûte enchantée*," *Dix-huitième siècle* 10 (numéro thématique "Qu'est-ce que les lumières?"), 435–449.

Steffahn, Harald (1998) *Bertha von Suttner* (Reinbek bei Hamburg: Rowohlt).

Steuten, Ulrich (2001) "Feridun Zaimoglu: *Liebesmale, scharlachrot*," *parapluie* [Elektronische Zeitschrift für Kulturen – Künste – Literaturen], 1 November, <https://parapluie.de/archiv/kommunikation/aufgelesen/> (accessed 23 April 2020).

Steyerl, Hito and Encarnación Gutiérrez Rodríguez (eds) (2012) *Spricht die Subalterne deutsch? Migration und postkoloniale Kritik* (Münster: Unrast).

Stieg, Gerald (2010) "'Grenzfälle' ou à qui appartient à la littérature autrichienne?," *Études Germaniques* 258, 2, 307–318.

Stoker, Bram (1897) *Dracula* (Westminster: Constable & Co).

Stokes, Martin (1992) *The Arabesk Debate: Music and Musicians in Modern Turkey* (Oxford: Clarendon Press).

Strasser, Alfred (2011) "Snobismus und neue deutsche Popliteratur am Beispiel von Benjamin Stuckrad-Barre," *Germanica* 49, 135–144.

Strasser, Alfred (ed.) (2006) *Voix étrangères en langue allemande*, *Germanica* 38.

Sturm-Trigonakis, Elke (2007) *Global Playing in der Literatur: Ein Versuch über die neue Weltliteratur* (Würzburg: Königshausen & Neumann).
Szondi, Peter (1956) *Theorie des modernen Dramas* (Frankfurt/M.: Suhrkamp).
Tantow, Lutz (1984) "In den Hinterhöfen der deutschen Sprache: Ein Streifzug durch die deutsche Literatur von Ausländern," *Die Zeit*, 15, 4 June. Online at: <http://www.zeit.de/1984/15/in-den-hinterhoefen-der-deutschen-sprache> (accessed 10 March 2019).
Tantow, Lutz (1985) "'aber mit ein bißl einem guten Willen tät man sich schon verständigen können': Aspekte des 'Gastarbeiter'-Theaters in der Bundesrepublik Deutschland und West-Berlin," *InfoDaF*, 3 December, 208–221.
Tawada, Yoko (1993) *Ein Gast* (Tübingen: Konkursbuch).
Tawada, Yoko (2000) *Spielzeug und Sprachmagie in der europäischen Literatur: Eine ethnopoetische Poetologie* (Tübingen: Konkursbuch).
Tawada, Yoko (2008) *Sprachpolizei und Spielpolyglotte*, Literarische Essays [2003] (Tübingen: Konkursbuch).
Tawada, Yoko (2012) *Yoko Tawada: Fremde Wasser*, ed. Ortrud Gutjahr (Tübingen: Konkursbuch).
Terkessidis, Mark (2010) *Interkultur* (Berlin: Suhrkamp).
Thieme, John (2001) *Postcolonial Con-texts: Writing back to the Canon* (London and New York: Continuum).
Thirouin, Marie-Odile (2007) "Deleuze et Kafka: l'invention de la littérature mineure," in *Deleuze et les écrivains. Littérature et philosophie*, ed. Bruno Gelas and Hervé Micolet (Nantes: Cécile Defaut), 293–310.
Tibi, Bassam (1998) *Europa ohne Identität? Die Krise der multikulturellen Gesellschaft* (Munich: Bertelsmann).
Tibi, Bassam (2017) "Debatte nirgends, Geschrei überall," *Cicero*, 17 May [online], <https://www.cicero.de/kultur/leitkultur-Debatte-nirgends-Geschrei-ueberall> (accessed 22 April 2020).
Tiffin, Helen (1987) "Post-colonial literatures and counter-discourse," *Kunapipi* 9, 3, 17–34.
Totzke, Ariane (2013) "Nationalismus und Völkermord in Emine Sevgi Özdamars Theaterstück *Perikizi – Ein Traumspiel*," in *Sprachen und Kulturen in (Inter)Aktion*, ed. Elke Sturm-Trigonakis and Simelia Delianidou (Frankfurt/M.: Peter Lang), 107–120.
Traxler, Hans (1963) *Die Wahrheit über Hänsel und Gretel: Die Dokumentation des Märchens der Brüder Grimm* (Frankfurt/M.: Bärmeier und Nikel).
Trojanow, Ilija (ed.) (2000) *Döner in Walhalla. Texte aus der anderen deutschen Literatur* (Cologne: Kiepenheuer & Witsch).
Trojanow, Ilija (2008) "Voran ins Gondwanaland," in Zaimoglu and Trojanow, *Ferne Nähe. Tübinger Poetik-Dozentur 2007*, ed. Dorothee Kimmich and Philipp Ostrowicz (Künzelsau: Swiridoff), 67–94.
Trojanow, Ilija and Feridun Zaimoglu (2008) *Ferne Nähe. Tübinger Poetik-Dozentur 2007*, ed. Dorothee Kimmich and Philipp Ostrowicz (Künzelsau: Swiridoff).
Turgeon, Laurier (2004) "Les mots pour dire les métissages: jeux et enjeux d'un lexique," *Revue germanique internationale* 21 [online], <http://rgi.revues.org/996> (accessed 22 April 2020).
Turgeon, Laurier, Denys Delâge, and Réal Ouellet (1996) *Transferts culturels et métissages Amérique/Europe, XVIe-XXe siècle. Cultural Transfer, America and Europe: 500 Years of Interculturation* (Paris: Presses de l'Université de Laval and L'Harmattan).

Uerlings, Herbert and Iulia Karin Patrut (eds) (2011) *Postkolonialismus und Kanon: Relektüren, Revisionen und postkoloniale Ästhetik* (Bielefeld: Aisthesis).
Uerlings, Herbert, *"Ich bin von niedriger Rasse." (Post-)Kolonialismus und Geschlechterdifferenz in der deutschen Literatur* (Cologne: Böhlau).
Vaydat, Pierre (2002) *"Les Nouvelles Souffrances du jeune W.* de Ulrich Plenzdorf: négation contestataire et littérature," *Germanica* 30, 91–99.
Wagner-Engelhaaf, Martina (2006) "Autofiktion oder: Autobiographie nach der Autobiographie. Goethe – Barthes – Özdamar," in *Autobiographisches Schreiben in der deutschsprachigen Gegenwartsliteratur, vol. 1: Grenzen der Identität und der Fiktionalität*, ed. Ulrich Breuer and Beatrice Sandberg (Munich: Iudicium), 353–368.
Wallraff, Günter (1985) *Ganz unten* (Cologne: Kiepenheuer & Witsch).
Walser, Martin (1999) "Erfahrungen beim Verfassen einer Sonntagsrede," in *Die Walser-Bubis-Debatte*, ed. Frank Schirrmacher (Frankfurt/M.: Suhrkamp), 7–17.
Weber, Angela (2009) *Im Spiegel der Migrationen. Transkulturelles Erzählen und Sprachpolitik bei Emine Sevgi Özdamar* (Bielefeld: Transcript).
Weber, Mirjam (2001) *"Der wahre Poesie-Orient." Eine Untersuchung zur Orientalismus-Theorie Edward Saids am Beispiel von Goethes 'West-östlichem Divan' und der Lyrik Heines* (Wiesbaden: Harassowitz).
Weidemann, Volker (2006) "Abgeschrieben? Streit um den Roman *Leyla:* Özdamar gegen Zaimoglu," *Frankfurter Allgemeine Zeitung*, 1 June.
Weigel, Sigrid (2006) *Genea-Logik: Generation, Tradition und Evolution zwischen Kultur- und Literaturwissenschaften* (Munich: Fink).
Weigel, Sigrid (2008) "Phantome der Kulturnation," *Die Tageszeitung*, 8 April.
Weinmann, Frédéric (2010) "La réconciliation de la masse et de l'élite autour des Contes de Grimm," in *Canon et identité culturelle: Élites, masses, manipulation*, ed. Fabrice Malkani, Anne-Marie Saint-Gille, and Ralf Zschachlitz (Saint-Étienne, Publications de l'Université de Saint- Étienne), 161–170.
Weinrich, Harald (2008) "Lieux et non-lieux d'un écrivain franco-allemand: Adelbert von Chamisso," *Le Genre humain* 47, 1, 269–278.
Weissmann, Dirk (ed.) (2011) *Littérature et migration: Écrivains germanophones venus d'ailleurs*, Allemagne d'aujourd'hui 197, July/September.
Wieland, Christoph Martin (1786–1789) *Dschinnistan oder auserlesene Feen- und Geistermährchen, theils neu erfunden, theils übersetzt und umgearbeitet*, 3 vol. (Winterthur: Steiner).
Wild, Bettina (2006) *Rafik Schami* (Munich: DTV).
Williams, Raymond (1958) *Culture & Society 1780–1950* (New York: Columbia University Press).
Williams, Raymond (1961) *The Long Revolution* (London: Chatto & Windus).
Wrobel, Dieter (2008) "Interkulturelle Literatur und Literaturdidaktik: Kanonbildung und Kanonerweiterung als Problem und Prozess," *Germanistische Mitteilungen* 68, 23–35.
Wysling, Hans and Yvonne Schmidlin (eds) (1997) *Thomas Mann. Ein Leben in Bildern* (Frankfurt/M., Fischer).
Xu, Wenying (2012) *Historical Dictionary of Asian American Literature and Theater* (Lanham, Md.: Scarecrow Press).
Yeşilada, Karin E. (2012) *Poesie der dritten Sprache: Türkisch-deutsche Lyrik der zweiten Generation* (Tübingen: Stauffenburg).

Yildiz, Yasemin (2009) "Kritisch 'Kanak:' Gesellschaftskritik, Sprache und Kultur bei Feridun Zaimoglu," in *Wider den Kulturenzwang: Migration, Kulturalisierung und Weltliteratur*, ed. Özkan Ezli, Dorothee Kimmich, and Annette Werberger (Bielefeld: Transcript) 187–205.

Young, Robert J. C. (2003) *Postcolonialism: A Very Short Introduction* (Oxford: OUP).

Zaimoglu, Feridun (1995) *Kanak Sprak. 24 Mißtöne vom Rande der Gesellschaft* (Hamburg: Rotbuch).

Zaimoglu, Feridun (1997a) *Abschaum. Die wahre Geschichte von Ertan Ongun*, Roman (Hamburg: Rotbuch).

Zaimoglu, Feridun (1997b) "'Ich kriege den Hunnenzorn:" Feridun Zaimoglu über das Verhältnis von Kanaksta und Dschörmans," *Die Zeit*, 12 December.

Zaimoglu, Feridun (1998a) *Koppstoff. Kanaka Sprak vom Rande der Gesellschaft* (Hamburg: Rotbuch).

Zaimoglu, Feridun (1998b) Talk show interview (Alfred Biolek), *Boulevard Bio* (ARD Fernsehen: Westdeutscher Rundfunk), 20 January, available at the Historisches Archiv des Westdeutschen Rundfunks, <http://www.koelnerarchive.de/index.php?id=36> (accessed 7 May 2020).

Zaimoglu, Feridun (1998c) Talk show interview (Gaby Hauptmann, with Wolf Biermann, Norbert Blüm, Harald Juhnke, Heide Simonis), *3 nach 9*, dir. Giovanni di Lorenzo (ARD Fernsehen: Norddeutscher Rundfunk), 8 May, online at: YOUTUBE, <https://www.youtube.com/watch?v=wrV7adgbcMc> (accessed 7 May 2020).

Zaimoglu, Feridun (1999) "Knabenwindelprosa. Überall wird von deutscher Popliteratur geschwärmt. Aber sie ist nur reaktionäres Kunsthandwerk. Eine Abrechnung," *Die Zeit*, 18 November.

Zaimoglu, Feridun (2002a) *German Amok*, Roman (Cologne: Kiepenheuer & Witsch [KiWi]), 2002.

Zaimoglu, Feridun (2002b) "Niemand wird geschont. Interview mit Feridun Zaimoglu über German Amok auf den deutschen Kulturbetrieb," (Olaf Neumann), *Jungle World* 41, <https://jungle.world/artikel/2002/41/niemand-wird-geschont> (accessed 20 April 2020).

Zaimoglu, Feridun (2002c) *Liebesmale, scharlachrot*, Roman [Hamburg, Rotbuch, 2000] (Cologne: Kiepenheuer & Witsch [KiWi]).

Zaimoglu, Feridun (2004a) *Zwölf Gramm Glück*, Erzählungen (Cologne: Kiepenheuer & Witsch [KiWi]).

Zaimoglu, Feridun (2004b) "Lebenswut, Herzhitze: Der Berlinale-Überraschungssieger kommt ins Kino: Fatih Akins herrlich maßloses Liebesdrama 'Gegen die Wand,'" *Der Tagesspiegel*, 3 December.

Zaimoglu, Feridun (2006a) *Leyla*, Roman (Cologne: Kiepenheuer & Witsch [KiWi]).

Zaimoglu, Feridun (2006b) "Guter Bimbo, böser Bimbo: STANDARD-Interview mit Feridun Zaimoglu," (Stefan Gmünder) *Der Standard*, 22 April.

Zaimoglu, Feridun (2006c) "Infiltration durch Penetration," Interview (Henryk M. Broder), *Der Spiegel*, 18 March.

Zaimoglu, Feridun (2007a) "Ein Gespräch mit Feridun Zaimoglu," in *Entgrenzungen. Vierzehn Autorengespräche über Liebe, Leben und Literatur*, ed. Olga Olivia Kasaty (Munich: Ed. Text + Kritik), 431–464.

Zaimoglu, Feridun (2007b) "Feridun Zaimoglu über seinen Ausstieg aus der Islamkonferenz," Interview, *Islamische Zeitung*, 24 April. Online at: <https://www.islamische-zeitung.de/

interview-autor-feridun-zaimoglu-ueber-seinen-ausstieg-aus-der-islam-konferenz/> (accessed 6 August 2018).

Zaimoglu, Feridun (2007c) "Interview: 'Ich bin ein Skeptiker der Aufklärung,'" Feridun Zaimoglu und Vito Avantario, 2 June, *Zeitschrift der Kultur* 68. Online at: <https://www.e-periodica.ch/cntmng?pid=dkm-003:2007:67::44> (accessed 6 August 2018).

Zaimoglu, Feridun (2008a) *Liebesbrand*, Roman (Cologne: Kiepenheuer & Witsch [KiWi]).

Zaimoglu, Feridun (2008b) "Feridun Zaimoglu im Interview: 'Ich bin ein begeisterter Deutscher,'" *Wirtschaftswoche*, Oktober 12.

Zaimoglu, Feridun (2009a) *Hinterland*, Roman (Cologne: Kiepenheuer & Witsch [KiWi]).

Zaimoglu, Feridun (2009b) "Die Flammen der wahren Hölle," Marion Tiedtke im Gespräch mit Feridun Zaimoglu und Günter Senkel, 1 October 2009. Online at: <https://www.thalia-theater.de/beitraege/59> (accessed 21 April 2020).

Zaimoglu, Feridun (2009c) "'Mehr Inbrunst bitte!': Der Autor Zaimoglu fordert Mut zum Reaktionären," Interview von Elmar Krekeler, *Die Welt*, 24 September 2009.

Zaimoglu, Feridun (2011a) *Ruß*, Roman (Cologne: Kiepenheuer & Witsch [KiWi]).

Zaimoglu, Feridun (2011b) "Feridun Zaimoglu im Gespräch," (Walter Arnold), *Kiel Maritim*, 1 September. Online at: <http://www.kiel-maritim.de/index.php/stadt-kiel/90-feridun-zaimoglu-im-gespraech-walter-arnold> (accessed 6 August 2018).

Zaimoglu, Feridun (2012) "'Ich bin nicht modern'/'I'm not modern': Interviews with Feridun Zaimoglu," in *Feridun Zaimoglu*, ed. Tom Cheesman and Karin E. Yeşilada (Oxford, Bern, Berlin, etc.: Peter Lang), 39–70.

Zaimoglu, Feridun (2014) *Isabel*, Roman (Cologne: Kiepenheuer & Witsch [KiWi]).

Zaimoglu, Feridun (2016) "Wir haben eine Krise des muslimischen Mannes," *Die Welt*, 29 January.

Zaimoglu, Feridun (2017a) *Evangelio. Ein Luther-Roman* (Cologne: Kiepenheuer & Witsch [KiWi]).

Zaimoglu, Feridun (2017b) "Feridun Zaimoglu über die Muttersprache: 'Ich kann nicht anders, als es auf Deutsch zu machen'" (Anja Reinhardt), *Deutschlandfunk*, 21 February. Online at: <http://www.deutschlandfunk.de/feridun-zaimoglu-ueber-die-muttersprache-ich-kann-nicht.691.de.html?dram:article_id=379539> (accessed 6 August 2018).

Zaimoglu, Feridun and Günter Senkel (2003) *Othello*, Theaterstück (nach Shakespeare). Stage manuscript (Reinbek: Rowohlt Theater Verlag).

Zaimoglu, Feridun and Günter Senkel (2005) *Lulu Live*, Theaterstück (nach Wedekind). Stage manuscript (Reinbek: Rowohlt Theater Verlag).

Zaimoglu, Feridun and Günter Senkel (2006) *Romeo und Julia*, Theaterstück (nach Shakespeare). Stage manuscript (Reinbek: Rowohlt Theater Verlag).

Zaimoglu, Feridun and Günter Senkel (2007) *Molière – Eine Passion*, Theaterstück. Stage manuscript (Reinbek: Rowohlt Theater Verlag).

Zaimoglu, Feridun and Günter Senkel (2009) *Nathan Messias*, Theaterstück (nach Lessings Nathan der Weise). Stage manuscript (Reinbek: Rowohlt Theater Verlag).

Zaimoglu, Feridun and Günter Senkel (2010) *Hamlet*, Theaterstück (nach Shakespeare). Stage manuscript (Reinbek: Rowohlt Theater Verlag).

Zaimoglu, Feridun and Günter Senkel (2011) *Julius Caesar*, Theaterstück (nach Shakespeare). Stage manuscript (Reinbek: Rowohlt Theater Verlag).

Zaimoglu, Feridun and Günter Senkel (2015) *Siegfried*, Bühnenbearbeitung der Nibelungensage. Stage manuscript (Reinbek: Rowohlt Theater Verlag).

Zaimoglu, Feridun and Günter Senkel (2018) *Siegfrieds Erben*. Stage manuscript (Reinbek: Rowohlt Theater Verlag).
Zantop, Susanne (1997) *Colonial Fantasies: Conquest, Family, and Nation in Precolonial Germany, 1770–1870* (Durham: Duke University Press).
Ziani, Safia (s.d.) "Müslüm Baba: Der Vater der Einsamen und Armen," *Terminal Y* [online], <http://www.terminal-y.de/muesluem-baba-der-vater-der-einsamen-und-armen/> (accessed 5 February 2018).
Zierau, Cornelia (2009) *"Wenn Wörter auf Wanderschaft gehen..." Aspekte kultureller, nationaler und geschlechtsspezifischer Differenzen in deutschsprachiger Migrationsliteratur* (Tübingen: Stauffenburg).
Zipes, Jack (1983a) *Fairy Tales and the Art of Subversion: The Classical Genre for Children and the Process of Civilization* (London: Heinemann).
Zipes, Jack (1983b) *The Trials and Tribulations of Little Red Riding Hood: Versions of the Tale in Sociocultural Context* (South Hadley, MA: Bergin & Garvey Publishers).
Zipes, Jack (1988) *The Brothers Grimm. From Enchanted Forests to the Modern World* (New York: Routledge).
Zipes, Jack (1993) "The Struggle for the Grimms' Throne: The Legacy of the Grimms' tales in the RFG and GDR since 1945," in *The Reception of Grimms' Fairy Tales: Responses, Reactions, Revisions*, ed. Donald Haase (Detroit, Mich.: Wayne State University Press), 167–206.
Zschachlitz, Ralf (2007) "'Blocage canonique,' 'espace des possibles,' 'dialectique à l'arrêt.' Éléments d'une théorie du canon chez Assmann, Bourdieu et Benjamin," in *Canon et mémoire culturelle: Œuvres canoniques et postérité*, ed. Malkani, Saint-Gille, and Zschachlitz, *Études germaniques* 243, 3, 543–557.
Zschirnt, Christiane (2002) *Bücher: Alles, was man lesen muss* (Frankfurt/M.: Eichborn).
Zymner, Rüdiger (1998) "Anspielung und Kanon," in *Kanon Macht Kultur*, ed. Renate von Heydebrand (Stuttgart: Metzler), 30–46.

Index of Names

A-Maaly, Khalid 54
Abel, Julia 217f., 221
Ackermann, Anton 268
Ackermann, Irmgard 29
Adelson, Leslie A. 8, 278, 294
Adenauer, Konrad 34
Adorno, Theodor W(iesengrund) 37f., 301
Akın, Fatih 214, 303
Améry, Jean (= Hanns Chaim Mayer, AKA) 38
Amodeo, Immacolata 4, 8
Amossy, Ruth 1, 15
Anderson, Benedict 5
Andries, Lise 60f.
Aristophanes 269
Armstrong, Louis 269
Arnim, Achim von 49, 75, 155, 161, 304
Aron, Paul 16, 276
Artaud, Antonin 176, 200
Aschcroft, Bill 26
Assad, Bachar 90
Assad, Hafez 87, 90
Assmann, Aleida 10, 31
Assmann, Jan 147
Atatürk (= Mustafa Kemal) 259
Ateş, Seyran 124, 220
Atkins, Susan 183
Austen, Jane 13
Ayhan, Ece 128

Bachmann, Ingeborg 40, 59, 126, 217
Bakhtin, Mikhail 11
Bardoph, Jacqueline 23, 26f.
Barthes, Roland 243, 245f., 256–258, 264
Becker, Lars 216
Beethoven, Ludwig van 24, 63
Benjamin, Walter 10, 38, 44, 50, 88, 92, 105, 295, 306
Benn, Gottfried 33, 36, 197, 248
Besson, Benno 172, 180, 189f., 201
Biermann, Wolf 189, 216, 222
Biller, Maxim 19, 297
Biondi, Franco 4, 11, 17, 85

Bloom, Harold 27, 31, 57
Blüm, Norbert 216
Blunck, Hans-Friedrich 38
Bonn, Charles 45, 213
Börne, Ludwig 34, 165
Bourdieu, Pierre 8, 14, 28f.
Braun, Eva 176f.
Brecht, Bertolt 32f., 41f., 55, 61, 74, 76, 93, 125, 127f., 130, 141, 161f., 169, 172f., 184, 189f., 194, 198, 201, 306f.
Bredel, Willi 85
Brentano, Clemens 49, 75, 155, 161, 304
Brinkmann, Rolf Dieter 295
Broch, Hermann 38
Brontë, Charlotte 11, 13
Brussig, Thomas 11, 295
Brutus, Marcus Junius, Caepio 176f.
Büchner, Georg 33f., 46, 51f., 55, 59, 77f., 128, 155
Bukowski, Charles 281, 288
Bürger, Gottfried August 281f.
Burroughs, William S. 295
Butler, Judith 11, 215
Byron, Georges Gordon, Lord 24, 35

Caesar, Julius 51, 176
Camus, Albert 11
Canetti, Elias 33, 54f., 67, 82
Celan, Paul 33f., 38–40, 43, 52, 54, 63f., 81f., 128
Çelik, Neco 48, 214
Cervantes, Saavedra, Miguel de 51, 92
Césaire, Aimé 51, 81
Chamisso, Adelbert (= Louis Charles Adélaïde de Chamissot de Boncourt, AKA) von 3f., 6, 33f., 50, 55, 59, 65–72, 74–77, 81f., 92, 99, 213, 289, 302, 307
Cheesman, Tom 48, 127, 219, 284, 288f.
Child, Francis James 109
Çirak, Zehra 11
Cleopatra 176
Coetzee, John Maxwell 11, 26, 53

Conrad, Joseph   13, 24
Cronenberg, David   144

Daimagüler, Mehmet   214, 300
Dante (= Durante degli Alighieri, AKA)   51
Danton, Georges Jacques   52, 176
Daoud, Kamel   11, 220
Daudet, Alphonse   24
Dayıoğlu-Yücel, Yasemin   126
Defoe, Daniel   11, 13, 26, 269
Deleuze, Gilles   1, 8, 16, 53, 77, 133
Derrida, Jacques   8, 10, 25
Detue, Frédérik   38
Disney, Walter Elias (Walt)   107
Do Paço, David   147 f.
Döbler, Katharina   228
Dobrindt, Alexander   2
Dorn, Thea (= Christiane Scherer)   301
Durzak, Manfred   4

Ecker, Gisela   173
Eckermann, Johann Peter   49
Eichendorff, Joseph Karl Benedikt   49
El Hissy, Maha   11 f., 134
Ellerbach, Benoît   19, 58, 87–90, 105, 108
Emmerich, Wolfgang   4
Engels, Friedrich   65
Enzensberger, Hans Magnus   61
Espagne, Michel   5, 15, 169, 301 f.
Ette, Ottmar   5, 128, 191, 198, 212
Ewers, Hans-Heino   88 f.

Fachinger, Petra   10–12, 280, 288
Fassbinder, Rainer Werner   98, 265
Fichte, Johann Gottlieb   48
Flaubert, Gustave   24
Fleischmann, Lea   11
Foucault, Michel   8, 10, 24, 235
Freiligrath, Ferdinand von   165, 167 f., 304
Frischmuth, Barbara   10

García Lorca, Federico   128
García Márquez, Gabriel   41
Gauvin, Lise   16 f.
Geiser, Myriam   6
Gendolla, Peter   32

Genette, Gérard   14, 56 f., 60, 79, 228, 268, 275
Gide, André   92
Gilleir, Anke   200
Ginkel, Emil   85
Ginsberg, Allen   288, 295
Goethe, Johann Wolfgang von   6, 32 f., 35 f., 38 f., 44, 46 f., 49, 51, 57 f., 62–65, 78, 81 f., 89, 92 f., 110–114, 116–122, 154, 172, 217, 226–230, 234–238, 240–244, 246, 248–250, 253–256, 262, 264 f., 267–278, 283, 288 f., 291, 296 f., 301–303, 307
Goldt, Max   295
Götz, Rainer   295
Gramsci, Antonio   25
Griffiths, Gareth   26
Grimm, Jakob & Wilhelm   40, 44, 50 f., 58, 81, 101, 103 f., 106–109, 152, 156, 164 f., 195, 208, 210, 212, 306
Grün, Max von der   86, 106
Guattari, Félix   1, 8, 16, 53, 77, 133
Günter, Grass   214
Gürses, Müslüm (= Müslüm Akbaş, AKA)   260–262, 264
Gutzschhahn, Uwe-Michael   44, 110 f., 114, 119

Habermas, Jürgen   10, 101
Hacks, Peter   269
Hafez (= Khwāja Shams-ud-Dīn Muḥammad Ḥāfeẓ-e Shīrāzī)   62, 87, 119
Hall, Stuart   5
Handke, Peter   295
Harnoncourt, Nikolaus   151
Hauff, Wilhelm   51, 58
Heesters, Johannes   162
Hegel, Georg Wilhelm Friedrich   48, 114, 120
Heidegger, Martin   36, 48
Heine, Harry, *then* Christian Johann Heinrich   23, 34, 46, 52 f., 65, 69–73, 75 f., 81 f., 92, 114, 120 f., 128–130, 140–142, 162–169, 194 f., 201–204, 207 f., 211 f., 268, 302, 305–307
Herwegh, Georg   165
Heym, Stefan   176
Heyse, Paul   46

Hikmet, Nâzım 128
Hillgruber, Andreas 101
Himmler, Heinrich 38
Hitler, Adolf 32, 52, 100, 162, 176 f., 197
Hobsbawm, Eric 5, 16
Hoernle, Edwin 105
Hoffmann, E(rnst) T(heodor) A(madeus) 49, 58, 140, 228, 282
Hofmann, Michael 42, 59, 228
Hölderlin, Friedrich 34, 46, 48 f., 62–65, 70, 226–228
Homer 35, 51, 56, 81, 236, 262, 269
Honecker, Erich 268 f.
Honigmann, Barbara 11
Hoskoté, Ranijt 8
Houellebecq, Michel 219
Hugo, Victor 52
Hwang, David Henry 144

Iser, Wolfgang 10
Itzenplitz, Eberhard 265

Jacoby, Georg 161
Jauß, Georg 10
Jean Paul (= Johann Paul Richter, AKA) 49
Jelinek, Elfriede 61, 198
Jens, Walter 41, 61
Jessen, Jens 41 f.
Joyce, James 53, 57
Juhnke, Harald 216

Kafka, Franz 1, 32–34, 36, 50, 53, 55, 57, 77, 81 f., 92
Kaiser, Georg 41 f., 111
Kant, Immanuel 35
Kara, Yadé 214
Karaman, Fatih F. 259 f.
Kelek, Necla 124, 153, 220
Keller, Gottfried 80
Kermani, Navid 8, 11, 14, 34–37, 44, 49, 53, 213, 301
Kerner, Justinius 165
Kerouac, Jack 295
Kleist, Heinrich von 49 f., 53, 59, 77, 128
Klopstock, Friedrich Gottlieb 46, 283
Kohl, Helmut 296
Kracht, Wolfgang 295

Kraft, Helga 130, 241
Kurt, Kemal 11, 14, 57, 134, 269
Kuruyazıcı, Nilüfer 4

Lacan, Jacques 8
Lammert, Norbert 2
Lamping, Dieter 6
Langhoff, Matthias 172, 174
Lasker-Schüler, Else 53 f., 57, 81, 128, 191 f., 194–201, 211, 248, 302
Lebert, Benjamin 295
Lecercle, Jean-Jacques 27 f.
Lenz, Jakob Michael Reinhold 33, 46, 51 f., 55, 77, 246
Lérès, Guy 262 f.
Lessing, Gotthold Ephraim 32–34, 36, 38, 48, 81, 213, 268
Liebeskind, August Jakob 147
Lorbeer, Hans 85
Lubrich, Oliver 95
Lucian of Samosata 60
Luserke, Matthias 248, 256
Luther, Martin 3, 42, 63, 142, 219
Luxemburg, Rosa 183

Macpherson, James 109, 261
Maingueneau, Dominique 15
Malkani, Fabrice 28
Mann, Heinrich 32
Mann, Thomas 35, 45, 50, 62
Manson, Charles 183
Maron, Monika 153
Marquardt, Fritz 172, 192
Marx, Karl 99, 114, 120, 131
Maupassant, Guy de 24
Mayer, Hans 36, 44 f.
Mecklenburg, Norbert 132, 173, 187 f.
Mede-Flock, Hanne 10
Meizoz, Jérôme 1, 15, 123
Merkel, Angela 123, 220
Merz, Friedrich 2
Messalina 176
Metternich, Klemens Wenzel von 71, 208
Millöcker, Carl 140, 161
Minnaard, Liesbeth 8, 296
Mörike, Eduard 38
Morley, John 117

Motte Fouqué, Friedrich Heinrich Karl Baron de la 50
Mozart, Wolfgang Amadeus 24, 129, 140, 146f., 149–151, 154, 202, 305
Müller, Heiner 35, 61, 80, 128, 130, 141, 171f., 179f., 183–187, 192, 212
Müller, Inge 183
Murnau, Friedrich Wilhelm 93

Napoleon I (= Napoleon Bonaparte) 68, 304
Neruda, Pablo 128
Nerval, Gérard de 24
Nestroy, Johann 46
Nietzsche, Friedrich 39, 114, 120f.
Nobel, Alfred 116
Nolte, Ernst 101
Nora, Pierre 28
Novalis (= Georg Philipp Friedrich Freiherr von Hardenberg, AKA) 49

Okay, Erman 134
Oliver, José F(rancisco) A(güera) 11
Özdamar, Emine Sevgi 11, 14, 17f., 44, 51, 53–56, 58f., 61, 73–80, 123–135, 137, 139–143, 146–148, 150, 152–156, 158, 162–164, 166, 168–175, 177–179, 184–187, 189–192, 194, 196–205, 208, 210–213, 217f., 265, 301f., 304–307
Özdemir, Cem 214, 300
Özdoğan, Selim 214
Özoğuz, Aydan 214

Percy, Thomas 109
Perrault, Charles 58, 101, 103, 140
Pfizer, Gustav 166
Pieck, Wilhelm 268
Pinkus, Theo 172
Pirinçci, Akif 14, 265, 279–281, 283–294, 296f.
Plenzdorf, Ulrich 217, 265, 267–278, 280, 283, 285, 287–291, 295–297, 303
Polanski, Roman 93
Propp, Vladimir 101, 156
Proust, Marcel 53, 286
Puccini, Giacomo 129, 139f., 142–147, 305

Reich-Ranicki, Marcel 33, 277
Reif-Hülser, Monika 10
Rhys, Jean 11
Richard III, King of England 176
Rilke, Rainer Maria 34, 39f., 82
Rimbaud, Arthur 39, 176
Robespierre, Maximilien de 176
Rökk, Marika 162
Roth, Moses Joseph 34
Rushdie, Salman 13, 72

Safranski, Rüdiger 301
SAID 11, 14, 47, 49, 61–65, 69, 307
Saint-Gille, Anne-Marie 28
Salinger, Jerome David 269, 273, 275, 295–297
Sarrazin, Thilo 124f., 154, 300
Schäfer, Wilhelm 38
Schami, Rafik (= Suheil Fadel, AKA) 4, 14, 17–19, 43f., 47, 50f., 53, 57f., 61, 65–73, 85–111, 113–122, 213, 301f., 304–307
Schelling, Friedrich Wilhelm Joseph von 48
Schikaneder, Emanuel 147
Schiller, Johann Christoph Friedrich 32, 34, 36, 46, 48, 161, 268
Schlegel, August Wilhelm 79f., 141, 179
Schmidt, Arno 61
Schneider, Manfred 30
Schneider, Richard Chaim 11
Schopenhauer, Arthur 114, 120
Schubert, Franz 154
Schwab, Gustav 165
Schwarzer, Alice 153
Senkel, Günter 48, 51, 213
Şenocak, Zafer 8, 11, 14, 39f., 44, 54, 82, 213, 301
Seyhan, Azade 8, 132
Shakespeare, William 13, 26, 35, 51, 78–81, 128f., 136, 138, 140–142, 157, 162–164, 169, 171, 173, 176, 178–180, 185, 204, 213, 269, 306
Simonis, Heide 216
Sloterdijk, Peter 301
Smetana, Bedřich 129, 137, 139f., 152, 154, 305
Socrates 131

Sommer, Theo 2
Spivak, Gayatri Chakravorty 25, 187
Staël, Germaine de 50
Stanislavski, Konstantin Sergeievich 76
Stein, Heinrich Friedrich Karl Reichsfreiherr vom und zum 38
Stendhal (= Marie-Henri Beyle, AKA) 192
Sterne, Laurence 49
Sternheim, Carl 41f.
Stoker, Bram 86, 93–95, 100, 305
Stuckrad-Barre, Benjamin 295
Sturm-Trigonakis, Elke 6
Stürmer, Michael 101, 285
Süreya, Cemal 128
Suttner, Bertha von 111, 115f., 118

Tawada, Yoko 11, 14, 49f., 54, 142, 213, 301
Tibi, Bassam 1f.
Tieck, Ludwig 49, 140
Tiffin, Helen 13, 26
Toller, Ernst 41f.
Topcu, Özlem 214
Trakl, Georg 43
Trojanow, Ilija 8, 42–44, 55
Tschinag, Galsan 11, 14, 47
Tucholsky, Kurt 36

Uhland, Ludwig 46, 165

Valentino, Rudolph 24
Van Gogh, Vincent Willem 176

Verdi, Giuseppe 24
Vlad III, Prince of Wallachia, AKA Vlad the Empaler 94–97, 99f.

Walcott, Derek 51, 81
Waldenfels, Bernard 10
Wallraff, Günter 86, 98, 300
Walser, Martin 37
Walser, Robert 33f., 55
Weigel, Helene 74, 194
Weigel, Sigrid 2, 74
Weinrich, Harald 3f.
Werner, Michael 5, 15, 98, 265, 301
Wieland, Christoph Martin 46
Wilhelm II, King of Prussia and German Emperor 111
Wolf, Christa 93

Yeginer, Murat 132
Yeşilada, Karin E. 48, 219

Zaimoglu, Feridun 11, 14, 19, 34, 40–42, 48, 51, 59, 126f., 213–229, 231, 234, 236, 238–240, 243f., 246–252, 254–259, 261–265, 270–279, 283f., 290–297, 301, 303, 307
Zelle, Carsten 32
Zipes, Jack 104, 106
Zschachlitz, Ralf 28f.
Zur Mühlen, Hermynia 105

Index of Notions

acculturation 9, 27, 55, 160, 197, 209, 284
agency 25 f., 291
alterity 10, 25, 54, 122
ancestors (literary) 67 f., 74, 76, 82, 98, 128, 156
Arabesk (music) 262, 264, 278, 293
Arabesk (music) 259, 261, 264, 293
Arbeiterliteratur 85
Aufklärung (*see also* Enlightenment) 35, 38, 44, 48, 72, 107, 222, 254
Ausländerliteratur 4
authoriality (*see also* posture, ethos) 1, 88
autobiography 49, 191 f.
autofiction 127, 191
avant-garde 32 f., 54, 57, 59, 124, 132, 189, 197, 289

Beat Generation 288, 295
Betroffenheit (Literatur der) 4, 86
Biedermeier 58
Bildungsroman 59, 194, 201, 212

canon
debate 31 f.
wars 30 f., 33
carnivalesque 11, 59, 127, 130, 146, 177
center and periphery 7, 302
Chamisso-Literatur 6
Chamisso Prize 3 f., 65, 74, 77, 289
counter-canon 31, 105
counter-culture 206 f., 215, 259, 267, 288, 295, 297
counter-discourse 13, 93, 121, 298, 304–306
cultural transfer 5, 15 f., 76, 135, 301

deterritorialization 16, 77 f., 128 f., 133–135, 290
diaspora 7, 90, 212

Empfindsamkeit (*see also* pre-Romanticism) 37, 42, 228, 245, 293

Enlightenment (*see also* Aufklärung) 1, 35, 58, 116, 121, 124, 147, 222
epic theater 74, 138, 169
ethnocentrism 6, 10, 170, 200
ethos (authorial) (*see also* authoriality, posture) 1, 15, 89, 127, 219–222, 281, 300, 302
Eurocentrism 81, 86 f., 117, 122, 124 f., 130, 147
exile literature 4, 32
exoticism 19, 88, 143 f., 147, 162, 199
Expressionism 37, 41, 191

feminism 10, 18, 25, 30 f., 54, 106, 116, 127, 153 f., 177, 183, 301
filiation (*see also* ancestors, genealogy, transmission) 10, 67, 303
folk
– culture 50, 59, 81, 152
– songs 155, 160, 282
– tales 41, 104, 132, 134 f., 139, 165
folklore 51, 54, 106, 108, 138, 156, 161, 164, 209–211, 222, 305

Gastarbeiterliteratur 3 f., 17, 86, 89
gender
– performativity 11
– relations 93, 221
– roles 153
– studies 8
genealogy (*see also* ancestors, filiation, transmission) 1, 14, 85, 127 f., 279
genocide 54, 64, 299
Gothic fiction 94, 98, 100

hegemony 10, 25, 29, 81, 251, 278, 301, 304, 306 f.
Historikerstreit 100
hybridity 5, 8, 11, 25, 59, 82, 95, 192, 227
hybridization 2, 92, 132, 158, 192, 295, 305

identity
– cultural 19, 26, 36, 123, 304

– national 34, 152, 170
– politics 129
integration debate 1
intertextuality 26, 56, 166
Islam Conference (*Deutsche Islamkonferenz*) 90

Jugendstil 37, 200

Kanak
– generation 220, 303
– identity 215
– movement 215, 218, 303
– posture 254 f.
karagöz (Turkish shadow theater) 59, 130 f.
Kulturnation 2, 32, 34, 82, 161 f., 170, 298, 302, 304
Künstlerroman 59

Leitkultur 1 f., 34, 37, 301

masculinity 146, 150, 221, 230, 251–254, 256, 259, 261, 290, 303
Migrantenliteratur 4
Migrationshintergrund 6, 42
Migrationsliteratur 4
mimicry (postcolonial) 11, 25, 59, 89, 298
multiculturalism 2, 27, 87, 129, 154, 214

Neue Innerlichkeit 38

Orientalism 18 f., 24, 54, 89 f., 120, 142, 146, 167, 191, 199, 305
othering 8 f.

Pietism 255, 278, 293, 296
Popliteratur 295 f.

postcolonial
– literature 10, 13, 81, 298 f.
– studies 5, 9–11, 24–26, 298
posture (*see also* authoriality, ethos) 1, 15, 19, 40, 42, 67, 88, 121, 123–125, 146, 168, 178, 199, 207, 210, 216 f., 219, 221 f., 229, 231, 237, 255–258, 290 f., 293 f., 297
pre-Romanticism 223, 283, 303

race 129, 145, 165, 223, 300
Romanticism 3, 32, 37 f., 40, 42, 49, 59, 109, 141, 165, 170, 228, 262, 293 f., 304 f.

scarification 262–264
Shoah 11, 54, 64, 200
stigma
– appropriation 290
– inversion 215
Sturm und Drang (*see also* pre-Romanticism) 37, 42, 51, 217, 226–228, 250, 254, 275, 281, 288, 291, 293, 295–297, 303
subalternity 8, 25, 51, 251
subculture 216, 268, 288, 294
Sufism 255 f., 278, 293

transmission (*see also* ancestors, filiation, genealogy) 1, 16, 29, 31 f., 68, 74, 103, 121, 194, 301

Volk 62, 71, 113, 304
Volkslieder (*see also* folk songs) 160, 304
Vormärz 32, 52, 165, 203, 208, 211 f.

Weltliteratur 6, 47, 128

www.ingramcontent.com/pod-product-compliance
Lightning Source LLC
Chambersburg PA
CBHW020219170426
43201CB00007B/261